POLAND
Land Taken by the Soviet Union, 1939
Land Assigned to Poland by the Soviet Union, 1945
N
UNION OF SOVIET SOCIALIST REPUBLICS
Riga
Vitebsk
Smolensk
Dnieper
Wilno
Wilejka
Minsk
Suwalki
Grodno
Lida
Nowogrodek
Narew
Bialystok
Baranowicze
Bug
Luniniec
Pinsk
Pripet
Brest
Biala Podlaska
Kock
Lubartow
Lublin
Wieprz
Chelm
Luboml
Turzysk
Kowel
Stochod
Lityn
Styr
Sarny
Włodzimierz Wolinski
Zamosc
Lutsk
Rowne
VOLHYNIA
Tomaszow Lubelski
Jarczow
Belzec
Bykow
Rawa Ruska
San
Krzemieniec
Zhitomir
Berdichev
Lwow
Tarnopol
Zbaraz
Trembowla
MTS.
Buczacz
Stanislawow
Zaleszczyki
Kolomija
Worochta

THE LIBERATION OF ONE

THE LIBERATION OF ONE

ROMUALD SPASOWSKI

Harcourt Brace Jovanovich, Publishers

San Diego New York London

HBJ

Library of Congress Cataloging in Publication Data

Spasowski, Romuald.
The liberation of one.

Includes index.
1. Spasowski, Romuald.
2. Defectors—Poland—Biography.
3. Defectors—United States—Biography.
I. Title.
DK4435.S63A34 1986 943.8'05'0924 [B] 85-24899
ISBN 0-15-151276-0

Designed by Michael Farmer
Printed in the United States of America
First edition
A B C D E

To Wanda

God held me before Him like a little lantern
Shielding me from wind, illuminating His face.
When I faded, He rekindled the flame
As if fearing what would come to pass if I began to sputter,
Flicker, and fail, extinguishing His name . . .

Ernest Bryll

Contents

Acknowledgments

I am grateful to my publisher, William Jovanovich, for his understanding and support, and for his profound caring for Poland.

I was fortunate to work with Marie Arana-Ward, editor of this book. Her professional excellence equals her qualities as a warm human being, and I wish to thank her wholeheartedly for her contributions.

My wife Wanda was constant companion to my writing, sharing my life once again as the story unfolded. Together we convey sincere thanks to our American friends who made the effort easier.

The Defection

DECEMBER 19, 1981

I knew when I dialed the U.S. State Department that I would reach my party immediately. There would be no secretaries in at that hour—two-fifteen—on a Saturday afternoon.

"Yes?" A familiar voice. It was Jack Scanlan, Deputy Assistant Secretary for Eastern Europe, and exactly the person I wanted to speak to.

"Jack, it's Romek" . . . I hesitated, then let it spill out all at once. "I'm asking for protection, Jack; I want the president to grant me and my family political asylum."

It was as if a great weight had fallen from me, as if I were suddenly free of the clutches of the Polish secret police, their constant shadowing, their insinuations, their Byzantine parlor games. I would no longer be subjected to Warsaw's coded cables and their deceit and duplicity, their churning out of excuses for the obscenity of martial law. I was liberating myself from that forever. It was as if the shackles were spinning away, receding, diminishing, and all of my past, so tautly woven into People's Poland, was spinning off with them. It had taken me forty years to come to this. But only as I put down the receiver was my decision before me in its naked reality.

I turned to my wife, Wanda, whose eyes were filled with anxiety. "The die is cast," I told her. Like a little girl, she flung her arms around my neck.

My first thought was that there was no more to be done; the long battle was over. Only in the next few minutes did I realize the implications of my presence in the ambassadorial residence. The house was extraterritorial property. I was not on U.S. soil. If I were to stay and set a precedent, who knows what invasions and violations might occur in Warsaw in the name of reciprocity. Wanda's concerns were of a more primal nature: she feared for my life. Violence had become something of an art for the Polish secret police, the SB, as it had always been for their Soviet mentors, the KGB.

We began packing, stopping now and then for a glance out the window. My secretary had just called from the embassy to say that staff members were waiting to see me. Her bold insistence that I come immediately had set me on edge. Why were they so determined to get me there? It was just a matter of time before they put two and two together.

Most important for me was my diplomatic diary with all its secrets. It was in a safe in the bedroom closet. I went there immediately and spun out the combination on the lock. It did not open. I struggled with the dial a number of times, before I realized that I was using the combination from the embassy safe. It was, perhaps, the first sign of my internal agitation.

Fifteen minutes went by. The doorbell rang. Two District policemen stood at the front door. They were there to protect me, they said.

Within half an hour five unmarked black cars slipped into the driveway and turned off their engines. Three men and a woman got out. A tall man with a bushy mustache, obviously the senior, flashed a radiant smile and an FBI badge. I understood that they would stand guard until we were ready, then escort us to an unknown destination. They seemed odd to us, these secret police people—amiable, warm even; not at all like the gruff and sullen megalomaniacs of the Polish SB. The only feature that gave them away was the unnaturally loose fit of their jackets. Taking up sentry positions in the basement, behind the house, and out front, they began a regular patrol, their walkie-talkies crackling.

We ran from room to room continuing to gather our things, our daughter, Misia, and her husband, Andrzej, helping us. From the windows we could see as the sharply lit winter afternoon slid into dusk. In the half-dark, we could make out a line of ten or fifteen police cars rounding our corner, their headlights forming a chain.

Mustache, who had been so affable, was now pressing us to hurry.

His gait became stacatto, his voice insistent. American friends arrived and ended up helping us pack; one, who had come for an appointment, found himself elbow-deep in packing boxes instead. Scrupulously, we separated all that was mine from all that belonged to People's Poland. We did, in fact, leave many things behind, but in a sudden urge to preserve some scrap of memory, I picked up a few things reminiscent of prewar Poland that I had rescued from the ignominy of the embassy basement: a statuette of King Zygmunt III, a small oil painting of Warsaw, and some old pieces of silver with the crowned eagle. Carefully, lovingly, I laid my father's bronze gladiator beside them. He had borne witness to too much of my life to be left behind now.

It was close to eight o'clock when we finally set foot outside. The air had turned cold and raw; the snow that had melted in the afternoon sun was now ice. Headlights on, motors running, the cars had assembled in one continuous string. As we walked to an FBI limousine, we saw that they were all loaded down with telephones and radio equipment, portable sirens and flashing lights. We rolled down the hill. Behind us the stone house was ablaze with an unnatural light. Every window and spotlight shone, and in the rising fumes of many cars' exhaust, the place had the bewitched glow of a storybook palace. As it grew smaller in the distance, I realized we were truly leaving Poland behind. I took Wanda's hand. We were both trembling.

In a caravan—police cars followed by FBI cars followed by police cars—and with top lights whirling, we sped through the city and into the night. It was a trip none of us remembers well, staggered as we were by the long step it represented. I remember only looking back to make sure that the car containing Misia and Andrzej was still with us.

After half an hour or so we stopped in front of a new but unfinished-looking building. Mustache politely directed us to follow him inside, where we were greeted by other FBI people. These temporary quarters were comfortable and we felt secure.

I did not sleep that night, however, despite a great weariness. The harrowing events of my life kept crowding into consciousness, denying me any possibility of rest. And there I was, after all, sitting on the edge of a bed somewhere in a quiet suburb of Washington while in Poland tanks were crashing into the mines, killing workers as they went. But I had broken with the infamy, betrayal, and deceit, and now my protest would be heard around the world. I sat on that unknown bit of American property, feeling for the first time in many, many years, an honest man. I had crossed my last Rubicon.

The next afternoon Wanda and I made our way in another FBI caravan to the State Department, where I was to make my public statement. The cars slipped into the underground garage, through the concrete entrails of that space, directly toward the elevators. I was a veteran diplomat and had crossed the State Department threshold hundreds of times before, but I had never come in this way.

The corridors struck us as empty, desolate; then we entered the press briefing room and saw that that place was bursting with life. About a hundred people sat facing the podium, with television cameras jutting out about them. I saw journalists, U.S. Information Agency people, State Department staff, and foreign press representatives. In the front row, smiling sardonically, was the representative of the Polish press agency; beside him, rather more somber and staring into his lap, was the man from *Trybuna Ludu*, Poland's Party-operated newspaper. What I was about to say to that audience was never to be reported or printed in the pages of that or any official Polish publication.

After a brief introduction, I mounted the podium, drew out my English notes, looked through the glare of lights and down at the metal tangle of microphones, and began at last to speak my heart.

"Ladies and gentlemen, I am the ambassador of Poland to Washington. I am the most senior Polish diplomat and this is my fifth ambassadorial post. I am also for the second time posted in Washington as ambassador. I wish to talk to you about recent events in my country.

"A week ago, a state of war was imposed upon Poland, a state of war against the Polish people. Under the umbrella of the military, specially trained units and security police began an unprecedented reign of terror. Factories were stormed, workers defended themselves. Solidarity members have been arrested in their offices and, at night, at home. All communication lines have been cut to isolate the country and to confuse the world.

"The death penalty has been introduced for not reporting to work. With unique precision, the police undertook all feasible steps to extinguish every ember of freedom, trying to eliminate independent-minded people. The professors from the Academy of Science have been put in prison. The activity of the religious and Catholic organizations has been forbidden.

"The cruel night of darkness and silence has spread over my country. Now, thousands of best sons and daughters of the Polish nation are faced with the ordeals of imprisonment. In prisons, in camps, in the open air, without heating, in freezing temperatures, my brothers, old and young, men and women face brute force and are exposed to enormous sufferings.

"There are even indications that some are being transported to camps in neighboring countries. This carefully orchestrated and directed crackdown is not an internal Polish issue. This is the most flagrant and brutal violation of human rights, which makes a mockery of the Polish signature put under the Final Act of the Helsinki Accords.

"I, ladies and gentlemen, cannot be silent. I cannot have any association, not speaking about representation, with the authorities responsible for this brutality and inhumanity. I decided this the moment I learned that Lech Walesa, the most beloved leader of Solidarity, is under arrest and kept by force.

"This, what I am doing now, is my expression of solidarity with him. I have decided to make this statement, to stand up openly and to say that I will do everything possible to assist the Polish people in their hour of need. I have asked the government of the United States to give shelter and political asylum to me and my family. Both have been granted, and I wish to express my thanks to the president of the United States and to the secretary of state, and to many of my friends in the Administration for allowing us to stay in your country.

"I turn now to you Americans who are listening to me and watching me now. At this very moment, when you sit in front of your TV sets, evil forces crash on Poland and its deeply patriotic and religious people. Think about those Poles, try to imagine their lot when you listen every day to the news. Remember, they are best sons and daughters of my country, those workers, those students, those intellectuals.

"A new chapter of Poland's struggle for independence and human dignity opened a week ago. We will never give up. The only solution to the tragedy is a political solution, by dialogue. Nobody can put in prison thirty-six million people and make them slaves in the very center of Europe. Violence and oppression will only aggravate the situation, and history proves that they are bound finally to collapse.

"The road to peace is the only road. The Catholic church in Poland represents a great moral force, the soul of the Polish nation. Solidarity has close to ten million people. It is natural that through the three-party talks—the church, Solidarity, and the authorities—a real effort should be made to find accommodation and peace. That is, to my mind, the only road to follow.

"Whatever the future will be, don't be silent, Americans. To defend freedom is in your tradition. Show your solidarity, show your support and humanitarian assistance to those who are in such need at this hour.

"I wish to say also good-bye to the many ambassadors and their wives, my colleagues in Washington. Thank you for your understanding. I will not forget your friendship. We—I and my wife—will not forget the warmth many of you have shown to us.

"I wish to thank also wholeheartedly all my American friends for their cooperation. Thank you for your assistance and understanding of my country.

"Let me turn now to the people of Poland. All Poles abroad salute you. We will never stop struggling until Poland be Poland and you are allowed that dignity which should be a part of every human being, so help us God!

"Let me turn now to the Polish-Americans. The Polish people have confidence in your strong bonds with the country of your forefathers. Let everybody know that, in your hearts and minds, you are with the people of Warsaw, of Gdansk, Krakow and Poznan, with the heroic workers of the shipyards and with the brave miners of Silesia.

"Let me turn now to the Polish diplomats in foreign missions outside Poland. Be Polish and true to yourselves. Remember, this is the hour. Do whatever your conscience dictates you do in order to assist our brothers and sisters in Poland.

"There is only one morality in the human family, the morality of people who live according to the principles of truth and justice. It is this morality which shall prevail. Long live Poland!"

Within two days, Wanda and I were in the Oval Office. There, I appealed personally to President Reagan for aid to the Polish people, making a clear distinction between the nation and its rulers. I told him I had made my decision out of love for my country; I had removed myself from a government that was permitting the Soviet Union to use it to crush its own people. In light of that, I suggested an agenda for an American response to martial law. Last among my requests was a simple show of support: that every American home light a candle for Poland, in the name of freedom.

The president listened closely and responded with words of compassion. Tears were in his eyes.

We expected a simple good-bye then, but the president indicated that he himself would show us out. At the front door, he took an umbrella and stepped out into the drizzling rain. I moved to take it, but he wouldn't allow it. He put his free arm around Wanda, I held on to his elbow, and we went across the lawn to the car. As we drove away, we looked through the rear window and saw the U.S. president standing in the rain, waving good-bye.

That evening we continued our journey, traveling a road that led us to a sprawling house nestled in snowy woods. We were now in the hands of the CIA.

It was in that house, deep in the countryside, that we heard Reagan's Christmas message, a speech devoted almost entirely to Poland. We rejoiced. America was with us in our dark hour. Christmas Eve we saw this for ourselves when millions of Americans showed their concern for Poland by lighting the candles I had asked for. They gleamed from windows coast to coast with the coming of night.

But even as Americans showed great support for my protest, the act was beginning to draw a markedly different response from Warsaw. Within a day of my statement, Minister of Foreign Affairs Jozef Czyrek requested that the Polish military take punitive actions against me. A ministry spokesman presented the junta's official position. It arrived at the State Department in English:

"The defection by Spasowski is an act of betraying the interests of the Polish State, deserving universal contempt and condemnation. In November of this year, Spasowski was recalled from the function of Ambassador in Washington as from the end of January 1982 with the intention of retiring him—and he knew this. He took measures to extend his stay. These were not accepted in connection with a critical assessment of the results of his work and his increasingly frequent incompetence, which was made worse by conditions of psychological depression connected with his personal affairs.

"In his propaganda enunciations Romuald Spasowski is trying to slander Poland and to dupe both employees of the Polish foreign service and also Polish and world public opinion. He is posing as a patriotic fighter. As payment for the asylum that has been granted, he is voicing his views which, not by chance, happen to coincide with anti-Polish and antisocialist theses of his American principals. He is doing this for his own egoistic and narrow-minded interests, although he was indebted so much in the past to his former fatherland.

"At present, when it has become clear that there will be no more privileges, he renounced his fatherland for Judas-like silver. This testifies to the fact that this renegade has abandoned all elementary theses of decency. This fact has met with condemnation of employees of the Polish foreign service. This act of betrayal will be assessed by the competent organs of the administration of justice as it deserves."

A Judas and a madman. I could have expected little else.

Not long after, the junta presented two demands to the State Department: that one of their representatives be permitted to meet with me, and that I return the things that I had "stolen" from the residence. The State Department officials had to tread carefully; in a similar situation, if they were told an American had defected from a foreign post, they, too, would want to meet with that person to reassure themselves that he had not been coerced. After some thought, I asked the State Department to respond in the following manner: Yes, I would meet with Warsaw's man, but since I had been a deputy foreign minister, it made sense for me to meet with no one lower than minister, and my meeting with the foreign minister would have to take place in public. To the accusation about the things missing from the residence, I presented the list of five items I had salvaged from the embassy cellar, and asked that in turn the Polish government present a list of all my family's possessions confiscated in Poland. The subject was never raised again.

As the brutalities in Poland raged on under the scourge of General Jaruzelski and his regime, I took to long walks in the snow. I had much to consider. In the evenings I would read the letters that were pouring in, many from people I had never met. Their expressions of friendship and support moved me. One sailor, as a gesture of welcome, sent an American flag.

I wanted to keep my protest alive, to let my voice be heard; I wanted to write. I began what seemed a hundred books—in my head, in endless permutations, on scores of crumpled sheets of paper. Should it be a political essay? An anti-Communist tract? A history of the Polish people? Yet another book concluding that Communism went wrong? These promised mere reflections that related little and convinced less. It is Polish lives that tell Poland's story, the human tragedies that have been played out on Poland's stage for as long as all of us who call ourselves Poles can remember. To relay a sense of that story to the rest of the world I need only describe my own life, I decided. I need only start at the beginning and tell it absolutely as it was.

BOOK ONE

Youth and War

1920–1945

CHAPTER I

My mother used to tell me that when she was in St. Zofia Hospital, on Zelazna Street in Warsaw, awaiting my birth, she could hear distant artillery fire in the night. Those were eventful days. The battle for Warsaw, which would decide Poland's fate, was under way on the other side of the Vistula River. It was August 1920. Sowing panic and plundering the Polish countryside, Russia's Red Army was approaching the Vistula along a wide front. In Bialystok, a city a hundred miles northeast of Warsaw that was already occupied by the Red Army, Bolshevik commissars were waiting to set themselves up as the Polish government and claim Poland for the Soviet Union.

Anyone able to rushed to defend independent Poland—civilians and youths alongside soldiers. With Jozef Pilsudski at the helm, Poland was victorious and halted the Red Army in what became known as "the miracle on the Vistula." The country remained an autonomous state, and the victory saved Europe from Soviet domination.

Because I was an only child, my parents devoted a great deal of time to me. I can still see my mother's slender silhouette in the little out-of-the-way spots in Warsaw's parks where she taught me names of flowers and watched while I looked for colored pebbles in the gravel. I was told that I cried when she would not let me take them home.

I was seven years old when my father decided that I was growing up spoiled. He enrolled me in a boarding school for orphans in

Spala, a little town about fifty miles away, where I spent six months of tearful nights. I came to resent my parents for several years as a result, but my stay in the orphanage did toughen me, and I returned home a changed boy. I had learned independence.

My father's tutelage did not stop with the orphanage, but continued in a painstaking program to educate me to the realities of life. Soon after my return from Spala, he took me off to the Warsaw suburb of Powisle, the city's slums, to a dark and grimy room—the home of an unemployed man and his extended family. It was the gaunt children with vacant eyes that made the most profound impression on me: I had been thrust into the heart of poverty, and I would never forget it. I began taking food packages to the poor. I would beg my parents for money, buy food, and make up the packages myself.

My parents' milieu became my world. I had no playmates my age; my only friend, Piotrus, had gone to live in France. A tall, thin, awkward boy, I was socially old for my years and I preferred adult conversation. My young life thus was filled with the people of Father's intellectual circles. I heard poetry for the first time in the living rooms of the poets Kazimierz Przerwa-Tetmajer and Tadeusz Boy-Zelenski, roamed the world by sitting at the desk of the great polar explorer Antoni Dobrowolski, heard foreign tongues from the lips of the linguist Tytus Benni. Benni was, in fact, my godfather—a Calvinist, as my father had once been. I was baptized in a Calvinist church in Warsaw at the age of ten, but only because a certificate of baptism was required for school. My father was an atheist, and I embraced atheism as fervently as another might have embraced religion.

Father did not keep up relations with my mother's family, which was originally from the Borderlands, Poland's eastern territories. Her family had been landowners in the province of Volhynia, and her parents, Stefan and Emilia Sumowski, of Lityn, were deeply patriotic people of conservative views. They believed that their twenty-year-old daughter Dziunia had encountered a cruel fortune when, while vacationing in Menton, on the French Riviera, in 1912, she met and fell in love with Wladyslaw Spasowski, a married man fifteen years her senior, who espoused revolutionary ideas, subscribed to no religion, and had even broken with his family. Dziunia's infatuation was understandable; Father was a handsome man with bold, romantic aspirations. But it was all too predictable, too, that her traditional Volhynian family rejected a radical philosopher of that stripe. Mother's father, Grandfather Sumowski, detested my father so much that once, when told in jest that Spasowski was approaching the estate, he grabbed his double-barreled shotgun and steamed out to the road to wait for him.

My father's family was from even farther out in the Borderlands, from an area that had been Polish in the eighteenth century. One of thirteen children, he had been born in 1877 on a small estate, Jakubowszczyzna, not far from Vitebsk. After the Russian Revolution, all that remained of that area was memory.

Father had lived a turbulent youth. As a student at the University of Warsaw, he was thrown out for participating in student demonstrations and sent back to Vitebsk. He later attended universities in Wilno and Lwow, and subsequently in Switzerland, at Geneva and Berne, from the last of which he received his doctorate in philosophy and sociology. In Switzerland he came to know many Polish and Russian revolutionaries, including Georgi Plekhanov and Feliks Dzerzhinski.

He owed the opportunity to study and travel to an accident. While in secondary school, he had been shot by a weapon as it was being handed to him on the rifle range. The bullet was not removed, and he was classified as unfit for military service. His brothers had served many years in the army and while he was preparing for his doctorate they were stuck in trenches along the Amur, in Siberia.

Father did not like stories about war and never repeated them. He considered war a barbarity, and military commanders criminals for whom murder was a specialty.

In 1929, for spreading atheistic and left-wing ideas, Father was dismissed from his post as director of a teachers training college and pensioned off. A few years later he published his major work, *The Liberation of Man,* in which he presented his radical views on the world, society, and education. By then he was a decided advocate of materialist philosophy and a recognized intellectual force in Poland. In a copy for me he wrote: "My son, may this book be as beloved a brother to you as it was for me a second child who grew and matured alongside you." I was thirteen at the time.

My parents separated when I was nine, and I became apathetic, introverted, uninclined to study. At first I lived with my mother in

Milanowek, seventeen miles from the capital, where, with money she had inherited from her father, she had bought a house called "Villa Rose." I went to school there, and did poorly right from the start. I didn't like the classroom environment; the buzz of activity grated on me. The tests I was given indicated conflicting abilities: a memory considerably worse than average and a surfeit of imagination.

Marshal Jozef Pilsudski died on May 12, 1935. To us he was the Commandant, the Chief, the Old Man. The news of his death reached my mother and me in Milanowek the following day. I remember the church bell ringing, and a national state of mourning being announced. No one spoke of anything else; we all felt as if something had broken within us, as if hard times were at hand. Those fears were difficult for a boy of fifteen to understand.

I remember, too, that, seeing the large black letters of the newspaper's front-page obituary, my mother covered her eyes with her hands, and stood in silence. I asked if she had known the marshal well.

"Your father and I were often invited to the house of a friend of his. That was right at the beginning, after the war. When the Old Man entered the room, everyone would stop talking and rise to their feet. His greatness was palpable; his very presence had an effect on people.

"Listen, but listen closely," she said, taking the opportunity to teach me some history, "and I'll tell you what I remember from the old days. Maybe then you'll understand what we owe the Chief.

"It was in 1896—I was four years old and living with my parents in Lublin. One fall day I went with my mother to visit a family who lived on the main street. It was an upstairs apartment, and, as usual, I ran out onto the balcony and watched the traffic while the grownups talked in the living room. Suddenly, I heard strange sounds coming from the distance—groans, clatter, and the low thunder of a thousand feet. I turned to look and spotted distant figures moving in time to those hollow, clanging sounds. I watched, staring hard. After a while I could make out people with chains on their hands and feet, long beards on their faces. Haggard and unresisting, they shuffled along in gray sheepskin coats, driven by Cossacks who shouted and whirled about on horses. Behind them came wagons loaded with dark, hunched figures.

"Son, I have never forgotten that sight and the sound of the chains on the cobblestones. That memory is as clear to me as if it had happened yesterday." The muscles in her face quivered, and I felt a lump rise in my throat to see my mother like that.

"They were going," she continued, "into the unknown, to distant Siberia. My mother told me that, when she brought me back into the living room from the balcony. I couldn't be calmed. I was a little girl but had understood that a terrible procession had just passed before my eyes. I remember my mother kneeling, crying, praying into the silent room.

"Romek," Mother said to me more firmly, "Pilsudski was a man who fought for a free Poland. He did more than anyone else to break the chains. There might never have been a free Poland were it not for him. Do you understand now why he is so missed?"

"I do," I whispered soberly.

On the final day of the funeral ceremonies, the marshal's coffin was placed in the cathedral in Krakow's Wawel Castle. Then, for the first time, and over the radio, I heard the largest bell in Poland tolling, the bell called Zygmunt.

A few days later, as always on the weekends, I went to see my father in Warsaw. He, too, had been touched by the marshal's death. "I valued him highly," he said, "until 1920, and then our paths diverged. Pilsudski's Poland is a country of landowners and capitalists. Last year he rounded up the brave people who spoke the truth about that and had them locked up. Those are fascist methods. Things reached such a point that even a man like Joseph Goebbels was being received in Poland." The thought of Adolf Hitler's Germany operating within our borders clearly galled him.

"People in official circles," he continued, "boast about what a wise foreign policy we have, that we have nonaggression pacts with the Soviet Union and Germany. But nonaggression pacts are not mutual-aid agreements. Poland cannot build a future on pacts like those. Moscow has concluded aid agreements with France and Czechoslovakia. We need agreements like that; Poland is standing all alone.

"Look at Germany. They've already introduced universal military service, they're rebuilding their army, and you should know that, no matter what, the Germans will succeed in this because German militarism has a long tradition. The art of killing is a talent with them. I tell you, son, dark clouds are gathering over Poland, and fascism will not spare us. Hitler is not aiming merely to frighten, but to plunder. If things continue like this, there'll be a war in a few years and, as usually happens, one country after another will be drawn in, and millions will lose their lives. Mark my words, the world will run with its own blood and tears."

Sitting across from my father, I concentrated, trying to understand what he was saying to me. He spoke with great confidence, as if these things were all apparent. "The French, English, and others are giving Hitler money for arms; in other words, the capitalists are subsidizing the fascists because they would like to destroy Communism and strangle the Soviet Union. They are not concerned with what Hitler will do with those arms. Their goal is only to destroy Communism! What is obvious to me is that in order to accomplish their aim, Hitler must first conquer Poland."

My father looked at me wearily. "Work hard, son, and study diligently, because nobody knows how much time you'll have for that. One must have an education, and a good one, in order not to be blind."

From everything my father said, it was clear that his faith in the Soviet Union was complete, and his abhorrence of Hitler's Germany immutable. I accepted that faith and that abhorrence as fact. The assumption was to become the basis of my world view and a standard of measure for evaluating the chaotic events that followed.

My father read French newspapers as well as Polish, and often listened to the radio. We had a good radio, a Philips, which could pick up many European stations. During the day we would listen to Warsaw broadcasts and in the evening we would listen to French radio, Paris in particular; on the other hand, my father never attempted to hear German broadcasts, even though he knew the language and I was studying it in school. He considered it a waste of time to listen to the fascists.

Every night at ten o'clock he would switch the dial to long wave in order to pick up Moscow. First there would be the sound of bells, the chimes of the Kremlin, then the clock on the Kremlin tower would slowly toll twelve midnight and the Comintern radio station would report the latest news. My father would listen closely, somctimes making notes on a pad of paper that always lay beside the radio.

I grew used to the sound of those chimes; their low tones conveyed a certain dignity and gravity. I usually kept my father company when he listened to the news, because by the age of fifteen I had begun to understand Russian. He would translate instantly any word I didn't know. I took the news reports solemnly, literally. Sometimes, however, I would argue with my father. The long descriptions of the kolkhozniks' record-breaking farming achievements seemed preposterous. Stalin was always referred to and quoted as if he were an ultimate authority, a deity. Something about that rang false in the Communist context.

In the years that followed, I would frequently, after listening to the news on Radio Moscow, express my comments and reservations to my father. He was pleased to hear them, because they demonstrated, as he put it, that I was thinking and had my own opinions.

One such evening is etched in my memory. Moscow broadcast Stalin himself, speaking with that strange Georgian accent of his. He attacked Hitler personally and called him a "spawn between bull and wild boar." I hated Hitler with all my heart, but that was the kind of expression drunkards in Milanowek hurled at each other—I couldn't understand what it was doing in a speech by Stalin.

My father did not question the validity of my reaction and only attempted to explain Stalin's remark by the different mentality of the "people over there," to whom such statements could speak volumes. I did not accept that explanation, and my doubts about Stalin began to increase in the next few years. Later, I reminded my father of those first unpleasant feelings of mine, that alarm that had gone off in me. The accounts of the purge trials, in which the accused always admitted to having committed crimes and actively participated in the counterrevolution, were to come later. That subject, too, caused us to debate, debates that sometimes took the form of open arguments. Then, too, he attempted to explain the trials and the behavior of the defendants by a mentality that was different from ours. He maintained that "people over there" could admit to crimes they had not committed in order not to impair the authority of the Communist Party and undermine confidence in communism in general. I would not accept that at all and, in the end, my father admitted that such behavior went against the grain of our nature and was, by and large, abnormal. However, he emphasized that I ought to remember that the Soviet Union was under fire from the intrigues and provocations of the capitalist world, which could not reconcile itself to Communist success.

An event occurred at the beginning of 1937 that shook me deeply. One winter evening a few of my father's friends came to our house, and, over tea, there was the usual wide-ranging conversation on events at home and abroad. The main topic was the Soviet Union's new constitution, which had just been adopted. My father contended that this was a great achievement and a giant stride in strengthening Soviet power. Capitalism had been eliminated in the Soviet Union, and socialist ownership of industries established. I remember how hotly he contended that the constitution granted equal rights to all citizens and assured everyone opportunities and freedoms unknown in the capitalist world.

Of course I believed what I heard. Like the others who took part in that meeting, I was swept up by the historic importance of the moment.

Toward the end of the evening, Tadeusz Strzalkowski, who was very active in the Communist Party, gave a report on local matters and said in conclusion, in a subdued voice, that he would like to share some sad news that had been received through Party channels.

"Professor," he said, "your student and our colleague Roma Hirsz has been sentenced to death in one of the trials in Moscow as a Polish spy. No doubt she has already been executed."

I couldn't believe my ears. Roma, a spy?

He continued. "We know that many members of our Party have been put to death, and the trials of others are now in progress. Terrible things are happening, Professor, beyond explanation."

He lowered his head, ran his hand through a thick mane of hair, and fell silent. He was about to say something else, but the words caught in his throat; he only waved his hand. For a long time the room was silent.

"I don't understand this at all," added Izaak Wajsbrot, a mathematician with a large forehead. "Those were splendid people, our *best* people."

My father said nothing. I could feel that he was pained by the news.

That evening I went to my room fairly early. I wanted to digest what I had just heard and think about Roma. Of my father's students, she had been one of my favorite tutors—a woman with a pretty face, the pleasant, almost playful smile of a young girl, large dark gleaming eyes, and smoothly brushed raven black hair. Hers was a wealthy family; her father was a laryngologist, well known in Warsaw.

I could not fall asleep. I could see Roma's face in full detail, as I had years ago when I was writing out my first clumsy sentences. She had sat beside me, her hair almost touching my head as she watched for the crooked letters to appear from under my pencil.

When I heard the sound of the Kremlin chimes in the next room that night, I did not get up to listen. I found myself drawing my quilt up over my ears.

In 1937 I graduated from the school in Milanowek and moved in with my father in order to continue my studies at the Lyceum of Natural Sciences, part of the Warsaw Merchants' Council School. It was a private institution maintained by an association of Warsaw merchants, and was probably one of the best secondary schools in the capital.

I was in entirely new surroundings, in no way reminiscent of the small, quiet school in Milanowek. The young people were primarily Jewish. Of the forty or so boys in my class, three were Catholics, one was Russian Orthodox, and one—me—was a supposed Calvinist.

Once a week I went to a religion class attended by a dozen or so Calvinist boys brought together from all over Warsaw. Pastor Zaunar, who gave the class, knew that I was an atheist and attended only because we were required to receive a grade in religion. But he was a tolerant man and understood that I wanted to learn the history of the Christian church.

My father and I quickly grew closer. He could see that not only did I accept his teachings and want to achieve a deeper knowledge, but also I was, in a way, becoming his partner in his reflections on and evaluation of current events. Noting my interest he set to work to provide me with intensive education in those areas he considered essential and in which school could be of no help. I was to read selected works of Polish literature, as well as Russian and French books aloud, to familiarize myself with their content and to get practice in other languages. Often he would read aloud, and I would listen and note down what I had not understood. Using that method we read Plutarch's *Lives* in French in 1938.

We also read *The History of the Communist Party* in Russian not long after it appeared in the Soviet Union. It was supposed to have been written, my father said, according to Stalin's instructions and in part by Stalin himself. I liked the book for its clarity and logic. For a number of years it was considered the Bolshevik bible in the Soviet Union, but after Stalin's death it was censored, for being based on falsifications.

All the walls of my father's room, which was both bedroom and study, were lined with books, a few thousand in all. The more valuable first editions and the antiquarian publications were kept in a bookcase with a glass front. He called them his most faithful companions.

The books and notes he was working with were always spread across his spacious desk. To one side was a rack with cardboard boxes containing his notes, assembled and arranged according to a system he strictly observed. At first glance the desk might have appeared disorderly, but in fact everything was in its place and carefully organized. My father immediately noticed—and bitterly complained—if any of his books or notes had been moved.

In the middle of his desk was a heavy glass inkwell, which would refract the rays of the sun during the afternoon, making the colors of the rainbow appear in various places in the room. The inkwell's two glass containers were always full and in constant use. When my father finished writing, I would hear the familiar click of the round brass covers sealing the wells tight.

On either side of the inkwell were miniature copies of famous sculptures. On one side was a mortally wounded lion, which, as I recall, commemorated the heroic men of the Swiss Guard who had kept their agreement and died as mercenaries in defense of the King of France; on the other side was the sculpture that most impressed me—a bronze gladiator dying on his shield, his sword already fallen from his hand. Beside the green-shaded brass lamp was a much-loved small, squat silver mug; it was all that remained to my father from his family home at distant Jakubowszczyzna.

In those years my father's views underwent further radicalization. He considered himself an avowed communist by conviction, but never did belong to the Party. His book about the Soviets, *The USSR: The Development of a New Social System,* was published in 1936. I could see that it had been based on official Soviet publications, whose reliability, I later realized, he had accepted without question. It was an apotheosis of the Soviet system. That same year the Polish authorities took it out of circulation for containing Bolshevik propaganda, and further sales were prohibited. He immediately began work on two new books: *The Philosophy of Self-Education*, an up-to-date version of *Principles of Self-Education*, published in 1923, and *Socialist Revolution in Poland*. He finished both books in mid-1939.

His activities, from writing books to contributing to journals, made him one of the leading communist intellectuals in Poland toward the end of the thirties. He was in frequent contact with leftists throughout Poland, and many activists, workers from various parts of the country and students, came to visit him. My father had become something of an institution. He was attacked fiercely by the right-wing press, defended and respected by the left. The Catholic press condemned him as a dangerous, soulless man. I remember that he helped reduce the bail set for communists who were facing long sentences by making good use of his many former students, some of whom held positions of influence.

But his relations with his old friends began to wither or simply to die. Some of them broke with him. He was becoming intolerant, thinking there was no need to listen to the ideas of stupid, narrow-minded people. At times he would react violently, and this disturbed me, even though I understood his motives entirely. One day a young assistant lecturer in economics from Poznan University came to our house, sat in my father's study, and began to contend that there were certain interesting elements in the Nazi program worth knowing about. My father cut him off, rose, and barked at him to leave the house at once.

With some of his friends, things sometimes reached the point of heated altercation. He maintained that only the Soviet Union could defend Poland and Europe from Nazism, that only communism could liberate people from exploitation and prejudice, that dialectical materialism was the only scientific method of investigating all phenomena, and that Lenin's works were the sole valid assessment of contemporary imperialism. For the Poland of that period, those were extreme, bold views, demanding great personal courage.

Naturally, the government viewed his activities with increasing aversion and suspicion. Our home was subjected to constant police surveillance in those years. I was always running into strangers fidgeting in our gateway.

I was with my father one hundred percent. His beliefs, his ideals, were mine. Like him, I hated fascism, and was contemptuous of all that was obscurantist or reactionary. In my view, world events later confirmed the validity of my father's predictions. He continued to listen to Radio Moscow at night, and the chimes of the Kremlin were constantly in my ears. I would sit beside my father and vow silently never to depart from the path he had taken or betray the hopes he had invested in me.

By mid-September of 1938, Warsaw was abuzz with excitement. Events were being hotly debated, and the European situation was becoming increasingly volatile. After occupying Austria in March of that year, the Germans had stepped up their pressure on Czechoslovakia and clamped down on the Sudetenland. Britain's prime minister, Neville Chamberlain, traveled to Berchtesgaden for talks with Hitler, and London and Paris called on Prague to yield in the name of peace in Europe. Czechoslovakia's survival hung in the balance.

It was at this time that the Polish government presented its demand that the city of Cieszyn, which had been divided between Poland and Czechoslovakia in 1920, be reunited and incorporated into Poland.

In the last days of September, at a four-power conference in Munich, Hitler finally compelled the leaders of Great Britain and France to accept his plan to sever the Sudetenland from Czechoslovakia and make it part of the Third Reich. That meant that Germany would be given the border fortifications and that the rest of the country would be at Hitler's mercy. On October 1 German troops entered the Sudetenland. The next day Polish troops crossed the Olza River and occupied Cieszyn.

Feelings ran high among the Polish left. My father thought that Czechoslovakia had been crudely betrayed and thrown into Hitler's maw. He speculated that this might mean the end of independence for Europe's smaller states, and he characterized Poland's role in Czechoslovakia's demise as villainous.

I remember well the preceding events. A mass meeting of youths representing various organizations had collected on Jozef Pilsudski Square, the largest such space in the capital. The demonstrators gathered to demand the return of Cieszyn and the neighboring part of Silesia beyond the Olza. By dusk, an enormous crowd filled the square. People arranged themselves according to their city district or school in columns of many thousands. I stood alongside my own schoolmates.

The dense crowd waited tensely, and as darkness fell over us, torches were lit, dozens, then hundreds and thousands. A band struck up the national anthem, and we all stood at attention. Searchlights glided across the blackness overhead. The speeches began, and the masses responded with applause and cheers. Gradually, the atmosphere became heated, and chanting began: "Si-le-sia, Si-le-sia, Si-le-sia," and "Cie-szyn, Cie-szyn, Cie-szyn."

A spectacle was unfolding: the great square illuminated by thousands of torches, a sea of human heads, a thrilling unity of action, the pulse of human voices chanting in unison. I shuddered. Was what I was hearing any different from chants of mass hysteria? My mood changed suddenly and unequivocally, as if I had been snapped out of a trance. I remembered what I had seen three months before as I sailed into the port of Gdansk on a Polish cruise ship. As we approached the port, I caught sight of banners bearing swastikas. Boys dressed in brown shirts with swastikas on their sleeves drew their hands across their throats with slitting motions. They had shouted with that same level of hysteria.

Now, here in Warsaw, I looked around me. The chanting continued. As the excitement reached a peak, I felt more and more alienated and confused. Even a long talk with my father that night could not dispel my bewilderment.

The authorities had appealed to all Poles to support Poland's right to occupy Cieszyn. All institutions and schools received copies of that appeal. The government required that it be read at school assemblies and that teachers express their support by signing it. I did not go to school that day. The next day began with two hours of physics, and, as usual, we filed into the hall. I took my seat in the third row and waited for our lecturer, Franciszek Zienkowski, to arrive. He was late that day; it had never happened before. After half an hour's delay, he entered the hall with his usual brisk march, but with a distinctly troubled expression on his face. He planted himself firmly in the center of the dais and began to speak. "My dear students, I want you to know why your physics teacher is tardy. This morning Principal Pawel Ordynski summoned all the teachers and, after reading us the appeal about the Cieszyn affair, which you all know about, he asked us to sign it. There was a discussion; various things were brought up. I refused to sign. I don't know what will happen to me. I may have to stop teaching in this school, although I've been here for twenty-five years now. I want to repeat to you what I said to the principal: I am no expert on politics. I am a physicist, a scientist, and a teacher by education. I have never been a politician. I cannot sign something of which I know nothing and understand less. In my opinion each of us is responsible for what we do and for our specific area of knowledge. I am responsible for teaching you."

He stopped, rubbed his close-cropped hair in his characteristic way, with the palm of his hand, and stood before us silently, as if considering whether there was anything else to say. The silence continued for a good while, until it was suddenly broken by a storm of applause. Zienkowski smiled in awkward gratitude and raised his hand. "And now to work," he said, "for we've lost a lot of time with this and we have experiments to do."

On his way to his desk he abruptly turned to face the front rows and addressed our classmate Ludwik Bryskier with a smile: "No doubt you can already see the results before I have even turned anything on!" The room burst into laughter. That was his favorite joke with Bryskier, who had sworn to an amazed Zienkowski that he could see the needle moving on an instrument even before the electricity had been turned on.

Zienkowski liked us as much as we liked him, so his subsequent fate was a particular blow to me. He survived the siege of Warsaw. During the occupation he was a lecturer in physics at a technical school in Warsaw. I worked with him there for a couple of months, repairing equipment.

After the war he was offered the physics chair at Warsaw Polytechnical. That was a distinct honor for the man and his work. I was told that he enjoyed the affection of his students and had great authority with them.

He continued, nevertheless, to be plagued by appeals. The events of his demise were described to me in detail by one of his former students at that school. It happened much later—in 1950. That March the World Peace Congress in Stockholm ratified the so-called Stockholm appeal on the banning of atomic weapons. Everyone in Poland was required to sign it, and the authorities boasted that it had been signed by eighteen million Poles out of a population of twenty-five million.

Professor Zienkowski refused to sign in 1950 for the same reason he had refused to sign anything political in 1938. He did so publicly and just as bravely. However, in 1950 the forces of coercion were more sophisticated. That was the period of Stalinist terror, compared to which the constraints imposed in Poland in 1938 were child's play. A campaign of slander was launched against Zienkowski, and "students" were produced to testify that he was a warmonger. False witnesses recalled that as a teacher he had tried to poison the minds of their colleagues.

Zienkowski had neither the ability nor the desire to defend himself against the slanders. Dismissed from Warsaw Polytechnical and banned from any other institution of learning, he was alone, abandoned. He and his sister, with whom he had always lived, suffered bitter poverty. They both died soon after, I was told, from simple hunger.

On Saturdays in the autumn I always went to school in green army denim for military training drills. We drilled at Bielany, immediately beyond the city limits. After regular school, we took a streetcar with an army lieutenant and were met at the other end by a couple of army sergeants. Rifles were issued, and we exercised strenuously for a couple of hours on the broad meadows and in the thickets alongside the Vistula. We were being prepared for winter camp in the fortress at Modlin.

One day at the end of October 1938, after the exercises were finished, when we had handed in our rifles, and groups of boys had set off toward the streetcar, I stopped for a minute to clean the mud off my uniform. Suddenly I heard shouting and saw a crowd on the other side of the road. Curious, I walked over and, through the arms of the boys in the circle, saw one of my schoolmates staggering from the blows of a husky boy, also in uniform, who was shouting, his voice hoarse: "I'll teach you, you lousy Jew!" He pummeled the boy wildly on the head, in the stomach, on the arms, while his victim made useless efforts to protect his face, which was covered with blood.

I rushed forward, shouldering my way through, and put myself between my schoolmate and the other boy. The bully, older, was a broad-shouldered athlete. Seeing me standing in his way, he howled, "Jew lover, you dare defend that . . ." and a stream of obscenities followed. He began swinging at me, and seconds later we were both going at it. The boys standing around us, students from the bully's class, cheered him on: "Teach him! Give him a lesson he won't forget!" I knew that he was stronger and that my only chance was to attack blindly. Perhaps if I could strike a few well-placed blows, he would be persuaded to stop. But I had never liked fighting, and that predisposition showed: one good punch from him and I was down. I lay with my face in the grass, and then the worst happened. The boy stood over me, enraged, spitting and kicking in a frenzy. When he was through, and my classmates came to help me, I could not get up. They wanted to call an ambulance, but I wouldn't let them; I told them to wait until I could take the piercing pain and drag myself along under my own power.

Finally, I managed to stand. A group of Jewish boys from my class pulled me onto the streetcar, escorted me home, and helped me climb up to the fourth floor. Afraid of my father's reaction, I begged them not to mention the incident, but he was not home. I washed, cleaned my clothes, and went right to bed. When my father came, I told him that I had caught a cold and had the shivers. The pain passed, but my spine had been damaged—for life.

Later that winter I spent almost a month in the Modlin fortress, that forbidding place that had once been occupied by the tsarist army in their effort to keep a tight rein on the Poles. The officers had promised that there we would learn what a real army was all about. There were many exercises and drills in the snow-covered fields, and the schedule was arranged so that we were nearly always running from one place to another. At the start, I attracted the company sergeant's attention, perhaps because he was my opposite—short, stocky, with piercing little eyes and coal black hair that had begun to thin. He gave me a tongue-lashing on the very first day when I tried to move my plank bed away from the blazing-hot stove. Having made a mental note of my, to him, high-handed behavior, he began bearing down on me during field exercises. He pushed snow over my face with his huge boot, shouting that only then would I be well covered and safe from enemy bullets. I bore his abuse patiently and never dreamed that there might come a time when the sergeant's trying instructions would save my life.

On the first Sunday I again drew attention to myself when at roll call I stepped out of line and refused to go to church. I was sent directly to clean latrines and work in the kitchen, while everyone else enjoyed their free time. The same thing happened again on the following Sunday. I gritted my teeth and refused to go to church, as I did every Sunday after that. I returned to my father's home as determined as I had left it.

CHAPTER II

Every day before five in the morning the light would go on in my father's room and, if I was not asleep, I would hear the faint scratch of his pen nib on paper. He used neither a typewriter nor the fountain pens that were then in fashion, but only ordinary pens, an inkwell, and pencils.

On winter mornings at seven o'clock, he would light the stove, throw in a bucket of coal, and then slam the airtight doors shut. We would eat breakfast together, and when I rushed off to be at school by eight, my father would resume his work.

In the years just preceding the war we no longer visited my father's old friends. The people who came to see us were members of either the left wing of the Polish Socialist Party or the Communist Party. Two people stood out among the Communists: the writer Antonina Sokolicz and the historian Stefan Rudnianski. These were idealistic people, with much knowledge and experience. Both, in different ways, touched my father's subsequent fate and my own.

Stefan Rudnianski, fifty years old, was a lecturer in history at the Free University of Warsaw. I did not like reading his essays. To me, it was like parsing sentences. His affiliation with the Communist Party dated back to the twenties. He was a Jew married to a woman of German descent. Gray-haired, bent, an expression of concentration on his face, he always gave the impression of being lost in thought. During the first months of the war, his daughter and I were joined by suffering.

Antonina Sokolicz was a worthy leftist activist. She always used the pseudonym Sokolicz, though her married name was really Merkel. At this time she was close to sixty. She had belonged to the Communist Party since the early twenties and had spent a number of years in prison. She was very active in MOPR, the International Aid Organization for Revolutionaries, and frequently traveled abroad on its behalf, primarily, as I recall, to Canada. She knew English well. She wrote novels and magazine pieces, but was principally known as an orator.

There were, during this time, two women novelists in Poland with decidedly Communist views—Antonina Sokolicz and Wanda Wasilewska. There was something of a professional and personal rivalry between them, and, as I was later to see for myself, their attitudes toward Poland were fundamentally different. During the war Wasilewska left for the East and became an obedient tool of Stalin; Sokolicz never left Warsaw.

My father respected Antonina for the clarity and logic of her ideas. However, as early as 1937, disagreements between them were evident, particularly in discussions of the Moscow trials and subsequent purges. At the beginning of that year a group of Soviet Communists, including Karl Radek, had been put on trial and later, it was reported, executed. Antonina had known Radek and liked him. To her mind, a monstrous crime had been committed.

As the year wore on, the press continually reported new purges, sentences, executions, and told of the terror whose range was growing and whose victims were those least expected. Nothing was known about the fate of a large number of members of the Communist Party of Poland who were in the Soviet Union. They had simply vanished without a trace, "particles of dust in the wind of revolution," as someone had put it.

Antonina and my father were fond of each other, trusted one another, and shared many of the same views. But by the beginning of 1939, they were at absolute loggerheads over Stalin. I remember Antonina shouting, "Forgive me, Professor, but you are blind! You won't accept the facts. Stalin has blood on his hands. You don't see it and, what's worse, you refuse to see it because you *want* to go on believing in him. I'm telling you, Stalin is a criminal."

Gesticulating wildly, she demanded, "Where are they, the people who left to take refuge there? What's happened to those dedicated Polish Communists?" Then came a stream of names and pseudonyms I did not know. Long silences ensued. My father did not interrupt. When she had calmed down, when the gush of her emotions had passed—Antonina had been a stage actress in her youth—she restated the case of Karl Radek. "They can cut me up into little pieces but they can never make me believe that Karl could have betrayed our cause. He was a wise and genuine Communist."

"Antonina, my dear," said my father finally, "I will not defend Stalin, although his line for developing the Soviet Union has proven beneficial. On the other hand, I do maintain that the Soviet Union is in mortal danger today. You yourself know what would happen if it were weak now, *now precisely.* If we are communists then our duty is to defend the Soviet Union, not to level accusations at it. We cannot be hostile to Soviet power, the Soviet Communists, and everything else there. Tomorrow, my dear Antonina, the cannons will be roaring. . . . And it will be the Soviets who will stand eye to eye with the greatest danger, Nazism. They will decide whether or not mankind will be saved. Danger awaits us all, but it is they, the Soviets, who will decide the future.

"The entire capitalist world," he continued, "is waiting for that fight to the death between communists and fascists. . . . Today that capitalist world is finding it useful to hurl accusations at the Soviets. I tell you, Antonina, we shouldn't let ourselves be drawn into that."

Sometimes I was overcome by depression, by sadness, because my father felt obliged to defend the Soviets, to have such boundless confidence in them. I could tell by his face that he was upset, that he might have some doubts that he dared not reveal, even to me, and in my heart I was afraid that he might go so far as to break off relations with Antonina. At moments such as those I would go off to one corner of her apartment, to the desk where she did her writing. I pretended to examine her sleek Canadian typewriter; in fact, I would sit there and worry. If Antonina's dark premonitions proved true, I thought, I would surely lose my faith in my father's vision. And what would happen then?

Toward the end of 1938 I told my father that I wanted to take part in Communist youth meetings. My father's student Strzalkowski promised to help me. A couple of days later a young girl appeared at our door; as soon as she had entered and taken a chair, she pulled out her cigarettes and lighted one. She explained to me that she had been instructed by a comrade to take me into the advanced study group. My father and I agree to have the group meet in our apartment, and a few days later seven young people congregated there.

Called Dora by the others, this girl introduced me only as Romek, a new member of the group. I looked my guests over. The boys were older than I but considerably shorter and with dark black hair; they were Jewish. The girls, with one exception, were short, too, and seemed well developed for their age—they looked like grown women. That day two topics were to be discussed: the first was political—the significance of Luxemburgism; the second, economic—the achievements of the Soviet economy on the threshold of the third five-year plan.

After a few opening remarks by Dora, the discussion began. I was surprised by their knowledge of Rosa Luxemburg's works and Karl Liebknecht's positions, as well as by their evaluation of Lenin and other revolutionaries. They handled facts and ideas with great ease and argued over matters I could not understand. I felt ashamed and decided to keep quiet. Every once in a while there would be a moment of silence, as if they were giving me the opportunity to join in. The room became dim from cigarette smoke and I even began to feel dizzy. The way they clamped their cigarettes between their teeth and talked made me uneasy, disoriented. I had not taken part in such a seemingly worldly group before. I had prepared myself to speak up on the second topic, and I felt somewhat confident, having just finished skimming again through books on the achievements of the first two five-year plans. Unfortunately, the second topic was never opened; they discussed the first to the end of the meeting.

When it was over, Dora asked me why I had not said anything, and smiled indulgently. "Yes, I understand. You have to get used to it—like Judyta. You know Judyta? She just joined our group a couple of days ago. She's still shy, too. But you'll get over that, right?" she said bluntly to a tall girl who stood there looking embarrassed.

"I'm glad not to be the only new one," Judyta murmured.

When the door closed behind them, I went to my father's room.

"Well, how did it go?" he asked with interest.

"I don't like it," I answered frankly. "They're terrible chatterboxes. I think they get more pleasure from simply talking than from exchanging ideas. And why is it they must smoke constantly? Have a look yourself. I couldn't stand it."

My father went into the dining room, which was dense with smoke. We opened the windows a little and went out for a walk. As we were leaving the gateway, I noticed a man ducking into the darkness.

"Look, he's here again," I whispered. "Over there. He ducked into the hallway."

"You're seeing things," said my father.

"I'm *not* seeing things. There's no question, the house is being watched."

The next meeting of the study group was in someone else's house. After Dora's introductory remarks, the discussion on the Soviet economy began. At first I took no part in it; their remarks struck me as entirely too superficial. When the topic seemed exhausted, I launched into a systematic presentation of the achievements and the state of the Soviet economy. My report was detailed, covering the new hydroelectric plants in particular. In conclusion, I spoke about defense, and about the air force. I had based my talk on Professor Stanislaw Nowakowski's study. Speaking with authority, for Nowakowski was a friend of my father and I had learned his book by heart, I knew I was showing them a thing or two. I spoke for nearly an hour and could see that my talk was a surprise.

"Very interesting," Judyta said to me afterward. "How do you know all that?"

I told her about Nowakowski.

"You're lucky to be able to spend time with people like that."

I left feeling satisfied and accepted. I had no way of knowing that it was the last time I would meet with that group.

It must have been in mid-March 1939 when I went with my father to visit Antonina Sokolicz for the last time before the war started. They spoke of the fact that the Comintern had disbanded Poland's Communist Party. As I understood it, the entire affair was shrouded in some sort of mystery; severe accusations of fascist infiltration had been leveled by the Comintern against the Polish Communists, but no one knew exactly why that drastic decision had been made. The members of the Party had found themselves suddenly suspended in a void, abandoned, without support or assistance.

Antonina's spirits were low. After so many trials, sentences, and purges, she was anticipating some action directed against the Party as a whole, but it had not crossed her mind that the Comintern could order the entire Party disbanded in such times.

"This is a situation in which we have to keep together," she argued. "If things happen as you say, Professor, if there's a war, such a catastrophe would find us scattered, divided. We will all perish. What's the point of it, then?"

My father was glum, silent.

"Something's going on, something's happening," she said, "something we don't know about. I feel that. I have, as Ludwik knows," she said, glancing over at her husband, "a sort of Party intuition, which has not failed me yet. When a *provocateur* is in a hall where I am speaking, my instincts tell me there is something wrong. And I have been proved right, not once, not twice, but always. I feel something's wrong now, too, Professor. Something horrible is happening."

I studied my father, Antonina, her husband. So many years of struggling for their great ideals, so many years of study, prison, abuse—and now, near the end of their lives, they were at a loss. I felt sorry for my father, for his face and his large expressive eyes floating in bewilderment beneath his shaggy eyebrows. I felt a rage against those who, unwittingly perhaps, were doing him such injury. I walked to the window and looked out as they talked. The streetlights were on around Wilson Square, and their light fell with a cold gleam on the snow. In the distance I could see outlines of houses, lamps in the windows. A fine snow was falling, swirling white on the pavement. The world seemed peaceful enough.

During the early months of 1939, I used to return from school in a hurry, eat dinner with my father, and set to work with my books. The difficult examination, the *matura*, was approaching, but my thoughts were running in a different direction—toward the unfolding world events that were promising to influence my life profoundly. We had stopped going to the theater and out for walks by then. And so, when my schoolmate Prywer invited me to a pre-exam get-together in mid-May, I happily welcomed the opportunity to socialize. I was confused about Prywer: on the one hand, he was the son of very wealthy parents and had money to squander; on the other hand, he belonged to the Communist Youth Union and was a very active member. He was a smallish boy, even-tempered, outstanding neither in nor out of school.

He lived in a large, luxurious apartment building whose stairway was inlaid with white marble. The entrance to the elevator gleamed with polished brass; the heavy carved doors attested to affluence. When I arrived, a dozen or so boys and girls were already there. They seemed somewhat older than I, and when I remarked on this to Prywer, he told me that they were students in their first year at the university or the polytechnical. He had invited only a few from our school.

"Dora told me," he said with a smile, seeing my surprise, "that you're in her group, and so I thought you'd fit in with us. The conversation will be good." He introduced me, but somehow that conversation never materialized for me and, in the end, I found myself alone and outside the group. I watched with envy the freedom with which the boys spoke to the girls, laughing and joking. I did not know how to banter like that.

In time, Prywer opened the door to the dining room and invited everyone to take a plate and help himself to food. I could not believe my eyes, the table was so beautifully and lavishly laid. There was caviar and salmon, which until then I had seen only in the display window of the exclusive Pakulski Brothers' stores.

The young people took advantage of the opportunity, sweeping everything they could onto their plates. The table began to empty while I stood and considered Prywer. Was it possible to be a Communist and indulge oneself like this, to buy expensive food when there was so much poverty about, and when the Party itself needed money? The Party had, of course, been disbanded, but many of the comrades were living in destitute conditions, and beggars were to be seen on the streets of Warsaw.

Thinking those thoughts, I stood apart from the hubbub. Someone pulled at my sleeve, and I looked around to find Judyta beside me. We shook hands.

"I'm so glad you're here. I really hurried; our class ran long today," she said.

Looking at her I could not believe that she was the same girl. Her long chestnut hair fell loose to her shoulders and back.

"I wouldn't have recognized you, Judyta. You look so different."

"Really?"

"Yes. Today you're somehow . . . different."

"You like me?"

"Yes," I said, feeling awkward at the turn our exchange had taken.

"Is it true that you defended a Jewish classmate in a street fight?"

"Yes, it's true, and then I got it good."

"Do you regret doing it?"

"Not at all. I did what I should have."

Judyta looked at me inquisitively with her large eyes. She could feel my discomfort in that place. We stood side by side eating fruit and talking. She told me about the anxiety among her fellow medical students. A war seemed inevitable. Like me, she was incapable of making small talk.

"What do you think will happen to us?" she asked. "You have a wise father; you must know. Do you know in Berlin *they're murdering Jews in the streets?* And when the Nazis get to Poland, what do you suppose will happen to us here—to the Jews I mean? I can talk about this with you. . . . You'll understand me." She did not wait for a response. "Nobody can give me a straight answer. They either shrug their shoulders and say things will be very bad, but they don't know in what way, or they say that things won't be all that bad because Poland is a large country with lots of Jews, or they say they have no idea at all. Tell me what you really feel."

She waited, looking for the answer in my eyes. I said nothing for a long time. I was collecting my thoughts, but her gaze intimidated me. I lowered my eyes. Never before had a girl looked at me like that, with large, beautiful eyes that were warm and sad at the same time. Perhaps, I thought, I should say that things won't be so bad after all, that we will manage. It would be the opposite of what I felt.

"It's going to be bad, very bad," I said to her. "Hitler has occupied Bohemia and Moravia, but he isn't satisfied; he's got us covered in the south. Now he's demanding Gdansk. Mussolini has occupied Albania. It looks like Poland is next. Think what they did in Spain, Judyta. Two months ago, they took Barcelona and crushed its antifascist forces. That was fascism's testing ground—Mussolini with his expeditionary corps, Hitler with his Condor Legion."

I named rivers and cities that had been destroyed by Italians and those bombed by German pilots. I knew that war well because I had followed the movement of the front on a detailed physical map of the Iberian Peninsula.

Judyta listened. "How can you remember all that?" she asked when I was finished.

"You know why? Because the war in Spain is a prelude, a preface, to the rest of it here in Europe," I responded, quoting a line I had heard often from my father. "We'd do well to be prepared."

A boy sitting to one side and listening to my argument joined in, his voice confident. "Things won't be so bad here; don't exaggerate. There have been talks. Our foreign minister, Beck, has been in Berchtesgaden, and their foreign minister, Ribbentrop, has been in Warsaw. We're not the Czechs, you know."

We said nothing. The boy walked off. A moment later phonograph music came from the next room. Judyta was staring out the dark window into the night. She seemed solemn, pale, beautiful. My eyes feasted on her. Apparently she felt my gaze, because she raised her head, and we looked deep into each other's eyes. We continued gazing like that in silence, neither one relenting, neither one willing to end that communion. It seemed to me that I could read gratitude in her eyes for saying what I thought, but there was a heavy sadness there, too.

The music started again. Judyta whispered, "Will you dance with me?"

"I don't know how," I replied.

"What do you mean?" she said, thinking I was teasing her.

"I really don't. I've never danced before. People like me—" I broke off, searching for words—"shouldn't be dancing in times like these. There's no place in my life for dancing."

"I can't believe it. . . . You go to parties where there are girls and you don't dance?"

"No, I never go to parties. This is my first. And you're . . ." I didn't finish the sentence.

"In that case, grant my request," she said, and took me by the hand. We began to do something like dancing. I dragged my feet around clumsily and felt ridiculous. Fortunately, the record was soon over, and we went back into the next room. I glanced at my watch; it was nearly ten.

"It's time for me to leave," I said.

Judyta looked reproachfully at me. "Walk me home. Then we

can be together a little while longer." I helped her on with her coat, a well-worn light coat. She wound her scarf around her neck and put on her beret. "Let's go!" We ran down the stairs. It was cold outside, drizzling, and very few people were on the street.

"Romek," she said when we were on the street, "take me by the arm."

I felt her press my arm against her body. Neither of us spoke.

We walked for quite a while in silence. Tall streetlights shone on the wide street.

"I know much more about you than you know about me," she said. "I know you're the son of the famous Professor Spasowski, I know where you live, I've even been to your apartment. I know that you're smart, that you're a communist. I know that you're not an anti-Semite, that you defend Jews. . . . And I also know that you don't dance or date."

"And all I know about you is that you're very pretty and much too sad."

Judyta burst out laughing. "It's true I'm sad. I'm a Jew. My parents were poor Jews. Neither is alive now. My father died a year ago. . . . He was a tailor. He spent his whole life cutting and sewing. As far back as I can remember, he was bent over his sewing machine, with his yarmulke on his head. He was very religious, and only went out on Saturdays to go to temple. He spent all his time in the basement where we lived. Mama helped my father in his work, but she died before he did, when I was twelve. I had no brothers or sisters. I lived alone with my father and took care of him, as my mother had. As soon as I started going to school, I wanted to be a doctor. I was good in school, even very good. My father didn't have to pay my tuition—that's why I was able to go. We couldn't afford it. I did well on my *matura* and last year I was accepted in medical school.

"After my father died," she continued, "I had to give up those two rooms in the basement, but the landlord, a good man who had known my father for thirty years, rented me a private room on the fourth floor very cheaply. I live there with my cousin. She's a seamstress and a little older than I am."

Judyta broke off. It was still drizzling.

"Aren't you drenched?" I asked.

"No, and even if I were, it wouldn't matter," she said, her eyes gleaming.

"Let's make a date," I said all at once. "I take my *matura* around the twentieth of May."

"I have classes and exams, too. Maybe right after your *matura,* toward the end of May."

"Fine. It'll have to be before June, because I'm going to a work camp."

"And not in July or August, because I'm supposed to go with a student group to a camp in Poronin."

"Well, then, let's say May 25 at four o'clock."

We were already in her neighborhood. Even at this hour of the night, the place was noisy. Polish and Yiddish could be heard everywhere. Lights were on in basements, a sign that life was teeming down there, too. Judyta pointed out a narrow set of stairs leading belowground.

"That's how we used to live when my parents were alive. I'll show you where. There's a family there now, with four or five children."

We turned a corner and Judyta came to a stop on Gesia Street.

"It's here. That gateway," she said, pointing. "That was my home." We walked up to the narrow stairs that led below the ground. "They must be asleep already, since there's no light on."

"How many years did you live here?"

"Practically my whole life, twenty years."

I thought about our fourth-floor apartment with its balcony on Noakowski Street, about Villa Rose, about Lityn. I stood there in silence and, without thinking, took Judyta's hand.

"You're not put off by all this?" she asked.

"I am a communist. You must know how I feel about the poor and the exploited."

"And I know I can be completely sincere with you. Come. I want to make sure you know where I live," she said. "There are lots of doors in my hallway."

The wooden stairs, worn and in disrepair, were dark, lit only at each floor by a pale gleam from the hallway. Dirt covered the walls, and hobbled furniture lay in corners.

"You see how dark and shabby it is here," whispered Judyta. "The stairs, the walls—not like Prywer's. It doesn't repel you?"

"Don't worry about it," I answered firmly.

We went down a long, narrow corridor lit by a weak bulb hanging from the ceiling by a wire.

"Here it is," she said, "number seven. Will you remember?"

She walked to the door and knocked. A woman's voice answered in Yiddish; they exchanged a few words, and the door opened, releasing a swath of light.

"Come in, please, Romek. You can see our place; my cousin's not asleep yet. Come in. I'm not ashamed of how I live."

I went in. There were two iron beds against the wall in the small room and a table between them by the window. On one side was a bookshelf, a sewing machine, two chairs, and on the other a small cupboard. Nothing more. In Yiddish, Judyta was explaining me to her cousin, who seemed startled by my presence.

"Judyta," I interrupted, "I must go."

She nodded and saw me to the hallway, where we faced one another.

"Can I kiss you?" I asked.

She drew closer. I trembled, feeling her hands slip into mine. Just at that moment the door across the hall opened wide and illuminated us in the harsh light of a powerful lamp. People appeared in the doorway and disappeared down the hall.

I kissed Judyta on the forehead and moved toward the stairs. "Don't forget, May 25, four o'clock."

I thought of her as I walked home in the rain. Her worries, her poverty, her feelings about me.

When I arrived, my father opened the door looking worried. "Why are you so late?" he asked. "You're drenched."

"I'm sorry. The party went on until ten. I met a girl there and walked her home. It was a long way."

He looked surprised. "That's the first I hear of any girl."

"There haven't been any before."

"What do you know about her?"

"Just about everything," I said confidently.

I passed the *matura* without any trouble, though it was a difficult written and oral examination. Shortly after, I went to the university and enrolled in the department of mathematics and natural sciences, where I expected to begin my study of experimental physics. Some of the scientists there were acquaintances of my father.

When May 25 came I impatiently made my way to Judyta's. At four o'clock sharp I was in front of her building on Gesia Street. I ran breathlessly up to the fourth floor. Her cousin opened the door and handed me a letter. Judyta explained that she had to go on a two-week training course for wartime medical personnel. She assured me that she thought of me constantly and longed to see me again.

"But I'm off to camp myself in ten days—we'll miss each other!"

"Judyta *had* to go," said her cousin. "Everyone knows she's Jewish; if she had said no, they would have given her trouble."

I wrote Judyta a note saying I would not be in Warsaw when she returned, but that I would come as soon as I could, and that I would not stop thinking about her. I walked down the stairs sadly.

Within days I received a note to report for work service on June 10 at Central Station in Warsaw. Along with hundreds of other recruits who had just passed the *matura,* I traveled west toward Poznan on a special train. My threadbare knapsack was nearly empty, since we were to receive complete uniforms at the camp. My fellow recruits were all strangers, because the schools had been mixed together.

One of the boys had a large suitcase and made bets with everyone about what was in it. To the person who could guess what it was, he promised the entire contents. But the person who guessed wrong would get nothing, and that person would have to give half of his food to him. He made the same bet with everyone, including me. I was not risking much; I had about a dozen little sardine and sausage sandwiches my father had made for me.

The suitcase was finally opened. It contained a smaller, very dilapidated suitcase with a missing handle, which in turn contained a small and tattered canvas bag. Inside the bag was a cardboard box, and a smaller one inside that, and so on and so on. From the smallest box of all, the boy withdrew a small walnut; he pulled a penknife from his pocket, split the shell open, and ate it.

"An appetizer," he said, smacking his lips. "I love those little walnuts." Then he put out his hand. "Well, now give me what you owe me. I'll take the best of it, because I'm feeling hungry."

Spirits were high now.

"And while I'm eating," he continued, "I'll guess who fixed you your snack. No charge for that."

Eating half my sardine sandwiches, he remarked, "Mothers usually make such nice little sandwiches . . . but these must have been made by your father, because mothers almost always make them with egg. Fathers just take the fish out of the can and that's it."

We laughed, and amid jokes, to the monotonous clack of the wheels, the time passed. I could not tear my thoughts away from my father, from Judyta, and from the events that seemed to be dragging us inexorably into war. But the rhythm of the wheels soon hypnotized me, and my thoughts grew entangled and complex. What was the meaning of the German-Italian Pact of Steel? Why had the Communists been crushed in Spain? We Polish Communists were standing fast against fascism, but why had the Soviets had our Party disbanded? I fell asleep.

The stopping of the train woke me. We had pulled into the little town of Pyzdry, on the Warta River. On broad fields not far from town we found a large camp, where over a thousand boys gathered in clusters of army tents. I had been assigned to the thirteenth company, fourth battalion.

We got up at sunrise and worked nearly all day building ramparts of earth and stone along the river. On scorching days the work was exhausting and the wheelbarrows heavy. To quench our thirst we drank warm water flavored with mint. It was not long before the blisters on our hands turned into bloody scabs from the sand ground into them. When, at times, I felt pain in the small of my back, I had to explain what the problem was and I was given a day off. Some were unable to withstand such intense work, others suffered sunstroke. As a rule, the physical labor ended at four o'clock in the afternoon, but military exercises would begin immediately thereafter. Having no rifles, we carried shovels.

On Sunday the company went to church. Just as in Modlin, I spoke up at roll call and went to my tent. The duty officer soon came for me and led me to the kitchen to peel potatoes. This happened again every Sunday, as it had in Modlin, but here I did not clean latrines, because the facilities were out in the open air. I was always alone—no one else refused to go to church. The educational instructor eventually asked me why I refused to go.

"Because I'm not a believer," I answered.

"Oh, I see," he said. "How long has that been?"

"Right from the start."

"Well, but you must have been born into some religion."

"Yes. Calvinist."

"That's like Luther?"

"No, like Calvin."

"Aha."

He left me alone, but I could see that he did not like it one bit. And he often stared at me, although with no ill will. It occurred to me that he was checking to see if I had horns on my head.

There were two categories of recruits in camp: those who had passed the *matura* and country boys with little or no schooling. The mixed camps, which I believe were first introduced in Poland in 1939, were meant to break down class barriers. I liked that idea very much.

Our tent was half and half. The boy next to me, Antek, was a peasant from a village near Kutno. Almost a head shorter than I, he was stocky, powerfully built, and had hair as fair as flax. The first few days we just made small talk. I could see that he was being cautious. I tried in vain to engage him in conversation, but he had no interest in or feeling for any of the subjects I introduced. One day I told him that I was building a radio. His eyes lit up.

"I have a crystal set, too," he said proudly, "and I can pick up all sorts of stations, although some are weak and can barely be heard. I'd love to have a set with tubes."

I told him about my set, which was still not finished. That broke the ice, and it turned out that he was an avid ham and knew a great deal, but had no basic knowledge of electricity. From then on we never had enough time for the things we wanted to discuss. I was happy to share what I knew. I drew diagrams of simple tube receivers, and he absorbed my knowledge with passion. We became fast friends, and when camp was over we promised each other that we would keep in touch. The war never gave us that opportunity.

From camp I wrote my father a letter that is still among my papers:

> I have noticed that my feelings for you are very different from what others think and say about their parents. In you I see a spiritual teacher, one who deals with the great questions of life. Sometimes, when all are asleep, I imagine a boundless expanse strewn with heavenly bodies and one long trail of light, illuminating the darkness as a lighthouse lights the dark of night. That light is the sublime thought of mankind, the thought of Democritus, of Aristarchus of Samos, Giordano Bruno and many, many

> others who broke two sets of chains: the inertia of common uninspired thought and the social barriers that prevent us from seeing the true laws of nature. . . .
>
> You, my father, are one of those people capable of understanding a hundred times more than the rest of us . . . and I am infinitely grateful to you for teaching me to see glimmers of that light and understand a little. The rest depends on me. . . . If darkness overcomes me then I will fall into the ranks of those who block the light and continue the inertia.

I longed for solitude during that time. Few people around me seemed to understand that a storm was coming. I was irritated when the boys would shout, "We'll show those Huns!" or "Till we meet again in Berlin, brothers!" These met with applause and general merriment, but such remarks utterly depressed me. Those near me would ask me why I was so glum. How could I explain the port of Gdansk, the long red banners with the swastikas and the Hitler Youth skimming their fingers across their throats? They don't understand a thing, I told myself.

I was very critical of those young people. I thought the majority of them stupid, naive, and frivolous. Now, with hindsight, I know that it was a unique group, the first generation to grow up in a free Poland.

On my return to Warsaw, I went to see Judyta immediately. There was another letter for me. She wrote that she was having a good rest, but was worrying about the future more and more, and that she missed me. It was a pleasure to read those warm words; words I'd never known from a girl before.

In the fall I was to go to the military college. I went to live with my mother and her second husband, Tadeusz Drynski, in Milanowek until then, but at the end of August I made a special trip into Warsaw to see if Judyta might have returned earlier than expected. Her door was locked tight.

I decided to dedicate the last days of August to assembling the radio I had been working on and to finish the telescope I had not had time to complete during the last two years. I spent whole days in my workshop, grinding, drilling, assembling, soldering, and fitting the parts together. Finally, on August 31, the telescope was ready. The weather was beautiful, the night starry and warm. I pointed the lens up at the sky and saw the moon's uneven, crater-pocked surface and the boundless space dotted with stars. I had a feeling that space was drawing me into it, that I was slowly losing touch with everything around me. So that is how infinity affects a person, I marveled.

A locomotive's whistle and a train's brakes grinding to a halt snapped me out of my reverie. Having lived for so long near the railroad station, I was used to trains coming and going; I hardly heard them. But this time I listened, and heard the locomotive's puffing, the babble of voices, the neighing of horses. A military transport—they seemed to be common day and night. Would there really be a war? I strained my ears, and caught the sound of someone playing a harmonica. I knew the melody from somewhere. . . . Yes, a wistful Borderlands tune. It was being played beautifully. Suddenly the train started up, steam hissed noisily, and the wheels began turning with their measured clack. Slowly, the sounds grew dimmer. One last belch of steam and all was quiet again.

CHAPTER III

On the morning of September 1, my mother woke me, her voice different. "Romek, get up. It's war, war—do you hear me? The Germans are attacking. I've heard it on the radio. Oh, my God! What will happen? What will become of us? War again!"

I jumped to my feet and ran into the dining room. Tadeusz was sitting motionless in front of the radio. Through the door I could see a bureau open in their bedroom and things strewn about. Tadeusz's officer's coat was hanging on a chair and, beside it, his freshly pressed pants. So we were finally at war.

I did not have to wait long to be convinced of that. Before noon the first bombs were dropped near the Witaczek silk factory, the only industrial enterprise in Milanowek. Loud explosions shook the little town. The crater-furrowed ground attested to the war's having begun in earnest. For the first time I saw the death-dealing airplanes, silver points moving like so many little toys against the background of blue sky.

That day Tadeusz handed his new BSA motorcycle over to the community office and prepared himself for war. He put on his uniform and packed his things. Through our tears, we said farewell and wondered whether we would meet again. My mother and I accompanied him to the wicket. He walked away with a swift and resolute step, a small suitcase in one hand.

I decided to finish the air-raid shelter I had been making in the garden. My time here is limited, I thought, but when I go off to fight, Mama will have shelter at least. It was a deep ditch among some pine trees, made secure with planks, tar paper, and sod.

News from Warsaw was not good. The city had been bombed, people had been killed or wounded. My thoughts ran constantly to my father; I was afraid for him. And what of Judyta?

Early on the morning of September 3, I took my bicycle and headed for Warsaw. There were no trains. The tracks had been damaged, and Central Station had been shut.

My mother took my leaving hard, since she knew that in Warsaw I would immediately report to the army. I assured her that I would think of her always and begged her not to worry: I was strong and healthy, had had military training, and would manage. Between her kisses and her tears she asked me to take care of myself—implored me to—looking at me with her large, tearful, loving eyes. As I rode away, she stood by the porch and made the sign of the cross. I loved my mother very much, but, as a convinced atheist, I was indifferent to the gesture. The image was to return to me many times, however, always indissolubly bound with the figure of my mother on that September morning.

Milanowek is seventeen miles from Central Station in Warsaw as the crow flies, that is, following the railroad track, which was the route I attempted. When passing through the town of Pruszkow, I saw burned-out houses and bomb craters. By the time I reached Warsaw's suburbs, I could feel the frenzy. Sirens were howling, and the air-raid alarm had just begun again. But I kept on, and was close to our street when the ground trembled from explosions. I quickly turned into a side street and headed toward a shelter in a building called The Roma, which housed various Catholic institutions. Then came the reverberations from bombs. I thought with fear of my father, not far away.

When the all clear sounded, I rode home in a hurry. My father was in the apartment and greeted me with joy, pressing me hard against his chest. He had been as afraid for me as I for him. But a profound sadness had invaded his handsome face, and when we sat down on the couch, I was struck by the look in his eyes.

"It's started." He sighed. "Now nothing can stop this mad course of events—death, suffering, ruin." He paused. "The Soviet Union signed a nonaggression pact with Hitler's Germany. Do you know that?" It was a question for which he expected no answer; he fell silent, only shook his head. Then, with a pained voice, he went on. "They had to, perhaps, but for Poland it can mean only a death sentence."

Soon there was another air raid, but my father did not want to go down to the shelter. We stayed in the apartment listening to communiqués on the radio, following the war, as much as possible, on a large map of Poland spread out on the dining-room table. This reminded me of the times when a large map of Spain had been spread out on that same table and I had measured the distances between Madrid and the front line. How dispassionate I had been then!

In the early afternoon, the broadcasting of communiqués was cut off, and, after a minute of silence, a voice full of emotion reported the latest news: At eleven o'clock London time the British ultimatum to Hitler regarding Poland expired, and Great Britain was at war with Germany. My father and I embraced in tears. Poland was not alone.

"And so, my son," he said, taking my hand, "on to another world war." He lowered his head. "England is far away, after all, and not prepared for war. It is France's reaction that will be most important."

Within hours we had that reaction. The radio reported that France, too, was at war with Germany. That had a great effect on my father, who had a high opinion of that country, its people, and its culture. I had often heard him speak with feeling about the heroism and suffering of the French during World War I. We talked long into the night.

"Poland will be defeated by the Germans," he said. "We have no chance against the German war machine. England and France cannot possibly render us aid quickly enough. The dark night of Hitler's rule is descending over Poland. . . . All the hopes I pinned on the Soviet Union are dashed." He was mumbling now.

Late that evening we tuned in to Radio Moscow, and heard those familiar Kremlin chimes tolling out midnight. Hardly a word was said about the war. The news reported on record-breaking production by kolkhozniks in distant corners of various Soviet republics. Locales and villages were mentioned, Russian and Asiatic names; statistics and percentages were given. How is this possible? I thought, fuming. Hitler is bombing Poland; people are dying. How can they not care?

I woke at dawn the next morning with a firm resolve to make my way to Judyta. Despite the hour, the streets were full of people. They stood around the newspaper kiosks passionately discussing the declarations of England and France. Despite everything, spirits were high. People laughed and wished each other luck. An older woman who, like me, was waiting at the streetcar stop, wiped her tears away with a handkerchief. "Young man," she said, undaunted by the fact that I was a stranger, "I was so afraid that we would be alone. I've already gone through so much in my lifetime, and now, such happiness, think of it . . . they're with us. May God bless you . . . we're all going through these hard times together."

It was noisy on Gesia Street; the whole population of that part of Warsaw seemed to be outdoors. I squeezed my way through the throngs of people talking and gesturing animatedly—people who, it seemed, were arguing, although their tongue was strange to me. Most were men wearing yarmulkes or black hats. Only up close was I able to tell by their expressions and their laughing eyes that they, too, were as pleased with the new turn of events as everyone else.

I recognized her building from a distance, the worst-looking one in the row of tenements. I ran up the stairs, listened for a moment at the door, and knocked—once, twice. Nobody answered. I tried the door; it was locked. When I checked with one of her neighbors, an older woman, I was told that there had not been a sound out of her apartment for a week.

Seeing my sadness on my return, my father asked, "What, she hasn't come back?"

"No. The apartment's locked tight, nobody's there, her neighbors don't know anything."

"Yes," he said, "that's how war is." He put his arm over my shoulder. "Take care, son. There are hard times ahead. You must be rugged, tough—otherwise you'll go under."

The map was on the table. Clearly my father had been attempting to determine the movement of the front line.

"I don't understand any of this," he said, gesturing toward the map. "The communiqués report where the battles are, but they seem to be all helter-skelter. Dammit, could Hitler really have already reached Czestochowa?"

In the course of the day we listened to the radio nonstop, and I plotted on the map the places where battles were being fought. I had done the same with the map of Spain, but there the front line had been apparent. Now it was impossible to form a clear picture; perhaps, I thought, the communiqués are purposely giving imprecise information.

My father drew another conclusion. "The Germans," he said, "have a great deal of modern motorized equipment. I'm afraid that between their air force and their tanks, they are breaking through our defenses and driving deep into the country."

That evening we walked over to see our old friends the Falskis. There were quite a few people there; the house was noisy with conversation. Marian Falski—a prominent educationalist, author of Poland's best-known reader, and an adviser for the League of Nations—was an optimist and said that we would not be beaten easily. His wife, Regina, thought just the opposite: that, in spite of England and France, Poland's situation was hopeless. Someone else argued that he knew France well, that the Maginot Line represented the highest achievement of military technology, and that, safely protected by it, the French would be able to prepare to strike at Germany. "We only have to hang on for two, maybe three weeks—no more than that—and then you'll see," he said in a convincing voice, clearly another optimist.

Taking me by the arm, when we left the Falskis, my father said: "A pack of fools. Regina's the only one in the whole bunch with any common sense."

The next day, in the late afternoon, we were visited by Strzalkowski and, immediately after him, by Wladek Czekalski, my father's disciple and a favorite of mine. Both had news, from independent sources, that in many places German tanks had penetrated deeply. We pored over the map. The radio kept reporting that the fighting was becoming more intense. Czekalski, who at that time was working at an automobile factory producing Fiats, told us that from their service stations he had learned that a German armored column was advancing on Warsaw; it had already taken Czestochowa. Battles would probably flare up on the road to Warsaw, but the enemy would be at the outskirts of the city in a couple of days. Strzalkowski had tried to join the army, but he simply had been unable to find anyone to talk to.

We pondered the Nazi-Soviet nonaggression pact. My father argued that the Soviets probably could not have done anything else. They could not allow themselves to be drawn into the war, and had to ensure the safety of their borders. That seemed logical to me, but I could not reconcile myself to the thought that such a great government, a champion of the common man, had signed any sort of agreement whatsoever with a bandit like Hitler.

My father thought the situation so serious that he recommended that Tadeusz, Wladek, and I make decisions of vital importance before it was too late. "When the Germans begin approaching Warsaw," he said, "I advise you to go east and do everything you can to avoid falling into Hitler's hands.

"If you stay here, things will end badly for you, sooner or later. I'm too old now; I'm sixty-two and I don't have the strength to go wandering about. I'll wait for my end here in this apartment, but you who are young must save yourselves. And you should take your families with you. I doubt that our army will be able to offer resistance for very long; those Nazis have too great an advantage."

With heavy hearts we bade each other farewell. I never saw Strzalkowski again. Wladek Czekalski I met later, completely by chance.

September 6 seemed to fulfill my father's prophecy. From the broadcasts we learned that our troops were offering desperate resistance, but there was no stopping the Nazis. We visited the Falskis, if only to find out what we could do. But there, too, depression reigned. Falski looked bad; he was pale and apathetic, a changed man. When we returned home, I sat down on my bed and glanced through the books that so recently had been vital to me. My entire education, my love of astronomy, physics, geology, all seemed to evaporate, slip into oblivion, become unnecessary. I took my knapsack from my wardrobe and packed a couple of the books I loved most. But it's ridiculous to set off for war with books, I thought, and put them back on the shelf. I then set out the things that seemed most necessary: a slide rule, a compass, a large scout knife, a detailed map of Poland, a canteen, some camping utensils, a thick wool sweater, some underwear, and thick wool socks. I'll cut through to the east, I decided, and, if necessary, cross the border of the Soviet Union and volunteer for the Red Army. If fortune chose to smile on me, I would, in the end, plant a red banner in Berlin. And if fortune did not, then I would end up in some ditch, and that would be the end. But I was confident; fortune could not possibly disappoint me.

Those and other thoughts were interrupted by the doorbell. I heard my father open the door and invite someone into his study. It was our upstairs neighbors, the Szirmers. Their son, Robert, was two years younger than I, and although I knew him only slightly, I was sure we had similar interests. Every now and then in the evening I would see light in the courtyard and know that he was experimenting with his arc lamp.

"Professor," Szirmer began, "excuse us, but it's the times, you see. Please, sir, you are an educated man; tell us what we can expect." It had been Judyta's question.

My father did not lie to them. He set forth his predictions, harsh as they were, but promised to assist them in any way he could. They left, even more depressed.

The door had barely shut behind them when the bell rang again. I opened the door to some men in streetcar uniforms asking to speak with the Professor.

"We have just received bad news," said a burly, broad-shouldered man. "The Germans are approaching the city. Our people are preparing a defense at Ochota. They're building barricades out of whatever they can find. We have a lot of antitank guns, and civilians are helping the army. Professor, we're leftists, from the Socialist Party, as you know. We know your books and respect you. What should we do?"

"You must decide for yourselves," said my father. "There are two choices, both very difficult and dangerous, as is everything now. Either remain in Warsaw and join in defending the city, or, if you are young, leave for the east and don't let yourself be taken prisoner by the Germans." My father gestured to me. "The latter is what I would prefer for my own son."

That evening as we listened to the radio, Jozef, the janitor, rang us. All young people were to go that evening to Union of Lublin Square, he said. An important announcement would be made.

We left the house at ten o'clock. The streets were full of people streaming down the sidewalks and the roadway. It was pitch dark, and the houses seemed deserted. Dense crowds covered the square and the neighboring streets. With my eyes now accustomed to the dark, I began to see young people mostly, although older people and even women with children were milling about, everyone in a state of excitement and anticipation. Soon, an amplified metallic voice broke the hum of a thousand voices, and the crowd grew quiet. All Warsaw's able-bodied young men were called upon to join the army in Praga, on the Vistula's right bank, where they would receive further instructions. Warsaw would be defended at all costs. "The Polish soldier," the mechanical voice resounded, "is defending his fatherland heroically. He is fighting back bravely and exacting heavy tolls from the enemy. Long live Poland!"

The crowd did not disperse. People remained to talk, their voices hushed; and, like a desolate wail, from the entrails of some apartment building came the hysterical sobs of a woman. We returned home in silence. I had never seen Warsaw like this. The doorways and windows were as dark as eye sockets in a skull. Figures appeared and disappeared in the darkness like phantoms. A strong whiff of terror stalked the night.

Once home I glanced at my father, and saw his eyes sad and sunken, his face set. He was not crying, but he squeezed my hand hard, and I could feel the muscles in the palm of his hand.

"The hour has come," he said in a soft voice. "You have no reason to wait here now. You must fight for your freedom. If Poland loses to Hitler, cross the Soviet border; you will be accepted there as a worker in that great land. I ask few things of you: be intelligent and always act on principle; believe in communism, believe in your father, believe that the communists will triumph in the end."

We threw ourselves into each other's arms. I held my father like that for a long time, wanting to engrave that embrace on my memory.

My things were almost all packed. I added a field jacket, a flashlight; I gathered my eyeglasses and made up a sewing kit. I dressed as I had in the Tatra Mountains—knickers, thick socks, sturdy leather boots. My father brought me what money he had, Polish zlotys and three or four gold coins, but I had saved up seventy zlotys of my own (about fifteen dollars) and resolved to take only that money with me. Why would I need money? I asked. I would be joining the army, after all, or if I crossed the border and found myself among Soviet friends, I would be given everything I needed. In the end, my father persuaded me to take his favorite watch, old but perfectly good, an Omega in a steel case.

We said farewell with a long handshake; then my father pressed my head to his heart. I ran down the stairs and into the dark, turning around to look up at our floor, our windows. The courtyard was empty and quiet. It was almost two o'clock.

Years later my mother gave me a letter my father had written about that night:

My dear son, you must know how your father has felt since that dark unforgettable night, the sixth of September, when you and I kissed each other perhaps for the very last time. How suddenly, quickly, tragically, and irrevocably everything has changed. . . . My thoughts run to you, dear son, who went off into the unknown without so much as a crust of bread. . . . Only later did I learn what terrible conditions prevailed: the wretched victims of German bombings who lined the roadsides. I have mercilessly railed against those villainous Nazis for many years but mine was a voice in the wilderness. . . . Now everything is going up in smoke, the carnage will not diminish, the rivers of blood will not be stopped, people will die—fall like flies—until the blond beast has raised his armored fist against everything and everyone and destroyed us all.

It was a warm night. People were still out and about, but there were considerably fewer of them now. As I headed for the right bank of the Vistula, I thought about my mother, my father, Warsaw, Judyta. One thought kept returning with increasing persistence: Now, before this final farewell to Warsaw, I had to try to find Judyta. Perhaps she would come with me. She was no child; she was strong, healthy. We could go on the road together and brave the Nazis. I could see her face, her large beautiful eyes, her hair falling to her shoulders, her smile, so sincere, friendly, trusting. Yes, she would certainly come. No, I should go straight to the bridge and not yield to weakness. If I were sure that I could save her, that would be another story, but I was not sure I could save even myself. Yet the memory of her voice tormented me: "Tell me, Romek, what do you think will happen to us?" Instinctively I turned, and marched toward Gesia Street, her street.

As I approached, people were standing along the walls, whispering softly in Yiddish. The pale gleam of dawn had appeared when I reached Judyta's building. I ran upstairs. The bulb that hung from the ceiling was not on, and I groped around in the dark to find her door. I knocked tentatively once, then again. No one answered. I stood there in silence until, finally, I made out a whisper on the other side of the door. She's there, I thought, elated, and I thumped hard. A woman's voice spoke in Yiddish; it sounded like Judyta's cousin.

"It's Romek. I've come for Judyta."

I heard a key squeak in the lock, and the door opened slowly. "Wait a moment, I'll light a candle. We have no electricity," she said.

"Is Judyta back?" I asked anxiously in the dark.

"No, and I haven't heard anything from her. I'm very worried."

A match flared, and the candle was lit. "Pardon, I'm not alone," she said. "But do come in. I'm with my fiancé. . . . These times are so terrible, we wanted to be together. Who knows how long . . ."

"Thank you. I'll only stay a couple of seconds. Please tell Judyta I came. I'm on my way to join the army, and if I cannot do that, then to the Soviet Union to fight fascism. Tell her that I came to help her . . . because . . ."

Neither of us said any more. Someone stirred in the bed.

"Tell her—" my voice caught in my throat—"I must go. Goodbye . . ."

I felt my way down the stairs, almost falling on one broken step. It was black, the air thick with cooking smells.

As day broke, I made my way to the river. Alongside me were people carrying or dragging all their worldly possessions. In those early-morning hours, Poniatowski Bridge was swarming with travelers. Even women and children labored along, weighed down by sacks, suitcases, bags. Layers of clothing covered their backs. People would stop to wipe the sweat from their faces even though it was September and the weather was pleasant enough. I, on the other hand, was in excellent physical condition, and my Tatra knapsack was nearly empty and light as a feather. I walked with a long, even step and passed everyone.

When I reached Praga and the Lublin highway, there was no one there to tell me where to go to join the new volunteer army, as had been promised the evening before. The entire throng was headed toward Lublin. I followed the crowds.

In the daylight I could see the Warsaw skyline on the horizon. From there came a hollow rumbling, as when a storm is approaching. That was the front. It seemed to me that every once in a while I could see the sky brightening, flashing, in the west. And although the sky above me was cloudless, that distant thunder of war was to accompany me through many days and nights.

The reverberations of battle seemed to subside with every sunrise, but from time to time during daylight, the drone of airplanes could be heard. I would stop and strain to find those little silver points against the bright blue sky. People along the road searched for them, too, prepared to run for cover. Eventually they picked up their cases and bundles once more and continued to walk.

It grew hot, that first day, a real scorcher. Every once in a while I rested in a ditch beneath a tree, and those I had passed caught up. By now, many of them carried less baggage, having abandoned their possessions in favor of comfort. Nevertheless, they constantly ran their sleeves across their drenched faces. A family who, with the last of their strength, had lugged their bulging suitcases through Warsaw had left their things in a ditch somewhere; now, only the father carried a suitcase, the rest of them only their coats.

In the afternoon even I began feeling fatigue, but I decided to keep going, to get as close to Lublin as possible. I had covered over thirty miles; yet that was considerably less than half way. It was still daylight when I passed Garwolin, a little one-horse town. Around the wretched one-story wooden houses people were milling about excitedly. They were mostly Jews, the majority of that little town's inhabitants. It was obvious they were confused. They had stayed there this long, but now the road was swarming with people heading southeast. Perhaps they should go that way, too? I passed a man in the prime of life standing in the sun at the side of the road wearing a large black hat. His eyes seemed to ask: Why are you going *that* way? I know, I answered silently, why I travel this way; there is a new army up ahead. But what about these children, women, old people?

The sun had begun to set, taking the heat with it, when loud explosions sounded ahead. A dark blot of smoke shot up in the distance and remained there until night began to fall. When it was dark, the smoke was transformed into the bright glow of flames, and slowly that eerie light crept across the horizon.

I had had enough of tramping, so I turned off toward a village and walked into the first hut. Inside were several people who, like me, were looking for a place to spend the night. There were no rooms left, but I needed sleep, not comfort. I drank some water and went off to the barn, where I dug a place for myself in the hay and sank into a deep slumber.

Early the next morning I was awakened by the cock's crow. The owner of the hut was already up, and I was given a modest breakfast. A single picture hung on the wall—Christ with a crown of thorns. I offered the owner payment, but he refused. "Maybe tomorrow we, too, will be refugees," said his wife. "God be with you." She has the same flaw as my mother, I thought, utter reliance on God; much re-education will be needed here in Poland if communism is to win out.

I strode out to the highway and soon reached one of the little towns that had burned during the night. It was Ryki. Of the houses, all that remained were brick chimneys and a few walls amid the smoldering ruins and glowing embers. The stench of fire and death was in the air. It was my first such encounter.

People still walked among the ruins, searching dazedly. They picked their way through, looking, perhaps, for what remained of their belongings and their kin. People traveling along the highway stared at them in silence, the women making the sign of the cross. Mute stupor showed in the people's faces. Yesterday this had been a little town, a few centuries old at least; today it was nothing but corpses and rubble. This was no dream or vision. The Nazis were here, doing as they had done in Spain, in those little towns, small points on the map spread out on our dining-room table. At that time I had listened to my father and believed him, but had not fathomed the significance of his words. Here at my feet was an ember that yesterday had been a home or someone's well-worn boot. Today, tomorrow, who knew what fate awaited me?

With those thoughts I continued walking with the crowd that now poured along the road. The day was very hot, the sky pure, and up above us was that constant, unnerving drone. I crossed the bridge over the Wieprz River. It was from here that Pilsudski had struck in my birth year, 1920, and sealed the Bolsheviks' defeat. History could have taken a different turn, I mused, and perhaps, were it not for that war, were it not for that attack, we might today have a Soviet Europe, and a peaceful Poland.

It was well after noon when my thoughts were interrupted by the rumble of motors and the clatter of treads. From the parting sea of people, an armored vehicle pulling a heavy-caliber field gun emerged. A second, third, and fourth followed, an entire column moving in the direction of Lublin. The first stopped right in front of me. An energetic young officer peered into his map case, studying it closely.

Without thinking twice, I ran over to him. "Captain, sir, I am a recruit with a *matura.* Romuald Spasowski. I was trained at school, at the camp in Modlin, and at the work camp on the Warta. I was to report to the military college, but now I'm going to Lublin to join the army. Please accept me as a volunteer."

The officer looked me over wearily. I did not know whether he had understood me.

"*Matura* . . . military college . . . ," he mumbled. "All right. Hop on there between the tractor and the gun. Just watch out that your leg doesn't get caught in there; it'll turn it into jelly. Sergeant!" he shouted. "This one's coming with us."

And so it was that, completely unexpectedly, I joined the army.

I did not ask where we were going. There was no one to ask; I was all by myself between the tractor and the fieldpiece. But I did not care where we were headed. Whatever the direction, it was the right one.

The sun was on its way toward the western horizon, long shadows were falling on the highway, and I was happily counting the miles we covered. A drone broke my reverie, but, bouncing over the potholes, I could see nothing. It grew louder, and seemed to be coming from every side. The commander, who was riding in the lead tractor, raised his hand and brought the column to a halt. He listened intently, peered through his binoculars, and gave the order "Into the woods!" One after another the tractors swerved off the road and cut across fields toward the woods a quarter of a mile away. I held on tight, almost hanging by my hands. Soon the droning seemed to envelop us. We were just pulling in beneath the trees when the first bombs exploded with a deafening roar. A hoarse voice shouted, "Hide!"

I jumped off and ran for my life through the trees, but, stunned by an exploding bomb nearby, I fell to the ground at the base of a massive tree. Digging my hands into moss and grass, I pressed myself into the ground, forcing my head as hard as I could into the earth, just as my tormentor in Modlin, the sergeant, had taught me. But this position did not prevent me from seeing the extent of the bombing, the dazzling glares, nor from feeling the earth tremble beneath me. I passed out.

It was already dark when I felt a pull on my sleeve. "Hey, what's the matter with you? Are you wounded?"

"Don't know," I managed. Pain was shooting through my whole body—in the small of my back, legs, shoulders, arms.

A hand passed over me. "I don't feel any blood. It must be a concussion. He's right by the crater."

It was like hearing voices in a dream. Don't know, don't know, I kept saying to myself as I moved one hand mechanically across my head, neck, and shoulders. They were dry, no blood.

"All right, get going," said the same voice. "We're moving out right now. . . . They cut us to pieces, the sons of bitches." He left.

I began coming to. From the bushes I could hear moaning; one person was crying out for help, someone else grunted. People were moving through the woods, rustling the leaves and branches, as they collected the wounded.

Finally, a familiar voice spoke in my direction. "What's the matter, can't you get up?"

"No, I can't."

"Wait, let me help you." Someone's arms lifted me up, and I found myself standing under a tree. "We're getting out. They're collecting the last of them. You were lucky. . . . I'll be right back to help you. Just don't fall into that crater. You'd have been a pretty sight if it hadn't been for that old oak tree there."

As I waited, I could feel my whole body shaking; I could barely stand. After what seemed an eternity, the stranger returned and led me to the edge of the woods, where trucks were waiting. Through the din in my head, I could hear voices. "Hurry!" "Load the wounded!" "Be careful!"

"Are you all right, civilian?" Someone was addressing me.

"I just . . . can't move."

"Wacus! Check and see if he's wounded."

Wacus went over me carefully. "No. Lieutenant."

"Come on then, get up on the truck." I clenched my teeth and clambered on with his help. The tailgate banged shut, and the truck pulled away. I looked around. My companions were all wounded soldiers, their limbs askew. Their groans grew louder with every bump in the road. I crouched beside a soldier leaning against one side of the truck. Blood-smeared and making weak, plaintive noises, he looked at me imploringly. His arm was dangling at his side.

Whenever thc truck hit a pothole, white bones jutted from his torn skin. I took his hand, afraid that he might fall off, and we rode on like that, the road horrible and long. My hands were covered with that soldier's blood, its sweet smell everywhere. Violent nausea began to overcome me, and it took great effort to hold it back. But the trucks suddenly stopped. People ran around with flashlights arguing excitedly. The rear of the truck was opened, and a few people climbed in. I got up.

Someone asked, "What's wrong with you?" He didn't wait for me to answer. "Get off this truck! What the hell are *you*, a civilian, doing in here if there's nothing wrong with you? We're taking only the seriously wounded to the hospital."

I did as he said with no argument, watching as the trucks drove away and vanished into the black of night. A few steps and I began to vomit. My insides were turning inside out. I sat down and leaned against something.

Covered with blood and vomit, I may have slept. I do not remember.

It was still night when I came to. The stars were bright as diamonds above me. For the first time I felt broken, having lost sometime during that night my confidence, my spirit. I wanted nothing, thought of nothing.

Dawn came, and I sat staring, glassy-eyed, until a woman's voice snapped me out of my stupor. "Oh, my God! So much blood. He's all covered with blood!" She bent down and peered at my face.

"You're alive! Oh, my God! Wait. My husband and son are coming—we'll take you home with us."

She moved away. I watched her indifferently, stupidly. An old rusty farm wagon drove up, and I was taken to a little hut.

My hosts proved to be good-hearted. They took off my bloody, stinking clothes, washed me, and put me to bed. When I awoke at noon, my pants, sweater, and shirt were already drying in the sun. My entire body was gripped by pain, and I by a new sense of fear, which would claw at my stomach with every passing plane and every distant bombing.

At lunch the family said they had brought me home thinking I was seriously wounded, so deathly had I looked. Where had the blood come from?

I told them about my one hapless night with the army, and as I did, I felt the whole family looking at me warmly.

"Look," said the man to his family, "here's a student, no doubt from some well-to-do home, with educated parents. Now it's war, and he's out, not knowing where he'll rest his head from one night to the next. . . . What will happen to him; what will happen to *us*?"

His wife crossed herself and went off to the next room, where I heard her praying.

We said good-bye as if we were old friends. "God be with you," shouted my host, waving. I looked back as I walked off, wanting to remember those good people. Flowers of many colors clustered around the foundation of their whitewashed hut, and, suspended above them, sunflowers in the sunlight.

It was early afternoon when I approached the Lublin highway. The road was full of people who seemed somehow different from those I had seen nearer Warsaw. They weren't carrying heavy packages, and they looked lost and frightened. There were few vehicles; every once in a while a wagon or a carriage, a *britzka*, went past. From the west there were clear echoes of war, like the menacing rumble of an approaching storm, and, at times—at considerably closer distances—individual bombs punctuated that roar.

I stood by the highway in the shade of a tree and studied the crowd. To my surprise, many of them were headed in the opposite direction, toward Warsaw. I noticed a tall man in a rumpled railroad uniform going that way and asked him what he expected to find there. "Why aren't you headed for Lublin?" I asked. "They're forming a new army there!"

The man looked disbelievingly at me and shook his head. "Come," he said, pointing to a ditch by the road. "Sit down with me a while. My legs are killing me. I'll tell you what's happening." We squatted down together. "Lublin is being bombed nonstop. The train station was destroyed. I saw it burning with my own eyes. I was lucky to get out of there. That's no place to be." He nodded toward the people going by. "If they only knew where they were going . . . and what's waiting for them there."

"Where are you from?" I asked.

"Poznan. The Germans have it in their mitts already."

He seemed a decent man, and I told him a little about myself. "If it's as you say," I said, "the only thing for me to do is go east. I cannot risk falling into German hands."

He bobbed his head in approval.

"I'll cut my way through as far as I can. Who knows, maybe I'll even cross the Soviet border," I said, searching his eyes for a reaction.

That surprised him. "Are *they* any better?"

It was clear I was not talking with a Communist or a sympathizer. But I trusted the man.

"I hate the fascists," I told him. He nodded, and with this encouragement I plunged in further. "Maybe we could travel together? Two's better than one. We could skirt Lublin and see what's what. I have family out east, in Volhynia, not far from Kowel. Do you know Kowel?"

"Oho, do I know Kowel? I've been there many times. It's an important railroad junction. But how will we get there? Things will be getting hotter on this road. That way, to Lublin," he said, pointing, "is only trouble, and the other way, to Warsaw, it's raining bombs."

"I know," I said after some thought. "But I have a map. We can travel on the side roads, and if that proves difficult, we can travel at night, take shortcuts, follow the stars. I know the stars well, I can keep us going in the right direction." He looked at me incredulously as I took out my map.

"Here we are. I suggest we head toward Kock along the Wieprz and then cross the Bug between Wlodawa and Chelm. The Germans shouldn't be able to catch up with us if we head in that direction. Do you agree?" He nodded, encouraged now. "Good."

As he rested his legs a bit longer, he told me what news he knew. "It's not good, not good at all. The rail junctions are under constant bombardment, stations have been destroyed, trains damaged. The Krauts have taken Krakow and Kielce. They're outside Warsaw now. The Kutno region, west of Warsaw, is riddled with little skirmishes. Same thing near Radom. It looks like our men will withdraw to the Bug . . . where we're heading." He waved, disgusted. "You understand, Silesia, Poznan, the Baltic coast are all in German hands. Our men can't handle it all; everything's disorganized. Not only are they being bombed from the air, but those damned armored columns are tearing right through."

"Let's figure it out," I said. "If it's, let's say, about a hundred and eighty miles to Warsaw from the German border, and their tanks covered that distance in six days, that means they averaged thirty miles a day. And if the Prussian border and the old border with Czechoslovakia are *less* than a hundred and eighty miles, they could get here any time. We haven't got a minute to lose."

"You lead," he said, with an air of resignation.

It was good to travel in someone's company. He told me about his family in Poznan, and I told him about Milanowek and my mother. I said nothing about my father and Judyta; my feelings about them were too complicated and personal to share. The sun was already sinking behind us when we approached a large village.

In a modest hut we were given a friendly reception, and after a meal of milk with potatoes and bread, we headed for the hay in their barn. The railroad man fell asleep immediately, but the pain in my spine gave me no peace, and I sat for hours, weaving in and out of slumber.

I awoke, as planned, at two o'clock in the morning. The railroad man at first refused to be awakened. But we set off finally, following the stars. I gave him a simplified lesson in practical astronomy and told him about the constellations. He was quiet, thinking, perhaps, about his family in Poznan.

By the light of a half-moon we could make out trees, bushes, and uneven terrain. Behind us, to the west, the sky was lit by a flickering glow, and the sounds of night were accompanied by a distant rumble. But we were moving away from those echoes of war. Years later I realized that we had passed close to the places where, about a month later, in the first days of October, the last great battle, the battle of Kock, took place—a battle waged by Polish soldiers for whom there was nothing left to do but fight to a bitter end.

We did not go as far as Kock, but turned south, toward the town of Lubartow. The day was becoming as sunny as the previous ones; and because we were heading due east, the sounds of the fighting diminished. Planes could be heard overhead, but no bombing. It seemed a peculiarly normal day. My friend began to wonder if we had to go so far east, but I prevailed on him to continue to Lubartow and there make further plans. We arrived before noon. The town was calm; life seemed to be proceeding in its own small way. The clerk at the post office could not enlighten us with any news, knew less, in fact, than we did, and was not even in telegraphic contact with Lublin. The town's peaceful ambience had an influence on my traveling companion, who tried to convince me to wait a few days before deciding what to do next.

While having a meal in an inn on the main street, we held our final parley, however. My comrade was intent on staying, and I was firm about continuing eastward. It was not easy to say good-bye. I had come to like him and had felt solace in his company. We wished one another a happy reunion with our family. He stayed at the table where we had just finished eating, and I set off on my way.

Again I was traveling with only my compass as guide; sometimes on dirt roads, when they led in the right direction, and sometimes taking shortcuts through fields, villages, copses. Maybe it's better this way, I thought. I'll do only what I want to; things will be smoother, easier. The primary task was to plot a course to Lityn. I sat down on a tree trunk at the edge of a forest and worked out the way to Turzysk, the small town nearest Lityn—about ninety miles away. I figured that I could be outside Turzysk in three days, four at the most—that is, the thirteenth or fourteenth of September. If things went well, I might cross the Bug the next day and be on the territory of Volhynia—"our" Volhynia, according to my mother.

Perhaps it would be there, I thought, that the Polish forces would organize their resistance. It would not be easy for the Germans to fight in those trackless areas, in those wetlands. France by then would have entered the picture, and Hitler would have to fight on two fronts. But what about my father in Warsaw? Is it still under siege? Are they bombing the city? My heart shrank at the thought.

The next day, as I took off after a night in a peasant's haystack, I noticed that the sounds of war seemed to have abated. Maybe things won't be as bad for us as I had imagined, I thought. The road led through fields; far up ahead I could see a dark forest. I met few people, and those mostly near villages. The grass was splendid, high and full of flowers of many different colors. I lay down, placed my knapsack beneath my head, and looked up at the sky. I was enjoying the relative peace, when I was torn from that bliss by the growl of engines. I spotted two low-wing monoplanes flying over the forest, almost brushing the treetops, and swaying from one side to the other. Pulling my head back into the grass, I watched the planes fly right over me. Black crosses were on the underside of their wings. I stood and watched as they disappeared issuing a chatter of machine-gun fire in the distance.

So, I thought, it's not entirely safe even here. I had hardly hoisted my knapsack and headed for the forest when the sound approached again and the same two points appeared over the trees. I was right in the middle of a field. No bushes, no ditch, only a single small tree about fifteen meters ahead of me. I ran toward it and clambered into its branches. The planes whirred past seconds later, swaying from side to side as before; one of them flew very close and leaned to the side. I had a clear view of both the pilot and the man behind him. Wearing flying helmets and dark glasses, they were looking intently into the forest and at the field I had been crossing. They flew off, and moments later I again heard a burst of machine-gun fire. I decided to stay in the tree, but the planes did not return, and I climbed down and entered the forest calmly.

I did not reach the Bug that day; the marshes had made me detour too far and I lost time. Although hungry and tired, I continued on my way all night long, taking my course by the stars. Somewhere in the distance, in the far distance, was that roar.

When the sun had risen, I stopped by a hut. Pictures of Christ and Virgin Mary like those I had seen in the more hospitable huts hung on the walls. While devouring a hearty breakfast, I chatted with my host.

"The Bug is not far—maybe four or five miles, or less," he explained. "There's a ferry. If you walk straight down the road, you'll come out at it. The river is narrow, but deep. Don't try to swim across. And be careful when you're on the other side of the Bug; go only to Poles. Avoid Ukranians."

We said warm good-byes, and I wished them peace.

In two hours I was across the Bug and on Volhynian soil, the Borderlands where my ancestors had lived for generations. The town of Luboml was only about nine miles away, and in spite of sharp pains in my legs my enthusiasm kept me going.

I strode along the road through dense forest and a stretch of broad fields. Despite the distance I had covered and my lack of sleep the night before, I felt refreshed; perhaps the forest air was doing me good, perhaps the greenery was soothing my nerves. As I came out of another forest, I spotted a *britzka*, moving quietly in my direction. Two soldiers in Polish uniform sat on the box, rifles slung over their shoulders. They halted directly in front of me. The soldier sitting next to the driver snatched his rifle and aimed it at me menacingly.

"Who are you?" he shouted.

"I'm a refugee . . . on my way to my family."

"Don't move a muscle." He jumped down, walked over, and frisked me. Meanwhile, the driver had swung his rifle around and aimed it at me.

"ID."

I reached into my pocket and pulled out the ID I had received in Warsaw only the August before.

"His residence is Warsaw," the soldier shouted. "Of course we can't check that now, can we?"

He looked me over. It had obviously seemed suspicious for a tall blond to emerge suddenly from the forest, with nothing more than a sweater and a knapsack on my back.

"Other identification—work, school?" I handed him my school ID. He looked it over.

Keeping his rifle trained on me, he turned halfway to the one sitting on the box and mumbled something.

"You're coming with us. This has to be checked."

I reached for my ID, and he hesitated.

"Okay, take it. And come on, jump up on the box."

I sat next to the driver, with the sergeant perched behind me. As the *britzka* moved over the bumps in the road, I could feel his rifle firmly lodged against my spine. It had been bad luck to come out just as they were passing and not fifteen seconds earlier or later. Had I spotted them through the trees, with their rifles over their shoulders, I would probably have waited for them to drive by. Or maybe I would have come running out shouting for joy—who knows? One thing was sure: I knew how German saboteurs were dealt with.

After about fifteen minutes, the sergeant in back spoke up. "Franek, stop by the store. I'll buy a liter. We've got this one, might as well have that, too, right?"

I guessed that "this one" meant me, a good catch, and that was worth a drink. What should I do? I was all too willing to explain myself at whatever place they were taking me, but if they were going to drink, who knew what sort of trial they would arrange? My hair was standing on end. I glanced at the man beside me. He had the ruddy complexion of a drinker. Something had to be done, and as quickly as possible. My thoughts kept coming in flashes.

We drove up to the intersection of two dirt roads, where a white hut, our immediate destination, shone among bushes to the left. Over the door was a sign: General Store. There were bushes to my right, and, behind those, the forest, about a hundred or so feet away. The *britzka* came to a halt, and the sergeant sprang off, ordering the driver to keep me at gunpoint.

"You watch it," the driver growled at me. "One move and . . ." He confidently set his rifle down on the seat. "Don't you worry, Sergeant, I can handle this one," he boasted. He was a burly peasant with enormous hands. I sat there tensely watching as the sergeant vanished into the store, and I weighed my chances. The driver slid his rifle up against the seat beside me, reached into his pocket, and pulled out a cigarette and a lighter that appeared to have been made from a rifle shell. He jammed the cigarette into his mouth and lighted it.

Something in me went off. I grabbed the man's rifle and leaped from the *britzka*. The rifle fell out of my hands. But I didn't look for it. I raced into the bushes and tore toward the forest. There were shouts behind me. Then one shot rang out, followed by another. The bullets whistled by me, but by then the forest enveloped me. I made a sharp turn to deceive them and kept on running. Another shot rang out, but a good distance away. The underbrush in the forest was becoming denser and denser. I ran for I do not know how long. When I finally stopped, it was quiet. I sat down on the moss.

To go through that, I mused, and with my own . . . But they were primitive people. No doubt they were well convinced now that they had had a German saboteur in their hands. My heart knocked like a hammer; I was exhausted, finished—with war, with wandering, with all this adventure. I thought I felt my strength leave me, ebb away forever.

Despite my exhaustion I continued toward Turzysk through the night. As usual, the sky was studded with stars, which illuminated the road so clearly that I did not need to use my compass. Dogs barked in the distance. Carrying a strong stick, I walked until daybreak.

The first peasant I met told me it was ten versts and a hook to Turzysk. That meant little to me, but, hungry and tired, I kept stubbornly on. The next day, September 14, I arrived in Lityn. My grandmother, Emilia Sumowska, let out a cry when she finally recognized her grandson. Perhaps I had changed since she last saw me, and I was tired, thin, my face bronze from the sun. She told me to take a bath, wrap myself in my late grandfather's dressing gown, and sit down at her table. I was happy to be in my grandmother's home. It had a certain smell all its own. I remembered those rooms, with their low ceilings, and the strange old furniture that had been saved from fires in the family manors.

Sitting at the table, I told her about my trip. She was genuinely worried, but I could read in her a certain satisfaction and approval of my enterprise, resolve, and physical vigor. I did not tell her all I planned; she would never have understood.

Grandmother was the first to tell me that Warsaw was under siege. The Germans were also pushing forward to take the entire country.

"You will see Stefan tomorrow," she said. "He'll tell you everything. He's got a good radio, and he and Zygmus are always listening to it. But there's no more Polish radio for us," she added sadly.

"I'd like to rest up a little," I told her, "gather my strength and repair my boots. Maybe two or three days, then I'll be pushing on."

That genuinely disturbed her. "What do you mean, 'pushing on'? Can't you appreciate what you've been through? Times are bad, dangerous. Stay here with us. We'll manage even if the Germans come. I know those people from the other war; they may have been thieves, and cruel, but you can reason with them."

Looking at my grandmother, I felt sorry for her. She was remembering the Kaiser's army and thinking of the Germans as the same. The poor woman could not imagine what the German army had become under Hitler's swastika.

The next day after breakfast I went with my grandmother to see Uncle Stefan, Aunt Augusia, and their two children, in the newly constructed manor house. My uncle had sent a *britzka* for us even though the house was only a few hundred yards away. The house had been modeled after a stylish old Polish manor; its walls and the small columns supporting the dome of the porch were freshly painted white. There was a circular flower bed in front. Three fox terriers ran out to greet the *britzka* as we swung around the driveway.

"Welcome, welcome," my uncle said, coming through the doorway. "Your arrival is a surprise in times like these."

"I came on foot, straight from Warsaw."

"On foot?" My uncle looked me over in disbelief. His eyes stopped on my battered boots. "Now I see," he said. "Well, tell us the news, Romek. Is your mother well?"

He ushered me into the house. I told of my impressions and experiences in Warsaw and on the road, and as I spoke the rest of my relatives gathered to listen. News of my arrival had spread quickly, and a short while later another *britzka* drove up. It came from the Nyry estate, with Stefan's sister Lincia and her husband, Zygmus.

My story made an impact on all of them. They listened in silence, though every once in a while a woman would mumble "Oh, my God." Their spirits sank. It's one thing to hear about war on the radio, I thought, and another to hear it from me.

Uncle Stefan told us the latest news: Warsaw was surrounded by a ring of German troops, but the city was defending itself; a major battle had been raging near Kutno for several days; there was heavy fighting in the Radom region; Lwow had been cut off. Canada had declared war on Germany. The Germans had crossed the Bug.

A weighty silence was broken by Zygmus's squeaky voice. "Now we can only expect the worst—that the Bolsheviks will start moving. What do you think? You do know about Hitler's pact with Stalin, don't you?"

"Yes," I answered, "and I think that the signing of that pact was not a bad thing inherently. Obviously it will go no further than the pact. Those are two very different states, very different systems, different policies, mortal enemies. Believe me, I know what the difference between fascism and communism is."

The room was silent again; no one joined in.

But Zygmus persisted. "Well, may your calculations prove right. In any case, I would not want to fall into the Bolsheviks' hands. You think you know Bolshevism from your books. I don't need to read those books of yours. I have met people who were there during the Bolshevik revolution, during Lenin, Trotsky, Dzerzhinski, and, of course, Stalin. . . . Those people barely got out of there alive. I was there myself as a young man, and I don't need to go into what they did with my family. The Bolsheviks make medieval tortures look like child's play." He waved his hand and shook his head. His face was flushed with anger.

"We know all that, Zygmus," said Uncle Stefan, "but we don't get a chance to see Romek often. Tell us, Romek, what you plan to do."

"I'll leave the day after tomorrow," I said firmly, trying to control my agitation and my ill will toward Zygmus, whom I considered a dolt, an ignoramus, an obscurantist.

"Where are you rushing off to?" my uncle asked. "It's dangerous everywhere now, and you'll never reach our army. Wait a while, and let's see how things develop. Remember that there are many Ukrainians here in Volhynia. Many of them are good, honest people, but many are rabid nationalists, right-wing Cossacks who hate Poles with a passion. Soviet agents are also here. You must be careful, Romek. This is no game."

Generalizations were not fair, I thought, and were typical of Uncle Stefan's and Zygmus's class views. There had never been easy harmony between the landowners and the peasants. The majority of the peasants here were Ukrainians. My relatives' remarks required a class interpretation.

That evening Grandmother and I sat down to dinner in her little house. The light from the oil lamp was soft, and nothing troubled the calm of that meal. Her girl brought the samovar to a rolling boil and then brought in a loaf of home-baked bread, fresh butter, cheese, and smoked boar ham. From somewhere in the distance we heard the howling of dogs, but nothing else disturbed the peace of that night.

"What are you thinking about, Romek?" asked my grandmother, seeing my attention drift away.

"I have a favor to ask of you, Grandmother. Before I leave I'd like you to show me all those keepsakes you have in that old wooden trunk. Many years ago you said I could see them when I grew up."

She smiled. "You have a good memory, but does that interest you really? After all, you . . . I mean, you are your father's son, and he was never concerned about such things."

"It interests me very much. Those were our ancestors."

She nodded in approval. "Yes, those were our ancestors. Let's go and look at them together."

The large wooden trunk, covered with a dark spread, stood in a corner of her bedroom, hidden behind the wardrobe. It was full of all sorts of things that I was unable to distinguish in the faint light of the oil lamp. My grandmother pulled the articles out one by one. On top, there were beautifully embroidered tapestries and golden sashes. Then she handed me a wooden box of richly inlaid black wood, probably ebony, which contained letters my ancestors had written and received over the ages. Old yellowed paper, worn in places, frayed along the edges, but clearly legible. There was a letter from King Jan Sobieski III to Maciej Sumowski. It was written from a military camp in Podolia to warn Maciej of the Turkish menace and was signed briefly, "Jan—the king."

I folded the letter respectfully and replaced it in the box. There were also letters from Tadeusz Kosciuszko and many others whose names I did not know, licenses and charters signed by the last king of Poland, Stanislaw August Poniatowski. In a letter King Stanislaw apologized for taking a couple of days to reply but said he had been out of Warsaw.

Then my grandmother began handing me crosses, silver shields with images of the Virgin that members of our family had worn, goblets engraved with writing and coats of arms. I was drawn to a silver cup with an engraved monogram—Z C—and I asked her about it.

"That is probably the most valuable keepsake we have," said my grandmother. "It's from a family which doesn't exist any more but whose blood is in our veins. The Zawisza Czarny."

"The Zawisza who fought at Grunwald back in the fifteenth century?" I asked.

"Yes, the one the Polish gentry mean when they say, 'As reliable as Zawisza.' My father's mother, Marianna, was a Zawisza Czarny. She was, if memory serves me, the last."

I looked at the cup. It must have been very old, and it seemed somehow squat and ungainly.

"But that is ancient history," my grandmother said. "You see this prayer book? It's called the 'little Dunin,' because it was put together by our ancestor Marcin Dunin, who was the archbishop of Gniezno and Poznan and who died about one hundred years ago. Do you want this prayer book as a keepsake? It has served me for many, many years."

"No," I answered quickly. "I'm an atheist."

"Yes, yes. That's how your father raised you, but, who knows, the time may come when you'll change. Perhaps when you're old everything that was meant to flow in your veins will return to you."

"They must have been educated people," I said to change the subject, because it pained me to hear my own grandmother speak about my father as a bad influence.

"Yes," she replied, "both on my side of the family and on your grandfather Sumowski's side. He had five brothers; they all graduated from the university at Dorpat. This area has, my dear boy, produced many great Poles for centuries now. Land here in the Borderlands has been watered with Polish blood. To the east and south of us, past the Styr and the Stochod rivers, Polish blood has been shed for centuries. Our forefathers fought for Poland there, for all Poland. The Lityn woods are covered with grave mounds, and nobody knows who's buried there. For many centuries, the Tatar and Cossack hordes passed through Podolia and Volhynia burning the cities and the countryside and slaughtering Poles. The Turks were here, too, dragging Polish women and children off to Istanbul to be raised as Janissaries, the Sultan's infantry guard. It was here in the Borderlands that the fate of Warsaw and Krakow was decided. People were sleeping in peace there by the Vistula, but somebody had to guard the fortified settlements in this wild open country, somebody had to do the fighting. People here have Poland in their blood. I love these woods, this land. . . ."

She trailed off, and we sat for a while in silence before she stooped to put all the things back into the trunk.

"Take the prayer book," she said. "Maybe someday you'll learn to pray and you'll remember this evening with your old grandmother."

As I fell asleep that night I forgot entirely about the war, transported as I was into my family history. I decided I would look through all of that trunk carefully, unhurriedly, someday, if . . .

I was, later, to think of that evening often. It was the last truly peaceful evening I had for many years—perhaps the very last.

The next day I began my travel preparations. Grandmother was already dressed when I awokc, and at breakfast she told me that I should take my uncle's bicycle. She had a jacket of good, warm material ready for me. It did not fit me at all badly, though the sleeves were a little short. I was also to take a long, fur-lined leather coat with me, for, as she said, winter was on its way. She produced underwear, spare boots, and a money bag containing a large number of Polish silver coins: two-, five-, and ten-zloty pieces. According to her, paper money had meant nothing in previous wars. I accepted the coins with hesitation; after all, I intended to cross the Soviet border, although I had not mentioned this to my grandmother. That intention seemed almost a certainty to me now, because the front sounded nearer, and we had heard that the Germans were pressing east and had already been at Brest Litovsk, an important railroad junction on the Bug, one hundred and twenty miles east of Warsaw. Warsaw still refused to surrender.

The following day I rose early and got ready to leave. My grandmother came into my room and kissed me. I could see the emotion in her large, kindly eyes. I kissed her hand and assured her that I would not forget Lityn. I felt that her old prejudice against me as Spasowski's son had melted away entirely and that now she was treating me as her grandson. On leaving, I stopped to look back at her standing on the porch. I could see her fragile figure, dressed in dark clothing, her head wrapped in a black shawl. Then she bade me farewell just as my mother had, in that backward, obscurantist, Volhynian style, with the sign of the cross.

That was the last I saw of Lityn. I never saw that large wooden trunk again either. Only the prayer book, the little Dunin, survived the storms of war, and it lies before me as I write.

CHAPTER IV

On my uncle's bicycle, the miles passed swiftly. Each time I was about to come out of woods into a clearing, I slowed down and listened hard. The din of war from the west was constantly in my ears, and at times I even thought I could distinguish single explosions. I had decided that there was no reason to go to Kowel, which lay to the north, and that I would pass that city and turn off to the east, heading for Sarny, the last railroad station before the Soviet border. From Sarny, the border was no more than forty miles away. I kept to dirt roads, even to paths, avoiding the little towns and villages. The area was only sparsely settled, and I rode mostly through woods and alongside bogs covered with a dense growth of rushes and cane, which surely could slow the Germans. And if only a couple of days were cloudy—rather than clear, dry, and beautiful—their air force might not pose such a threat.

I passed the little town of Holuby, crossed the railroad tracks connecting Kowel with Lutsk, and a few hours later was on the narrow bridge over the Stochod. There seemed to be fewer people on the other side of the river; yet once in a while I passed small villages where, among the dozen or so cottages, peace reigned and people acted as if nothing at all were happening.

I was riding past large leafy trees when weariness swept over me. As I turned off the hot road into the cool underbrush, the afternoon stillness was broken by the sound of engines. Something flashed past above the trees and then I saw two airplanes roar by. The wings flared up like birds', and their undersides were emblazoned with large red stars.

I jumped to my feet. Soviet planes! So the Soviet Union was striking against the Germans, confirming my deepest conviction that there could be no peace between fascism and communism, that there would be a fight to the death, and that, in the end, the world proletariat would emerge victorious. Tears welled in my eyes as I thought of my father vindicated at last by those beautiful silver planes flying overhead. I remember the day well—it was September 17.

Excited, invigorated, I pushed on. As the sun was setting I crossed the Styr. It was not long before I spotted a good-size village that seemed a promising place to spend the night. There were no people to be seen as I rode through an orchard and up to the first hut. I called out. No one answered. I knocked at the door, but the place looked abandoned. The door squeaked open when I pressed on the latch, and peering in I could see that people could not have been gone for long. Pots still stood on the stove, chairs were overturned, things were strewn on the floor. I called again, disturbed by the desolation. There was only silence.

Then, from one corner of the hut came a man's soft voice: "Are you Polish?"

"Yes."

"Me, too," said the man, rising from behind the bed. Though the light was dim, I recognized a railroad uniform as he approached me. His hair was disheveled, and his eyes anxious. What do you want?"

"I'm bicycling to Sarny and I'm looking for a place to spend the night."

"To Sarny?" His voice was almost fearful.

"What's the matter?" I asked, not understanding his reaction, not understanding the strangeness of the whole encounter. "Do you live here? Is this your house?"

"Don't you know anything?" he asked. "My family lived here, my sister and her husband and children—Polish settlers. This whole settlement is Polish. Until yesterday . . . Yesterday was terrible, really terrible. . . . Ukrainians came into the village; they shot people, murdered them. . . . What didn't they do! As I was coming into town I met a man who had gotten out of here, and he told me about it. Whole families were slaughtered in these huts. Everyone! Women, children. I think my family must have escaped, the house being right at the edge of the woods. They probably took what they could, and ran out of here. I slipped in from the woods a couple of hours ago. I thought I'd wait here to see what happened. . . . They bombed my train in Kowel and . . . I came back on a bicycle. What's going to happen to us Poles?" His voice began to break. Then he burst into tears, and his whole body shook.

Without speaking, I gave him my hand. He squeezed it with trembling fingers. We sat down.

"It's still very dangerous here," he said after a moment, wiping his nose with his handkerchief. "We shouldn't go outside. They could come back. And as for you, you can't go any farther. Past here are only Ukrainian villages. They'll torture you first, then kill you. Why are you heading that way? Do you have family there?"

"I didn't want to be caught by the Germans," I told him, leaving out any mention of Lityn.

"We've got to get away," he interrupted, "but not at night. My family knew these woods and bogs, every tree. They would know it well enough at night, but not us. The place is full of marshes; one splash and you're gone. The best time's early morning. Those Ukrainian hoodlums will probably be asleep then."

I considered my options. If things were so bad, perhaps I should really give up on reaching Sarny. In any case, Soviet planes were flying over us; at least we could assume that there were no Nazi troops here.

"Fine," I said at last. "You've convinced me. We can set off together as soon as it starts getting light. Is there anything to eat here?" I was wracked with hunger pangs.

We went out into the dark and began scavenging for food. Somewhere in the distance a sputter of rifle shots sounded.

"You see," he whispered, "they're still at it."

As we made our way to the farmyard, an ill-fated hen cackled in one of the cages. We snatched it, found a hatchet, and cut off its head. My companion searched through the pots and found some potatoes. Now we had food, but we would have to cook it so that no fire or smoke from the chimney could be seen from outside. We covered the windows with whatever was at hand, chose the driest pieces of wood, so there would be as little smoke as possible, and spent two hours waiting for the thing to cook. The hen had not been plucked well, the potatoes had only been half-peeled, but the broth that night seemed to me the most delicious I had ever had.

We barricaded the doors and lay down on the beds, the hatchet by mine, a pitchfork by his. There we lay, half dozing, half listening, until the first light of day.

As soon as the road could barely be glimpsed, we got on our bicycles and left that sad, eerie place. When we had put some distance between us and the settlement, my companion stopped to breathe a sigh of relief. "Those Ukrainians have been threatening Poles here for years, but now that they see the Poles are defenseless, they have a chance to do their worst."

Meaning to raise his spirits, to assure him all was not lost, I told him about the planes with the red stars. He froze.

"That's the end, the end of us! A knife in the back!" he cried. "They'll finish us off now. Oh, God, there's no help for us, no help. . . ."

I did not argue. I could see that my words had broken him, that he, like the railroad man on the Lublin highway, had no grasp of the difference between communism and fascism, or any idea of what the Soviet Union could mean to us.

After a while we set out again, bicycling straight ahead. The thought of returning to the comforts of Lityn kept haunting me, but I could just imagine Zygmus's smile of derision at such defeat. No, never. There was only one way to go, to Lutsk, fifty miles off, but away from those Ukrainian villages. I told the railroad man my idea, and he agreed.

Toward evening we stopped at a hut in a large Polish village. The owner received us warmly, and over supper we talked. He told us that the Soviets had entered Poland, and he was disturbed by it. "I know the Bolsheviks and what they're capable of; you don't need to tell me. If they were to come here, I'd harness the horse, and my wife and I would get as far away from them as possible, even if that meant going where the Germans are. I'd rather be killed by the Germans than have those barbarians torture me here."

My dreams were bad that night.

The next day we were no more than twenty miles from Lutsk when we heard bursts of machine-gun fire, a string of rifle shots, then sudden silence. A moment later a column of trucks full of soldiers approached us on the road. They were not Polish; nor were they German. It was the first Red Army detachment I had ever seen.

I watched it with great emotion as it hurried westward. The soldiers rode in ordinary civilian trucks painted grass green. Some stood, some sat, some were even lying down; many of them were holding short submachine guns with large round drums, others had long rifles with thin bayonets fixed to them. I did not spot any officers. Each truck was pulling a very long barreled antitank gun. White and red banners were fluttering from them. Snatches of Russian reached our ears as they passed; some of the men were singing, and I thought I heard the sound of an accordion. They didn't look like an army at all. Their uniforms were simple; instead of jackets, they wore long green belted tunics that came down over their pants. Their headgear varied—some wore field caps, others wore strange peaked hats, still others wore caps with visors. We looked on silently, each keeping his emotions to himself. Soon the entire detachment vanished in a cloud of dust.

We reached Lutsk before evening. I knew the city, having been there a few times on the way to Lityn. I remembered its clean streets, its painted fences, its whitewashed one-story buildings, the churches, and Lubart Castle on the hill, at the foot of which flowed the broad swollen waters of the Styr.

But the city seemed different now, alien. We crossed a square by a park where Polish soldiers were lying under the trees or sitting by columns of trucks and cars; some of them were cooking food on sticks. There was something ponderous about the way they moved.

"What's going on here?" my companion asked a soldier who was kneeling and blowing on a smoking stick.

"Can't you see? The Russians have surrounded us."

A sergeant lying close by sat up and muttered through a sneer, "There was no reason to defend ourselves. . . . There were hordes of them, and look at what's left of us! We could barely drag ourselves here after a round with those Germans. We managed to cut our way through and cross the Bug with whatever was left. . . ." He broke off and looked around. Tears had flooded his eyes. "You see us here—just soldiers. They took the officers off somewhere, confiscated our arms. They'll probably disband the army. But what do I know? Meanwhile, we're forbidden to leave the area, and so here we are, just sitting. They told us we're prisoners of war."

He seemed mortally weary and indifferent, but others were in worse shape. Many had bandages on head, arm, or leg. Their faces were dark and sallow, eyes sunken. These were Poles who had been fighting against the fascists, but they had ended up without their arms and abandoned, their officers taken off somewhere. I convinced myself that they had been taken off to rest and be debriefed about the Wehrmacht.

Thus did my wanderer's stay in Lutsk begin. A couple of days later my companion said that he was fed up with the sight of the Soviets and was going to return to his family in Sandomierz. He headed west; I ended up in a shelter for homeless refugees, people who, like me, had little or no money. There was no place to lie down; we spent the whole night perching in rows of chairs. The lucky ones who arrived early got folding chairs. By midnight people would collapse in heaps on the dirty floor.

Each night I would resolve that it would be my last in this place and that tomorrow I would find something else, no matter where, but doors were slammed in my face wherever I went. I even tried to see the authorities, but that, too, was hopeless. Members of the city government were disoriented, gruff, always shrugging their shoulders. The Soviet authorities were not receiving anyone. The houses where they lived were guarded by soldiers, who let no one pass. "Wait a while," I heard everywhere. "What's your hurry?" Word got around that a refugee-aid committee would soon be formed, but before it opened its doors the building was surrounded by hundreds of displaced Poles begging for help of any kind. Getting in was an impossible proposition.

Days passed, and I did not succeed even in telling anyone who I was or what I wanted. I lived on bread and went hungry most of the time. There was nothing in the stores, and for the first time in my life I languished for hours in long lines. I did, of course, have the silver zlotys my grandmother had given me, which people were glad to accept, but prices had soared, and I calculated that I would be out of money in a few weeks.

September passed while I went from one house to another searching for somewhere to lay my head. But everywhere I went I saw refugees like me who had been hurled to the Polish Borderlands by the war; no one wanted or could afford to take in a stranger and feed him. I spent hours wandering the streets, depressed and increasingly consumed with the idea of returning to Warsaw. Such were my thoughts as I walked to the outskirts of the city one day. The area was distinctly poor; people were living in one-story huts jammed along both sides of the road—tumble-down wooden shanties with collapsed roofs, sunken walls, warped doorframes.

Perhaps I'll have better luck here, I thought, remembering the houses with gardens, the apartments, and the villas where the doors had been slammed in my face. I stopped in front of one shanty. Sunflowers were being dried by the door on a plank. I took a deep breath and knocked. A voice answered in Yiddish, "Who's there?"

The door was not closed. I saw a short woman's outline in the half-darkness. "May I talk with you for a minute?" I asked.

"What do you want?" she answered in Polish with a thick Yiddish accent.

I hesitated. It would be the same story again—there's nothing we can do, please leave, no shelter here, maybe somewhere else, we're full up. . . .

"What do you want?" she repeated.

"For many days now I've been looking for somewhere to live. I'm a refugee, from Warsaw, a student. Please, just give me a place to stay. It doesn't have to be much of anything." I said it almost in one breath, before she could cut me off.

The woman looked at me in silence. A moment later she came and opened the door wide. "Please come in."

We sat down at the table. I told her about myself, that my father was a writer, that I did not want to fall into the hands of the Germans. She listened. She might have been forty, but looked spent. I imagined I could read a glimmer of compassion for me in those gentle eyes. "Would you like some tea?"

When she went to make it, I heard movement in the adjoining room. The door opened, and two dark little heads peeped in.

"We have no room here," she said, "but if we put the children on straw mattresses, maybe that would free a bed. My husband'll be home soon; we'll talk it over."

Only on drinking the tea did I realize how much I had wanted something warm to drink and a place to rest. Had I ever been so tired? The woman still rustled about, and the smell of fried potatoes reached me. She brought out a tray of potato pancakes and set it before me.

"Please," she said, "have something to eat."

To me those simple pancakes tasted like rare delicacies.

Finally her husband, Moishe, arrived. Together they whispered in the next room for what seemed hours. I thought I could discern displeasure in his voice, excuses. I was resigning myself to having to look for shelter again, when the door opened and Moishe came in. He offered me his hand and sat down heavily at the table. He looked a great deal older than his wife.

"This isn't good," he began. "We are poor people, there's a war on, times are bad . . . and then you appear."

He fell silent. I waited. I cannot explain any more, I thought, I cannot ask any more; it had been my last chance. I moved to rise.

"Such trouble," said Moishe, throwing up his hands. "Well, you stay here with us—but God only knows how we'll manage."

I slumped back into the chair. Moishe must have read the gratitude in my face, because he reached out and placed his hand on mine.

"All right, all right, don't worry . . ."

"I'll help you as much as I can," I assured him. I felt as if a stone had fallen from my heart. How little a person needs if he has nothing at all.

Living there, I saw for myself how truly poor these Jews were. Moishe was a cobbler in another man's shop; he worked from dawn to night to support a family of four. They did not eat well—mostly potatoes and potato- or rye-flour pancakes fried in oil. They had never had meat on their table. They said that before the war they had eaten herring often, but it was now as unavailable as everything else. What they had, they shared with me. I tried to repay them by bringing back what I bought after hours spent in the city's lines. In the evenings we sat around the table in the room where Moishe and his wife and daughter slept. I told them about Warsaw and Poland. After the ice was broken, they began to feel comfortable with a man of the world such as I must have seemed, and they asked many questions. Their little boy would crawl into my lap and listen to our conversations. The little girl would gaze up at me with wide-open eyes; I was probably the first stranger she had seen up close.

By mid-October I still had not managed to get through to any of the authorities. At last I learned that once or twice a week a *komandir*—a name used by the Soviets for officers of all ranks—a man who dealt with "special" matters, was on duty in the city hall. Although I did not know what that meant, he seemed the right sort of person to help me do the two things uppermost in my mind: join the fight against fascism somehow and rescue my father from Nazi-occupied Warsaw. It was no easy matter getting in to see this komandir. Ten times I had to tell various people who I was, where I was from, and what I wanted. At last I was granted an appointment.

As usual there was a throng of people in city hall that morning; the corridors and rooms were jammed to the limits. The place was dirty, and the offices stank. I reported to the room assigned. A young Soviet soldier took my numbered ticket and noted my personal data in his book—name, father's name, date of birth. Then he went into the next room, which, as I had expected, was the komandir's office. I was told to wait.

I waited and waited, rehearsing my words in endless permutations. After quite some time a civilian went into the office with a bundle of papers under his arm, and through the open door I caught a glimpse of a figure in full uniform sweeping the floor with a light-colored broom. Peculiar, I thought, but illuminating: a Soviet officer does not look down on work of any kind; such is the way it should be in a communist society.

The door closed, leaving me waiting again until a voice rang out: "Petya!" The soldier jumped up, went into the office, and reappeared to wave me in. Behind the desk was the komandir I had seen with the broom. Like everyone else, he wore a belted green shirt, but red geometric shapes fastened to his collar indicated his rank, which I was unable to decipher. He gestured for me to be seated and looked me over closely. Once again I gave my name, my father's name, my date of birth, and it was only after these formalities that I was able to present my case. I spoke in textbook Russian, awkwardly, ignorant of colloquialisms. As he listened, he scribbled. He asked no questions, but kept his eyes riveted on me; I had the uncomfortable feeling that his evaluation did not depend in the least on what I was saying. Even after I had finished speaking about myself and my father, he continued to take stock of me. Finally he asked, "But how is it you know Russian?"

I told him that my father had taught me and that I had practiced by listening to Radio Moscow every day. He seemed surprised by that simple explanation, but became more so when I told him that I would be willing to fight fascism as a sailor in the Soviet Red Navy. He spoke little, asking only a few casual questions about my father, my family, Warsaw.

He then asked me where I was living. And there I hesitated. Almost instinctively I was reluctant to give him the address of my Jewish hosts, and so I told him I was staying at the shelter for refugees. I also deliberately did not mention Lityn, having noticed the detailed notes he had made about my family in Warsaw; I was apprehensive that Lityn would draw too much attention. Later, I often thought about how, although I had not planned it, that omission was my salvation.

In conclusion the komandir said that mine was a difficult case, that he would try to help me, and that I should report to him again in exactly one week.

I had a fever and chills on the day I was to report again, but I went to the city hall all the same. It turned out that no one was expecting me, and it seemed that the entire process would have to be gone through again. I walked away from the little window somewhat resigned, but with a firm resolve to see through to my goal.

I returned to Moishe's with a high fever and literally collapsed onto my bed. How lucky I am, I thought, to be here and not sleeping on a chair in the refugee shelter. The next day Moishe brought me powders from the drugstore, but nothing helped; I was utterly weak, my appetite gone entirely. Moishe's wife would come and put her hand on my forehead several times a day and say: "Oi, not good, not good!" She brought me tea and asked me to swallow a teaspoonful of sugar to give me some strength. I was in bed for several days, in a delirium, my head spinning. Time went by in a blur.

One evening, when I at last felt a little stronger, I ate dinner with the family, and Moishe talked about the election.

"What election?" I asked.

"You don't know? For the last few days all they've been doing in Lutsk is going around with those megaphones, shouting that the people demand freedom. They've covered the whole city with posters. Today, every citizen was required to go and vote in front of the commission. They gave you a card with some names on it, and you had to toss the card into a box. That's all there was to it. They warned that there'd be trouble for anyone who didn't vote; that would mean you were against the people, against the Soviets, against *good*. So, naturally everyone tossed in his card, and so did I. . . . What kind of election was that? Tell me, please."

"What were the names on the card?" I asked him.

"How should I know? I didn't even read them. What difference would it make? They said you had to vote or you'd be in trouble, so how could reading it make it any better? Everyone voted like that. What else could we do?"

It was already nearing the end of October when I made my way again to the city hall. Lutsk was all in red; red bunting and posters hung on houses, fences, posts, everywhere. The city hall, too, was covered with red. The posters were evidently there to attest to the revolutionary mood of the populace, and, in Ukrainian, they demanded that the Western Ukraine be incorporated into the Soviet Union's great family of nations.

That day I was luckier. With my numbered ticket in hand, I proceeded to the floor above, where I did not have to wait long to see the komandir. He began the conversation himself as I took a seat in front of his desk.

"Your case requires further consideration," he said, "and so I've made an appointment for you with other komandirs, who will deal with your case. There's no more I can do, but they will try to help you."

I was to report to a certain address immediately after the holiday celebrating the Bolshevik revolution. On bidding the komandir farewell, I looked into his eyes, and I seemed to see some cold, malevolent glint in them. It's an illusion, I assured myself; it's the fever, and I'm seeing things.

It was late in the day when I returned from the city. The whole family, including a bearded man in a hat whom I did not know, was seated at the table. He was introduced to me as a relative who had fled Krakow, where he had been a rabbi. First, he told us, he had gone to Lwow, but things had become too dangerous for refugees there. I felt I was in a difficult spot, because his arrival seemed to signal my departure. There was no room for another person.

"I probably ought to be leaving." I must have said that with some sorrow, because Moishe and his wife exchanged glances.

The rabbi spoke first. "I know things are hard, but where are things easy now? It's hard everywhere. Just so they don't get any worse," he reasoned with himself. "I know what it means to go from one place to another," he said finally, turning to me. "We can share the bed."

And from that day on, for several weeks, I shared a rabbi's bed.

Every morning and evening I was witness to his religious rites. First he would rapidly mumble prayers under his breath in what must have been Hebrew; then he would wind a black band, to which something like a small box was fixed, around his arm. I did not ask him what it was, guessing that it contained holy books, perhaps the Talmud. He would again whisper something, unwrap the band with the little box, and finish, in a changed voice, by reciting another prayer or singing some lament.

At night the rabbi would fall asleep quickly, and I would soon follow, worn out from days spent roaming the city. Or I would lie awake, with an eerie feeling that my father was in grave danger.

The city grew even redder in the few days before the celebration of the revolution. Loudspeakers announced that the Fifth Special Session of the Supreme Soviet of the USSR, in session between October 31 and November 2, had decided to grant the request of the national assemblies elected by the populace of the Western Ukraine and Byelorussia and incorporate those territories into the great family of Soviet republics. On the main street, where a parade was to take place, Ukrainian signs expressed gratitude for the incorporation of those lands into the Soviet fatherland. There were no signs in Polish or in Yiddish, as if the city had neither Poles nor Jews, and yet, in traversing the streets, almost the only language I heard was Polish.

My morale sank even lower when I saw that new banners had been hung with anti-Polish slogans: "Down with the Polish lords"; "The oppressed Ukrainian people will at last be able to breathe free." The stores, too, were decked in red. In one display window paper bags full of sugar lay on a red cloth, with a sign suspended above: "The Soviet Union gives the children of the Western Ukraine sugar, which lordly Poland had refused them." I could not believe it. I had been in these parts many times over a number of years and I knew well that the stores here were as well supplied as anywhere else, that there had never been a shortage of sugar in Poland, and that it had always been cheap. And, what was more, back then there had been no lines spilling down the streets in front of the stores.

The red posters, signs, and banners had been hung by Soviet soldiers, assisted by Ukrainian police sporting red arm bands. They drove through the city in small, creaky, green trucks stacked with bales of red cloth. I could not help but reflect that for a couple of days now I had not been able to buy even a handkerchief to replace the one I had lost. Watching as red Lutsk came into being, I listened in on what the Poles were saying. An older man said to a younger one: "You see this logic? They hang up some red cloth and think the whole thing's settled. . . . Just look at their horrible faces. We've got to get out of here. Nothing good'll come of this. . . ."

I went back to my Jews.

"Why are they plastering the whole city with red cloth? There's enough there to make everyone a shirt!" said Moishe. "What a waste of good cloth, oi . . . and such nice red cloth, too."

On Revolution Day I left for the city early. Police were everywhere, and soldiers patrolled the area to keep people from gathering on the streets where the parade would pass. Loudspeakers mounted on green trucks shouted instructions to people forming lines for the parade. The trucks had obviously brought people in from the countryside. Many women wore kerchiefs on their heads, and the men looked like they had come straight from the fields. Most of them were speaking Ukrainian. Before I knew what was happening, the people around me began to form ranks, and soon I was walking with them, part of a group. I must have attracted attention in that crowd of country people, since the women surrounding me were all small and squat. There I was, a lanky guy in a leather coat and a strange cap towering two heads above the kerchiefed peasant women. At moments, I was ready to turn and flee. Yet I was restrained by the thought that this was a test of the strength of my principles, of my internationalist beliefs. Over there, on the other side, people are not parading, I thought. Over there, the Nazis are destroying us. I studied the faces around me. There were no expressions except, perhaps, curiosity; they had simply been brought in to march, and so they marched. In the distance, on the main street, where a platform had been set up, the loudspeakers were relaying marches I had never heard before. But the sidewalks were empty. A strange parade, I thought, with no people watching. The music from the loudspeakers grew louder as we passed the platform, and every so often there would be a cry of "Haj zywe!" (Long live!). The crowd would respond mechanically, "Haj zywe!" and keep on moving. There was a row of about fifteen people on the platform: some Soviet soldiers, some civilians, a few women, whom no one seemed to know. The street was drowning in red, and there were even more banners and signs than there had been in the late afternoon of the previous day. Those right by the platform were the largest and expressed gratitude to Stalin for liberating the Western Ukraine. A banner spread between buildings across a street cried out: "Long live Stalin, leader of progressive humanity!"

I returned to Moishe's in low spirits. I had not expected communism to have such trappings. Perhaps Ukrainian nationalist instincts were still mired in capitalist thinking; perhaps they needed time to mature into internationalism. I did not dare allow the scene to influence my thinking. I put it out of my mind.

As arranged, I reported to the Red Army komandirs, this time in a new location—an old manor house surrounded by a garden wall. The soldier at the gate must have been notified of my visit, because, when I told him my name, he let me pass. In the entry hall another soldier met me and led me up to the second floor, where he instructed me to wait, pointing to a chair. Time crawled as I waited. I had begun to squirm impatiently when a tall komandir in an overcoat clomped up the stairs and slipped into the doorway across from me. He was followed by a soldier, who disappeared behind the same door carrying files. Again an interminable wait. Little did I know that I was in the quarters of the NKVD—the secret police.

I was beginning to suspect that there had been some sort of misunderstanding, when the door opened and the komandir beckoned me. He began the interview, squinting from time to time at the papers on his desk. To my dismay, we started again from the beginning—last name, first name, father's name, date and place of birth—though in more detail this time. Preliminaries done, the door swung open, and a second komandir entered. He was shorter and younger. He seated himself to one side and fixed his eyes on me. I had the uncomfortable feeling that the meeting had become an interrogation, but I restrained my discomfort with the thought that at last I had accomplished what I had been trying to do for weeks. Perhaps I could persuade our Soviet comrades to assist my father, who might well be in danger by now. Without the slightest trepidation or nervousness, I presented my father's case and my own. I spoke boldly, with conviction; I had nothing to hide and quickly answered the increasingly detailed questions.

"You say that you always lived in Warsaw," continued the komandir at the desk. "And where did you go to school?"

I told him about my school in Warsaw, lying for the first time and concealing my schooling in Milanowek, for that would have opened a new and endless subject for them.

"What street is the school on?" he asked.

"Prosta Street, on the corner of Prosta and Walicow."

I began to be angered by the komandir's endless recording of details. I had come to them for help, and they were persecuting me in error, just as the soldiers on the *britzka* had.

The younger komandir now joined in, and began asking more and more questions, until eventually I was speaking with him only. He demanded to know whom I knew in the Polish Communist Party, wanting first names, father's names, addresses, dates of birth. The other komandir scribbled madly. I gave them a few names, but I did not know addresses. This extended interview was plainly more than just an inquiry into my own case. And I was by now angry and concealing information.

The younger komandir began to question me about my knowledge of Russian. "Really," he said, "how is it you know Russian?"

"I don't know it well," I explained. "I've already told you that my father, who does know Russian well, taught me. And I listened to the radio."

"You are not fluent, but your accent is Russian. Where does that accent come from? Have you spent time with Russians?"

"No, not at all." I repeated, "From the radio."

"The radio . . . the radio," parroted the komandir, glancing meaningfully at the older one.

"But didn't you study from a textbook?" asked the one at the desk.

"No, never," I answered impatiently. Once again I was concealing the truth, because I *had* gone through the standard textbook for Polish officers, which my father had purchased for me. My lie was instinctive; I was trying desperately to keep the conversation on some relevant course.

"Did you study other languages?" hammered the young komandir persistently.

"Yes. Eight years of German in school, and four of Latin."

They exchanged glances once more.

"You say you know German," continued the older one. "Do you know it well?"

"I do. One learns a lot in eight years. I can recite German poetry."

"Maybe you know some other languages, too?" he asked.

And here I committed a grave mistake. "Yes, of course. I studied French, Italian, and English."

This was too much for them—they exchanged significant glances openly. I was obliged to tell them about each language in turn, and with undisguised amazement they asked me whether I spoke each of them as well as I spoke Russian. I corrected that impression by saying that I knew only German well and was just a beginner in the others. That was quite beyond them, as was the fact that to learn them I had simply bought the language manuals in a bookstore. They were obviously surprised that in Poland one could buy foreign-language textbooks so easily.

The interview had become protracted, and I was feeling tired. "What will happen with my father?" I asked. "How will you help him slip out of Warsaw to the Soviet side?"

"Don't worry, it'll be arranged. These things can't be rushed," the older one chanted without a trace of sincerity in his voice.

"We'll talk again. Come see us in a week, in exactly one week, on Tuesday, and we'll continue then. Be sure to come, because that will be the important meeting, maybe the decisive one."

Crossing the street the next day, I heard a voice call out my name. Wladek Czekalski, my father's disciple, stood in front of me. Eyes radiant, he threw his arms around me. We kissed each other so many times that passers-by turned to stare, and with good reason. Wladek was the first person I knew whom I had encountered in Lutsk.

"Where did you get that leather coat?" he asked. "Your father told us you left wearing nothing but a sweater." Without waiting for an answer, he continued. "But you look awful. Have you been sick? How are you doing? How's life been? It's so good to see you, so good we met!"

We had always been close and fond of one another. He saw me as the son of the professor who for years had been his mentor—the one person, as he repeated often, who had changed his entire life. Now he was not letting me get a word in edgewise.

"Let's have a talk! What a coincidence!"

Wladek reported that he had seen my father a few days after I left Warsaw. He spoke of the shelling of the city, and said that he had barely been able to get out himself.

I told him about my efforts to come to my father's aid, and about my most recent interview with the komandirs. Wladek's expression darkened.

"We must discuss this, Romek," he said gravely. "That doesn't sound good at all. I want you to share some information given me by Wajsbrot."

"Wajsbrot?" I asked. "The man who used to come see my father? Izaak Wajsbrot?"

"Yes. You know him. The best thing would be for us to go see him now—he can tell you everything himself."

In less than fifteen minutes we were at the other end of town, where Wajsbrot was living at the home of a local teacher. Catching sight of me, he cried out, and asked immediately, "Where's the professor?"

"Still in Warsaw," I replied.

"If he could just be here with us . . . if he could just be here," he repeated, "maybe things would be different. They'd have to reckon with him; he'd get through to see the right people. . . ."

"You know, Comrade Wajsbrot, how much I respect the professor," interrupted Wladek. "He is the only person who really mattered in my life, but even he would be beating his head against the wall in this place. Romek's been doing just that. Romek, tell him about your interviews with the komandirs."

I told Wajsbrot about the Soviets and my impressions of them. When I had finished, they, too, exchanged glances.

"Why are you looking at each other? Was I wrong?"

"No," Wajsbrot assured me, "but we have information from our comrades here, from the Party. They say things are bad, very bad. You see, Romek, from what we know, it appears that the Soviet authorities not only have no interest in what happens to Communists here in the so-called Western Ukraine, they are even killing them. That means Poles and Jews, not Ukrainians. Here in Lutsk there was one Party member, a good man, a Jew, a Polish Jew like me—they took him in for interrogation, once, twice. The third time he never came back. The Soviets finally told his wife that it would be better for her if she stopped pestering them with questions about her husband. One of them was even brazen enough to advise her that this was a splendid opportunity to find herself another husband. The same thing is happening with non-Jewish Poles, here as well as in Kowel. Families are trying to find out what happened to their kin, but they can't learn anything."

"Who are they?" I asked, bridling.

"What do you mean *who*? The NKVD!" answered Wajsbrot. "Tell me, where did you speak with those komandirs? . . . What kind of caps were they wearing?"

I gave him the address and described their caps, whose flat tops were bright green.

"There you are," he proclaimed. "They must have been NKVD. Did they tell you to come back in exactly one week, and did they try to impress on you that it would be an important meeting?"

"They did."

"This is very serious, Romek. You go back there and . . . you'll disappear like all the others."

"But what can they do to me? I didn't conceal anything. I only wanted to save my father and to join their side in this war!"

"I'm afraid that's not how they see it," said Wajsbrot. "They are a suspicious lot."

"Do they know where you're living?" asked Wajsbrot.

"No," I answered. "I'm living with a poor Jewish family, but I told the komandir that I was in the shelter for refugees."

"Good," he replied. "Who knows what might come into the NKVD's mind before you're to report to them again."

"Why do you keep saying NKVD?" I objected. "They're Red Army."

"Romek, in the Soviet Union under Stalin, the NKVD leads the pack."

"But how can I *not* report to them? You think I'm going to let all my efforts go to waste? Forget it. That makes no sense at all."

"Do you remember Rudnianski?" asked Wajsbrot. "Stefan Rudnianski from the Free University, your father's colleague?"

"Of course."

"Rudnianski is at the University in Lwow, lecturing on dialectical materialism. I think it would be best for you to attempt to work through him and not through people here. . . . He might have good connections. He may be in contact with Moscow University or with Wanda Wasilewska. I hear that she's already in Moscow, that she's been appointed to a high position." In fact, this novelist, in some unexplainable way, had become Stalin's protégé.

"But what if Rudnianski isn't in touch with Wasilewska and can't do anything? What then?" interjected Wladek.

I returned to Moishe's confused. All my hopes for arranging something with the Soviets had been shattered. If that's really how things are, I thought, if they're persecuting Polish Communists, then why should they treat me any differently? And if they sent me off, I would be unable to help my father, I would be powerless. I could not allow that to happen.

The next morning I met Wladek and told him I would go to Lwow to see Rudnianski. I would cross back over to the German side, where my father was, as a last resort.

"To go to Lwow is smart, but to cross over to the German side?" Wladek had misgivings. "You could be shot at the border by either Germans or Russians." He looked around, for we were standing in the street and people were nearby. "Romek, the Russians are just as cruel as the Germans; don't forget that. They may have a different line, but that's the only difference."

I looked at him reproachfully. He was well aware I was my father's son and did not like to hear remarks like that.

"I'm leaving for Lwow tomorrow at the latest. I'm not wasting time," I told him.

"I'm going with you then."

I returned to Moishe's and looked wistfully around that cozy hut where I had been given shelter. At the table I announced my decision. They were truly surprised and saddened.

"If I don't succeed in helping my father in Lwow, I'll cross over to the German side. It's hard and risky, I know, but there's nothing else I can do."

Moishe was disturbed by this. "No good," he kept repeating. "You said yourself that you knew what they were like, that you didn't want to fall into their hands . . . and now . . ."

"Yes, but my father's survival is at stake."

"I understand—a father is very important—but can you really save him from the Germans? He'll die and so will you. Such a decision, made so fast—it's no good."

Moishe's wife looked at me, her eyes filled with fear. "Do you think these are the old days? There's nothing easier than dying now. Stay here with us."

A moment later the rabbi, even the children, joined in the chorus. But I could not be dissuaded, although leaving that little hut would be hard for me. I promised to leave them my bicycle to remember me by.

It took me a long time to fall asleep that night. My thoughts were agitated, as if by a premonition that considerably more than a trip to Lwow lay in store for me.

I rose early the next morning and repacked my things, putting only clothing, my sweater, my spare pair of boots, and my grandmother's "Dunin" into my knapsack. In my pocket I hid a section cut from my map showing the "border" rivers, the San and the Bug. I left the rest of my things with my friends in the event that I returned.

Wajsbrot was alarmed by the swiftness of my decision, and even tried to convince me to postpone it, to think through this step that might prove a crucial one in my life. But I was determined.

"I will try to settle my affairs in Lwow," I said, "but if that does not succeed, I have no other choice. Yesterday you convinced me that I cannot depend on those komandirs. Today you are trying to dissuade me from following my only other option."

"Romek," said Izaak, "listen. I'm trying to think what your father would do if he were here. He certainly wouldn't want you crossing over to the German side. There are serious dangers in that: you could fall into German hands, or you could get killed. Both the Germans and the Russians at the border shoot to kill. Your plan is close to madness. Only people with nothing to lose take risks like that. . . . Your father would never allow it."

"I don't agree," I protested. "I've always been revolted by heroics and by unnecessary risks, but I'm in a different situation now. My father's fate depends on me."

I left Lutsk with a heavy heart, reflecting bitterly that things there had reached such a point that I was fleeing from Soviet authorities. It was a travesty indeed.

The train was teeming with people, some of whom stood right between my feet. The trip dragged. The distance of one hundred miles, which we could normally have covered in less than three hours, was promising to take that train many hours more, because it stopped at every way station. We kept dozing, the train kept stopping, more passengers kept boarding. . . .

The station in Lwow, too, was mobbed. Polish refugees weighed down with bags seemed lost among the surging crowds of Ukrainians in their peasant boots, faces sunburned and ruddy. There was no information available, and people simply floated about in confusion. Inside the station, Soviet patrols with red arm bands on their overcoat sleeves and long bayonets fixed to their rifles walked in fours through the crowds. The marble floor was muddy. People were perched shoulder to shoulder on the benches; others lay on the floor by the walls.

Wladek knew Lwow and led the way. I had only a hazy memory of the city, since I had been there only years ago with my mother. But everything looked different now—gray and dismal. Even Wladek had trouble finding his way around; he complained that the names of the streets had been changed. The signs were all in Ukrainian now. Nevertheless, we soon reached the university, and found it swaddled in its own red bunting and bearing a different name.

"Yes, Stefan Rudnianski lectures here," a clerk informed us in Ukranian. "Dialectical materialism. He should arrive in half an hour."

We took a seat. I was seething. "They may have changed the name of the university to something Ukrainian and covered it with red bunting," I told Wladek, "but they cannot alter the fact that Lwow Academy was founded almost three hundred years ago by the Polish king Jan Kazimierz."

Wladek shrugged his shoulders. "I told you what I thought of them. Don't you remember? What does any of this have to do with communism? It's the exact opposite."

Rudnianski walked in, hair white as snow, stooped. He seemed smaller and somehow nervous. At first he didn't recognize me.

"Spasowski, Spasowski," he repeated, evidently thinking of my father, and unable to reconcile the name with the tall young man before him. "Oh, yes," finally, "please come in. What brings you here and how is your father?" he asked.

I told him about myself and of the need to rescue my father.

"Those aren't easy matters," he said. "If he were here, that would be one thing, but he's in Warsaw, on the German side. My own family is there, too, you know, my wife, both children. . . . There's nothing I can do for them."

"What do you mean? Can't the people here help you?"

"Maybe they could; there are all sorts here," he said, lowering his voice involuntarily, his eyes darting around. "You see . . . . these are complicated matters." He was weighing his words carefully, his voice a whisper. "This is Lwow, you see. The authorities are Ukrainian . . ." He was about to add something to that, but hesitated. A moment later, he continued. "It's the central authorities in Moscow who decide these questions."

"But the university must have some connections with Moscow University. They could be an avenue . . ." I argued.

"Yes, there are connections, but only Ukrainians are going to Moscow." He lowered his voice again. "In Lwow it is considered a great honor to be admitted to Moscow, not to mention *invited*. . . ."

"Have you been there?" I asked.

"No, I haven't had the chance. Maybe next year . . ."

I felt sorry for him. Could this be the same Rudnianski who had criticized the Polish gentry, the capitalists, and the government with such energy and eloquence?

"Maybe Wanda Wasilewska can help?" I said as a last resort, "I heard she was here."

"Oh, Wasilewska," he said dismissively. "She's in Lwow often, but she spends most of the time in Moscow. Well . . . she could do a great deal . . . but you would never get through to her. . . . She's become very important since she was received by Stalin, as you know. . . ."

Listening to him, I could feel my hopes of achieving something in Lwow dwindling. Rudnianski was changed, frightened. My only option now was to try to rescue my father myself. When I told him that, the old professor looked surprised. But he did not try to talk me out of it.

"When will you cross over?" he asked.

"As soon as possible—tomorrow, the day after . . ."

His brow knit. "Maybe you can bring Lucylla with you on the way back," he said pensively. "I would be grateful. Would you take a card to my wife?"

He wrote a few words on a card, gave me the Lwow address of Boy-Zelenski, shook our hands, and said good-bye.

"You know," I said, as Wladek and I walked along the corridor, "I had no idea it was going to be that bad. . . . He wasn't the slightest bit interested in us, whether we'd eaten, where we would spend the night. Let's go see Boy and then cross over."

"Romek," Wladek said, "the rich don't understand the hungry. Even under communism."

Boy-Zelenski lived in the center of the city, in a large luxurious apartment building that reminded me of Prywer's building in Warsaw: a wide gateway, a beautiful staircase with banisters of intricate metal sculptures, doors made of heavy oak with large bronze doorknobs. But these were all signs of past glory, proof that what once had been was no longer, for the place had not been swept or cleaned in weeks. Like the rest of Lwow, it was littered with trash, mud, and cigarette butts.

A tall woman opened the door and led us through a large foyer into a living room, where she knocked on another door. The room, in semidarkness, was furnished with fine heavy furniture: a credenza, bookcases, a desk with a high-backed chair. Heavy curtains hung ponderously on either side of the glass doors.

A voice reached us from the next room, and the woman opened the door. An old man in a frock coat and linen trousers rose from an armchair and moved slowly toward us.

"My name is Spasowski, Romuald Spasowski, and this is my friend," I said. "I am Wladyslaw Spasowski's son."

Boy nodded, seeming to make the association.

"Perhaps you remember me from many years ago. When I was little, I used to go with my parents to Tetmajer's house—you remember? You were there often."

Boy smiled dimly. "Sit down, please. What can I do for you?"

I told him briefly about myself and asked him whether he could help me bring my father to the Soviet side.

"Me?" he said with genuine surprise. "Believe me, in these times no one knows what can happen to one or how things will turn out." He shook his head in resignation. I looked closely at him. His eyes were cold, peering at me glassily from a large flat face. I told him my plans. He listened without interruption, his mind elsewhere.

"Please give your father my respects," was his only response.

There was nothing more to say. My eyes wandered around the room. Here, too, the furniture was stately; there was a large couch by the wall, on which I assumed he slept. Books, papers, and figurines crowded one another on his desk.

"We'll be going then," said Wladek, breaking a long silence.

We walked out, troubled by the old man's indifference. Outside, a cold and gusty wind was blowing.

"I'm angry and I'm hungry," I said, putting my arm around Wladek's shoulder.

"Me, too. We're in a bad spot. I thought for sure he would put us up for the night. In an hour or less the curfew starts. We'll have to find somewhere to spend the night or we'll get picked up by a patrol, and God only knows what will happen to us then." The streets were already nearly deserted.

Rounding a corner, we came upon a hotel. A group of people at the desk were pleading for rooms, but all were taken. A large man shouted through a door that people who were not registered should get out, because the military patrols would be by to arrest loiterers. Our situation looked hopeless.

"Romek, give me one of your silver coins," said Wladek. He walked over to the large man, whispered something to him, and handed him the coin. It would not have occurred to me to do that, to bribe someone. The man spread his hands apart, palms up, and began a harangue of some sort.

"He insists that we give him two silver five-zloty pieces for a room," Wladek came back and reported. "The scum!"

I gave Wladek another coin, and in a moment he was back. "All settled. He says we have only to go outside and wait in front for a little while, then he'll bring us in through the other side. Here there are too many people, too many eyes."

We went out. The man appeared a short while later. He took us through a gate and upstairs to the second floor, where he opened a door that led into the rear of the hotel. We walked up to the fourth floor to a normal hotel room with two beds. I pulled out a few of the flat cakes Moishe's wife had given me for the road. These, with a little cold water to drink, and we were off to bed. What luxury! I mused. Alone in a bed for the first time in weeks. And I had worried that things would end badly.

It was drizzling the next morning when we left the hotel. We had some luck on the way and were able to buy bread and sausage, since the stores had just opened and the lines were still short. Eating our bread and sausage and drinking hot tea in a little tea shop, we made further plans. We pored over the piece I had torn from my map and came to the conclusion that I ought to make the crossing at the nearest point, which meant somewhere in the vicinity of Rawa Ruska, only about thirty miles from Lwow. Wladek insisted on accompanying me as far as he could.

On the street we ran into my schoolmate Leon Lis. He and I greeted one another warmly, but he spoke contemptuously of the Soviets, and we were soon arguing. He accused me of blindness, and I accused him of a certain smallness of mind. He seemed able to see only the petty shortcomings and idiocies, not the greatness of the Soviet revolution. But I could not refute his arguments well, and, furious, we parted. Had we been told at that time what lay in store for us, neither of us would have believed it. Leon spent the entire war, five years, on the Soviet side, and ended up serving in the Red Army. Mine was a very different fate.

My farewell with Wladek in Rawa Ruska was emotional. As he asked me to give his love to his wife, Murcia, and to his son, his voice broke. We embraced, shook hands, and parted, I turning to see his figure vanish among the little buildings.

I passed a few villages and in one stopped at a hut that seemed to me the best kept. This method, recommended by someone in Lutsk, did not fail me. The broad-shouldered Ukrainian who came to the door said, "Might get you across tonight. What will you pay me with?"

I held out a silver five-zloty coin. "I have only three of these," I said.

"Fine. Let me have that one, as payment in advance. Wait here. We'll leave together as soon as word comes that there's going to be a crossing."

"We're crossing the river?" I asked, assuming that at that place one could cross on foot.

"Yes, a little river that runs into the Bug. Sometimes they shoot," he volunteered. "And sometimes the Germans nab people and turn them over to the Russians; the Russians do the same thing, and people are bounced back and forth. Fewer people are trying now, because it's more dangerous. But a month ago they were crossing in droves. Some of them were even driving through the water in their wagons."

"Sit down," he said, "or lie down there on the floor. It's going to be a couple of hours."

I lay down in the corner of the room with my knapsack under my head and fell asleep. It must have been after midnight when he shook me awake. "Time to cross. Let's go."

There was no moon, no stars. First it was just the two of us, but soon we were joined by others, carrying bundles. I gathered from the loud breathing that their baggage was heavy. Once or twice I passed what looked like refugees from the Soviet side teetering under all their belongings.

We walked for a long time, stumbling from holes in the road, but careful to keep up and not go astray in the dark. Our leader would stop and listen intently from time to time, and then we all would stop, the silence broken only by tired gasps. The hike was so long that even I, with my light knapsack, began to feel weary. About then the leader ordered us to sit down; we had come to the river. I could hear little splashes, like the sound of boats in the water, and voices speaking in a whisper.

Then suddenly, and very close by, a shrill Russian shout, "Stop! Stop!" The shout was repeated from the other side. The leader and the few men assisting him began to bark commands at us. "Quick, quick, into the boats, or they'll get us. . . ."

People rushed to the boats. A few tried to carry their things, but the leaders tore them out of their hands, cursing and shouting that there was no time, that the Russians were right behind us.

I jumped into a boat. A moment later we were moving with the current, the banks on either side gliding past us. No one in the boat said a word, and the only sound was the soft lap of water as the boatman withdrew the long pole he used to push against the bottom. Only minutes later the underside of the boat brushed land.

"Go on, get out," ordered the boatman. People began scrambling onto the shore, feeling their way with their hands.

"Where to?" I asked the boatman.

"Straight ahead," he answered, pushing himself back into the water. Empty now, the boat slipped away and vanished in the darkness.

I was on the German side.

CHAPTER V

People from the boat began to vanish, melting away into the black of night. I could hear soft whispers and muffled weeping; some of them had left all their worldly goods on the other side of the river. Those guides were thieves, I thought; the Russian shouting had been nothing more than a show put on to fool those people and rob them of their belongings. No question about it, by now the guides would have gathered up their loot and were probably on their way home to divide it.

I walked alone into the darkness. Since there were no stars and I did not have my compass with me, I could easily lose my way. I tried instinctively to move perpendicular to the river, to the northwest, toward Tomaszow, the largest of the little towns on my route and only about twelve miles from the crossing. Not another soul did I see that night. I walked slowly, cautiously, stopping to listen every so often. For all I knew, I was heading right for a German sentry. My only protection was to listen hard, to move like a cat. I spent the night crossing fields, overgrown paths, ditches, bushes. When the first light of day appeared in the sky, I was surrounded by meadows and fields.

I sat down in a hollow to rest for a while. Studying my strip of map, I figured that everything indicated I was somewhere between Belzec and Bykow. Things might be safer here, I thought, now that I'm past the "border" area. When it grew lighter, I took out my wallet and examined my ID card. I began to regret that, on Moishe's advice, I had registered as a refugee in Lutsk. They had put a

Ukrainian seal on the first page: "Refugee Aid Committee, Lutsk, October 4." Now, if I were stopped by Germans, there would be no denying that I had been over there. I would have to lie and say that I had fled from the Soviet side. But what chance did I have against the Nazis anyway?

It was probably some time after nine when I came to a road that seemed to lead in the right direction; I was able to know that from the color of the bark of trees. The bark and the moss indicated I was going north. The road led through a cluster of green growth and then through a wide, open field; I could see whitewashed houses and peasant huts in the distance. I was happily striding toward the little town when a string of men came around a bend, heading directly toward me. I saw at once that they were marching in step: a German patrol. I kept on walking and collected my thoughts, knowing I would have to run the risk; the moment had come, and luck would be either with me or not. I balled up the strip of map in my pocket and tossed it under a bush.

The Germans were close now. They looked like front-line troops: field caps, short uniform jackets, pants tucked into high-topped leather boots, rifles over shoulders, leather belts, cartridge holders. I walked along the edge of the road, leaving them plenty of room to pass, but I did not stop. As the noncom who led the patrol passed, I ran a quick glance over his face. He was staring at me, and I was sure he would shout "Halt!" any second now, but he did not make a sound, and I walked on past. A strange anxiety then crept over me that they might have stopped and pointed their rifles at my back. But I restrained myself from looking around. If they were going to shoot, I decided, I would have heard some sort of command. Only as I entered the town did I turn around. They were already far away. My first test was over.

I spent the night in that little town, Jarczow, and the next day traveled to Tomaszow with the innkeeper's brother. It was in the Tomaszow station that I grew accustomed to the sight of German soldiers.

On the train to Warsaw, jammed in one corner of a crowded compartment, I dozed, thinking of the time I had spent on the Soviet side. Suddenly I roused myself. The train had halted at a station, Zamosc. I looked out on the mobbed platform. A squad of German soldiers across from the station stood at ease in a perfect line. Reporting to an officer, a noncom clicked his heels sharply and saluted. A command was shouted; the squad snapped to attention and did a right face in absolute unison. They marched off in orderly rows of three.

The ragtag crowd, some of them Polish soldiers still in crumpled uniforms, watched them in stiff silence. The Germans' hobnailed boots stamped evenly along the platform. Their faces, sunburned and ruddy, emanated health. As they marched off into the distance a patch of bronze on each of their knapsacks glinted in the sun.

The Warsaw to which I returned now was not the same city I had left ten weeks before. It was badly crippled; the results of war and siege were evident everywhere: homes burned or destroyed, walls ragged with bullet holes, roads pocked with craters, streetlights broken, streetcar wires snarled and dangling. As I walked, I studied the people—tired, tattered bodies bent in half against the cold, moving furtively. The more I saw, the greater the pain tearing at my heart. Would it not have been better to have stayed in Warsaw, to have been here with them, to have taken care of my father, and perhaps even see Judyta return? Throughout all this suffering, as the city was turned into a shell of its former self, I had wandered far, to no avail. Warsaw, my city, whose streets were my home, whose squares knew my feet, was gone forever. What, then, of my father?

The closer I got to home, the more anxious I became. I was afraid to turn onto Emilia Plater Street, because Noakowski, our street, would be visible from there. Shattered houses were everywhere. I walked, instead, by way of Piekna and Koszykowa streets. One more corner . . . I made the sudden turn and faced my destination, Number Twenty-two.

I ran through the familiar gateway and courtyard, noticing the aura of neglect. Clearly no one had swept it out for weeks. I bolted into the stairwell and raced up the stairs. The bell, my father's footsteps, the opened door . . . In the dark I could not see his face, but I knew his shape. We threw ourselves into each other's arms.

"Son, my son . . ." he whispered again and again.

Immediately I asked about my mother and Judyta.

"Nothing's changed in Milanowek," he said, "and no news of Judyta."

That day I spent hours telling my father about my experiences. I concealed nothing, letting all my negative observations and feelings about the Soviets, particularly about those komandirs, spill out. He listened attentively, without interruption, noting his questions on a slip of paper. I could see that my words caused him a great deal of pain, but he made an effort to control his agitation.

My eye was not blind to the traces of his own recent experience. Considerably more gray hair was noticeable around his temples, and more wrinkles lined his face, but most of all it showed in his eyes, so recently vital and brilliant, acute and piercing, now full of sadness and resignation. But it was clear that his views and ideals had not changed; rather, they had congealed in him despite all his trials.

I closed my report to him by saying, "No one helped, Father. Not the Soviets, not Rudnianski, not Boy-Zelenski. It seems no one can be counted on for anything. Wladek and Wajsbrot are powerless. It's all up to us, only us, what we do. We have no other choice but to gather our strength and cross to the Soviet side as quickly as we can. Here, with the Nazis, there will be only death.

My father kissed me. "Yes, son. It grieves me that you were treated so inhumanly by the Soviets. I neither understand them nor forgive them for that. But I am glad you are willing to try again with me."

We began to prepare immediately for our crossing to the East.

Walking to Judyta's the next morning, I saw the enormity of Warsaw's destruction. The war had spared nothing; the Nazis had either turned the city upside down or snuffed the life out of it. In many parts where there had once been lawns and flowers, the ground was dug up and marked with crosses. The streets were crawling with people, since all public transportation was effectively stopped. Germans in uniform and helmets—military police—swarmed through the main streets with newfangled machine pistols—Schmeissers, I learned later—around their necks.

The more I walked, and the more I saw, the more I was shaken. Messages had been posted on lone walls of collapsed buildings, in gateways that now led nowhere, by courtyards littered with rubble and smoldering wood. Cards spoke to relatives telling them that So-and-so was alive or that someone's parents had been killed and that a child was now living with someone else at Such-and-such address. Saddest of all, a superintendent announced to whomever it concerned that an entire family had been killed in the bombing on September 25.

In the Jewish quarter, gone were the noisy crowds of talkative, gesticulating residents. People crept by, some exchanging words in whispers, some with gaze fixed ahead, all of them poised, waiting for something to occur, some new danger to strike.

I turned onto Gesia Street; another forty feet to go. Almost there, I stopped, rooted to the ground. Of Judyta's building, only scorched walls remained. One building next to it was entirely in ruins, the direct target of an aerial bomb. Not believing my eyes, I drew closer. The gateway to her building was still there, but it led nowhere, only to rubble, brick, and charred wood. There was nothing but empty space between the walls high up where her room had been.

Memories rushed cinematically through my mind. It was there a few months ago that we had said farewell and I had pressed a timid kiss to her forehead. She had asked so many times, "What will happen, Romek, when they come?" Here was her answer. I lunged toward a wall with the messages; all were names I did not know. A few people stopped, watching me curiously as I pored over the cards.

I felt helpless, vanquished. My search had found nothing. I stood before the ruins of her building remembering our walk, her warmth beside me, our farewell. . . . Would I never see her again?

I walked home with my head still filled with Judyta, my eyes with the sight of Warsaw crippled. The Royal Castle's walls were scorched, its roof caved in, its paneless window frames like black eye sockets, through which I could see the gray sky. King Zygmunt III still stood on his column, but it was jagged by his feet. The war had reached even him.

My father saw my despondence when I returned, and did not try to console me.

"This is war, son; this is the madness we must face. Think how many sons have lost their fathers and how many fathers have lost their sons because of the capitalist-bred monster of Hitlerism. It could have been prevented. There was a time when the capitalists could have put a stop to the Nazis in Germany. It was a gradual thing, after all—murdering the opposition and nurturing the monster. Only the communists fought them."

I asked my father to tell me more about what he had been through in Warsaw. He had been in the makeshift shelter in the cellar only twice during air raids, having come to the conclusion that if a bomb hit, the building would collapse into the cellar, and no one would survive. Later, during the heavy bombing at the end of the siege, he had stood in the doorway to the balcony gazing out as the German planes disgorged their bombs, until Jozef, the janitor, who had known him for twenty years, forced him to go down to the cellar by refusing to leave without him.

"I thought of you as I watched those barbarians," my father told me. "Some intuition told me you were in danger, and so I, too, wanted to be. Besides," he added with a flick of his hand, "what good would it have done to hide? You've seen what it's like out there."

My father also related an experience he had before the bombing of September 25. He had opened his door to find a group of Polish police and soldiers, who thrust themselves unceremoniously into the apartment. They went through all the rooms, glanced through his books, and ordered him to get dressed. To my father's protests, the officer replied unequivocally that he would be taken to the front lines, where he would get what he deserved for his communist activities.

"And I said," my father continued, "that they could take me only by force, and that if they wanted to kill me, they could do it right there on the spot and save themselves trouble."

I could see the muscles in his face quivering at the very memory.

"They shouted, they jammed a hat on my head, and they pushed me out to the stairs, making me walk in front of them like a condemned man. We walked like that as far as Sniadecki Street. They had a military headquarters established in one of the buildings there during the siege. And there they took me to face the authorities—a colonel in uniform who sorted through papers and inspected me closely. He ordered everyone to leave the room and then said to me: 'So! They have brought you here to me, Professor, as an enemy of Poland.'

"He asked me to sit down and then introduced himself to me as one of my former students at the Konarski School. Not only that! He said I had been his favorite teacher." My father's voice was fraught with emotion.

"I told him about myself, about my beliefs, and what I thought of our government—its lethal flirtation with the Nazis, which had led to everything now happening in Poland. Now that Warsaw is dying, I said to the colonel, now that I don't even know if my beloved son is alive, you can do with me whatever you wish.

"The colonel must have been moved by this meeting. He asked only one thing—did I know anyone in a position of authority. I told him that I had carefully avoided such acquaintances, having parted ways with them long ago. 'But,' I said, 'there is one student, one who went to the Gorski School, with whom I spoke a couple of months ago—Colonel Krawczyk.' That perked the colonel up, and he said that that would settle the affair. 'I'll make a note here,' he said, 'that you were released on my say-so, because of your ties to Colonel Krawczyk, who was, after all, Marshal Pilsudski's adjutant and a powerful army man.'

"When I left, the soldiers and policemen were surprised. They had thought, of course, that their threats were real, that the fate they had promised me here in the apartment would come to pass."

My father lowered his head. The sorrow in his eyes broke my heart.

"The heaviest bombings took place after that," he continued, "and I decided to try to save the manuscript of my book. I went to the Soviet Embassy and handed the manuscript, in three packages, to a Soviet diplomat by the name of Chebyshev, who told me that he was the highest-ranking officer. He promised that the work would be dispatched to Moscow as soon as circumstances permitted, and he assured me that he would report to Moscow the vulnerability of the Polish communists."

After Warsaw had fallen, my father went again to the Soviet Embassy. It remained undamaged. There he spoke with an employee in charge of the building whose Polish was immaculate. He could only tell my father that Chebyshev and the other Soviets had left before the heavy bombing had begun and that some documents had been shipped out at that time.

"But now read these letters, Romek," my father said. There were three:

My dearest son,

I have already written you a dozen or so letters, being kept by various people. No doubt they will reach you by and by. I hope you will receive this final letter. You know how deeply I love you, son, how much I want to see you and embrace you again. My selfish little desires do not, however, make me blind to the distant horizons of your future. From the depths of my heart I feel only joy that you made a manly and brave decision—the only right decision—to remain on the other side, not to return to this cursed hell. . . .

Now nearly everything depends on you alone, on your skills, your diligence, your zeal, the breadth of your intellectual horizons. . . .

What a great shame it is that you never had time enough to read through either volume of my *Liberation of Man*; it treats many burning issues comprehensively, substantively, and in detail, and would have helped you in these times to find your bearings on a number of points. Perhaps you will come to study those ideas, if not in book form, then in manuscript in the Lenin Library.

Russian, English, Polish, and German ought to suffice you in life and in your studies. Don't waste time on other languages. . . . Dedicate all your energies to acquiring real knowledge and to performing real, creative work—practical work in the spirit of revolution and liberation. . . .

I delight in the thought of your last two years in Warsaw, years full of harmony and love—you and I working together toward your exams calmly but with passion, I finishing the second volume of *The Liberation of Man.* And those free moments when, either at home or out on endless walks, we struggled with the basic problems of philosophy, of society . . .

My heart is full of pride because you understood me so deeply; you so ably appraised my principles; you were a student infinitely grateful to your teacher. That is my greatest reward in all these years of teaching.

Son, try to find Tadeusz Strzalkowski, Wladek Czekalski, and Izaak Wajsbrot. Keep in contact with them.

If all of this is pointless, if your good, subtle, sensitive, and noble heart has ceased to beat, if your bright, clear, intelligent eyes no longer look upon this world, if your quick, vital mind no longer pursues that lightning ideal, then your father's life is truly useless, truly over, and I go preserving your bright and beautiful image in my memory until the final beat of my heart.

Human life, thus far, has been a miserable enterprise. Humanity must be spared the hell of capitalism.

October 15, 1939
With deepest love,
Your father

In the second letter, addressed to my mother and dated October 27, 1939, my father wrote at the end:

> . . . And what would Romek have done seeing scoundrels and fools taking his father out to be shot? . . . Reflect on this for a moment and you will thank fate that our son was not here. Now that perhaps his greatest dreams are being realized, that he may have entered a naval academy somewhere in that great Soviet land, shouldn't our parental blessing support his important and bold decision? A decision that promises him a rich and beautiful future delivering working humanity into a life of goodness and happiness . . .

The third letter had no date and was really only notes for a letter that was to have been written in November, the current month.

> Be sensitive to good and evil in society, to what is noble and what is base. Be sensitive to pain, poverty, suffering, and misfortune, to falsehood and lies, honesty and justice.
>
> Have principles of your own. Have no truck with fools. Make your own friends and give to them of yourself. Be a friend to them, be sensitive to their troubles and misfortunes.
>
> Be persistent in the pursuit of your goals, emulate the example of great men.
>
> Don't be conceited, take council with wise people and wise books. Study hard, read a lot.
>
> Look closely at life and love sincerely that which is deserving of love but do not love life more than the integrity of your mind, heart, and actions.
>
> I embrace you with all my heart for the last time, you, my only and beloved boy.
>
> *Your father*

When I had finished, my father said, "Where Poland is concerned, my thoughts couldn't be bleaker. You know I've always said that in the end we, too, would have to face Nazi cruelty. The Germans have proven that we Poles mean nothing to them. What they have already done to Warsaw is unprecedented barbarism. Just think of the victims, the suffering. They simply surrounded the city and bombed it. In mid-October they set up some sort of bizarre administration, called the 'General Gouvernement.' Note there is no mention of Poland in that term. A sinister omen. Ten days ago the Nazis arrested many of the professors at Jagellonian University, in Krakow. They've been torturing them. This is only the beginning, son. . . ."

Several days later I went to Milanowek. At the sight of me, my mother shrieked and burst into tears. Regaining her composure, she explained that she had cried out not only from happiness and surprise, but also because I looked exactly the way someone had told her I would look.

"In that leather coat and cap! I was so worried, and when people asked if there had been any word or sign of you, I couldn't hold my tears. No word! No sign! I couldn't help but think the worst. Only one person reassured me, told me you would surely come back. Even told me what you'd be wearing!"

"And who was that?" I asked curiously.

"But tell me," continued my mother, ignoring my question, "where did you get that coat and cap? You never had a leather coat like that before."

"From Grandmother in Lityn."

My mother was thin and pale, her eyes larger than I could remember. Nothing had changed in her house outwardly; it, like nearly all the buildings in Milanowek, was undamaged. No fighting had taken place in that area.

Tadeusz and I kissed warmly. He had returned home a few days after leaving, having failed to join up with the army because the events had moved so swiftly. He asked me not to mention to anyone that he was an officer in the reserves; he was concealing that fact from the Germans, because they had ordered all Polish officers to report. His brother Ignas, of whom I was very fond—we had built radio sets together—had been killed in action during the siege of Warsaw. We fell silent in our sorrow.

At dinner I told them of my adventures. Tadeusz spared no bitterness in his remarks about the Soviets. He was merciless: they were murderers, traitors who had plunged the fatal knife in our back precisely when our army's sole salvation lay in a retreat to the East.

They were thieves, too, he added, who had stolen land and priceless centers of Polish culture like Wilno and Lwow, where Polish universities had been founded in the sixteenth and seventeenth centuries. What brute in all of Russia would have even the faintest idea of what the word "university" means? As for the agreement between the Soviets and the Germans, it was nothing but a plot made by a pair of bandits.

I spoke of my father's and my plans to travel east.

"In the middle of a war?" My mother was clearly shaken. "You'll both be killed!"

Tadeusz was of a different mind. "Let them try it," he said. "If Romek hasn't had enough yet, if he really wants a taste of more, let him get it."

The next day my mother asked me to go with her to visit the parents of a classmate of mine who had been very kind to her.

"You'll meet someone there," she said, smiling playfully, "who always cheered me with assurances that you would come home. Someone who even knew what you'd be wearing . . . Little Wanda, your classmate Czeslaw's sister. You wouldn't recognize her, she's changed so much. She's gone from girl to young lady."

"The same Wanda I remember sitting in the sand and making pies?"

"Yes. It was Wanda who predicted you would come home to us in that light-colored, fur-lined leather coat and that cap. And she would tell me that nothing could possibly happen to you, because she was praying for you constantly. Such a nice girl."

The Sikorskis were overjoyed to see me, and I had to relate all that had happened. We sat around the table, all but Wanda, who leaned against the white tile stove and never took her eyes off me. I indeed would not have recognized her. Although she was only twelve, she was a child no longer.

A few days later I bid my mother farewell once more. She wept, knowing that soon my father and I would cross over to the East, to the Soviet side.

The destruction of war had not spared the Zoliborz area of Warsaw; walls were pocked by shrapnel and bullets, but there seemed to be less serious damage. Wilson Square, where my father's colleague Antonina Sokolicz lived, was no longer the same clean, well-kept place it once had been. Her building was almost deserted; the windows on the staircase were shattered, and the wind came howling through to rattle her door.

Visiting there with my father, I went over the long litany of what I had been through. Antonina and her husband, Ludwik Merkel, listened in silence, and asked but one question: How are the Soviet authorities treating Poles, Polish refugees, Party members? I tried to speak as objectively as I could.

My father told them of our plan to head east and asked if they had a similar resolve. Antonina thought for a long while, then spoke cautiously. "Things are only going to get harder here. I *do* think you should go. But don't forget that it's Stalin's Soviet Union you're headed for. Remember the Molotov-Ribbentrop Pact. Didn't the Red Army go into action on September 17 and occupy all of eastern Poland? There had to have been an agreement there, and there are probably others. Remember, Professor, that many of our Polish comrades have vanished without a trace in the Soviet Union. You," she said, looking at him, "have your own unshakable convictions. Russia has never liked that trait in its people, maybe less now than ever. Still, you have written so many anti-Nazi pieces that you have no choice but to go. . . . No, I won't be going. I'll stay in Warsaw; my place is here.

"Look at Romek," she continued. "His experiences speak volumes. No one took an interest in him, no one helped him, and no one will want to arrange for you to cross over to the other side. Romek's description of Rudnianski, his metamorphosis, his fear—that's Stalin's influence. People mean nothing over there; only the cause is important, the cause as *they* perceive it. One life alone has no relevance."

She broke off. I could see that she, too, had changed. Her features were more pinched, her movements more nervous, more impulsive.

"And, please, Professor," she said with some exasperation, "don't go on defending those pacts with the Germans. They're a disgrace, and the world proletariat will never forgive the Russians, no matter how they try to explain them away. . . .

"I doubt you'll like it there. I consider it my duty to warn you. But it's clear you cannot stay here."

Dusk had fallen, and it was too late to return home. The German occupiers had imposed a curfew almost immediately, and people found on the streets after hours were shot on the spot without ceremony. My father and I had to spend the night at Antonina's. Looking from the window, I saw a deserted Wilson Square, a wilderness of stone.

We began to prepare for our journey. It was already December and there had been some snow, so we were pressed for time. I decided to do Wladek the service he had requested in Lutsk. We would travel to his wife's home, not far from the Bug. I wrote and asked whether they would be able to help us cross the river. They answered that they would expect us any time.

One day the doorbell rang and a group of men in workers' clothes asked to see Professor Spasowski. I took them in to my father's study and stayed to hear what was said.

"Professor," began the leader, "we have come to you as to a father for advice. We know your books, and we know about you from our beloved Professor Nowakowski. We are workers from the Cegielski factory in Poznan—all Party members once, before they disbanded our Party. The Germans are driving Poles out of Poznan. We're treated like cattle, worse than cattle. We don't even have the right to walk on the sidewalks any more. And the Germans can beat us whenever they like. Lately they've been arresting more and more of us leftists, and no one knows what becomes of them.

"We've decided to go east, to be with our own. We're leaving our families. They could be deported—we don't know—but it may be easier for women and children to survive. We want to cross the Bug. . . ."

My heart rejoiced. I looked at these tough Polish workers—strong, brave, assertive—and I was proud.

My father mentioned that I had just returned from there. I told them everything, concealed nothing, and warned them that things would not be easy. I described the wounded Polish soldiers in the park, their weapons gone, their faces bewildered, their officers mysteriously taken away.

"I didn't meet anyone I would call a true communist," I said. "I met only with Ukrainians and Soviet komandirs, who probably intended to arrest me in the end. It's a completely different world. But you have to expect that—it is the first of its kind."

They asked about crossing the Bug, and I told them about the greedy guides, the importance of money. The workers were obviously poor, having left all their savings with their families.

My father opened his desk drawer and withdrew a bundle of paper money. He divided it in half. "Here, this is for you and this is for us. And here, a gold coin."

The men were silent, on the verge of tears and uncertain how to react. "We can't accept the money, Professor," said the leader.

"Not only *can* you accept," said my father firmly, "but you *must* accept. Your plan will come to nothing without money."

The leader rummaged through his pockets and drew out a watch on a thick chain. "Professor," he said, "we love you and respect you like a father, you have showed us the way, now you even want to help us with money. . . . We thank you and we accept, but please take my watch in return. I am an ironworker. I was given this watch by my father on my first day of work. My father was an ironworker, too."

My father took the watch in his hand, studied it, fondled it, and set it on his desk. He was deeply moved. "Thank you." He spoke slowly. "I will always treasure this gift from workers." I had to leave the room.

When they had left, we examined the thick silver Omega, a watch we called an "onion," because of its size. How could I know, as we turned that watch in our hands, that it would survive all the subsequent storms and lie before me now, a treasured relic of those terrible times and those courageous souls.

The next day we went to old Professor Rudnianski's home. His wife, a tall, slender woman who appeared to be of German descent, questioned me in detail about her husband, and after reading the slip of paper I had brought from him, passed it to her daughter.

The girl's face lit up. "Father wrote this? Yes! I recognize his writing! He wants me to go see him!" she said joyfully.

"Only," answered her mother dryly, "if the professor and Romek will take you along. But you'll have to make up your own mind. It's a very risky business. . . ."

Lucylla insisted that her mind was already made up. If we would take her with us, she was ready to pack her things quickly.

Looking at her, I asked myself whether she could withstand the rigors of the crossing; I had intended to concentrate on helping my father. I asked her how old she was, and she replied that she had already turned sixteen. She did seem strong and healthy. She must have sensed that I was sizing her up, because she began attempting to convince me that she was physically up to it.

Shortly before we were to depart, Szirmer, our neighbor upstairs, visited us unexpectedly, once again asking for advice. Since the first of December the Germans had been forcing the Jews to wear arm bands with the Star of David. Did not that mean that persecution was not far behind?

We did not conceal the fact that we were leaving for the other side. He scurried off to get his wife and returned a moment later with her.

"We have a great favor to ask of you, Professor, a truly great favor," they blurted out together in their excitement. "You're crossing over and you know what to do. Please take our son, Robert, with you. We're worried about him. He's already seventeen, a very gifted boy, but he's wasting away here under Hitler. My wife and I are old; we might not have long to live anyway. But why should he die?"

My father's eyes met mine.

"Do you realize how dangerous it is to cross to the other side?" he asked Szirmer. "We may be risking our lives, but my son and I have decided to take that risk. It would be a great responsibility to take your son. We can guarantee nothing, nothing at all. . . ."

"But Professor," persisted Szirmer, "what's in store for him here? I know Hitler's ways; I have friends and family in Germany." He nodded toward his wife. "She still doesn't fully realize what's going to happen here. There is only death. Just so we don't suffer too long . . . You know well, Professor, that for young people there's no other choice but to go. . . ."

"If that's the case," said my father with finality, "your son should prepare to leave immediately."

Joy flashed in Szirmer's eyes; his wife burst into tears. "When will you go?" she moaned.

"In three days," I answered. "Make sure that he has everything he needs in his knapsack. And don't make it heavy, because no one will be carrying it for him."

It was nearing the middle of December, and the frosts had come, but fortunately these were light; the days were overcast and there were frequent snow flurries. On one of those cloudy gray mornings

Lucylla and her mother appeared at our door. Small knapsack in hand, Lucylla was all smiles and determination, but her mother was clearly sad and frightened. The doorbell rang again. It was Robert and his parents, both on the verge of tears.

My father and I were ready. He had put on his winter coat with the black fur collar and a tall black fur cap, the sort older men wore in those days. The farewells, the final words of warning from parents, the tears, and then we were alone. I checked the knapsacks. Robert's was much too heavy, but he said everything in it was essential. Let him carry it, I thought; I had seen people trying to lug heavy bags down the highways and I knew what came of that.

On the stairs, I realized I was leaving behind forever the place where I had lived for nearly twenty years: the staircase with its polished wooden railing, its metal supports of interwoven leaves. Those stairs I had learned to take as if I were skiing. And there was the courtyard and its gateway, always dim, a favorite haunt of police informers in recent years. It was soon all behind us.

We set out across the Poniatowski Bridge to reach Praga, where we would take a train to Biala Podlaska, a small town about ninety miles east of Warsaw. From time to time, I looked over at my father to see how he was faring with his knapsack. I knew it was not heavy, having succeeded in taking out some of the heaviest pieces of clothing by pretending to be repacking it. My own knapsack was bulging with his things, but my father had not noticed. He walked on resolutely, and my only concern was to watch that he did not slip on patches of frozen snow.

Our journey was uneventful. When the train dragged itself into Biala Podlaska, luck seemed to be favoring us—there were no Germans at the station apart from a disinterested squad of the Wehrmacht. We roamed the city looking for the address Wladek had given me, and soon came on the well-kept house where his wife's family lived. We were happy to see Murcia herself open the door. So the first stage of our expedition had passed with good fortune. Now we were to await a signal from our guides.

Days went by before a peasant drove up in his wagon to report that for the last few days both sides of the border had been closely guarded, by Soviets and Germans. Recently, the patrols on the German side had been reinforced. We would have to wait longer for the crossing.

My father and I spent the time laying further plans. What I feared most was not the crossing itself, but my father's first encounter with the other side. How would he react to Ukrainians who breathe hatred for Poles? How would he receive the indifference of Soviet komandirs? How would the flagrant propaganda affect him, the towns swimming in red, the slogans on the streets?

Lucylla and Robert kept together, talking, and often laughing so heartily that I could only be envious. I had never been able to laugh like that, and now, after all I had been through, I could not remember laughing at all.

Early each morning I checked to see if the heavy frosts had come, which could make crossing the river difficult. Fortunately, the river was not frozen, but snow was constant, and everything was white.

Late one morning a sleigh pulled by two horses drove up, bringing us the good news that we would cross that night. We would have to be ready within the hour. The sleigh was crowded with the four of us and the driver, but we were warm sitting in the hay, covered with thick saddle blankets. It was a long ride through the white wilderness. Night was just falling when the sleigh came to a stop in front of a country hut.

"Wait for your guide here," said the driver. "The people inside know everything, and they'll give you some food."

It was warm inside. Our host encouraged us to feel at home. His wife brought us hot tea and bread. I took a look around, and, by now a connoisseur of Polish huts, knew that these were poor peasants. The table, chairs, and bench were modest—nailed planks of hard pine, no paint. The place was spare, but neat and clean. On the wall hung the usual picture of Christ with a crown of thorns.

As we sipped tea from rough cups, our host said, "So far we've only had people escaping from the Bolsheviks. . . . You're the first ones going the other way."

"Yes, we're heading in the opposite direction," said my father, "away from the fascists, to the land of the Soviets. Don't you know the difference between the fascists and the workers' and peasants' state?"

I shot him a glance full of reproach for lecturing the peasant at a time like this. But he went on, as if to me. "People should at least know what the Soviet system is."

The peasant replied, "Yes, that's so. But what the people escaping from over there say can break your heart. They deport people, and nobody knows where to. They round up all the Poles and loot the cities. . . . And they jail more people than ever before; treat them terrible, too." He paused and asked, almost rhetorically, "So why go there?"

Lucylla and Robert were listening intently. My father appeared ready to continue the discussion, but I broke in. "We have a hard night ahead and we'll need all our strength. Let's get some sleep now, even if it's on the floor. Would that be all right?"

Our host nodded. "Please rest. My wife will bring you something to lie on right away."

My father was given a pillow and a blanket; the rest of us used our coats and our knapsacks. I soon heard my father's heavy, tired sighs, then I, too, dozed off.

Near midnight someone knocked at the door of the hut. In the flickering light of an oil lamp I saw a tall man in a sheepskin coat brushing snow off his arms and cap.

Our host said something to him and then turned to me. "Thank God, you'll be crossing tonight. Get ready."

"You must pay now," said our guide, an older man with a walrus mustache. "As agreed."

I had the money ready. "Here. Two hundred zlotys and twenty dollars in gold."

The man took the money and examined it by the oil lamp. "Good," he said curtly. "We'll cross." He stood looking at the four of us. "The night is very dark, and though everything is white with snow it's hard to see. That's good and that's bad; good because the Krauts and Ukrainians won't see us; bad because you'll stumble and fall. I have a thick piece of rope with me. I'll go first; you follow in any order you like, but hold the rope tight. I know the way, every bush. Just watch your hold and don't get lost in the dark."

The night was black. Our guide handed me one end of the rope. I gave it to my father and took my place behind him; then came Lucylla, with Robert bringing up the rear. The path we took was circuitous, the ground uneven; every so often one of us would fall to our knees in the snow.

We walked for a long time before our path took a downward turn. We must be approaching the river, I thought. We moved soundlessly except for the soft stirring of powdery snow. Suddenly the peasant stopped and whistled softly. He was answered by another soft whistle, which seemed to come from below. He began moving forward again, and we followed. My eyes caught sight of a dark swath, which I knew must be the river. Another fifteen steps and we were on the shore.

Our guide whispered with someone, no doubt the ferryman. Then a short figure came out of the dark toward us and said very softly: "All right, get into the boat. . . . Easy does it, one at a time. Put your things in the bottom."

My father clambered in first and the rest of us followed. At last, I thought, now, no matter what happens, we are free of the Nazis. I looked around. The ferryman was pushing against the shore with a long pole. The boat shuddered, scraped against the bottom, and then began moving freely. I could feel the current bearing it away, speeding along as the ferryman's pole thrust against the river bottom. Water splashed against the sides, and the white snow-covered stretch of shore receded. It grew darker and darker; I could barely see the outline of my father's cap ahead of me. And the night was still; there was only the sound of the boat skimming the river and the water dripping from the ferryman's pole. We were slipping across like phantoms. How safe it was here, how free!

Suddenly the boat lurched to one side, and water began flowing in. The ferryman cursed. "We're sinking," my father gasped. The water was whirling around me, mounting and piercing me with cold. The boat floor disappeared from beneath my feet. Instinctively I began swimming. I could see nothing, and no one uttered a word. Up to my chin and drifting with the current, I thought I could see my father's cap moving above the water, but then it would vanish. Caught and turned by eddies, I lost all sense of direction—and time.

Suddenly my foot struck something; then both feet. "Father," I cried, the word almost freezing in my mouth, "I'm on land. It gets shallower here."

"Here I am, son." His voice was close.

The water became shallower, and I tried to stand, but my clothing and leather coat were too heavy with water. After two more tries, I was standing knee-deep. The shore looked white. I took a few steps, and my feet sank into snow. Splashing sounds came from behind me.

"Father, Lucylla, Robert, where are you?" I shouted. Voices responded, and I caught a glimpse of my father's tall hat.

I helped him onto the snow. Lucylla came next, stumbling and falling. I grabbed her by the waist and carried her out. Robert clambered up on his own; the ferryman was last. Weighed down with water, our knapsacks were heavy as lead, with the ferryman's help I dragged them onto the shore.

We were on a sandbar no more than fifteen feet wide and long.

"Look, the boat washed up, too," said the ferryman.

I squinted through the dark and saw the prow of the boat against the snow, borne there by the same current. "Can we keep going?" I asked.

"No. It's full of water. The water has to be tipped out. Maybe two of us together can do it."

"Let's get to work then," I said. "Robert, give us a hand."

Somehow we managed to tip the boat back and forth, the water splashing out both sides. Then we scooped more out with our hands. It took a long time, and my body began warming up but my hands nearly froze. Finally, the ferryman announced that enough water had been drained, and two people could probably set out in it. I turned to my father.

"Father, go with the ferryman to the Soviet side and try to find help for us quickly. We'll stay here and hold out as long as we can."

My father got into the boat immediately, with no argument. Together, the ferryman and I shoved the boat off the sandbar; he jumped in, and a moment later it vanished into the darkness.

Absorbed by the boat, I had forgotten Lucylla. She was sitting motionless, bent forward, on a knapsack. I leaned close to her, but she did not respond. I gave her a little shake, but she seemed to be asleep. Then I began shaking her violently, pumping her arms up and down. I told Robert to do the same with her legs. She pulled herself together long enough to get out a few words: "It's all over."

"It's *not* over. It's just beginning. . . . Stupid girl, you'd like everything easy, wouldn't you? Stupid idiot . . ." I heaped her with all the abuse I could think of.

"How dare you talk to her like that? What's the matter with you?" shouted Robert indignantly.

"Lucylla, get up, don't give in, don't be an ass, get up, show you can move," I shouted.

Slowly, heavily, she rose to her feet.

Just then there was a flash and a rifle shot from the direction my father had taken. The shot echoed along the river and was followed by a second and a third.

"*Stoi!* Stop!" cried voices in Russian. "Come here." The echoes rebounded off the shore. "Stoi . . . Stoi . . . Stoi . . ."

Another flash, another shot, then silence. My heart was pounding. I listened intently. Could they have been shooting at my father? I kept trying to hear something more, but now there was only silence, the dark of night, the soft sound of water.

A flare shot up on the German side, followed by a bang. A penetrating yellowish light spread through the darkness and illuminated the river and the shore. It hung in the sky momentarily, and then slowly sank to earth. More bangs, and then red flashes and another pair of flares lit up the Soviet side. It became bright as day; I could see both shores. We were on a sandbar in the middle of the river.

While we stood there helplessly, lit by flares from both sides, I thought of lying down, in case they opened fire, but my feet were deep in snow and I had grown resigned. The last flares fell, and it was pitch black again. Now it was I sitting on a knapsack, silent, motionless, feeling the icy cold overcome me and thinking it would be best, easiest, to die.

Yet my mind struggled against the idea of freezing to death. I sprang to my feet in some last instinct for life. No, I would not give in. Dying for a cause is one thing, but not like this, from the cold, in the middle of a river. I ran around in a circle waving my arms until I fell, exhausted. But I pulled myself up and ran, falling again and again until I reached the limits of my strength. Warmth began to surge through my body. Fumbling in the dark, I found Robert and Lucylla motionless. Robert did not respond at all. I began punching him and, out of desperation, walloping him as hard as I could. I took off his cap and rubbed his face with snow. He pushed me away, flapping his hands at me, begging me to leave him alone. "Why are you hitting me?" he cried. Finally he began to defend himself and even tried to hit me back, rising angrily to his feet.

"Come, let's take care of Lucylla," I shouted. "She's in bad shape. You take one side, I'll take the other, and we'll run her around."

Lucylla was a dead weight and could barely put one foot in front of another. We sat her down and rubbed her face and hands with snow. I had begun to lose hope, at the end of my own strength, when she started to react. She was clearly suffering from exposure and shock, and her words were incoherent.

"We've got to save her," I repeated insistently, not knowing whether I was talking to myself or to Robert. In saving Lucylla we had been saving ourselves, for now I could feel warmth throughout my whole body.

Then I heard something splash in the water and then another, louder, noise, as if made by an oar. There was a flash, a blinding light, and harsh yells. "Halt! Halt! Schnell!"

Two men in German uniform hopped onto the sandbar and grabbed Lucylla and Robert. I was numb, in a trance. By the light of their flashlights I could see my friends limp in the soldiers' arms, their feet dragging across the snow. I scrambled over to the boat with my last ounce of strength. It was large and wide, like a pontoon. The Germans threw our knapsacks into the boat cursing at their weight. Then we pulled away. Now it is really all over, I thought, coming to my senses. Maybe it's better this way, faster.

As the boat approached the western shore I could hear several German voices. I felt weak. What had it all been for? The boat struck shore, and several flashlights were trained on us. The Germans carried Lucylla and Robert out of the boat and set them down like sacks in the snow. I got out by myself, my legs shaky, and stood by Lucylla.

A German in a cap with earmuffs walked over to me and shone his flashlight in my eyes. "Who are you?" he shouted in German. "What are you doing here? We'll teach you, you filthy smuggler! What do you have to say?"

I did not answer. A bland indifference had settled over me.

"Don't you understand me?" he yelled. "Talk . . . We'll teach you how to talk. . . ."

I began swaying, and would have fallen had it not been for the tree behind me. I leaned against it. The German drew closer, still yelling, his light still in my eyes. I understood nothing more; weakness was invading me. As the light moved away I could see him, as if through a mist, reach for his holster. He brought the muzzle of his pistol up to my nose and pummeled my frozen face with it, shouting furiously, "Talk! Talk! Talk!"

I remember nothing else. I must have collapsed.

I learned later what had happened from some peasants who lived near the river. The German patrol left us lying on the snowy riverbank. Good front-line soldiers, they would not waste bullets on unconscious people. One of them went to the nearest hut, spoke with the peasant there, and pointed in the direction of the river. The peasant understood that there were some people out there and that it was all right for him to take care of them. When the Germans left, he and his neighbor dragged us to his hut, took off our wet, frozen clothing, and put us to bed.

The next day, my face and head were bruised and painful and I was trembling, but, to my surprise, I was alive. Robert was in worse shape, and looked like he had pneumonia. Pale and weak, he had a high fever, a cough, and an ache in his chest. Lucylla was much worse. She was delirious, her head on fire. I did not know what to do. We have to stay right here for now, I thought, but what next? Try again to cross or return to Warsaw? I shuddered at the thought of attempting a second crossing. Better to stay here; at least I know who I'm dealing with.

The owner of the hut returned. A warm, kindhearted man, he told me that he and his wife had been distraught about our condition when we were dragged in. They had given their home over to us and gone to stay with their neighbor.

It occurred to me that the Germans might return, so I unpacked all our knapsacks. In my father's I found the book he had written about the Soviet Union, as well as some notes. I tossed the book into the snow and burned the notes in the stove.

I gave my attention to Lucylla, who was talking to herself, constantly repeating that she was scared. I stayed close to her and kept my hand at her temple, which seemed to bring her some relief, since she grew calmer. She stopped mumbling and moaning when I spoke to her, though she gave no sign of having understood what I said.

Nights were hardest. Robert tossed and turned but could sleep. I sat by Lucylla, keeping my hand at her head, speaking to her whenever she moaned, though I was exhausted myself and could not help nodding off.

My closeness seemed to calm her, and there soon was a certain improvement in her condition. She regained consciousness, and looked at me with eyes warm with gratitude.

No Germans came for us. Only once, looking through a spot I had scraped on the frosted window, did I see a German patrol moving along the bank of the river.

I lost track of time. The man whose hut we were staying in came to see us every day. His wife cooked for us—soup with potatoes seasoned with crackling, mostly, but sometimes she made dumplings, or noodle soup.

"It's Christmas Eve," said the peasant one day. "My wife's cooked potato pancakes and some fried fish. Just watch out for the bones."

That day passed like every other. It soon grew dark, and Lucylla and Robert lay quietly in their beds, asleep. Only days ago we had been on a sandbar a few feet long. Hitler on one side, Stalin on the other. Three people freezing—a Polish communist, a Polish Jew, and the daughter of a Jew and a German. No government reached us there. It had been the last patch of earth between salvation and hell.

I felt an irresistible urge for fresh air and open space. I jumped up, threw on my leather coat, and went outside. The air was sharp and damp, the night full of stars. They were still, beautiful, mysterious, so clear they seemed within reach. I looked up with envy. There was peace out there in the universe, no Germans, no Soviets, another world, ruled by the laws of nature. What was that universe? Did what was happening on this little speck of earth have any significance? Was it of any account out there in the vastness?

CHAPTER VI

Days passed. Lucylla was finally out of bed and walking around, and even keeping things tidy. She was, however, still talking to herself. At times she would sit and stare out the window as if detached from the world around her.

The frosts had become strong, and the bitter cold penetrated the hut. Fortunately, our host had a good supply of wood stacked out back, and he allowed us to keep a constant fire going in the kitchen. We saw no one apart from him and his wife. When going out for firewood, I would peer through branches at the river, which wound like a black ribbon through the white snow. In a little while, I thought, the river would be frozen solid, and we would be able to walk across to the other side. But to what end?

At dusk one day before the New Year, there was a loud knock at the door. I glanced over just as someone opened it, and found my feet rooted to the floor. My father was in the doorway. He was still wearing the tall fur cap I knew so well, the coat with the big black fur collar. Only his glasses and his long, frost-covered mustache were visible beneath his cap. His coat was crumpled and dirty, and he was not moving steadily. I ran to him and threw my arms about him. Removing his fogged glasses, the words fell from his mouth as if in disbelief: "Is that you, son?"

He spoke, but his words made little sense. I could see a mortal weariness in his face and pain in his tired eyes. He sat down heavily and looked blankly at me. With time he became conscious of where he was.

"You're alive, you're alive?" he whispered, his lips trembling nervously. Tears streamed down his cheeks into his bushy mustache, which still glinted with bits of ice.

I removed his coat and hat, and took his hand and stroked it. "How was it there, Father?"

He dismissed the question with a wave and glanced up at me with the sorrowful eyes of a man bereft. "I'll tell you, I'll tell you everything, but not now. Tell me how you three have been."

"We were half dead when the Germans took us," I began. My father sat bolt upright. He looked first at me, then at Lucylla and Robert.

"The Germans?" he whispered.

"Yes, the Germans. They brought us back from that sandbar; they even brought our knapsacks. . . . Things might have ended badly if we hadn't been so exhausted. I just collapsed onto the snow when they were questioning me. . . ."

"The Germans, the Germans," he repeated as if to himself.

I sat him on my bed, where he drank a little hot tea before he lay down and closed his eyes. But his lips were still moving: "The Germans . . . the Germans . . ."

After a few days my father regained some of his strength, but still did not wish to talk about what he had seen on the other side. He would only make that same gesture with his hand and ask me not to insist.

I saw no reason to remain in that hut any longer, and prepared for our return to Warsaw. I felt we should pay our host, who was glad to return to his own home, since he had been feeding us from his own modest supplies. We sorted out things—socks, sweaters, shirts, pants—from our knapsacks, which contained considerably more than we were now able to carry in our weakened and demoralized state. It made for decent compensation. Our hosts were satisfied, grateful.

We traveled by sleigh to Biala Podlaska without incident. There were military police at the station there, and the train was packed. None of that, however, mattered to us. We were now resigned to fate.

I tried to cheer Robert. "Why are you so quiet?" I asked. "Don't give up. . . ."

He explained that he had not given up. "What can they do to me?" he said. "The most they can do is kill me." Lucylla was silent, too, and could not be coaxed into conversation.

Finally, we were home. Robert ran upstairs to his family; I took Lucylla home to Zoliborz. I never saw her again.

It was only after several days that my father was able to tell me what had happened to him on the other side. In describing his ordeals, he lived through them a second time, and he would pause every so often, as if wishing to digest what he himself had just said. I felt that he wanted to tell me everything in detail, so that I would know that he had done all he could to come to our aid.

"It was very dark," he began. "I don't know how the ferryman was able to get his bearings. The current was stronger than before, and he seemed to be having trouble steering. It wasn't long before we saw the white of the other shore, and the boat struck a rock. I waded to land, up to my knees in water. That's when the first shots were fired, about thirty or forty yards from us. They must have been firing blindly, since it was pitch black, but both the ferryman and I heard the bullets whistling close by us. Then we heard the shouts 'Stop! Come here.' Maybe they'd heard the boat strike the shore or the ferryman's pole knocking against the wood. The shots seemed to be coming from the side now. They shouted once more. 'Stop! Come here.' We stood still until they began to approach us with their flashlights blazing. It was then that the yellow flares went off, lighting everything—us, them, the river. They were Red Army soldiers, and they ordered us to follow them. It was hard to walk—slippery. And they prodded us with their bayonets.

"A little later there were more flares, but much closer this time, red ones. They made a horrible light—the first ones, that cadaverous yellow, and then those red ones. I stumbled and fell and saw those soldiers in their peaked caps learing over me. . . . I tried to explain that my son was still in the middle of the river, but my entreaties meant nothing to them. They told me to shut my mouth. Their language was foul.

"I could hardly move; my coat was soaked with water and felt like lead. My strength was just about gone. If the ferryman hadn't helped me along, I don't know how I would have managed.

"We drove in an open truck for a long time. I kept thinking I would freeze to death. Finally we arrived at what I found out later was the old tsarist fortress of Brest. We were thrown into a dungeon packed with people who had been picked up the same way we had. They all must have been Poles. It was hard to breathe, but the round stove in the middle made it warm, even hot. People were lying on the stone floor or sitting on their bundles. There were no benches or chairs, only dark walls covered with faded scrawls.

"One man, who must have seen that I could barely stand, gave me his place by the stove. After a couple of days my overcoat and clothes dried out.

"I immediately demanded to speak with the komandir, but aside from having me write my name and my father's name on a slip of paper, as everyone else had, they took no interest in me. I insisted, and tried to leave the cell to go to the next room, where there were some Russians, but the soldier at the door shoved me back with force. No one would speak with me. The Red Army soldiers treated everyone"—a momentary silence—"like cattle.

"Every day they gave us a bowl of soup—sometimes there was even a little meat in it—and a piece of bread, and we waited to see what they'd do with us. Every day new people came, and every day soldiers read out the names of those who were being taken out.

"I made another attempt to state my case when a high-ranking officer, who appeared to be the komandir in charge, entered our cell. I jumped up, ran to him, and grabbed him by the arm. He stopped and gave me a strange look.

" 'Comrade Komandir,' I beseeched in Russian, 'take pity on me. My son may have frozen in the middle of the river. . . .'

"I was unable to say any more because he tore his arm away and said, 'And who are you, a Pole?'

" 'Yes, I'm a Pole, a Polish communist.'

" 'Go to hell,' he bellowed and marched out of the cell.

"Believe me, son, there was no more I could do. Finally, one day when they were calling out names I heard my own, Wladyslaw Stanislawowicz Spasowski. This time I demanded a talk with the komandir, but they shoved the ferryman and me outside, where, with a group of about a dozen people, we were put in an open truck and taken back to the river. There, soldiers with bayonets on their rifles ordered us—and none too politely either—to get into a pontoon boat, which took us back to the German side.

"You know what I felt as we were approaching the German side and I saw Nazi soldiers again? I was certain that you were no longer alive, and I had no idea what to do. I thought perhaps the time had come . . . But by then the pontoon boat had reached shore. There was a squad of Germans waiting for us. We were delivered to them, and they lined us up. Then one German, who must have been a noncommissioned officer, walked in front of us, looking at each person to decide what was to be done with him. I was standing at the end of the line with the ferryman, and I noticed that the German was choosing the young men and ordering them to step out of line and wait on the side. When only the older people were left, he ordered us to disperse. We could go wherever we wanted, but he warned us that if anyone was caught a second time attempting to cross the border between the Third Reich and its ally the Soviet Union, that person would live to regret it." My father fell silent. It seemed that unburdening himself of all this had brought him some relief.

When he was alone with the ferryman, who had had enough of everything and just wanted to go home, he told me, he asked to be accompanied to the point where the crossing had been attempted, to find out what had happened to us. They walked for several miles, my father's strength ebbing quickly. But they managed to reach the place, and the first hut they found proved to be the one we had been taken to.

I was shaken by my father's story and felt broken in spirit. For a few days my future seemed black as night. Now I thought no better of the Soviets than I did of the Nazis, who, I had heard, at the end of December had dragged one hundred and six innocent people from their apartments and from the streets of Warsaw and murdered them in cold blood.

Life in Warsaw, however, had its own exigencies; to keep alive you had to eat. I began to take charge of obtaining food. My heart bled at the sight of my father, and I resolved to do everything within my power to save him. We had no money; all our savings were gone. I sold our last twenty-dollar coin, and with that money we were able to live for a few weeks, eating potatoes and potato pancakes, as Moishe's family had in Lutsk. Then we sold my father's cuff links and a pearl tie clasp, a present my mother had given him on the French Riviera. After that it was a mineral collection that friends of my parents had given me before the war. I sold the gold nugget first, then thc crystals. When they were gone, I loaded my knapsack with books and went to the Arct Bookstore, on Nowy Swiat, which took them on commission. And thus did my father's library—all the fine commemorative works of Polish literature, the first editions, the old books, many with dedications, collected with great care throughout his life—vanish day by day.

We often dropped by to see the Falskis, on Lekarska Street, where we would read the underground bulletins that reported news of the General Gouvernement and the former Polish territories, as well as world events. There were constant accounts of new Nazi atrocities, persecution, beatings, people shot on the streets. There was only pessimism. The West was silent. France was saying nothing, betraying no sign of preparing to act against Germany. Reports from London and Paris provided no consolation. In any case, listening to the radio was a dangerous proposition. The Germans had outlawed the possession of radios, and Poles in violation were subject to a death sentence.

The meetings at the Falskis' became gloomier.

"Hitler still has the initiative," said my father one day.

"Well, that's thanks to that great Soviet Union and Stalin of yours," Marian responded caustically. "That same Soviet Union which gave you a splendid, proletarian reception. The Soviets have been helping the Third Reich so much since they partitioned Poland with Hitler that now there is no likelihood that Germany will collapse economically.

"We have information that there are trainloads of raw materials constantly moving west and, for the most part, returning empty. The railroad workers say that train after train is going to Germany with crude oil, iron ore, lumber, grain, anything you can think of, and that there are more and more of them all the time. That's how much Stalin loves Hitler now, dear Spasowski."

The Soviet-Finnish war drew lively comment and elicited both repugnance and pity for the Soviets, who had attacked little Finland and been unable to subdue it.

"But this time the world spoke up for justice," said Marian, "when it threw the Soviet Union, that repulsive aggressor, out of the League of Nations. It's no great achievement to conquer Finland. That war is another shameful page in Soviet history. Let them try the same thing with the Germans! The only reason Stalin is currying their favor is because he's afraid of them."

At the beginning of March 1940, Antonina Sokolicz informed my father of the tragic situation of those former comrades and sympathizers who had remained in Warsaw.

"I do not maintain," she said, "that they would have been better off over on the other side. What Romek has told us is impressive and reveals just how vile Stalin is, but that does not alter the fact that here, under the so-called General Gouvernement, everything is heading for catastrophe. We have many good people in Zoliborz who feel completely lost, and we have to do something to convince them that Hitler's Reich won't last forever and that, in the end, Communists can count on the anti-Nazi forces throughout the world.

"Our people have been overcome by pessimism," she continued; "they don't believe things can change for the better. I have decided to do something. . . . It occurred to me to ask Romek to give a talk. He's one of the few of our people who have been on the other side, seen the Soviets with his own eyes, and can speak on this subject from his own experience. The point is not to excuse the Soviets, but to demonstrate that the land of the peasants and the workers, such as it is, has a power of its own. I know that Romek is familiar with the subject. He could kindle a hope that Communism can fight fascism whether Stalin wants to or not."

I was surprised by her suggestion, as was my father.

"But if I were to rely on my firsthand encounter with the Soviets," I said, "say what I actually have seen, that would be worse than saying nothing at all. I told you about the komandirs, the way they treat Polish soldiers, the marches, the elections, the propaganda, the university in Lwow. I can speak about the industrialization of the Soviet Union only on the basis of Nowakowski's book and from the few Red Army vehicles, tractors, and other equipment I managed to catch a glimpse of."

Antonina tried to persuade me. "This is truly important. It would give you experience you could not get otherwise. I'll try to make things safe. Only old, proven Communists will be at those meetings."

Despite my father's objections, it was decided that I would report to Antonina on a given afternoon and be taken to an apartment where I would give my talk. The first time, I was quite nervous. An older woman, who was introduced to me only by her first name, took me from Antonina's apartment. She did not know who I was; Antonina had introduced me only as Comrade Romek. We circled around the old part of Zoliborz until we arrived at a corner house, where we walked up to a two-room apartment on the third floor. There were about fifteen people, mostly men, sitting on chairs, the couch, the floor, and against the wall. Looking around, I was reminded of the faces of those workers from the Cegielski factory who had come to see us from Poznan. I felt more sure of myself, encouraged by those rugged faces, those work-hardened hands.

I spoke of my own experiences and the great emotion I had felt at my first sight of planes with red stars on their wings. I told them about the powerful tractors produced in the Soviet Union and how modern industry had arisen in the land of the workers and the peasants through hard work, despite poverty and isolation. Now Hitler will have to reckon with that industry, I added. I concluded by saying that the day would come when the Communists would liberate Europe from fascism. The talk took more than an hour, and afterward I was asked pointed questions about the behavior of the Soviets on occupied Polish territory and about the Soviet-Finnish war. I made no secret of my impressions, but I kept my personal experiences to myself.

I gave that same talk four more times, always after being taken to a new place with great caution, and always being given a sign before leaving that the coast was clear.

Boarding a streetcar on my way home that first time, I ran into some German soldiers standing with a German civilian and an officer. A sign reading "Nür für Deutsche" (Only for Germans) prohibited Poles from entering from the front. I glared at them; if my antifascist harangues would come to anything, they were doomed.

The news of German arrests and brutalities continued. We knew only what was happening in Warsaw, but it was safe to assume that all the Polish territories, and the General Gouvernement in particular, were in the Gestapo's grip. The Falskis told us how friends had been taken during the night by military police in patrol wagons and Gestapo men in black Mercedes-Benzes. They had vanished without a trace. People were apparently being taken either to the Gestapo headquarters on Aleja Szucha or to Pawiak Prison.

One day, on my way to Aleje Ujazdowskie, the avenue down which I had marched each year to celebrate Poland's independence, I crossed Aleja Szucha and saw the scowling German guards in front of the building that once had been our Ministry of Education. Helmets on their heads, legs thrust wide apart, they sported moon-shaped metal plaques suspended on chains on their chests and machine pistols in their hands. The entrance to the courtyard was barricaded by crossbeams covered with barbed wire. It was a hostile place. Rumor had it that it was here that the Gestapo tortured.

Szirmer was worried. The Jews of Warsaw were being terrorized, and people he knew had been arrested by the Gestapo. Violence in the Jewish quarter was more and more common. "What should I do?" he asked.

My father spread his hands, saying that he no longer knew, and that no doubt we would all die at the hands of those murderers. It was a matter of time.

One day I visited my mother in Milanowek and learned that there was no peace there either. The Nazis had conducted a pogrom against the young people. She begged me not to visit again; Milanowek had become a dangerous place.

Upon my return I searched through my father's desk drawer, where, beneath all the papers, I found a tube sealed with a cork that contained several bronze-colored sticks the thickness of a pencil. The label read: Potassium cyanide.

"What do you want with those?" my father asked.

"To protect you and me against the Nazis. Do you want to fall into their hands?"

My father did not answer; he merely nodded his head.

I knew from chemistry class that potassium cyanide was a potent poison. Opening the tube with great care, I shook the sticks into a mug and dissolved them in a little warm water to make as concentrated a solution as possible. Then I poured the tea-colored liquid into two phials that had secure glass stoppers.

From that moment on, my father and I carried those phials in our pockets at all times. I fully intended to use that deadly potion if I fell into Nazi hands.

On April 9, 1940, Hitler's Wehrmacht launched its invasion of Denmark and Norway. Denmark surrendered that same day. The fighting in mountainous Norway was to last much longer, with support from British landings. Events were now moving with terrifying speed. We were going to the Falskis practically every day to read the latest communiqués.

At the end of April our upstairs neighbor came running to tell us that in a number of places walls were being constructed around the Jewish parts of the city. "Could the Germans be walling off the Jews because they're planning to exterminate them?" he asked. "Tell me, Professor, building walls to separate people, is that something a normal human being would do?"

One day in early May my father and I were crossing Poznanska Street, where the Soviet Embassy had been before the war. The front door was ajar, and from it came Zelman, the man with whom my father had once spoken about the manuscript he had left at the embassy. Zelman, who was now caretaker of the building, recognized my father and seemed pleased to have run into him. He said he was living alone in that empty building and had no one to talk to. Eventually, we were asked in, and sat in the waiting room.

"Do you have any information about my manuscript?" asked my father.

"No. I don't know anything about it," answered Zelman. "In general I have no information to give anyone. No one has even bothered to tell me what my responsibilities are here."

"Have you heard anything about Chebyshev? Do you know where he is?"

"No. I don't know anything about him either, though he promised me that I would be given instructions and he would arrange everything for me. I've phoned the Soviet Embassy in Berlin a few times to ask what is going on, but they don't tell me a thing."

My father told him what had happened to us. Zelman did not seem surprised.

"That's war," he said. "What do front-line soldiers know about anything? It was your misfortune to run into them first, Professor. In my opinion," he said, pausing for a moment to think, "the only path for you is to try to obtain official permission to leave for the Soviet Union. There have been a few such cases; a few people have already been granted permission and gone. It has to be done through the Soviet Embassy in Berlin, however, through the consular division. Here's the address.

"Some people have written to the Soviet Consulate in Gdansk or Königsberg. I don't know what success they've had. . . . Best straight to Berlin, I'd say."

The rooms of what had been the Soviet Embassy were dark and gloomy, the windows covered by curtains that clearly had not been touched for months. A thick layer of dust covered the heavy, monstrous furniture; the windows were fortified with bars.

"And so you really advise me to write to the embassy . . ." said my father thoughtfully. "But that would surely attract the Germans' attention."

"But what do you have to lose?" responded Zelman. "Sooner or later the Germans will 'remove' you, along with all the other leftists. . . . Not only the leftists now, mind you; everyone—Jews, Poles. And the war will last a long time. The Soviets are sending the Germans raw materials at a terrific rate. Anyone who thinks Germany is suffering shortages is wrong. But do as you wish, Professor. I can't predict anything, I can't guarantee anything. . . . My job is to take care of the building. You know, I've been working here for several years, and they promised to help me leave. But I haven't heard a word from them. Germans come here from time to time; I show them a letter, in Russian, signed by Chebyshev saying that they left me here to watch the building. The Germans look at the paper, discuss it among themselves, then leave. They haven't done anything to me yet, but how long can this go on?"

Zelman spoke with resignation, as if he were now at the mercy of fate. I ached to ask him if he was a Communist, but I restrained myself. Surely they would leave no one but a Communist in charge of their building. But why had he been abandoned like this?

After our talk with Zelman the idea of applying for official permission to leave for the USSR never left our minds. There was the obvious danger involved in using the German mail, but what other choice did we have?

Subsequent events accelerated our decision. On May 10, the Germans shattered the relative calm by attacking Holland, Belgium, and Luxembourg. Another blitzkrieg. Despite their fortifications and defenses, the Dutch army capitulated on the fifth day, and by May 20 armored Wehrmacht divisions had reached the Atlantic coast at Abbéville, in France. Holland and Belgium had been cut off, and Hitler's armored divisions began pouring into France. The Western Front seemed doomed.

The communiqués from the Wehrmacht high command reported by the *Warschauer Zeitung*, the German daily we called the "reptile paper," provided the quickest accounts and the most precise information on the areas taken by the Germans. France's defeat had been inevitable. The fabled Maginot Line had proved useless. General Heinz Guderian's armored columns had simply gone around it by breaking through the Belgian defenses to the north. All this took place in the dizzying course of two weeks.

I was still feeling bitter about Poland's defeat in September, but the capitulation of Holland, Belgium, and France was staggering. Two weeks into the invasion of Poland we were still fighting furiously, and Poland was, after all, surrounded by Germany on three sides; our mobilization had been paralyzed, we had had no time to prepare, we had had no Maginot Line. The French had had time to get ready, their army could not have been any smaller than Germany's, they had to defend themselves on only one side, they had the Maginot Line, no one was attacking them from the rear, as the Soviets had done in Poland. In addition, they had England on their side. Comparing their defeat with Poland's gave me harsh and bitter satisfaction.

For my father, too, whose faith in France was unshakable, all this came as a colossal blow. He said little at the Falskis'; he read the clandestine reports with a certain indifference. All seemed lost; fascism was triumphant.

I noticed a similar sense of resignation in Marian Falski, who by nature had been an optimist. He argued that there was but one consolation in the tragic May of 1940: Neville Chamberlain had resigned, and the prime minister was now Winston Churchill, a name I had not heard before.

Influenced by this turn of events, my father and I decided to make official application to the Soviet Embassy in Berlin. We began writing letters, the first of which was sent on May 31; the second, on the same day to the Soviet Consulate in Gdansk. A letter went to Moscow on June 1 addressed to Vyacheslav Molotov, the commissar of foreign affairs. We sent out two more letters in June, one to the Commissariat of Foreign Affairs in Moscow, the other to Stefan Rudnianski in Lwow. Meanwhile, the German army was scoring triumphs in the West, its tanks driving toward Paris at the beginning of June. Events moved with lightning speed: Benito Mussolini's Italy declared war on the Allies, Paris fell in the middle of June, and on June 22 France agreed to surrender unconditionally.

Poland was seized by fear, its last hope dashed. Despair could be seen on the faces in Warsaw's streets. And it was precisely at that time that the Nazis stepped up their repression, as if wishing to break the nation once and for all. The reports of Nazi persecution and cruelty spread through Warsaw like wildfire. Mass arrests were common, as Polish intelligentsia were herded to concentration camps at Dachau, Buchenwald, and Sachsenhausen. No big camps had yet been readied on Polish soil, but they came later. The Germans busily demolished houses in the ghetto and accelerated the building of a wall around it. We all, by now, felt certain that the Nazis intended to exterminate the Polish population.

I immersed myself in work to keep my mind off the future. Every morning I studied English from an old German textbook with Gothic script. My father had just reviewed his notes and again was reading excerpts from *Plutarch's Lives* to me in French. One day in early July, the doorbell rang. Loud knocking followed. I froze when I opened the door and saw who was there. I was facing an officer with the death's-head on his cap.

He was my height and had some sort of decoration pinned to his uniform. He shoved his way into the apartment without a word. A civilian came in behind him, shorter, thickset, his hands in the pockets of his brown leather coat.

"Spasowski?" asked the Gestapo man.

I nodded, dumb with fear.

"And who's that?" he asked, striding into the study. My father had just risen from his desk.

"My father."

The officer glanced around the room as if checking to see that nobody else was there. Then, turning to me, he shouted, "Move!" He pointed to the front room. I understood that he wanted me to show him the apartment. He followed me; the civilian stayed with my father. The officer checked the dining room, took a quick look into my room, and crossed the hallway to the kitchen, checking the bathroom on the way. In the kitchen he ordered me to open the door to the back stairs. Posted there was another civilian, hands thrust in the pockets of his leather coat. The officer nodded his head and ordered me to close the door.

Back in the study, he pushed my father out of the way and sat down at his desk. He picked up the Plutarch, a large, handsome volume with a red cover and gold lettering, turned it over, and passed it to the civilian, who held it upside down and shook it, to check if anything was concealed between the pages, then, satisfied, threw it to the floor. Meanwhile, the Gestapo man had opened the desk drawer and was rummaging through it. He pulled out some papers and handed them to the civilian, who tersely reported on their contents. They were old letters, photographs, notes. My stomach turned as I looked at all the telltale papers in my father's desk.

The officer emptied one drawer after another, throwing everything he considered unimportant to the floor. Every once in a while he would scowl up at us, checking our faces for some betrayal of anxiety.

I took a good long look at him. He could not have been more than thirty. I could not make out any insignia, but I guessed him to be a captain. His hair was light blond, already thinning; he had a Prussian head and penetrating blue eyes. He was frightening, but not ugly. "Grenzpolizei" (Frontier Police) was written on the sleeves of his uniform in black stripes. A circular badge with a swastika decorated his jacket pocket; beside it, a rhomboid-shaped badge was inscribed "Condor." So he had flown in Spain, gotten his training and experience there.

When he finished with the desk, he set to work on the table beside it. Each paper required a brief translation by the civilian, who then, upon a nod from the officer, tossed it to the floor. This took quite some time, the pile of papers on the floor growing higher and higher. At one point I froze, when the civilian translated: "What the Nazis are now doing in their own country proves that they will shrink from no cruelty. . . ."

He broke off. The Gestapo officer ripped the paper from his hand and peered at it closely. It was only a quarter of a page, printed in tiny penciled letters. He threw the piece of paper on the desk toward me and shouted, "Read!"

I took it. It was a note written by my father for his book. I was momentarily speechless, the piece of paper somehow heavy in my hand. Then, as I began to read, I could feel my hair stand on end. My father had written his assessment of Hitlerism and racism on that little piece of paper. He accused the Nazis of seeking to dominate the world, and he called on the world to defend itself with all the force it could muster. The last sentence was about Hitler: "Adolf Hitler is an ignoramus and a criminal, who, in his mad obsessions, is capable of anything, including the conflagration of war."

I read the words out, as I had been ordered, but they became little more than a whisper as I realized that I was reading a death sentence. The interpreter translated everything into German; making it sound even more ominous in that language.

When I was finished, the Gestapo officer rose and walked up to me. At first I thought that he meant to attack me, but he brought his face close to mine, our noses almost touching.

"Who wrote that?" he screamed.

"I wrote it," said my father, his voice calm but muffled.

"You!"

He spun around toward my father. I held my breath, sure they would begin beating him, knowing they would have to kill both of us if they did.

But the officer sat down at the desk once more and ordered the civilian to sit across from him.

"Write," he ordered. "The attached manuscript was found . . ."

My father interrupted him. "Our application to leave for the Soviet Union is at the Soviet Embassy in Berlin and has been sent on to Moscow."

The officer studied my father first, then me. He did not seem surprised in the least.

"I am a communist, a Polish communist," continued my father. "I have requested the Soviet authorities to allow me and my son into the Soviet Union."

The officer ignored his words. He ordered the civilian over to the bookcase to search the books. One by one they were flung to the floor. My father had a great many books, and I knew it would take hours to go through them all. Then I remembered that just yesterday morning we had brought home a bulletin from the Falskis'. I had hidden it in the spine of a book on that very shelf, despite my father's constant chiding that I was playing underground for no good reason. The man eventually came to it. He shook it, flipped through it suspiciously, but finally tossed it to the floor with all the rest. I sighed, relieved, but had anything been gained? I could see how pale my father's face had become, and I was afraid he might faint. I leaned forward to take the carafe from his desk and pour him a glass of water.

The civilian seized my arm. "Not allowed," he snarled. He picked up the carafe and the glass and passed them under his nose. "Wasser," he announced.

The officer permitted my father to have a drink of water, which seemed to cause the civilian some surprise. He turned his attention back to the bookshelves, casting malign glances at me.

Suddenly, the front doorbell rang twice. The officer barked at me, "Open the door and don't say anything!"

When I did, I was amazed to see my old classmate Ludwik Bryskier and his father. They were both wearing arm bands with the Star of David on them. Ludwik started, "We . . ." but he got no further, for I shouted gruffly, "They don't live here. Wrong floor!" Confusion flashed across their faces as I slammed the door.

"Who was it?" asked the officer when I returned.

"I don't know. They wanted the apartment downstairs."

The interpreter nodded to indicate that that was what I had said. I was afraid that Ludwik would ring again, thinking that I had not recognized him. But he did not.

The officer then signaled to the civilian that the search was over.

"You come with us," he said to my father. My stomach jumped. Would they make us part? My father looked so spent, so weak, like a condemned man whose time had come. I probably never felt more love for him than I did at that moment.

"I'll go with my father," I said, turning decisively toward the officer. He seemed astonished.

"You're both going; make it quick," he said dryly. We left as we were. In the gateway Jozef peered at us as we passed. A black limousine was parked near our building. The civilian got in the back with us, the Gestapo officer in front with the driver. As we went down familiar streets, past familiar buildings, people turned to stare. In a short time we pulled up in front of the headquarters on Aleja Szucha. A military policeman consulted the driver, the gate opened, and we drove into the inner courtyard and stopped in front of a uniformed guard, who checked their identifications. The officer and the civilian disappeared, and other men, with no silver on their uniforms, escorted us downstairs to the cellar. There, we were led behind a door made of thick iron bars, shoved into a long corridor, frisked, and pushed into a cell—"a tramway," as Poles came to call them.

"Sit down!" a German shouted in after us. "No talking and looking around." The door slammed with a loud metallic clang.

The cell, long and narrow, was half sunk in darkness. Chairs huddled against the wall, their backs to the bars; there was only a narrow passageway between them. A few people sat there, but I could not see their faces. My father and I sat down. Someone nearby not so much moaned, as whimpered softly.

I knew what this place was. People spoke of it as the cruelest in the city, the home of Hitler's expert sadists. That piece of paper—why had my father not destroyed it? How could it have been overlooked? I had traveled to the Soviet side and returned, only to find myself in Aleja Szucha because of a piece of paper, the iron doors slammed shut behind us and every glimmer of hope gone.

A whisper came from behind me; it was Polish but I could understand nothing because the voice was so soft. From the corridor came a yell: "Shut up! Filthy swine—we'll teach you."

The whispering stopped. It was quiet as a tomb, except for the sound of hobnailed boots tramping on the corridor's stone floor. My mind was racing. Why had I put the phials in the bathroom? I should have slammed the door on the Gestapo; we could have taken the poison before they shot off the lock and broke the door down. How could I have been so stupid as to let them in right away?

Footsteps approached in the corridor; a key grated in the lock.

"You two!" The man pointed at me and my father. "Make it quick!" he shouted, kicking our legs with his heavy boot. I gritted my teeth.

"This way," bellowed another. "Quick, you swine!"

Upstairs, he pushed us into a room, where he raised his arm in the Nazi salute and reported our arrival. Two men sat at a desk. I recognized one—the same tall officer; the other was a short, thickset man, also in uniform. A repulsive smirk curled across the short one's face. They herded us into another, larger, room, and sat themselves at desks. We remained standing in the middle; on a table next to us lay a thick whip. At another small table by the window, a woman sat before a typewriter. A blank sheet of paper was poised in the machine. She was young, a German, no doubt; her hair was pinned up in back. She stared at us as if we were inanimate objects.

First they asked for personal data: last name, first name, parents, date of birth. The typist interpreted and, at the same time, typed rapidly, the keys clicking and clacking under her skillful fingers. The men reminded me of the Soviet komandirs. They, too, had asked those questions, though in more detail. I answered now and then in German.

"Where does your mother live?" the tall officer asked me.

"She died before the war," I lied.

"Do you have brothers or sisters?"

"No, I'm an only child."

"And the rest of your family?"

"In Lwow."

"Admit that you wrote this filth," shouted the thickset one to my father.

"But I've already told you that I wrote it," answered my father calmly.

"And have you written a lot of filth like this?"

"I am a writer. I have written a great deal about society, philosophy, and other . . ."

The thickset one jumped up, ran over to my father, and slammed him against the wall violently. My father staggered from the blow.

"Who are you, swine?" the man thundered.

My father was dazed and for a moment did not seem to know what was happening.

"Who are you?" the man yelled again, shoving my father now toward the table.

"I am a communist," said my father, his voice weak and breaking, "and will remain one until I die. Our case is being handled by the Soviet Embassy in Berlin. I have written to Ambassador Dekanozov in Berlin and to Molotov, the commissar of foreign affairs in Moscow. . . ."

I do not know why I did not attack that ape. I stood rooted to the floor, my whole body tense. The typist banged my father's words onto her paper, and the tall officer rose from his desk to approach me.

"Are you a communist, too?" he asked, bringing his face close to mine.

"Yes, I am a communist," I hissed through my teeth. And for a long moment we stared into each other's eyes.

"And a Bolshevik?" he shouted.

"And a Bolshevik. I'm going to the Soviet Union with my father. I've written, too."

At this point, one of them must have rung a bell, because the door swung open, a man in uniform entered, clicked his heels, and shouted, "Heil Hitler!"

"Take them away," shouted the thickset one.

Once again keys clanked in two sets of iron doors, and we were back in the tramway. There were more prisoners now. I took a seat, and my father sat behind me. A howl came through the walls, stopped, then broke out again.

I looked around frantically and caught the eye of a young man. He whispered in my direction, "There's a torture chamber down there, in the cellar."

He said no more. Again the silence was ripped by an ear-splitting cry. I began to tremble.

Footsteps, the clank of the lock, and a man was hurled into the cell. I could hear him groan as he lowered himself into the seat beside me. I studied him over my shoulder. His eyes were red, and blood ran down his cheek. He was propping himself up with his hands at great effort.

I ran my eyes along the wall. Words were scrawled and scratched in a few places—a capital Z; the names Jan, Iza; a brief phrase, "I can't take any more."

Time went by, and a Gestapo man came to the door to call a few names, among them were my father's and mine. We were shoved and kicked outside to a courtyard in the back, where a few prisoners stood by the wall. Military trucks covered with green tarpaulins waited. We were thrust aboard these with curses and more abuse. Gestapo men sat on a bench in back, machine pistols in hand. I sat where I could see out a small window made of transparent material.

"No talking, no looking around!" came a hoarse shout from the rear as we pulled away. I could follow our course through the little window—Aleje Ujazdowskie, Aleje Jerozolimskie, a right turn onto Marszalkowska Street. We slowed and came to a stop, by the window of a streetcar only an arm's length away. Faces peered in at me—a young man, an older woman—they seemed to live in a world apart, the world of the living. They noticed me and smiled, not realizing what they were seeing. Our truck sped past.

We drove past Saxon Gardens, Bank Square, and made two sharp turns. A gate opened—Pawiak Prison. The truck lurched as it pulled in. "Get out!" The Germans pushed us into the building, down corridors, and into a large room with barred windows. Polish police, still wearing their navy blue prewar uniforms, frisked everyone thoroughly and demanded that we surrender all our possessions, including belts, suspenders, and shoelaces. My father handed over the apartment keys, his wallet, and pocket watch.

"A fine watch," the policeman volunteered casually. "Probably keeps good time. Those were good watches. . ."

We said nothing. It was the watch my father had been given by the workers from the Cegielski factory. The policeman tossed it into an envelope. That's the last time we'll see that watch, I thought, and the policeman, as if having read my mind, reassured me: "*It* won't go astray; don't worry. If only its owner could be so lucky."

We were taken below to long corridors lined on both sides by heavy, steel-clad doors with peepholes. A key ground in a lock, and we were in a cell, the metallic echo of the door slamming behind us. It was dark. A faint light beckoned from the other side. I walked forward and raised my head. There were bars, and past them some sort of long, narrow declivity, which seemed hewn into the wall and ran upward at an angle to another set of bars, the merest scrap of blue sky visible through them.

A man—another prisoner—sat up on his plank bed, extended his hand, and said in a flat voice, "I'm Zembrzuski, a lawyer from Warsaw. How long have you been in? Oh, just today. Sit down, please," he said making a place for me.

"A father and son," he repeated when we introduced ourselves. I could not see his face, only his nodding head. After a while my eyes grew accustomed to the darkness and I could see his large, gleaming eyes, so deeply sunk and darkly circled that they seemed like eye sockets in a skull.

"Have you been here long?" I asked.

"I don't know any more; I've lost count. But I've been here quite a few weeks. At first they kept taking me to Szucha and beating me there. I kept count of the days. Then they stopped. Who knows what'll happen next, tomorrow, today, a minute from now. Time stands still here. For some it stands still forever—they slaughter people in these cells. Sometimes you can hear it. . . ."

He fell silent, his fingers twitching nervously. There were no further questions, neither from him nor from us.

A while later more people were crowded into the cell. I could hear the lawyer's breathing become labored; his lungs wheezed. I knew what that meant, because I had suffered asthma attacks as a child. He was suffocating.

I lay down beside my father on another plank bed. It was crowded, for there were three of us on it. No one said anything, but my mind was in a tumult. I thought of prewar Warsaw, evening strolls with my father, the peace of those days, our conversations about the Greek philosophers. Oh, if I could only turn my mind off like a radio, one snap and darkness, stillness. What good were all those memories to me now?

The next day we were taken back to the Gestapo headquarters at Szucha. The same truck, the same men kicking us, the same tramway. This time I noticed a pile of stretchers behind an iron door. A man was carried out as we were coming in. Blood stains seeped through his rumpled clothing, and he lay motionless. Another person was carried by. I managed to get a look at him, although I was trembling with fear. He was an older, bearded man. In the cell someone whispered that he was a professor, and had been singled out for torture.

We were interrogated again by the same Gestapo officers. The same young woman gazed indifferently at us.

"Did you belong to the Communist Party of Poland?" asked the thickset man.

"No," my father said. "I have never belonged to any party, but I supported the Polish Communists' program, and I still do."

"Did you have any contacts with Communists?"

"No. Contacts never concerned me. Philosophy was always my main concern. Ideas interest me, not individuals. Ideas endure; individuals don't."

"Don't try hiding things. We know how to get information out of people. You didn't know any Communists, you say?" The man placed a hand on his whip.

"I have told you," my father said evenly, "I'm a philosopher. I'm not interested in people."

"You were born in Jakubowszczyzna?" interrupted the tall one, mangling the word. "Where is that?"

"Near Vitebsk, in what is now Soviet Byelorussia."

"Weissrussland?" asked the thickset one. "White Russia?"

"Ycs, Weissrussland in German."

"So you're Weissrusse?"

"No. We're Poles. I was just born there."

The two Germans conferred, and I could hear Weisrussland repeated again and again. Then the session was over. We were returned to Pawiak and again a heavy iron cell door closed behind us. It was a different cell this time.

Two days passed, though it seemed longer to me than that. I tried to assess our situation calmly. We had not been tortured yet, but why should they bother? They already knew enough to hang us; they knew what my father had written about Hitler and that we were both communists. That was plenty. Still, I thought, something was staying their hand. Probably those letters we had sent to Berlin and Moscow. I was sure they knew about those letters before; perhaps they were what had prompted them to seize us. If good relations with the Soviets were important, they might feel compelled to be cautious with us; but should the circumstances change, we would be finished.

I whispered these thoughts to my father, who said I was probably right. "You shouldn't be here, son," he said to me. "You could be killed any day. How could I have known that our fate would depend on relations between the Soviets and these barbarians? And that the better those relations, the better our chances of surviving. There's something terrible and ironic in that."

It was curious. The Gestapo, being German and orderly perhaps, were being careful not to exterminate those who were making appeals to their "partners." Germans love order, said my German teacher at school. "Ordnung muss sein," she would repeat, while I nodded off to sleep in class.

My father said no more, feeling the new burden placed on him by his experience of the past few months. He was resigned, but I knew, I felt, that he was not concerned with his own fate; he was able to rise above himself. But his trust had been shaken, if not broken. There, in that cellar in Pawiak Prison, his thoughts were with the people by the Bug, and in Brest Fortress, where he had met his defeat. He did not say that; he did not have to.

Again the lock clanged in the heavy iron door, and again we were taken back to Szucha. This time the tall Gestapo officer was accompanied by another, who, judging by the silver on his uniform, was of higher rank. The new officer sat at the desk reading while my father and I stood before him. After a moment he raised his head from the paper and gave us a long, searching look.

"Sign this statement," he said sharply, his eyes boring into us. "You will report here every two weeks." He addressed only my father. "You realize that your past activity and this," he sneered, indicating the piece of paper, "are enough to sentence you to death. But if you receive permission from the Soviet Union, you are to report here immediately. We are the only ones who can grant exit visas."

He handed my father the statement. My father read it and gave it to me. It contained everything we had said, neat and tidy. A copy of my father's condemnation of Hitler was attached to the record as evidence. They handed my father a pen. I signed after him.

As a policeman led us out, I glanced over at the tall Gestapo officer. I looked hard into his eyes, but met only a cold, vacant stare.

We were taken downstairs to the tramway again. I closed my eyes and began thinking. Now there was some hope of escaping this hell. An hour ago it would have seemed impossible. From somewhere within me an instinct for life awoke again.

They took us back to Pawiak, but not to the cellar. Our possessions were returned; one Polish policeman wrote out two release forms while another brought the envelopes with our things. They watched us curiously as we replaced our shoelaces. "You two were lucky, very lucky," they said. "It's rare for people to get out of here alive."

We did not answer. There was nothing to say. A moment later we were free, as free as one could possibly be in the General Gouvernement.

The next day, I insisted on caution. Making but one visit to our friends the Falskis, I told them we would not risk their safety by visiting them again. My father requested that no one come to see us.

Our existence was marked by constant uncertainty, since the next hour could well bring us the end of our lives. What to do next? We could simply leave our apartment and seek shelter elsewhere under assumed names. Many people had done just that. But my father hoped that soon, maybe even tomorrow, a letter would arrive from Berlin informing us that we has been granted permission to go to the Soviet Union. To disappear meant to forfeit that opportunity forever, and, worse yet, to ensure that our names would find their way onto the Gestapo's search list. We would be doomed to a life of constant hiding outside Warsaw and without means. I could not imagine my father surviving such a life. He was exhausted and in poor health.

His features sharpened now, he absolutely forbade me to accompany him when he reported to the Gestapo every two weeks, and he made me promise that if he ever failed to return after three hours, I was to leave the apartment at once and go into hiding. I knew too well that if he were detained, he would never come out alive, and the days on which he reported were sheer torture for me, every good-bye seeming like our last. Each time, I would wait for him by the door, sick at heart and straining to hear his footsteps on the stairs. I knew the sound of his step so well that I could recognize it the moment his shoe struck the floor of the downstairs hall. That instinct never betrayed me. When he was late, I was overcome with despair, my heart hammering. I would ask myself what I could renounce or suffer in exchange for his return.

Thus we resolved to hold on, to wait things out. In July my father again wrote letters to Soviet Ambassador Vladimir Dekanozov in Berlin, to the consulate in Königsberg, to Stefan Rudnianski in Lwow, and also to Wanda Wasilewska, informing them that we were being interrogated and insisting on an immediate decision.

We were always alone during the months that followed. I would have gone to see Ludwik Bryskier to explain the circumstances that forced me to slam the door in his face that fateful day, but I had no address for him. We visited no one and went outside only to sell books and buy food. I did not like going out; it meant having to see German uniforms and those arrogant caps. Sometimes, on the little side streets, I would come upon small groups of street musicians playing old Polish songs, some of which had been popular before the war. The musicians wore dilapidated Polish army uniforms without shoulder straps; often they were cripples. They played those melodies with true feeling while people stood around them in silence, many of them wiping tears from their eyes. Poland would reappear among us. I, too, cried. I was a communist, but my eyes would well with tears. I felt I was hearing a farewell, a requiem for a world gone.

The hopelessness of our situation was only a reflection of the general hopelessness. After the fall of France, nothing, it seemed, could reverse the course of events. Hitler was preparing to deal with England; the Luftwaffe was attacking English ships in the English Channel and bombing the British Isles.

Our only source of information was the *Warschauer Zeitung*. Every day brought new communiqués of Luftwaffe successes over England. We trembled lest that last bastion of Western resistance be overcome.

Weeks passed, and the German invasion of England did not materialize. Then the Germans began a furious bombardment of London, Bristol, Coventry, and many other cities in southern England. In Poland nothing changed.

One evening we were visited by Szirmer, his wife, and Robert. They reported that the German housing supervisor of the area had ordered them to vacate their apartment the next day, leave all their possessions behind, and move into the ghetto.

"Professor"—Szirmer's voice quavered—"this will be the end of us. . . . We've come to say good-bye. . . . We know what your own life's been like; you wanted to help us, to save Robert, and we thank you. Now we are headed for that hell behind walls and barbed wire. There Hitler will finish off the Jews; he will slaughter us all."

From Szirmer we learned that the walls around the ghetto were almost up. In a matter of days, the Jewish population would be entirely cut off from the rest of the city.

"Such high walls, three yards or more," he said. "Barbed wire on top, as if they intended to keep wild animals there. Except that it's for people—for us, for her"—he pointed at his wife—"for Robert."

We sat in my father's study, unable to look at one another. I felt great pity for them. Was there really no way out? But why not go to Milanowek, to my mother's, to the little white caretaker's cottage by the garden?

As I spoke excitedly, old Szirmer's eyes began to gleam, and Robert smiled the way he used to when we ran into each other on the stairs before the war. My father approved without hesitation.

The next morning I traveled with the Szirmers to Milanowek. I was glad it had become cold; it was November, rain and snow fell in turn, and the women wore coverings on their heads. Robert's mother was so heavily wrapped that her face—a clearly Semitic one—could not be seen. The trip passed without incident.

My mother took them in with her typical warmth. The first night, they moved into the little house. It had one room and a small kitchen.

I returned to my father's the same day. In discussing the Szirmers, we thought of Professor Benedykt Bornstein. He was a close friend of my father's, an idealist philosopher, and—more important, it seemed now—a Jew. Surely his family would need help, too. I hurried to their place, and arrived just in time. The Professor and his wife were in a quandary. Someone was extorting money from them, threatening to report them to the Germans. They were torn between fleeing or moving into the ghetto. I suggested Milanowek; I knew my mother would gladly share her house with them, too. Two days later Benedykt and Jadwiga were in Villa Rose. There they lived with my mother in their own room with a separate entrance from the veranda.

Winter set in. We felt we were in our death throes. Everything had come to an end; not only our strength, but our resources, since all the best books had been sold. There was still some coal in the cellar, and the temperature in the apartment was bearable, but food had become a serious problem. My father's letters remained unanswered.

During those long winter evenings, I would sit and think of my father and how he had behaved with the Gestapo. He had been so calm, so noble. I had seen him hike up his pants, because his suspenders had been taken from him; and shuffle along like all the other prisoners, in shoes without laces. But even this he did with great dignity. He was prepared to die, but never once expressed fear or regret. There was only determination.

The first letter, from the Consular Division of the Soviet Embassy in Berlin, arrived toward the end of December. My father tore it open, confident that it contained approval, finally, for us to travel to the Soviet Union. It was written in Russian.

Mr. Spasowski,

We have received your letter concerning travel to the Soviet Union. However, the formalities involved (filling out applications and so on) absolutely require your presence here. Upon arrival here, you can take your appeal to the Consular Division of the Embassy of the USSR in Germany at this address: Berlin, Kurfürstenstrasse, 134.

Treshina
Secretary of the Consular Division
December 7, 1940

I saw the blood drain from my father's face. He said nothing.

After all the letters he had sent and after everything that had happened, he, a persecuted communist Pole, was to report to the Soviet Embassy in Berlin to fill out forms. How was he supposed to travel there, and on whose permission? Not only did this letter force us to deal with the German authorities, but it alerted them that the Soviet authorities were handling our case as an inconsequential, routine matter. It took the heart out of us.

But my father refused to give up; he was intent on delivering me from this hell. In January he wrote again to the Soviet Embassy in Berlin, insisting that our request to leave for the USSR be dealt with swiftly.

Toward the end of that month he received a thick envelope from the embassy. A stack of forms was attached to a brief, formal letter. We filled out the forms and sent them back, along with several photographs of each of us.

I went to Milanowek in February. Things were hard there, too, but I brought back a little flour, some potatoes and peas, and a small piece of pork fat for flavoring. Tadeusz told me that he was teaching in Warsaw, at the Technical School, and that Professor Zienkowski, my old physics professor, was lecturing there. I went to see Zienkowski, and was given employment in his laboratory. This provided me a small but daily meal at the school.

Yet our situation continued to deteriorate. Everything we owned of value had been sold. There remained only books that the bookstores refused to take on commission and my father's furniture, modest and of little value. I had grown weaker, and carrying coal from the cellar to the fourth floor had become a problem.

At the end of March, when our situation seemed entirely hopeless, we were visited unexpectedly by a man named Karol Batorski. He introduced himself as an admirer of my father, having read all his books, but he had never dared see him in person. Now that times had become so difficult, he had decided to pay him a visit, to come to his aid. Batorski ran a restaurant in Piastow, just outside Warsaw. With him he had brought a package of food containing butter and pork fat, items we had not seen in months. At last I was able to cook my father a decent meal.

Batorski had come out of the blue. It was ironic that a stranger had come to my father's aid, when not one of his students had appeared. We were profoundly grateful to him, and he proved a true friend, bringing us packages and restoring our failing strength.

In the early spring we began taking walks, mostly in the early-morning hours. One day, on returning, we found a relative of ours from Molodeczno, Janina Mieczkowska, waiting for us. At the end of 1939 she had fled Soviet-occupied Poland, where her husband had died tragically. I learned later that Russians had stormed her house one night and beaten my uncle's face to a bloody pulp. She had then gone to live with relatives in Kielce, but they, in turn, had been arrested by the Germans. She lived with us from that day forward, and ran our modest household, despite the dangers of my father's having to report to the Gestapo. She had no fear of the Gestapo, she said. Janina never spoke of her husband, and asked us never to utter the word "Bolshevik" in her presence, for the memory of what she had lived through with them would bring her to the verge of hysteria.

I visited my mother again at the beginning of April, and heard from Tadeusz the rumor that the Germans were preparing to strike at the Soviet Union. They were busily concentrating Wehrmacht units and ammunition dumps in the territories between the Vistula and the Bug.

In Warsaw that rumor was confirmed by the Falskis. Someone they knew reported that the forests were stacked with barrels of fuel, and that the Germans had dug enormous holes to store bombs and artillery shells; new Wehrmacht units, arriving in droves, were being quartered in tents.

May passed uneventfully, but I remember June 22. It was a Sunday, a sunny one. As usual, we rose early, my father up before six to heat water for tea. Janina was still in bed. We each had a slice of black bread and margarine and, as usual, set out for our walk. The streets were empty. On Aleja Niepodleglosci we were stopped by the only other pedestrian, a man unmistakably jubilant.

"You must have heard the latest news," he said, chortling. "The Krauts and the Rooskies have finally gone after one another."

We were stunned. Despite the rumors, it came as a surprise.

"Ye-e-s-s! Hitler's gone for Stalin's throat; he's got his teeth into it. . . . *Now* the show's getting interesting." He went on his way.

We stood there.

I did not doubt that it was the truth. I took my father by the arm. "We've run out of time, and they never helped. They treated us like the Nazis did, no better. I hate them . . . for your sake. . . ."

My father took my hand. "Don't say those things, son."

"Forgive me, but I hate them. . . . I hate them! They're not communists. They're just scum!"

He was looking at me helplessly. "Let's go home quickly, get our things."

"No, Father," I shouted. "Let me decide for us this time. We won't return home, we can never return."

His eyes widened with surprise. "Why is that?"

"Because the Gestapo will be there any minute, if they're not there already. Don't you see? We're the enemy now—and we've let them know it! I won't permit you to return. . . . Our home is finished. We'll go to Batorski."

We ended that walk by boarding a local train at the Chalubinski Street station. It was only when we were well on our way that I realized that all I had with me was my prewar ID and the phial of cyanide. Besides his phial, keys, and ID, my father had the silver watch the workers had given him and enough money for our tickets.

Faithful Batorski received us warmly and vacated the room above the restaurant for us. No one knew who we were, and he told everyone that some relatives had come to stay. There was more than enough food, but after satisfying my initial hunger I lost what appetite I had. I did, however, sleep better, no longer straining to hear the gate in the courtyard or footsteps on the stairs.

People talked only about the war. German newspapers, formerly scorned by Poles, were being snatched up. We heard that crowds were now forming in front of the German loudspeakers in Warsaw. Only days before, Poles had spit when crossing those places. The crowds now waited for the latest communiqués from the high command. It was announced that German armored columns were driving eastward, cutting through the Soviet army like butter. Lwow, Wilno, Minsk, and Riga had fallen in the very first days, and on the central front Guderian's armored columns were heading for Moscow. By July 1 they had crossed the Berezina River. The Soviet air force had been dealt a shattering defeat. The *Warschauer Zeitung* reported enormous spoils—vast numbers of weapons had fallen into

German hands, and prisoners of war had been taken by the hundreds of thousands. "The Bolsheviks are trembling," wrote the Nazi press, "and the victorious German army presses on toward Moscow."

Within ten days the Wehrmacht had seized an area considerably larger than prewar Poland, on a front that extended fifteen hundred miles.

Those were bleak days for my father. "Hitler could defeat the Soviet Union," he would say sadly; "Hitler could dominate the world; there would be no knowing if and when the Brown Shirts' rule would end. I don't want to live to see that happen," he would tell me. "I prefer to die. I'm already bone tired, I've had enough of life."

I could see that staying with Batorski, though he was friendly and generous, had changed nothing. My father still felt sick at heart.

On the third of July we went to Milanowek and spent the afternoon sitting with my mother and the Bornsteins on wicker chairs in the shade of the lime and pine trees. Bornstein commented on the latest reports from the front with his innate sense of calm and measure, but my father, always a lively, interested person, now sat silently in his chair, in some other world. I thought that perhaps he was thinking of his youth, images and memories passing through his mind, for at times his expression would soften. I felt, sitting under the trees that day, that he was preparing for death. That evening he locked himself in a room and spent hours writing.

Nor did I want to go on living.

The Germans continued driving forward with the same momentum. On the evening of July 5, my father took me aside and told me that he had decided to depart from this world. He asked—implored—me to follow his instructions to the letter and not to attempt to change his mind. He wanted one last talk with me and asked me then to return to Batorski's with him. When he went to bed that night, I noticed that a thick red rash had appeared on his back. Much later a doctor told me that such rashes are caused by nervous strain.

The next day—Sunday, again—we took a train to Podkowa Lesna, a small place set in a forest of pine and oak two miles from Milanowek. It was there that my father wanted to talk.

"I am certain you will understand me," he said. "We've been so close; we've understood each other so well. . . .

"I am tired," he continued. "You know why. I can't survive this war. I don't want to watch them destroy the Polish nation, and the Soviet Union, too. I have decided to die as I wish, not as the Nazis wish. Don't stop me from taking this step. All my life I have preached that a person cannot place what is small and low above the values of his spirit. Do you remember I wrote to you once not to love life more than the integrity of your mind, your heart, your actions? My hour has come. I have decided it. I will live in you, for that is the nature of life, and in nature nothing dies. You are young; you must do everything in your power to survive these terrible times, so that afterward you can carry on the struggle for those ideals you and I together hold."

"We'll both go." I forced the words through my tears. "I won't stay alone. We have always been together, and we will be together even in this."

My father cut me off and looked deeply into my eyes. "But you love me, son. You can see how exhausted and weary I am—I have no strength left. You wouldn't want me to fall into their hands again. You've seen what it's like. . . . *You* be the continuation of my life, and fulfill what we began together. Remember, I will live in *you*, and we will always be together. . . . But now I am so very, very tired that I can't go on. I don't want to go on. I beg you, son, let me go; let me do what I want to do most of all; let me remain true to myself to the end, to the ideals I have always believed in."

His eyes entreated me to obey him. Heartsick, I didn't say a word. I looked at his beautiful head, his pale face, his wise deep-set gray blue eyes, his thick head of hair silvered at his temples. Then my eyes wandered past him to the green of the leaves and the pine trees, the sky, and I felt that everything within me had suddenly burst and broken. The moment I had dreaded most had come.

My father's voice shook the silence. "A person must know when to live, when to fight for what he believes in, and when to leave to keep his dignity."

We rose from the grass. I took my father by the arm, and we walked to the station. The train arrived in a few minutes. I sat across from him. He was lost in thought. We arrived at Malichy station, which was close to where Batorski lived. After walking only a few steps, my father stopped. "We will say good-bye here, son. I'll go see Batorski; I want to talk with him and thank him. Get on the next train for Milanowek and go to your mother's." We kissed and looked for a long time into each other's eyes.

"I will go to Warsaw from here," he said finally. "There, in the Botanical Gardens, on that same bench you and I used to sit on, I will end my life. . . . That's not far from Aleja Szucha and the Gestapo, so no doubt they'll find out about it. Maybe then they'll leave you in peace. You must live. . . . That is my last and only will. If you survive . . . think of your father."

He turned and began walking away, but spun around and came back, his hand fumbling through his jacket in search of something. He unfastened the silver pocket watch and chain from his vest and pressed it into my hand.

"Take it," he said. "You remember, they gave it to me, the workers from Cegielski. I won't be needing it now."

I searched his face—our final look. "I swear," I whispered, clutching the watch in my hand, "I will never be a disappointment to you."

He strode away with a quick, decisive step, and did not look back. I have only the vaguest recollection of standing on the platform, boarding the train. I saw nothing around me. I looked at a sign, able to see the letters but unable to make out the words. There was a trembling throughout my body.

My mother got the truth out of me that evening—that my father was no longer among the living. Professor Bornstein came and sat by my bed.

"I only want to tell you, Romek," he said evenly, "that tomorrow morning I'm going to Warsaw to retrieve your father's body. He deserves that—to be buried like a human being. I loved him very much even though we were such different men. Your mother told me it was to happen in the Botanical Gardens. Can you tell me any more?"

"Only," I said, barely able to utter the words, "that he would be on the bench beneath the largest oak tree—the tree under which we used to sit."

"How was he dressed?" he asked.

"In a brown suit," I said, and burst into tears.

Bornstein nodded, stroked my head as though I were a little boy, then left the room.

He returned from Warsaw late the next day, just before nightfall.

I was in bed, in a state of collapse. I couldn't reconcile myself to Father's death, refused to eat, and stayed locked up in my room.

Only after some time did I begin to consider what to do next. Instinctively I knew that the Gestapo would be after me. I had been well known in Milanowek before the war, and now the Germans were making constant arrests. My mother had even warned me once not to come. Now there was another factor to be taken into account: there were two Jewish families with us—Professor Bornstein and his wife, and the three Szirmers, all of them fugitives, all of them living under false names. I had to plan my life so as not to bring tragedy down on that house.

I decided that I had to leave. Remembering Lutsk, where I had found refuge with the poor, I decided on a settlement outside Milanowek where poor people lived in one-room wooden shanties built before the war. Anielcia, a maid who had worked for us before the war, had lived in one of those shanties; she had gone off and married a house painter.

She and her husband were glad to share their simple room with me. I decided to move there at once, but in a way that would attract no attention. Tadeusz gave me some stained, ill-fitting work clothes. Wearing those, and with a sack in one hand, I left the house early one morning and resumed the wanderer's life.

Anielcia showed me kindness and did what she could to bring me out of my sadness. The house painter followed her example, but, unable to utter a single word without prolonged stuttering, he sang words of encouragement and friendliness to me. He would lose his stutter when he sang; in a strong, fine voice he would croon conversations to the tunes of songs and operatic arias. The effect was so outlandish I could not help smiling.

My decision was soon proved to have been correct. Two weeks later, Janina, who was still living in my father's apartment in Warsaw, came to Milanowek and told my mother that the Gestapo had appeared between nine and ten o'clock on that unforgettable Sunday morning in June. They had shouted and stomped about, demanding to know where the two of us were. She told them the truth—that we had left the house for our walk and had never returned. They ordered us to report to them at once and threatened to come for her if we failed to appear.

They interrogated her. She explained that she was the maid and showed them her bed in the kitchen as proof. She went on to tell them that the Bolsheviks had murdered her husband. The Gestapo shouted and made threats but did nothing to her. After they had gone, Janina quickly went through my father's desk and bookshelves, stuffed his papers and letters into a bag, and took them to a neighbor's two floors below. It had been a wise move, because the Gestapo reappeared within the next few days and conducted another search, dumping all his belongings on the floor and going through all of them.

So Janina had brought the inkwell, a few other small mementoes from my father's desk, and the bag of papers from our neighbor's to my mother.

My mother was smiling as she spoke of this during one of her visits to me.

"Why the smile?" I asked, still sorrowful.

"You see, both Janina and I acted like old conspirators, just like we did in tsarist times. It's in our blood. Here are the papers she brought. Look through them and set aside the ones you want to save. I'll find a good hiding place for them. Maybe they'll survive and be of some use to you if we live through this hell.

"And here," she continued after a moment, "are your father's last words. Benedykt brought them back from Warsaw. Read them, but don't cry; you've cried enough. Your father was a courageous man—you can be proud of him.

"Would you like me to tell you what Benedykt said when he returned from Warsaw?" she asked, her voice uncertain. "Do you feel strong enough?"

"Yes, please," I assured her. "I have my strength back now."

"All right then, listen. On Monday, Benedykt went to Warsaw, to the Botanical Gardens. There was no sign of the tragedy. He decided to inquire at the administration building, near the entrance. There he met a Pole, the acting manager. Benedykt asked whether anyone had been found dead in the park the day before. The man invited him in and, after assuring himself that Benedykt was a Pole, too, told him that a gardener who had been working there had reported that a man was lying on the ground by a bench under the big oak tree and didn't appear to be alive. Indeed, the body was there on the ground, an empty phial on the bench beside him. They also found two notes; clearly, they had been written just before his death. They searched through the dead man's wallet and found his pension card: Wladyslaw Spasowski. The manager asked Benedykt if he had known him.

"I didn't say anything," Bornstein had told my mother. "I somehow could not get the words out."

The manager then volunteered that he knew who Spasowski was—"an important leftist, a great mind. They were after him. . . . He evidently had no choice."

"They didn't know what to do," my mother continued. "They couldn't hide the body and bury it themselves. So they informed the police. The police came, looked at the ID, and ordered that the body remain where it was until they returned. It was almost dark when the Germans arrived. They examined the body, checked the ID, and looked very closely at the face. Then they had a little discussion and, finally, they left. The Polish police stood off to the side until the Germans were through, then ordered the city morgue to come for the body.

"Benedykt asked the manager if he knew where the body had been taken, and the man gave him the address. Benedykt thanked him and, as he was leaving, told the man that he and Spasowski had been friends since their student days, and that he knew his family.

"The manager then admitted that he had not given the Germans the notes he had found on the ground. He asked Benedykt if he would pass them on to Spasowski's family. Of course, Benedykt agreed.

"Benedykt went directly to the mortuary, where Poles and Jews were brought in great numbers every day. He asked about the body of an older man in a brown suit, dead the day before. The people were not co-operative at first; so he offered bribes—good bribes. He was taken to where the bodies were kept. In the airless room, dimly lit, more than a dozen bodies were sprawled on the cement floor. He looked at them one by one until he noticed something brown by the wall. He walked over. Your father's face was there.

"Until then, Benedykt said, he had been calm, but suddenly he broke down and covered his face with his hands. It was difficult to reconcile that face with his old friend. When he got hold of himself, he asked where the body would be buried. Wherever there was room, he was told, in common graves. He gave another bribe and said that there was a plot for this man at the Evangelical Cemetery on Zytnia

Street and that if they took the body there right away, there would be no problem and more money.

"He went directly from the mortuary to the cemetery and arranged all the formalities. At around four o'clock they brought the body in a paper bag. There were no coffins, so they made a long box out of planks right there at the cemetery and buried your father in a new row of graves, close to the wall. He's resting there now. . . ."

When my mother left, Anielcia cleared the old square table that her husband had repaired and painted white. It was by the window that looked out over cropfields to a little village nestled among trees on the distant horizon. It was a peaceful view, an oddity in the terrible times in which we were living.

There were many papers in the bag Janina had brought. Once again I read with emotion the letters my father had written to me in September 1939, autobiographical notes he had written for me in 1933, and various notes and letters he had received, including those from Romain Rolland, George Bernard Shaw, and well-known Poles. Then I found in my hands a letter written to me on June 1 of this year, the last long letter I ever received from him:

> My dearest son,
>
> As you are well aware, after finishing my great swan song (which, along with Volume I of *The Liberation of Man*, constitutes my life's testament and is the only work of its kind in Poland), I lived only for you in my final years; lived in the hope of leading you from the house of bondage, from capitalist infamy, out onto the great highroad of hope and creative social struggle on the other side of the barricade.
>
> I have not bowed beneath the blows of bitter experience caused me precisely by those with whom we strove to co-operate. I am convinced that you, too, despite your experiences and hardships, will not break and will remain true to our ideology—one that is splendid and unrivaled, one whose goal is the complete liberation and unification of all working humanity.
>
> So be steadfast, and act dialectically in that direction, that spirit. You will find no goal better, more noble and worthy in this world—this work alone will bring you profound joy and happiness.

My dearest son, I am so proud of you. I love you and would want to be at your side always, training your spirit for the great struggles in life.

You are young and fresh like the dawn of a fair spring day; the whole world will soon open up to you—the bloody mist of war will soon roll away and you will spread your wings and fly like an eagle. Remember, human life is short, and works of lasting value require great effort and application. Plan your life as wisely as you can; change that plan according to conditions and circumstances but spare no efforts to carry it out. This is what all intelligent and courageous people have done, whether their creativity lay in theory or in practice.

As I am now—weak, suffering, constrained—I feel but a burden and hindrance rather than the aid I was before.

I will be at my post to the end, however, and only in the event of outright violence will I go, following the example of Brutus and Cato, whose hearts were true and brave though their spiritual horizons were more cramped than yours and mine.

My heartfelt love, my deepest thoughts, and my most fervent good wishes go to you, my son, as they will until my final breath. When I die I will live on in your mind and heart. I know that you truly love me and will bear our parting manfully, that you will grow deeper and stronger in spirit, that you will overcome all obstacles and difficulties to become what you and I dreamed of together—my greatest pride and joy, a son to astound the world.

I hold you close to my heart as I bless you and bid you farewell.

June 1, 1941
Warsaw
Your Father

I wept as I read that letter, and when the tears had dried on my face, I could not help but weep again.

It was only after a long while that I picked up the gray envelope that Benedykt had brought back from Warsaw. I opened it with trepidation. Within, I found a small envelope, the kind used for calling cards. My father had written, in pencil: "Romek, Milanowek, 17 Piasta Street, Villa Rose." How fortunate that the Polish manager of the Botanical Gardens had not let the envelope fall into the hands of the Germans; it certainly would have cost us our lives. My father had addressed the letter as he was dying; his only concern was that the letter reach me.

The little envelope contained a piece of paper with only three words on it: "I love you!" and it was signed "Your Father." His dying words. I kissed the piece of paper and gazed at the words, the handwriting hasty, out of character.

On another piece of paper he had written:

1. My body has not reacted although it has been half an hour since I took my first dose.
2. Accordingly, I have taken a second dose and am waiting.
3. If this does not work I will go to the Poniatowski Bridge and the Vistula.

My body is strong but I am stronger.

Farewell, world. Farewell, my son. *Moriturus te salutat*! My decision is unchangeable. Enough of this life! I am a citizen of the world (*cives universitatis*) and do not wish to be any other sort of citizen

These last words, too, must have been written in haste, for they were scrawled, as if his hand was weak. The text broke off at that point. I repeated his words: "I am a citizen of the world and do not wish to be any other sort of citizen." They had a definite meaning for me. The Soviet Union had demanded that we travel to Berlin, that we comply with a whole series of formalities—applications, photographs—in order to get Soviet citizenship. In his dying moments my father had made his declaration: he did not wish to be a citizen of any country, but a citizen of the world. And, in his final moments, he had returned to what is immortal.

Through my tears, I watched the paper float from my hands to the table.

There were a few other papers. I looked through them slowly. From one envelope I shook out everything that remained of our more than year-long effort to cross over to the other side: a letter from the Soviet Embassy we had received a couple of months before, a letter we got at the end of 1940, and a great many postal receipts, which I had carefully collected each time my father mailed a letter that referred to our case. There were twenty-six of them, sixteen for letters sent to the Soviet Embassy in Berlin. Two of those had been personally addressed to Dekanozov, the Soviet ambassador. My father had written as one communist to another. He had never received a reply.

With my father's death, my youth was over. I alone was now the sailor, the helmsman, the ship.

A few days later my mother and Tadeusz came to visit. We discussed my options. I asked Tadeusz to go see the Falskis in Warsaw, to tell them about my father, and to request that they obtain a forged ID with a name that had the same initials as mine. He was also to ask them to help me make my way to the West; there, somewhere, a Polish army no doubt would be formed now that France had fallen. Falski had told me earlier that young Poles were going west through Slovakia and Hungary and then through Italy. If that proved impossible, I wanted him to help me find work through his numerous friends and acquaintances. It did not matter where or what sort.

A week later Tadeusz returned with an ID for me made out in the name of Roman Sokolowski, and issued, supposedly, before the war, in 1937—in Bialystok, so that it could never be checked. All records there, we knew, had been destroyed during the fighting in September 1939. The description fit me perfectly; my profession was mechanic, as I had requested.

Tadeusz also gave me an address to which I was to report for work. I was to be employed as a manual laborer on an agricultural estate, Kociszew, near Grojec, about thirty miles south of Warsaw. Falski warned me that the estate was under German control, and so I ought to be careful, but, all the same, I might be safer there. As for crossing over to the West, routes had been blocked under the Third Reich's influence. That option was closed.

"I don't know what's going to happen," Tadeusz said. "Your mother and I want to help people because these are terrible times, but I'm afraid that we'll all go under. I wasn't able to refuse Regina Falski when she told me that her brother Leon had barely managed to escape from his apartment a few days ago. I brought him to Milanowek. He's living with us, sleeping on the floor. It's all right now, but should someone report us, the Germans will come."

After he left, I thought about Villa Rose. I reproached myself for possibly having acted rashly in bringing so many Jews there. I was about to go off again; if a catastrophe befell them, I would be spared. But my returning to Milanowek could only bring sure disaster to everyone.

Before my departure my mother visited me once more, accompanied by Wanda Sikorska, who, my mother told me, very much wished to see me. I was surprised by her now; she had changed again since I had last seen her. She was only fourteen, but had become a tall, good-looking girl, with slanted green eyes, high cheekbones, and a certain sweetness of expression. She asked me to take care of myself and assured me with a sincere naïveté that nothing bad could befall me because she would be constantly praying for me.

I wondered why this girl was so concerned for me. I had known her for years and remembered the first time I had seen her, a chubby little two-year-old. Later, we had gone to the same school, but I had paid no attention to a tot like her.

CHAPTER VII

Saturday, August 2, 1941, was an overcast day. I left Milanowek on the same local train I had taken with my father less than a month before. Apprehensively, I counted the stations that separated me from the stop where our farewell had taken place. As I approached it, my emotions took over. I went out onto the platform, pressed the silver watch between my palms, and looked through my tears at the tree-lined road down which my father had vanished forever.

It was raining, and dark, leaden clouds rolled across the sky when I arrived in Grojec, and by the time I walked to the estate, I was dripping. The storm had only been a reflection of my mood.

The manor looked as though it had been built shortly before the war; its architecture bespoke both modernity and expense. I stopped the first person I saw and asked about the owner, only to learn that the man with whom I was speaking was Hlasko himself.

"I'm Roman Sokolowski," I said.

"Oh, you're the student I was asked to take on here." He looked me over curiously. I was still soaking wet.

"Yes, I'm Sokolowski," I repeated.

"Oh, I don't pry into names and things," he said. "I was asked to take you on, and that's enough for me. In bad times like these it's better not to know. . . ."

There was something childlike in his eyes. He was about fifty, and judging from his soft, velvety hand, had led a comfortable life. Before the war he had been a very rich man, chairman of the Carpathian Oil Company, with oil wells of his own.

"I had thought of keeping you in the manor house, like one of the family, but I have so many relatives living with me right now I simply can't do that. Better not to anyway. You see, this estate, even though it's my property, is being run by the Germans. We have a trustee here, a Volksdeutscher. I get along with him because I've known him for years. He used to be an all right fellow—lived in Grojec. He was a petty official then. But now he's a new man, a real Hun. Watch out for him! He still does what I say, because he remembers that I used to have a lot of power and he's not sure how things will turn out. But who knows what might come into that head of his. . . .

"I've decided," continued Hlasko, "that you'll live in one of the administration buildings, not far from here. You can be the night watchman in the orchards. You're not afraid of the dark, are you?"

When he saw me, the German in charge, Linke, knew who I was immediately. "Herr Student, ja?" He took my measure with a single glance, noting that I was soaking wet. "Yes, yes, these are some times; people must work rain or shine. Poles must work and work well—that's the most important thing. These are great times. . . . In a couple of days the German Panzerwaffe will take Moscow." He rubbed his hands.

I surveyed his fleshy body, his sports jacket, his officer's jodhpurs, his tall black gleaming boots. The ruddy, flushed face was radiating joy. My hatred for him was immediate.

The next day the gardener showed me around the orchard, which contained hundreds of fruit trees, mostly apple, pear, and plum. It bordered the farm buildings on one side, and, on the other, abutted a cemetery, whose moss-covered gravestones were lost among weeds, bushes, and towering old oaks.

"You afraid of ghosts?" the gardener asked me.

"No. Why?"

"There's ghosts in there . . . in the old cemetery. No one comes here at night, at least before midnight. But you have to keep a sharp watch. People like to shake fruit off the trees by the cemetery; they're the best." He was taking malicious pleasure in trying to frighten me; that was clear.

That night was to be my first on the job, so I armed myself with an oak stick to drive off any thieves. I was to have a mean-tempered dog for company, but he had nearly destroyed his cage at the sight of me. Until the dog grew used to me, I stood watch alone.

I felt safe beneath the vault of night, beyond the reach of the Nazis. I thought of the cell in Pawiak Prison where only a scrap of sky could be seen shining between the bars. That first night I spent a long time sitting on a gravestone. I felt secure in the dark, with the stars, the solitude. I was free there to give myself over to the memories of my father—the despair and regret—which swept over me in waves.

One fall day I was summoned by Linke. He rose heavily from a desk covered with stacks of paper and, after a few casual questions about how things were, began talking as if he wanted to confide in me—or perhaps only to boast.

"You have to admit," he said, "the Polish economy was never good. No plan, nothing worked. In Kociszew there's a lot of land, good land, too, but it's still the same old Polish economic system—no plans, no machinery. I do the best I can, but tell me, do you really think anything can be done with these people? It's wartime, and, in spite of all my efforts, there are problems with the few machines there are, with everything. It's the people. . . ."

He poured himself a glass of vodka and set another in front of me. "Drink, Herr Student! Times are tough for Poles. When someone gives you a drink, drink it." He began moralizing. "People have to learn how to work. You, too. Believe me, the Germans will teach the Poles how to work; oh, they'll teach them all right, even though it may be bitter medicine. We must establish order. Germans love orders; Germans are clean, you understand. Look at me, clean-shaven, hair short, the way it should be. I start work early and work from morning till night."

He poured himself another vodka, polished it off, and poured another. His voice was becoming hoarse and loud.

"The German war machine is a precision machine. Well oiled. Splendid—wunderbar! Do you speak German? Wunderbar. It drives on and on. They'll take Moscow, then Siberia, the Caucasus, the oil, all that Russia has to offer. That's how *I* see it, a greater Germany!"

His mood was improving by the minute. His face was even more flushed than usual; sweat stood on his forehead. "What a soldier the German soldier is! Who can resist him? Listen to me, I've heard it from the soldiers who've fought at the front. . . . What soldiers, what *men* they are!"

He lowered his voice, as if to confide in me. "When they go into a city, or a village, all that lives trembles. There's no joking around with Germans. If they have to, it's bang-bang-the end. That's how things are, that's what a soldier does. This is war, total war. Old, young, children, women . . . doesn't matter. . . . This is total war, this is the army. . . . What discipline, what organization!"

Linke took another drink, his eyes bleary now. I was sure he could only barely see me. I picked up my glass, pretended to drink, and, when he wasn't looking, poured the rest on the floor.

"Where's the discipline in Kociszew?" He spat disgustedly. "People here are good for nothing. . . . Pigs, not people. Schweinerei! But I, Linke, will teach them. They don't know Linke yet, but they'll come to remember his name. . . ."

He continued mumbling to himself, sprawled in his chair. His head eventually fell forward to the table, and his fat brutish body slumped down. I left quickly.

The weather was becoming increasingly cold, and there were light frosts in the morning. My time at the Kociszew estate was over. There was no more work for me—the fruit in the orchard had either been gathered or had fallen. I went again to see Linke.

"Have a seat, Herr Student," he said, polite for some reason. "So now you know that working on an estate's not easy. Not easy, like life."

He went on about the estate, and I waited for him to start lauding Germany and berating Poland again. But he took a different tack.

"There are bloody battles going on now outside Moscow. The Germans can see the towers of the Kremlin through their binoculars, but the Bolsheviks are putting up a stubborn resistance. It's a crazy war. The front is thousands of miles long, and those Bolsheviks are dying by the thousands, but there is no end to them. And the winter in Moscow! Spit freezes before it even hits the ground!"

My heart leapt with joy. This was no longer the old cocksure, arrogant Linke. He must have heard that the Germans, too, were freezing, were *dying*, at Moscow's doors. I was in excellent spirits.

My only route back to Milanowek was via Warsaw, as I had come. I left carrying my food allowance: some flour, sugar, peas, and a piece of salt pork I had been given. The train was mobbed. Like me, everyone was carrying as much food as he could.

I listened to what people were saying. They were talking about German atrocities, roundups and shootings in Warsaw and the provinces. I began to feel anxious as we approached Warsaw, and made my way out between two cars to watch the station come into view. Just then I saw a series of long green trucks pull up in front of the station and military police come pouring out of them. Germans! The train came to a halt. Cries of panic broke out among the passengers. Through holes in the concrete wall on the other side of the track I caught a glimpse of a military police uniform. We were surrounded.

Meanwhile, a streetcar had stopped at the adjoining square, but seeing what was happening at the station, no one got off. It will pull away in a minute, I thought; it's my only chance to break out of the trap. A column of police was already forming in front of the streetcar, as if in preparation for an attack. It would soon be too late to do anything: I would be up against the station wall, my hands up, a policeman checking my papers. They would take people like me.

I let the sack of food slide out of my hands, hopped off the train to the station platform, and began running. Out of the corner of my eye I could see the streetcar pulling away and making the turn. It would be right in front of the station in a minute. I jumped over the wire fencing and ran as fast as I could, feeling certain I could catch up and hop on. Behind me, police were yelling and motors were roaring, but I had only a single thought in mind. The streetcar had turned onto a straight track and was gathering speed. I headed for its rear platform. The handle was almost within reach when the streetcar picked up speed again. With one last burst of energy, I drew close enough to grab the handle, first with one hand, then with the other. But my legs could not keep up and my boots were dragging along the street. I held on but lacked the strength to pull myself up onto the steps. Just then a strong hand grabbed me under the arm and pulled me up. I could barely breathe. The streetcar was speeding away from the station; the police were diminishing into doll-size figures. I looked up to see who had saved me, and froze. A uniformed German was bending over me, a death's-head on his cap. He was shouting good-naturedly, "You've got a real runner's legs. Bravo!"

When I struggled to my feet on the platform, he gave me a too-friendly whack on the back. I went into the car, my heart pounding. The Poles there sat quietly looking at me as I slid into a seat.

"You made it," said the quiet voice of the man sitting opposite me. "That German brute got all excited when he saw you make a run for it—like it was a horse race or something."

Everything was pretty much the same in Milanowek, though my mother was thinner, more worn out from work.

It was December; the morning frosts had started and the strong winds would soon be bringing us blizzards. I felt a great need to see my father's grave. My mother, who knew the cemetery from before the war and had already visited the grave twice, wanted to go with me.

She found it without difficulty. For a moment we stood before that small mound of earth, its sides overgrown with withered grass and dusted with snow. The grave was marked with a black metal plate on which there was a cross and the words: "To the sacred memory of Wladyslaw Spasowski. Born December 28, 1877. Died July 6, 1941."

My mother felt my eyes on her and, knowing what I was about to say, took my hand. "Don't make a fuss about the cross," she whispered. "It's better this way."

I did not protest, though I felt pained. How could she have allowed it—that cross, that "sacred memory"? He had been an atheist, and had remained true to himself to the very end. How could she have done it?

"I know what you're feeling," she said. "I used to be a nonbeliever myself. But isn't his memory sacred for you? And the cross? You're still young, but someday you'll remember what I'm telling you now: We all have our own cross to bear. Christ's cross has no equal; his was the greatest life the world has known. Don't deny me that cross on your father's grave. . . ."

I looked down the long row of graves. There were no metal markers, only wooden sticks with gray cardboard nailed to them. The rain had nearly washed away the words. I bent down to read the one next to my father's: Ludwik Merkel. Died July 1941. It was the husband of Antonina Sokolicz, my father's Communist colleague. I remembered my father's words: "Ludwik is not communist; but he's an honest, respectable man, and I consider him my friend." Now fate had decreed that they would lie side by side.

I turned to look at the grave on the other side of my father's. There, among the prickly hawthorn, was a grave marker with the words "Roman Sokolowski. Age 19, a tragic death."

It was my assumed name, and my exact age.

They needed me in Milanowek. That consideration seemed to me more important than anything else. I decided to stay.

We were well into winter, the snow deep, the frost thick, when my uncle Zygmus from Volhynia appeared at my mother's house. I had seen him last two years before, in Lityn, when his loathing for the Bolsheviks had gotten on my nerves. He and three other members of his family simply trudged into the kitchen in their heavy, fur-collared winter coats and caps with earlaps, so thick with frost that we did not know who they were at first. I recognized Zygmus by his voice. They had come from Lwow, a long journey. The four of them were clutching bags containing the little that remained of the once prosperous family of Zygmunt Chmielowski and his wife, Lincia Sumowska, my mother's sister. They were exhausted and rested on our beds while my mother prepared our usual supper—dumpling soup—though this time, in honor of their coming, seasoned potatoes, pork fat, and onions were added. Tadeusz tossed some more wood into the stove, and a pleasant warmth began to radiate through the room. On the table he readied an acetylene lamp he had made himself, because the Germans would turn off the electricity come nightfall.

"Stay with us," said my mother when we had all sat down at the table. "It's crowded here, it's dark, and we don't have much, but this place is our very own, bought with Lityn money. This should be home for you, too, in times like these. We don't have enough beds for everyone—Romek's sleeping on the floor on a pallet—but we have a couple of other pallets and plenty of hay, and there are sheets, blankets, and quilts. We have potatoes for the winter, enough for you, too, so we won't die of hunger as long as they leave us be."

"It's all turned out the way I said it would," said Zygmus sadly. "The Soviets have taken your mother," he said. "Your brother Stefan and his family, too. Probably to Siberia; there's no trace of them."

We were overcome. My mother began to weep. "Oh, my God. Oh, my God," were her only words.

"You have no idea, Dziunia," interjected Aunt Lincia, "what's been happening in the East since the Bolsheviks arrived. It's sheer savagery. A sane mind couldn't imagine it."

A few days after Soviet troops had crossed the border, Zygmus learned that Soviet commissars were at Lityn and had arrested my Uncle Stefan. Zygmus wasted no time. He packed what he could into a peasant wagon, and they left the estate within an hour.

They had been in Kowel and had seen what was taking place there. "They also killed people right on the spot," said Lincia wanly, "our best friends. . . ."

Speaking chaotically, they both continued the story. "We fled to Lwow. Perl, the innkeeper, came to see us and brought the news that everyone had been deported. Everyone, from your grandmother"—he looked at me—"down to the newborn baby. They were all packed into a cattle car and taken off to Siberia in the middle of winter.

"By the end of 1939, every Pole in Lwow was in danger. The NKVD made lists and arrested people at night. Some simply vanished, perhaps murdered, perhaps put on trains. No one knows. Prisons were overflowing. The stories made our blood run cold. Cells were so crowded people had to stand; there was no air, only a horrible stench. People fainted, people died; they stood in their own excrement. Many, especially soldiers and policemen, were tortured to death, many committed suicide.

"I don't know where we found the strength and the nerve to hang on. Finally the Germans came. That was June 30. And what happened then? It's hard to describe. The Bolsheviks were caught by surprise. They fled in a panic, abandoning everything, even their families. The Ukrainians who had been wearing red arm bands and helping the Soviets suddenly did an about-face and greeted the Germans ecstatically as their liberators. Blood started flowing again. The Germans killed mostly Jews, but the Ukrainian nationalists killed whomever they could get their hands on—Jews, Poles, Bolsheviks. There's no describing it.

"The only reason we got out of Lwow was because Lincia still speaks the German she learned as a young girl. She finally obtained German permission for us to leave for Warsaw. Things may be no different here, but at least we'll die with the people we love," Zygmus said, sighing.

I went to see the Sikorskis. Czeslaw was gloomy. I had noticed that their life was increasingly hard. Wanda's father, Jan, had been earning little and had decided to go to relatives near Kielce to get help. They lived mostly on potatoes and turnips, and Wanda had had to leave school. She was thin and pale. I would bring her apples from our garden. Though she was seven years younger, I enjoyed talking with her. I would tell her about my peregrinations. She would listen wide-eyed, and I had the feeling that she was reliving it all with me. I, in turn, would listen to her music, though the lighter things in life did not appeal to me. She would play the piano and sing for me in a lovely soprano, which later matured into a fine singer's voice.

One day, Wanda's mother, Melania, asked me to help Wanda bring up some potatoes from the cellar. The old rusty padlock was stuck. We went down to the cellar with a candle. Wanda held it while I tried to open the jammed padlock. As I worked she moved closer, and I could feel her hair touching the side of my head. I lifted my head, and her lips formed a kiss on my forehead. She did not say a word, but withdrew, as if ashamed and frightened. I rose to my feet, somewhat startled myself. When I took her into my arms, the candle fell from her hand. . .

I finally managed to open the padlock, and we took the potatoes upstairs. Wanda's mother was surprised that it had taken so long and apologized for causing me so much trouble. What had happened in the cellar became our secret, and I could regard Wanda as a child no longer.

One afternoon at the Sikorski dinner table Wanda spoke of how sad it was not to have a Christmas tree on which to hang the Star of Bethlehem. "They have such a nice foresty smell," she said with regret. The German authorities had forbidden Poles to cut down trees.

I decided she would have one. The day before Christmas Eve I told her that I would come by for a little while after curfew, so she should not be disturbed if she heard someone knocking at the door. She and her mother thought I was joking. It was no secret that the police patrols shot without warning.

Late that night I cut down a beautiful spruce and carried it to their house. The streets were deserted; I did not see a soul. A strict blackout was in force, and all the houses were dark.

I knocked at the Sikorskis' door. Wanda's father opened it in terror. My reward was in Wanda's eyes.

That night was a turning point for me. From then until the end of the war, I disregarded the curfew and visited that house every night I could, though not without at least one close call.

Toward the end of 1941 I constructed a small radio, one equipped to pick up shortwave. It was made in two parts, and thus was easier to hide. Our method for changing stations and bands was quite primitive—we used an alligator clip. We used a condenser with a tuning knob, and a short wire as an antenna.

In mid-December I listened to that radio for the first time. Those were the days when German propaganda crowed about Berlin's and Rome's declarations of war against the United States, and showered America with threats and insults. But older Poles rejoiced that the United States had entered the war. They remembered World War I and considered America's entry in 1917 to have been the decisive factor in the Allies' victory. "No one has yet defeated America in war," they said, recalling the tall doughboys in the wide-brimmed hats. I was glad to hear that the entry of that distant nation was a good thing.

Then, too, London was broadcasting reports that the Germans had been beaten back from Moscow and had suffered heavy losses. The Red Army had recaptured an important strategic point at Rostov-on-Don that led to the Caucasus and had retaken several other cities as well. Leningrad was putting up a desperate defense. Winter was raging along the entire Eastern Front.

In Africa, Tobruk, which had been under siege for nearly eight months, was relieved by troops composed partly of Poles from the Carpathian Brigade led by General Stanislaw Kopanski. The BBC said that the Polish soldiers had displayed great fortitude and valor. Our spirits were raised by that news. There was, however, bad news from the Far East. The Japanese had attacked Pearl Harbor. It was a world war now, and Japan's successes were dimming any Allied progress in Europe.

No end could be seen to the war. We did not see, either, much chance of surviving the coming year, which seemed an abyss into which we all would fall. Perhaps because there was just such an abyss before us, the older people decided to celebrate the New Year together—it might well be our last. It was a potluck affair, everyone bringing what they had on hand. There was the traditional red borscht, dumplings with crackling instead of mushrooms, and a piece of meat that Wanda's father had brought from Warsaw.

After dinner I placed three records on the hand-cranked phonograph: the Polish national anthem, Chopin's *Polonaise,* and "The American Patrol." Surprised to hear the national anthem, everyone rose, despite the fact that the record was old and the melody faint behind the scratches and static. My mother wiped a tear from her eye, probably having remembered something from her childhood, when Poland existed only in the hearts of Poles, as it did again now. Tadeusz wiped his nose, Sikorski made no attempt to hide his tears, Benedykt Bornstein's walrus mustache quivered.

"I want to say a few more words about the Soviets," piped up Zygmus. He paused, filled his lungs, and continued in his high-pitched voice. "The Bolsheviks have introduced their own system, one in which the very base of existence crumbles; all desire is lost, everyone is turned into a beggar. People are sent to labor camps for having possessions; others are removed from their jobs, not able to buy food, forced to become informers for the NKVD; neighbor is afraid of neighbor; children are persecuted at school and encouraged to denounce their parents.

"You go outside, patrols check your papers, you never know whether you will see your home again.

"It's not much better here on the German side. But here Poles know what's what. The Germans don't pretend to be our friends."

Zygmus's pronouncements grated on me. Of course there had been abuses—I had no doubt the Soviets had permitted crimes to occur. But how could people be so blind to the greater fact that it was that same Soviet Union that was bearing the brunt of the fight against fascism?

Sikorski spoke up. "We have our own share of trouble here in Warsaw. Yesterday, at the Lodzinski pharmacy, where I work, I was making up a compound when I heard shooting nearby. I looked out the window but didn't see anyone except a couple of German gendarmes by the ghetto wall. Zelazna Street, where the pharmacy is located, is the boundary of the ghetto, and they've built a high wall, with broken glass and barbed wire on top. When the Germans left, I saw the mutilated bodies of two teen-age Jewish boys slumped against the wall. They had attempted to escape. That's what we can *see*; what's going on *behind* the wall, I'm told, defies all description.

"A few days ago, an elderly man was climbing the steps to our store. The stairs were icy; he slipped, fell, and dislocated his knee. No sooner had we carried him into the store and bandaged his leg than the Polish police arrived, claiming we were hiding a Jew. Our explanations did no good, and they were about to call in the Germans. It was only after they pulled down his pants and saw that he wasn't circumcised that they left us in peace. . . . Ours are incredible times."

At midnight that New Year's Eve, Sikorski raised his glass and proposed a toast to the victory of our own soldiers as well as that of our allies. Only years later did I learn that he was a cousin of General Wladyslaw Sikorski, prime minister and commander in chief of the Polish armed forces in England.

And so 1942 began. The winter was exceptionally hard; there were long periods of bitter cold and much snow. The temperature fell almost to freezing inside Villa Rose at night, and the windowpanes were constantly covered with frost flowers.

Living so close to the railroad tracks, we were able to observe increasing numbers of trains marked with red crosses heading south and west. Those trains had the right of way, and there were days when they would come one after the other bearing wounded and frozen German soldiers back from the front, especially from Moscow, where, according to Wehrmacht communiqués, pitched battles were being fought in ice and snow. Sometimes when one of those trains halted briefly in Milanowek, waiting for a signal to change, I would throw on my coat and run down to the tracks. The steam rising around the train gave it a ghostly look. Icicles hung from the locomotive, and the cars were glazed with a silvery frost. Occasionally, through half-open windows, I caught glimpses of bandaged heads, arms, legs, soldiers piled on top of one another in layers. Polish onlookers would gaze at the trains silently, neither compassion nor satisfaction on their faces. They probably were thinking what I was: These are the same men who, two years ago, attacked us, killed our soldiers, murdered our civilians, bombed our cities.

For us those trains were the first real harbingers of German defeat, and for me they were bittersweet vindication of my father's and Antonina's insistence that the workers' and peasants' state was the only force capable of halting Hitler.

Just before daybreak, when the electricity came back on, Tadeusz and I would remove the radio from its hiding place and wait impatiently for the Polish broadcast from London. The news from the front confirmed our railside observations: the Germans had been stopped.

But the whole world was at war, and that war might go on for decades, while Poland confronted the specter of extermination. Tadeusz kept repeating that we had been condemned to death by two archcriminals—Hitler and Stalin. This caused us to quarrel constantly, which often turned into long, bitter arguments.

Everywhere, I heard open hostility about the Soviets. My views had worked to isolate me, and that isolation in turn congealed my opinions.

Uncle Zygmus and Tadeusz believed that the Soviet successes were only temporary. The winter had caught the Germans by surprise, they said, the way it had Napoleon in 1812. "We'll see what happens when the winter's over, whether or not the Nazis move farther east and start routing the Bolsheviks." They thought this time the Germans might direct their strike to the south and occupy the Ukraine, the land of milk and honey. They argued that Hitler would certainly want to control the Black Sea coast, and that his next goal would be the oil-rich Caucasus. I considered all that naive chatter, but subsequent events proved them right.

It was a cold and hungry time. We ate the same things, chiefly potatoes, day in and day out. I considered a piece of sallow ration-card bread spread with ration-card beet marmalade a great treat. I hung a little piece of pork fat from the lamp over the table so that we would not forget what it looked like. Tadeusz laughed at me, saying that I was even capable of eating a stick while gazing up at that little piece of pork fat.

I could never shake my anxiety that someone might report us to the Germans. We heard of Nazi brutalities nearly every day—roundups, searches, shootings of Poles who were hiding Jews. Nor could I imagine surviving my mother if anything happened to her.

I took comfort in knowing that if worst came to worst, there was always the phial. I kept it with me at all times. But I had resolved that we would survive, and I hit on the idea of constructing hiding places we could use in the event of a raid.

My plans met with full support. Between March and June 1942 three well-disguised hiding places were constructed. I built the largest one, with room for ten people, under the floor of the room where our workshop and steel lathe were located. We had to remove several tons of earth, carry it out through the window to the garden and dispose of it there without attracting attention. The garden was, however, under intensive cultivation, and the sight of us carrying buckets of earth did not seem unusual to people passing by on the street. That hiding place was supported by wooden beams, so that it could not be discovered by knocking on the floorboards. The entrance was impossible to see. When bolted shut from the inside, the hiding place could be found only by tearing up the floor. We laid in an electric line and concealed ventilation. To make the camouflage even better, we covered the trapdoor with a table constructed so that it had a shelf close to the floor, on which we kept various cans and bits of paper we used in the workshop. With the table in place, the trapdoor was invisible.

We organized drills at various times of day. The hiding place was only for certain ones of us. The number of people in the house had to correspond, after all, with the number of beds. The shelters had room for the young people and the older ones whose papers were not in order. As the owner, my mother would remain in the house in the event of a raid; Tadeusz would either stay with her or use the hiding place, depending on the situation. We sprinkled naphthalene all over the floor, and we had to train ourselves not to sneeze. This, to protect us from being sniffed out by dogs. It seemed to me that all precautions had been taken to prepare us for the worst.

I constructed two other hiding places, outside our living area. One was under the roof and exited on the second floor. The other, a small two-or-three-person hiding place, was in the garden, near the spruce trees not far from the house. It was to be used in the event we were caught by surprise in the garden.

Tadeusz went to work in Warsaw every day. One day in March, he arrived home accompanied by a junior colleague, an assistant professor at Warsaw University, Bernard Buras and his wife, Marysia. Those were false names, since they were Jews. The two of them did not look well at all. Bernard told us how they had managed to buy their way out of the ghetto.

"And how many Jews are there in that place?" someone asked.

"I don't know," he answered. "No one knows for sure, because no one's bothered to count. There are a lot of people there living 'wild,' as they say—young people in hiding who aren't registered anywhere. The Germans deport them as fast as they catch them. I've heard that there may be four hundred thousand or even more. Who knows? People are dying all the time."

He told us that he had worked as an assistant and lathe operator at a watchmaker's, fitting the watches into cases. But even that did not ensure him subsistence. Food was prohibitively expensive in the ghetto, and he and Marysia had grown weaker and weaker. They were, in fact, dying.

I glanced over at Marysia. Before the war she had graduated from the university with a degree in chemistry. She was perhaps twenty-five years old, small, thin, haggard, with huge dark eyes. She had obviously been a good-looking girl, but now she was emaciated, and fear haunted her eyes.

My mother emptied out the servant's room off the kitchen for them. Bernard and I quickly became friends, and he at once joined us in the building of hiding places.

The Bornsteins decided that it was time to leave us. Villa Rose was crowded now, and they had found another place to stay. I was very fond of both Bornsteins and was sorry to see them go. I thought of my father every time I looked at Benedykt.

I was at the lathe one day in April when I heard strange voices in the kitchen. Poking my head in the door, I saw Ludwik Bryskier speaking to my mother. Beside him was a small woman, a kerchief around her head. I had not seen Ludwik since the day the Gestapo had been in our apartment and I had slammed the door in his face.

He cried out my name, but was unable to utter another word before my arms were around him. He drew back and looked me in the eyes.

"Ludwik," I said, trying to dispel his fears immediately, "I'll do everything I can to help you and your mother."

"You're a good person," he whispered. "I knew you wouldn't leave us to die. We are at our rope's end—I came here feeling you wouldn't fail me."

He and his mother sat down on the couch and drank tea, and we all pulled up chairs around them. They seemed to relax, although, a few minutes before, they had not known whether they would find me or any of my family here, whether someone would slam the door again and sentence them to death.

I explained what had happened two years before.

Ludwik embraced me. "You couldn't have done anything else," he said. "I can only be grateful to you. We felt crushed as we walked away from your door, but I felt that there had to be more to it than that; it had been too—" he hesitated for a second—"too brutal, not like you at all. My father had seen you only a couple of times before the war; he kept saying that he couldn't understand it. He, unfortunately, didn't live long enough to find out the truth.

"When things became unbearable in the ghetto, I would sit down and look through my old notebooks from school. I would forget the present for a little while thinking about the good old days. Anyway, once, when looking through old notebooks, I came across a slip of paper on which you had written your address in Milanowek. From that moment on that address became our only hope, our anchor. We decided to try; we had nothing to lose.

"You have no idea what's happening in Warsaw. People are dying by the thousands. They cover the bodies with newspaper, put them on wagons, and toss them in heaps. The rations are always being reduced. Recently they were giving out two kilograms of gummy bread, which was supposed to last a month. People would stagger and fall—just fall in their tracks—from starvation. And hunger brings out the worst in us. It's a struggle for existence, every day, every hour.

"How did you get out of the ghetto?" someone asked Ludwik.

"I paid off the Jewish police. They got everything they asked for, almost all of my father's life savings. They promised us that when we left the ghetto there would not be any German police around, only Polish police, who would let us pass because they in turn would be paid off. But there was no guarantee that they wouldn't just take our money and then let us be killed. This morning the Jewish police let us out. We went through a gateway and were on the other side when a Polish policeman caught sight of us, but he turned the other way. We crossed the street in a hurry, our knees trembling. I ripped off our Star of David arm bands and threw them away, and we tore into the unknown, with only an address as a destination. All the way here people seemed to be looking at us, recognizing us for what we were—Jews on the run. . . ."

Ludwik and his mother lived with us for several months before settling elsewhere under false names. We often saw each other.

My mother was glad to lend a hand to my schoolmate and his mother. Neither she nor Tadeusz ever complained that we had been exposed to greater danger by them, although we constantly heard of tragedies that had befallen entire families for hiding Jews. My mother thought our actions entirely natural, simply what decent people did.

She rarely went to church, and I don't recall ever seeing her pray. When asked if she was religious, she would reply that she prayed in her own way. She was entirely unbiased and treated all people the same, whether they were deeply religious or not. But she could not bear to hear faith or religion mocked or joked about. Two things were sacred to her—Christ and the cross—that was never to change.

Tadeusz, on the other hand, went to church often and spoke out against atheism. He considered me a soulless communist who would only learn how much he had sinned and how far he had strayed when it was too late. I heard him reproach my mother for having a son who had grown up without any religion, telling her that "there's a devil somewhere in Romek."

For my mother's sake and for the sake of peace in the house, I avoided conversations about religion with Tadeusz. I considered him a decent man but a narrow-minded one.

At the end of April, I met a young man who worked as a "fish farmer." I was intrigued by him. He was probably a bit older than I, but had had little education. His family owned several ponds, and, he reported, they lived well off the fish they bred.

"It's a very interesting line of work. Not much is known about it here," he said, "but it has a great future. . . . You know," he added, lowering his voice, "as a fisherman, it's easier to escape from Hitler. All you have to do is make your way to the Baltic, then to Sweden. You can cross over in your boat. That's why I signed up for this really good school. They give you an ID with a German 'crow' on it. During roundups, they don't touch people with 'crows' on their IDs."

He withdrew his wallet and showed me his ID, which read: "Fishery School, Fischereifachschule." There was a German eagle at the bottom, beneath his photo and the signatures.

"Where is this place?" I asked.

"On Pankiewicza Street, right across from Central Station. Don't even think about it; hurry right over. They reject most everybody, but they're taking in a new class right now."

That conversation stuck in my mind after the young man had left. What nonsense, I thought; me, a future physicist, a person with plans and goals . . . On the other hand, it might be a good idea, might help me survive, and could even come in handy later on. It couldn't hurt to learn the fisherman's trade. I decided to pursue the matter.

The school was located on the upper floors of an ordinary apartment building. At the office I was informed that registration had just ended for the coming year and there was no chance of admission now. The secretary let me know that they did not take people off the street; there were few places, so references were needed, good references. I asked her who the director was.

"You don't know?" She sniffed. "Professor Franciszek Staff, the world-famous ichthyologist."

"Is he related to the poet Leopold Staff?" I asked.

Flabbergasted by my ignorance, she trumpeted, "His brother!"

Just then a door opened and revealed an old man with bushy gray hair. "Is this everything?" he asked the secretary.

"May I speak with you briefly, Professor?" I suddenly found myself saying, not the least convinced that I was behaving properly.

To the secretary's chagrin, he agreed.

I knew the poetry of Leopold Staff and was quite fond of it. Even today I know a few of his poems by heart. Leopold was religious and patriotic, and I assumed his brother would be as upstanding, so I did not hesitate to tell him the truth. I spoke of my father. Staff knew of his death. He took a livelier interest in me upon learning that I had graduated from the Merchants' Council School in 1939 and had studied with Pawel Ordynski.

"What mark did you receive in biology?"

"An A for the year and on the final exam."

"You're accepted then," he said. "Give your name to the secretary. I wish you luck."

In the summer of 1942 we listened to the radio broadcasts from London with trepidation in our hearts. The Germans were advancing and seemed to have seized the initiative everywhere. In Libya, at the beginning of June, Rommel had effected a sudden turnabout, inflicting heavy losses on the British forces. The Germans took Tobruk, which was not defended by Poles this time.

Rommel was made a field marshal; his Afrika Korps was moving swiftly toward Egypt. It seemed only a matter of time before they would take that country and move to conquer the Near East from the Nile. Axis planes were already bombing Alexandria and even Haifa.

Tadeusz and I pored over the map, following the German panzer columns as they took hundreds of thousands of prisoners in their drive eastward along the Black Sea coast. The Germans again conquered Rostov-on-Don and began their march to the Caucasus, the oil fields, and even Astrakhan, on the Caspian Sea. Was it Hitler's plan to connect the armies fighting on the Eastern Front with Rommel's troops in the Near East? As it happened, Rommel's offensive forces were foiled in Egypt, but we took no comfort in this.

In August planes were again seen over Warsaw. People insisted that these were Allied planes. At the beginning of September the Soviet air force bombarded the city in a night raid. Wanda was sick at the Red Cross hospital in Warsaw, and as soon as I learned of the bombing, I left for the city in a state of anxiety.

Warsaw looked grim. To the ruins of 1939 and to the ghetto walls was added new destruction. The smell of burning was in the air.

I approached the hospital with apprehension, but it had been spared. Wanda was up and about, and glad to see me. She told me that it had been a trying night for the patients, bombs fell close by, and anyone able to move hid with the hospital staff in the cellars.

We crossed the hospital lawn and went out through the gate to a little side street, looking for a quiet place to talk. Spotting a narrow glass door with a sign that read, "Café-Restaurant," we went inside.

"We don't have anything today," a waitress said. "Terrible times. We don't even have bread. Tea is all we have, without sugar."

"Then we'd like two teas," I said. "We just want a quiet talk."

Wanda described the night of the raid. "I didn't go down to the shelter because there were patients in my ward who couldn't walk. It all happened so fast, the explosions. . . . There was no time to get those patients down to the cellars. So I stayed with them; someone had to. We prayed together. I recited a prayer aloud, and they repeated it after me. . . . Maybe that's what saved us. . . ."

Prayer as a defense against bombs! She actually seemed to believe it. I took her hand. "That was a fine thing you did," I said.

She looked up at me as if surprised, and her little fingers squeezed my large, rough paw.

The fishery school had surpassed my expectations. It was a creation that could have been spawned only in those tragic times amid the rubble of independent Poland, where Poles were now forbidden nearly everything, and higher and middle schools were nonexistent. In that milieu Professor Staff had come up with a vocational school, whose pretext it was to prepare fishermen so that the economy of the General Gouvernement could put the ponds to use and produce fish for the Germans to sell in the stores designated "For Germans only."

Staff had employed professors who two years before had been the heads of departments at universities. These men knew how to divert us, if only momentarily, from the barbarity we witnessed each day. They transported us to a world of benevolent creatures, a world that lived by the laws of nature, free of all evils.

I was fascinated by both the lecturers and the students. Some subjects, land surveying and triangulation, for instance, in my opinion were taught in too much detail. It was said that knowledge of these was necessary for planning fish ponds. Only later did I discover the real reason they were taught with such special attention. They were subjects indispensable to military training. The whole school was a cover for the Home Army (AK), the patriotic underground organization whose commanders reported to General Sikorski in London.

By fall of 1942 the Germans were constantly staging roundups on the streets. Every trip to school became a gamble. I learned to keep my eyes and ears open for the warnings Poles exchanged. Trains would signal German roundups with their lights or whistles as they passed one another. After such a signal, the engineer being warned would slow down, so that all the young men could jump off into a field before the next station. But it was not possible to slow down if German soldiers were on the train. Those who knew how would jump off a train going nearly full speed. A few times I fell and was badly bruised. Once, I calculated poorly and almost went slamming into a post. This was not the typical schoolboy's route to school; it was more like running the gauntlet.

A couple of months later the Germans evicted the school, and the building was taken over for offices. The school was facing total liquidation, but the indefatigable Staff unearthed a new home for it in an apartment building that had until recently been part of the ghetto—a sweatshop where Jews had labored for the Germans. I was only there a few times, helping to clean out the building, but the experience left an impression on me. Jewish holy books were strewn all over the floor, as were a great many little books printed in minute Hebrew letters and attached to black ribbons like those the rabbi with whom I shared a bed in Lutsk, had wound around his arm. The building was a place from which everything living had fled. From the windows on the fourth and fifth floors the ghetto was visible—streets, encircled by walls, where the sun gleamed off broken glass and barbed wire.

Did the world, the world beyond the reach of Hitler and the Gestapo, know what was going on here in Poland? In Warsaw? It seemed impossible that it could be unaware that so many were dying here. Yet there was no indication that it did know or care. That realization was dispiriting. At Villa Rose, in our little "community of the persecuted," we felt abandoned. It was no easy task to carry on, amid anxiety and uncertainty, in the face of the human tragedies to which we were witness. The Polish motto, "For your freedom and ours," seemed suspended in a void.

Tadeusz had been insisting since the summer that I dedicate more time to gathering firewood for winter and to working in the garden while the ground could still be turned for next year's crop. He also needed my help at the lathe.

"You spent a lot of time constructing those hiding places," he said, "which haven't proved to be necessary. It's time you did the work that keeps us alive. You know how many people our garden is feeding."

He himself was working very hard. He spent every free moment he had at home working in the garden or at his lathe. His hands were worn, and I noticed that he was going gray at the temples. The constant tension and uncertainty were taking their toll; an alien look had invaded his eyes. My mother, ever thinner, her features sharper, was often upset and said that she had no strength to go on. Coming across a picture of her as a young woman once, I could not believe it was the same person. She had been truly beautiful, this lovely girl, with enormous eyes, in an old-fashioned dress and hat.

Bernard Buras confided in us that he was afraid for his wife, who was in a constant state of anxiety about her mother in Wolomin. Each time they received news, Marysia would be reborn; she would grow talkative, even merry. When she was in good spirits, she would dye her hair a striking red. But then a lack of further news of her mother would sadden her again and she would not leave her room.

One snowy winter day, a letter arrived for Marysia. Bernard was down in the workshop with Tadeusz and me. When he returned to their room, he found Marysia unconscious on the floor. The letter, written anonymously, described how, a week before, German military police had broken into the building where her mother was hiding. They had known Jews were there; they had not even needed to conduct a search. They led everyone from the building and shot them. The building was then doused with gasoline and burned to the ground as a lesson to others who were hiding Jews.

Marysia was never herself again. We were unable to bring her out of her apathy; she would sit and stare for hours on end, oblivious. One day she disappeared. Tadeusz, Bernard, and I ran outside. She was there by the gate, staring silently at the railroad tracks to Warsaw, where her mother had perished. She offered no resistance as we led her back to the house.

Late one evening, sometime after that, we sat around the table after curfew waiting for the electricity to be turned back on so that we could listen to the radio. Bernard did not feel like waiting, said good night, and went off to his room. Seconds later his door slammed against the wall, and he returned, his face white as a sheet. "Marysia's gone."

We ran out. It was a dark, icy night. Marysia was nowhere to be found. Where could she have gone? What was happening to her?

She might be dying at the hands of the military police, or being interrogated and beaten, and forced to reveal the address of her hiding place. She's sick, she doesn't know what she's doing, I thought, and it's not just she but all of us.

"Bernard," I nearly shouted, "we must go look for her."

He was surprised. "How? Where?"

"Get dressed," I said, issuing an order. "Put on your warmest clothing, immediately."

I threw on my leather coat and slipped a pair of wire clippers into my pocket, as I always did when going out at night.

"Be careful," my mother implored. "Remember, at night they just shoot."

A fine snow was falling. The night was so dark that it was a long while before we could make out the railroad tracks. I stared at those tracks and listened intently. There was only blackness and silence.

"Let's walk along the track toward Warsaw," I whispered, feeling instinctively that she had set off in that direction . . . to her mother, and to certain death.

We walked for a long time through the snow, Bernard holding on to my belt. How far could she have gone? Perhaps she had fallen into a ditch by the tracks, and we had walked past her. Maybe we should call her. No, we couldn't risk that. I quickened my pace. The snow was thicker now, and we stumbled on the snowy ties. Perhaps I was wrong, I thought; she might have run straight ahead from the house. We could be losing time. I caught a glimpse of something. We stopped and strained our ears, but the night was profoundly still. A light glimmered up ahead, and I was certain now that it was no illusion.

"Let's go," I whispered, "but be quiet."

We moved slowly, stopping every so often. The glimmer appeared and disappeared through the snow. Finally, I could see the orange glow of a lighted window. It was the trackman's hut. I stole up to the window quiet as a cat and peered in. The glass was frosted over and dirty. A railroad lantern hung from the wall, and a potbellied stove glowed in the corner. I could see two dark-uniformed figures—Bahnschutz, railroad police—one by a table, rummaging through something, the other on a bench. Then I recognized the small hunched figure on the opposite bench—it was Marysia. The Germans were discussing something. Rifles leaned against the wall.

The man sitting opposite Marysia began to shout and wave his hand as if threatening her.

It would be quite straightforward, I reflected, if we had some sort of weapons, but with our bare hands . . . ?

"Marysia's in there," I whispered to Bernard. "There are also two Bahnschutz with rifles. Listen carefully. We must take them by surprise. We'll pretend to be Germans. I'll burst in shouting 'Heil Hitler' and grab Marysia. You come in right behind me and shout in German at the top of your lungs like they do—'Verflucht,' 'Schweine.' Just use your best German accent and make it loud, so they'll think there are lots of us, understand? As soon as we've got her, we run. If they begin to suspect us, grab their rifles and let them have it with the butts. But that's a last resort, remember."

We stole up to the door. "Now!" I hissed. I pressed down the latch, kicked open the door, and burst into the room, saluting vigorously and shouting loud, "Heil Hitler! Wo ist diese Judin?"

I bounded toward Marysia, grabbed her by the arm, and dragged her, staggering, toward the door. The two men were flabbergasted. Meanwhile, Bernard was outside shouting in German at the top of his lungs: "Verflucht! Schweinerei! Raus!"

Marysia was light and slender, and a strong shove had her out the door and into Bernard's arms. The whole thing had taken seconds.

When I slammed the door shut behind me, the faces of the two men were dumbfounded, even full of apology.

We quickly put distance between ourselves and the Germans, practically carrying Marysia. We were able to see even less than before as we slipped over the icy ties. Moments later voices rang out behind us, real German curses. The men must have come to their senses and run out of the hut, but they were bewildered and unable to find our tracks. The danger was past. No German was going to stick his nose outside for long on a night like this.

I was absolutely exhausted when we reached Villa Rose, but only then did I surrender myself to the fatigue and the tension.

Marysia made no more attempts to run away, but she remained apathetic. She took poison twice, unsuccessfully, during the next year.

I began to suffer from poor health for the first time in mid-December. Abscesses appeared on my body; I ran a temperature and felt very weak. I thought I was nearing my end, especially since I did not have the strength to get into the hiding place quickly. My mother and Tadeusz did what they could to provide me with nourishing food, for they were all agreed that my sickness was the result of malnutrition.

Wanda visited me often. I was ashamed of the ugly running abscesses on my body and tried to hide them from her. My mother had, however, described my condition to her in detail, and she was genuinely concerned. Wanda always wore a muffler she had been given by her old grandmother. Each time she visited she would bring me something hidden in that muffler, usually a little cup containing whipped egg yolks and sugar, *gogiel-mogiel*, we called it. She insisted that I eat whatever she brought while she watched. Then she would wrap the cup up in a napkin and hide it in her muffler again. Her visits were my only bright moments.

We did not celebrate New Year's Eve in 1942–43; the night passed like any other. Early that January we were paid a visit by the cousin of my father's colleague Antonina Sokolicz. Antonina had been arrested by the Gestapo, brutally beaten and sent to Auschwitz.

Antonina's premonitions had been right. At the time, I had thought her overly dramatic. But of the four people who had engaged in those passionate discussions before the war, only I remained: weak, sick, covered with running sores. What would happen next? I was losing hope, and our small community of survivors in Villa Rose was becoming desperate. Every day seemed poised on the brink of death and oblivion.

CHAPTER VIII

By early 1943, the Russians had seized the initiative on the Eastern Front. Surrounded at Stalingrad, the German army was being driven into an ever diminishing area. The Red Army was making progress on the front near Moscow, and, fearing encirclement, German troops were withdrawing from the Caucasus and retreating toward Rostov-on-Don. In the north, the siege of Leningrad had been breached. At the end of January, Hitler conferred the title of field marshal on Friedrich Paulus, but two days later the new field marshal's 6th Army surrendered, and in Stalingrad the Soviets took ninety-two thousand Germans prisoner. This news came as an enormous relief to us all.

My strength returned with the coming of spring. The abscesses healed slowly. I started going outside into the warm sun in March; soon I was doing a full day's work in the garden.

In mid-April Tadeusz brought home a copy of the *Warschauer Zeitung*. The headline story trumpeted the discovery of an atrocity committed by the Soviets against Polish officers taken prisoner in 1939. According to the paper, ten thousand Polish officers had been shot, each with a bullet behind the ear, and thrown into mass graves in the Katyn forest, near Smolensk.

Tadeusz was enraged. "Romek, I don't want to hear one more word about the Soviets being any allies of ours. I've had enough."

I felt an unbridgeable abyss open between us. To me this was only German propaganda. The Germans obviously were accusing the Soviet Union knowing full well that the Poles hated the Soviets.

Tadeusz was simply blind, easy prey for Joseph Goebbels's cunning propaganda.

That day Wanda's brother, Czeslaw, came to see me. He told me that Wanda would not be coming by that day, that she had been crying a great deal and did not want to leave the house. Besides, she had lessons to do. I recognized the logic that excuse indicated: Katyn, Soviets, Communists, me.

The argument with Tadeusz flared up again, and Uncle Zygmus joined in. He and my aunt were to leave within a few days, and perhaps that had made him especially volatile.

"Those murders were committed by the NKVD. It's their style," Zygmus proclaimed. "Here, the Germans kill in an organized fashion, German style. But over there the terror is more insidious. Not only does it destroy the body, but it poisons the soul. The Germans may be murdering Poles, but if the Soviets come, Poles will begin to destroy one another."

"How?" asked Tadeusz.

"Slavery, endless slavery, that's how. We'll all curse the day we were born," said Zygmus with a sneer. "I would rather die than see that day, but Stalin is the essence of cunning. If he manages to deceive Britain and America . . ."

"He won't succeed in that!" interrupted Tadeusz with conviction. "London and Washington know full well what the Kremlin is all about!"

"I tell you they don't," countered Zygmus. "No one really knows. To know, you have to be there, be on the inside. The world has never known lies such as these—people simply can't imagine. The Russians are schooled in deception. Don't forget the Potemkin villages. The West doesn't understand that kind of behavior. For them it's only theater." He was referring to the story that Potemkin had had sham villages built to impress the empress Catherine.

Zygmus's face was flushed; veins stood out on his temples. He rose to his feet and paced the room, back and forth, back and forth.

Then Tadeusz turned to me and said, "You are young, and so you trusted your father, you believed that he knew everything, understood everything. But the truly sad thing is that you still have no God in your heart. You're happy that the Soviets defeated the Germans at Stalingrad, you're glad that the Communists are winning, that Bolshevism is strong. But do you think about Poland, about the Polish people? What will happen to us, to the Poles, to Poland, when the people who murdered our officers arrive? Sometimes I get the impression that you're not really a Pole, that we have some foreigner living among us here."

My mother stopped her husband, upset. "I must ask you not to speak that way to my son. I forbid it in my house."

I felt sorry for her. This tension only added to the daily deprivations, worries, and danger she was forced to endure. Tadeusz was aware of this, of course, but he had been unable to restrain himself, especially with Uncle Zygmus at his side. Since I had made no attempt to answer him, and only regarded his anger with irony, he was more incensed than ever.

Finally, everyone left. Mother stayed with me and stroked my head.

"I understand you," she said. "You're the image of your father. Always a man of principle, never yielding. But you should realize that these people are Poles, not cosmopolitans. Tadeusz's parents were simple people who taught him to believe in God and to love Poland. Please don't goad him. He'll always be what he is. You have much to learn and understand." Her distress was evident. She was caught in the middle and suffering.

When alone, I realized that there was no reason for me to stay in Milanowek. As soon as I was fully recovered, I thought, I would take to the woods and fight the Germans. Let these people be whatever they like; I'll be who I am—a revolutionary, an atheist, and a friend of the Soviet Union. The score I had to settle with the Soviets on my father's account was my business, and if I survived the war, I would surely even that score. But that was on a secondary, lesser, agenda. For now, I would take to the woods.

On a sunny April day Wanda's father returned from Warsaw and announced: "It's started. . . . The Jews in the ghetto are fighting. . . . There's shooting, bombing, burning, smoke. . . ."

I went into Warsaw for the next few days. I could smell the smoke as the train approached the city. From the streets along the walls of the ghetto I heard the chatter of machine-gun fire and the odd, isolated shot. The hell that had devoured thousands was now in flames. I dropped by the fishery school. Classes were still being held, but only as a matter of form; everyone either ran around in a state of confusion or watched from the windows. Conversations were animated.

During the course of one lecture, Professor Waclaw Roszkowski walked over to a window, stopped speaking, and gazed in silence at the ghetto. He stood there for a long time until the end of the class. We could hear flies buzzing. When the bell rang, Roszkowski left the room swiftly, silently, his head hanging. He would meet his death within a year—murdered in his own bed during the Warsaw uprising.

One day I walked toward the sound of fighting. Black smoke hung over the ghetto, and the smell of burning made me cough. I found myself near Nalewki Street, wondering why I had chosen that route. I continued walking straight ahead toward the heart of the raging battle, and it was only then that I realized I was only yards from Gesia Street, where Judyta had lived. It was now behind the walls. I stopped. That had been a lifetime ago—four years, to be exact, four years during which the world had turned upside down.

Few people walked the streets; every once in a long while a figure would hurry past. The acrid smoke tore at my throat, and the closer I got the more my eyes smarted and teared. I walked to the gate of the ghetto. I leaned against a building and peered in at the smoking houses, at the Germans standing guard, and at others, probably Ukrainians, in gray green uniforms, and Polish police in dark blue.

The apartment buildings on the other side of the wall were scorched, the windows black. Past them, other houses were consumed by smoke and fire. Every so often I would hear a grenade, followed by a burst of machine-gun fire. Hollow explosions shook the ground under me; they were dynamiting the houses.

Engines roared behind me, and I looked around to see a column of soldiers riding down Nalewki Street. I ducked into a gateway and watched them drive past—two armored cars followed by an SS detachment on motorcycles with sidecars, and finally a few truckloads of SS regulars. The armored cars and motorcycles passed through the ghetto gates, came to a stop, and the men jumped from the trucks prepared to attack, as if they were at the front. They wore steel helmets and goggles, and carried long submachine guns. Cartridge belts were slung over their shoulders. A few had flamethrowers. Their faces were ruddy from drink, their voices hoarse; their commands sounded like the barking of dogs. More trucks pulled up, with another unit. The uniforms of this group were a dull ocher, the color of rotting leaves and, instead of high SS boots, they wore black puttees.

"Who are these people?" I asked the man who watched beside me, obviously a tenant of the building in whose entranceway I stood.

"Red Army turncoats, probably Ukrainians," he muttered. "Always going in there with the Krauts to kill Jews. They're the same as the SS, no better; people say they're even worse, crueler."

The men in the black puttees were not armed like the Germans. They carried rifles, large leather ammunition pouches, and long bayonets attached to their belts. They wore field caps, not helmets. Next to the Germans, they looked like marauders, their faces hard.

They walked into the ghetto, toward Gesia Street. I moved closer and peered in. The SS men and the other troops had disappeared from sight, but the sound of gunfire had grown louder. I found myself morbidly fascinated. Suddenly, I saw four diminutive human figures leap from the balcony of a building and fall to the ground. The balcony was distant and the fall noiseless amid the gunfire. Had they jumped to their deaths rather than fall into the hands of the troops who had just entered? They had fallen close to each other; perhaps they had even held hands.

I closed my eyes and pulled myself away, took a few steps, and stopped. Before me were small tables under a canvas awning, a café. Two civilians sat at one table, slurping drinks and staring vapidly at the fighting within the ghetto walls. I whirled and marched off in the opposite direction.

Back at Villa Rose at night, I recounted what I had seen. In the faces around me I thought I could see fear, surprise, and admiration all at once that their fellow Jews were fighting back against such overwhelming odds.

A few days later I set off on foot into the country, toward Brwinow, which lay in the same direction as Warsaw, to buy a sack of rye. I ground rye at home in a hand mill, and we made flat cakes from the flour. The sky was clear, transparent, as I emerged from my transaction, but looking up at it I came to a halt. Fifteen miles away, Warsaw was not visible, but I saw a steady column of smoke rising vertically against the horizon—a narrow, sharply etched column that looked as if it had been pasted to the sky. That dark specter thrust itself up at the clouds above, producing a mushroom shape. The air was still. I recalled the sight of Nalewki Street, Gesia. That apocalyptic form was probably rising from that very place. In the light of the setting sun the form turned a muddy red, rendering it all the more sinister.

The sight haunted me. What had we come to? It was clear to me that the whole world system needed changing; humanity itself needed to change. For me, the only answer was communism. Despite their good intentions, Uncle Zygmus and Tadeusz were, in all their naiveté, obstacles to human progress.

By the end of April, Poland's future seemed more complicated than ever. Radio London reported that Moscow had broken off relations with the Polish government-in-exile, apparently over the accusations of Soviet culpability in the massacre of Polish officers at Katyn. The Soviets considered the Polish government's appeal to the International Red Cross to investigate the murders a provocation.

Tadeusz was quick to comment, "Now they hate us just for being Poles. We can't even investigate the murder of our own people."

Wanda's mother was in the Red Cross hospital in Warsaw at the end of May. She had undergone two serious operations and now needed to recover her strength. Every week we brought her food, usually chicken broth. That was no simple matter. The Germans were grabbing people off the streets; one had to be watchful and one had to be lucky. Wanda and I took the food together one day. As we walked from the hospital after the visit, I suggested that we drop by the little café we had stopped at last year and sit for a while at the same table. This time they served a thick soup with home-baked bread, quite a luxurious meal.

I saw Wanda anew as I looked at her over the table, a lovely young woman—barely sixteen now—with those slanted, greenish eyes. We sat silently; only our eyes were eloquent.

"I want to tell you that I love you," I said finally. "I want to be with you always; I want to take care of you." I took her small hand in mine. "I know that you're still young, that it's too early to talk about the future . . ." I broke off. Wanda had begun shaking her head until her curly hair covered her face.

"Do you want me to be your wife?" she asked guilelessly.

"I do, of course I do," I said, surprising myself.

"I want you to be my husband," she said emphatically, "and I want to be married in church."

"Yes, but what will your parents say?"

"Leave that to me," she said. "First I'll have a talk with my father. You know how much he loves me. . . . What about your mother?"

"I'll have a talk with her," I said decisively.

I took Wanda's arm as we left the café and could feel that this brought her pleasure.

When, after so many years, I recall us sitting in that shabby little café, I cannot resist thinking how strong is love and the instinct for life—spreading roots even into the volcanoes on which we then lived.

During the summer I worked in the garden from early morning. I mounded potatoes, weeded, and gathered wood to burn in the winter. My strength had come back; my hands were like a lumberer's.

At the beginning of July, Radio London broadcast the news of the tragic death of General Wladyslaw Sikorski. Returning from the Middle East, his plane had crashed into the sea immediately after takeoff from Gibraltar. The general's death grieved us all deeply.

"The worst calamities always befall Poland," moaned Tadeusz. "No other country has lost its leader. No other capital has suffered as Warsaw has. In no other place have the Nazis slaughtered the way they have here. It's been almost four years now. And no other country has a future as uncertain as ours. A person could really lose faith, even in God." He ran off to confession that same day.

How convenient, I thought. He confesses, his spirits are renewed, and he feels a changed person. Whereas I have only myself; but I would never want it otherwise.

It was at that time that I decided to do what I had thought to earlier—join the fighting. It would be hard to part from my mother and Wanda, wrong, maybe, to leave them in such great danger. Yet the memory of the flaming ghetto convinced me that what really counted was bullets and bayonets. I felt a certain blood lust and did not care if I died as long as my life cost them dear. I was envious of the younger boys at the fishery school, who belonged to a military organization that prepared them to take up arms.

Fate seemed to lend me a hand. My great-aunt Emilia Langiert and her daughter came to Villa Rose for a summer's respite from the ordeals and emotions of life in Warsaw. Aunt Emilia was over seventy and was having trouble breathing. She spent a great deal of time in our garden, surrounded by flowers, delighting in the pure, fragrant air. From time to time I would take a break from work to sit with her and hear stories of the Borderlands. My rapt attention gave her pleasure. During one such talk, just before she was to return home, I confided that I intended to join the Home Army's partisans. I asked her if she could help me arrange this through her contacts in Warsaw, since I was certain that either she or her daughter was in touch with the Home Army, their entire family having always been bound up with the cause of Poland's independence.

"Is that what you really want?" she asked intently.

"Yes," I said. "I am even prepared to die."

"To the best of my knowledge," she said, "you grew up under your father's influence. He was a communist and therefore somewhat of a foreigner in his thinking. The Polish underground army is a patriotic organization. Won't that be an obstacle for you?"

"No, it won't. I want to fight the Nazis, and the Home Army is doing just that." She asked me no more questions and promised to bring it up "if she happened to meet the right person."

Two weeks later she returned to Milanowek and immediately invited me into her room for a talk. "Romek dear, I spoke to someone and I have an answer for you. The Home Army will accept you if, in addition to the oath that everyone must swear, you provide an additional declaration that you will never have anything to do with the Soviets. The decision is yours. Think it over. It's important."

I went out into the garden. Even in the name of fighting the Germans I could not in one stroke cancel my beliefs, my goals. I was and I remained a communist. I did not require long for reflection.

"I've thought it through," I told my aunt. "I want to fight the fascists, but I cannot declare that I will never deal with the Soviets. I am a communist, after all."

In her large, kindly eyes, I could detect a glimmer of disappointment and, perhaps, even anger. "Don't tell me who and what you are. I know you and love you like a grandson." She looked at me, but her voice seemed to address someone else. "My son, Stas, died a hero's death fighting Bolsheviks for control of the Borderlands. I have the Order of Virtuti Militari he was awarded posthumously."

She paused, then continued in that reportorial voice. "My daughter, Wanda, too, belonged to the Polish Military Organization in the Borderlands; her code name was Flycatcher. She was caught by the Bolsheviks, tortured, and shot in Vinnitsa in 1919. I have the Cross of Valor she was awarded." She turned her face away. I left the room. The matter was settled for all time.

That same day something occurred that temporarily obscured all else. Wanda came running to our house to say, between gasps, that her father had barely escaped the Germans, who had come to the pharmacy to arrest its owner. I accompanied her home, and her father told me the rest of the story.

"The Germans must have realized what we were up to," he said. "The owner, Antoni Lodzinski, works for the underground and was supplying Jews in the ghetto with medicine. After the ghetto was destroyed, he moved his store of supplies to another part of town. That must have caught their eye; they must have gotten a whiff of something. They arrested him while I was out today. As I was returning to the pharmacy, people on the street warned me. I came right home. What should I do? Go to work tomorrow as usual or go into hiding?" I suggested that he and his family come to Villa Rose. The house was full, but we would make room.

Lodzinski was sent to Auschwitz. Several months later his wife learned that he had died there. Wanda's father was interrogated, but miraculously escaped Lodzinski's fate.

Toward the end of summer the Germans began prowling more often in Milanowek. Military police, frequently accompanied by Gestapo men, came daily to search house after house for people working for the underground and for Jews in hiding. Young men in particular were being arrested. We were in a constant state of alert, but life had to go on, and it was impossible to foresee every eventuality and to avoid being caught by surprise.

It was a surprise indeed when my mother's voice called out one day, quite suddenly, "The Germans are coming into the garden! Hide!"

She had been ironing clothes by the window and had seen the Germans as they passed through the gate. I opened the trapdoor hurriedly, and the others came running.

"Quick!" I shouted. "All the way to the back. Faster!"

Marysia was the first one in, followed by Bernard, Tadeusz, and those who happened to be at our house that day: Mrs. Szirmer and Wanda.

My mother stood ready to slide the table back over the trapdoor. "Hurry!" she cried fearfully. "They're at the house."

I heard their boots on the front steps, their fists on the door. I jumped in and quickly pulled the trapdoor down over me. My mother had already begun dragging the table, scraping its legs across the floor. Then her footsteps grew fainter as she went to the door, on which the Germans were now pounding violently. The trapdoor had not been evenly closed. So I raised it slightly to straighten it out. Tilting my head back, I looked through the narrow gap between the floor and the bottom shelf of the table. I had just begun to lower the trap door into place when the door to the workroom burst open and black high-topped boots marched toward me. They seemed immense. I gently lowered the trapdoor and slowly screwed in the well-oiled screws. I had not made a sound. The stomping of boots and German shouts were directly overhead. I trembled for my mother.

Tadeusz lit a lamp and made a sign that no one talk or sneeze and that everyone have a handkerchief ready just in case. In the dim light the faces were pale, tense, expectant, the eyes fearful.

Time seemed to have stopped. What was going on up there? What were they doing to my mother? And what would happen to old Szirmer, left above in the gatehouse? Had they started to interrogate him? Had they learned he was a Jew? Would they wait for the "other members of the household" to return?

About an hour passed before I heard our signal. The three knocks were followed by three scratches and three more knocks. The table was being slid to the side.

"We're safe!" I shouted.

I unscrewed the trapdoor and raised it. My mother loomed above, pale and calm, though her hands were trembling.

"They're gone. I made sure," she said. "We were saved by the iron."

Indeed, we could smell something burning as we climbed out. We hovered around my tiny mother and thanked her, some with tears in their eyes.

"The Germans searched the whole house from top to bottom," she told us. "They ransacked everything. The wardrobes are still open and the suitcases still out from under the beds. But they didn't find a thing. They started questioning me, asking who lived here and where my husband was. I told them he was at work, in Warsaw. They asked if I had children. I said I had a son, but he didn't return in 1939 and must have died. They talked among themselves. I knew they had noticed all the beds. Just then I smelled something burning and screeched that the house must be on fire. They followed me into the next room, which was full of smoke. The iron was still on, a dress had burned, and the ironing-board cover and the little table were on fire. I burst into tears, pretending mostly. They studied me, milled around, talked it over, and left."

"But what happened in the gatehouse?" I asked.

"They went there. Old Szirmer was very brave. He pretended that he didn't understand a thing. He looked so old—he hadn't shaved—and they left him alone."

Tadeusz turned to me. "Romek should be thanked," he said, offering me his hand. "If it weren't for your stubbornness and insistence on building the hiding place, things could have been very bad for us. Who knows what might have happened?" He kissed me.

Our ability to endure seemed to be reaching its limit. We were exhausted from the occupation; making ends meet, alone, took an enormous effort. And the atmosphere of terror was unremitting.

Autumn had come, with foul rainy weather. The wind whistled outside, and the days were cold, gray, and sad. The Germans were grabbing more and more people off the streets. Walking around Warsaw or taking the suburban lines had now become, for young men especially, a lottery. Posters were pasted up all over the city listing the names of those taken hostage and declaring that all of them would be put to death if offenses against the German authorities did not cease. Days later, according to the ritual, some of the hostages would be executed by firing squad on an appointed Warsaw street. People would be herded there by force to witness it. New posters announced that the sentences had been carried out and promised that if incidents of disobedience continued, more executions would take place. It was a daily routine. Posters, lists, executions, blood, then new posters, new roundups, new lists, and more blood to course down Warsaw's streets.

One day Tadeusz asked me to deliver a small package containing a few dozen steel parts for balances—these we would produce on our lathe. By the time I reached Zlota Street, passers-by were warning one another that things were "hot," military police wagons had been spotted in various parts of the city. I tried keeping to side streets, but caught sight of them.

The streets were nearly deserted; the few pedestrians had either scattered quickly or scurried alongside the walls of buildings. As I went, I kept an eye out for open gates, so that, if need be, I could hide in a stairway or in an apartment. I finally reached my destination and delivered the package. But along the way, I had learned that the Central Station area was hot, so I decided to walk through the Old City.

Just as I was turning into the street that led to the market, a commotion broke out, and people began running and hiding. German patrol cars were approaching. I ran with the others, until I found myself alone across from the cathedral. I decided to take refuge behind its heavy wooden door. The interior, half sunk in darkness, seemed empty; every sound echoed back.

I'll sit in one of the stalls and wait it out, I thought, sinking into one. Echoes played as in a sea shell. I stayed perfectly still.

A loud noise came from the entrance, and then the sound of feet. I could make out the all-too-familiar German and the hobnailed boots on the stone floor. I reached into my pocket and pulled out the phial. Would they ransack the place? The hobnailed boots came closer. Now I could hear snatches of conversation, a gentle voice explaining something. The footsteps halted, then moved away. In a while there was only quiet.

I replaced the phial and took out my father's pocket watch. It was precisely one o'clock. I did not want to leave the cathedral yet, feeling at peace in that half-darkness with the echoes, the stained-glass windows, the lofty Gothic vaults.

I became lost in thought. How Warsaw had changed with the sight of Germans hunting down people in the streets! Even the Royal Castle was a burned-out ruin, and Poles, we Poles, were reduced to sneaking along our streets so as not to fall into the hands of the Gestapo. Only in the cathedral did it seem that all had not changed, that one could return for a moment to that other Warsaw, forget for a moment what was going on outside . . . though even the cathedral was not spared the sound of German boots.

I rose and headed for the door. As I did, a voice bellowed forth from the depths of the cathedral, making my legs tremble. "I saw you come in here, son, to get away from the roundup. Things are quiet again. You are safe. . . ."

I stopped and saw a priest in black, sitting in the half-darkness in one of the side aisles.

"Thank you," I called out weakly.

"May God guide your steps," he replied.

A couple of days later Rogozinski, who had kindled my interest in the fishery school, showed up at Villa Rose. He was agitated, and his voice quivered. "Your friend Kazik is dead."

Kazik Malkowski, eighteen, son of a former professor at Stefan Batory University in Wilno, and my dearest friend at the fishery school.

I finally managed one word: "How?"

"They grabbed him on the street. . . . He had a pistol on him, that's what someone said. He was walking along when the military police blocked off the street. The patrol wagons came to a screeching halt, and out came the SS with their Schmeissers. Kazik was caught in the trap. They shoved everybody up against the wall and frisked them. He had no choice. He was about to pull out the pistol and start shooting, but he didn't have time. One of the SS was faster on the draw. He went before a firing squad yesterday."

Neither of us spoke. I walked off, sobs tearing at my throat. "Kazik, Kazik," I repeated again and again.

Rogozinski continued. "I heard that they poured plaster in his mouth so that he couldn't shout anything before he fell."

I couldn't sleep that night. I kept seeing Kazik, his slender profile, his well-shaped head . . . and his hands bound behind his back with wire, his face twisted, livid, wretched, his hair matted with blood. I could visualize him in those last minutes of his life, his large dark eyes looking on his murderers with wild contempt. I was sure he would have wanted to cry out that he was not dying in vain. He would have shouted, "Long live Poland!" Those words in his voice rang in my ears like a bell, loud, deafening.

CHAPTER IX

As 1943 ended, the front line continued to move nearer to Poland's borders. The Germans were in full retreat in the east, and to the west Allied forces were bombing Essen, Hamburg, Frankfurt, Berlin. On New Year's Eve we gathered around the radio in the hiding place and listened to the BBC: "According to the latest reports from the Eastern Front, the Soviet troops of the 1st Ukrainian Front, led by Marshal Nikolai Vatutin, are now at the very borders of Poland."

Tadeusz removed his headphones. "All of Poland will be in a state of anticipation now," he said. "May God watch over us."

I sat and stared at the silver tubes of our radio and at the brown tuner, and thought of the Soviet komandirs who had questioned me in Lutsk. Who knows, I reflected, they could still be alive, they could even be on their way here. Their approach could well signal liberation from the Germans. With that thought, an unfamiliar burden of uncertainty settled on my heart.

Within the first days of January 1944, the Red Army crossed the Polish border and took Sarny, the same Sarny I had walked to from Lityn in 1939 hoping to cross the Soviet border to fight in the ranks of the Red Army. How illusory my plans had been. What would happen now?

Everyone was asking that question, and there was a general fear that the Soviets would continue to recognize the division of Poland they had effected with the Nazis in 1939. That fear was confirmed quickly. Just as the Red Army was taking Sarny, Moscow issued a statement claiming their right to our Borderlands, which they had occupied on the basis of the Nazi-Soviet Pact.

I was sick at heart. I thought that everything that the Soviets had done in collusion with Hitler should have been retracted, acknowledged by Moscow itself as an error. After all, I thought, true communists cannot admit the use of force and violence as a legitimate means of action. My father never would have tolerated such an admission. I concealed my misgivings and disappointments from Tadeusz and the others.

At the beginning of February, Tadeusz returned from Warsaw very excited. He said that the Home Army had assassinated SS General Franz Kutschera, the chief of police, whose offices were at Szucha.

"Warsaw is buzzing with the news, and the Germans are taking revenge. They're shooting hostages, but they're afraid. They know now that even the head of the Gestapo can be brought to justice by Polish hands."

We listened to the radio constantly. The Germans had increased their terror after the assassination of Kutschera. And perhaps it was precisely because no one knew what the next hour would bring that we fled from the familiar to seek news from places where tyranny was being defeated. It was then that the call signal of the station in London—that bum, bum, bum, buuum, like the letter *V* in Morse code—became united in my mind with that other world, not under the heel of oppression. The memory of the signal, and the glow of the tubes in the dark as we listened, I would never forget. Tadeusz often mocked me, asking why I was not listening to Moscow and its chimes. His ridicule irritated me. I had tried to listen to Radio Moscow, but had dropped it soon enough. I could not stomach those stiff communiqués glorifying the Red Army and those propaganda programs on Soviet achievements.

In mid-May, while sitting crouched in the hiding place, we heard that Polish soldiers had raised our white-and-red flag on the rubble of the monastery at Monte Cassino, in Italy. Polish forces had inflicted a decisive breach in the Germans' defense line on the road to Rome. The news about this victory spread like lightning, a brilliant moment in the darkness.

Two weeks later we heard a London report that Allied troops had entered Rome and, two days after that came the news of the Allied landings in France. People were unable to control their emotion; they simply laughed, even as they walked down the street alone, their faces radiant. The end of the war was at hand.

By the end of July the very air in Poland had changed. The Germans were liquidating their offices in Warsaw, and the traffic on the bridges over the Vistula grew frantic. A column of German trucks chaotically loaded with machines sped westward past us. Scores of German soldiers arrived in Milanowek, invading the homes and throwing the inhabitants out with only the clothes on their backs. Wanda's house was occupied, and she and her family moved in with us, naturally. Villa Rose thus was even more crowded, but I was happy to have her so near.

It was at that time, in the last days of July, that one of Wanda's relatives, Ryszard Ryszkowski, an officer with the Home Army, came with news. "Do you know what's happening in Warsaw? The Germans are fleeing in a panic. The Bolsheviks are advancing toward Warsaw at full speed. If they keep it up, they'll be in Praga in a day or two. They've probably already crossed the Vistula in the south."

"And how are they treating Poles?" asked Tadeusz.

"Things aren't good," he said briskly. "In fact, they're very bad. The Bolsheviks are treating us like enemies. The news from Volhynia is that the Soviets are trying to disarm our Home Army divisions by force. We have reports of wounded men being finished off. In some places Soviet troops have shot our officers. In Wilno they invited our leaders to a meeting, supposedly so they could all confer and reach some consensus. Not one Pole ever returned from that gathering."

Two days later, on August 1, Warsaw erupted. The uprising began at five in the afternoon. People returning to Milanowek in the evening reported that the city was roaring with gunfire. At first I did not have an accurate sense of the scale of the events taking place there; few people did. The Germans were in the panic of retreat, and the insurgents were intent on seizing control of the city.

By the second or third day we knew from Radio London that the armed uprising had spread throughout Warsaw and that battles were in progress in every quarter. We looked along the railroad tracks and watched the smoke clouds as they formed on the horizon and grew from day to day.

Travelers began to tell the terrifying tale. Atrocities, bestialities were being committed by the Germans and the Ukrainians in the Wola district. The Germans were not so few or so weak that they could not throw significant weight into crushing the uprising. Tanks and SS units armed to the teeth advanced on the city, and Warsaw was, again, under the siege of artillery fire and aerial bombardment.

Because I was a communist and a Soviet sympathizer, I was often asked what would happen when the front and the mighty Red Army reached the Vistula. I argued that although the Soviets had covered hundreds of miles in their offensive, I had no doubt whatsoever that after some necessary regrouping they would lend Warsaw a hand. The taking of cities had proved very important in this war. The Germans had wanted to seize Moscow, Leningrad, and Stalingrad. The Russians had taken their cities—Rostov, Kharkov, and Kiev—back by heavy fighting. Why would they not want to wrest Warsaw from the hands of the Nazis now?

But as the end of August approached, Warsaw was fighting still alone. The Red Army did not budge. The days were blisteringly hot. On the horizon, a broad umbrella of smoke hung over the battling, dying city.

In the afternoon of just such a day, German police burst into our garden. I was picking tomatoes with Wanda and Bernard when I heard Tadeusz's voice rasp from the window, "Germans! Hide!"

I ran to the bushes and peeped through to see an entire squad in helmets pour through the gate. There was no time to hide in the house.

"Quick! Behind the spruce trees," I shouted. For an eternity I was unable to find the trapdoor to the garden hiding place and could only grasp at handfuls of soil.

"Look and see what the Germans are doing," I snapped, finally raising the hatch.

"They've surrounded the front of the house," whispered Bernard. "But they're coming to the rear, too."

Within seconds, Bernard and Wanda disappeared beneath the ground. As I lowered myself in, I raked some soil and shrubbery over the hatch and closed it.

The hiding place was pitch dark and permeated by a musty, earthy smell. It was cramped, and we had to squat. The only sound was that of our own breathing. As time passed, I could feel sweat begin to bead my forehead. It felt like being buried alive. There was no ventilation, and breathing grew difficult. Bernard began to wheeze, and Wanda was gasping and moaning softly.

"I can't . . . I'm suffocating," Bernard's husky voice said.

"We can't leave before we get the signal," I answered, barely able to breathe.

"Let me out," he moaned. "I can't take any more."

I reached for Wanda's head; it hung inert. Hunched against the wall, she did not respond. Every second crawled. Feeling blindly along the ground, I found a small stick and began picking away at the ground above my head, hoping to make a small hole for some fresh air. But I only knocked dirt onto my face and into my eyes.

"Open the hatch," rasped Bernard, his voice desperate now.

"Out there we have no chance," I shouted, my voice dying as I spoke, since I was suffocating, too.

Bernard had begun to struggle with Wanda, who was in his way. I reached out and grabbed him by the throat. "We'll die here, you understand? You're leaving over my dead body."

Bernard gurgled, and a shudder shook his body. Wanda's shoulders jerked convulsively. She was still moaning. It had now become so intolerably hot that I reached for the hatch and was about to open it. But my hand fell. A sharp pain pierced my chest, and I began to urinate. Wanda and Bernard were deathly still. I, too, lost consciousness.

When I opened my eyes, I saw stars overhead and felt grass beneath me. Slowly, I recognized voices—my mother's, Tadeusz's, Wanda's father's. She lay to one side of me, Bernard beside her. My mother was holding Wanda's head in her hands and wiping her face with a wet towel. Her father was giving her artificial respiration. Marysia and Tadeusz worked on Bernard.

We lay there for a long time under the spruce trees.

The next day my mother told me what had happened. Tadeusz, Marysia, and Czeslaw had gotten into the hiding place in the house in time. The Germans were searching for young men, but were apparently taking young women as well. They had shoved my mother around brutally. They ransacked the house but found no young people. Then they had gone out into the garden, stacked their rifles near the spruce trees, and ordered my mother to make some coffee.

"They sat down not far from where you were," said my mother.

"I was trembling with fear that you might come out before the signal. If you had, you would have found yourselves right in front of them. It would have meant certain death. What a good thing you were able to hold out!"

The Germans who were occupying houses in Milanowek left at the beginning of September, and the Sikorskis returned to their wrecked, looted home. But their thoughts, as ours, were with Warsaw, whose streets continued to run with blood. The Red Army never did come to Warsaw's aid, as I had predicted it would. While our hopes burst like soap bubbles, the cloud over the capital grew more and more ominous. Warsaw was in flames. The news from the city was worse every day—carnage, destruction, fire, hunger.

One day in mid-September our neighbor came running, shouting hoarsely: "Allied planes are over Warsaw. They're dropping aid, weapons. . . . I always said our allies wouldn't let us down."

We ran outside. The September sky was beautiful. From high above us came the roar of engines, although it was hard to tell how many airplanes there were. It was a different sky from the one I remembered in September of 1939; the rumble of German planes had been louder.

While people lifted their heads and searched for Allied planes, trains hurtled through Milanowek bearing people from Warsaw. The freight cars were locked tight, but through the bars of the tiny windows we could see gaunt faces. Sometimes the trains slowed down or stopped, and we saw eyes filled with terror and heard muffled voices crying, "Water! Water!"

By every car a German military policeman stood guard wearing a helmet and holding a rifle. A car of police armed with automatic weapons was always coupled to the end of the train.

We waited for those trains every day, our hands loaded with pails and watering cans, with baskets of apples and tomatoes. By then, the Sikorski family was living with us, having been driven from their home yet again, this time by Hungarian soldiers billeted in Milanowek. We would all go down to the tracks together to meet the trains from Warsaw. People—whole families, including children—brought whatever they could, forming dense lines on either side. We tossed apples, tomatoes, or other fruit through the bars and into the cars, or we splashed the haggard, suffering faces with fresh water.

But the openings were small, and much of the fruit missed the mark.

One day we stood on the platform beside a train that had stopped for a signal. I rapidly tossed the apples and tomatoes Wanda handed me. I had just grabbed the bucket and was about to begin splashing water into one of the cars when my mother, who was standing nearby, shrieked, "Look out! He's going to shoot!"

I jerked my face to the side and dropped the pail. A policeman at the end of the car was aiming his rifle directly at me and Wanda. But he didn't fire. As the train pulled away he kept his aim and stared, as if to say, "I could have killed you had I wanted to." He continued to stare long after the car passed us and he had become a little figure in the distance.

The annihilation of Warsaw before our very eyes broke many a spirit. We grew mute and lost interest in following events on the various fronts. The worst had happened, and we would all share the fate of Warsaw when the front rolled through. We took our meals wordlessly. Unprovoked, my mother would often wipe away tears, and Wanda would go off to a corner to conceal her emotion. Tadeusz changed more dramatically than anyone else. He stopped listening to the radio and sat hunched over his desk, his head in his hands.

The uprising collapsed after sixty-three days. Warsaw was forced to surrender. No one had come to its aid, and hoping for help had only prolonged the agony. The Germans and their hirelings murdered as many residents as they could. Later I learned that the Germans had thrown two brigades into battle against the Polish insurgents: one composed of German criminals fresh from prison, the other of Red Army turncoats who had distinguished themselves by their sadism. Poles who survived were herded out of the city to a special camp in Pruszkow. There the young were taken for forced labor; the older people were let go once they had been picked clean of their valuables. Aged women would pass through Milanowek on foot, rejects from that camp.

My great-aunt Emilia and her sick daughter arrived, both barely able to stand. Many friends and relatives came. And the subjects of conversation were always the same: What will the future bring? What are the Germans' intentions? Would the entire population be deported and all able-bodied people herded out to dig antitank ditches?

Daily, the uncertainties grew. So Wanda and I decided that there was no reason to put off getting married. The Sikorski family was now back home again, after the Hungarian troops had suddenly left Milanowek. The day the family moved back, I helped and stayed on to ask Wanda's parents for her hand. I felt uneasy, but Wanda's father's response was unequivocal.

He said he had known me for fifteen years and that it was a person's character that mattered, not his beliefs. Beliefs could change. "Your beliefs are foreign to me," he added with some emphasis, "but I know why you are the way you are. I appreciate your attachment to your father. I know you will be good to Wanda—that's the most important thing.

"We've known now for a long time that you've given her your heart. She's still very young, seventeen, and, if times were normal, I would ask you to wait. But these are terrible times—we have no idea what fate awaits us. Who knows, maybe it will be easier for the two of you to survive if you're together. All I ask is that the wedding take place in church, for this family has been Catholic for generations."

He went on, evidently wanting to clear the air about my politics. "I will be straightforward. You're going to be my son-in-law, and it's only right that I share my thoughts with you. I am not a political person, and to tell the truth I don't have much of a grasp of such things. I'm a pharmacist. But life has taught me much. In 1918 I was in Russia with my young bride. The Bolsheviks began murdering the Polish and Russian intelligentsia there, and the Dvina ran literally red with blood. I think you know what I'm leading up to: I know the Bolsheviks and what they're capable of, and I wasn't surprised to see them stand by and watch Warsaw burn."

I wanted to argue and leaned forward to do so, but he continued. "What I think, my dear Romek, is that Stalin knows what he's doing. Warsaw's destruction is in Stalin's interest. Now he has cunningly arranged for the Germans to do it for him. His army has lined up on the other side of the Vistula to watch the Germans do their work. No victim, no suffering means anything to Stalin. We know how he's dealt with his enemies in the past. His mentality is that of the schemer.

"And where are the Allies now? Where are the Americans? Hadn't they already taken Belgium when the uprising broke out? Weren't

My mother at 20

Wladyslaw Spasowski, my father, at 35

Three years old

At the orphans' school in Spala with my mother and father

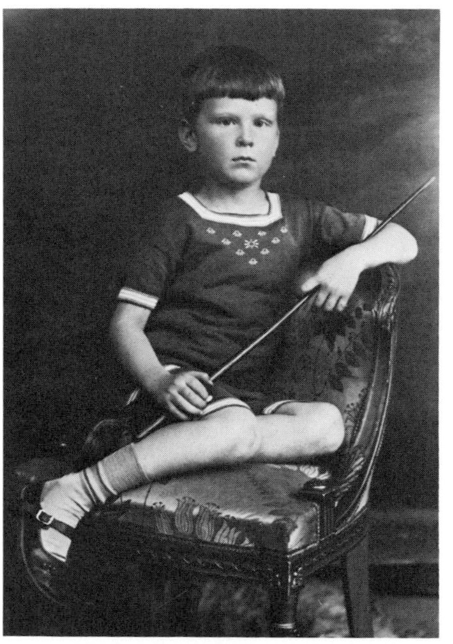

At about five, when my father decided I was growing up spoiled

With the Spala orphans; I am the one with shoes and glasses

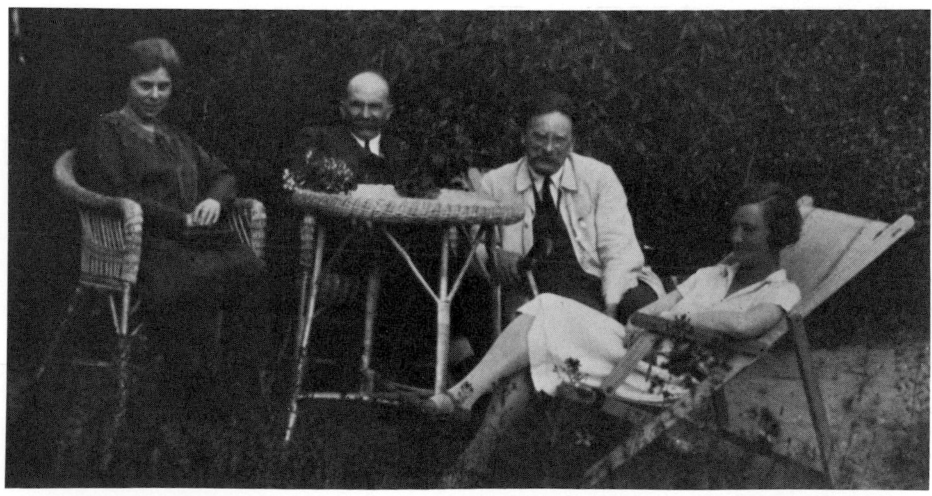

Jadwiga and Benedykt Bornstein with my father and mother at Villa Rose, 1930

In Lityn with Uncle Stefan Sumowski and his Daimler, later appropriated by the Polish military police

After the *matura* examinations, May 1939, when I knew Judyta

With Father in Gdynia, 1933

My sketch of Father listening to Radio Moscow

Train station at Milanowek in the thirties

Villa Rose in summer . . .

. . . and in winter

Sitting room in Villa Rose just before the war, with portrait of Grandfather Sumowski and our radio on the side table

Grandmother Sumowska and Aunt Emilia Langiert

Tadeusz Drynski, my mother's second husband and my most bitter critic

Grandmother Sumowska in 1947

1941 photographs of me and my father sent to Berlin with our applications to emigrate to the USSR; recovered in Moscow more than twenty years later

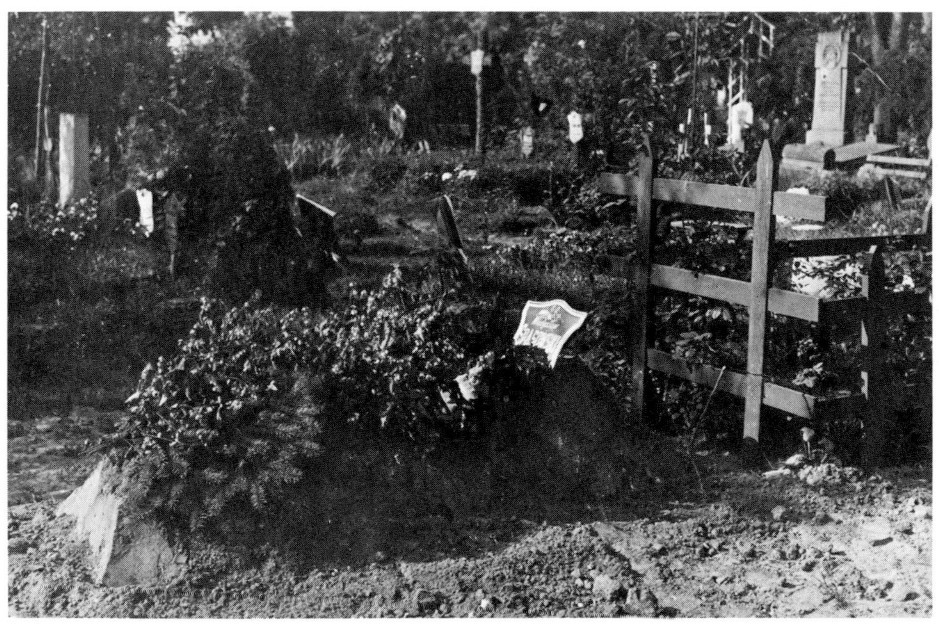

My father's grave shortly after his suicide; behind the fence is the grave of Roman Sokolowski, whose name I bore on my false ID

In 1941, after the death of my father

My first sight of five-year-old Wanda, third from left, playing in the sand

Wanda in 1943

Jan and Melania Sikorski, Wanda's parents.

Wanda in spring 1944, before her family was evicted by the Germans

At School for Political Officers, Lodz, April 1945; I am the tall one; Head Sergeant Gieleta is in front of me

As a lieutenant in Bad Salzuflen

Polish War Crimes Mission in Bad Salzuflen, Germany

Wanda in Milanowek with our newborn Misia

their planes flying across Germany? How could they allow the uprising to fail so tragically? For those who know the Bolsheviks, this comes as no surprise at all. Either the Allies are too weak or Stalin has simply tricked them. They do not know the Bolsheviks.

"Now I'll tell you something Ryszard told me before the uprising. He told me that there is proof that between 1939 and 1941 the NKVD worked hand in glove with the Gestapo in wiping out Poles. To me this is no revelation. It seems quite natural. And Ryszard tells me it's one-hundred-percent certain that it was the Bolsheviks who murdered the Polish officers at Katyn, and I have no doubts that's true."

"How can he possibly know these things?" I interrupted.

"Well, I'll tell you something, but this is in confidence. You must give me your word you won't tell a soul. As you well know, Ryszard is an officer in the Home Army. He learned this directly from headquarters.

"Now, let me tell you about my family. My father owned an estate by Skalbmierz, near Krakow. It was there I was born. The man who raised me was my uncle, a canon in Kielce. And you know about our relative General Sikorski. Romek, my dear boy, you can see the sort of family you want to marry into."

Several days later I noticed Wanda looking sad; she had been crying. "Your great-aunt Emilia invited me to come see her," she finally confessed in a voice trembling with emotion. "She told me that I was a child she loved and that you were a Bolshevik by conviction—that she considered it her duty to warn me against you. She asked me to think about it before it was too late.

"There's more," Wanda continued. "Your other relatives have been telling me that leftists like your father have no principles. They ask, 'Did he bring your mother happiness?' They tell me I should marry a religious man who shares my values." Wanda burst into tears again and begged, "You won't leave me! You love me! I know you do. . . . I've prayed so often for you."

So, even *my* family was against me. I tried to console Wanda and assure her that I loved her very much and that we would always be together.

"But if you want to marry me, you must do me one favor."

"I agree even before you ask it," I said.

"You always carry that little phial. It's not Christian for a person to take his own life. Take it out of your pocket and give it to me. I don't want any husband of mine carrying such a thing around."

I was taken aback. I had grown accustomed to that phial and always had it on me. I often held it in my hand. I hesitated. The phial was integrally connected with memories of my father, of our experience together in Szucha. But she kept looking at me, determined and expectant. It was her first request of me, a decisive one.

"All right," I agreed. "But I don't want you to have the phial. I'll give it to my mother, and I promise I won't so much as touch it again without your permission." We kissed.

That same day I gave my mother the phial. Gladdened by my decision, she hid it far from harm's reach.

By mid-October, the weather was turning cold. The rains came often, and the ground was covered with leaves, yellow and brown. One cloudy day Wanda and I left her house and, holding hands, headed for the church. I felt ill at ease, finding it difficult to imagine talking with a priest; I was determined to tell him the truth about myself without offending him or causing Wanda distress.

At the large rectory, the door was opened by a priest in a well-fitting cassock, an impressive man wearing horn-rimmed glasses. At first he was unwilling to speak with us because we had not come during regular hours, but when Wanda explained that we had deliberately chosen this time of day so as not to run into anyone, he let us in. We sat down at a round table, and he signaled us to begin explaining ourselves.

"We've come," I began, "because we wish to be married. My fiancée's name is Wanda Alina Sikorski. She is seventeen, a Catholic, and lives in Milanowek. I also live in Milanowek, but I'm not registered; I've been in hiding from the Germans since 1941. I am twenty-four, a Calvinist by heritage but in truth an atheist. . . ."

Here he flung me a quick, pointed glance.

"My real name is Romuald Spasowski," I went on. "She"—I indicated Wanda—"is the sister of one of my classmates."

"I have my parents' permission," Wanda volunteered brightly.

The priest ignored her and shot me the question, "Are you by any chance related to Wladyslaw Spasowski, the leftist?"

"Yes. I'm his son. He and I were arrested by the Gestapo; he committed suicide. . . ."

There was clear animosity in the priest's eyes now. "But she's too young," he said, after pausing for reflection. "Do you really have your parents' permission?"

"Yes, I do, Father," said Wanda. "I have both my parents' permission. They've known Romek and his family for many years, from before the war."

"I would like to speak with your father," replied the priest, "but I won't marry you."

We were stunned.

The priest turned to me and added dryly, "Before you think about marriage, you should bring me a document from the Germans saying you have their permission. The Protestant churches, the Calvinists, are, after all, under their jurisdiction."

My face drained, and my body stiffened. I could not believe my ears.

"Perhaps you *have* to get married?" His voice alone was an assault on Wanda. She blushed and glanced at me with fear in her eyes.

"We'll be leaving now," I said without looking at the priest. I wanted to tell him a thing or two, but seeing that Wanda was barely holding herself together, I gritted my teeth. We left without offering him our hands.

I was furious. The priest had virtually implied that I should report to the Gestapo. Such behavior only confirmed my view that the Catholic church was a reactionary organization. We walked home in silence.

At one moment we both said the same thing at the same time: "I don't want to be married by him even if he agrees to."

I looked into Wanda's eyes. "So you see," I said, "we think alike even though I am not religious. I want our marriage to be the most beautiful memory of our entire lives. That priest can't do that for us."

Wanda's father spoke with the priest, who insulted him by saying that he did not know what sort of person would give his daughter in such a marriage. Sikorski responded that he knew perfectly well what he was doing. In the end the priest said there could be no question of his performing a marriage for any Spasowski.

Our marriage seemed more doomed with each passing day. At the end of October, I took Wanda some apples. She was sad and suggested we go for a walk. We walked far into the fields outside Milanowek.

"I'm taking you the way I used to go in the fall of 1939," she said, "when I brought hot food and fruit to the Polish prisoners the Germans kept behind barbed wire."

It was a dark fall day. We talked about the possibility of our being separated by the force of events, for there were ever more persistent rumors that the Germans would be evacuating the population and taking all men for forced labor. We were afraid that fate would separate us forever.

We came to bare ground. It was there, on those flat wet fields, that the Germans had set up their prisoner-of-war camp in 1939.

"Here," said Wanda, pointing. "The camp was right here. Now there's not a trace left. Only trees . . . Once, I was walking along the barbed wire carrying a small pail of soup when I spotted a familiar face. I stopped, and the man held out his mess kit; I poured him some soup. 'Are you Mr. Jerzy Pichelski?' I asked. He nodded, apparently moved that he had been recognized in that mass of humanity when he was so dirty and shaggy. I had never met a movie star before. So I did what any twelve-year-old would do—I asked him for his autograph!"

She leaned into my arm, and we continued walking like that until we reached the end of the little village of Zukow. There, among the trees, we spotted a small church, its wood blackened by time, so old it appeared to have grown into the ground.

"Let's go in," said Wanda, searching my face, as if afraid to hear that I had had my fill of churches.

"Fine," I said, somehow attracted by the antiquity of the church.

We were surprised by the beauty of the interior, which was painted a light blue, the gilding, the statues carved from wood. The church was empty except for a sacristan in a surplice busy near the altar. We sat down. Wanda was soon on her knees praying.

"Isn't it beautiful here?" she whispered. "Shall we go see the priest?"

The question shocked me from my reveries. I assumed that all priests would act the same as the first one. "We can try. I don't want to make you sad, but I don't see much hope."

"Let's try it," she implored.

The sacristan told us that the priest was in the rectory, a small dilapidated single-story building beside the church. Crossing a well-worn wooden threshold, we entered a low whitewashed room with a plank floor.

"Praised be Jesus Christ," said Wanda softly.

"For ever and ever," the priest replied, smiling when he saw that I said nothing. "What can I do for you, my children?" he asked, studying us. He had gray hair, though he was not old, probably little more than fifty. There was both surprise and encouragement in his gray eyes. Something about his face, I thought, inspired confidence.

"We've come to ask a great favor of you, Father," said Wanda, her voice trembling. "We have met with disappointment and great sadness because, Father, we wish to be married and the priest in Milanowek treated us unfairly. Romek, tell him what happened."

The priest turned his head to me. "Please sit down. You must be tired. It's a long walk from Milanowek."

I told him the story in detail, and he listened in silence. When I had finished, he took Wanda by the hand and said warmly: "Don't worry, my child. I can see that you love each other and want to be together in these tragic times. And God sees it, too." He thought for a moment. "I can also see that you are tired. Let me offer you what little I have. Will you drink tea with me? What is your name?"

"Wanda Alina . . ."

"And so, Wanda, you must like cherry preserves?" He rose and went into the kitchen to prepare the tea.

Wanda wiped tears from her eyes with her handkerchief. "You see," she whispered, "God is with us."

I tried to control my own emotions. There was something about this priest that I could not quite find words for. He was simply a good man, I decided.

The priest soon reappeared. "My name is Sienkiewicz. . . . We're living in horrible times. There seems to be no rest for us Poles." As he spoke I glanced at his cassock, faded from age; the cuffs were worn and ragged.

"Our little church," he said, pointing out the window, "has witnessed a great deal. It was built in the seventeenth century, even before Jan Sobieski saved Vienna from the Turks. It's a miracle that it survived so long, being wooden. . . . So many wars, uprisings, tragedies, and now again no one knows what the future holds. The front has reached the Vistula; the Bolsheviks are thirty miles away. Who knows . . . ?" He crossed himself. "May God protect us and keep us in his care."

He sat down. "So you're in hiding, since 1941, you say," he said to me. "That's a long time," He broke off, then continued. "I understand that you want to be married without any public announcement, any posting of the banns."

I nodded my head.

"Yes, yes," he said. "God will be your witness. He is always the witness. I can see that you love each other and I can feel that you are telling the truth. God expects us to be good and truthful. Yes, yes, truthful, as befits human beings, God's children."

Once again he paused, leaving us breathless. "I can marry you on a Sunday, when High Mass is over and the people have left. But since you are an atheist," he said, with a glance at me, "as you were honest enough to tell me, you must not make confession. I'll arrange that with the bishop. He'll agree."

An old woman, no doubt the sacristan's wife, shuffled into the room carrying hot tea, bread, and cherry preserves that were dark, almost black, like the sort I had eaten long, long ago in Volhynia.

"Ask your husband," said the priest to the woman, "to check when we can perform a marriage."

Within moments the sacristan had entered the room.

"Can we perform a marriage in a week?" asked the priest.

"No. There are two already. And there can't be a marriage if the banns are not posted."

"In this case," interrupted the priest, "banns will be posted only on the day of the wedding. So it will be on Sunday the twelfth, right after High Mass, when all the people have left."

The sacristan looked in surprise from the priest to us. "And the names?" he asked.

"I'll tell you them when we post the banns," replied the priest. He glanced at the window. "Now, my children, may God be with you as you speed home. It'll be dark soon, and it's a long way.

"Oh, one more thing," he said to Wanda. "Since you're only seventeen, my child, I would prefer your father to come to see me for a little talk."

The way home seemed short, happiness lending us wings.

Sunday, November 12, 1944, was a gloomy fall day. Rain mixed with snow had fallen during the night, leaving puddles on the dirt roads and patches of white snow here and there. Gusts of wind wrinkled the puddles' surfaces. Wanda and her father rode in a *britzka* with a carriage top. The scraggy horse had difficulty pulling it over the sopping-wet ground. Tadeusz and I walked beside the carriage. The road led through pinewoods and fields with a few clusters of trees, mostly willows. Dark clouds swept across the sky, and rain fell every so often. In places, Tadeusz and I would be up to our ankles in mud and water.

As I walked alongside the *britzka* I could see the hem of Wanda's light blue dress protruding from her coat and her feet in old-fashioned galoshes.

We kept a lookout for the German police; after all, we were in a zone that bordered the front. The driver, however, was optimistic and assured us that it would be hard to kick a dog out of the house in such weather and the Krauts would not be out running around the fields on a day like this. He was right; we did not come upon anyone.

My happiness was not in the least impeded by the mud splashing into my shoes and my wet pants sticking to my legs like cold compresses. I must have been a sorry sight, looking not for a moment like the happy groom.

The streets of Zukow were deserted, everyone having gone home after Mass. At the church, Father Sienkiewicz received us and gave us his blessing. After I handed him our rings—my mother's and father's wedding rings—he asked Wanda's father to join him for a moment. The sacristan lit the candles and disappeared into the organ loft to play.

Father Sienkiewicz emerged before the altar, and we stood facing him. He glanced at my mud-spattered pants and smiled good-naturedly, his handsome profile and kindly eyes radiating warmth and assurance. We knelt as he prayed in Latin, and then, in Polish, he blessed our union. We rose and repeated the marriage vows.

Wanda, the beautiful girl I had always been so fond of, was now beside me, now my wife, rapt in prayer. She stared, wide-eyed, at the priest and at the altar, over which Christ hung, spread on the cross. The chords of the organ reverberated and drowned out the wailing of the wind. I was happy.

After the ceremony, Father Sienkiewicz turned to Wanda and said,

"I want to speak with you alone for a moment, my child." The two of them walked off to one side. Wanda honored the priest's request never to tell me what he had said. But many years later she confirmed that everything the wise and beloved Father Sienkiewicz had told her had come true.

I spent the night at my wife's house. At mine we would not have been able to be alone together. There could be no honeymoon then, and there never was. I could not believe that this beautiful girl now belonged to me, as I belonged to her. Delighting in each other and confiding everything that had remained unsaid, we never closed our eyes that night. My happiness was complete but short-lived: at daybreak I was seized by the fear that everything could shatter like some ephemeral dream if fate chose to separate us.

The Germans, like dogcatchers, were rounding up people every day and sending them out to build earthworks, to dig trenches and antitank ditches. The people simply disappeared. Only days later would some news, or a few words on a scrap of paper, come trickling back. Thanks to our hiding places, we had so far managed to escape the roundups, but it was now a time of deportation, and the situation was increasingly tense.

One day when I visited Villa Rose, my mother opened the door in tears.

"They took Tadeusz," she said. "He didn't even have time to say good-bye. They just took him. . . ."

"How come he didn't hide?"

"It came as a surprise; he had no time," she said, sobbing. "We knew they'd be rounding people up today, because they've been doing it every other day. We were careful—Tadeusz had even opened the trapdoor. Around noon he saw that there was no water in the pail and went to fetch some from the well. . . . The poor man had no way of knowing that that very moment the Germans were coming through the garden on the way to our house. He ran into them right by the well. I was waiting for the water, and when he didn't come back, I ran out to see what had happened. The truck was just pulling away from our gate. . . . He had to have been in it. . . ."

I began living in Villa Rose again to help take Tadeusz's place, while Wanda stayed with her parents. We were all only biding time until the Germans drove us from our homes.

Tadeusz returned in mid-December, having managed to escape from a hard-labor unit after two weeks. He was emaciated, his large forehead more prominent than ever. He attributed his escape to help from the Virgin, to whom he had prayed constantly. Taking advantage of a moment when the German guarding him had turned away, he had slipped, unseen, into some sort of cave, where he remained until night fell. The people in the countryside had given him food and shelter on his two-day journey home.

One day Rogozinski showed up. "I stopped by," he said, in his chronically hoarse voice, "because you're the only one who'll understand how I feel. . . . You knew them all. . . ." He looked odd. I didn't understand.

"Romek, we're the only two left. . . ."

"What do you mean?"

"I met someone from the underground who escaped from one of the train transports. We got to talking, and I told him about the fishery school. He had been with them in Warsaw during the uprising. There had been a lot of them, and they had created their own unit. Right at the beginning of the uprising they had fought in Zoliborz, and fought well, down to the last bullet. Not a single one survived. . . ."

I was speechless, the faces of those young men swarming through my memory. We said no more.

The new year brought no changes. The fronts on the Vistula and the Narew did not budge. Day after day passed, and the fronts remained at those rivers. Radio London reported heavy Allied bombing of Germany.

On January 17 I walked to a village near Grodzisk to order some grain from a farmer we knew. On the empty highway, I heard distant rumblings that seemed to come from several directions at once. There had been no indications that the front line was approaching; I had not known that five days earlier the Soviets had launched an offensive, creating a bridgehead on the left bank of the Vistula and on the Narew. In the course of a few days Soviet tanks had covered more than sixty miles. On that very day, the Red Army entered our ruined, deserted capital, accompanied by Polish detachments that had been formed in the Soviet Union.

When, after buying the grain, I was preparing to leave the farmer's hut, I heard the growl of a motor. The farmer and I ran to the window in time to see a German motorcycle with a sidecar pass. Three soldiers were perched on it. The driver wore a helmet, but the one behind him rode bareheaded. They all looked lost. I waited a while before setting out for home.

Crossing the fields to the highway, I saw that it was streaming with people now. I watched for some moments before I realized that what I was seeing was Soviet troops mopping up the last remnants of the Wehrmacht. One extended line after another swept past, little more than a dozen paces apart. I had no choice but to move through them. A burst of machine-gun fire and a series of individual shots sounded close by. Waves of people approached, and I saw, with some alarm, that one soldier was heading directly for me. I recognized the winter cap with earlaps I had seen in Lwow in 1939, the long sallow-colored overcoat, the felt boots. He was holding a rifle with a fixed bayonet; his face was dark, eyes sunken. He had a menacing look about him—the sort that would shoot and keep on going without so much as blinking an eye. As he neared, he barked at me, "Stop! Who are you?"

"I'm a Pole," I answered in Russian. He looked me over from head to toe and then motioned with his rifle to one side.

"Pass!" he said. As I trudged on, I remembered my weeping in 1939 at the sight of planes with red stars on their wings. My feelings had changed. Why? I asked myself. After all, they had liberated Poland from the bloody German occupation. Wasn't this the moment I had waited for these five long harrowing years? The nightmare of Nazism was disappearing. But Poland's day of liberation was not the event I had fantasized. I could not rejoice.

A group of people gaped at a ditch. Inside three dead Germans were sprawled, the motorcycle with sidecar beside them. Two Red Army soldiers had just finished going through the dead men's pockets, and one was brandishing a watch. Within minutes they were stomping on the Germans' stomachs, chests, heads. Blood seeped through the uniforms.

I hated Germans with a passion and had I had a weapon I would have killed many during the war, but the wantonness of this sight disgusted me. I turned away. The old peasant beside me also plodded off. As he did, he mumbled, "The Germans were criminals, but these are no better." Words I was to remember.

Later that day Soviet troops passed through Milanowek. Wanda, Tadeusz, and I went to watch. The Red Army soldiers seemed strange, haunted, their faces endlessly weary. They moved lethargically, a gray mass that little resembled an army, their earlaps flapping, their eyes voids, their gray overcoats almost down to their ankles. They wore quilted jackets and trousers, and clumsy, misshapen felt boots. Some of them carried rifles with protruding bayonets; others carried submachine guns with cartridge drums, a piece of rope where the strap should have been.

The Poles smiled at the Soviet soldiers, but they did not respond. Seeing how weary they were, Poles handed them food. They ate without stopping or even slowing their pace. Trucks followed pulling long-barreled antitank guns. "On to Berlin" signs were scrawled in Russian on their sides. Then came a shabby Cossack cavalry detachment. From beneath large caps stared feral eyes.

Wanda watched in silence. I could sense her fear.

"There's your grand Red Army," Tadeusz threw at me ironically. "Marauders would inspire more confidence."

I did not respond. I, too, had forebodings.

That night I was unable to fall asleep and kept asking myself what my next step should be. Can I stay at home while Nazism is collapsing and a new, postwar world is emerging? Can I really choose a warm bed beside my beloved wife and forget entirely the vows I made to my father? Was I to renounce those "streaks of light" about which I had written to my father in 1939 and, now that the hour for action had come, remain here listening to the Soviets being mocked, jeered, and cursed?

I decided to take action: to go to Warsaw; to find the Polish authorities, the Polish detachments formed in the Soviet Union, and join the Polish Communists at last.

Wanda was afraid for me. She asked me not to go. Soon, however, she relented, when I found others willing to accompany me. We set out early on the piercing cold morning of January 19, the snow creaking underfoot. We took the path along the railroad tracks. Electricity was out everywhere, and the railroad ties were torn up closer to Warsaw, the tracks warped and useless. A railroad worker walking with us advised, "Never walk along undamaged track. Keep to one side. Undamaged tracks are certain to have mines under them. You'll be blown up before you know what hit you." It was good advice: bodies along the tracks and blood on the snow were proof enough.

The closer we drew to Warsaw, the more ominous the scene. The entire rail system was either rubble or burned. Skeletons of buildings jutted up where the city had once been. In place of Warsaw's streets we saw only debris. The city was deserted, a wasteland. From time to time we spotted a shadowy figure hurrying through the snow-dusted wilderness.

Where am I? I asked myself. I knew Warsaw well, but I had lost my bearings in this place. It was a ghost of a city, a moonscape. We paused. My companions were looking anxiously at me, their leader, who had assured them I knew the city like the back of my hand.

"Let's go." I pretended to have gotten my bearings, so as not to dishearten them; surely I would recognize some landmark along the way. In time I did. First we went to my father's apartment on Noakowski Street; I was deluding myself that we might be able to spend the night there. Of the building, only half of a collapsed gate remained. Where our apartment had been, a few stairs hung from a free-standing wall, and from the floor above a sink dangled precariously in the air.

We set off again, and I did not look back. It was more than I could bear.

The Falskis' house had been burned, the roof smashed, the windows blown out. We continued down a short street, checking each of the two-story connected houses on it. At the far end one seemed in better shape. We went inside, glad to have a roof over our heads even though it was as cold inside as out.

The house had been looted. The furniture was overturned, and the floor was strewn with bureau drawers, broken glass, bits of porcelain. We stood amid the shambles staring mutely as the light began to fade outside. Suddenly the silence was broken by the chatter of a machine gun, very close. A moment later it was answered by another round of fire.

"We'll camp here," I decided. I chose a small room on the ground floor to the rear of the house. It would be easy to cover the one window so that our light would not attract attention. We brought a piece of sheet metal up from the cellar and built a fire, throwing in chair legs and bits of the period furniture. Soon the room was bright and warm; the snow in a pot had melted, and we made a meal of hot water and the bread we had brought with us.

Early the next morning we were awakened by the piercing cold. Day broke as we finished eating our meager breakfast of bread and water. We went outside—above us, sun and blue sky; before us, rubble and smoldering ruins as far as the eye could see.

Where would we find the authorities, the soldiers, the Polish Communists? Ever watchful for German mines, we made our way to the Old City through the snow and along paths already tramped out. On Nowy Swiat, in front of the ruins of Staszic Palace, a bare pedestal thrust out from a heap of rubble; Thorvaldsen's statue of Copernicus was no longer on top. The burned-out Church of the Holy Cross loomed over the ruins of apartment buildings, and the statue of Christ bearing the cross now lay on the ground amid the rubble. I searched for Zygmunt's Column, but only the base remained. Some distance away, the heavy bronze figure of the king lay smashed beside its cracked column. The thick walls of the Royal Castle had collapsed. The Old City was a terrifying labyrinth of bare ragged walls.

Where the cathedral in which I had taken refuge in the fall of 1943 once stood was a hill of rubble and a solitary fragment of one of the Gothic arches. We slipped on the snow as the path rose and led us to where the Old City Market had been. As we stood staring dumbly at the wreckage, two soldiers emerged from the ruins. They wore green overcoats and carried submachine guns across their backs. Polish eagles were on their field caps.

"Are you Polish?" I asked as they walked past. They did not reply and passed without stopping.

"Hey," I shouted after them, "are you Poles?"

The soldiers continued on their way without looking back.

Something's fishy, I thought. Poles surely would have answered. Perhaps they were Russians, volunteered one of my companions.

As we made our way to the Vistula, we ran into some people from Praga. Both of the bridges across the river had been destroyed, and they had had to cross on the ice—a risky business because it was still thin and cracking above the main current. I asked them about Praga. It was still standing, they answered, if you could call it that. But there was no information whatsoever.

Sick at heart and chilled to the bone, I looked around at Warsaw, a dead city—a burial ground for people and hope. There was nothing to be done but return to our survivors in Villa Rose.

BOOK TWO

Career and Conscience

1945–1970

CHAPTER X

Although the idea of joining the army was never far from my thoughts, I and a few others founded a Communist Party committee in Milanowek. I had learned that outside the Party there would be little opportunity to influence events.

At the beginning of March, once the Party committee was well established, I walked to Warsaw again and crossed the Vistula to Praga by boat. There I spoke for the first time with a representative of the military, who informed me that the Polish army's main political headquarters, which had been formed in the Soviet Union, was now located in the town of Wlochy, not far from Warsaw. On my way home, I walked to Wlochy, where I applied as a volunteer. I made it plain that I wanted to fight against the Germans. A decision, I was told, would take two weeks.

When I reported again, I was instructed to travel to Lodz, where I would be enrolled in the School for Political Officers. I protested that I wanted to go to the front, not to school, but it was to no avail. Either go or remain a civilian, they told me. They simply were not recruiting volunteers for the army.

On Wednesday, April 4, Wanda and I stood on the railway platform waiting for my train. This would be a trial for us both—she was saying good-bye to her husband after only four months of marriage, and I was leaving a young wife behind in very uncertain times.

The train was so packed that there was no question of getting into a compartment. People sat on the roofs. I kissed Wanda, hopped on a step, and clambered up onto the roof. She stood alone on the platform, her eyes brimming with tears. The train pulled out, leaving most of the crowd on the platform behind. The throng receded into the distance, and with it the small figure of my young wife in a blue coat with a gray fur collar and a round white woolen cap. Finally, it all vanished from sight.

The train swayed mercilessly from side to side, and I had to hold on for dear life although my hands were numb from the cold. The dangling electric wires flashing past forced me to lie flat. I was reminded of scenes of people on train roofs during the Russian Revolution as depicted in Soviet films. Was this my 1917? I asked myself. After two hours, the train pulled into Lodz. I could barely straighten my frozen fingers.

Two days later I was admitted to the School for Political Officers. Led by a sergeant, we left the assembly point—a long column of civilians walking four abreast and badly out of step. The column passed through a gate into a spacious courtyard surrounded on three sides by barracks and by a high wall on the fourth. I seemed to be the only one with any military training. We were issued denim uniforms, clean but faded and frayed in places. My pants were too short, and the beet-colored puttees were not long enough to cover my long thin calves. On the other hand, I was issued an excellent pair of boots; they were used and roomy, but unlike those of my fellow soldiers, they never caused me one blister or any pain. The others made good-humored fun of me, claiming I could execute an about face without so much as budging my boots.

Intensive drills began. All our weapons were Soviet, the familiar rifles with their long skewerlike bayonets, submachine guns with round cartridge drums, and light semiautomatic rifles with detachable clips. There were heavier arms, too, mortar and antitank rifles.

My company was part of a battalion commanded by Captain Onufreev, a tall, slender man with light hair and a long face; he did not look Russian, even though his last name made it clear that he was. He wore high Russian-style boots with tops made of soft pleated leather. He came only to formations and was always accompanied by his political deputy, Captain Ruda, a thin man around thirty who spoke Polish with no accent and who turned out to be from Warsaw and an alumnus of my school.

Most of our day-to-day contact was with our company leader, Sergeant Gieleta, and the platoon leader, Corporal Giemlik. They were both from Silesia and had been mobilized by the Germans into the Wehrmacht after Poland was seized in 1939. After they were taken prisoner by the Soviets on the Eastern Front, and after experiences they refused to discuss, they were placed in Polish detachments formed in the Soviet Union. They spoke Polish with thick German accents peppered with many Russian words. They swore in Russian and German, barked their commands in very loud voices, as if they were still in the Wehrmacht, reviled their men for any infraction, and generally maintained strict Prussian discipline.

The trainees were mostly rough country boys who had been associated with the Communist partisans during the last year of the war. Some hailed from the Polish Workers Party (PPR) or the People's Army, others from the Peasant Battalions, a conglomeration of various left-wing groups. Although quick-witted, they had had no higher education, and some had had no more than a few years of elementary school. Many of them had lost loved ones in the war; some had been orphaned. The great majority were well built and used to physical work. They had been seasoned by the hardships of partisan life and found little difficulty in carrying out our intensive drills.

Evening roll call each day ended with the singing of the patriotic song "The Troop," composed in the early part of the century as a protest against the Germanization of the Polish people. Every time the words "we won't abandon the land of our fathers" burst forth from four hundred throats, I would rage inwardly at the thought of all those—starting with the boys from the fishery school—who had died at the hands of the Germans.

On the first Sunday after service dress was issued, the entire battalion was to attend Mass. I resolved to do just as I had done before the war; I waited for the moment I could step out of formation. Finally the command came: "Those on duty and the sick, forward!" I stepped forward.

"What's the matter with you?" snapped Sergeant Gieleta.

"I am an atheist. I do not attend church," I replied.

"I see. All right then, there's cleanup to do, march."

As the battalion passed through the gate singing "Oh, sea, our sea," I returned to the barracks to clean latrines and preserve my convictions.

It was the same story the next Sunday: I was the sole resister.

Henryk Zygier, a fellow who had come to the school from the Red Army sidled over to me and volunteered, "You've probably guessed I'm a Jew. I don't believe in those superstitions either, but I'd rather let it slide and spend a little time in church than clean latrines. Think it over. You'll never change anything by yourself. The stakes are high here, brother, and it looks like church is part of it."

"I have principles," I replied, "and they are important for me. Do you understand? I will not be an opportunist. I have my opinion of how a Communist should act."

He shook his head. "Why make such a show of principle right off? Krakow wasn't built in a day."

In mid-April Vienna fell to Soviet troops, and the drive on Berlin began. Polish detachments formed in the Soviet Union stormed the left bank of the Neisse, while U.S. forces raced down the Danube and Russians swept up it.

News soon arrived from Moscow that the Polish provisional government had, on April 21, signed the Provisional Treaty of Friendship and Aid with the Soviet Union. Our instructors emphasized the historical significance of this agreement, which was to provide great support for People's Poland for twenty years. They said that the Soviets had never forgotten about Poland even in the darkest hours, that the Soviet Union had always come to Poland's aid and had always had a hand of friendship to offer Poland. That friendship had now guaranteed Poland's international position, which was recognized at the Allied "Big Three" conference in Yalta, and would continue to remain, because Polish affairs would be seen to by our great friend Generalissimo Stalin.

Such words always produced unpleasant associations for me, since I could not help thinking of 1939, the Nazi-Soviet Pact, and the fate of Poles in the Borderlands. But I was persuaded that the past was over and done with, that now the Soviet Union wished us well, since Poland was following their example.

Toward the end of April word spread through the companies that the Political Section would be calling us each in for a little talk. Those who had already been called said that the officers asked various personal questions and required further information for the biographies and forms that had to be filled out yet again.

My turn came soon enough. I filled out the detailed questionnaire while I waited to be summoned into a room where three officers sat at a table covered with red cloth. Captain Malko sat at the center and indicated that I sit opposite him.

"What prompted you to apply here?" Malko began.

"I didn't apply," I answered. "I tried to volunteer for the army—I have personal accounts to settle with the Germans. But I was sent here, probably because I am a Communist."

Malko rummaged through his files. This session irritated me, bringing back memories of past interrogations. The difference was that here I felt sure of myself, almost defiant.

"What does that mean; 'I am a Communist'? After all, the Communist Party of Poland was disbanded."

"I know well that it was disbanded," I replied. "For me it's not a matter of belonging to the Party, but of my convictions."

"You are the son of Wladyslaw Spasowski, is that right?" interrupted Malko. He knew more about me than I had expected.

"Yes, he was my father," I answered. "A communist, too, even though he did not belong to the Party."

"All right," said Malko, "And during the occupation did you belong to the PPR, the Polish Workers' Party? Or to its military arm, the People's Guard—the People's Army?"

"Neither. My life was such that I was unable to belong to any party. For a short time in the spring of 1940 I gave lectures at meetings for workers in the Party. I spoke to them about the Soviet Union, because I had been in the Borderlands in 1939, on the other side of the Bug. But that was long before the other groups existed."

"And why did you cross back over to the German side?"

"Primarily to try to save my father. And I must say the Soviet authorities gave me no help in that," I said emphatically.

"And afterward, what happened then?"

"Then the Gestapo arrested my father and me. They knew about the letters my father and I had written to Moscow, Lwow, and Berlin . . . to Dekanozov."

"And then?"

I told my story. It was difficult for me to speak of what was painful and intensely personal to strangers such as these. Perhaps Malko noticed my agitation. In any case, he did not pursue that line of questioning.

"Well," he said, "that was 1941. Then what?"

"Then I hid and protected Jews in my mother's house. They were friends of ours, my mother's, my father's, mine, from before the war. There must have been ten altogether."

"So that means you have never belonged to any organization or political party?"

"No, I haven't," I replied.

"And since the liberation?"

"I have been working on the Party committee in Milanowek."

"Indeed you have," said Malko. "I have here in front of me a letter from that committee concerning you. They recommend you very highly." Malko rummaged through his files again, and no one said a word.

"We'll be asking you in again in a couple of days," he said in conclusion, "after we've seen everyone."

I started back for my company, immersed in thought. The whole thing had the same smell as the scene with the Soviet komandirs in Lutsk, except that now I felt fortified by experience. They're not going to intimidate me, I thought. I passed my test in 1940. I proved my dedication to communism well enough then.

It was not long before I was summoned by Captain Malko for a second time.

"Sit down, Spasowski," he said in a friendly voice. "The Political Section has decided to entrust you with the position of deputy company commander for political matters. A great responsibility will be on your shoulders—the company's political attitude. Nevertheless, you will remain a trainee like all the rest. You will participate in all classes and drills. It is the lot of a Communist," he said with a smile, "to have more work and more responsibilities. Your duties will include keeping an eye on the level of political instruction in your company as well as preparation for front-line service. So you won't have a moment to waste. You'll be on the run like everyone else, and you'll have to prepare your other work in the evening, when everyone else is relaxing or sleeping. Your position, though it will carry no rank with it, will be equivalent to that of company leader. If need be, but only in extreme situations, you can countermand officers' orders and report to your superiors; either to Captain Ruda or to the Political Section, directly. In turn, the political deputies of platoon leaders will be subordinate to you. They, too, will be appointed by us."

Malko looked directly at me, and for the first time I seemed to detect a certain warmth in his eyes.

"Our army, Comrade Spasowski, is similar to the prewar army only exteriorly. In reality, this is an army that answers to political decisions and is strictly dependent on its political officers. Clearly, the better the military training this army has, the greater its political value. You can see that, I'm sure. I will provide you with precise instructions for your prescribed duties and authority. Here are the school's internal orders." He handed me a few printed sheets. "Read them right here and learn them by heart. In fact, your authority is greater than indicated there."

That day, after the list of political appointees was read off at roll call, Sergeant Gieleta walked over to me and offered me his hand.

"I admit I wanted to kick your ass for the way you acted about church. . . . But now I want to bury the hatchet, Comrade Deputy Company Commander," he said stressing his final words and giving me an ironic smile.

Just after our arrival in Lodz, I had noticed a young man who kept aloof and seemed constantly pensive and morose. His name was Michal. We became friends despite the fact that he had been assigned to another company, and we continued to meet in the courtyard.

"It's started," he said one day.

"What's started?"

"You don't know, and you're a political deputy? Well, I'll tell you, but keep this a secret, or it could cost me my head, and maybe other people's heads, too. I can't keep silent any longer."

Michal began tentatively. "I was sent here to inform on people." He looked at me. "I'm not here to go to school. In a couple of weeks or months, when they're done with me here, they'll send me somewhere else."

"Who sent you?"

"The Russians, the NKVD . . . I work for them."

"The NKVD? But you're a Pole; you told me so yourself—from Volhynia."

"Yes, I am a Pole. My father was an officer in the Polish army. He disappeared in 1939, and we haven't been able to find out his whereabouts, or anything, not from the Krauts and not from the Rooskies. My older brother was in the Home Army during the occupation. When the Soviets came last year, they disarmed the entire detachment and tortured my brother so that he would name names."

Michal's voice was trembling, a sign of deep sorrow within. I took his hand.

"I wasn't a member of the Home Army," he continued, "but they took me, too, and beat me. Then they promised me that they would release my brother if I would inform for them. I agreed to." He stared straight ahead. "Now I report to the captain, the tall one. You must have seen him crossing the yard on the way to that door there," he said pointing. "He has his own office on the fourth floor. He speaks only Russian but he understands Polish."

"You said it's started. What did you mean by that?"

"I'm not the only one they sent here to inform. I don't know how many there are, but there are quite a few, maybe even a dozen, and they're recruiting others right here on the spot. There must be a lot of them, because that captain has a very strict schedule and sees me only on Fridays, always at the same hour. If there's some emergency, I can phone him from the guardhouse and give my first name. So be careful. Even the walls have ears around here. . . .

"During the few weeks that we've been here," he continued, "the captain ordered me to act like everyone else, not to attract any attention. He treated me to chocolate, wanting to indulge me, to make friends. When I was at his office yesterday he told me that we're getting down to work now. My mission for this week is to present my opinion, in writing, of everyone in the platoon, of everything I know."

Weeks passed, and I did not see Michal again. Later I learned that he had been in the infirmary for a while, and then he simply disappeared.

During political classes, which always took place after drill, the instructors devoted considerable time to discussing Poland between the two World Wars. They spoke at length about the "fascist" prewar government and the "Polish reactionary camp," composed of various "right-wing" groups.

The way the lecturers treated the Communist Party of Poland (KPP) left me uncomfortable. The nineteen-twenties were discussed in a normal enough fashion, but the situation in the thirties became, with the approach of the outbreak of the war, progressively hazy. Their comments on the KPP also became increasingly unfavorable, up to the time the Party was finally disbanded and ceased to function in 1938.

They devoted considerably more time to the "Polish left," the Socialist Party in the cities and the peasant movement in the countryside, from which, as they put it, the "healthy" antifascist front was formed during the occupation, facilitating the creation of a "broad" front of workers and peasants connected with the best revolutionary traditions of the Polish people, reaching back as far as Kosciuszko's 1794 uprising.

On May 2 the Red Army took Berlin. Units of the Polish First Army, formed in the Soviet Union, marched into the capital of the Third Reich along with them. I envied them and would have given much to have been among them.

The Third Reich surrendered on May 8. Once again our instructors outdid themselves in lavishing superlatives on the invincible and omnipotent Red Army and the genius who led it, Generalissimo Stalin.

Why do they say so little about the Western Front? I wondered, and why don't we hear a single word about the British and American air raids that pounded the Germans day and night. I knew from Radio London that more than a thousand bombers had been involved in those raids, which left the cities of the Third Reich in a sea of flames. After all, those bombing raids had been going on for two years now, and alone could have broken the Nazis.

During those days of intoxication with the Red Army's victories, the school was visited by its head, General Melenas. A large, thickset man, he stood before us in his Polish general's uniform resplendent with silver braid. His first words to us, "Hello, cadets!," were spoken with such a thick Russian accent as to leave no doubt about his nationality. The next dozen or so words of his greeting to us proved that he had no knowledge of Polish. The floor was then taken by his political deputy, Colonel Schleyen, who spoke fluently and without an accent. It was said that he had been a Communist before the war and had fought in the International Brigade in Spain but had spent the war years in the Soviet Union. In his speech he called on us to work; despite the war's having ended, People's Poland would need a firm footing in its People's Army to protect it from enemies both without and within.

That May, the Yalta agreement was still being quoted by our lecturers as a great victory. They were trumpeting Soviet propaganda expertly. I never shared my feelings, though I was gnawed inwardly by the falsifications. Throwing myself into the building of a new Poland, I had begun to compromise with the lies. I took part in all classes and exercises, and often worked late into the night to prepare the briefings I made to my company each morning. I grew thin, weak, and soon fell ill.

In June, suffering from an infection in my leg, I was admitted to the infirmary. There were several cadets there, with a variety of complaints. They were all glad to see a new face.

"Don't be afraid," said one. "There's been no serious or fatal illness here so far, with one exception."

They asked me what was wrong with me and began betting "how many he'll get." I did not understand. "You'll find out," they said good-naturedly, and continued to argue.

"For a leg," said the boy to my right, "the least you can get is twelve, because gangrene can spread."

"You don't know what you're talking about," said the one to my left. "There was a guy here with a finger that was pitch-black and he got only six."

"How can you compare a leg with a finger?" replied the one on my right. "If a finger's six, a leg's got to be twelve, minimum."

"I'm having problems with one lung, and it could be serious," said another, "and I got only four."

"Only four!" spouted a boy by the window. "I have headaches—they said I had a stroke—and I got only two."

It made no sense to me. The doctor came late in the day, examined my leg, and scribbled on the chart at the foot of my bed. No sooner had he gone out the door than everyone ran to my chart and started shouting, "He got twelve! He got twelve!" Then the boy to my right boasted, "I told you so. I'm an expert in these things. A leg is *not* the same as a finger, not even the *blackest* finger."

Then they explained it to me. "You see, they only prescribe one kind of medicine for us here, little red powerhouses. If you gave a horse one too many, he'd keel over and die. Wait and see. The orderly'll come any minute and bring you four for the night. But he won't just hand them to you. You have to swallow them while he watches. . . ."

"When you take them," another said, "your head will rock like a boat and your piss will turn blood red."

"We all piss red," trumpeted the boy across from me. "I get four pills, but I piss just as red as they do.

"They say that if you piss red, the pills are working," intoned a connoisseur. "There was a guy here who couldn't piss red—he died. The first night is the worst, because you don't know what your piss will look like in the morning."

The next morning I entered the bathroom with some trepidation and breathed a sigh of relief when I saw that what I was producing was red. I left the infirmary, "fully restored," two weeks later.

A new and important event had occurred while I was there. Great Britain and the United States recognized our Government of National Unity, which had been formed in Moscow. I was exultant. It meant that the Allies were offering their support for a program for social justice in Poland. Only years later did I understand the true meaning of Yalta and of that recognition. Stalin had achieved his goal. The truth was such:

When Germany had invaded the Soviet Union in June 1941 and Stalin had allied himself with the Western democracies, Moscow established diplomatic relations with the Polish government-in-exile in London. But after the German defeat at Stalingrad in January 1943, Stalin began preparing in earnest for the conquest of Central Europe. Poland was a key country. A master plan was worked out by Stalin and Lavrenti Beria, the chief of the NKVD. To convince the West of his good intentions, Stalin first dissolved the Comintern. Then Moscow ruptured all relations with the Polish government-in-exile, in order to allow itself a free hand in that country. The NKVD selected a group of prewar Polish Communists to become leaders in the newly established Union of Polish Patriots (ZPP) and in the hastily mobilized Polish military units. Among these leaders were Wanda Wasilewska, Edward Ochab, Aleksander Zawadzki, Jakub Berman, Hilary Minc, Stefan Jedrychowski, Piotr Jaroszewicz, and Marian Naszkowski. All of them, with the exception of Wasilewska, became top leaders of People's Poland. And most I would come to know personally.

The NKVD was also busily preparing the ground in Poland. In Warsaw, a Soviet agent of long standing, Boleslaw Bierut, and his associate Zenon Kliszko formed the National Homeland Council (KRN), an underground "parliament," which was to lend credibility to the Soviet-sponsored Polish authorities after the Red Army's entry into Polish territory.

In July 1944, when the first piece of Polish land was "liberated," the KRN established the Polish Committee of National Liberation (PKWN), the first governing body. It, too, consisted of Polish agents prepared by the ZPP. When, a few days later, the uprising against the Germans started in Warsaw, the Red Army stood by as the city was destroyed and the Home Army was eliminated.

At the end of 1944, the KRN made the Committee of National Liberation into the Provisional Government of the Polish Republic (RTRP). When Churchill, Roosevelt, and Stalin conferred at Yalta in February 1945, Stalin held two trump cards: the Red Army was occupying Poland, and Moscow's "Polish" government was already functioning in the ruins of Warsaw. At Yalta, the Big Three essentially handed Poland over to Stalin, who promised to create a coalition government and carry out democratic elections. A few weeks later sixteen Polish underground leaders were invited for talks with Soviet Marshal Georgi Zhukov, but when they appeared for the meeting, they were abducted to Lubyanka Prison in Moscow, where they were tortured for three months. Among them was the commander in chief of the Home Army, General Leopold Okulicki.

In June, Poland's Provisional Government of National Unity was formed in Moscow, led by the figurehead premier Edward Osobka-Morawski and two vice premiers, Wladyslaw Gomulka and Stanislaw Mikolajczyk, the former premier of the Polish government in London. Bierut became president. On July 5, 1945 the West recognized this government. At about that time, a show trial was held in Moscow for the sixteen underground Poles. Sentences were passed. General Okulicki was murdered the following year in a Soviet prison. The West was silent.

When I returned from the infirmary, the lecturers were jubilant. Our diplomats were getting ready to depart for London and Washington, they said. They kept repeating that the Polish London-based government was, since Mikolajczyk's departure, considered by the Western powers to be a liability. They heaped abuse, calling it "a bankrupt clique," "the dwarfs of reaction," "the forces of darkness," and claiming that all these "scheming" reactionaries were connected by the "class interests of the bloodsuckers" and by the "poisonous seeds of anti-Semitism." They spoke with particular venom of General Wladyslaw Anders, Polish leader at Monte Cassino, and the leaders of the Home Army and the Warsaw uprising.

They accused General Tadeusz Bor-Komorowski of having the blood of hundreds of thousands on his hands.

The Polish people had now "thrown them overboard," cried one lecturer in a fury, and now the Western world had broken all relations with them and they were "on the garbage heap of history." The same fate was in store for all representatives and agents of the London clique here in Poland who had been "fairly tried in Moscow as rebels against the nation."

I felt extreme confusion as I listened to all this. I told myself that, after all, the history of revolutionary movements showed that there was no standing on ceremony in the class struggle; it was either us or them, either the Communists or the counterrevolutionaries. But the trials of Poles in Moscow, the reviling of Poles who had fought against the Nazis on every front, the creation of an atmosphere of hostility and mockery—all that gave me no peace, and, staying up late to prepare my briefing, I would experience moments of deep perplexity.

When I gave my briefings to the company, I spoke my mind as I thought a Communist ought to, the way my father and Antonina would have spoken, always with dignity, without mockery and derision, keeping the good of the cause constantly in mind. I often referred to the history of Poland and to the experiences of other revolutionary movements—the French Revolution, the Paris Commune, the October Revolution of 1917—presenting the importance of the changes occurring in Poland against that background.

These briefings were given before five in the morning, with the trainees sitting on their plank beds or on the floor, their backs against the walls. The room was quiet. I could see their heads turn toward me as I passed them, for I never stood, but always paced through the room. Sometimes I would see someone's eyes closing, and I would stop and wait silently until the boy beside him poked him awake. I knew they were not getting much more sleep than I was.

Why was I so fond of these meetings? For me, those boys were the true sons of Polish soil. There was not one lazy, reluctant malingerer among them; they all did the best they could and seemed ready to undertake all and any problems. And it was clear to me that all of them hated the Germans as passionately as I did.

Yet I felt that something stood between us. I reflected on this until I realized that it was the difference in our memories of prewar

Poland. For the majority, their memories were of the villages and little towns they came from, where everything was small and daily life was difficult. My memories were primarily of a variety of splendid people, the beauty of the land, the soaring Tatras, and the smell of iodine by the blue Baltic Sea—all things outside their experience. And those memories were also bound up with the monuments to Poland's long history, the Borderlands, and my own ancestors, and those, too, they neither knew nor could fathom. At times, giving in to my imagination, I would speak to them about this and watch their eyes glaze over, proof that they did not understand a word of what I was saying.

There was one other important difference between us. For them, primarily the sons of peasants of the Kielce area, the Soviet Union was a fresh chapter that promised only good—liberation from the Germans. For me, that chapter had already been written in a very different way. Although I kept telling myself that the past was over and done with, that there must be reasons and explanations, I could not blot out that chapter, nor did I wish to.

One scorching July day, just as we returned from drill, the duty officer told me that someone was waiting for me in the guardroom by the gate. Weary and dirty, I dragged myself over and saw my wife, Wanda, there. My appearance must have shocked her: my denim uniform—faded, sweat-stained, too short—my red puttees, my enormous and shapeless boots. As we ran to each other's arms, joy and sorrow both were in her eyes.

"You look awful," she said. "Did you really have to do this?"

I could only gaze at her. She seemed more beautiful to me than ever, though she had grown thinner; her prominent cheekbones and slanting green eyes were now more sharply defined.

"I came in a truck from the silk factory. And I'll go back the same way. I've arranged everything," she said all in one breath. "If they'll give you leave, we can stay with your aunt Kossakowska. She'll give us a room; she's a very dear woman, your aunt."

I succeeded in arranging leave, thanks to Malko. An hour later I was on my way to see my wife, clean and more or less freshened up. We walked through the streets, stopping for a moment, and Wanda pressed herself to me. The feeling of her breasts filled me with desire. Our kisses were so long, so passionate, that people turned to stare.

"This will be our honeymoon," she whispered. "We didn't have one and we probably never will. Let this be it."

As we walked, she told me about her trip from Milanowek.

"I was very afraid," she began. "Soviet soldiers have been raping women. My father didn't want me to travel, but I insisted. He finally agreed, but only because my friend who works in the silk factory helped me out. The factory sends a truckful of silk to Lodz every week or so. She persuaded them to hide me in the truck."

I was growing more alarmed as she spoke.

"At first I rode with them in the front, but they stopped along the way and told me to get in the back, where they had made a little hiding place for me among the bales. They stacked the bales around me, and we were off again. You can imagine how scared I was when the truck stopped later and I heard voices—Russian voices. I could understand "What've you got in there? Where're you from? No girls in there? Let's have a look." And then I heard them pawing through the bales. My heart nearly stopped. The drivers gave them some vodka. Later they told me they always keep a little on hand for the Rooskies. And that was the end of that. I was drenched with my own sweat. I didn't get out until the truck drove up to your aunt's house. People stopped and stared to see a dirty slant-eyed girl coming out from under those bales of beautiful silk."

She cast me a playful glance, but I was furious that she had exposed herself to such danger.

At my aunt's house, she told me the rest of her news. She had won first place in her singing class at the conservatory. So she would be able to finish her musical studies quickly. A radio station rising out of the ruins of Warsaw had offered her a job.

"As you know, all my life I've dreamed about becoming a singer," she said. "Now my teacher, Julia Mechowna, says I will. . . . She knows; she sang at La Scala. Anyway, everything would be fine if it hadn't been for May Day."

"What do you mean?"

"Some people from your committee told me," she said gravely, "that since you're in the army, I should march in the May Day parade. So I did. There were only a few of us, maybe twenty people in all of Milanowek. We walked behind the red banner, and the sidewalks were packed with people hissing us. Since then I've been a pariah." She was holding back tears.

"Has anyone done you any harm?" I asked, disturbed.

"No. It's worse than that. Everywhere I go, literally everywhere, people turn away from me. Even in church, the seat beside me is always empty. What did I do that was so wrong? I wanted to do the right thing for you. But thanks to dear Mechowna, who, as you know, treats me like a daughter, I haven't had any trouble at the conservatory, even though people have told her that the "red" with the "Bolshevik" husband should be thrown out. Professor Boleslaw Woytowicz stood up for me, too, but other people who used to be nice to me now keep giving me nasty looks. . . ." Her little face looked up at me sadly. Grieved, I could not speak.

"My brother's turned away from me," she continued. "Czeslaw told our parents he didn't want anything to do with me, because I had disgraced the family. And so my mother, who does everything to avoid hurting her dear little son's feelings, shouted and yelled at my father for allowing me to marry you and ruin my life. But Father says you're an honest person. He says a man with a father like yours could have made himself a career in Communism right off. You didn't have to be a soldier. . . .

"And Tadeusz is so furious at you now that just before I left he said that you're so crazy you'd probably be happy if the Russians raped me, because then you'd have a real Russian wife. Your mother can't bear to listen to such talk, and the two of them are always at odds now. The atmosphere in Villa Rose is so tense they're both saying they'll have to separate. And I'm right in the middle," she said, her tears flowing freely now.

We sat side by side in silence. I took my wife in my arms, and when we turned out the lights the whole world slipped into the darkness leaving only the two of us.

Our honeymoon came to an end the next morning. Wanda returned to Milanowek by train in the care of some Polish soldiers whose help I had enlisted at the station. And I went back to the barracks, vowing that I would make something of our life and my plans.

I was summoned by the Political Section at the beginning of August. The other deputy company commanders, as well as some civilians, were already there when I arrived.

"Things are not going well in the city," Malko began. "Our comrades on the Municipal Committee tell us that strikes might break out at any moment in the Geyer and Scheibler textile factories, and they have asked us for help. They say they can't deal with the women factory workers; they're too hysterical. The women refuse to obey orders; they just keep complaining that they have nothing to feed their families. Comrade Secretary," said Malko, turning to one of the civilians at the table, "give us a sense of the situation."

"We're at our wit's end," began the secretary. "We thought the wave of hysteria would pass, and we'd be able to calm the staff down. It wasn't the first time this has happened. A few women, the most vocal ones . . . well, our office managed to shuffle them out of there, but that didn't help. All it did was promote more hysteria, because—dammit, no one knows how—but the word spread that this had been the work of Security. That was the last straw. We keep telling them that if they don't work, there won't be anything to eat, and they keep insisting that they're starving and won't go on working under those conditions. Of course we're not giving them any food. . . . Today the leader of the group asked to talk with the factory manager. But then they yelled at him and kicked him out, as they did with our propaganda man. We thought perhaps if some of our soldiers came and talked with them . . . Uniforms always seem to have an effect on women. . . ."

"That's the situation, comrades," said Malko. "We think we should lend them a hand. It's for the cause, after all. We should send our noncoms, our political deputy company commanders, right from drill, so the women can see that these are real soldiers. That ought to create a bond between them. I propose that Spasowski be the first."

"Speak to them simply . . . from the heart," interjected the secretary. "The women are edgy; let one interrupt and start shouting or crying, and they'll all join in. It's something awful, I tell you. Men are easier to work with."

I did not have to wait long for this assignment. We had just returned from the field the next day when a runner arrived yelling, "Spasowski to the Political Section, on the double!" My uniform was covered with dust, my boots with mud, and my hands were smeared with the oil I had been using to clean the barrel and bolt of my rifle. We had been on a forced march again that day, and I was dead tired.

The civilians from the committee were waiting in the office.

"Things are jumping at the factory again today," said one of them. "And it looks like it'll get worse. Delegates from other factories are talking with them now. We dragged them out of there in a hurry, but who knows what'll happen. You'd better be ready."

Moments later I was on my way down a street packed with factories. What could I say? I asked myself.

"There's gonna be an awful lot of them," said the civilian, interrupting my thought. "They'll pack the spinning room."

We pulled up in front of a large iron gate hung with red banners. The gatekeepers let us pass, and the car bumped over the cobblestones of the courtyard. We entered the factory by a side door. Through a half-open door inside I caught a fleeting glimpse of a dense crowd of people and heard shouts but could not make out the words.

"Wait here," said the civilian. "Remember, the heart . . . that's all they understand. No reading from a paper. As soon as they see paper, they'll start shouting that it's all propaganda. They drove the last one out."

I tried to collect my thoughts. I'll simply tell them about myself, I decided. I would tell them that I had come close to dying, that my life had turned into a hell, that I was from Warsaw. That I had volunteered for the army because I wanted to settle accounts with the Germans, that I was a soldier and would defend the government of the working people. Many of them had sons like me, and I knew mothers as worn-out from work as they. But our common effort would build a new, socialist Poland. I had come straight from drill, I'd say, and I hoped they would return to work tomorrow, just as I intended to go back to the field.

People kept entering and leaving the room, and the roar of the crowd poured through the door. I heard what must have been someone delivering a speech, followed by another roar. A man finally shouted, "The delegations have finished, but the crowd is still there. Where's that soldier? Let's send him out there now. . . ."

A moment later I was in the large factory hall, facing a dense crowd of standing women, a sea of heads.

"Let us through, let us through!" shouted the man. "A soldier wants to speak to you. Let us pass!"

The women's faces were weary and gaunt; some were older and wrinkled, others young, but all were haggard, all watching, anticipating. When I walked up to the small metal platform, the light was so blindingly bright that I could see only the faces of those nearest to me; the vast mass of people was sunk in darkness. I stepped to the microphone. Nothing to lose now, I thought, and as I gazed straight ahead, I felt my anxiety slip away.

"Women workers of the Geyer textile factory!" I began sonorously, every word echoing and reverberating. "I, a Polish soldier, am appealing to you, the workers of the Lodz textile industry . . ." And then I said just what I felt. The reverberations created the impression of endless space in front of me. I could feel thousands of eyes staring at my crumpled denim uniform, my tall, thin body, me. What would my father have said had he seen me thundering before that crowd of workers like some sort of tribune?

I spoke for a long time, perhaps too long, improvising on the outline I had sketched out in my mind earlier. At one point I told them that surely they, too, had sons like me, and I paused. A voice shouted, "My son has tuberculosis, and he's hungry all the time." Then an uproar broke out, and it seemed to me that all the women were shouting. The pandemonium went on for some time before I could speak again. I appealed to them to resume work, and concluded by saying that socialist Poland was calling on everyone to work and defend what the workers had struggled for. There was scattered applause.

The next day I was again summoned to the Political Section.

"It appears that your speech had a calming influence," said Malko. "The Municipal Committee sends you its thanks. Except . . . you shouldn't have talked about socialism. We know what you meant and, of course, we think as you do, but—and this is just between us—it shouldn't be talked about. People aren't ready for it yet; and it irritates a lot of people abroad. It has to be like a school assembly: talk about patriotism, about democracy. A lot about democracy. The word 'communism,' which, fortunately, you didn't use, should never be mentioned at all, nor the Party. You know that. Instead, more general concepts should be employed, like those of the Polish left, which has rich democratic traditions. Democratic, that's the point."

Malko had been satisfied with my speech and was now offering me friendly instruction.

"Aside from that, it was very good," he concluded. "You spoke directly, from the heart, and that's the right way."

I spoke in one more factory after that, and then devoted myself entirely to the coming examinations. The end of the war and the establishment of People's Poland had had no effect on our course of studies; on the contrary, it seemed to me that our instruction had been accelerated, as if to cram as much material into our heads as possible, in the shortest time. We had to be able to dismantle and reassemble every kind of weapon used on the firing range, and drills were constantly taking place in the companies: a blanket on the floor would be heaped with a mixture of parts from a pistol, a rifle, a submachine gun, an antitank rifle, a mortar. We had to pick out the parts of one weapon and assemble the whole thing in less than five minutes. My grades were especially good, perhaps the best.

The graduation of Captain Onufreev's battalion took place on September 15, 1945. The barracks courtyard was decorated with white-and-red flags and the entire battalion, wearing newly issued officers' uniforms, stood waiting to take the oath. The ceremonies were led by General Marian Spychalski, deputy commander of the People's Army.

One of the first to stand before him, I called out, "Cadet Romuald Spasowski," and knelt on one knee.

Then the general said in a flat, weary voice, "I promote you to officer in the Polish People's army," and he touched my shoulder with his saber.

I rose, stood at attention, and cried out, "For the glory of the fatherland!"

He walked along the ranks and repeated the same ceremony after each name was called. Then he stood before all of us and droned away. "Officers: This course is now graduating the last of the officers who began their studies during the war, when we had to work as rapidly and intensively as possible to create political and ideological cadres for the country. You must serve democracy. . . . You are people who know how. Thanks to it, to democracy and democratic policy, a great victory has been achieved. . . ."

Was he going to be using the word "democracy" everywhere, I wondered. He went on to say that it was thanks to democracy that the Western Territories and the Baltic had been returned to Poland, that the reborn Polish army was a mighty pillar of Polish democracy, that we were building the road to lasting peace, that it would be necessary to fight for democracy just as in wartime, that even today we had to sacrifice our lives.

"You must be on your guard," the general shouted, his voice raised now, "so that no external enemy, no part of that international fascism forever laying in wait, dares threaten the peace, and no internal enemy, no reactionaries, will undermine what we have accomplished." He repeated his warnings about international fascism and domestic reactionaries, hammering the point that every true democrat must honor the Polish officer.

Why the masquerade, I wondered. Democracy again and again, but not a word about socialism or communism. I had never heard anything about democracy from the lips of any Communist before; they always said straight out that it was the dictatorship of the proletariat that was needed: a conscious, intelligent, just dictatorship, imposed by the best of the best. Not these foggy ideas of democracy. What was his point? He had said twice that international fascism would not dare threaten the peace. What fascism was that? Nazism had fallen; Hitler was dead. Italian fascism had collapsed, the Italians having strung up Mussolini by his feet. So who did he have in mind? Franco? But Franco was not a force that could threaten the powers that had defeated fascism. Where, then, was that "international fascism" exactly?

That evening I walked over to my fellow new officer Henryk Zygier, my Red Army veteran friend who, I had noticed, had a nose for what was in the wind.

"Tell me, did you understand everything Spychalski said?"

He looked at me questioningly. "What do you mean?"

"All that democracy, democracy . . ."

He smiled, "Simple," he answered. "I know that word from 1944. They were using it all the time then, too, and changing it around every which way." He nodded his head, indicating we should sit.

"This is better; we're closer, and I can whisper. I know who you are and I know I can talk to you. You're honest," he said with a friendly smile. "You won't go running to report me. You see, in their vocabulary, democracy and dictatorship mean the same thing. And they both begin with D. It's more convenient to use the term 'democracy' right now because our 'democratic' allies are giving us a lot—vehicles, food, *good* food, everything. But you have to make the distinction and say that here, which means in the Soviet Union and Poland, we have a people's democracy. A 'people's democracy' speaks for itself. But over there in the West they have a 'decadent democracy,' the sort that can breed fascism. You know the expression a 'poisoned seed'? They don't use it here much, but in the Red Army that's what they call the West, a poisoned seed."

He glanced over at me and smiled amiably through squinting eyes. "You are very good at your job, Second Lieutenant Spasowski, and you're an idealist. You lack only one thing: you didn't spend enough time with them over there. I don't mean the short while you were there in 1939, but a *long* time, living there. It's a school of dialectics no philosopher ever dreamed of, brother."

"And what did you take that threat of 'international fascism' to mean? Was he thinking of Franco's Spain?" I asked.

Zygier interrupted me impatiently. "Franco? You've missed the point again. Didn't I tell you? Decadent democracy can breed fascism, Nazism, Mussolini, whatever you like, any devil. He was talking about decadent democracy. That means the decadent imperialist powers can breed anything. . . . But no one says that now, at the present stage. You see, that's what dialectics means; every stage has its own vocabulary and themes, and woe to him who doesn't understand that. For me, it's clear as day. Watch out; two times two may be four for you, but for them, at this stage, it's five. . . . Remember this conversation, Second Lieutenant, and don't you dare say a word of it to anyone."

He put on his cap, stood up straight, and saluted me. I did the same. We said our good-byes and I never saw him again.

The new officers received assignments to various military units, chiefly as deputy battalion or regiment commanders. I was assigned to the armed forces' political headquarters in Warsaw, GZP for short, and the next day traveled by train to the capital. I found myself on my way back to Warsaw wearing a new uniform made of good material, leather straps across my chest, and a holster containing my heavy Tetetka pistol. The other passengers regarded me with a certain reserve but without animosity, and I felt I was an object of some interest.

Warsaw had changed. I remembered it as snow-covered ruins, a wilderness devoid of people. Bricks and rubble still jutted out, but now the centers of the streets were clear, and people were walking in all directions. They were living wherever they could find shelter, in the filthiest, most unexpected places: in undamaged parts of buildings, even on the nearly inaccessible upper floors; in little huts attached to protruding walls; in gateways whose arches had not collapsed; in cellars that could be reached only through tunnels in the rubble. It was even possible to find food there amid the ruins—flat cakes cooked on a real campfire, homemade soup cooked on bricks. "Restaurants" were springing up, too, primitive sheds that, under the circumstances, seemed oases of comfort.

The ruins were crawling with survivors searching for their loved ones. It reminded me of 1939, except that now the little pieces of paper were everywhere—on bits of wall, the remains of gateways, broken streetlights, bricks, but always near former homes, though they were recognizable no longer.

I went straight to the political headquarters, which was located at the corner of Krakowskie Przedmiescie and Krolewska in a large arcaded building whose walls had been cracked by shells but which had miraculously escaped fire and explosion. I was directed to a Colonel Grosfeld, who received me coolly and officially. He was slightly stoop shouldered and nearly bald, with a high, sloping brow; his small piercing eyes scrutinized me through old-fashioned pince-nez on his aquiline nose. After a brief conversation he sent me to the Propaganda Department, headed by Major Korta, who said that he was unable to assure me a separate room for me and my wife; he had only a room to be shared with another officer. It was decided that I could live in Milanowek and commute to Warsaw.

My heart pounding. I went at once to Milanowek, and from the train station there, I walked quickly, nearly running. Wanda, who was living with her parents, could not believe I had returned so soon and was as delighted as a child by the figure I cut in my new uniform.

She had passed her *matura,* and a career in music was now open to her. We talked excitedly, each of us wanting to share everything immediately. Life seemed to smile upon us and the sight of the other gave us new strength.

"Your mother," she reported, "is well. She looks better now. All the people she was harboring have left, but your grandmother from Lityn and her whole family have come back from Russia. It must have taken a miracle. They've been through terrible things. Krzys, your nephew, runs around the garden all the time nibbling the bark off the birch trees, and little Basia is eating everything in sight; that's what they learned in the Siberian taiga, that's how they ate. Tadeusz's mother and sister have also come back; the Germans deported them to Ravensbrück right after the uprising. . . ."

At Villa Rose, my mother burst into tears when she saw me, then spent a good while scrutinizing my uniform, unable to accept me as a soldier.

Tadeusz made no effort to conceal his enmity. "Yes, yes," he repeated, "they've made a commissar of you. We should have expected that you'd become a Bolshevik commissar in the end. . . . But it's been nothing but hardship here, terrible hardship." He showed me his toil-worn hands.

"What can I say?" he said, looking at me coldly, as if I were an alien object. "They're still arresting people from the Home Army, deporting them. Poles are dying, even here in Milanowek. . . . As if there hadn't already been slaughter enough during the German occupation. Even the families of your old colleagues are now behind bars."

I took a good look at Tadeusz. He was a changed man; he looked spent and embittered. Very little remained of the prewar Tadeusz who had helped me build my telescope, the jolly, good-natured young scientist who had aspired to become a professor, who always had a smile on his face when he returned from church on Sundays, humming to himself, at peace. He doesn't understand anything, I thought; he has no sense of world currents, of the historical meaning of a People's Poland.

Uncle Stefan suddenly appeared. The deportation to Siberia had left him unrecognizable; he had aged, and was nearly bald and very thin. He came in with his wife, Agusia, who was even thinner, her eyes sunken and lifeless. We embraced, and they gazed at me with mouths open, unable to reconcile me with the nineteen-year-old who had once traveled to Lityn on foot. "You're in the army?" he asked, looking me over. "Maybe you've gotten what you wanted. . . . As for us, we've been through a lot. Too much to tell."

I urged him to recount their experiences, but he did not want to speak of them. "I can't do it. It has cost me too much already. I can't go through it again. Maybe Agusia will tell you. Her nerves are stronger than mine."

"It was a nightmare," began Agusia, "and I can't believe that I'm here with you now. Romek, you left Lityn on the same day we heard that the Bolsheviks had invaded Poland. We lived in a state of anticipation. Zygmus predicted the worst and began preparing to flee, but he didn't know where to run. A few days passed in peace, maybe a week. Then suddenly the political commissars of the Red Army arrived. They called a public meeting. They herded everybody on the estate together and announced that the 'landowner,' meaning Stefan, would be tried.

"People were terrified," interjected Stefan, "old women wailed, children clung to their mothers. . . . They tied my hands behind me and led me out like a criminal to face that crowd. At a table off to one side sat the commissar in charge; he was all in leather. Next to him were a couple of other Red Army men, scribbling away. . . ."

"We all stood up for Stefan," continued Agusia. "I had two-month-old Basia in my arms, and beside me Krzys, who was five then, and my mother, already seventy. It was a terrible sight, I tell you. The commissar wore a peaked cap, which he never took off. He screeched at Stefan in Ukrainian, calling him names, saying that he was the hated exploiter, that he had personally tyrannized the peasants, that he had beaten and abused them, and stolen bread from the mouths of children. He said that everybody in the district knew about it, even in the faraway Soviet Ukraine. 'Look at this pig, this bloodsucker!' he shouted. 'He won't escape the punishment that you, the people, are going to mete out to him now. He called on the crowd to speak their piece and punish Stefan. He goaded them on, but no one responded. He told them not to be afraid, saying that the day of the Polish lords was over. 'Soviet power is protecting you now,' he shouted. 'You must come forward with whatever wrongs have been done to you.' Still no one said a word.

"There was a moment," she said, "as I watched the farce, that I almost broke out laughing hysterically, because those peasants just stood there, silent, and the commissar was at a loss. But he kept trying to egg them on, screaming that the people's justice must be done, that monsters like Stefan had to be excoriated, that such crimes were punishable by death. . . . But the crowd remained as silent as stones, and finally the commissar sat down.

"We stood there counting the minutes we had left to live," continued Agusia. "Basia was whimpering, and I was wondering how they would murder us. Suddenly someone in the crowd began to speak. We froze. The commissar shot to his feet and yelled for the person to speak louder so that everyone could hear. I recognized him—it was one of the peasants from Lityn, a Ukrainian, who, people said, was a nationalist. He had his cap in his hand and fingered it as he raised his voice. 'Why put *him* on trial? He never did us any harm!' No sooner had he said that than there was an uproar. A lot of people spoke up, a lot of the women. They said Stefan wasn't a bad man, that things hadn't been bad in Lityn, that he had never done any harm. The commissar tried to shout them down. His face was red with fury. He bellowed that they were defending a 'landowner,' a known exploiter and abuser of peasants; that if they insisted on carrying on like that, Soviet power would have to mete out justice itself. And then he screamed that the people's court was over."

Agusia shook her head. "We just stood there, stunned and touched. I could see the tears in Stefan's eyes. The peasants shuffled off with their heads lowered, the women's covered with their kerchiefs.

"They took Stefan away at once and loaded him on a truck. His hands were tied, and he couldn't get up himself. Red Army soldiers stood over him with those long bayonets of theirs. Then they drove away. . . . Later I learned that they had been holding him in prison in Turzysk and then had taken him to Kowel."

I noticed nervous tics tugging Agusia's gaunt face. "They deported you all together?" I asked.

"I was in prison while they prepared their case against me and gathered 'witnesses,'" said Uncle Stefan. "A show trial, because Lityn was a large estate, so they had singled it out. But a couple of weeks later a group of people from Lityn arrived in Kowel and submitted a petition on behalf of the peasants who were demanding my release. That came as a surprise to the Soviets, and my case was postponed. Agusia, Mama, and the children were in the gamekeeper's lodge, living under arrest, but the peasants of Lityn wouldn't let them go under. They brought them food from the farmhands' quarters. They themselves weren't free to leave the estate."

Agusia carried the story on. "The Red Army apparently created a village committee in our house, supposedly to manage the estate, and they promised the peasants that everyone would have plenty of everything. They hung red banners and plastered the walls with posters. But the committee still didn't know what it was supposed to do. The peasants brought in tables and planks and sat on them because the soldiers had taken away all the furniture right at the beginning. When they saw what was going on, the people from the village and the farmhands started taking whatever they could back to their own homes. And so the cows disappeared from the barn and only a few pigs were left in the pigpen. They made off with all the equipment and farm machinery and left only a tractor so damaged that it was useless. There weren't any more horses because the Red Army took them right at the start, even before they absconded with the furniture. To make a long story short, the estate was gone; all that remained were the walls."

"What about the car?" I asked, remembering my uncle's prized automobile.

"The Daimler was confiscated at the beginning of the war." He smiled wanly. "How I cared for that car! There wasn't a single scratch on it. One day the Polish military police came and ordered me to hand it over to them. They needed it, they said, to help motorize the army. As they were leaving, they almost knocked over the fence, because the driver didn't know how to shift and had put the car in reverse. When he slammed on the brakes, his rifle poked a hole through the canvas top. They drove away somehow. That was the last I saw of it."

"It was already cold and had started to snow," continued Agusia, "when, one day—it must have been in December—they brought Stefan by truck to the estate, but they didn't allow him to get out. His hands were tied. Russian soldiers came into the gamekeeper's cottage and shouted for everyone to prepare to travel at once, to gather up their warm winter things. We all ran from one corner to another grabbing and packing whatever was closest to hand, while they stomped about the house hurrying us. Then they said that we had enough and led us out to the courtyard. Suddenly Mama ran back into the house as if she had forgotten something, but a moment later the soldiers brought her back out and put her in the truck first. She had something wrapped up in her shawl. They put me, Basia, and Krzys in, tossed in our things, and took us straight to the train station in Kowel. There was a freight train waiting there, guarded by Red Army soldiers. It was made up of cattle cars, those brick-colored cars with bars on the windows. They crammed us into a crowded car, in which people were sitting packed together on the floor. Others stood. They were all dirty and miserable, many straight from prison, as Stefan had been. The soldiers closed and bolted the doors, and the train pulled away.

"We rode and rode. Conditions were too horrible to describe, but you can imagine for yourself. We went on for weeks in that car. Once a day they would open the doors and throw in food and water. Russian peasants standing at stations so small they didn't even have signs would sometimes pass us what little they had. But the Bolsheviks would open fire on them, as if they were dogs.

"A few people died there in the car. Others passed out or froze to death; the little stove couldn't heat the entire car in weather like that. It was a miracle of God that we came out of it alive. We had no idea where we were being taken.

"Finally, one day they slid open the door and ordered us out. No station, nothing. Just the tracks and the snow and the taiga . . ."

She broke off.

"You've never seen the taiga, Romek. It stretches forever. We lived in sheds we built ourselves, from the trees. We didn't know where we were. Later we learned that the nearest settlement was Yoshkar Ola, a town with a Tatar name. But it was a world away.

"You're surprised that Krzys and Basia eat birch bark? If it hadn't been for that bark . . . I ate it myself when there was nothing else. Everyone did. . . ."

Agusia trailed off, and I went into Grandmother's room. Against the pillow, her face was gray and wrinkled now; she looked as she had in 1939 but smaller and dried out. She was awake, and her eyes sparkled at the sight of me and a faint smile crossed her face. I kissed her hand and forehead. She looked at me in silence, too weak to speak, and then a single word came from her lips: "Romek."

Some days later, Wanda and I visited my grandmother again. She was sitting in an armchair. "Do you remember," she started in weakly, "when you were in Lityn, that I showed you everything I kept in my trunk?" She paused and looked at me, her face wan but her eyes alive. "Everything's gone. Into the hands of people who haven't any idea what those things mean . . .

"When the Bolsheviks dragged us out of the gamekeeper's cottage, I tore away and ran back in. I knew I had no time, that they'd grab me and throw me back into the truck, so I snatched the first thing I came across. You remember the clock that used to sit on the mantelpiece, that old gold clock? I had had it since childhood. I snatched it and wrapped it up in my shawl before they came to drag me back out."

"Bring me that little package from the windowsill." She undid it and drew out a small bag.

"Open it up," she said, "but carefully, on the table, so that nothing goes astray."

I poured the parts of the old clock onto the table—the hands, the pendulum, the screws, the small gilded columns, the feet from its base, the porcelain dial. I squinted at the dial and read the inscription: A. Chopin. Paris.

"My last keepsake, Romek. The last of the memories . . . Everything else is lost and gone. I leave this to you."

CHAPTER XI

Our first home together was a small room in a house on the outskirts of Milanowek. The furniture consisted of a small table, two chairs, an iron bed, and a cupboard, half of which had been cleared for our use. We had everything we needed and were happy.

I rose each day at five o'clock and returned late in the evening. I spent my days at a desk drafting short propaganda pieces, mostly concerned with the historical significance of our western border and the economic value of the territories that had been incorporated into Poland. There was never a request for a propaganda piece on the areas that Poland had lost in the east—the Borderlands, Volhynia, Wilno, and Lwow. Any mention of them was always crossed out.

My work at the political headquarters afforded me no satisfaction. I was immersed in propaganda, and my superiors had no desire for anything else. I had the constant feeling that the true picture of what had occurred after the war was being concealed, the true aims passed over in silence.

Our department consisted of two small rooms. Major Korta, a blond, chubby-cheeked man of around fifty, of whom it was said that he had left the priesthood to marry, sat with the junior editors, at a desk facing the door. A young captain with dark, bushy hair and thick glasses, sat across from me, and beside him Leopold Lewin; a lieutenant poet with a lively disposition. The next room was a studio, through whose open door I could always see Witold Kalicki, a young artist and painter, bent over his drafting table, and his colleague Lieutenant Bojko.

Colonel Grosfeld, who had assigned me to propaganda, dropped by rarely and was apparently writing a great deal himself for his chief, General Swietlik. I saw the general only a few times.

One day was like the next. We were forever receiving new orders for articles and forever complaining of the lack of material, statistics, encyclopedias. Sometimes the monotony would be broken by the hot-tempered Lewin, who would come running into the room shouting at the top of his voice, "He can kiss my ass!"

And to our inquiring looks, he would respond, "Grosfeld! He can kiss my ass! I'm not gong to write anything more here."

Then Bojko's head would appear in the doorway. His frightened eyes would only make Lewin more excited. "Let him go ahead and throw me out! I'll gladly go back to civilian life. I've had it up to here!"

On the train back to Milanowek I often felt unfriendly glances, looks of outright hostility, especially from young men. I learned soon enough what those glances meant. Late one evening when I got off the train, a fellow walked up to me on the platform and blocked my way, saying, "So! Didn't you like the way I was looking at you?"

I made no response and stepped to one side, but he drew nearer and thrust his nose practically into my face.

"Get out of my way, Russian stooge!" he shouted.

"No, *you* get out!" I volleyed back, unfastening my holster.

A little crowd had gathered around us, and I heard someone murmur, "Big shot, he's got a gun." I stood under a street lamp with my hand on my opened holster staring straight into the eyes of that young man, a thin, pale blond wearing a shoddy jacket.

He must have seen in my eyes that I was not joking, for he swore, turned on his heel, and strode off. The crowd dispersed, grumbling.

I returned home agitated. "Why did you reach for your pistol?" Wanda said, disturbed and anxious. "That could have made him even angrier!"

"What was I supposed to do? Wrestle him there on the platform? Actually, I did the right thing—it scared him off."

"I'm worried about you," she said. "I don't know who that was—maybe just some street kid. Let's hope so. But he might have been Home Army. I know them, Romek. Oh, yes, I know those boys." Tears welled in Wanda's eyes. "All they have left is their honor;

they would keep their oath to God and the fatherland even if it meant dying." Wanda looked at me despairingly.

"They can't shoot the entire nation, can they?" she went on. "Uncle Olek—you remember my sweet uncle with the pince-nez? They shot him, Romek; the Bolsheviks murdered him at Katyn." She was blubbering now, and I did not try to stop her. Little did I know that my own flesh and blood had been victim at Katyn—cousins Jozef, Michal, Witold. Wanda continued, "We want a free Poland, one free of *them*. I want us to have a son, Romek, but I won't allow him to become like you. He'll be a true Pole. I know what your Communists are doing with the Home Army boys. Maybe the boy you ran into today at the station had the right to talk to you like that!"

As I listened I thought of young Kazik, my friend who had been caught on the street and executed by the Gestapo. Life was becoming more and more confused. That blond boy at the station may well have been Home Army.

Back in control now, Wanda announced decisively: "I'm going to come to meet you at the station every evening, and we'll walk home together."

"That's absurd."

But she insisted vehemently. "After everything we've been through, if we're going to die, we'll die together, and that's that."

Thereafter she would wait for me at the station, sitting in the smoky waiting room if I was late. We would head home together through the dark, empty streets and down the paths through the pine woods. I would walk with my hand on my pistol, ready to defend us if I had to. Often I was so tired that I would almost be asleep on my feet, and Wanda, who knew the way through the woods by heart, would lead me, so that I would not stumble on spruce roots protruding from the ground. In later years, we would think often of those treks through the night together.

Being together brought us happiness. The window in our room looked out onto a small garden and the street beyond it. At night the moon would peer through our window, and when it was full, would make our room glow. We needed little apart from one another.

We visited our parents on Sundays. I enjoyed talking with my father-in-law. I would tell him about my work and Poland's recovered territories, but he was always of another opinion.

"I don't see what there is to be so happy about. Poland has fixed borders, the prewar borders, and that's what we have to demand, no more and no less. Listen to me, Romek. Those borders contain our old cultural centers, Wilno and Lwow, with their centuries-old universities. That's where our ancestors lived and worked. That must not be changed, even for a fortune in gold. My dear young man, Poland is not money, not merchandise; it can't be bought and sold, exchanged. . . . You do agree, don't you?"

He would rise and pace the room. "I know that what I say may irritate you, even pain you, but we tell each other what we really think. Our allies have betrayed us in a most disgraceful fashion and when we least expected it—after they had won the final victory. Why did they enter the fight against Hitler in the first place—a fight that began in Poland—only to leave us worse off? We were the first people in Europe to say no to Hitler. Sure, our allies said no, too. But after five years of bloody war, when Stalin occupied Poland, like Hitler, the Western Allies ended up saying yes to him at Yalta, and without so much as a word to us. They handed Poland over to him, they handed all of us over to him. I don't know *why* they did it. That's what eats at me—I don't know why. I don't know what price the Russians paid so that the West would consent to the subjugation of our country, which for centuries has been a rampart of Christianity."

He sat down and took me by the hand. "I'm speaking to you as I would to a son," he said. "I know you are not guided by self-interest; I know you're not plotting a career for yourself as others are now. But mark my words. You won't escape the truth. No one does. The truth will come to you, or, rather, you will come to the truth. I don't know when, but you'll see it and you'll look truth in the eye, and then you'll know you have to make a decision . . . to choose between what is true and what you only thought was true."

Why should I argue? I thought. He wouldn't understand me anyway. I knew that his intentions were good and that he was an honest man, though one of limited horizons. He was not able to rise above the average ideas of the Polish bourgeoisie. A solution to those problems could be found only through a class approach and a dialectical understanding of the historical processes, as in Lenin's works. Sikorski's views would prove narrow and false, and very parochial when seen against the background of the economic and social changes that were taking place now. I was confident, convinced I was in the right, and perhaps more obstinate than ever before.

Autumn began in full earnest. The wind drove fallen leaves down the streets of Milanowek, and there was white frost on the ground when I left the house in the mornings. On Sundays we would stay in bed late, and I would dream with Wanda about resuming my studies in physics.

But life took an entirely different turn. I received a new assignment, an interesting one this time. I was to compile the Soldier's Pocket Yearbook for 1946. There was little time. I was told that I would have to do a lot of writing, that there would be conferences at various institutions—especially at the Military Institute of Geography—and that I might also have to travel in order to collect material. I told Wanda about it excitedly.

She listened with interest, but distantly. At breakfast I asked her if something was wrong. She looked at me enigmatically for a moment and then blurted, "I'm going to have a baby!"

Logical as it was, I was caught completely by surprise. "Are you sure?" I asked.

"Yes, entirely sure. But don't worry; I'm not afraid. The most important thing for me is that we be together when the time comes. We *will* be together, won't we?"

"Of course we will," I answered with conviction.

I tried to coddle her then. I forbade her to come meet me at the station, but she insisted that she needed the exercise and continued to wait for me.

Publishing the yearbook by the deadline proved difficult, because the institute had not finished the map of the new Poland. I went to see its head, Colonel Naumienko, a man so fat he had trouble passing through the doorways. It turned out that this would be the first map of Poland's new borders that the institute produced. Obtaining the names of the places in the Western Territories would be difficult. I found myself spending considerable time at the institute, where I became privy to an interesting profile of Naumienko.

Before the war, the institute's graphics sections had made and printed high-quality ordnance maps in several colors. The cartographers were excellent, and the machines were modern, imported from abroad. After taking Warsaw, the Germans had thrown out the Polish workers, keeping only a few from the lower technical levels, including Naumienko. The workshops remained practically idle until 1941, since the Germans had already long since prepared all the maps they needed for waging war in the east. However, Operation Barbarossa, launched against Russia in June 1941, changed that situation. It turned out that the Wehrmacht's maps of the Ukraine and Byelorussia were based on misleading Soviet maps, prepared specifically for disinformation purposes by Soviet intelligence before the war. The Germans had to supply accurate maps as quickly as possible. The institute went into full operation and began printing maps based on captured Soviet maps.

It was then that Naumienko made his career. Nobody knew whether he had been in contact with Soviet intelligence before that or whether they had searched him out at the time. In any case, he told them precisely which maps, and in what quantities, the Germans were printing at the institute. That, of course, was a signal as to what military operations were to be expected in the east. Once the Red Army entered Warsaw, Naumienko became head of the institute with rank of colonel. I was intrigued by that story and made a note of it, thinking that it might come in handy at some point.

The yearbook was ready at the beginning of February, and the first copies went around to the editors. It was then that my fate was determined. That day a soldier on orderly duty came and said I was wanted in the Personnel Department. He took me to the head of it, Colonel Garbowski, a thin, rather tall officer with an intelligent face and a large shock of gray hair.

"Be seated, Lieutenant Spasowski," he said politely. "I know you from your file, but you don't know me. Before the war I was a teacher and a Communist. I know who your father was, and, of course, I know his books . . . excellent books, especially *Liberation.*

"Looking through your questionnaire," he continued, "I noticed that you know German and Russian. But it's German that's my main concern. We have to delegate one officer from the political headquarters, someone with a good knowledge of German. How well do you know the language?"

"I know it well," I replied, "but I must tell you, Colonel, I dislike that language very much. You know my life story; I'm sure you understand why."

"Well, who likes Huns? They're not for liking. Of course you don't like them. . . . Well then, how's your English?"

"Weak. I've had a little practice in conversation; I know that my pronunciation is very bad."

"But you know the basics?"

"The basics I know."

"Good. Now I'll fill you in. Our military mission will be leaving for Germany in a couple of weeks to hold talks about extraditing those German war criminals that Poland is demanding for punishment. This is being done in conjunction with the international tribunal in Nuremberg.

"The mission will be subordinate to MON, to the Ministry of National Defense, and will be composed of officers with backgrounds in law, some of whom will be given military rank, as a matter of form. But since this has been causing a good deal of trouble, it's been decided that we send one political officer, too. You fill the bill. We'll be sending you to Germany for a few weeks, two months at the most. Do you agree? I'm asking because we won't 'force' anyone to go abroad. . . ."

"I agree," I replied without thinking, fascinated by the chance to see Germany and thinking only moments later about Wanda, about our baby.

"Good, very good," the Colonel nodded.

"I'd like to know what my duties will be there," I asked, too late.

"To tell you the truth, I don't know," he answered, laying aside the file. "You'll do everything that needs to be done for the success of the mission. The leader will be Colonel Zapolski, and there'll be both Party and non-Party people. The assignment begins at once, and you're to report to two places: to the Chief Commission for the Investigation of German War Crimes, and to MON, to Colonel Muszkat; he's the one running the show. You'll receive your orders tomorrow."

My assignment created a sensation back in my department.

"He's a lucky one," timid Bojko said. "He no sooner arrives here than he puts out that yearbook. He'll probably get a citation for that, maybe even a promotion, and now he's going to Germany.

Maybe farther—who knows? Meanwhile, our asses will grow into these rickety chairs here. Nothing will come of all this."

"No, no," interjected Lewin. "Something will come of this. I'll tell you what—hemorrhoids, that's what. I've already got mine."

But I could not smile; my thoughts were on Wanda. What had I gone and done? What was she going to say?

"And so you decided all by yourself, without asking me," she finally said when I told her. She was close to despair. "And you'll be leaving me all alone again."

I tried to calm her by explaining that it was only for a few weeks, but large tears streamed down her cheeks uncontrollably. I was about to promise her that I would cancel out. I would remind the colonel that he himself had said they did not force anyone to go abroad. But just as I was about to make that promise, Wanda dozed off from exhaustion. Once again I began to reflect that this might be my only chance to see the world and that I should not withdraw, not only for me, but for her sake and for our child's. There was no future in walking home together through the dark each night, a pistol in my hand.

I did not sleep that night. Wanda kept waking up every so often from her anxious dreams. She rose early the next morning as usual to make me breakfast, even though I asked her to remain in bed after her sleepless night. I had just finished my tea when she threw her arms around my neck.

"All right," she said, "go, if you think you have to. But come back quickly, and let this be the last time. I can't keep you from going. I saw how your eyes sparkled when you started to tell me about it yesterday. But remember that you must return and be with me when my time comes. Three more months. Remember!"

The chief commission was located in two rooms on the ground floor of an old apartment building, on Aleje Jerozolimskie, which one entered from a dark, narrow courtyard heaped with rubble. In the director's office, a short, thin man with smoothly combed and parted hair rose from his desk, which was stacked with papers. A look of pleasure crossed his face when I told him who I was.

"How good to see you, Lieutenant," he said. "I don't know what to do any more." He indicated his desk. "And now that military mission is here, too. Everyone's asking when they're leaving. I'm all by myself and I keep calling everyone and trying to find out. It's a mess. . . . I'm Gumkowski, Janusz Gumkowski. Well, two heads are better than one." He filled me in rapidly on the commission. In the adjoining room, which had no windows and was lit by a bulb hanging from the ceiling, he began to tell me about his archives, which looked more like stored wastepaper than a record system. But he knew where everything was, what paper was on what shelf, what was up by the ceiling or down on the floor, what was under the table or under his desk. He explained that provincial commissions were at work in other cities and had their own premises and personnel. It was only in Warsaw that the chief commission was working under such calamitous conditions. He was there by himself.

"There's nothing in this wilderness, Lieutenant, no offices, no people. We're starting from scratch, like cavemen, but I'm an optimist. You'll see what we do here. Did you suffer under the Germans?" he asked.

I told him about myself.

"Then I'm a lucky man," he said. "You see, what this work needs is people who can see the victims behind all these papers. Take this poster, for example." He unrolled it. "A list of the hostages who were executed in Radom. See, there are the signatures, and it tells whose order it was and the date. Do you know how much human suffering this poster represents? Believe me, it's not a question of vengeance. . . . Six million people died in Poland during the war—Poles, Jews, soldiers, civilians, children, old people. No vengeance could match that crime. And besides, we're not a vengeful nation; read Polish history. But there is something called 'justice.' The hand of justice will reach out and continue to reach out, so that in the future others will remember that there is no such thing as impunity. It's a question of mankind, of not losing confidence in humanity."

He walked over to his desk, rummaged through papers and a moment later drew one out and read out: "Muszkat . . . He's in MON and runs the show there. The trouble is that he's never there. An important man, but I tell you, he's like a Fata Morgana; he appears and then he disappears. I receive letters from him all at once, with all sorts of instructions—do this, do that, and be quick about it—in spite of the fact that I am not his subordinate. And to top it all off, I can never find him. Wherever I go, they always tell me that he just left. Maybe your luck will be better. An officer was here, a lawyer, too, and when I uttered Muszkat's name, he couldn't say a word; he raised his arms as if he were surrendering, and the only sound that came out of him was: Aaaaaaa. Perhaps you can tell me what it means when an officer says Aaaaaaa."

That was how it all began. Gumkowski proved to be a sober-minded and intelligent man. I spent many days in his "storehouse," reading a variety of documents in preparation for my trip.

I tried to meet with Colonel Marian Muszkat several times, without success. One day, my luck changed. As I entered his office and reported, the curly-haired man rose from his desk and looked me over with quick, restless eyes. "Lieutenant Spasowski. So what have you accomplished by now? How many members in the mission?"

"I know nothing about that, Colonel," I replied.

"What! Just what are you doing, Spasowski?"

"I'm working with Director Gumkowski on documents."

"With Gumkowski? Why? What does Gumkowski need you for? He can't help you. Let him give you the documents you need, and that's that!"

He threw me a rancorous look and was about to say something else, but the telephone rang.

"Jakub?" said Muszkat. "It's a good thing you returned my call. I'm leaving for Szczecin. Put some pressure on Justice to get that mission organized—you know, the one to Germany. Right. So far we have only one officer from Swietlik. Where are the others? They know how to make promises but not how to keep them. Fine. Goodbye." He replaced the receiver and pressed a button on his desk.

Within seconds his secretary was at the doorway. "Yes, Comrade Colonel."

"Make a note to call Comrade Jakub tomorrow, Jakub Berman. It's urgent." Berman was the nation's most powerful Communist.

Then he turned to me and said, "Are you by any chance related to that Spasowski the writer?"

"I'm his son."

"Unbelievable . . . I remember hearing your father speak. He was held in high esteem by the left. I know he's no longer alive. Listen, I have no time, I have to run."

The phone rang again.

"See you," said Muszkat, and turned away as he lifted the receiver.

I left with my mind in a whirl.

Despite Muszkat's disparaging remarks, I spent most of my time with Gumkowski and began to get my bearings on the work he was doing. I learned that the mission would take documents to Germany to serve two different purposes: first, supplemental materials to be given to the international tribunal in Nuremberg, our principal indictment having been in its hands for quite some time; and, second, co-operation to be established with the British occupying forces.

Gradually, matters connected with the trip began to fall into place, so I went to the Ministry of Foreign Affairs (MSZ) to get my passport. The ministry was located in a building on Aleja Szucha adjacent to the one that had been Gestapo headquarters, which stirred bad memories as I entered the front door. I walked into an entry hall full of paint-spattered women workers and scaffolding. Repairs were being made, and the stairs were covered with planks.

I requested to see the personnel director, and a moment later was in her office. She took my papers and looked through them.

"Fine. We'll arrange it. But you didn't fill this part out," she said, pointing.

"I filled it out down below." I bent over her desk and extended my hand. My wide sleeve caught on her ink stand, and blue ink streamed onto her desk, her papers, my form.

She bristled and threw me a murderous look. "This is intolerable. Leave. We have nothing more to talk about."

It was my first encounter with the institution that would become my life. At one point years later, when I told this story, someone remarked that sometimes you can see the end in the beginning.

Two days later, however, I received my passport, though it was handed to me by the director's secretary. I went immediately to MON to be outfitted for travel by the quartermaster.

"You can't go in that uniform," said the General Staff's supply chief.

"Why not? This is a perfectly good uniform," I replied. "Practically brand new."

"You don't understand," he said. "General Spychalski's orders are to outfit you like a prewar officer. Well-fitting uniform, silver braid. The proper colors will be on your collar, and your four-cornered cap will be correct. Everything first class. The belts have already been ordered from the leather shop."

Two weeks later I was unrecognizable. Muszkat held a briefing for the officers traveling abroad, and we looked like members of another army entirely, not at all like those to be seen in the streets of Warsaw. Nearly all had four-cornered caps trimmed with the same dark red that was on their collars—the color for prewar military attorneys. Only I and two other junior officers wore infantry officers' uniforms.

"The military mission of which you all are members," began Colonel Muszkat, running his eyes over us, "was convened by order of the Minister of National Defense, Marshal Rola-Zymierski. He has placed me in charge, and although I will be remaining here at home, I am your leader. I have appointed Colonel Zapolski to be your leader in Germany."

Then we were assigned our tasks, in very general form. When my turn came, I heard: "Lieutenant Spasowski will be responsible for the documents and their correct use, and for the money for your maintenance, which he will pay out to you." Thus Muszkat, in a single sentence, saddled me with a responsibility that was to have far-reaching consequences.

I had my first inkling of the awesomeness of my duties when, a few days before our departure, soldiers dragged a few large suitcases full of money into the chief commission office. Gumkowski and I spent several hours counting that money, and finally I wrote out a receipt for half a million German reichsmarks.

"How should I transport the money?" I asked Gumkowski. "Not in those old suitcases. They could come apart any minute."

"I don't know," he said, with a shrug of his shoulders. "They've handed you quite a problem."

But a few days later he somehow acquired a large wooden chest banded with good solid iron and with an old-fashioned lock, whose key was as long as a pencil. It was an antique and belonged in a museum, but it was in good shape and strong and we pressed it into service as if it were the latest thing for storing money and documents.

On March 19, 1946, at seven o'clock in the morning, four men carried the chest from the chief commission and loaded it onto a two-wheeled cart, which they pulled to the railroad station. I walked behind them. My eyes never left the chest. It barely fit into our compartment and filled all the area between the seats. Our leader, Colonel Zapolski, decided that I was to ride alone with the chest, and that the compartment would be kept locked at all times; arms were to be used if anyone attempted to break in.

As the train pulled away, I began my work for the foreign service of People's Poland, work that would last thirty-four years, nine months, and one day.

CHAPTER XII

I gazed out the train window at the passing landscape. The war had left its scars everywhere. Twisted steel girders jutted from the ruins of train stations, and a solitary chimney in a bare field suggested where a hut had once stood. I closed my eyes and saw my wife's tear-stained face, and then her anxious father's.

The officers passing down the corridor would glance into my compartment, their faces cheerful. They must have been swapping jokes, for peals of laughter erupted every so often above the clack of the wheels. I was happy to be alone, but that solitude drew some attention, and later on I heard that the officers had scornfully nicknamed me "The Political."

We arrived in Czechoslovakia that afternoon. There were no signs of destruction; it was as if there had been no war at all. Red bunting and banners hung from the buildings, as they had in Lutsk in 1939. The train halted at the station for a long time. Czech railroad workers said that Yugoslavia's leader, Marshal Tito, had just passed through, and the station had been decorated for him. Later, when I saw Prague, my heart bled for Warsaw. Prague had houses, stores, people; it was a normal city. One of our captains muttered bitterly, "Golden Prague."

When the train stopped at the border station in Bavaria, I saw American soldiers for the first time—a Military Police patrol on the platform. No one checked our papers; the train continued on its way. Two hours later we pulled into Nuremberg—a forest of burned-out houses.

American soldiers saluted us at the station, especially our captains, whom they took for three-star generals because of the red piping on their caps. My strongbox created a commotion—it was such an unwieldy piece of baggage.

That same day we went to the international tribunal, where the leaders of the Third Reich were being tried. The hall was as bright as a theater. The defendants sat in two rows on the right side with a row of American MPs behind them. I recognized most of them. I was unable to take my eyes off Hans Frank, sitting there as motionless as the others. He had been the one in charge of murder in Poland. He had lived in Krakow—in Wawel, the castle of the Polish kings.

"You should read this, Lieutenant," Gumkowski had said one day, handing me a photocopy of a German newspaper. "Read what this scum had to say back in February 1940 after a visit to Czechoslovakia." I bent close to the lamp on his desk and read Frank's words: "In Prague red notices were posted that seven Czechs were executed today. If I wanted to order notices posted every time seven Poles were shot, there wouldn't be enough forests in Poland to make the paper."

That afternoon we visited the prison—long, brightly lit corridors, MPs everywhere, cell doors armor-plated. The MP accompanying us urged us to have a look through the peepholes. I wanted to see Frank; the others were of no interest to me. Finally I found him, sitting at a small table, his back to the door. He turned on hearing us in the corridor and looked over at the door, at me, with cold, fishlike eyes.

At the hall again the following day, I looked around at the judges, the prosecutors, the clerks, and noticed Soviet uniforms. My immediate association with that sight was troubling—I could think only of the abandonment of Warsaw.

From Nuremberg we traveled to Frankfurt am Main, where we were quartered in a hotel for officers. In the morning we had breakfast in a separate part of the dining room. The table service gleamed—the knives, forks, and spoons were silver, the dishes white porcelain. Zapolski was in excellent humor. He told us stories about World War I. You can see he's a man of the world, I thought, sitting at one end of the table with the two other junior officers. Suddenly the swinging doors opened and out came a line of waiters in white jackets. They sliced open small paper boxes and sprinkled some brown flakes into our plates. The colonel finished a story. It must have been funny, since it was followed by a burst of laughter. Then silence. Everyone sat still, as if waiting for an order, the younger men ready to follow the older.

"Officers," said our leader, "what are you waiting for?"

"Maybe . . ." began one of the captains.

"No 'maybes,' " said Zapolski in a voice that brooked no contradiction. "I order you to eat."

The air was filled with the sounds of cornflakes crunching. Strange American food, I thought, but I was hungry and it didn't taste bad. They were sweet and crunchy and good, but they were dry and kept getting lodged between my teeth. Most of us had already finished when the swinging doors flung wide again and in came the waiters, carrying trays with pitchers on them. With great calm, they poured milk into our empty plates.

The chief cleared his throat, realizing, to his dismay, that he had given his order prematurely. His deputy, a tall, gray-haired, jovial colonel, was making such a preposterous face that it took all the self-control I could muster not to burst out in a loud guffaw.

Late that afternoon our train pulled into the small station in Bad Oeynhausen, headquarters for the British Army of the Rhine. There we were met by an English captain who spoke fluent Polish, and we were taken to two-story houses from which German tenants had been expelled.

While we were there, I rarely went outside, because I truly became a prisoner of the chest. But I took every opportunity to observe the British and was surprised by their discipline and demeanor. The men always looked alert and saluted snappily. I saw no drunken soldiers, as I often had at home, especially among the Soviets. Like their soldiers, the British officers wore battle dress most of the time; only in the evening did they wear service dress.

My knowledge of English proved entirely inadequate, and eventually we had to hire an interpreter, Second Lieutenant Ostrowski, who had been in a POW camp for officers and who, before the war, had worked as a geographer at Warsaw University. It was from him that we learned there was another Polish War Crimes Mission in Bad Oeynhausen, one convened the previous year by the Polish government-in-exile in London. I met the leader of that mission at the club. At first he recoiled at the sight of me, and I, too, tensed, but after a while we were able to converse normally. I reported our meeting to Zapolski, who calmly said that it would be better if we could settle the matter among ourselves, with them ceding to us. However, the others in our group learned of the existence of the London mission, and this led to our first internal discord. Major Podlaski, from the Military Prosecutor's Office, let everyone know that we could have nothing in common with "traitors," that the only path to take was to demand that the British immediately throw them out of their occupation zone and hand all their documents to us. Our quarrels grew intense. Podlaski threatened that the entire matter would be examined in Warsaw; he succeeded in intimidating some and turning them against Zapolski. Soon, real trouble broke out, and the British authorities stepped in.

I was in my room one evening when I heard shouts and the stamping of feet outside. I ran to the window and saw Ostrowski running down the middle of the street shouting, "Help! Save me! He's after me!" About fifty feet behind him was Podlaski, bellowing, "Halt! Stop!" As they disappeared around the corner, I ran outside. Officers from all the other missions were pouring into the street.

Within a few minutes Podlaski returned, panting. He stomped into the building and slammed the door furiously behind him.

The next day the British summoned Zapolski and told him firmly that there were to be no more such incidents.

I ran into Ostrowski in the park. He said hello but was nervous and clearly did not want to talk. It took some doing to convince him to sit down with me.

"I've had enough of you Warsaw people. I'm leaving for Australia. That's it for you! That major of yours lured me to his place, saying he had something for me to translate. And then he started questioning me, moving in on me. I ended up in a corner, but he kept shouting, 'Who sent you here? We know your sort! Come on, out with it!' I'd had it, I couldn't take any more. I jumped out the window and started running, but he ran out the front door after me." Ostrowski was very distressed and rubbing his hands. "Oh, yes, Lieutenant, I've had enough. Forgive me for saying this, but I find all of you strange. You may speak Polish, but you don't act like Poles. At the end of last year some Warsaw people came here to discuss repatriation. Some little redhead runt of a major—he looked ridiculous compared to the British—he came here and began the talks. That was something, let me tell you!"

Ostrowski clutched at his head and continued. "The British had just found me; the Warsaw contingency didn't know a word of English. Warsaw was demanding the immediate repatriation of all Poles—they wanted them all forcibly expelled from the British zone. The British calmly reiterated their position: every Pole should decide for himself. And that went on until one day the little redhead came to a meeting drunk and started yelling at *me!* I didn't know what to do. He said, 'Tell that son of a bitch that he has to expel all the Polish military and civilian DPs from their zone or else . . .' Of course I translated that as 'The colonel respectfully requests that you repatriate the DPs. . . .' So on it went. Sometime after that, the British called an urgent meeting; the man from Warsaw came late. Again he began speaking crudely. At that point the head Englishman interrupted my translation and began speaking in Polish, beautiful Polish. He said that he had had enough of these talks, because now he was certain with whom he was dealing, that this would be their last meeting, and that the runt would have to leave the British zone at once. When he was through, he rose and left the room with all the aplomb in the world; the little guy from Warsaw just sat there like a clod. That happened at the end of last year, but I kept holding out for the lawyers, the educated people, to come. I was sure that with the riffraff gone it would be a different story. And then that Podlaski shows up.

"What's happened to Poland, Lieutenant?" he asked in all candor. But he did not wait for an answer. We said good-bye.

A few weeks later most of our officers were recalled to Poland. And Zapolski received two letters: a summons to return home and orders to investigate the possibility of hiring Polish legal officers who had spent the war in POW camps in Germany. He ordered me to deal with the matter, and left for home. Our work seemed to be coming to an end.

I had met a lieutenant at the repatriation mission and requested that he send me any legal officers reporting to be returned to Poland. I had several applicants after a few days, and a week later a number of them were hired and at work at their desks. I had informed Muszkat and Gumkowski that I had hired legal officers and that I was trying hard to make the investigating teams of the London mission subordinate to ours, since only then would we be able to go into action.

I was soon summoned to Berlin to our military mission at the Allied Control Council for Germany in the British sector of the city. I reported to General Jakub Prawin, a short, thin man, who rose from his desk with a frown and offered me his hand. "Be seated, Lieutenant. We have a lot to talk about." He cast me an appraising look before he started. "Here is your promotion to full lieutenant and here is a letter from Muszkat. Read it, and then we'll have more to say."

I scanned the letter. Muszkat informed me that I was to remain in Germany all summer, perhaps even until the end of the year. He gave me a free hand to hire as many officers as needed and encouraged me to take over the other investigating teams in the zone. The letter concluded with the statement that I was to be head of the Polish mission in the British zone.

"It's no easy task you have before you," said Prawin when I was through reading. "I wanted to meet you because I'm the one in charge of Polish interests throughout Germany, and you'll be reporting to me. I approve of the general line you are following, but would urge you to act judiciously. Great responsibility is resting on you. Concentrate on executing these tasks." As the general rubbed his bald spot, I suddenly realized that I would not be with my wife when she gave birth.

"The situation at home is very tense," the general continued. "There's going to be a referendum. We're mobilizing all our strength, but it's no easy thing to do. If it weren't for the help our Soviet comrades are lending, things would be sorry indeed.

"Any special requests?" asked the general as we said good-bye.

"Yes. I must be in Warsaw when my wife has our baby."

He shook his head. "I'll try to let you go, but your assignments are important. It won't be easy."

That summer I began work as head of the mission. Meantime, the British had moved all foreign missions to Bad Salzuflen, a town less than a dozen miles to the south. We were given a house by a park. I invited the officers from all war crimes teams to the new headquarters for a meeting. To my delight, everyone in the zone from Lübeck, Braunschweig, Paderborn, and Iserlohn came, about twenty officers. Despite my promotion to full lieutenant, I was still the most junior officer there, and the youngest. I was somewhat overwhelmed and decided to speak briefly.

"I thank you for coming, gentlemen," I began, my voice trembling. "Your views are not my concern. The main thing is that you're Poles, and that we are united in the will to punish those who inflicted such suffering on our nation. I don't know why I survived the war; I can't explain it. I'm from Warsaw, and you know what that means. I swore that if I survived, I would avenge the blood of those who were murdered. I made no efforts to come to Germany. It was fate that brought me here."

I looked around. They were all pensive, no doubt thinking of their own families, whom they hadn't seen since before the war.

"I have no intention of concealing anything from you," I continued. "I am a Communist and the son of one. I am not motivated by self-interest. MON has granted me the authority to head this mission and to make use of its means. This wooden chest contains funds that I brought here from Poland, which should last us a long time."

Everyone agreed to co-operate and acknowledged me as their leader. Those were memorable moments for me. A large mission was coming into being, one with investigative units in important cities in the British zone, one composed of savvy officers who could boast law degrees and a knowledge of foreign languages. I was proud to be a part of it.

I informed Muszkat and Gumkowski, as well as Prawin, of this latest development and then we went into action, often working late into the night. In no time we created a central card index published in book form for use by the investigating officers. It came to be known as Spasowski's List.

Work was in full swing at the mission when Wanda gave birth to a baby girl in Milanowek on July 1, and wrote me a letter of bitter reproach. On the day I received the letter I was preparing to leave for Berlin to deliver an important war criminal—the first German mayor of occupied Warsaw. I decided to compel Prawin to give me leave. He did.

From Berlin I traveled by train to Warsaw. As usual, Muszkat was not easy to find. But when I did locate him, I spent a long time describing the mission's activities.

I ended our conversation by insisting that, if I were to remain in Germany past the end of the year, my wife and child would have to come live with me.

Despite her bitterness, Wanda welcomed me with joy. She had changed, grown more serious. She was cheered by the prospect of our being together after the New Year, but I could see regret in her eyes, too, because she would have to postpone her studies and singing career until some time in the future. Apprehensively I picked up my little daughter, Misia, who seemed almost microscopic to me, even though she was already a month old. Her head was covered with reddish hair, and her sky blue eyes looked at with curiosity. I felt proud and happy.

The family had been waiting for my return before the baby's baptism. I offered no objections—I had promised Wanda that she would have the final say in such matters. The christening took place in Milanowek, and my daughter was given the name Maria Grazyna. The young priest regarded me with some interest, since I was in uniform as I carried in my daughter. My father-in-law was pleased with me and may even have thought that I was finally beginning to straighten out.

"Now when the world is finally breathing free again, night is falling over Poland," he told me. "We're crammed in between the Soviets and the Soviet zone in Germany. Nothing can save us. There's no hope."

I tried to argue with him, but he wouldn't listen.

"You're far away, but here the terror is real and growing. They held a referendum. A farcc! There were three questions. Listen to what they were. Do we want the present western border—that means the Oder—to be a permanent border? Tell me, what Pole doesn't want a permanent border after all the changes and resettlements. That was a mockery. The second question: Do we want the nationalization of industry and agricultural reform? They distributed the land to the peasants and they took away the factories, and now they ask if the peasants want the land. They've already taken our family estate, and now they ask. Another mockery. And the third question: Do we want the Senate abolished? Things will be more democratic without it. Yet another mockery, for that wasn't the point. You can't imagine how much propaganda there was to vote yes three times. The opposition was put in prison, people were beaten, some died. They won that referendum of theirs," he continued wearily, "they won because they falsified all the results. It's already known abroad that everything was rigged. Here in Milanowek, people voted no but the results came out yes. You see the people: sad, helpless, weak, exhausted, and sick from the hell they've been through. And the West? They've only abandoned us to certain doom here."

I returned to Germany with a heavy heart. Certainly, I had pictured the postwar world differently.

Several months later, at the beginning of December, I received orders from Berlin to remain and direct the mission during the coming year. So I set off for Warsaw in the middle of a winter blizzard to get my wife and child.

Wanda was delighted by our living conditions in Bad Salzuflen; everything seemed wonderful to us after what we had been through during the war. We made our home in two small rooms in the attic of the building where the mission was housed.

"You've been promoted to captain," General Prawin announced when I next reported to his office in Berlin. "You're advancing quickly, Captain. And now that your family is with you, we'll be keeping you longer in Germany."

He was in a chatty mood. "We've won the elections in Poland. The West has been silenced. They have to accept the fact that the Communists are in the majority. . . . They wanted to discredit it, but they couldn't. . . . The Soviet generals on the Control Council have sent us their congratulations and assured us that we can always count on their help."

"I hear that a lot of people in Warsaw are being put in prison." I said it directly.

"My dear man, there's a struggle on. Didn't they put us in prison before the war?" He stroked his bald spot for an instant, then added, "Yes, yes, I remember how it was myself. It's always like this when the people are reaching for power. The most important thing is that the West has been silenced. The election is behind us; people have been put in power. President Bierut has already proven himself, and people say that Premier Jozef Cyrankiewicz is a very good man.

Now we must correct the economic picture somewhat and keep power firmly in our hands. . . . The elections are a fact. It's victory that counts in this world; the losers don't get a say. Our Soviet comrades are always saying this, and they've come a long way. Yes, yes, they know only too well you have to seize power with your own hands."

After a long conversation, the general instructed me to report for a new assignment to the military attaché, Colonel Kazimierz Sidor.

His office was higher up, on the fourth floor. The colonel greeted me with an ingratiating smile "Have a seat. Perhaps you'd be more comfortable on the couch by the table," he said, brushing back his shock of hair. His uniform had lapels, like those of Western officers, and his shirt and tie were an identical green.

"We have a lot of work to do, Lieutenant Spasowski," he began, and then corrected himself. "*Captain* Spasowski. I know about your promotion. Congratulations." He asked me about my family, our accommodations in Bad Salzuflen, my work, and the officers I had hired.

"You're in a unique position, Captain. You have access to information few other people have. We want you to co-operate with us. When I say 'we' I don't mean me, Kazimierz Sidor, in some sort of *pluralis majestaticus,* but the Second Section of the General Staff, or, to put it simply, military intelligence. I'm not asking whether you agree or not, because, as a regular officer, you cannot refuse. Your principal assignment with us will be to make a detailed study of the location of all British units making up the Army of the Rhine, to which you have been accredited. How you go about it is your own business, but it shouldn't prove difficult with officers on the spot. As far as the larger units are concerned, I'll fill you in right now."

He walked over to a map and pointed out the places where the headquarters of the corps and divisions of the BAOR were stationed.

"We need to know where all the units are," he said, stressing the point, "even the very smallest. We also need information concerning their numerical strength and equipment. No information on those subjects is to be considered superfluous. You are to send all reports, maps, everything, by couriers in special packages addressed to me. Remember this: for you, my name is not Sidor, but Gustaw, and you are to use the name Karl when signing reports. You are to enlist all the officers you need and pass on their names to us, but not by mail. That you will do in person the next time you're in Berlin. I don't need to tell you, Captain, that we require you to be cautious, circumspect, and shrewd; in short, don't get yourself in any trouble. You don't have a diplomatic passport.

"Military intelligence," he continued with a smile, "is rather an extraordinary thing. After all, you get to use your mind, and that in itself is a bonus."

He paused, then continued with conviction. "You see, this isn't a job for policemen. This is more than just keeping an eye on our own and turning in reports," he said with a significant smile. "This is something else entirely."

On my way home on the autobahn I drew out some paper, placed it out of the driver's view, and surreptitiously made notes of the signs that indicated where BAOR units were stationed. And so I began working for intelligence. It was a very intense period at the mission and difficult for me to find time to carry out the task assigned by Sidor. During the next few months, I managed to speak with only a few officers and enlist their co-operation. The results, however, were paltry, and I received a reprimand from Berlin. Then news came that Sidor had been recalled and replaced by Colonel Smal, who began an outright campaign of badgering me for reports. However, I knew that I had to act very cautiously, for were my recruiting efforts for intelligence to come to light, all our work would be ruined and result in the mission's downfall.

As leader, I decided to give life to my convictions, and so I made my mission's salaries equal: all would have just enough to live on. Later on, when the British authorities introduced special vouchers for the BAOR, I held to my principle that our officers should earn only one-third as much as those in the other missions. There was grumbling here and there, but no one protested; after all, I had imposed those regulations on myself, too. Our officers continued to work with devotion, and it was only years later that I fully appreciated the warmth that existed among our staff during that unique time in my life in Bad Salzuflen.

In the middle of 1947, our team in Lübeck informed us that they had come across the trail of SS General Wilhelm Koppe, who, as the chief of the SS and the police in the General Gouvernement, was one of the most sought-after war criminals. The mission was in an uproar at the prospect of snaring such an important Nazi. I sent my best investigative officers to Lübeck. In a few days they confirmed that Koppe was hiding in the Lüneburg area and that he had an enemy in his close circle who was willing to betray him. He was, however, difficult to apprehend, because as soon as things got hot for him he would cross over to the Soviet zone, and then, after a while, return to the British zone, a maneuver he had already repeated a few times successfully. Now he had prepared a plan of escape to Argentina, by ship from Denmark. Our informant warned us that Koppe was always armed and accompanied by armed SS men. I went to the Haystack, the British special investigation unit, to see a major I had met there, and informed him that I would be leaving for Lübeck to arrest Koppe. He was very much interested and promised us any help we needed.

The trip to Lübeck and along the Danish border was full of surprises. At the exact time we had set for Koppe's betrayer to deliver him into our hands, we waited outside Flensburg, by the road that led to Denmark. The car with Koppe never appeared. We returned to Lübeck disappointed. Captain Bigda, the head of the Lübeck team persuaded me to stay in his house for the night. I was tired and anxious to get to bed, but Bigda's wife was having problems finding clean sheets. "Why haven't they brought the laundry back yet?" she complained.

"You send out your laundry?" I asked casually.

"Yes," interjected her husband. "They usually bring it back within a couple of days."

"And who picks it up?" I was only making social banter.

"The British. They have a laundry here for the entire region. They pick up the laundry in their trucks."

He walked over to a desk, withdrew a piece of gray paper from a drawer, and handed it to me. "Here," he said, pointing. "See? We're on the list of British units."

I glanced at the list, and my jaw almost swung open. That piece of paper listed all the British units in the Lübeck military district, as well as the intelligence sections and special liaison units.

Bigda was pleased with himself. "We're in a very good position," he added. "We're treated just like any British unit in every respect—rations, clothing, food, everything, including laundry."

"I'd like to hold on to this list," I said. "You're treated well here. All our investigative sections should be so lucky."

"Perhaps you'd like the old lists as well?" asked Bigda.

"If you don't need them. I'll show them to some people who are bound to be interested."

Within a few weeks, all our branches were either using the British laundry or had acquired the British laundry lists. My subsequent report, which included a map of the various British units, looked impressive, since I was also able to estimate the number in each unit. Missing was the amount of arms they had, since, unfortunately, arms were not routinely sent to the laundry.

The British, I learned later, had duped me and whisked Koppe away from us, but they might as well have handed me that first intelligence report on a silver platter.

In our mission's branch in Braunschweig we had a certain Lieutenant Przybylko, a very friendly and sociable officer, who was doing absolutely nothing, as far as we could tell, but making German friends and visiting them frequently to play cards. One friend turned out to be an engineer who, before the war, had worked on designing the large steel mill the Germans were constructing in Salzgitter, about a dozen miles south of Braunschweig. This Hermann Goering Steel Works was to produce millions of tons of steel from the inferior local ore. The war interrupted the construction of the colossus, but the engineer had a complete set of the plans, and he was now offering to sell them to the Polish lieutenant.

I informed Berlin, and Smal, my new superior in intelligence, immediately expressed interest. The affair dragged on for several months as we haggled over the price. Finally, a figure of a few thousand dollars was agreed upon. The engineer handed over the plans and files thick with documentation in a series of deliveries. I drove to Braunschweig the evening the last and most important documents were to be transferred in exchange for payment in full, and attended the opera, just to throw off anyone who might be watching. Though my eyes and ears were on the performance of *Aïda*, my mind was firmly on the exchange about to be made.

Late that night we set off quietly for a destination outside Goslar. The German was waiting in his car at the appointed place. He was given his money, and he handed over the last of the documents.

Spotlights suddenly flashed on behind us. A chase began. Our American Ford, despite its speed, could not shake our pursuer. We decided to risk cutting across the fields, trusting our powerful engine and high suspension. Our driver turned off the lights, and the car sped maniacally through the dark. We left the other car in a ditch. The documents were dispatched almost immediately, and I informed Smal of the completion of the operation. About twelve years later I learned, quite by accident, that the plans for Salzgitter made their way to the Soviets, and they, in turn, presented them to Poland as a general blueprint for the steel works at Nowa Huta.

Toward the end of the year, I was summoned to Berlin, and General Prawin handed me my promotion to major.

"You may well be the fastest-advancing officer we have in this army," he said, with a friendly smile. "People get promoted here in Berlin, too, but those are only titular ranks. You're getting real promotions. Congratulations, congratulations!"

I reported to the general's deputy, Colonel Hubert Meller.

"Well, here you are at last. What are you doing over there in the zone, that godforsaken hole? It's high time we had a talk. There's a great deal to be done, and all you do is chase after war criminals. What's the point of all that?" He made a face and lit his pipe. "You have to think dialectically. Imperialism is trying to resurrect the spirit of Nazism in Germany, and we have to stand up to that whole gang, to its propaganda especially. That's why the Cominform has been created. In Poland the reactionaries must be beaten with their own weapons. That's a law of history and dialectics. Always with their own weapons. If they want elections, let's give them elections; if they want terror, we'll give them terror and more terror . . . until they lose their taste for it. It's always like that. Now we have to take the offensive and connect with forces that can offer us support in the West. What does that mean?" he asked rhetorically. He rose and walked over to the window. "It means a great deal. The initial steps have already been taken, and this is where you come in, Comrade Spasowski. It has been decided to create military missions in the western zones that will co-ordinate the activities of specialized missions like your own. The Ministry of Foreign Affairs in Warsaw will choose a chief, and we have recommended you to be his deputy, because you know what's going on and—why hide the fact?—you've proven yourself. We must go into action. The seeds of a party must be planted in West Germany. You have been appointed our Party plenipotentiary in West Germany, Comrade Spasowski. There are many mine workers of Polish descent there. They must be politicized. You'll be given detailed instructions."

I left Meller's office with an aching head.

Soon after, I went to see Colonel Smal.

"I must congratulate you at long last, Major Spasowski," he said to me. "Warsaw expresses its appreciation to you for the plans of the steel works, an important affair. Your reports on the placement of British units are also very good. We've already received confirmation that your reports were accurate. You see, we asked Warsaw's help, and our Soviet comrades informed us which units were stationed in which towns. Of course everything checked out, except that you supplied more details. You did quite a thorough job. Your officers must have been on the road a great deal of the time."

"Actually, they traveled very little."

"What do you mean? How could you get your hands on all that information then?"

"Dirty laundry." I opened my briefcase and withdrew the lists. "Here's the evidence, supplied by none other than the British themselves," I said.

Smal looked through the lists, shook his head, and sighed. "You know something, Spasowski? You're promising intelligence material all right."

While I was in Berlin I received letters from Muszkat informing me that my nomination as chief of the war crimes missions in three zones—British, American, and French—had been approved, and I was instructed to pay visits to Augsburg, Munich, and Baden-Baden.

I felt sick at heart and utterly confused; everything was descending on me too suddenly. I ran into Meller, who had received correspondence from the Ministry of Foreign Affairs, and who dragged me into his office. He was in a state of great agitation.

"Can you imagine—they're sending Zaleski, a prewar diplomat, to be your chief. He'll have the titular rank of colonel. He's not one of us; before the war he served in Paris and Tokyo. There are certain questions about him, but Warsaw insists that we need an experienced man."

He studied me through his steel-rimmed glasses. "You'll have to be very careful with him. Stay on your toes. I don't envy you."

Colonel Zaleski turned out to be as tall as I was. He was a gawky sort of man. I paid him a visit upon his arrival in Bad Salzuflen. We began 1948 working together.

"Ah, so it's you," he said, his eyes opening wide as he looked me over with a smile that might have been taken as friendly, but I chose to take it as ironic. "I've heard a lot about you, good things, all sorts of things; you know how people are. I have my own sources and my own secrets, Major," he said with an enigmatic squint. "And you've no doubt heard about me: a diplomat of the prewar regime, experienced, but a dangerous ex-intelligence agent who needs to be watched. Isn't that so? Don't deny it."

I was taken aback by his words, but Zaleski was comfortable, in his element.

"You see, the people's government . . ." he said, casting me a sidelong glance, "I'm expressing myself right, aren't I? The way you're supposed to? If I make any mistakes, please point them out to me. I want to correct them and learn. After all, that's why you're with me, to be my political commissar. What was I saying? Ah, yes, the people's government has some need for expertise and knowledge. That is of course why suspicious types like myself still have jobs. But when they learn how to do it themselves, they'll throw us out as quickly as they did the landowners."

Zaleski disarmed me. I had never met anyone like him before. At times he seemed childishly direct and naive, but that was for appearances only. In reality he was an educated and experienced diplomat who only posed as a great cynic. After a few weeks of sniffing one another out, we established friendly footing and I realized that there was a decent person behind that crust of cynicism.

Shortly we were both summoned to Berlin. The Russians were stopping everyone in Helmstedt, poring over their documents, and turning many cars away. They finally allowed us to pass but not before a good deal of wrangling.

"You see, it's interesting," said Zaleski. "Something's in the wind. I can feel it in my bones."

I traveled to Berlin by car only once more. Toward the end of

July the Russians set up a full blockade, halting all vehicular traffic to Berlin. From then on we went by plane.

Once, when Zaleski and I were flying together and the pilot announced that we were over the Soviet zone, Zaleski began laughing to himself. "You know, it would be funny if those Migs shot us down. A dedicated Communist like you and a cynic like me shot down together by Soviet Migs over Germany three years after the war in a plane belonging to His Royal Highness of England . . . No, that's too funny."

I considered Zaleski something of an eccentric and made allowances for him. He was my diametric opposite, but we treated one another with humor, and I returned the affection that I felt from him. He taught me an invaluable lesson: how to maintain a certain distance from political events.

In October 1948, the British military authorities granted me permission to serve as consul in Düsseldorf, and I moved my family and work there. The Berlin blockade was still in effect, and tension was mounting; the Russians were claiming the right to the entire German capital. Communication with Berlin had become quite difficult, but I knew what I was supposed to do. I went about establishing the first Communist Party cell. It was joined by a few German citizens of Polish descent who lived in Westphalia and by a few of our own workers. Each member of the cell was assigned the task of creating similar cells, thereby increasing the size and influence of our network.

In the spring of 1949, I was permitted my first postwar leave and traveled with Wanda and three-year-old Misia to Austria, where in the resort of Ehrwald, BAOR had a leave center for its officers. Wanda, who was pregnant again, delighted in the views of majestic, snow-covered Sonnenspitze as it caught the first rays of the rising sun.

But within a week a telegram arrived from Düsseldorf. Zaleski ordered me to return at once—a car was on its way. When we got back, Zaleski immediately handed me a sealed envelope. It was from Smal. He ordered me and my family to vacate the British zone immediately. A Polish officer had defected. Although the man had not worked with me, he could well have known about my activities. All the positive things I had done were suddenly undone by my espionage connection, and I was having to abandon my post and rush away like a fugitive. I was categorically ordered to leave all my personal belongings behind and to depart, drawing as little attention to myself as possible. Following Zaleski's advice, we went in two cars.

The autobahn in Helmstedt was backed up with cars waiting to be cleared to cross over to Berlin. The word was that British MPs were not allowing any vehicles out of the British zone because "Ivan" was still maintaining the blockade. It took some doing, but finally, after hours of arguing, the senior MP officer yielded and ordered the gate raised.

"You're proceeding on your own responsibility, Major. There's no coming back," he said.

We pulled up to the Soviet sentry post. Sloppily uniformed soldiers blocked their gate. They walked over to our car and looked inside, their eyes hostile, their submachine guns clutched in their hands. I got out and began to explain. "Nyet. Go back." Undeterred, I continued my explanation, but to no avail. They only repeated, "Nyet. Go back," and cursed among themselves. I soon lost patience with them and demanded to speak to their commanding officer. That got me nowhere at all.

We remained there for hours, without water or food. Every once in a while they would allow us to go down into a ditch to answer the call of nature. Wanda was frantic, little Misia wouldn't stop crying, and I was losing hope with every passing minute. Straining my eyes toward the British zone, I thought I saw them observing us through binoculars.

Years later, when thinking back on this and my obstinacy, I came to the conclusion that at that time I was probably the only person in the world who would have waited so stubbornly, and with a devotion worthy of a better cause, until he was graciously allowed behind the "iron curtain."

It was dark by the time the commanding officer arrived on the scene. I explained everything to him from the start. He, too, said, "No. Not allowed," but he made a note of General Prawin's name—perhaps it sounded Russian to him. He told me he would make a call. After a while he returned to say that his commanding officers had never heard of that general. No amount of threats or entreaties made any difference.

It was very late when one of the Russians appeared and said we could pass, but we were not to leave the autobahn before we reached Berlin. The gate was raised. There wasn't a soul or a light to be seen. We drove through a desert of darkness. I was heartsick for my wife and little daughter, who were huddled in the back seat, asleep.

After an hour or so on the road I thought I smelled something burning. Within moments smoke poured from under the hood, blocking visibility. We stopped, and our driver jumped out and threw open the hood. Flames leaped out at him. Clawing up dirt with our bare hands—Wanda, too—we heaped it on the fire and managed to extinguish it. Misia lay crying in a ditch. I realized then how wise Zaleski had been to advise us to take a second car. Towing the charred car behind us, we limped into Berlin the next morning. Wanda had miscarried during the night. Our three-year stay in Germany was over.

When we arrived in Warsaw we encountered a sad city; despair was written on its people's faces. Their clothes were worn and colorless. Drunks wandered the streets.

"What's left for me?" cried a young man to himself as he reeled down a sidewalk in the dark. I walked up close and saw a refined, likable face in the light of the street lamp. "They've taken everything. . . . There's nothing left for me," he shouted. He waved one hand and continued swaying down the street. I trudged away gloomily; I had never run across a youth so desperate, so obviously wasted—even on the streets of vanquished Germany.

I learned when I reported for duty that I had been transferred to military intelligence, which was located in prewar military buildings on Aleja Niepodleglosci that had now been repaired. I began working there, and a few days later was introduced at a seemingly endless meeting of the Party organization.

First, the secretary read a report on rightist deviation in the Party. Then everyone took turns condemning Party First Secretary Wladyslaw Gomulka and Vice Minister of Defense General Spychalski. I said nothing, but listened closely. I had confidence in the Party and knew from experience that such deviations did in fact exist and had to be combated. But I found myself disliking the people at that meeting. They were mostly young, and their speech was vulgar and punctuated with Russian. The low-ceilinged room, with windows barred and closed, was filled with a cloud of cigarette smoke. I left the place feeling suffocated.

It was the duty of every Party member returning from abroad to report to the Foreign Department of the Central Committee of the newly formed Polish United Worker's Party, the PZPR. It had been in December of 1948 that the Polish Workers' Party, headed by Gomulka, had merged with the Socialist Party, headed by Cyrankiewicz. When I went to the PZPR offices, the encounter turned out to be a pleasant one. My name was well known there because of my father, and one of the women officials had been a pupil of his. It was then that it occurred to me to request employment there. I did so, and a few days later was summoned to see the department head, Ostap Dluski, who, toward the end of our conversation, said that they wanted me and were already in the process of arranging for me to be transferred from the army. The Party was all-powerful and able to arrange these things, and I concluded that my days in the army were over.

I was assigned to German affairs, which meant that I would pore over West German publications, make brief summaries of them, and indicate anything with which I did not agree in a final note of my own. In one, I wrote that I saw the situation differently—that the Ruhr was not in a state of revolutionary ferment. My remarks caused some consternation, and a short while later I was told that this type of work suited neither them nor me. After that, I was transferred to the Ministry of Foreign Affairs.

Thus it was that I ended up in the institution where three years before I had so unluckily knocked over the ink stand.

Wanda was furnishing our first Warsaw apartment as best she could, standing in lines from five o'clock in the morning for several weeks to buy the basics. Daily life was proving hard, but I firmly believed things would get better.

My convictions were unshakable. So I was not so dismayed as other Poles when Soviet Marshal Konstantin Rokossovsky was nominated marshal of Poland, minister of defense, and commander in chief of all of Poland's armed forces. But Warsaw was seething, and people trembled at the thought of Poland being incorporated into the Soviet Union as another of its republics. In Milanowek at that time, I had a conversation with my father-in-law, who was very ill and weak, suffering from leukemia.

"My days are numbered, but that's not the only reason there's no place for me in this postwar world," he said. "I'm glad you've come. There's something I wanted to ask you about."

It was a gray Sunday afternoon in fall. He was lying on a couch, his pale face lit by the lamp on the table.

"I'm of the belief," he said softly, "that I'm departing an evil world—evil because people have made it so. A world heading for a catastrophe because it has destroyed goodness and truth. A splendid person and patriot like Wladyslaw Sikorski is killed in Gibraltar . . . He would have made a fine leader. But the Bolsheviks have made Rokossovsky our marshal, Rokossovsky, whose army stood and watched while Warsaw fought, burned, and died.

"You remember I told you that I would find out why we were sold out." He sighed. "Now I know. You know why?" he asked, pulling himself up onto his pillow. "Out of stupidity—stupidity! Because the West has no idea what Bolshevism is all about. Neither do you, for that matter." He paused and stared deep into my eyes.

"I've never said this to you before, but now that I'm dying, I will not hold back. I don't understand you. I know you're a decent person. I know your love for family traditions, your love for Poland. I remember that New Year's Eve during the occupation when we listened to the national anthem. . . . But how is it you are so quick to sell us out to Communism and Moscow?"

We looked each other in the eye, his gaze frozen and glassy. I knew that I had to respond from the depths of my heart.

"I am executing my father's will and testament," I replied slowly. "I gave him my word when we said our last farewell. He believed that only communism and the brotherhood of all men, no matter who they are, could save the world and mankind from the curse of endless war, crime, and suffering. When he died, he took my promise with him. I will follow his path until the end of my life."

"Brotherhood." He whispered the word as he gazed steadily at me. "And was it brotherhood that led the Bolsheviks to slaughter the priest who married you? He survived the terrible years of the war only to be tortured to death by the Communists."

"What are you saying?" I interrupted him, seeing Father Sienkiewicz's kindly face bobbing in my memory.

"That's right, tortured. They wanted him to betray people in the underground. He'd been their chaplain."

We sat together in profound silence. My father-in-law died a few days later, on November 18. Until the very end he was a man dedicated to his country.

Life continued to spare us no sorrows. When I went to visit my mother after my father-in-law's funeral, I found her alone. She told me that Tadeusz had suffered a severe nervous breakdown that had been causing him lapses of consciousness and memory. The treatment he had received had done something to his mind. He had become a changed man and had left her.

I learned then, too, that my aunt Emilia and her daughter had died. They had starved themselves to death, unwilling to live in a Bolshevik Poland. They had locked themselves in their apartment, and were found only when the building was scheduled for demolition.

"Think of it, son," my mother said. "After all we've been through, after living every single day as if it were a gift from God, I've been deserted by everyone. In the evening I walk around the house and I hear voices from beneath the floorboards, from that hiding place you built. Sometimes I wake up in a sweat in the middle of the night hearing a pounding at the door and the stomp of boots. Now that I'm all alone here, the local authorities have insisted that some woman live in the little house where the Szirmers hid. As it turns out, she's a prostitute. It must be my fate to suffer everything to the end."

One day Wanda ran into the sister of one of my former teachers in Milanowek, Leon Dziubecki, and learned that he had been arrested and tortured. Wanda ran at once to see my old boss Muszkat and his wife, whom we had since befriended, and made a scene, demanding the release of that innocent man and saying he was an excellent person and a patriot. She attacked me when I returned home that evening, hotly describing the government's brutal treatment of prisoners. I told her that there was a struggle going on in Poland, a struggle for a better future, and an argument broke out between us.

"You believe in those half-cocked ideas, but you're as unfeeling as a stone and blind to what's happening around you. Can't you see what's been done to the best people we know? The true Poles?"

"But, Wanda, you know that we lost millions of people," I said to reproach her for being so narrow-minded and stubborn. "The last system condemned millions of people to death, not thousands. Do you want history to repeat itself, and Poland and all of Europe to run with blood again? You throw crimes in my face as if I were guilty of them. You must be aware by now that I am not a petty criminal and my beliefs are not frivolous pretensions. I'm a Communist and I'll die a Communist like my father."

At the ministry I was appointed head of the section that dealt with relations with East Germany, and I was also elected secretary of one of four Party organizations operating there. I often spoke at meetings, condemning rightist deviation in the PZPR and all nationalistic "distortions" of Communism, such as that in Hungary.

An agreement with the Germans concerning the Oder-Neisse border began to reach a final shape in the spring of 1950. This was to be the permanent Polish-German border. At my level I only executed decisions that were already made; I devised the prepared text of the agreement. The difficulties attending the creation of that text were overcome by Soviet pressure on both sides. The agreement was to be signed at the border, in the small town of Zgorzelec (Görlitz), with a crowd of Poles and Germans who lived on either side of the frontier. The corrections were entered only at the last minute, and on the day of the signing I found myself speeding by car from Warsaw to Zgorzelec with the final version of the document.

When I handed the folders to General Secretary Stefan Wierblowski, he threw me an evil look, for Premier Cyrankiewicz had already bawled him out for the delay.

Years later I was often to think of that day in Zgorzelec. Then, it had seemed a historic victory for peace, for both Poles and Germans. With time, I saw with increasing clarity that it was Soviet foreign policy that was the actual beneficiary there, because the treaty helped them consolidate their hegemony over Central Europe.

In June of 1950 war broke out in Korea. The papers kept reporting the successes of the "Korean Liberation Army," but the situation soon turned around with the landing of American forces at

Inchon in September. Then the press began to sound the alarm and condemn imperialist aggression.

It was in that psychotic atmosphere that the Party committee at the ministry received the instruction to root out alien elements that had managed to infiltrate. Sentence fell on Comrade Gawrak-Czeczot, among others, and the committee called an emergency meeting to demonstrate how a healthy Party purges its ranks of class enemies.

I chaired that meeting, and the hall grew still when, late in the evening, I brought up the Gawrak affair. "The ranks of our Marxist-Leninist Party have been insidiously infiltrated by alien class elements," I began. "Looking at Gawrak's profile, we have to ask ourselves: What connects this man to the Party?"

The hall was silent, the witch hunt was on. I laid bare all that was opportunistic and bourgeois in the victim. The condemned Gawrak sat to one side, head lowered.

Then members of the committee took the floor, hurling biting accusations. Gawrak did not defend himself; in a weak and resigned voice, he said that he had not measured up. I called for an open vote, and Gawrak was expelled unanimously.

I flung him the order, "Return your Party card at once." After taking his card from his trembling hand, I insisted he leave the hall then and there.

Gawrak was dismissed from the ministry as a result of his expulsion from the Party. The so-called good comrades congratulated me for being so decisive in throwing a class enemy out. I noticed that several rank-and-file Party members began giving me ingratiating smiles, in an effort to curry favor with me. To them I was now a "powerful" figure in the Party. I was satisfied with myself; at last I had power I could wield for the good of the Party. Yet, deep within me, though I would never have acknowledged it at the time, I was pricked by an awareness that it had been a nasty, well-rehearsed spectacle, and that I had played the role of inquisitor. Those stirrings of conscience never quite disappeared after that; on the contrary, over the years I thought of that affair more and more. It became a threshold—the time when, blithely bandying the latest catchwords, I had lost my humanity.

The campaign against nationalistic deviations, the purges, the anxious atmosphere caused by the war in Korea, all created a general nervousness, and the Party retaliated by demanding iron discipline.

People were dismissed from work for being a few minutes late; no excuses were accepted. They would arrive panting to check in for the day. The good comrades introduced the custom of staying late at the office, some for whole days and nights on end. The person whose window was lit up the latest was the one most dedicated to the cause. I started going home late, too.

Two of the officers who had worked with me in Germany were hired by the ministry upon their return to Poland. One of them, a prewar lawyer, had lost his entire family in Warsaw. He had returned to Poland only because I had so advised him, and he had confidence in me. Now he was horrified by the state Poland was in, and regretted having returned. One morning, I dropped by his office and found him greatly excited.

"Have you seen the paper?" he asked. "Look. Read this. They've made it a capital crime to possess foreign currency and gold."

The bulletin was perfectly explicit: "The punishment for possessing foreign currency and gold coins includes the death penalty."

"Do you remember that I told you I was keeping all my savings in gold coins? What can I do now? I have no place to hide them—I live in a tiny room. Could you hide them in Milanowek?" he asked, looking helplessly at me.

I could not refuse. I felt responsible for convincing the man to return. A few days later he handed over his gold coins, which I took to Milanowek and buried in the garden one night. But when he needed the money a few years later, I could not find it. I felt terrible, and the next time I went abroad I bought gold and gave him as much as he needed. He is dead now, but his treasure remains buried somewhere under a tree in Villa Rose's garden.

Toward the end of the year I was summoned to the Foreign Department of the Central Committee.

"We have an important assignment for you," Comrade Feder, the deputy director, started in with her quiet but authoritarian voice. "Things aren't going well for our diplomatic service. Our embassy in London is falling to pieces. Only the ambassador and his deputy are left, and we're recalling the deputy. Everyone else has defected, apart from a few clerks. We want to send you there to rectify the situation."

Feder told me about the defections and said that the deputy ambassador was a dedicated comrade but simply didn't know how to get along with people.

"You will replace him, have the rank of first secretary, and be our permanent representative; that means secretary of the Party organization. The army, too, will be turning to you for help—after all, you have old ties with them. Once you know your way around there, write us a report, and we'll recall anyone you feel shouldn't be there.

"One more thing," she continued. "Your predecessor knew a wide range of people in London, including a certain 'Williams.' We want to preserve that contact, because we have been receiving interesting material from him."

As Feder predicted, military intelligence—now called Z-II—got in touch with me. At first I spoke with junior officers, who treated me not as a diplomat, but as their man. They made it clear that they considered me still an officer on active service.

"Your diplomatic post in London," I was told, "should enable you to reconnoiter their main defense installations. We want to know what British capabilities are against an invasion from the Continent. Get to the heart of their defense tactics and inform us if any changes have occurred since the war years, since their defense against the Germans."

I was taken later to the chief, Colonel Bielski. He was tall, and his hair was graying at the temples. In his air force uniform, he looked quite distinguished.

"On the basis of your reports from Germany," he said, "we have added to your responsibilities—you are to give your attention to science and technology, too. That is very important for us now. In Germany you came up with those valuable plans for the steel works. In England try to make as many acquaintances and contacts as you can. If you're active enough and look in the right places, things of interest to us will turn up by themselves. We want to know about political affairs, but only as background. Take the official ministry line on such matters, of course."

He paused for a moment to look me over.

"If the SB, that is, Security, comes to you for anything," he said, "inform us immediately. They are to leave you alone."

"After a year," he said slowly, deliberately, "you will have developed friendly relations with a few potential informers. Then you can start really probing. Our cryptographer will supply you with photographic equipment, cameras, and accessories. For now, learn only one code, the one with which you will communicate with us. It's an easy, weak code, but can quickly be made hard to break. There's one more thing: our military attaché in London. You will not report to him in any way, but in time he might be of some use to you. In a while we'll send you one of our secretaries through the ministry. You can trust her for all your typing." His eyes were calm but intense. "I wish you luck."

CHAPTER XIII

March 1951. I crossed the threshold of the embassy on London's Portland Place firmly resolved to make it into a good diplomatic outpost serving the cause of Communism in Poland. Ambassador Jerzy Michalowski received me with a formal cordiality in which I detected both curiosity and suspicion. It was clear that he looked on me as a plant who would be policing him and everyone else at the embassy.

I began by having talks with what was left of the staff and saw for myself how riddled with intrigue and suspicion the place actually was.

I inherited a corner room on the third floor, which was significantly larger than the ambassador's and contained a large desk, bookcases, deep armchairs, and a safe with double doors. My office could be entered only through my secretary's, whereas the ambassador's office opened directly onto the corridor. While straightening up my room, I came across a series of locked drawers in a bookcase. I tugged open one of them. It was stuffed with bits of paper. I picked up one scribbled messily in pencil: "Today the commercial attaché's wife and the consul's wife were talking in the car. I heard them say things were bad in Poland, and they lowered their voices so I wouldn't hear. The Gadfly." So, this was the denunciation drawer. Disgusted, I made my way through a few more scraps; there were notes from Mosquito, Fly, and an assortment of other insects. I burned them all.

Life was not easy at first in London, especially for my family.

We were lost in that great metropolis. With two children—our second child, Wladyslaw, was born there on June 27, 1951—we found it difficult to get a comfortable apartment, and made five moves in three years. I took enormous pleasure in my son, who was a beautiful and unusually peaceful child, but, unfortunately, I had less and less time to spend with my family.

In keeping with accepted practice, our Consular Division wanted to register our son as having been born in Warsaw, something required by the authorities so that, as they put it, "the child's record will not be spoiled." I was unable to convince the clerks that my wife and I wanted London to be listed. Finally, I had to issue an official order to that effect. It was probably then that I was denounced to Warsaw for the first time.

My first secret action was to meet with the mysterious Williams, a meeting that had been arranged before my arrival in London. Significance had been attached to him as a contact; I had been carefully told not to "burn" this valuable source of information. Our first encounter took place in the British Museum, by the Rosetta stone, a venue that lent appropriate mystery to the exchange. He was a soft-spoken, professorial man with an enigmatic air. He had important papers with him and slipped them to me quickly.

I met with Williams many times thereafter, most often in restaurants. He was always punctual and conscientious in delivering his reports, and from him we received incisive accounts of Great Britain's domestic situation: of behind-the-scenes developments in Parliament, of the labor unions and the economic difficulties. He was a prolific writer, and would bring several papers at a time, for which he was paid five pounds apiece. The Foreign Department of the Central Committee set an especially high value on any materials concerning the Labour Party's left wing, its leader, Aneurin Bevan, and his group in Parliament. We saw in him a force that perhaps at some future point might play a decisive role in British politics.

I grew genuinely fond of Williams, whose real name I never knew, but our meetings began filling me with anxiety. Though I took every possible precaution—changing taxis several times on the way to a meeting—I was haunted by the vague notion that something was wrong, that I was being followed, or that Williams was working for British counterintelligence. I began to observe him closely, and noticed that he displayed no anxiety; he simply did not look around nervously, like a man afraid of being recognized. I decided to break off contact with him.

Soon enough Colonel Bielski in Warsaw had another covert project for me. A Polish atomic physicist, Marian Danysz, had been invited by Cecil F. Powell, of Bristol University, 1950 winner of the Nobel Prize in physics. Danysz would report to me. Powell was one of the leading atomic physicists in the world, studying the disintegration of the nucleus when bombarded by the high-energy particles of cosmic rays. The most advanced technology for conducting such experiments was in Bristol. Specially prepared emulsions were sent up to the stratosphere by balloon, where intensity of cosmic rays is high; the emulsion would then be subjected to microscopic scanning. This method produced results similar to those achieved with the aid of expensive accelerators.

On the basis of my talks with Danysz, I would send reports to which I attached sketches and detailed descriptions of every novelty in Professor Powell's laboratory.

I began attending sessions of Parliament, and when, at the end of October, Winston Churchill became prime minister, I found myself at those sessions often. The debates in the House of Commons were interesting. I was especially fascinated by Churchill's clashes with the leftist Bevan. Our ambassador had made a point of advising me to attend "question time"—when the government had to take questions from the floor.

One day, when nothing particularly important was in the offing, I took a seat in the middle of the first row of the diplomatic gallery, which faced the speaker. It was entirely empty. Churchill began to take questions, and I marveled at how freely and fluently he spoke. He offered a rather laconic explanation to a question concerning, as I recall, British armed forces in the Far East, but then, pressed by the Opposition, who, with a great hubbub, demanded an exhaustive reply, Churchill made a theatrical gesture to stop the uproar. Why was he being forced to reveal secrets, he asked, when there could well be a Communist spy in the gallery just dying to get his hands on that very information. He pointed sharply up in my direction. All heads turned toward the gallery. I could feel hundreds of eyes upon me. I left when the debate resumed, and never returned.

We received news that First Secretary Gomulka had been arrested. Soon after, Wanda returned from Warsaw with grim news to tell. An officer we had known in Germany "asked me to tell you," she said, "that there have been a great many arrests in the army, even in Z-II. He warns you not to go to Poland if you can help it, and to refuse to return home if you are summoned."

Her words troubled me, but I was all too used to her hypersensitivity. I also knew that she had friends and acquaintances in the underground and had inherited their sense of doom. I paid little attention to the warning.

In mid-1952, I was in Warsaw again and reported to Colonel Bielski. Great Britain had just conducted a successful test of its own atomic bomb in the Monte Bello Islands, and he was vehement in insisting that I quickly become more active in matters relating to science, and atomic research in particular.

He seemed exhausted; his inner calm was gone; he spoke disjointedly. "In our line of work the only person you can trust is yourself." He was looking me in the eye too directly. "Remember, on one side of you you've got British counterintelligence, who are very experienced, and on the other, Security agents, Polish and otherwise. Our people have a variety of aims, a great variety. . . ." He was about to add something, but fell silent for a moment. "Watch out for Security. They shouldn't have any idea what you're doing."

I was anxious to change the subject—though later I came to regret it—and asked, "What do you think about the reports from Danysz?"

"Good . . . better than good. It's a shame that he's left England. Why don't you get in touch with Bristol yourself? Or with Harwell—England's leading scientific center? You seem to know a great deal about physics." With that, our meeting was over.

Bielski's office led out through a reception room, where a lieutenant sat at a desk; beyond that was a wide hallway with doors on both sides. The corridor was odd: at a certain point it narrowed so that only one person at a time could pass. The fat dark-haired sergeant who monitored traffic there would have had trouble squeezing through himself. I wondered what its purpose was, but that was the sort of institution where it was better not to ask questions. Its purpose became all too clear six months later, when I was in Warsaw again.

I had been scolded sternly by the Central Committee for not having yet made contact with the British Communist Party, and especially with its foreign section. So upon my return to London, I met with Robert Stewart, the section head. He was a short, stocky man of about seventy, but he held himself well; he had a ruddy, expressive face, an aquiline nose, and a large gray mustache. He spoke with a thick Scottish brogue, which I could barely understand, but I liked the man. He had the bluff ways of a real worker. We continued to meet, usually at his home or at mine.

At Stewart's, I met the heads of the Communist Party in Britain. They congratulated me warmly on the passage—as they put it—of the new constitution that confirmed Poland as a people's republic. When will that happen here, they wondered, and took consolation in the hope that it might occur during their lifetimes.

My work seemed to be progressing smoothly, and on weekends I took Wanda and the children to Hyde Park, where we could listen to the Sunday orators, who, on chairs or wooden boxes, spoke whether anyone was listening or not. Those were rare moments we spent together, with Misia running around and paying her inevitable visit to the statue of Peter Pan, and Wanda behind the carriage of our baby son, whom we had nicknamed Kaytus. I loved my family very much, but was keenly aware of my inability to be as free and easy as the people around us: the grown men sailing boats on the pond, the boys running across the beautiful grass pulling kites.

Just after I broke off contact with Williams, events occurred that were to draw me in deeper and deeper. I had made the acquaintance of a British architect who knew a great deal about the areas I had been ordered to investigate by Z-II. He was an older man who had spent the entire war in England and had taken part in planning the coastal defenses that had been hastily installed to protect the island from an invasion by Germany.

On the basis of his descriptions, I made sketches of underwater structures whose purpose was to make German troop landings impossible. I did not succeed in obtaining from him the general plan of defense for the British Isles, but I did learn something about the various stages through which it had evolved. It was clear that the best military and civilian minds had been employed.

My meetings with that engineer were infrequent, but they continued for quite some time. Even with him, I was not entirely certain that I was not dealing with a plant.

One day, Bob Stewart, taking great precautions, informed me that two young scientists from the nuclear study facility at Harwell had decided to leave England permanently with their families and devote themselves to the cause of socialism. To my complete surprise, I now had access to a place that Bielski had singled out as a prime place to gather intelligence. I immediately dispatched a "lightning bolt"—a coded, top-priority telegram that had to be hand-delivered at once. That same day I received a "thunderbolt"—a telegram that had to be replied to through our constant radio contact.

Z-II insisted on more information. I was unable to answer a number of their questions about the physicists, but dispatched the information I did have. A lightning bolt arrived that evening, instructing me to look into the matter in detail. My orders were unequivocal: complete secrecy is essential. Your behavior must not cause the slightest suspicion. You must act in strict accordance with our instructions. Inform us when they are ready to leave.

The ambassador had just left on vacation and was later to attend a session of the United Nations General Assembly. Thus a variety of diplomatic duties fell on me. It was I who, in the name of the Polish mission, had to greet the new Soviet ambassador to London, Andrei Gromyko, a dour man of few words and a face of stone. Yet despite the fact that I was busily attending receptions and organizing Party meetings at the embassy, my mind was constantly whirling with plans for the Harwell scientists—my "Operation Bob."

One day, I was disturbed to find that someone had tampered with the seal that I broke off each day from the wooden panel on my safe. I remembered Bielski's warning. The new employees, who had just arrived, were all representatives of Security, and, even though relations were formally correct, I had noticed that they were taking unusual interest in my activities. I decided to establish a hiding place for Operation Bob that would be known to me alone. At night, with my office doors securely locked and the curtains carefully drawn, I improvised a hiding place under the floor, a miniature version of the one we had made during the occupation; this one was reached by removing the old brass screws in the parquet floor. I eventually kept all my secret documents there. No one ever learned of that hiding place; no doubt it is still there.

Stewart came by the embassy from time to time bringing various official Party publications, which I would pass on to Warsaw. One day when he brought the latest issues and we had sat down at a table, he drew a blank piece of paper from his pocket and wrote a date on it. I understood that this was the date the scientists would be ready to go behind the iron curtain. I rose and burned the piece of paper in the fireplace while he watched, nodding approval. We had not exchanged a single word.

I notified Z-II by lightning bolt and received an answer that I would get detailed instructions for the physicists in the next diplomatic pouch. I was also ordered to meet with them in order to check them out one last time and establish the latest plans for their journey. We order you, read the last line, to make every possible effort to avoid surveillance.

The diplomatic mail arrived one week later, and late that same day our cryptographer brought me a gray envelope innocently addressed: Comrade R. Spasowski. Deliver in person.

I waited until I was alone, and could lock myself in my room, before tearing open the envelope. Inside was a somewhat smaller envelope marked "For Karol"—for me. That envelope contained yet another, sewn at all four corners with coarse thread and then sealed with wax in the middle and at the corners. I broke the seals and read my instructions. I was to memorize them and make no notes. The instructions, quite detailed, divided Operation Bob into phases. Both married couples were to travel to Bern, Switzerland, for what was supposedly a short vacation in the Alps. A story should be fabricated and put into circulation; it should be spread around, for example, that the women's health made the trip necessary, but it should not be overdone. A few dates and flights from London to choose from were listed, with the explanation that there would be connections with flights to Warsaw on those days. If the plane from London was delayed, the Polish flight would wait for them. Both physicists were to wear something by which they could be recognized; a password and response were also to be established. When the flight from London arrived, a man would be waiting by the exit with a raincoat over his arm (a short description of him was given); he would have dealt with all the formalities already, and the travelers would be able to proceed with him at once to the Polish plane. They were advised to bring only hand luggage with them, but if they insisted, they could ship heavier things themselves or these could be sent on the next flight. I was to keep Z-II informed at every step. In conclusion, I was told to return the instructions by the same courier as soon as I had memorized them.

I was in a state of agitation. It was clear that the success of the plan depended on me alone. I read through the instructions a few times and committed them to memory. Then I phoned Wanda and told her I had a lot of paperwork and would not be home until morning. She answered that that made no sense at all, that I was ruining my health for no good reason, and that one day I would regret it. Sad and weary, I tossed the envelopes into my fireplace and watched as they glowed in the fire and burned to ashes.

I decided to read through the instructions one more time, but I could not find them. Had I burned all the pages along with the envelopes? I sat down and immediately wrote out all the instructions from memory. I would have some explaining to do. Day had just begun to break as I fell asleep on my couch.

Toward the end of that week an Englishman brought a note to me at the embassy. It was an invitation from Stewart to come to his house for dinner. I knew I would be meeting the physicists there.

On the appointed day, I returned home as usual from the embassy and went shopping with Wanda. In the evening, I went out for a walk and caught a cab to Hyde Park; from there I took a second cab to Trafalgar Square, and then a third to Stewart's house. His daughter let me in. Sitting beside Bob in the living room was a young man—Campbell, one of the physicists.

"His colleague couldn't come," said Stewart. "His wife's not well. But everything's still on. Both couples are ready to leave."

I looked at Campbell long and hard. Did he really look like the sort of person who would want to devote himself to socialism? Did he have any idea what life was like in Warsaw?

"Have you planned this for a long time?" I asked.

"Yes, for a few years now." He looked over at Stewart, as if at a witness. "I don't see any place for me here; there's no future here."

"Does anyone know about your plans?"

"Only my wife and Comrade Stewart. And of course my friend who's going with us."

"And are you prepared for certain inconveniences . . . in the beginning?" I asked.

"Oh, yes. We're not living in luxury here. We're ready." He paused. "I want to dedicate my work to the good of mankind. I don't want it used for imperialistic purposes, for exploitation."

He sounded sincere. For a moment it seemed I could hear myself speaking, the person I was before the war, the idealist. He, too, had a great shock of hair, as I had once had, and he looked me straight in the eye. A decent man, I concluded.

"How do you plan to travel?" I asked.

He shrugged his shoulders.

"I suggest Switzerland. I've heard that you've already been there once, skiing. A trip to the same place will attract the least attention. Perhaps you could go together, both couples. And perhaps you can say that you're traveling for health reasons."

"That's all taken care of," he replied with a smile. "The doctors have already advised my wife to spend some time in a dry Continental climate."

I questioned him about Harwell, and from his answers it was clear that he knew the place well.

"I don't want to work for the extermination of the human race," he said. "The future of the world belongs to socialism, to equality and peace, not to war."

He reached into his pocket and drew out what looked like a fountain pen, but was, in fact, a small Geiger counter that all the staff at Harwell carried to detect whether they had been exposed to harmful levels of radioactivity.

"With your permission, I'd like to bring along certain small instruments like this," he said. "They might come in handy, and they'll never be missed here. I don't know whether you have such things over there."

It was the first time I had ever seen such a device that size and I examined it with interest.

We settled on a date for their departure. Stewart sat listening in on the conversation, looking like a Scot happy to have poked the British imperialists in the eye. He fiddled with his mustache and sipped hot tea, smacking his lips. Though pleased with it all himself, Campbell was clearly growing more and more nervous. His fingers drummed the table.

"Will we meet in Poland?" he asked as I rose.

"I can't really say," I answered. "I'd like very much to see you in Warsaw, but I can't make any promises."

Now that the die was cast and everything settled, perhaps he felt uneasy, I thought. He was probably wondering what it would be like living among strangers.

I said good-bye to him and wished him success. Before leaving I asked Stewart to phone me at home as soon as their plane took off. He need not say anything; the call itself would be indication enough.

It was late when I left Stewart's house. I walked part of the way and caught a taxi on Kilburn Road. Pleased that such an important affair was progressing so smoothly, so secretly, I leaned back and felt myself begin to relax. The taxi was moving fast, and when it took a corner, I felt a spring in the seat jabbing into me. Strange, I thought, a new taxi and the seat is already broken. I felt it again at the next turn and reached between the seat and the back. Something was stuck there. I pulled it out and found myself holding a large pistol. I froze. My fingerprints were on it. Who would believe that the gun was not mine? It might have already been used in a crime. A trap?

I looked out the window. The best thing to do would be to open it quietly and toss out the pistol. Just then we passed two policemen, under a streetlight. If I tossed it right at their feet, the chase would be on. The driver might be a plant; he might be watching me to sound the alarm as soon as I tossed the pistol. I looked through the rear window and saw the headlights of a car following us at a distance. Damn it, I thought, we're being followed; there's no point in tossing it out the window. I took out my handkerchief, wiped the pistol clean, and then used the handkerchief to push it back between the seat and the back. I could think of nothing else to do.

We had reached Regent's Park and approached Portland Place quickly. I glanced at the embassy, on the corner. No one was around. I looked around again as I pulled out my money. Weymouth Street was deserted, too. I reached back for the pistol, slipped it into my pocket, and got out.

I breathed a sigh when the sleepy watchman turned on the light in the embassy's side entrance and peered out at me through the peephole.

"Oh, it's you, Comrade Secretary. So late and you're still working." I detected a touch of flattery in his voice.

I locked myself in my office and took out the pistol. It was a large Browning that had clearly seen a lot of service, maybe during the war. I removed the clip, opened the bolt, and a cartridge popped out of the chamber. The gun had been loaded and ready to fire. One of the cartridges was gone. I could only guess at the circumstances that had caused the gun to be abandoned. I sniffed the barrel; it smelled of a recent firing, and the characteristic bluish deposit was in the chamber.

I sent a lightning bolt to Z-II: "Operation in process. Will confirm when they are on their way."

On the critical day I nervously waited at home for the phone to ring. Scheduled departure time had already come and gone. Finally, after what seemed hours, the phone rang. I snatched up the receiver, but the caller said nothing. The physicists were in the air.

I went at once to the embassy and dispatched a thunderbolt: "Operation executed. They're in air." I indicated the time and the flight. "Rest is up to you," I said; "I await confirmation."

A reply arrived quickly: "Confirmed. Remainder of operation in progress. Everything prepared." The next day I received a lightning bolt that read: "Operation concluded."

I did not see Bob Stewart for several weeks, until one day he stopped by the embassy unexpectedly with some party publications and asked if I would like to meet Harry Pollitt, the general secretary of the Communist Party of Great Britain. I was delighted; I knew that he rarely saw anyone in private. It was arranged that Pollitt and his wife would come to my home on Bayswater Road for dinner.

The Pollitts were warm and pleasant. Harry was over sixty, bald, with tufts of gray hair at the sides of his head. He asked about Poland, the reconstruction of Warsaw, the Polish Communist Party, but after those questions he grew reticent, taciturn. This was the time when Rudolf Slansky, the general secretary of the Czechoslovakian Communist Party, was on trial. Our conversation made its inevitable way to that subject. In the last mail from Warsaw I had received a sheaf of materials from the Central Committee denouncing in the harshest possible terms the "treacherous conspiracy" Slansky had headed. I told Pollitt about Slansky, reciting the Party line's litany of the man's crimes. He gazed at me with his large bulging eyes, but did not respond; it was as if he had not heard what I said.

Years later, in 1963, Slansky was posthumously rehabilitated. But Pollitt did not live to know it. Only many years later, too, did I learn that on Soviet instructions Party prosecutors had offered an array of "traitors," in Hungary, Bulgaria, Rumania, Albania. In Poland they had singled out Gomulka.

I delayed calling a meeting about the Slansky case and only did so at the beginning of December 1952, after he had been executed.

I chaired that meeting, but the main report was delivered by someone else. In keeping with the materials sent by the Central Committee, Slansky was depicted as a monster for whom any condemnation would have been too mild. Even there, in the embassy's Chinese Salon, our little group caught the whiff of menace in the air and dutifully heaped Slansky's corpse with a long list of accusations and abuse. The excoriation was followed by praises sung to the "Land of the Soviets," which, under Stalin's brilliant leadership, was carrying out the great program that would lead from socialism to communism. We in Poland, concluded the speaker, are protected from errors and distortions because our Party and our government are now led by a new man, Boleslaw Bierut.

I left the meeting with a sense of shame at having chaired and lent myself to that sort of display, although it was not the first time I had witnessed—even thundered—a denunciation. How had it come to happen, I wondered. How could a person with such high ideals as mine find himself among such people, taking part in such a charade?

That meeting was to have consequences. A few days later, the trade counselor came to see me in a state of indignation; the doorman, a member of the Party, had been so disturbed by it that he had simply quit working.

"Just imagine," he said. "Yesterday I had a meeting with some important British industrialists, some of whom came from outside London. Our doorman, who *always* opens the door graciously and hangs up the visitors' coats, sat in the cloakroom as if he were deaf. When I asked him why, he said it was high time he stopped waiting on those capitalist snakes, and that he wasn't going to lift a finger for them any more. He said he'd been fighting in the class struggle for forty years and he wasn't going to lower himself one minute more. I had to hang their coats myself. He's *still* not doing anything today!

"But do you know what he's really up to? It's not too difficult to figure out! He probably feels there are traitors like Slansky right here in our embassy, and it's time he put an end to them, too. Maybe he has me in mind and—who knows?—maybe you, too. I know for a fact that the staff thinks you are not the least bit concerned about them."

I called an executive meeting to defuse the situation, but it turned out that the doorman was not the only one to have caught the scent of counterrevolution.

"Yes, the doorman did not behave properly," said our military attaché. "No one should quit work without notice. And yet I think that he was motivated by healthy class instincts. He was only employing what he learned at our meetings."

It was a stormy exchange leading nowhere. In the end the doorman went back to work, as a favor, but missed no opportunity to crow that a counterrevolution was afoot.

At the beginning of 1953, official Polish-British relations were nil. Our embassy devoted itself exclusively to intelligence work and propaganda. Contacts with the Foreign Office were a pure formality. The situation was only a reflection of the mood in Poland at the time, as well as of East-West tensions caused by events in Korea.

In January, Churchill paid a visit to Washington, where he warned against any further Chinese involvement in the Korean war. At the end of the month, news of the "Doctors' Plot" was made public in Moscow. A group of Jewish physicians was accused of plotting to murder Stalin. Once again meetings were held in which everyone was condemned: counterrevolutionaries, imperialists, capitalists, nationalists, cosmopolites, Jews, doctors.

In the frenzy of those days, a telegram arrived from the ministry informing the ambassador that he was being recalled. I was summoned to Warsaw. In the ministry, I was instructed to make sure that the change of ambassadors proceeded smoothly.

I called Z-II to report in. "We'll pass on the message," said the voice at the other end of the line dryly. "Where can you be reached?"

Days passed without a word. I called again and demanded to speak with the officer in charge of British affairs. I could sense confusion at the other end. After a wait, a voice came on the line speaking Russian. "This is Major . . ." I didn't catch the Russian name.

I repeated my name and said that I would be in Warsaw only a short time and would like to speak with someone. The major knew who I was and told me to report in two days.

That conversation gave me pause; I was reminded of the warning that Wanda had passed on to me, but I was not particularly worried, merely miffed at having been put off so curtly.

Two days later I presented myself at the guard office at Z-II.

There had been changes: there was a different entrance now, and passage into the building was allowed only after a thorough checking and rechecking of identification. The duty officer accompanied me upstairs. Automatically, I turned down the hall toward Colonel Bielski's office, but the duty officer pointed me in the opposite direction.

"Colonel Bielski has a new office?" I asked.

He gave me a look of utter surprise. "He no longer works here," he replied. "This way please."

He opened a door that led to a reception room where an officer in Polish uniform whom I had never seen before sat behind a desk. Two Soviet officers, a lieutenant colonel and a colonel, were standing beside him.

The Polish officer rose and introduced me, speaking Russian. It was difficult to get a conversation going. The Russians did not try to mask their scrutiny of me. A moment later two more Soviet officers entered the room, with a major in Polish uniform, a man I had dealt with before. The phone rang.

"Everyone's here, Comrade General," the officer at the desk said into the phone. He indicated the door behind him; I passed through and was astounded by what I saw.

The office was significantly larger than any I had seen in that building. The curtains were half drawn; lamps in the corners cast a dim light. On the wall hung a life-size portrait of Stalin in his generalissimo's cap and uniform, against a background of unfurled red flags. A Soviet general rose from behind the desk, the gold stars on his shoulder boards gleaming. A row of Soviet officers seated at a table perpendicular to the desk also rose to their feet.

The general strode up and extended his hand. "Hello, Comrade. Take a seat," he said in Russian, indicating a place at the table across from him. "How are things, Comrade Major?" he asked, switching to something that he supposed to be Polish. "You've done well," he said. "But tell me, are the Conservatives really going to rule Great Britain for long?"

"That's difficult to judge," I began carefully, and went on to give him a measured report. The general nodded, the gold on his uniform flashing with every movement. The officers around me, most of whom were colonels, looked intently at me, some nodding seriously.

"All right," interrupted the general after a while. "You've done good work, and you should be commended for that. So, for work well done, a present for you, on behalf of the Polish army. . . ."

He leaned forward ponderously and handed a red box to the officer seated nearest to him. The box passed from one officer to the next until it reached me. I opened it. A German camera—a Leica—sat inside.

"For you . . . To remember us by . . ." said the general, rising. I rose, too, at a loss for words.

"Well, we wish you more success," he said, coming from behind his desk and offering me his hand.

I left the room followed by all but a few of the other officers.

"We'll talk later," said the Polish major, the only other Pole there. "He wanted that meeting; all of his assistants were there."

"A lot has changed. . . . I don't recognize the place," I said.

The major gave me what seemed an odd look.

"And whatever happened to those physicists?" I asked.

"Oh, them. They went east. . . . Well, I'll be seeing you," he said and walked away briskly.

I was seen out by a fat, swarthy sergeant in a Polish uniform.

"What happened to Colonel Bielski?" I asked. "Where's his office now?"

My question so astounded the sergeant that he came to a full stop halfway down the stairs. He pointed skyward with his thumb. Then he continued down the stairs without a word more.

At the bottom, I asked him: "What do you mean? Dead?"

"They're still repainting his office," replied the sergeant, lowering his voice. "The stains keep coming through. When he blew out his brains, they splattered all over the wall."

We were right by the exit. Suddenly the pupils of his eyes shrank—he was clearly frightened he had said too much. He saluted, spun around, and walked away.

Years later I learned part of that story. Bielski had flown back to Warsaw from an assignment. There was a car waiting for him, and it went straight to Z-II. Secret police followed him. He locked himself in his office—perhaps he hoped to elude them—but he knew they were waiting for him at the point where the corridor narrowed. They wanted to take him alive; he denied them that pleasure. No one was ever able to explain what he was afraid of. As far as I could determine, he had been a devoted Communist.

After my return to London, Ambassador Michalowski left for a short vacation before his departure. And while he was away, a real bomb went off: March 5, Stalin died. We received a note to that effect from the Soviets, indicating the days their ambassador would be receiving condolences.

At the Soviet Embassy the young woman who opened the door for me had a tear-stained face and a wet handkerchief in her hand. The place was as silent as a tomb. The embassy workers moved on tiptoe, their faces frozen into grim expressions. Ambassador Gromyko was receiving in a small sitting room; on the wall was a portrait of Stalin wreathed in black crepe. We exchanged greetings, and I took a seat across from him. The funereal atmosphere was contagious, and I was able to utter only a short formal expression of condolence, all in one breath. Then we simply sat facing one another in silence. If only his eyelids would move, if only his lips would move, I thought. But his cold gaze told me neither what he was thinking and feeling nor whether I should leave or remain. I rose and left the room.

When I told Wanda my impressions, we agreed that there was something atavistic about their behavior, some whiff of old Russia, with all its groveling before the tsar. Mistakenly, I thought that the people in our embassy would behave differently from the Soviets. But a committee was immediately formed to prepare a commemorative ceremony, and they vied with one another in concocting ways to honor Stalin's memory.

The commemoration was held in the Chinese Salon, always dark because of the goldbronze color of the walls. Only one lamp was on. Candles flickered on either side of our crepe-wreathed photograph of Stalin, as before an altar. Upon entering, I heard women weeping plaintively; the men sat wiping their noses. Theatrically, the Security employees were leading the pack. I could not believe my eyes and ears. Just as I took my seat at the chairman's table, I saw Wanda enter the room, but I soon lost her in the crowd.

The ceremony dragged on, and though it would be difficult to describe all the speeches, they were united in their regret and despair. One person's voice broke with emotion as he said that our father was gone and now the children were all alone. I was anxious for the masquerade to end.

On the way home in the car I asked Wanda: "Where were you?

I couldn't find you. You shouldn't walk out like that. You know how people watch."

"I had no intention of leaving," she answered. "But as soon as I went into that room and saw those candles burning in front of the picture of that monster and heard people crying, forgive me, but I couldn't restrain myself. It all struck me as so funny that I almost burst out laughing. Thank God, our friend from the shipping office ran over to me and led me out of the room, so people couldn't see. We went upstairs to your waiting room, and he explained to me that such behavior could be dangerous. Had anyone noticed, it would have been the end of you. Forgive me."

The new chief, Ambassador Milnikiel, arrived. A large, coarse man, he often used vulgar language. But beneath that surface was a kindly man, probably the most decent person I encountered in our diplomatic service.

Immediately after his arrival, the newspapers broke a sensational story: Captain Cwiklinski, of our passenger liner *Batory*, left the ship in Newcastle, where she was undergoing repairs. The ambassador received instructions to assign me to save the situation; they feared that the entire crew might want to defect.

I had a conversation with the ambassador before leaving London.

"I told them I didn't want you to go," he said. "I was counting on you to have enough time to acquaint me with what's been going on here, but they insisted that it had to be you. They're afraid that if they send anybody from the secret police, the crew will get scared and stay for sure. Those Security people are a no-good bunch; they've done enough harm already."

I was taken aback to hear a Party member speak so candidly. Milnikiel smiled at my astonishment. "All right, go," he said. "My only request is that you phone me at least twice a day. I know those people in Warsaw—they'll be demanding a report before you even get there. They're about to get mud in their eyes over there in Newcastle, and they're worried about it."

"And what if there's no news?"

"Call twice a day every day no matter what."

It was rainy, damp, and cold when I arrived in Newcastle by train. Even from a distance, I recognized the *Batory*, a fifteen-thousand-ton ship with many decks. I climbed the ladder to the main deck just as the first officer strode over to introduce himself as the captain's deputy. The crew regarded me with a certain hostility. I ordered the deputy to take me to the captain's cabin and explain the situation to me in detail. Within that room, I could get a sense of the captain—of the man. Memorabilia cluttered the desk: framed photographs, souvenirs, paperweights. A row of certificates hung on the wall, and, above them, the crowned Polish eagle.

"I don't know what's happened to him," began the deputy. "He simply disappeared, and then his statement showed up here. I knew something was going on. He had become impatient. It was obvious he was suffering through some decision. Nothing's missing. He took only part of his own personal belongings and, as you can see, even left his photographs behind."

We talked about the morale of the officers and crew, and the deputy said, "I feel I can tell you in confidence that the captain couldn't stand that officer in charge of cultural and educational affairs—you know who I mean, that political instructor. He was always butting in everywhere. You know who he works for. . . . The captain just couldn't bear him." He hesitated for a moment. "You see, not everyone would understand this. You'd have to know Cwiklinski. He's a prewar man. He had his faults, like everybody else, but he had great virtues, too. He was a real person, knew the world—a true patriot, and the crew knew that and loved him for it. His presence permeated this ship. As soon as he entered a room, all eyes would turn. He spoke beautifully. Oh, he was a *real* captain. You can understand what that means, can't you?"

I nodded. "I understand it very well. Tell me more."

"So, what do they do? They send somebody on board to sniff around and listen at doors." Suddenly he stopped. "Maybe I've said too much."

"I thank you for your straightforwardness. You don't have to worry; it won't go any further. But don't mention it to anyone else; not everyone's the same. Tell me now, how many of the others want to stay here in England?"

"None of them, as far as I know."

That day I met with the other officers, and the next day with the crew. The Security officer seemed to be gloating, pleased that the captain, against whom he had written a good deal, had confirmed his opinions by deserting.

I spent a week in Newcastle and telephoned Milnikiel every day to assure him that everything was in order and that the ship would return to Poland as soon as the repairs were completed. Toward the end of the week he asked, with some impatience, "And nobody else has deserted?"

"Nobody," I replied.

"And the crew's morale?"

"They're taking the captain's disappearance hard, but they have families; they'll be going back."

"And the officers?" He was being persistent.

"They're going back, too. What are you so upset about?" I asked, having become impatient myself.

"And who's hanging around? You know what I mean. Any émigrés, Poles, strangers? Potential agents?"

"Not that I noticed. There are a few local Poles lounging around the dock in front of the ship now and then, but that's normal."

"Listen," said the ambassador, his voice losing all patience, "you must give me something more definite than that. The man with the sour face—you know who I mean—is bombarding me with greens, and won't leave me alone."

I knew who he meant: the general secretary of the ministry, Wierblowski. "Green" meant coded telegram.

"Well, then," I responded, "write him that Spasowski reports that the ship will be sailing home, and aboard it will be all the crew. If they need something more definite than that, tell them it's been pouring the whole time here in Newcastle, and that it's cold."

"Go to hell," he barked, and hung up.

The ambassador summoned me as soon as I returned to London. Without so much as a word, he handed me a stack of telegrams that had passed between him and Wierblowski during my absence. They were arranged chronologically: on top was the notice of my departure and Milnikiel's calm report of what I had learned in Newcastle. Toward the middle of the stack, Wierblowski's tone began to betray increasing impatience. The demands for further information became categorical and terse, and the replies more and more laconic. The ambassador's final reply read: "Kiss my ass."

I shook with laughter, unable to restrain myself.

He, however, remained serious. "Well! What can you expect? That idiot was not about to let up with those questions of his." Milnikiel knew Bierut, and was safe. He did not have to mince words with anybody—because of his connections, of course, but also because he was that sort of man.

The *Batory* did in fact return to Poland. With, I believe—at least on that occasion—all its crew on board.

I threw myself into my next intelligence assignment—the penetration of an institute doing research on germ warfare—but when I successfully passed some material on to Warsaw, new orders arrived: I was not to involve myself with this matter any further. I understood from this that someone else would be taking over my contact, and that I would be leaving the country shortly. This proved true.

We left London for good soon after we attended Queen Elizabeth II's coronation. But before departure I chaired a final Party meeting. News had spread that I was being recalled, and the Party members did not hide their hostility toward me now that they did not have to. As the meeting progressed, their speeches startled and pained me. When I had arrived in London, the embassy was falling apart. I had had no small part in its reconstruction. And now some doorman or driver was taking the floor and braying: "You know, comrades, as soon as I came here, I could see things weren't right. Working people aren't appreciated in this embassy. Comrades, the ambassador and the Party secretary have separated themselves from the masses. They're diplomats, they're *heads.* And it's the fishhead that always starts stinking first. . . ."

I turned cold and hot by turns. I thought of how much work I had put in there, how many sleepless nights . . . and to have it all end like this. The entire group listened in silence, a good many nodding their heads.

Security had clearly taken control of the embassy, and many were afraid. I recalled Bielski's warning to me and his miserable self-immolation. It was with such thoughts that I returned to Poland with my family in the summer of 1953.

CHAPTER XIV

In July of 1953 the Council of State appointed me envoy to Argentina. Several years before, an envoy had been sent there, but he had defected soon after his arrival in Buenos Aires.

"I'm telling you in *deadly* earnest, you must leave as quickly as possible," Foreign Minister Stanislaw Skrzeszewski said to me as he scribbled a note and tossed it into his desk drawer. He had been a teacher before the war, and indeed looked comfortable at a desk. In fact, behind his desk he seemed a great deal larger than he was. His head was huge, his eyes swift and darting. He was known for his mentorial pronouncements, and as soon as I left his office, one of his staff asked me, "Did he say that what he was telling you was in 'deadly earnest'? And did he make a note and then toss it in his drawer? Better watch out; that means he'll remember."

The fact that we had not had an envoy in Argentina for years, Minister Skrzeszewski told me, was something that did not please "our friends" at all. Haste was essential. So, we were in Buenos Aires by autumn.

I visited Soviet Ambassador Rezanov while waiting for the opportunity to present President Juan Perón with my credentials. A massive man with a bloated face and small shrewd eyes, the Russian surprised me by his praise for the Argentine president.

"Warsaw considers Peronism an Argentine version of fascism," I began, dutifully parroting the foreign minister's words to me.

Rezanov grimaced. "Yes, people think that because Perón himself cites Mussolini as his mentor. But the situation has changed, and that's no longer the point. Mussolini is gone; only Franco is left, and he and Perón aren't very fond of each other. That's not what matters to us, not what's useful to us. The main thing is that Perón is anti-American. He can't be otherwise; he has to be anti-American and anti-imperialist to exist. That's his platform, that's his appeal here. And *that,*" said Rezanov, drawing on his cigarette, "is the key thing for us. We can mount that platform with him." He smiled, winked, and poured us some vodka.

"Yes, but he persecutes the Communist Party," I said firmly.

"He does and he doesn't," replied Rezanov, wobbling his head on his corpulent neck. "And besides, what military government in Latin America *doesn't* persecute Communists? But Perón changes his tune from time to time. It depends which way he's facing. If he wants to show Washington his teeth, he lets the Communists out of prison and delivers an anti-imperialist speech, but if he wants something out of the Americans, he locks the Communists back up. . . . Lately he's been leaving them alone. . . .

"You see," said Rezanov, lifting his glass, "Perón understands that the Soviet Union is his ally against America. The other socialist countries, too," he added. "So let's drink to that. Perón's no fool. If he acts properly, we'll help him. Na zdorovye." He toasted me.

"I wonder what sort of reception you'll get from him," Rezanov continued. "Of course you'll tell me about it later on."

I did not have to wait long for my meeting with Perón. On the day my credentials were to be presented, two carriages drawn by beautiful horses and a cavalry detachment in tall caps appeared in front of our mission on Avenida Libertador San Martín and took me to the Casa Rosada, the presidential residence.

I was surprised by the palace's rich and traditional decor, the beautiful period furniture in its drawing rooms, the sculptures, mirrors, gilding, and paintings. Juan Perón received me in military dress, wearing a sash bright with the national colors, and supporting himself with a cane. Behind him were the minister of foreign affairs, whom I knew from preliminary visits, and the head of protocol.

After the ceremonial presentation of credentials, Perón gave me a friendly smile, offered his hand, and indicated a little table and chairs off to one side. Once the polite formalities were over—my telling him that I wished to develop an exchange of Poland's coal for Argentina's grain, and his assurances that I was welcomed in friendship—he lit a cigarette, and the conversation became more relaxed.

"Congratulations on your splendid speeches at the United Nations," he said at one point. I pricked up my ears. "Your representative, Andrei Vishinsky. He's been making very good speeches, strongly condemning American imperialism."

Should I correct the president? I took a subtler route: "Vishinsky, who is the Soviet Union's representative, has done a fine job of presenting the position of the largest among the socialist countries."

I do not know whether Perón understood the point I was making, but I did notice the ministers exchanging glances. Perón was in a good humor and blazed ahead.

"Our revolution," he said, "is a genuine Argentine one. For that reason, what we're doing here has a powerful and lasting basis. The imperialists don't believe that, but time will prove their error. . . ." He broke off and calmly finished his cigarette.

"I'll tell you about an exchange I once had with the American ambassador," he continued, a big grin spreading over his face. He lit another cigarette with his gold lighter and inhaled deeply.

"He was sitting in the same chair you're in now. We were talking. At one point in the conversation he reached into his pocket, pulled out a coin, and turned it over and over in the palm of his hand, like this. 'This is a twenty-dollar gold piece,' he said. 'I'd like to give it to you, Mr. President, as a souvenir of our first meeting.' He proffered the coin. For a moment I wondered what to do. However, I extended my hand and took the present."

Perón smiled, his eyes gleaming with amusement. "Do you know what I said? I said that I was taking that twenty dollars because any money used to counteract American imperialism is good money."

We both guffawed.

I had been in Buenos Aires for a little more than a year and was quite satisfied with the way our mutual relations were developing. Trade was at an unprecedented level, and there was every promise of continued success. Wanda and I had acquired great affection and feeling for Argentina. The children were quickly learning Spanish. But just as we were beginning to feel at home there, I was suddenly, in November of 1954, summoned to Warsaw.

"We're recalling you at once, said Skrzeszewski to me when I arrived. You'll have just enough time to get your affairs in order. I want you back in Poland before the end of the year. We'll be sending you to another post . . . to the United States. You'll have to move quickly." He picked up his pen, dashed off a note, and tossed it into his desk drawer.

On our return, I was struck by the contrast between life in Warsaw and the vibrancy of Buenos Aires. Warsaw was sad and gray; hunched, shivering people stood in lines in front of stores. In the center of the city, on an enormous square, the Stalin Palace of Culture, a spired tower given to us by the Soviets, dominated the city. A bitter-cold wind roared through the square. People said it was the ghost of Stalin huffing and puffing, freezing us all to death.

My mother was still living in Villa Rose, working nights at the hospital caring for patients with tuberculosis. She was dejected because the local administration had forced her to take in more tenants and she no longer felt at home in her own house. I tried to tell her about Argentina, but it was of no interest to her. She still looked at me with love, but now those large sky blue eyes seemed to have faded. Living in two different worlds, we had no words to bridge the gap.

"The first thing we saw from the plane was the Palace of Culture," I said, to have something, anything, to say.

She went to the kitchen and made tea. "They're building such useless monstrosities," she trumpeted from there, "but Poles have nothing to repair their homes with. I can't even fix my leaky roof. If things go on like this, Villa Rose will surely collapse. Perhaps that's precisely what they want: for all private homes to fall to pieces."

Milanowek had the edge of hardship about it; it was a place forlorn and abandoned.

I spent entire days at the ministry preparing for my new post. My predecessor's reports and greens seemed quite intelligent to me. I wondered if I would be able to manage in that great world that made everything I had experienced seem provincial. Everyone kept telling me that Washington was the most difficult and the least pleasant post: the United States was an imperialist, warmongering nation that lived by sheer exploitation. They told me that the Pentagon, which had the world in its military tentacles, was so huge it was visible from an airplane.

Ambassador Jozef Winiewicz soon returned from Washington.

"First of all, stay in constant touch with Georgi Zarubin, the Soviet ambassador. He's a wonderful person, the best diplomat I know. Contact with him is invaluable, but, that aside, he demands it of you. My wife, Marylka, saw Zarubin's wife all the time. Your wife will have to cultivate her. Zarubin's wife is the one who decides what's fitting in matters of protocol.

"As far as Americans go, accept beforehand that you're going to get to know only a few of them, even though there are a great many people at the State Department. They won't allow you any high access. It's simply a policy of discrimination—the cold war, you know. George Lister is the man in charge of Polish affairs; at what they call the "Polish desk." There are many, many levels above him, reaching to the secretary of state. Better be careful; most of them are unfriendly, difficult, sometimes malicious. And it's a Republican administration—Eisenhower—and things are always much tougher with the Republicans.

"The Polish-American community is very reactionary." he went on. "There's no one to talk to at the Polish-American Congress. But there's a progressive Polish community that you should look into. There's former state senator Nowak, from Detroit, Stanley Nowak, a great friend of ours. He's the editor of a paper, which is to be supported. The ministry will give you instructions on that. I recommend Nowak.

"One other thing, Comrade Spasowski: Contact with the Communist Party of the United States is very important, but you have to watch out. Best that you arrange this through a third person, because the FBI keeps an eye on them."

Minister Skrzeszewski did not discuss these questions in detail with me. "I realize that you're familiar with the situation and know where you're headed," he said, shuffling his index cards. "It's an awful place, but, as they say, work and pleasure are two different things. The most important thing is to keep your eyes and ears open, and to follow our instructions to a T. This is in deadly earnest, you realize. Winiewicz is an experienced diplomat—it'll be hard for you to fill his shoes, but we'll take that into account. Do your best."

By mid-April 1955, we were at our Washington, D.C. embassy on Sixteenth Street. In my office, large portraits of Bierut and Dzerzhinski hung on the walls. I called the doorkeeper and ordered him to take them down. All that remained was a tapestry with the national emblem. Soon I heard muttering among the staff, but no one dared raise the question at a Party meeting: I had come with the reputation of being a powerful person.

The reception rooms were lovely, with antique furnishings, valuable paintings, prewar china, and old silver. Many of the objects bore the prewar national emblem: a crowned eagle. We were fond of those reception rooms, feeling in them a breath of the past. Again a certain duality kept re-emerging in me: for all my devotion to the cause of Communism and my involvement in the Party, I felt a strong kinship with the traditions of old Poland.

My first contacts with the American administration were not encouraging. The visit to Secretary of State John Foster Dulles did not augur well for the future. When I was shown into his office, he raised his head but did not rise to greet me. I stood awkwardly to one side and waited. Finally, he turned toward me and, after scrutinizing me from head to toe, said, "You're a very young man, Ambassador." Silence. I wondered how to reply, how to behave. I managed to get something out: "Good afternoon, Mr. Secretary. I know I have a difficult mission ahead of me, but in my judgment my age should not render it any more difficult."

Dulles came out from behind his desk and indicated a chair by a small table. He sat down beside me.

"Oh, no, don't misunderstand me. I don't have any prejudice against youth." He regarded me as if I were a specimen from another planet. Eventually, the conversation got around to where I had been during the war and about my family, but it was strictly a protocol visit, and after this short exchange I handed him the envelope containing a copy of my credentials. Winiewicz had been right to warn me about the Americans, I thought.

While waiting to present my credentials to the president, I paid visits to the socialists. Zarubin received me with a sort of bluff cordiality. He was a large man, as tall as I, with a severe face; beneath his beetling brow were cold, narrow eyes. Coffee, tea, vodka, cognac, and Miszka chocolates were proffered from his table. He quizzed me about Argentina and Germany.

"You're a person of experience," he said, "despite your age. It's rare for someone so young to be sent to Washington. Here the ambassadors are usually fifty, often over sixty. And experience is what you *need* here. You have to have your wits about you."

He stared intently at me, assessing every feature. "To be brief, the situation is this: the cold-war mentality prevails in the Administration and, above all, in the State Department. They're all Dulleses; the country's being run by imperialists of the first order. These are hostile and dangerous forces, of course, but there are ways—there are ways. Even among the fattest industrialists there is a decent person here and there who can understand us and attend to his own interests at the same time. A great deal can be done through them, sometimes a very great deal, but the opportunities are rare."

He continued as we drank tea. "You see, as a people the Americans are very hard working. They've built a lot, but they live in ignorance. They know little and they understand less. They're naïve . . . they're little children. Something is said, something is done, they get wind of something, and they are all up in arms. Give them a few days, and it all blows over; they forget all about it, and everything is as it was before. It's amazing. We Communists have long memories, but these people live from one day to the next. Better for us, of course, but it makes it hard to work with them." He raised a glass of cognac. "To your health and success.

"Well," he went on, savoring his role as adviser, "it's a great and rich country; they have everything. But there *is* poverty, mostly in the South. Terrible poverty. You'll see for yourself when you travel to the South how black people are treated here. Simply shocking."

He poured himself another glass. "It's not easy to work here because this isn't one country, one neat and homogeneous place. This is the entire world. Everything that happens in the world is echoed and focused here: events in Europe, Africa, Latin America. . . . But you'll see this soon enough. How are things in Poland?"

"Tough, very tough," I answered. "Warsaw was destroyed; life is hard."

"What do you mean 'life is hard,' " he mimicked me. "You Poles got your freedom for nothing, served to you on a platter by the Red Army. Who liberated Poland?" He waited for my answer. I remained silent. "Things are tough—hmph! You didn't have to fight; there was no revolution. How is it things are hard?"

Now Zarubin's bushy brows were meeting firmly over his nose. He sat stiffly, awaiting my answer.

"I spent the entire war in Warsaw. I know what the Polish people have been through. Warsaw was destroyed; six million died. What other nation lost twenty percent of its population?" My voice was growing alien to me.

"I'm not saying Poles didn't *die*," replied Zarubin. "Of course they did. But now there's only one thing for Poland to do: rebuild. That's a great deal easier than fighting a revolution, dying, and *then* rebuilding. We had to destroy before we were able to start building anew. And one thing more: you don't have to worry about counter-revolution; the Red Army is standing guard for us both."

He poured more cognac into the squat crystal glasses. "I remember those years of revolution—hunger, cold, no boots. We managed. We'll win this time, too. You understand. We'll take care of the Americans and the rest of the imperialist bastards, too. To your health, Ambassador, to your success." We each took a good sip of the cognac.

Zarubin wiped his lips with the back of his hand. "Now, have a little caviar please," he said, moving a plate toward me. "They go so well together, cognac and caviar." We munched, and he continued. "Americans aren't as tough and strong as we are. They're children . . . *children.* We'll talk often, you and I. I want to be kept closely informed of everything. It'll make work for both of us that much easier. Winiewicz came to see me as soon as he had something important, sometimes directly from the State Department. The sooner Moscow knows, the easier our work, much easier."

I only smiled, nodded, and kept quiet. His views on Poland had grated on me. I would not serve as his informant.

On May 5 I went to the White House to present my credentials to President Dwight Eisenhower. It was a formality, but Eisenhower made a good impression on me. He was surprisingly and disarmingly direct, unpretentious, human.

My next visit was to the speaker of the House of Representatives, Sam Rayburn. He asked me abruptly, "Are you a Communist?"

"Yes, I'm a Communist," I replied, and he regarded me with surprise.

"Let me tell you what I think about you Communists," he said. "I dislike you—most of all because you're preparing for war. It's obvious, isn't it? Isn't that the reason you formed the Warsaw Pact a few days ago? As if there hasn't been enough war already in this world."

"We're not preparing for war," I insisted. "We only want to defend the peace."

"Doesn't matter," he said, with a wave of his hand. "We'll never agree on who wants what. So be it. But I want you to know how all this looks from my vantage point; I'm over seventy and you couldn't be forty yet."

"Thirty-five."

"There, you see, I'm twice as old as you. You people have lost your sense of reason and we've lost it, too. We're all heading straight for disaster. If it comes to war, we'll devastate each other: the Americans, the Europeans, the Russians, the Poles—we'll all be wiped out; we'll annihilate each other. And who'll be left? The Chinese."

"One man is as good as another," I said. "Wars are terrible because they kill human beings; it doesn't matter what sort."

"Yes, yes," he said. "I know you people, always saying that you defend all of humanity, but in life, in practice, that's not at all the way you act. You'd like nothing better than to see our destruction."

He voiced those grim sentiments with conviction and with the stubbornness of an old man, but also with a sense of rancor, as if I were to blame for the imminent destruction of the white race. No doubt he was sincere; the complaints he lodged against me he had applied to himself, to everyone.

Those first meetings convinced me that America was not what I had imagined. I had not perceived any undue military influence, no policy imposed by the Pentagon; everyone I had met was very much himself, natural and direct. My image of America had begun to come apart, and month by month it would grow more and more disorganized.

I was made painfully aware of a Communist ambassador's special difficulties when, a short while later, I received instructions from Minister Skrzeszewski: I was to demand of the American government that it expel all Poles who had come to the United States during and after the war. I realized the absurdity of such a *démarche* and wrote back to the minister expressing my reservations. His reply offered no reasons or explanations; he confirmed the instructions. Again I wrote that I did not understand his purpose, only to receive orders to do what I was told and stop asking questions. Thus it was that I found myself facing Under Secretary Robert Murphy. He regarded me coolly, as befit a conservative Irish Catholic across the table from a young Communist.

"Mr. Secretary, I'm here on order of my ministry, and what I have to say will be in strict accord with the instructions I have received," I began, thereby providing him with advance notice that I was not a madman.

Murphy tilted his head with curiosity. After a few preliminary sentences to mitigate the shock, I hit home: "The Polish government demands that all Poles residing in the United States return to Poland. . . ." I watched as Murphy's eyes opened wider and wider, followed by a disbelieving grin, then a wild laugh.

"That's a good one," he roared. "I never heard anything like that before. You say all Poles—*all* of them? Write to your Mr. Sks—however you say it—and tell him that you've informed me and that I stated that the United States has a different view of these matters. The more Americans there are abroad, the more America is pleased—American influence is only increased that much more. That's all you need to tell him."

On my way back it took all the control I could muster not to burst into the blackest curses at Skrzeszewski, who no doubt had composed those instructions in "deadly earnest." I described the ridiculous exchange in a telegram to Warsaw, but received no reply.

Wanda had seats for concerts at Constitution Hall, to which she took her mother and the children. One Sunday in the fall, Artur Rubinstein performed; we sent him flowers, and after the concert Wanda went backstage to meet him. He was very moved by her visit; it was the first time anyone from the new Poland had made the effort. Wanda immediately invited him to the embassy, and two days later he was our guest. We sat in the Blue Room, with its imposing portrait of Bierut, at which Rubinstein looked askance.

"This is the first time I've been here in many years," he said. "Thank you for inviting me. I was here as the guest of Ambassadors Potocki and Ciechanowski. And I played this piano—Paderewski's piano—before the war." He stroked the keyboard.

"You're a young woman," he said to Wanda, "but there's a Polish soul in you. There have been so many changes in the world, but my heart is still Polish. I suppose I'm a romantic, like Chopin." Rubinstein turned to me. "The war changed everything. Terrible things happened. I will not travel to Germany and Russia now. I will not play there. Did you have any contact with Jews during the war?"

"Yes. Quite a lot," I replied, wondering whether I should elaborate; those are difficult things to put into words.

"And what did you do after the war?"

"I was in the army."

"The Communist army?"

"Yes, the Communist army. Since 1945."

"That was when Poland's fate hung in the balance," he said, "I remember it as if it were yesterday. The United Nations was being founded in San Francisco, and I was invited to play at the ceremony. The opera house was full of dignitaries—Stettinius, Eden, Molotov—but there wasn't a Pole to be found. Just imagine, the war had begun over Poland, and we were the first to offer Hitler resistance, yet there were no Polish representatives there, not even a flag. Had I failed to spot them? I asked my wife. She looked all around carefully: no, there were no Poles there. I went out on stage to meet the applause, but I kept thinking that I couldn't let this just pass. So I announced that, on behalf of the Poles who were *not* there, I would play the Polish national anthem. Everyone rose—they had to—and "Dabrowski's Mazurka" filled that room with Poland."

In the fall and winter of 1955–56 I participated in United Nations General Assembly sessions for the first time, as a member of the five-man Polish delegation. I took my duties very seriously. I delivered speeches, held talks, got involved.

There was one person there whose presence disturbed me deeply: Vyacheslav Molotov, the head of the Soviet delegation. Every time I saw his large bald head, his upturned nose, and those little eyes behind his pince-nez, I could not help but think of the Nazi-Soviet Pact, of the start of all the suffering and ruin in Poland that diabolical marriage had engendered. Molotov's presence alone started my critical weighing of the UN.

The People's Republic of Poland's delegation was a show in itself. Our speeches oozed with rhetoric and platitudes. Every year, at the end of each session, all the diplomatic mail and documents that had accumulated were supposed to be shipped to Poland. In reality, the stacks and stacks of wooden crates, sealed before shipment with the emblem of state, were used by our high-ranking officials to ship—both for their own use and for resale in Poland—bales of fabric, fur coats, radios, phonographs, and anything else that could be bought at a good price in New York; things people living under socialism never saw. My colleagues encouraged me to avail myself of this "opportunity," most likely because anyone not involved in the game presented some danger. Wanda and I thought of my mother and our family and friends, but we never used this means.

In February 1956, the American press carried revelations from the Twentieth Party Congress in Moscow, and I heard the expression "personality cult" for the first time. I was glad to see Stalin condemned, as he had been. People arriving in Washington from Poland told us of the confusion this had caused in Warsaw, the various rumors that were making the rounds, and the general nervousness among high dignitaries. Not a word came from the ministry, however. Then news spread that Boleslaw Bierut had died suddenly during a visit to Moscow, and Nikita Khrushchev had gone to Warsaw to attend his funeral. Edward Ochab, a prewar Communist who had spent the war years in the Soviet Union, was appointed first secretary of the Party. I was summoned to Warsaw.

It was already past mid-March, but Warsaw still lay under snow, which melted by day and froze by night. I had never seen the foreign minister so on edge as on the day a number of ambassadors gathered in his office to be briefed by Franciszek Mazur, the secretary of the Central Committee, who had just returned from Moscow. I sat beside Milnikiel. Mazur's account was disjointed, and he looked exhausted. It seemed to me that he was purposely confusing the issue, pretending to report on Khrushchev's speech, but constantly digressing and inserting his own opinions.

"Many of these things were already known by our Soviet comrades in various circles," he said. "What can you say? Communists suffered great losses for a long time from the unjust policy that emanated from the cult of the personality. That cult caused enormous damage; before the war it cost the Red Army five thousand of its highest-ranking komandirs. They perished as a result of that cult."

"What does that mean—they perished as a result of that cult? *How* did they perish?" asked Milnikiel.

"They were executed," answered Mazur calmly.

"Who executed them, the cult?" asked someone. The room went silent.

"And how did Bierut die?" asked Milnikiel.

"Bierut?" said Mazur. "Bierut got sick. . . . I wasn't there. How would I know?"

He went on to mention other victims of the cult, trials, counter-revolution, false accusations; but the cult was always the villain. He also spoke of the rehabilitation of the Communist Party of Poland, which had been condemned and disbanded before the war on the basis of false accusations.

"And who was responsible for that?" I asked, thinking of Antonina.

"Everything was possible under the cult, even that," answered Mazur.

"When will we have the full text of Khrushchev's speech?" asked someone.

"I doubt you ever will," he replied. "I've explained the most important aspects here today. Now every cell of our Party should concentrate on overcoming the personality cult."

"And just what does that mean?" asked Milnikiel impatiently. "Will you finally *explain* to us what that means?"

"You saw for yourselves what the cult led to. It's self-evident," replied Mazur dryly. "We'll require honest criticism—self-criticism—from all comrades, and especially from you, the top activists in the foreign service. That's the only way we can overcome the evil caused by the cult."

The meeting did not last long. Milnikiel and I walked together in silence down Aleje Ujazdowskie, the frozen snow crunching under our boots.

"You know," I said, to break the silence, "I've been through a great deal in my life, but what I'm hearing now confirms my worst suspicions. Mazur was trying to wriggle out of it; he didn't want to reveal the whole truth. But there is no doubt that those people were simply murderers. I don't see any place for myself. . . ."

"Do you think *I* do?" he said, and came to a stop. "Bierut might have just dropped dead in Moscow, as they say he did, or maybe they gave him some help. Who knows?"

"My father died because of them, because of *them* only. *They're* responsible for his death," I shouted.

"Calm down," he said. "You're going to change them? It's too Byzantine for one little person to change. It's one great Byzantium."

"What's the alternative, then?" I asked. "For us."

"For us? I don't know. There probably isn't one. Strange things are happening. I've been in Warsaw a couple of days, and, as you know, everyone runs to the ambassador to find out what's happening. The ambassador doesn't know shit. I heard that people are starting to flee Security and the Military Prosecutor's Office like rats from a sinking ship. Did you hear about Podlaski?"

"I knew him in Germany." I recalled the sight of the major chasing the translator through the streets. "A sadist and a degenerate."

"Well, apparently he bolted to the East," he said, and then paused, as if searching for words. "I have nothing in common with the Bolsheviks, but I'm not suited for emigration. . . ."

"I'll put it to you straight," I responded, taking him by the arm. "If I'm guilty, truly guilty, of anything, let them shoot me in the head, but let them do it here, in Poland. . . ."

"But," he interrupted, "there aren't many like you and me in this shitty Party of ours. How many Spasowskis were there before the war? One. You believed in the Party before it was the vogue. Now all sorts of people are pushing their way in through the doors and the windows, and if they keep coming, things here will end up like they are in Moscow: rotten to the core. Do you know that Khrushchev *demanded* that Ochab be the new first secretary? And so we elected him. We had to, because the Russians always know what's best for us."

We had already been along the street twice, and it was time to stop. We embraced and went our own ways.

I was still in Warsaw when the news spread that Hungarian Foreign Minister Laszlo Rajk had been cleared of all charges in Hungary. But they had murdered him in 1949. What good could the whitewash do now? And I had spit on him, too. . . .

The cherry trees were in blossom along the Potomac when I returned to Washington, and I went with my family for a look at them. The United States seemed the happiest, the luckiest of all countries, and it was with envy that I observed the carefree people around me. The memories I had brought back from Warsaw gave me no peace.

The ministry was stingy with its information, so I followed the Western press closely and missed no opportunity to talk with people who had just come from Poland. The couriers were in that group, and although they were part of Security, they were also affected by the changes in the political wind, and that loosened their tongues. They felt free to report that their chiefs, who until recently had sadistically been torturing prisoners, were now under arrest, and that the powerful Jakub Berman had been removed from office. They told me what was happening at the ministry, too. Skrzeszewski had left, and a new foreign minister, Adam Rapacki, had been installed.

An amnesty was proclaimed in Poland, and thousands of people were released from prison. The couriers were worried that power might slip out of Security's hands. "What's the Party anyway?" they said, in sum, condescendingly. "It has no power. In Poland, the power is in our hands, and if things keep on like this, that'll be the end of People's Poland, because the rabble won't tow the line, they won't be afraid of us any more." I did not debate the point with them; I wanted to know what was going on, not to change their minds. They were repugnant to me—lording it over the very people they had come from, the very peasants and workers whom they now called rabble.

From the beginning of 1956, Warsaw constantly sent me directives, and I was called on often to lodge protests with the State Department. This began with the balloons that were launched from West Germany and landed in Poland with publications from Radio Free Europe. Then came the case of the potato bugs that supposedly had also been sent by balloon to Poland to destroy our potato crop and sow starvation. Later on, U.S. planes violated state borders by flying so high they could not be spotted and recognized. Each time something like this happened, I received detailed instructions and was ordered to lodge a protest at the "highest level." At the State Department they knew a new protest was coming the moment Spasowski appeared.

Amid all these unpleasant activities, there was, however, one of a different sort. The State Department raised the question of Poland's lend-lease debt. The talks did not last long, because the sums involved were not great and we came to an understanding quite quickly. I informed Warsaw at once, and later sent a telegram to say that the agreement was ready for signing. Rapacki had by that time been in office two months, and, to my satisfaction, the answer was swift and positive. Signing that document at the end of June afforded me a sense of gratification; this was really the first agreement that contained a promise of improved ties.

Soon after this, Soviet Ambassador Zarubin and I had an unpleasant exchange. He was irritated.

"What is this?" he said. "You barely started your talks and now you've already signed? I was never informed of any of it. You did it on your own? What am I supposed to deduce from this?"

"No, I didn't do it on my own," I replied. "I acted strictly in accordance with instructions from Warsaw. When they order me to protest, I protest, and when they allow me to sign, I sign."

"Warsaw, Warsaw," he repeated. "But *we* didn't know about it. That's simply not allowed."

"I have one boss, and he's in Warsaw," I answered. "I have to assume that he knows what he's doing."

Zarubin's eyes were glinting with malice. "It's not right," he said firmly. "After all, *we* also have to deal with the lend-lease question. There's been a major oversight here."

Our conversation was foundering. "How's your family?" he asked, in a feeble attempt to revive it.

"Fine, thank you."

"My wife tells me that you're sending your children to an American school. Is that true?" he asked.

"Yes. They went to public school for a short while and now they're in private school. The Maret School. A very good school. It's expensive—too expensive—but we want to give our children the best education possible."

Zarubin shook his head. "That's not good, that's not right. The older children should stay behind and go to school in their own country, and you know *our* school is always open for the younger ones."

"Thank you," I said. "My children studied Spanish in Argentina, and we want them to master English here."

"Do what you think best," he replied. "But you're not acting properly. Remember, you're supposed to set an example." Zarubin would not let me rest, thereafter, on the subject of the education of my own children.

Toward the end of June 1956, trouble erupted in Poznan. For the first time since the war, factory workers—particularly those of the

Cegielski factory, which produced heavy railway equipment—took to the streets, demanding bread and freedom. Those demonstrations were suppressed with an iron fist. Speaking on the radio in Poznan, Cyrankiewicz threatened that the people's government would "cut off" the hand of anyone who acted against it. The Party's propaganda machine went to work, and I began receiving telegrams explaining that the workers in Poznan had allowed themselves to be deceived by the "reactionary underground" and had taken part in an "imperialist conspiracy." Wanda kept telling me not to believe the lies that I was being sent from Warsaw and not to engage in any public condemnation of the workers. I heeded her advice, and never regretted it.

Only twenty-five years later, when I was ambassador to the United States for a second time, did a friend send me documents, compiled by Solidarity, that revealed the plan used by the people's government to settle accounts with the workers during that period in 1956. The story was as follows.

On June 28, the day the demonstration began, Premier Jozef Cyrankiewicz (a former socialist with a liberal reputation), Secretary of the Central Committee Edward Gierek (later Party first secretary), and General Stanislav Poplavsky (a Soviet general attached to the Polish army by Moscow) flew together to Poznan. Late that day, Poplavsky issued an order: "Use full infantry and armor and, if necessary, artillery."

Between midnight and four the next morning, the battle against the workers and students raged in the streets, gateways, cellars, alleys, and attics. More than seventy people were killed, and several hundred were wounded. The dead were hustled away and buried quietly under police supervision in various cemeteries in the vicinity. The funeral of a single Security official was marked with great ceremony, and Gierek stressed his "heroic demeanor." Then the repressions, the roundups, and the explusion of young people from the city began.

The documents reveal that among those killed were two boys under the age of fifteen. One of them was Romek Strzalkowski, a thirteen-year-old music student and boy scout. That morning Romek, with a white-and-red flag, marched at the head of the demonstration alongside the workers. People saw Security men run out of the gates of the Security building and tear the banner from his hands. It is unclear what happened next. There is no question, however, that at noon he was shot and killed inside the building. Later, Security tried to force his parents to remain silent: there was an attempt to abduct his mother by car, and shots were fired at his father while he was praying at the grave of his only son. Little Romek became the hero of the city.

It was a very hot and humid summer in Washington. Sometimes, toward the end of the week, I would go for long walks after work. I had a special liking for East Potomac Park, across from the airport. I would drive to the Jefferson Memorial and then walk as far as Hains Point and back, delighting in the long view and the light breeze. During one of my walks there I ran into Zarubin, who, surprisingly, also strolled there a couple of times a week. We walked together.

"What's going to happen in Poland?" he asked, looking around. "We can talk freely here. They haven't gone so far as to teach those birds"—he pointed to the gulls—"how to eavesdrop. The trouble is that you Poles never went through a revolution like we did; you still have a lot of counterrevolution to deal with. We finished ours off." He drew a deft finger across his throat. "They can have their say in heaven. But in Poznan they showed you what they're capable of. I read the speech Premier Bulganin delivered at your Seventh Plenum. . . . It was a fair assessment of the situation. All your trouble boils down to the work of imperialist agents. You should be done with them once and for all. You have to show your fist"—he raised a thick paw—"so that they never forget. Instead of that, you people are searching for causes of what you perceive to be your own errors. You're blind to the class enemy—the agents of imperialism. Even Ochab, an old Communist, is falling into that trap. That's plain wrong. You don't build socialism like that."

I stopped in my tracks, and Zarubin halted, too. "You know," I said, "I was in Warsaw after your Twentieth Party Congress. I know what Khrushchev said—maybe not all of it, but a lot. Those were terrible revelations. And do you think that hasn't had an influence everywhere in the world? You speak of enemies. But it turns out Stalin destroyed perfectly decent people, claiming they were enemies. How can you possibly criticize our Communist Party?"

Zarubin dismissed me with a wave of his hand. "If it weren't for

Stalin and the others like him, there'd be nothing left of us." Once again he raised his hand and made a fist. "You'll see. People won't forget Stalin. What counts is what was built, where the power is."

"Our Party has admitted," I said, "that it committed errors against the working class. We will correct those errors."

Zarubin glanced at me with a look of pity. "Oh, Spasowski, Spasowski. I'll tell you again: power is what counts. You should be wiping out your enemies, not looking for your mistakes. Mistakes can be corrected later. Nothing can be built without effort and error; victims and sacrifices are part of it. You know how we built our heavy industry and what happened during the war, and yet you're telling me about the mistakes made in Poznan! It pains me to hear it. Your country's weakness lies in the very fact that you cannot understand what it takes to be powerful."

"Comrade Zarubin," I interruped, "you talk about building, but can our little country be compared with your continent? I read about Soviet development before the war. You have enormous resources; we . . ."

"And you don't?" he asked, impatient with me now. "Stop drumming on how much you lost. Forget about the past, understand? Forget about it! What you need is to think for the long term. What you need is heavy industry. Twenty-five million tons of steel a year, no less. *Then* you'll have a good foundation. And then you'll have the right sort of working class, too. How much raw steel do you produce a year?" he asked.

"Four million tons."

"There! You see? You should be producing six times that. And to reach that level there have to be sacrifices. The Soviet Union will definitely overtake the United States, maybe in fifteen years. And Poland has to overtake France, England. It'll be more difficult with West Germany, but you *must* overtake the others. Not only in steel, but in coal, cement, energy—all those important areas on which further development depends."

We began walking again. At Hains Point, Zarubin stopped and looked down at the Potomac.

"In our line of work we may not produce steel, but we have other responsibilities." He shot me a glance. "We find out where the capitalists are ahead—be it in science or in technology—and we grab it for ourselves. Just as in wartime, intelligence assures victories. We must do a lot of looking and a lot of grabbing to ensure the victory of Communism in the world. And that, my friend, requires experience, patience, and a good head on your shoulders."

We stood by the water leaning on the iron railing. Zarubin was staring straight ahead, weighing whether he should say more.

"I'll tell you one thing," he said after a while. "In this sort of work you can't leave any loose ends. That can be fatal. All loose ends have to be thrown in the water, always thrown in the water, so that no one will ever discover what really happened. We must be the only ones to know. When the time comes, we'll go back for what we threw in." He glanced at his watch. "Time for me to go." He motioned for his car, which had stayed nearby.

I was left alone by the Potomac pondering his words. One thing I knew: I did not share his dream of conquering the world.

CHAPTER XV

In October 1956, the couriers were bringing news of mounting dissatisfaction in Poland.

"The students!" exclaimed one of them. "They're a hundred percent volatile. To think we lived to see the day."

All signals indicated that some sort of crisis was approaching. I ordered an Associated Press teleprinter to be installed in the office, since I was receiving less and less information from the ministry. By mid-month, communication with Warsaw was almost nil; only the press department was sending articles from newspapers.

We stayed up all night on October 18 reading repeated reports of Soviet troop movements within the country and at the borders. It was after midnight when I tore off a report, and Wanda and I read: "Flash. Columns of Soviet tanks are pressing toward Warsaw." One "flash" followed another. The Eighth Plenum was convening in an atmosphere of tension. Khrushchev had flown to Warsaw, followed by Soviet Marshal Ivan Koniev. Gomulka and his comrades had been unanimously voted into the Central Committee. The plenum had broken off. Talks were now being held with Khrushchev. . . . And then there was the commentary, the speculation, the rumors.

By morning we all sat in silence, Wanda's mother stealing in a comment now and then, the children frightened that something terrible was in store. Suddenly there was a knock at the door, and my secretary burst in excitedly.

"Robert Murphy's secretary just called. You're to go see him at once, Mr. Ambassador." She gasped for breath, having just bolted up the stairs. "Can I confirm?"

"Yes." I telephoned the cryptographer and turned to Wanda, who stood motionless and pale. "Not a word," I said. "Damn them. When you need them, they don't say anything, and when things are fine, they shower you with all sorts of nonsense."

"Don't worry; news from the ministry would only be lies, as usual. My concern is with Warsaw, with Poland, with the people," she said, her voice breaking.

"You're right, of course. . . . But I feel so alone, so completely alone. I'll tell the Americans the truth—that I don't know any more than what I read on this."

"No, you're not alone," responded Wanda. "You and I are always together. I'm asking you, Romek, if you learn from the Americans that harm is coming to Poland, beg them to help us." Tears streamed from her eyes. "God be with you."

In the car I glanced through the AP news. Molotov had flown to Poland. Could he be hatching some new plot?

In the conference room at the State Department, I saw a collection of men hunched around a table. Murphy rose from his chair; dark circles framed his eyes. "Please take a seat." Lengths of tape and pink paper that looked like telegrams covered the table.

"As you see," he said, "we've been poring over the news from Poland. Our embassy can't keep up with events. The teletype keeps up only because it runs nonstop. The situation sounds drastic. Soviet tanks are moving on Warsaw. And you know about Khrushchev, I'm sure. . . .

"Mr. Ambassador," he said after some hesitation, "you realize the gravity of the situation." He looked searchingly into my face. "However, before we move to discuss Poland, I would like to ask you a question. Your answer will determine the course our talk will take. Tell me, is the fact that Soviet tanks are moving on Warsaw something you consider an internal affair . . . an internal *Polish* affair? Or an international affair?"

I was surprised by that question. I had prepared for something else entirely—a talk about the situation in general. But Murphy was a seasoned diplomat. My thoughts came like lightning. To say it was an internal affair simply would not be true; I would be lying. To say it was an international affair was to admit that the Soviets were committing aggression. The year 1939 flashed through my mind: Molotov, Volhynia, Soviets driving west, Polish soldiers betrayed. Oh, no, no hypocrisy this time. I heard myself say, "This is an international affair, Mr. Secretary." Murphy smiled at me, probably for the first time.

"If so," he said, "then we can talk. Had you taken the other position, our conversation would have been over."

Murphy said the U.S. Embassy in Warsaw had reported that a plenum had begun that morning and had been broken off. Apparently the talks with Khrushchev had been marked by sharp exchanges; Warsaw was waiting for the Soviet response. We assured one another that our offices would remain in touch.

Immediately upon my return to the embassy, I sent a telegram to Warsaw. I received a terse reply only many days later: "You instinctively took the correct position." An uncommitted response.

Thus, the next phase in Poland's postwar history began. Everyone was thrilled with October's outcome, which had put an end to the nightmare of Stalinism in Poland. Gomulka and the Communists in his camp were happy because the people had stood behind them and shown their courage. Gomulka was installed as first secretary and surrounded by the halo of victory over Moscow.

But the people had different reasons for their happiness. Poland had stood up to the Soviets and had won. Many came to the station in the fall when Gomulka was leaving by train for Moscow and brought food for him. They implored him not to risk his life by eating with the Russians. Most important, after October, Poles felt they could start breathing more freely. They had convincing reason on October 28, when Stefan Cardinal Wyszynski returned to Warsaw from three years of enforced isolation. He was greeted enthusiastically, with joy and love. Poles felt as one.

Soviet Marshal Rokossovsky and others in the pro-Stalin group were removed from office. The Central Council of Trade Unions adopted a resolution providing for the complete independence of the unions. Later, with some perspective, I understood that the Kremlin was also satisfied, because power was back in the hands of the Communist Party. In addition, Moscow was now free to deal with Hungary, where, near the end of October, the nation had demanded the same things the Poles in Poznan had: freedom and bread.

Soviet troops had just left Budapest. Hungarian Premier Imre Nagy had assured the people that he would hold free elections and appealed to the UN for help. A few days later, however, the Soviet army swept back into Budapest, and a massacre began. The Hungarians' resistance was broken in the course of ten days. When the sound of battle died down in Hungary, young people were deported in cattle cars for parts unknown. Even our couriers who were in Budapest at that time spoke of Soviet methods with disgust. Who could conceal their indignation at the fact that shipments of blood that Poles had donated to help wounded Hungarians were seized by the Soviets for their own purposes? In the middle of the following year, Nagy was executed, following a secret trial. And the West? It condemned, and quickly forgot. Zarubin had been right.

I met the new foreign minister, Adam Rapacki, at a UN session in the fall of that year. He was a cultured, intelligent man with a winning appearance, and he knew how to listen. I was charmed by him, and that first impression lasted throughout our acquaintance. By nature he was an idealist, an optimist who, after October, saw Poland's future in bright colors.

At the end of January 1957, I began receiving telegrams instructing me to solicit U.S. aid; Poland was unable to feed itself. The Stalinist administration had brought agriculture to ruin, and we urgently needed to import at least a million tons of grain, mainly wheat, to feed the population. I was ordered to make cautious preliminary probes, to avoid publicity in the press.

After many talks, chiefly at the State Department, I realized that our needs were understood and that the post-October climate was favorable, but it was clear that detailed negotiations would be required.

A month later, a team of negotiators, led by the general director of the Ministry of Finance, arrived from Warsaw. I had cleared the way for their intensive talks as best I could.

The arrival of the team and the talks on food purchases did catch the attention of the press. After the Polish October, I had become something of a media personality. I came to know many journalists, chief among them Walter Lippmann, who always listened closely and asked difficult questions. I had great respect for him.

Another was Chalmers Roberts, who asked me to lunch at his house one day. He explained that he was also inviting a high-ranking CIA official, because the grain deal with Poland was now being weighed, and the Central Intelligence Agency had a question for me. I agreed on condition that the meeting be kept secret.

At lunch, the CIA representative came quickly to the point. "I'm wondering if the agricultural items you want from us aren't going to be sent farther on, to the Soviets."

"I'm certain that they won't be. We need them ourselves," I answered.

"Fine, but where are the guarantees?"

"We didn't buckle under in October—we won't be giving away what is rightfully ours, what our people need to live on. If the Soviets try to take it by force, there'll be such an uproar, you'll find out about it immediately."

"All right. But we're also wondering whether we're doing the right thing in extending credits to you," he said. "After all, in helping you, we're helping Communists, and it's no secret you want to destroy us."

"You're not helping Communists in general; you're aiding Polish Communists like Gomulka, who want to be independent."

"But can you *maintain* your independence?"

"Of course we can. There are thirty million of us. Poles *are* for independence. That's the truest guarantee." The CIA man gave me his card and assured me that no one would learn of the meeting. Roberts, too, promised me the same.

I did not inform Warsaw, reasoning that my authority included contact with all agencies of the U.S. government. I realized that even my most general report on a meeting with a CIA official would cause a storm in Warsaw and do a great deal of harm. And there existed another and greater danger. I was certain that Moscow possessed a complete set of all coded messages I sent back to Poland. Zarubin's behavior left no doubt in that respect. Contact with the CIA would certainly have been judged by Moscow as exceeding the permissible limits of Polish independence, and the consequences could have been dire. Talking with the CIA had been risky, but it had ended well. It was my one and only contact with that agency.

In that period I spent many an hour walking alone through the rooms of the embassy talking to my conscience, weighing my actions, which, after all, represented a departure from proletarian internationalism, from my loftiest goals. At times I was torn, because it seemed to me that I was breaking the promises I had made to my father. I had concealed my contact with the CIA, that thoroughly counterrevolutionary agency. I was sending the ministry telegrams supporting the idea of taking credits from the United States, which meant closer ties with the capitalist world. Where would it all lead? Washington was making a major play by encouraging Poles to seek greater independence. Moscow, however, would seek to subject Poland to increased dependence. Where did I fit in all this, as a Pole and as a Communist? At times I thought of proposing that I be recalled to Warsaw.

I thought about my past experiences, turning them over in my mind, and I felt that it was Poland's interest that was voicing itself in me with increasing strength, while that enigmatic "proletarian internationalism" was fading like morning haze.

At about that time, Stefan Wierblowski arrived in Washington. It was he who, with others, produced the July Manifesto—the basic document in the creation of People's Poland. I had learned it by heart when I was in the army.

Now he headed the Polish UNESCO committee. He was bitter at having had to leave the ministry less than two months after Stalin's death. Our conversation forced its way through discussions of UNESCO, literature, and Polish writers. I mentioned that Stefan Zeromski was my favorite writer and watched as Wierblowski's eyes opened wide.

"Zeromski? How can that be?" he asked, his ugly face contorted.

"Zeromski's the closest to my heart," I replied. "No other writer has caught the longings and the sufferings of the Polish soul as he has."

He regarded me with indignation. "What kind of talk is that? The Polish soul? You have some way with words," he sneered. "Zeromski was a precursor of Polish fascism. It was he who sowed the poison seeds of nationalism and romanticism."

I bridled. "Fascism? The poison seed of fascism? I can see that you don't know what fascism is. . . ."

"And how do you fit all that into a socialist Poland," he asked disgustedly, "which, after all, sooner or later will become a Soviet republic and be ruled by Communists. How does that fit in with Communism? And internationalism?"

I quickly replied, "Oh, no. Poland will always be Poland. It will never lose its identity. I am a Communist and so am against exploitation in Poland, but yours is a terrible vision—Poland losing its independence, personality, traditions, everything that makes it what it is. In the name of what, I ask you?"

The conversation did not last long. After he left, I said to Wanda,

"If that's what the authors of the July Manifesto are like, then it's no wonder that People's Poland is falling apart, the way it did in October of last year."

I had not ceased to think of myself as a Communist, but as a Polish Communist who acted on behalf of his nation. I walked the embassy's dark corridors thinking of these things and talking to myself.

At the beginning of June 1957, the first credit agreements were signed, and, soon after, grain was loaded onto ships in ports on the Gulf of Mexico. Poland was now able to purchase U.S. food surpluses under very favorable conditions, and it could also buy agricultural and industrial equipment on credit and pay with its own currency. The agreements also dealt with the settling of past claims and left open the possibility of further food surplus purchases. In the fifties and sixties, those shipments exceeded three hundred million dollars. In 1960, the United States granted Poland most-favored-nation status.

In mid-July of 1957, just before the Polish People's Republic's independence day, I called the janitors and told them to rearrange the furniture in the reception rooms and rehang the pictures.

At our reception, Zarubin sidled up to me and said, "It feels different here now . . . new furniture. And the pictures seem to be in different places. Where's Gomulka?" he asked, squinting even more narrowly.

"There's no portrait of him here, and there won't be any. No cults. That way, there'll be no picture to take down next time, Comrade Zarubin. We'll keep things just the way they are."

From that moment, our relations grew even cooler. I had seen the congressional documents on the massacre of Polish officers at Katyn. There was no doubt that their blood was on Soviet hands. I could not stand the sight of Zarubin.

That summer I traveled to Poland for consultations. Warsaw greeted me with lovely weather and August sun. Even on the airplane I could sense a change. People carried themselves differently; there were not soldiers and rifles everywhere. On Sunday a huge crowd of people, who could not all fit into the Church of the Savior, clustered in front of it, singing. I was told that the economic situation remained severe, and that there were shortages of many basic items, but that people felt freer. The Soviets were less and less in evidence.

Rapacki expressed his satisfaction about the way relations with the United States were developing in general and with the credit agreements in particular. I was just leaving when he suddenly added with a smile. "The premier wants to see you."

I did not have a high opinion of Cyrankiewicz. I had met him only casually a few times, but I knew a great deal about him. He was a slick orator, an opportunist, and a cynic. I found such traits alien. Perhaps he had a right to some cynicism, since he had spent two years as a prisoner at Auschwitz. But he was Moscow's man, the executor of its orders, and an informer on the highest level. In the Party he had the reputation of being a liberal, but during the strikes in Poznan, he had shown himself to be a merciless brute. He was known to throw himself into binges of debauchery; all Warsaw knew about his womanizing and his drunken revels. He had a weakness for toys and ingenious Western gadgets, which his friends would bring from abroad. Those toys and gadgets inhabited an entire room in his apartment, and it was said that he played with them for hours.

He saw me in his office. And there he was as I remembered him, a pleasant, talkative, and reflective man, whose quick darting eyes, with abnormally large circles beneath them, betrayed the sensuality of his life. His large bald head appeared to have square corners—I could not help but stare at the curiosity of it. He asked intelligent questions about the United States and the American way of life. Then, precipitously, he asked me, "Tell me, Comrade Ambassador, *why* are they helping us?"

I was prepared for that question and had been waiting for it. Here was my opportunity to support the idea of accepting the credits as convincingly as I could.

"Comrade Premier," I began, "for me this is a simple matter. I know how they see us. There is no one point of view in America; there are three. The Administration is extensive; it has no unified perspective. Its policy toward Poland comes from the interplay of those three philosophies."

Cyrankiewicz knew how to listen. And I had interested him.

"The first approach says don't give the Communists anything; let them starve if they can't produce enough for themselves. That's the point of view of the military-industrial complex." Cyrankiewicz nodded approval.

"The second approach, on the contrary, says the United States should give to the Communists and give them a lot—billions, if need be. Because only then can they tear Communist states like Poland away from the Soviet Union. That's the point of view of U.S. intelligence." Cyrankiewicz seemed to be finding this point convincing as well.

"The third approach," I continued, "says give them a little bit and see what happens. That concept avoids any extreme moves and treats Poland as an aim in itself—not as a means for realizing other goals. That's the State Department's position.

"I think," I said in conclusion, "that only that third line is politically acceptable for us, and it is for that reason that I support taking the grain credits and the Exim Bank loans."

I knew with whom I was speaking and that my objective would backfire if he could detect any "naiveté" in my assessment of the United States, or if I engaged in any special pleading in the name of the Polish people.

He listened to me carefully throughout, and it appeared that my presentation had won him over. I had neglected neither imperialism nor counterrevolutionary plots and yet had recommended the credits on an intellectual level. He was satisfied and wished me further success in my work for People's Poland. As I rose to leave, I saw on his desk a pistol-shaped cigarette lighter I distinctly recognized from Times Square.

I went to Milanowek. Czeslaw, my brother-in-law, surprised me with the warmth of his welcome. Our paths had diverged after the war; he had never been able to accept and forgive my having become a *politruk*, a political instructor. Now, our old friendship seemed to have come back to life. He was working for Polish Radio as an editor of programs for overseas Poles, and had much experience with Polish censorship. In him, his life, and his work, I saw a Pole in his own land living as if he were in a foreign country. It was a sad sight. He was a beaten man. He had continued to live in Milanowek with his wife and his son, who was four. He had not joined the Party, even though I had made efforts to talk him into it in the best of faith. He had not joined a trade union either, because, he said, they, too, were part of the tyranny, part of the lie. And because he could not claim affiliation with any of the "right" groups, he had been deprived of all amenities: vacations, medical attention, etcetera.

I tried to tell him to change his attitude, that he was working too hard, overspending himself, but he would not hear a word of it.

"You'll see, old man," he said when we were saying good-bye, "your day will come, too. Your eyes have already been pried open a little; a person can talk to you now. But it's just the beginning. When you know the whole truth, you'll renounce the whole thing. You live far away now, and from there things here look better than they are. Maybe in America you might do Poland some good."

I found my mother in tears at Villa Rose. My uncle Stefan had just died. On the way back from the funeral I thought of Wanda's hankering for a family plot of our own, and I was soon at the Calvinist cemetery seeing about it. Nothing had changed: grass covered my father's grave and a few faded flowers jutted from the mound. The caretaker had become a little hunched but was still working, gardening there. He greeted me like an old friend.

"I remember you, I remember you!" he crowed. "You were skinny back then. I remember your mother and those strangers who came here asking if anyone visited Spasowski's grave regularly. How're your wife and daughter? The three of us planted flowers on the grave together a long time ago.

"You're lucky; your timing is good," he said when I asked about a family plot. "There's something beautiful for sale. An old tomb, one of the oldest, on the main path. It was destroyed during the war. The family died out a long time ago, and we're selling it. I'll show it to you, if you like. Beautiful spot. Perfect for resting."

We went to see it. I could not have imagined anything better. On the grave beside that patch of grass was a large granite slab into which two words had been cut: Stefan Zeromski. My favorite writer. I immediately put a down payment on the plot, and returned later to pay for it in full. It was the only property I bought in People's Poland.

When I returned to Warsaw next spring I had to face the painful ordeal of having my father's remains exhumed and transferred to our new family plot. I arrived at the cemetery early one morning and stood with a few friends while two workers dug up the ground. Their shovels unearthed pieces of rotted wood, brownish bone, and finally a small, brown, sallow skull. All the remains were placed in a new coffin and reburied in the new plot. The experience left me utterly shaken.

At the beginning of October 1957, at the UN, Minister Rapacki presented a plan to create an atomic-free zone in Central Europe. The proposal enjoyed considerable popularity, and was attractive in its terse simplicity.

In 1957 I did not yet understand Moscow's strategic plans, that long-term series of political initiatives designed to give them advantages. The ultimate target, clearly, was not Western governments, but Western societies.

It was only during the seventies that I realized it was no accident that the most important and insidious initiatives were launched from Poland. We were the largest, most prestigious, of the satellites. Campaigns begun on Polish soil had the best chance of being accepted by the West, either as authentically Polish or as a collective effort, that is, undertaken by all the members of the Soviet bloc. I was to learn that Moscow never treated matters of form and propaganda lightly and was scrupulous in preserving all appearances of authenticity and legality. When the truth is absent, appearances must be especially strong, taught Machiavelli. And thus to all eyes it was Poland making and endowing what was in the Soviets' best interests: the Cominform had taken shape in Poland in 1947; the World Peace Movement was begun in Wroclaw in 1948; the Warsaw Pact was created in our capital in 1955; and it was Rapacki who put forward an important European proposal at the UN in 1957.

The Rapacki Plan to create an atomic-free zone was supposed to be an advantageous agreement for all the European states, but Moscow had only one goal in 1957: to isolate and neutralize Germany. They have continued to pursue this aim in various ways for more than a quarter of a century. But at the time, I had no understanding of any of this.

I was putting considerable energy into improving Polish-American co-operation in agriculture. I began with Senator Allen Ellender, the chairman of the Agriculture Committee, with whom I was on friendly terms. Offering caramel candies that he made himself at his home outside Washington, he would voice his views of socialist agriculture. "It's a matter of give and take," he would argue, his hands waving. "You can't be taking all the time. The Soviets have been doing it ever since the revolution, but they'll soon learn that even the richest soil can be exhausted. Wait and see; their harvests will only decrease, and in twenty or thirty years they'll have a famine. I don't think they'll change." He would pour tea and push the caramels my way. I ate them gladly, since they reminded me of Milanowek candy.

I heeded Ellender's advice to learn more about American agriculture, flew to Des Moines, and drove to Roswell Garst's farm. Garst spent several hours showing me around and telling me about the hybrid seed corn he was raising. I learned a great deal and realized how complex indeed was the process of making the earth yield up the simplest staple.

Back in Washington, I found myself at the Department of Agriculture often, working out my obsession and talking to Secretary of Agriculture Ezra Taft Benson. He was a wonderful person, entirely willing to aid Polish farming, and I applied myself diligently to preparations for a trip to Poland by him.

Khrushchev arrived in the United States that September, and, surprising to me, his official visit included Garst's farm. It was toward the end of his stay that the premier held talks with Eisenhower at Camp David, and out of that blossomed the optimism we all called the "spirit of Camp David." The day after Khrushchev's departure, Secretary Benson left for Warsaw on an official two-day visit, and so took off in the glow of that positive atmosphere. It was a time of highest hopes for me.

I was, however, to be utterly disappointed. No agreements were reached in Warsaw, even though the Americans told me on their return of the friendly reception and great hospitality they had been shown. Mostly they spoke of the splendid Polish food, the liberal quantities of vodka. They had even learned a little Polish: *do dna*, bottoms up. They told me that they were either at parties or paying visits, so very little time had remained for talks. Wanda was furious, horrified. Benson, after all, was a Mormon and did not drink coffee or tea, let alone vodka. "Apologize to him," she beseeched me. "Explain that these are new socialist customs, that they are imported from those people to the east of us. They have nothing in common with our tradition and our culture."

But I had not lost hope. Our minister of agriculture, now Edward Ochab, was due to arrive in the United States within a few days. Although I had been somewhat disenchanted by him in Warsaw, I was counting on his acting differently in Washington; I would have ample time to explain everything to him in an unhurried atmosphere.

But Ochab was distracted and gruff. He listened to what I had to say in his hotel room, expressed a modicum of surprise, and then, nodding his head, only said, "I see." His visit to Benson was a disaster. Ochab visibly bristled; he spoke stiffly, saying that the only thing Polish agriculture lacked was farm machinery; otherwise things were in good shape. His visit with Secretary of State Christian Herter was even worse. Ochab pulled a stack of papers from his briefcase and began reading a speech on the dangers of West German revisionism. He kept quoting various West European publications, stumbling over their names. The interpreter was fearless, translating long paragraphs into English from the abbreviated notes he could manage to scribble. Herter's eyes became glazed; finally they closed, and he dozed off.

My hopes for aid to Polish agriculture had evaporated into the air like the erstwhile spirit of Camp David. My disappointment was all the greater when the spring visit of our vice premier Piotr Jaroszewicz failed to produce something tangible between the two countries. Then U.S. pilot Francis Gary Powers, on a U-2 reconnaissance mission over the Soviet Union, was forced down and captured, and the cold war crept back in to finish off my hopes for good.

Despite the political tensions, however, cultural exchange was in full swing, and my embassy became known for its "musical evenings." Americans flowed in to hear Chopin played on Paderewski's piano in the Blue Room, and to hear violinist Wanda Wilkomirska, pianist Ruth Slenczynska, and composer Boleslaw Woytowicz. Wanda was in her element.

Wanda, her mother, and the children attended St. Matthew's Cathedral, which I, too, was glad to visit even though I took no part in the services. Wanda also loved the convent and church of the Franciscans, especially in the spring and around Easter. Christmas was a festive occasion for us. Wanda insisted on preserving Polish custom. The children would plead for me to come listen to them sing carols with their school groups in various churches. Dressed in white robes, they would stand in front of the altar and sing. I must admit that I was always moved. I wondered what the future would bring them. With their more frequent questions about Poland, there seemed to be more they simply could not understand.

Wanda was scrupulous about teaching the children Polish history from prewar textbooks or from those published outside the country, because, she said, they had to know the truth. So I had informed "opponents" to contend with. But still, they could hardly picture life and conditions in Poland as they really were; they had been abroad for so many years. Wanda and I gave increasing thought to how they would adapt after their return. We decided to let them see Poland for themselves, since I did not want to tell them anything that was not true. What seemed to intrigue them most was the "iron curtain" that was so often talked about on U.S. television. We would hear them murmuring behind our backs, discussing what that curtain was like—big, thick, long . . .

At the beginning of August in 1960, I left for my first vacation with my family in three long years. We were to drive through the United States, an idea Wanda and the children had been planning meticulously, tracing out the route and doing research on points of interest. Suddenly, in Santa Barbara, I received instructions from Rapacki to return immediately, in order to be in New York in time for the arrival of Gomulka, who was leading the Polish delegation to the Fifteenth Session of the UN General Assembly.

I cut our vacation by three weeks, and disappointed my family bitterly. Greeting Gomulka at the airport, I was optimistic; I took his laughing eyes as a sign of good humor and bonhomie. But while we stood waiting for baggage in the Pan-Am terminal, Rapacki, laboring to find something to talk about, said, "Comrade Spasowski was on vacation with his family in California when he got word of your coming."

Gomulka looked at me closely. "That's far away. Were you traveling by train?"

"No. By car," I answered.

"And how long does a trip like that take?"

"Almost a week from Washington to California, Comrade Secretary, and that's driving fast."

"Is that so?" He was surprised. "This really is a big country. Once, I drove from Szczecin to Przemysl in one day, but that was nonstop."

"The United States has excellent roads," I remarked. "One can travel fast."

"And had you been on vacation long?" asked Gomulka.

"Five weeks. I cut it short to be here for your arrival."

"Ambassador Spasowski has already been in the States five years," explained Rapacki, "and hasn't had one vacation yet. He has a few months coming to him."

"And how much does a vacation like that cost?" asked Gomulka.

"I haven't figured it out exactly yet," I answered, "but I suppose it will add up to two thousand dollars or more."

"*How much*?" shouted Gomulka.

I glanced at Rapacki, who shook his head, meaning I should not say more.

"Yes, it has to cost that much," I said. "Motel, gas, and food for a family of four."

"And you can afford that?" asked Gomulka, looking with irritation from me to Rapacki and back. "You, Comrade Rapacki, you're the one constantly telling me that salaries are low and that you'd like to raise them!"

Rapacki shrugged his shoulders. "Comrade Spasowski had a vacation coming, and he saved up five years for it. It's a good thing, too—he's finally getting a look at America."

"*Two thousand dollars* for a vacation!" shouted Gomulka again, but just then we were told that our car was waiting.

"Why did you tell him how much it cost?" whispered Rapacki into my ear on the way to the car. "Gomulka won't forget. He'll keep needling you about it. He's a penny-pincher—always calculating salaries and prices. . . ."

It was only the beginning. A few days later Rapacki returned to Warsaw. I wanted to get in to see Gomulka for a talk, but nothing came of my efforts; he had no time for me.

I spent a couple of days in New York listening to the speeches at the session, and I saw Khrushchev bang his shoe on the table. Such vulgar behavior had never been seen there before. I was appalled, but to my surprise I learned that some Americans thought the Soviet premier refreshingly original and spontaneous. Finally, I returned to Washington, where I learned from the State Department that, accompanied by Winiewicz, Gomulka had met with Herter in New York. I had been deliberately left out. Several days passed before word arrived that Gomulka wished to see me. I flew to New York. When I entered his room he was writing in a small notebook.

"What can you tell me about Polish-American relations? How do you assess them?" he asked me straight out.

I told him that during my tenure in Washington there had been growth in good relations. I spoke of the political and economic benefits that had accrued to Poland, the agreements that had been concluded, and the opportunities for agriculture that had gone ignored. As he listened, Gomulka drew a pack of Polish cigarettes from his pocket, pulled out one, broke off half of it, and thrust it into a glass holder.

"And how is the American working class doing?" he asked, lighting his cigarette.

"It's hard to compare it to ours," I responded. "It's a different country, different conditions, different standard of living. There was no war here."

"That," he interrupted, taking a drag, "I know. Tell me about life for the average American worker. For example, how much does a kilogram of meat cost and what does that figure mean in terms of salaries?"

I was surprised; I hadn't expected questions of that sort.

"America is a great producer of food. Feeding people is no problem here; no one goes hungry."

"Yes, yes. But how much does a kilogram of meat cost?" he insisted impatiently.

"Well, I don't remember exactly; my wife does the shopping. And besides, it depends what sort of meat."

"Pork. How much does a kilo of pork cost?" he snapped, opening his notebook and picking up his pencil.

"I'd say a pound of pork costs around a dollar, perhaps a bit less, depending on the store. . . ."

"What does that mean—around a dollar and depending on the store? Prices are prices. A *pound*, what's a pound—how much?"

"Two pounds is a little less than a kilo."

"Two dollars a kilo then. Impossible. How can they live with prices like that?"

He began doing some calculations. I could see that he was figuring the dollar amount in Polish zlotys and was discovering that meat was dirt cheap in Poland compared to prices in the United States.

"Very expensive. Considerably more expensive than in Poland," he repeated. "Things are no easier here than at home." He sharpened his stubby yellow pencil in a round pencil sharpener and made an entry in his notebook. Then he looked up and reproached me. "Comrade Spasowski, you have to be aware of the prices of basic foods like meat, lard, potatoes, bread, sugar. I can see that I won't be getting any information from you. You've been here almost six years and you still don't know these things."

I left disappointed. Had I known that was what he was interested in, I would have brought a price list with me. But that was not really the point, I thought. How could he, the Party's first secretary, be so obsessed with such petty details, and, on top of that, draw the wrong conclusions from them? How did that reconcile with the great responsibilities he was shouldering? And that little notebook, the yellow pencil . . . I went out into the city and walked the streets trying to regain my calm.

At the mission the next day, I was just passing the chief of mission's room when the door opened and out came Gomulka, followed by Winiewicz. Gomulka saw me, flushed, and bellowed at the top of his lungs, "You say the working class isn't bad off here and you don't even know the basic prices!"

Astounded, I froze.

He continued shouting. "The workers told us about their life. . . ."

"What workers?" I found myself shouting back, so he would hear me.

"Yes, they told us, and they told us about *you.*" His face was now beet red. "They say that you don't care about anything."

"Is that right?" I barked, fed up with him.

"I know it all. You pay no attention to them. You don't care about the working class." He was shaking his fist and raving so loudly that doors were opening and frightened faces were peering out.

"Don't raise your voice to me!" I shouted. "You don't know anything. You have no bearings here; you've been fed fairy tales." I spun around and started down the stairs.

I was on the ground floor when I heard Winiewicz's voice, in a gentle, unctuous register. "Don't get yourself so upset, Comrade Gomulka. Your health is too precious. Let's go have breakfast."

Outside I took a deep breath. I had had enough of that maniac Gomulka. My hopes for bringing some improvement to Polish agriculture had burst and vanished like so many soap bubbles. But something larger, more ominous had broken as well—I had lost confidence in the leader of the Party, in the Party itself.

After Gomulka's departure, our brawl was much discussed, and a number of pundits were sure I would soon be recalled. Apparently Gomulka's entourage had no memory of anyone ever having raised his voice to him.

I later learned the background to this incident. The evening before, Winiewicz had arranged a meeting with a delegation of progressive Polish-Americans headed by former state senator Stanley Nowak, of Detroit. Nowak had complained that I was neglecting the workers and the Communist Party. It was this that had aroused Gomulka's fury. Winiewicz had taught me a lesson in internal politics.

I had nothing to do with intelligence in Argentina or the United States, a situation entirely to my liking. Only once did intelligence work overtly touch on my life, and it was while I was in New York for that meeting with Gomulka. When I returned home to Washington, Wanda told me reproachfully that one evening after dark she had heard something moving on the other side of the garage. Kaytus, who was only nine, took a flashlight and went to see what it was, thinking it might be a raccoon. It was no raccoon, no person, only a small package stuck between the trash cans. My son carted it into the house. Moments later the doorbell rang, and in marched the military attaché, Colonel Henryk Ladon, in a state of outrage. He snatched the package from my son and scolded him for being out in the dark and for not minding his own business. Ladon warned Kaytus to stay away from our trash cans. Hearing that, Wanda reviled him and said that he should be ashamed of himself for putting up contraptions to spy on America, which was aiding Poland. Angrily she showed him the door.

I called Ladon in the next day. "What do you think my residence is—a drop?" I asked brusquely.

"I thought you would help me," he answered.

"I know you're involved in intelligence. That's your business. But I forbid you to implicate me like that."

"I'll report this," he hissed.

"Very good. Just so this was the last time."

Peace reigned with the trash cans after that, and we never brought up the subject again.

I had met Senator John F. Kennedy in 1957, but it was only in mid-1959 that I went to see him, to request his support in providing Poland with further grain credits. After I had told him the purpose of my visit, Kennedy asked about the source of Poland's economic problems.

"Our greatest problems are with agriculture. We can't produce enough grain. . . ."

Kennedy interrupted. "Why can't you? You could before the war. I have Polish relatives. I know Poland was an exporter—you even exported to America."

"Yes, but the situation's changed," I explained. "Now we have socialism, and the emphasis is on rebuilding industry."

"That's just the point. It's socialism that's causing the problems," he said.

"No. The war did tremendous damage in Poland," I began, but he interrupted me again.

"It's been almost fifteen years since the war," he said impatiently. "Look at Western Europe; it's rebuilt by now. But you wanted socialism, and you got it."

"Our agriculture has always been behind the times," I said.

"So you want us to cover the cost of your failure—failures that are directly due to your system."

"Capitalism's faults are no secret either." I was on the offensive; the conversation had taken a bad tack.

"Yes, but you want to use *us* to save *you*," he slammed back directly. I could see that his hackles were up. I, too, was feeling resentful and decided to end the conversation.

"I didn't come to see you, Mr. Senator, to point out the faults in your system; neither am I interested in hearing about the faults in mine. That's not productive." I rose and moved to say good-bye. Kennedy, too, rose, and seemed to regard me with surprise. We stood like that for a moment.

"No, no," he said. "I didn't mean to offend you. It would be foolish to part like this. After all, we both belong to the generation that suffered through the war. I was in the Pacific. I was wounded;

that injury still gives me trouble. Where were you?" he asked lowering himself into his chair.

"In Poland," I replied, returning to my chair. "With the Germans and with the Soviets. I wasn't wounded, but I had many close calls."

Now, as Kennedy listened, he seemed to regard me differently. I was emboldened to continue. "You see, Mr. Senator, things were very hard. I was young and a Communist—a devoted Communist. I was nineteen years old then; I *believed* in Communism."

"And now you don't?" he asked.

"I do," I said, confused by my own slip, "but as a Pole I have suffered a great deal. I am a Polish Communist."

"Were you arrested?" asked Kennedy.

"Yes."

"And you got out?"

"I did. I survived it . . . but my father didn't. It's hard for me to speak about that, even though many years have passed."

Kennedy moved closer to his desk and rested his hands on it. "You see," he said, "people like us shouldn't be at odds. We've been through a lot, endured a lot. Now the world is in our hands. The future depends on us, on our generation. How old are you?"

"Thirty-nine."

"Young for an ambassador." He smiled. "You must be among the youngest in the diplomatic corps."

"And how old are you?"

"Forty-two."

"You must be the youngest man in the Senate."

"Probably." He smiled again. "But the pain has made me old—" He leaned back in his chair. "You and I should talk like people who have an eye to the future . . . Do you agree?"

"Of course I agree, and I'm grateful to you for this conversation," I said, "although I came to see you about something very different—credits."

"I support credits for Poland and I will continue to. I have great affection and respect for the Polish people," he replied directly.

We spoke of Polish history, of Poland's connections with America, my work in Washington, and about our families. We said goodbye warmly, and when I was at the door he asked me to come see him again.

I liked the man and was grateful to him for having made me stay after our initial disagreement. I did not meet again with the senator. He soon launched his election campaign. And it was with genuine satisfaction that I sat with the diplomatic corps at the steps of the Capitol to watch him take the oath of office during the presidential inauguration. Recalling our conversation and his vision of the future, I was firmly convinced that he was a man capable of doing a great deal of good in our complicated world.

Early that spring I was recalled—by the usual brief, laconic cable. A few months had passed since the run-in with Gomulka, and I had been counting on it being a thing of the past. The cable truly saddened me. I had come to be fond of the United States, and more important, I felt that it was only now that I could be fully useful.

During the time we were paying farewell visits and packing to leave, an incident occurred that electrified many. In the Soviet spacecraft *Vostok*, Yuri Gagarin became the first man to orbit the earth. As it had in 1957, the press once again began writing about Soviet superiority in science and technology, and many Americans began reading Russian textbooks and taking classes in the language.

A few days after this, the courier arrived. He was surprised that America was making the space shot into such a sensation. In Poland people had taken the news about Gagarin calmly. Only the press played it up.

"I wonder why that was," I said.

"Simple," he answered. "Whatever the press does, the people do the opposite. There's a joke going around Warsaw. At some construction site or other, a worker on the ground hears about Gagarin and calls up to his friend on the scaffold: 'Janek, I heard on the radio that the Soviets are in space.' 'Really?' says Janek animatedly. 'All of them?' 'No, just one.' 'So why bother my ass about it.' "

Many people attended our farewell reception. Wanda, the children, and I stood side by side in the Blue Room, all of us feeling that we would be leaving many friends and a significant part of our lives behind. But somehow, I felt I would see America again.

I requested a visit to the White House, and soon received a positive reply. I prepared myself carefully, because for me this was not a mere matter of protocol. I wanted to tell the president of my feelings on leaving the United States.

As I entered the president's office, he reached for his crutches and rose from his chair, a smile across his face.

"Mr. President, I've come to say good-bye. Thank you for having found time for me."

His gesture told me it was all understood. "I remember you well," he said. "It's a shame you're going back. Do you have to?"

"Yes. I've been recalled. Maybe the time is right. I've spent six years in this great country. . . ." I could feel all the words I had prepared fly away, and I began saying what was uppermost in my mind.

"It was hard for me here at first," I said. "But I gained confidence, I learned how to act the way I thought a Polish ambassador should act. I treated my instructions from Warsaw as a matter of form; maybe that's why I achieved something here."

Kennedy gazed at me. He did not interrupt.

"Polish-American relations are normalizing, developing even, and I'm glad of that, but I take no credit for it. There have been a lot of changes in the world. Some say the cold war is over and we are in a period of thaw, in a 'spirit of Camp David.' "

"Yes," interjected the president. "But both sides must truly want a thaw. The American people have always wanted to live in friendly peace with other nations. We are a nation of immigrants—a people who came to this continent to live in peace and freedom. And it is peace we want today. But there are forces in the world with other purposes in mind. Moscow's purpose is to impose its system on other countries by force. We may want peace, but we're not about to abandon our commitment to freedom and democracy by stepping aside and allowing Moscow to achieve its objectives. No, never," he said emphatically, grimly. "Communists would do well to remember that we will always defend freedom in every corner of the world, and with all the force we have."

He raised his hand and pointed a finger directly at me. "I want you to remember that the reason I value Poland is that Poles love freedom and will fight for it. I know that a great injustice has been done you, and I'm confident that a time will come when you're free again. Do you know what I mean? I'm not saying these things to offend you; I am being as direct as I can be."

He looked straight into my eyes, checking to see that I had not misunderstood him.

"You don't offend me, Mr. President," I replied. "To be frank, I came to this country six years ago a confirmed Communist. And I'm leaving it as a Communist, but as a *Polish* Communist—just as confirmed, mind you, but my center of gravity has shifted. Poland comes first. And I would agree with you: no one should be permitted to strip anyone else of his freedom. I have always believed that Communists grant freedom, not take it away. Do you know what *I* mean?"

"Yes, I do. But that's a bold statement coming from a Polish ambassador."

"Very bold," I replied. "I will admit to you that I have learned a great deal here in the United States. I learned not to abide the demagoguery, the slogans. As ambassador, I wanted to deal with specific issues, to facilitate communication between two peoples, to obtain aid for our farmers. Poland can and must feed itself. We must be dependent on no one. Otherwise we cannot be free. Unfortunately, nothing has come of my efforts."

Deep in his chair, Kennedy listened as I told him about the first grain credits. I told him how essential I had thought them; that I had expected Gomulka to initiate a program to upgrade Polish agriculture. I related my disappointment in Ochab's visit, in the behavior of his successor, in the visit of Vice Premier Jaroszewicz, and finally in Gomulka himself.

"One can only conclude that our leadership doesn't want us to be self-sufficient or independent," I said resignedly.

"You made great efforts," he murmured pensively. "Perhaps these things are more complicated than we can imagine."

"I'll be leaving soon, Mr. President," I said. "And I'll admit that it's with a heavy heart. Much has improved, I know, but I must say I've lost confidence in our rulers." I was being searingly candid, and my voice trembled with those words. "Thank you, Mr. President, for the aid, for the understanding and friendship, for all the good things I experienced in America, but first and foremost for your attitude toward Poland, a country that has suffered much."

Kennedy seemed genuinely moved. "You've understood the United States well, and you've done much to improve relations. I thank you, as president of the United States. Always remember: the Polish people have a true friend in the American people."

"That means a great deal to me," I said, trying to restrain my emotion. "I wish you health, good health, and success, genuine success."

That was my last talk before leaving Washington. I remember the president wedged back in his chair, a young man with an open face, his crutches beside him.

I sent Warsaw a bland cable about my meeting at the White House. Only Wanda knew the truth about what had been spoken.

CHAPTER XVI

We stopped in Rome on our way home to Warsaw, and stayed to look at the sights, Wanda lingering over churches, relics, St. Peter's. In a few days the automobile I had purchased in Washington arrived in Genoa, and we began a trip through Italy I had long promised my family. I had not expected that this ancient, beautiful country would make such an impression on me, but I was transported backward in time, to the history lessons of my childhood. It had been in Italy, in 1797, that General Henryk Dabrowski had formed the first legions that were to liberate Poland. And it had been in Italy that same year that Josef Wybicki, a soldier and politician, had written the poem that would become Poland's national anthem.

Driving south, we entered the mountainous region of Abruzzi and strained our eyes impatiently for Monte Cassino. Finally, the white outline of the monastery appeared on the top of the mountain. I reminded the children that this ancient Benedictine seat had been changed by the Germans in 1944 to a fortress on the Gustav Line, guarding the way to Rome. The bloody battles to take the mountain and the monastery had lasted three and a half months, and soldiers from fifteen countries had taken part, including twenty thousand Poles. One hundred thousand had been wounded. Poles had accomplished the ultimate victory, and their flag, hastily stitched together from a Red Cross flag and the soldiers' handkerchiefs, had fluttered over the ruins.

We drove higher and higher, until we reached the Polish cemetery below the monastery, and there stood silently before the inscription.

We Polish soldiers,
For our freedom and yours,
have given our souls to God,
Our bodies to the soil of Italy
and our hearts to Poland.

Tears welled in my eyes.

Seeing that white forest of crosses I recalled the hope that had surged in me when I heard in 1944 that Monte Cassino had been taken. The news had come on the little makeshift radio in our dark hiding place under the floor.

We walked among the crosses, picked a few poppies, and remembered the song:

The red poppies at Monte Cassino
have drunk Polish blood instead of dew. . . .

It was hard for us to leave, but we began walking slowly toward the rebuilt monastery. Kaytus found a piece of metal along the way. "What's this?" he asked, handing it to me.

"A tap from a soldier's boot. You can see the nail holes."

"Could it be from one of our soldiers who was killed here?" he asked in a serious voice.

"Could be," I replied.

"I'll keep it as a souvenir. I can take it, can't I, Father?" he asked.

"Yes, you can, son. It's of no use to anyone any more." He put the piece of metal in his wallet, where he kept his little souvenirs.

In the monastery the new white marble gleamed in the sunlight.

We returned to Rome, and then our path led through the rolling landscape of Umbria to Assisi, and the grave of Saint Francis. As Wanda and the children prayed, I realized they wanted to spend more time there, but something urged me on. I had felt strange and alienated there, and was glad when, late in the day, we saw the blue of the Adriatic.

Finally, we began our drive north toward the Czech border. There were fewer and fewer towns as we went; soon all we saw were fields and the solitary road. As usual, Wanda sat in the front beside me; in the rear-view mirror I could see the children talking nervously to one another.

"We're getting closer to it," whispered my son. "Look how empty everything is."

"I'm scared," said my daughter. "They say there's really nothing there, that it's only an expression people use, but I have the feeling we'll see it any minute now."

"Of course we will," said Kaytus, nodding his head with conviction. "You'll see; there'll be an iron curtain, all right. They just tell us there isn't so we won't be scared. . . ."

It pained me to hear that conversation. I was just about to say something to them when a small booth by the side of the road came into view. I slowed down. It was Austrian passport and customs control. I presented our passports, but the official waved them away with a friendly gesture and asked if I had enough gasoline, because I might have trouble finding any on the other side. He waved goodbye, and we drove on. I was happy that that crossing had gone so smoothly, that the childrens' faces had seemed to brighten. But then we came on a fence, barbed wire strung between concrete posts, and behind that a stretch of plowed earth and more barbed wire, with white insulators on the posts. The wire was electrified. Lookout towers were perched in the distance, as in a concentration camp. Within minutes our car was passing through a ditch, and we came to a stop in front of a barrier of iron rails. The childrens' frightened faces flashed in my rear-view mirror.

"See! There it is," said Kaytus.

A Czech soldier walked up to our car and leaned in. "Passports," he said curtly and bent close to count us. "Four," he said, and walked away.

"Why did you say there was no iron curtain?" Misia reproached us. "We almost believed you."

"Because there isn't," I replied.

"What about those iron bars?" said Kaytus. "And the barbed wire, *all* that barbed wire. I remember seeing it in movies."

I was summoned into the border-guard booth for questioning and when I returned, Czech soldiers were just pulling a mirror out from beneath the car, after checking for stowaways. Madmen, I thought. I was furious as I drove away. How must I have looked in my own childrens' eyes? How must socialism have looked? We passed rows of posts, barbed wire, insulators, watchtowers, even a patrol with vicious-looking dogs. The children were silent. I knew what that meant. They were angry at me for having deceived them, and they were bewildered to find themselves actually behind the iron curtain, in a world they did not know. I caught sight of them in the mirror, holding hands to lend one another courage.

That was mid-July. A month later, the East German authorities began to build the Berlin wall.

Again Warsaw seemed changed, better than what we remembered. There were now stores in which one could buy various products made by domestic industry; there was just such a store—"1001 Little Things"—on the ground floor of the building where I was allocated a four-room apartment by the ministry. The building was still under construction, like everything in the area, and we took our first steps into that apartment on planks laid over rubble. Our sixth-floor windows, at the corner of Marszalkowska and Nowogrodzka streets afforded us a sweeping view of Stalin's monolithic Palace of Culture. "Stalin will never let us sleep in peace," said Wanda, but I argued that it would be hard to find a better, more central location and that we should be happy. So began our life in Poland after ten years abroad.

I went right to work, but not on U.S. affairs; I was appointed director of the Afro-Asian Department. I regretted putting my U.S. experience behind me, and I suspected that Winiewicz had had a hand in my transfer. But I had to admit that the change was auspicious; I could broaden my knowledge of the world.

Soon after my arrival, a modest ceremony took place in Minister Rapacki's office: he presented me with the silver Order of the Banner of Labor, awarded for outstanding service in building socialism in People's Poland. During the ceremony I thought of President Kennedy with a sense of satisfaction and felt confident that I was traveling the right road, the one laid out long ago by my father.

I had attained another zenith at that time, although I was blind to it. I had a wonderful family: a loving wife, two fine children. Things seemed to conform to my vision of a bettering world. With assurance I imposed my own, presumably infallible, formulas on everything. Only later did I see this as arrogance.

One thing was firmly embedded in me: I was a Pole. The history and tradition of my people were alive within me. It was in the name of higher goals that I reconciled what was happening around me in

People's Poland, though distant alarm signals sounded in me every so often. The loudest alarms became associated more and more regularly with the Soviets. Their crimes were at loggerheads with my beliefs. But I tried to avoid such thoughts, was afraid of them.

Looking back now, with some perspective, it is clear to me that the high point of my devotion to People's Poland was precisely during that ceremony in Rapacki's office. It was also the high point of my illusions. My faith in socialism and in the Party began to diminish thereafter—slowly but relentlessly.

I spent a great deal of time at the office, and Wanda got the apartment running and stood in line for hours in front of the stores. The greatest problem was finding schools for the children, and when we finally succeeded, both Misia and Kaytus were unable to adapt to their new surroundings. Misia came home from school disheartened, saying that the teachers told lies and that the students were not free to say anything; they were to listen and repeat things like parrots.

Kaytus was a big boy, bright for his years, and, most important, kind and gentle. He had no taste for mischief and fighting, but he often came home from school beaten and bruised. He did not complain; he gritted his teeth and persevered. One day the school called Wanda and told her to come for her son. She found him barely able to move. His schoolmates had thrown him downstairs. He was in a state of shock and kept repeating that he never wanted to go back. Wanda taught him at home thereafter. He had been traumatized by his peers, by adults, by life in general. He began to ask when we would leave the country again.

My immediate superior now was Vice Minister Marian Naszkowski. He was Moscow's man. He had come to the ministry in 1952 after serving as a deputy to Soviet Marshal Rokossovsky. He was known as a lout, a pompous, overbearing one, who brooked no opposition. People feared him. I had first met him before leaving for Argentina, and then later when he attended sessions of the General Assembly, as head of the delegation. I disliked him from the start. That September of 1961, I saw him frequently, since my department was hurriedly preparing material for President Aleksander Zawadzki, who had been invited by President Sukarno to visit Indonesia at the beginning of October, and I was to accompany him.

Naszkowski was a short man with a longish face and unpleasant, mocking eyes. He would grimace ill-naturedly when something displeased him. He did exactly that as he read the notes I had worked up for Zawadzki's visit.

"Out of all this," he said, picking up the stack of notes, "only the final communiqué has any real significance. After you arrive in Djakarta, you must take the first possible opportunity to deliver our plan for the communiqué. The point is that it be negotiated on the basis of *our* plan. Remember, deliver it at once; we must catch them off guard, before they have a chance to hand us their plan first. Do you understand me?" he said, nearly shouting.

"You must also conduct the talks," he continued, "so that until the end they won't have any idea what's most important to us. As you can see, I've added a series of new points; they're your bargaining chips. You can give them away, but only after a lot of haggling. Understand? It's this paragraph that's most important to us," he said, prodding with his pencil. "It concerns their recognition of the Oder-Neisse as our western border." His cheeks puffed as he issued the command, "Negotiate this point so that there are absolutely no changes in the wording." He leaned back imperiously.

"But what if they still don't want to accept the point?" I asked. "Only the socialist countries have recognized that border to date."

"What they want doesn't matter," he snorted. "They must—do you understand?—they must recognize it. That's why we're making an effort to go there: to make a breakthrough. We're not supporting their right to West Irian just for the fun of it. Their whole stand on anticolonialism is built around New Guinea, around Irian."

I accepted this as my guideline. It was, besides, one very much to my liking, because it concerned the consolidation of our claims to the Western Territories. I was even surprised that boorish Naszkowski took such a patriotic, such a Polish, view of things. I resolved to handle this assignment to the very best of my abilities.

The papers were drawn up by the end of September and forwarded to Belvedere Palace, the president's residence. I was summoned a few days later by Zawadzki. The director of his office warned me that his boss was sick, easily excited, and difficult at times. Everyone was afraid to talk with him, he said as he knocked at the door.

Zawadzki was pacing his office when I entered. He struck me as astonishingly short—a little man. A sandy blond, with impatient eyes, he looked to be over sixty. When offering me his hand, he peered at me closely.

"Sit down," he said abruptly, and sat down himself. His desk was covered with my papers. "I've read your materials and I wanted to meet you," he said. "I've known you only from the dispatches you wrote from Washington. I know who your father was; I read his books." He fell silent and seemed to be looking at me more gently.

"Your material is good, interesting," he said. "You worked hard. I can see you'll be useful to me. As soon as we take off, you will be subordinate to me, and me alone. Naszkowski is flying with us," he said, wincing as he uttered the name, "because this is handled through the ministry, but you and your people will be working for me alone. I don't like intermediaries, especially buffoons like him."

I was surprised by how freely he spoke of Naszkowski. He was very sure of himself. Even though he was president, real power was not in his hands.

In Indonesia, I negotiated the communiqué successfully, but not without a stormy struggle. Zawadzki made an attempt to speak to Sukarno in order to expedite things, but Sukarno merely dismissed him, saying he left such matters to his advisers. I finally had to handle the entire matter myself, and agreed to have Poland recognize Indonesia's "liberation" of West Irian in return for their official recognition of Poland's Oder-Neisse border.

Zawadzki was elated; his mission had been fulfilled. At the time, I was enormously gratified, but later, with increasing clarity, I saw this as an instance of Moscow's cold calculation; I had been a pawn, effecting nothing short of Soviet global strategy.

Nations had fought the recent war in defense of their freedom and for their borders. But after the war the Soviets thwarted attempts to return to old borders. They had occupied the very heart of Europe, and as a result, Soviet divisions could station themselves close to the borders of France, Belgium, Holland, and Italy. None of Russia's tsars had ever dreamed of such expansion. Is there anything surprising in the fact that Soviet Russia's foreign policy strove to win international recognition of these colossal gains? Most important in this struggle for recognition was that the Western powers acknowledge the Oder as the Polish-German border, because it was precisely that westward shift that made a great expansion possible.

The French president, Charles de Gaulle, took the first step toward international recognition of that border in a statement made in 1959. Other Western states did not follow his example, maintaining that only a peace conference could settle matters relating to borders. Between 1959 and 1961, Rapacki frequently instructed our ambassadors to put pressure on the Western governments, but the West simply did not respond. Moscow's ambassadors made attempts at persuasion, dictated by their "friendship for Poland," but they, too, proved of no use. It was in mid-1961 that the idea arose of having Indonesia break the impasse. And I had played the midwife.

At the end of 1961 I went to Africa, to take part in ceremonies in Upper Volta and Nigeria as an ambassador on special mission and also to visit our post in Mali. It was on my stop in Paris, as a result of a casual conversation on the street with a Frenchwoman, that I began to betray my wife. Our home life through 1962 became full of misgivings after that. Wanda felt something had happened; maybe she saw it in my eyes. That she suspected me was clear. The children could see that something strange was going on. They grew silent; their eyes filled with reproach. I became closed in, aloof, hard to get along with. We stopped being man and wife. I returned home from the office later and later at night. I had never paid any attention to women before; people had laughed at me for it. Now, in mid-life, I began looking at women on the street, and knew that I was doing it instinctively; I seemed obsessed by them.

There were other problems at home. Studying with Wanda now, my son would go into convulsions at the mere mention of school; he refused to set foot in a school in Poland again. We were at a loss and, in our search for a solution to this problem, we began considering a music school, in the hope that it would attract a more sympathetic, sensitive kind of child. By then Kaytus could play the piano quite well, and he had absolute pitch. But he needed to play two instruments to be accepted by such a school. He chose the cello and began preparing for the fifth-grade entrance examinations. By midyear he had passed the examinations effortlessly and began attending the music school on Miodowa Street, across from Cardinal Wyszynski's residence.

Our social life encountered its share of problems, too, caused by our situation at home. Wanda did not like Party people, and, though I was constantly hearing that a career depended on personal ties with highly placed people and toadying up to people in power, the idea was repellent to me. So we saw old acquaintances, mostly people who were not in the Party. Wanda knew a number of people who had belonged to the Home Army during the war and whose lives were extremely difficult now. My old schoolmate from Milanowek Bronek Sianoszek was one. I had last seen him before the war, in 1939. Our lives had taken very different turns. He had been in the Home Army from the beginning to the end and now lived very modestly in an old apartment near the Poniatowski Bridge. He was in poor health and usually in bed when we visited him, but he still had his thick head of hair, his sharp and penetrating eyes beneath bushy brows, his powerful jaw. During the war he had been in charge of guarding an underground factory that produced Sten sub-machine guns, and he had organized shock troops during the Warsaw uprising. In his threadbare gray sweater, he hardly looked the type to have been honored with the Virtuti Militari, the highest combat decoration, and the double Cross of Valor.

Bronek had told us once that in 1945, when the Soviets occupied Poland and were brutally liquidating the Home Army, he had been ordered to assassinate Dr. Alfred Fiderkiewicz, a prewar Communist and Soviet collaborator. But he could not bring himself to kill that old, balding doctor, who had, at some time or other, treated Milanowek's children. He went to his house one night to warn the old man that the Home Army had fingered him. When he got there, however, he was arrested by Security men who had been policing the place. They threw him into Rakowiecka Prison—death row. He managed to escape—the only prisoner in the history of that place ever to do so—but was recaptured. He then wrote to Fiderkiewicz and convinced him that he had meant no harm that night. Fiderkiewicz had his sentence commuted and, years later, during the amnesty under Gomulka, he was released.

I loved listening to Bronek's stories. He was a good and honest man, in stark contrast to the false personalities who surrounded me at work, especially in the Party. For a second time I began to grow close to this uncommon Pole. Wanda and the children, Kaytus particularly, lavished great friendship and love on him.

Two dangerous trouble spots flared up in October of 1962. The Chinese attacked India along the border in the high Himalayas, and Prime Minister Jawaharlal Nehru appealed to the United States for help. In Warsaw no one understood this war, which was happening on "my" terrain. I had become an expert in that area. At the same time, Khrushchev was attempting to arm Cuba with long-range missiles, and President Kennedy "quarantined" the island. I was no longer dealing with American affairs, but the dispatches I received from the ministry attested to the fact that anxiety prevailed throughout the world.

I was in Africa again at the end of the year; in Ghana and Guinea, and later on in Algeria. It had been in Niger that I had met Soviet Ambassador Pozhidayev, and it was from him that I received an official invitation to Moscow. At first Wanda did not want to go—she was not feeling well, Moscow held no interest for her, she was afraid of Russians. I, however, was curious and unafraid; mine was more an attitude of defiance.

With such disparate feelings we landed together in Moscow. It was freezing cold, and a snowstorm was in progress, but Moscow's smell was as distinct as ever. Wanda was trembling, and not only from the cold. She had been seized by a fear that left her only when she set foot outside the Soviet Union again.

Wlodzimierz Paszkowski, the ambassador's deputy, met us at the airport and took us to his apartment. As we drove in by car, we looked out at the city—immense, cold, dense, alien. The next day, I learned that at the Soviet Ministry of Foreign Affairs no one was an exception; soldiers examined everyone's documents scrupulously on the ground floor. Only those with passes were allowed in.

I was given a warm welcome by Pozhidayev. He, his staff, and I exchanged information about our relations with the African countries. I was surprised by their detailed knowledge of the smaller countries, especially of their natural resources and mineral wealth. The most interesting other meeting was with Mikhail Kapitsa, the official in charge of Chinese affairs. He was an enormously tall, athletic man with a large balding head and hard eyes. Our conversation was frank. He was excellently informed and sure of himself. About Peking's policy he was extremely critical. He outright loathed the leaders there.

That evening, I told Wanda about my meetings at the ministry and said that my last talk would be the next day, with Gromov, the head of Polish affairs and the power behind Soviet involvement in Poland.

"If he's so powerful," snipped Wanda, "then ask him why the Soviets didn't allow you to stay on their side during the war. And if he can do so much, ask him to give you back all the papers and photographs your father sent when he was trying to get their help."

Gromov greeted me confidently in his ministry offices. "Welcome to Moscow, Comrade Spasowski. You've finally come. You didn't have the time before? Or perhaps the desire?" he said, with obvious acrimony.

"I had no business here," I replied.

"No business here?" he asked in surprise.

"I'm sure you know what countries I've worked in. I always kept in contact with your ambassadors, with Menshikov, Zarubin, and the others."

"That's not the same," he interrupted impatiently. "Our Polish comrades are always paying us visits—in delegations, on business, and sometimes just to talk. That's the way things are done, and it's precisely that which makes the work go more smoothly. You've been working in your ministry for more than ten years, you've held important positions, even in the United States, and this is your first appearance here. How can that be?" He stopped, clearly waiting to hear my excuse.

"I have some business with you," I began. "That is, my father did, during the war, but you did nothing on his case."

"What's this you say?"

"You did nothing. You didn't allow him into your country, and because of that he died. That's history now, but I have a piece of business for you. We wrote to you; my father wrote to your ambassador in Berlin. We sent photographs with our application forms, a lot of photographs. Those were the last photographs of my father. I'd like to see them."

Gromov made notes as I spoke. "I'll see what can be done," he said. "And are you satisfied with the consultations?" he asked, changing the subject.

"Yes, very," I answered. "I didn't expect such insightful, comprehensive assessments."

Gromov smiled. "But you see, you lose in not coming to see us. Moscow is not just any capitol; it's the center of world Communism. We know a lot. The whole treasure house of Marxist knowledge is here. We have our people all over the world. You spoke with Kapitsa, isn't that so?"

"Yes, I did."

"That's the sort of people we have, people deeply rooted in their fields. We build policy based on their knowledge. Comrade Paszkowski has already seen that for himself, isn't that so?" he said turning to Paszkowski.

"Yes, Comrade Gromov," Paszkowski said obediently.

"But to know your field you have to have the facts. Our people have enormous documentation at their disposal. We know everything that's happening in every corner of the world. Well, all right, it's good that we met," he said in conclusion.

"Gromov wasn't as talkative as usual," Paszkowski said as we got into the car. "He'll talk more when he knows and likes you better. He once told me that politics was like chess. In fact, he has his people learn how to play chess so they can anticipate what'll come after the third, or the fifth move."

"Really?" This was news to me.

"It's true. Many diplomats come to the Soviet Union thinking they know everything, that Moscow is backward and primitive. But the Soviets are always a couple of steps ahead. They already have them and their countries where they want them. They're just waiting; they have time. Like they did with Napoleon. Remember?"

Paszkowski broke off. He never said much in the car, especially when the driver was there.

The next day I received word that Gromov wanted to see me.

"I have a surprise for you," he said cheerfully. "Please sit down. Here it is." He handed me a small envelope. I was struck dumb when I opened it. There were two photographs, my father and me, the very ones we had sent to the Soviet Embassy in Berlin at the end of 1940. I looked at my father's sad eyes, the shape of his head I so loved. I turned the picture over; my father had written his name on the back. The pictures had been cropped, no doubt to fit the spaces on the forms, and there were holes along the edges where staples had been removed. For a fleeting moment I relived that time, the hope with which we had mailed those photos, how we waited for word each day and strained our ears each night for the sound of heavy German boots on the stairs. I suddenly became furious. Those photographs proved that the Nazi postal service had delivered everything to the Soviet Embassy in orderly fashion, that the embassy had sent it all on to Moscow, and that it was in Moscow that nothing had been done. Why? Because before the war Spasowski had helped the Communists, whose party Moscow had disbanded. Moscow had sentenced him to death, and it was left to the Nazis to carry out the sentence. I had had no illusions on that score for some time, but here it was in black and white.

Gromov broke the silence. "Do you recognize your father? I recognized you right away. You haven't changed much."

"I recognize him," I answered numbly.

"Now that's what I call order, organization. Only the Bolsheviks could do that," said Paszkowski. "After so many years—they need something, they reach for it, and there it is. And those were from the war. That's efficiency for you."

"Oh, yes, our comrades are very careful to keep all documents in good order," said Gromov. "For every person there's a document; whether the person lives or not, the document does. . . ." He broke off as I rose.

"Good-bye, Comrade Gromov. Thank you."

"I can see you're very moved," he said. "I understand. A father is a father. . . . Good-bye."

In the corridor, Paszkowski took me by the arm. "You shouldn't take this so much to heart. That was the war. You can't change anything now."

"I know I can't," I answered harshly. "But I can change myself."

"And you shouldn't have left Gromov so abruptly. You might have offended him. He went and found the photos for you, after all."

He had no feelings, no idea what was going on inside me. Nor did Gromov.

Wanda and I left by plane for Warsaw the next day. We spoke little on the way.

At the beginning of 1963 I visited our friend Bronek quite frequently. The state of his health had taken a turn for the worse and he had undergone a stomach resection. Yet he was strong enough for talking, and we grew closer. I knew that now his purpose in life was to help people, especially former Home Army soldiers. At first that seemed utterly impractical to me. How was he going to help people from his bed when he had nothing himself? But I was to see it come about. He was able to aid his old comrades in arms, some of whom were in great need, and to aid them in very real ways. He began to be known as a one-man institution. There were days when a steady stream of people came to his apartment. They came for advice and aid from all parts of the country. Everyone who came to him had to offer something of their own. He would introduce them to each other, and they would then aid one another. Doctors would treat patients without charge, lawyers would provide legal counsel, and those from distant provinces would help find lodgings for others or bring food. Bronek wanted nothing for himself. I never heard a word of complaint from him, even though the authorities gave him no peace.

One day, however, he could not restrain himself and told me, "The police were here again yesterday. They come every few weeks, search the place, ransack it, and question me, sometimes quite nastily. Then they go down to the cellar and search for weapons."

"They're still doing that after all these years?" I asked. "Why haven't you said anything about this to me before?"

"Yes, it's still going on," he answered. "Why didn't I mention it? Why—what could you have done about it? I'm treated like a black sheep. I can't even get a permanent residence permit for Warsaw. I can be thrown out of this apartment at any time and resettled outside the city." I could read the sadness in his eyes. "And I fought for this city," he said. "It was within these walls that I organized the Baska, the shock troops."

Is there really nothing I can do? I thought bitterly. And what does that make me?

One day Bronek said, "You should think about your friendship with me. Keeping it up won't do you any good in your diplomatic career."

"How can you say that?" I responded bridling. "You're wrong if you think a career is what I'm after. You look around and see a lot of scum, and you think I'm the same, that every Communist is scum. And you say that our people's democracy has nothing in common with socialism, that it's only an imitation of the Soviet

Union. But remember what we had to build on," I said in an attempt at defense. "It's easy enough to criticize."

Bronek was in a frenzy when I visited him one fall day. "The squeeze is on," he said. "I'm a kind of bellwether. The police have started bursting in on me more often again. That has to mean something. Your Thirteenth Party Plenum is telling, too. They want to shut people's mouths. Gomulka is promising stricter censorship. He's forgotten all about October. He pretends to hold meetings on church-state relations with Cardinal Wyszynski, but everyone knows that the country's seminary students are being forcibly drafted into the army. . . ."

Before we had gone to Moscow I had taken my family to the mountains, to Bukowina Tatrzanska, where the High Tatras could be seen in broad panorama. The beautiful views and the chance to rest were wonderful, but with them came a meeting that was to bring more turmoil into our lives. There I met a woman, nearly twenty years younger than I. And she sent my head spinning.

I saw her for the first time when she took a seat in our train compartment. To me, she was breath-takingly beautiful. She had chestnut hair and green eyes. During the entire trip I could not rip my eyes away. She left as I unloaded our skis, and I thought I would never see her again. But, as luck would have it, I ran into her in a ski lodge. It was there I introduced myself. She told me her name, Zofia; that she lived in Warsaw, worked, was divorced, and had one child.

After returning downcast from our trip to Moscow, I felt hungry for some distraction. I remembered Zofia, looked her up, and we began to see each other. I fell into that vortex quickly, but I kept it secret, lying to Wanda as I had before, pretending to the children that nothing had changed. Our family drama intensified that spring and summer. I persuaded Wanda to take a cruise on the Mediterranean. It was then that Zofia and I became lovers. I was in a daze, insatiable. I cared about nothing but her and lost all interest in my home and my children. As this new life crowded everything else from view, I seriously considered divorcing Wanda.

Wanda had hardly been home a month when I persuaded her to travel again, this time with a group of ministry people who were going to Bulgaria and the Black Sea for the late summer. She went, but the unexpected happened: she fell ill in Budapest and, beset with severe pain in her spine, sought help from the only friends she had there, Americans at the embassy. Turner Blair Shelton was the chargé there. He and his wife had helped us once before, in Washington, when Misia had needed an operation on her eyes. The Sheltons took Wanda to a doctor and kept her for several days at their residence. She made no secret of where she was when she called me in Warsaw. But when the ministry was informed by the Hungarians that my wife had stayed with Americans, there was hell to pay. I was summoned to the Personnel Department.

"This is very compromising," argued the vice director with indignation. "The wife of a high official in our foreign service seeks help from American imperialists!"

I attempted to explain that she had been in great pain and had nowhere else to turn, but he was unmoved.

"There is no justification for this. This is intolerable. How do you suppose this makes us look to our Hungarian comrades? Others will hear about it, too, of course. If it weren't for your standing, there would be very serious repercussions." His tone was threatening.

I grew furious and let him know in no uncertain terms that I had no taste for lectures of this sort. He soon thought better of his position and quieted down. The incident had no other consequences. Minister Rapacki never raised the subject with me, though he had, no doubt, been informed of it. It did, however, leave a certain residue. I had fought back. The episode was duly noted in my file.

By this time everyone knew of my love affair with Zofia, and it was causing something of a sensation. It was clear that there were people in the ministry who had made a point of spreading the word. Things reached such a pitch that Rapacki summoned me to his office. I denied nothing and told him everything. He was surprised that my affair had attracted such attention that it was even being discussed among the diplomatic corps. Wishing to help, he suggested that I take a position far from Poland, but that meant I would have to break off with Zofia. I refused. If he transferred me, I told him, I would not take my family anyway. Gloomily, he counseled discretion and made it clear that he did not approve of my behavior.

My closest friend at the ministry was Milnikiel, now the American Department's director. I went to see him for some friendly advice. I complained that I was being gossiped about and confided that Wanda, a Catholic, was dead set against divorce. I had no idea what to do.

"Every man goes through a crisis of some sort," he said. "I'm no saint either. You know full well Jadwiga is my second wife. Remember, you have to keep your sense of responsibility. You can't put your family on the same level as some woman you've only known for a few months."

I responded emotionally. I said I could not imagine life without Zofia, I knew what I was doing, I had a right to happiness.

"I'm trying to understand you, but don't tell me you know what you're doing," he said, wanting to persuade me. "I know Wanda. She's a good person. You've been through so much together. I know your wonderful children and how much they love you. What do you want to do, ruin them?" he shouted.

I had not expected to meet with such vitriol from him. I recoiled, but he seemed not to notice and kept talking.

"You only *think* you love this woman. You're on fire, but that's not love; that's lust. There's a difference. You have no right to break up your family. Do something. Go away. Break off with her; come to your senses; don't sacrifice the people who truly love you, need you."

"So! You're against me, too!" I shouted. My stubbornness had clearly begun to irritate Milnikiel. He rose and paced his office.

"I thought you were a serious person," he said finally, "but I can see that I'm dealing with an idiot."

"I'll follow the dictates of my heart," I shouted.

"Your heart?" he yelled. "You're *worse* than an idiot. If you abandon your family, I'll have to think you're just a little shit, common scum."

I was running out the door as he said these words. I did not want to hear any more. I had the feeling I was being attacked from every side, and the assaults were only making me more resolute.

My behavior was slowly poisoning the entire family. Wanda had changed beyond recognition—she was thin, nervous. Her whole world, all she had built, was crumbling. Her husband, whom she had known since childhood and whom she had so loved and trusted, had suddenly proved to be a stranger, all too willing to leave her and the children alone in a hostile world where problems mounted with each passing day. Our son would no longer study; he abandoned the cello and became sad, listless. I felt desperate to do something to break this cycle of unhappiness. Ironically, at the beginning of October, Rapacki promoted me. I was appointed ambassador *ad personam.*

Rapacki rarely visited the embassies in Warsaw, but he did attend one dinner given by the Egyptian ambassador. Wanda and I had been invited, and it was our last dinner together for quite some time. The table was engaged in lively conversation about relations between Egypt and Syria when suddenly the door swung open and our director of protocol entered the room, walked over to Ambassador Michalowski, and whispered something in his ear. Michalowski rose and, in turn, whispered something to the minister. Like everyone else, I wondered what was going on.

Rapacki finally spoke, his voice quivering. "President Kennedy is dead. He was just assassinated in Texas. The report came over the radio minutes ago."

A hush fell over the room and the dinner was soon over. At the door Rapacki said to me, "Report to my office tomorrow morning."

When I entered his office the next day he had just finished one cigarette and was lighting another. His ashtray was piled; two empty coffee cups sat beside it.

"Where do you stand now?" he asked, getting right to business.

"No change. I still won't leave for a post outside the country."

"I see. But you must resolve things. There's too much noise. You're going to Vietnam. I've been planning to send you to Indochina for two or three years now. The conflict's widening. In fact, the situation is changing daily. We need informed people. I want you to leave immediately."

I was miserable. Unable to commit myself to my family and unable to give up Zofia, I was having to leave the country by edict. The future could not have seemed darker.

At the end of November I visited Bronek, who had just undergone another serious operation. He told me how good Wanda and Kaytus had been to him. He was no stranger to my dilemma. He was sitting up straight, leaning against a pillow, pale. His eyes seemed to reach into me.

"I dislike Communists very much," he said, his voice weak. "But

I always had a soft spot for you. Perhaps because we've known each other since we were little boys. I feel sorry for you. One day you're going to realize that you're on the wrong side. You're doing your family great harm, you know. To a wife like that, children like yours. I've gotten to know Kaytus. I envy you having a son like him. I worry that you really don't know him at all." His voice trailed off for a moment.

"Do you know why you're like that?" he asked all of a sudden.

I was regretting that I had come. I lowered my eyes. When I raised them again, Bronek seemed to be looking at me as if passing sentence.

"You don't have God in your heart," he said dully.

I could not have cared less what route I would take to Vietnam. Our airline representative at the ministry said it would be fastest to fly via Rome. I left Warsaw just before the New Year of 1964.

CHAPTER XVII

My eight months as head of the Polish delegation to the International Control Commission in Vietnam was a fine blend of emotional and physical torture. The commission turned out to be ineffectual. But being there, and bearing witness to that war, I came to feel deeply about the struggle undertaken by Ho Chi Minh and our fellow North Vietnamese Communists. I was wracked with guilt when Wanda wrote to tell of Kaytus's suffering; he was thirteen now, a sensitive boy feeling the bitter weight of our separation. He himself wrote to beg me to come back to them. So paramount was my ego, however, that I wrote Kaytus nothing, and Wanda only a short note to say that I was initiating divorce proceedings. Longing for Zofia and plagued with amoebic dysentery, I returned to Warsaw in September of 1964.

It was already beautiful autumn, the yellow leaves falling from the trees, when I arrived. Zofia had been waiting as impatiently for me as I for her; she wanted to be my wife. I moved into her two-room apartment in a ramshackle building. The shortages, the inconveniences of life in Warsaw, did not reach me in my honeymoon mood.

Some evenings Zofia and I would walk to the nearby Grand Hotel. There, on the top floor, we would dance to the music of a deafening band. I would press her close and move my feet gracelessly, pretending to dance. The air was heavy with noise, cigarette smoke, and the smell of vodka. I shuffled about among outlandish men—pockets stuffed with crumpled zlotys, pressed in close embrace to thickly painted, worldly young girls. I made believe I was in my own element in that bizarre, demimonde existence to which until then I had been only a stranger. In the apartment I would play with Zofia's five-year-old son from time to time. He would look at me now and then and ask me who I was.

I returned to my previous position at the ministry—director of the Afro-Asian Department. There my situation seemed at last to have been accepted; no one asked me about my private life.

At dinner once, I slipped and called Zofia Wanda. She reproached me roundly, complaining that I still had not forgotten that woman who had caused her so much suffering. It had been an accident, I assured her. That same evening I called her son Kaytus, and he ran to his mother crying that I was calling him names. A mistake, I explained. I did not realize that something was at work in my subconscious. What was deep within me, at my core, kept surfacing despite my will.

I had not seen Wanda since my return from Saigon, but I met with the children once. They had changed a great deal, grown up, and they talked with me as if they were my equals. Misia had graduated from secondary school, passed her university entrance examinations, and was studying English. Kaytus was still out of school and unwilling to talk about it. The meeting was painful, awkward, and neither one hid their sense of betrayal.

The date of the divorce hearing grew nearer. To Zofia I feigned resilience, but inwardly I cringed at the thought of a confrontation with Wanda, at which I would not be able to look her in the eye. Too, I feared my own son; I feared the words he had written to me in Saigon: "a time will come when it will be too late." Whenever I looked at Zofia's little son, I would see Kaytus, serious, sad, with a look of reproach in his eyes. At such moments I would flee Zofia's place and wander the streets, but there was no escaping my guilt.

The day of the hearing came. It took all the strength I had to look at Wanda. She looked back at me without recrimination, as if simply asking: Why? My mind was roaring through scenes from our life. What had happened to us? Where was I? What was happening here?

The voice of the woman judge brought me back to reality. "Do the parties see any chance of reaching an amicable arrangement in this divorce?"

My lawyer glanced over at me. "How do you respond to that?" he asked.

"I want an amicable arrangement."

"That can take a long time," he whispered. "And what if they start putting forward demands?"

"Do everything to arrange things amicably," I replied firmly.

"As you wish," he responded without conviction. Zofia had insisted to him that the divorce be arranged quickly.

The lawyers talked between themselves, and the hearing was adjourned. My lawyer shook his head, and one of the witnesses said outright that clearly I had lost the first round—the judge had not seen any determination on my part. Zofia scolded me sharply; it was the first time I had seen her angry. The next day, at my desk in the ministry, I felt an odd satisfaction at the thought that the fragile threads binding me to Wanda had not been broken.

Warsaw was immersed in conjectures concerning Khrushchev's removal, and the Party people at the ministry reveled in endless discussion. Most expressed satisfaction that Moscow now had a true leader, a statesman, Leonid Brezhnev; his knitted brows had produced the right impression. Khrushchev had weakened the Soviets, they said, and undermined the authority of the great socialist superpower with his revelations about Stalin at the Twentieth Party Congress. It was that and that alone that had caused the break with China. High time he was out. I knew that in saying this they were trying to catch the wind of the new line in their sails.

Milnikiel was one of the few of another opinion. "Khrushchev tore the scab off a festering wound," he told me. "That took courage and made him enemies. Nikita's ways were crude and simple. He wanted to make trouble abroad, so what does he do? One, he ships missiles to Cuba; two, he plots to create disorder in Europe."

"What! I don't know anything about that—about Europe."

"It wasn't talked about, even here. Gomulka didn't want any publicity about it. He stormed around here abusing people, throwing inkwells, stamping his feet. You know what he can be like. Well, he had a meeting with Nikita in January, in Lansk. . . . You know about Lansk?"

"No."

"You've been out of things, friend; you'll have to catch up. Security built complexes for Gomulka and our Politburo that supposedly were vacation resorts. One of them is in Lansk, north of Warsaw, by the lakes. A wonderful place, they say. Forests, lakes, deer, fish, and all of it surrounded, guarded, by the Internal Security Corps [KBW]. A submachine gun behind every tree."

"What happened?"

"So, Gomulka and Khrushchev met there, and Khrushchev confided his plans for Germany. He said he was traveling to Bonn to play the German card. He told Gomulka it was time for the unification of Germany, and that he had a simple formula. Everyone knew the Germans dreamed of unification. Well, he'd make that dream come true. And in turn they would make Moscow's dream come true: Germany would be neutral from then on. That is, neutral on the side of the Soviets, if you know what I mean."

"Disaster!" I cried.

"Well, it must have sent Gomulka's head whirling when he heard that," continued Milnikiel. "He could see himself caught between the Soviet Union and a neutral Germany; Ribbentrop and Molotov all over again. Fortunately, Khrushchev didn't succeed, though he *did* try. He sent his son-in-law, Alexei Adzhubei, to Bonn to sound out the Germans. Gomulka was so furious that he began talking about it publicly. They say that all this accelerated Khrushchev's removal. Can you imagine what would have happened if he had tried to unify Germany?"

"I don't like Gomulka, but he was right to fear another agreement between the Soviets and the Germans," I said gravely.

"Well, it could happen—if not today, then tomorrow or the day after. I might not live to see it, but watch out. Moscow keeps the German card in its pocket, and a time will come, has to come, when Moscow will throw that card on the table. Too bad Konrad Adenauer's out. He's an old fox; he would never be taken in by the Soviets. But younger ones might swallow the bait of unification."

Around this same time I was visited in my office by the director of the Education Section of the Personnel Department. A big, potbellied man with a full, bloated face and a red nose, he supposedly had once been a priest and had rejected the cloth after the war.

"I'd like to have a little chat with you. Some of the people who've been here a long time brought your name up to me," he began innocently. "About your education. . . . You don't have any higher education, and with your position and future some degrees would be all to the good. Many people in our ministry have filled up the gaps in their education. . . ."

"What do you have in mind?" I asked.

"I could arrange for you to acquire a master's degree. Later, a doctorate . . ."

"I have no time to study," I replied.

"Oh, there's a way around that. It won't take much time," he explained. "I'll give you a list of professors. You go see them. They'll give you some tests, but they'll just be formalities. Within six months you'll have your master's degree; the doctorate will follow."

I was stupefied, but he continued. "We're arranging degrees for all the active Party people. Everyone has degrees now, and some people have even become professors, permanent part-time positions. They find this arrangement very profitable. The Party supports this."

I could feel the rage in my throat. "No! I don't need diplomas."

"Are you sure?" He was looking at me incredulously. "A doctor of political science? Everyone I speak to takes advantage of it. They even thank me."

I was resolute, and the man did not raise the subject again. I remained the most stubborn, least-educated department director in the ministry.

The unsettling conversations only multiplied after that. The head of intelligence, Z-II, was General Tadeusz Jedynak. I had met him during my stay in Washington; he had questioned me once briefly on the U.S. political situation, but had never broached the subject of intelligence. I phoned him on my return to Warsaw, wanting to pass on my impressions of the Polish officers in Vietnam. Jedynak received me in his spacious, elegant office, complete with a large potted palm and a glass case containing crystals and silver athletic trophies. With a strong Lwow accent, Jedynak greeted me like an old friend, looking me over with a smile. "What rank are you, a major?"

"Yes," I said, "same as in 1949, when I came back from Germany and left the army."

"What do you mean *left* the army?" he said in surprise. "You're still a major on active duty; you've just been delegated to the foreign service."

"It's some sort of mistake," I said, disconcerted. "I've already served my time. If I am listed on active duty, I want to be demobilized as quickly as possible."

"I'll help you out of old friendship, but reluctantly. Give it some thought. But what brings you here today?" he asked.

Mincing no words, I presented my judgment of the military people delegated to Vietnam—primitive, materialistic intriguers. "Not only is it shameful, but it's harmful. Where do we get these fools? On what basis are they selected?"

Jedynak had been making notes, but he looked up at me and tapped his pencil on his desk. "You've struck a sensitive point. The truth is that morale is getting worse and worse in the army; in fact, it's rotten." He leaned toward me. "The worst of it is that it's cultivated from the very top."

"What does that mean, 'from the very top'?"

"It's that wretched Spychalski, who's been marshal of Poland for a year now. He's ruining our army. Only people with pull get sent to Indochina. The lists are made up a few years in advance and are based on the crony system. To get on a list like that, you need support in high places, preferably from Spychalski or from someone on the General Staff. Knowledge of languages, qualifications, the needs of the army—none of that means anything. Even here at Z-II we have problems sending out intelligence people. You can't get a toe hold. The qualifying commission is under constant pressure, and the people on the approved list are like sacred cows; they can't be touched. And that Spychalski—he only flies into a fury and screams at the slightest criticism."

"Like Gomulka," I interjected.

"Maybe even more so."

"So what's going to happen to People's Poland with men like that at the helm?" The impertinent question was out of my mouth before I could rein it in.

"I don't know," came the answer.

That conversation was quickly overshadowed by other events. One morning at the beginning of February 1965, I was sitting in my office at the ministry when the phone rang. It was Wanda.

"I must see you," she said, her voice weary, as if speaking cost her effort. "It's not about me; it's about Kaytus, his health, his future. Surely that still means something to you."

We had not spoken together since I left for Vietnam, more than a year ago. I could not answer her.

"If you don't want to talk with me, and you don't care about your son, just say so. . . . Nothing surprises me any more," she added, sensing my hesitation.

She sounded like she was about to hang up. "How can you say that?" I asked, collecting myself. "You know how much I love him."

"The boy's completely lost," she said, her voice quivering. "I don't know what to do with him any more, but I must do something. . . . I want to talk with you." She paused, and then hammered out phrases in quick succession: "Not about me. We don't want anything from you. You'll get your divorce; you'll be free."

"Of course we can meet," I said. "Just tell me when and where."

"The Church of the Franciscans?"

"All right. See you there at eleven."

"Thank you," she said in a near whisper.

I felt a sense of relief, too, as if a great weight had fallen from my heart. And yet an emptiness gnawed at the pit of my stomach. The new life I had built with such effort and suffering seemed to be teetering on the verge of collapse. I did not inform Zofia of this development and left for the meeting with a pounding heart. The church, like the entire Old City, had been rebuilt after the war; the walls looked freshly whitewashed, but the places for holy pictures and sculptures were conspicuously empty. I had always felt intimidated in such sanctuaries, but this time I was too nervous to be. I paced until Wanda entered. She was wearing a black coat with a hood.

"Thank you for agreeing to see me right away," she said, offering me her hand. She looked pale and thin but pretty. "Let me pray for a minute to Saint Anthony," she said, "the patron of lost things. . . . It was before his altar that the first High Mass was said in the ruins after the war."

I sat in a pew by a column and looked at her as she prayed on her knees. She had changed surprisingly little.

"I wanted to talk with you because I can't go on like this," said Wanda softly as she sat down. "You can't imagine what's become of Kaytus. He's not the same boy any more. He's grown a lot, but he's very thin. He doesn't study; he disappears. I know that he's been watching you, what you do, where you go. He's writing a sort of diary, and what I read in it made me afraid. We have wonderful friends who've tried to help us. But Kaytus simply can't stay here, so close to everything that's going on," she said, her voice trembling. "I have to make a normal life for myself, I have to save the children. And that can't be done through the court. Misia's having all sorts of troubles at school because of our situation, and she's grown bitter. We have to go away . . . far away. . . . Then, of course, there's the secret police. They follow us. Some civilians even threatened me on the street."

"What do you mean? That's impossible," I interrupted.

"No, no. It's true," she said, nodding her head sadly. "You must know it by now—anything's possible here. Well, we've had enough of what they call People's Poland. The country I love has been ravaged—it's simply not here any more. I beg you to help us make arrangements so that we can leave it."

My heart bled as I looked at her. What had things come to? This was my Wanda, my old love, whom I had cherished and shielded during the war. We stared at one another in silence, and I thought I saw her hand shaking as she wiped away tears. More people had come into the church, and the sacristan was standing in front of the altar.

"It'll be hard to talk here now," said Wanda.

It was bitter cold outside, so we went into a café at the edge of the Old City. The place was empty at that time of day, and we sat down across from each other at a small table, glad to be able to talk freely.

"You're well aware that I don't accept divorce," she said. "There is no divorce in the Catholic church. I've applied to the curia to have the marriage annulled, but the priests have warned me that that will take a long time." She looked at me with her green, upturned eyes. "That's what you want, and we won't stand in your way any more. I don't want to be any trouble to you, but you must know the truth. Kaytus doesn't want your name any more. I'm afraid that if we don't leave Poland, things will end badly."

"Where do you want to go?" I asked. "To America?"

She nodded yes. "I've already started working on it. You must try to understand; we're really at the end of our tether." She was whispering.

Old memories swept over me as I looked into her face. The waitress brought tea and pastries. "Will you help?" Wanda asked softly when she had gone.

"I'll help. I'll not only help . . ." I said; then my voice died in my throat. I was realizing that my life would cease to have meaning without her.

"You have every right to leave the country," I stammered. "But I know now I can't live without you."

Wanda sat motionless. I could see she was rent by emotion. She took a pen from her handbag and wrote on a paper napkin. "Remember! You needn't say things like that. I love you. But you don't have to see me any more, nor do you have to care what happens to us."

I read what she had written with joy in my heart, but I could not speak either. I took the pen from her hand and wrote my words on the napkin under hers: "I love you, too, I love you. Hang on till spring, I beg you! Either you'll leave the country or we'll be together. I love you more than life!!"

Wanda's eyes were warm and brimming.

"I . . . I . . ." I said. "I want to be with you. I can't go on like this much longer." A lump was in my throat, and the tears streamed down my cheeks. My hand slid over and timidly touched her small, delicate hand.

"Just give me a little time to arrange things. A little time. A couple of weeks. Please, please."

Wanda seemed not to believe her own ears.

"Please. I beg you. Trust me," I urged her. "I've had enough of that other life. I want to be with you . . . if you still want me. I'll leave it up to you whether or not to tell the children."

"I won't say anything to them now," she replied after consideration. "They're in another world, hoping to get out of here. You don't realize how much they've been through, how much they've suffered. They can't stand socialism, the hypocrisy of it, the crudeness, the vulgarity. The secret police started tailing Kaytus, too. They follow him everywhere. What do they want? What could they possibly want from a boy? It's more than the mind can bear."

"May I call you?" I asked.

"No, don't do that. I'll call you. When?"

"Three weeks from today, at the end of March."

I accompanied Wanda to the bus and watched her disappear among the crowd of passengers. For a moment I wanted to run after her. On my way back to the ministry it was hard to believe what had happened. It had been so sudden, so unexpected. I was happy and yet . . . derailed.

That evening Zofia saw that something was wrong; she tried cheering me up. I pretended that my mood had improved, and decided not to tell her for the time being. We went out for a walk in the snow; I had to get out in the open. Crossing the street from our building to Heroes of the Ghetto Square, we made our way through freezing wind and swirling snow. Zofia took my arm and began telling me about a coming business trip, while I pondered the twists my life was taking. I was crossing that square with a beautiful young woman whom I would leave, no question of that, to go back to my family—if they could wait and still wanted me. We turned into a side street, where there was more shelter from the snow.

"Why don't you answer?" I heard her ask.

"I'm thinking."

"Don't think so much. Thinking by itself doesn't get anything done. You have to act. Lately all you've been doing is thinking. You know I'm only waiting for the divorce. Waiting to be married. Waiting, waiting. I've already asked you twice if you would miss me, and you said nothing."

We came out onto the square again. The dark silhouette of the monument to the ghetto heroes loomed up faintly. Lighted windows flickered through the snow.

"Were you in this part of town before the war?" she asked, trying to draw me into conversation. "What did it look like then? Has it changed a lot?"

"Yes. A lot. Everything. There were narrow streets here, old buildings; mostly Jews lived here. Somewhere near here . . ."

"What?" she said, pressing the point.

"Somewhere near here the poor Jews lived. . . ."

Zofia listened with some disbelief, and I suddenly realized that she was doing so with good reason. We belonged to different generations; there were twenty years between us. She did not remember Poland between the wars. The war itself she knew only from stories about the little town where her father had been a craftsman. Two different worlds. I could not help but compare her with Wanda, who had grown up with me and who was connected to me by so much experience, so much life.

"Why have you stopped talking again?" she asked, her breath puffing white before her.

"I'm remembering things," I replied.

"Remembering, remembering. Let's go home, I've had enough of this cold."

Soon after an official trip to Cairo with Minister Rapacki, Jedynak invited me to see him. He greeted me with a pleasant smile and a handshake.

"I've been looking into your file," he said. "You have a very good reputation and you've risen high. The army wants to keep people like you."

"I have nothing in common with the army any more," I said brusquely. "I implore you again—please transfer me to the reserves."

"All right," he replied. "If that's what you really want I'll try to arrange it and have you promoted to lieutenant colonel at the same time. But it'll take a while. I have to wait for the opportune moment, when some replacement is needed. . . . How's your private life going?" he asked out of the blue.

"Very complicated—and all my doing."

"I know. I know more than you might think."

"Then I would assume you know I'm going back to my family?"

"You're leaving Zofia?" he asked in surprise.

"You know her?" I was taken aback to hear him say her name.

"No, I don't know her personally, but I do know a lot about her. Probably everything that matters."

A private life is impossible in this country, I thought, recalling Wanda's friends, who referred to Poland as a police state.

"So, you're going back home. Congratulations. I don't want to interfere, but it's a good thing, a very good thing. Can I speak to you frankly, man to man? You won't be offended?" he asked.

"No."

"Zofia is a pretty woman. She came on to you because she's ambitious. I'm not surprised. An ambassador, travel, the great world . . . And she's from one of those godforsaken holes, so it's no surprise she'd want to claw her way to the top. Don't take offense now, but you're twenty years older; you were infatuated. You weren't the first, and you won't be the last. It's a good thing you came to your senses in time. . . ."

I could not reply. Those were bitter things to hear.

"And what about Wanda?" he asked. "Does she know you're coming back?"

"She does," I answered. "I've made her suffer—she's been through a lot." I hesitated whether to say more, but I had grown fond of Jedynak and went on. "She's been threatened, you know. She's under Security's surveillance; even our son is."

Jedynak seemed to weigh his words as he spoke. "I know, I know, I know," he repeated, shaking his head. "But there are other forces at work here. Unpleasant ones. You know that when she was in Budapest Wanda went to the American Embassy there, and even stayed with Americans. News of that spread everywhere."

I said nothing.

"I'll tell you one thing." He spoke slowly, lowering his voice. "Our relations with the people from over there—you know, the *East*—are very thick and complex. We are penetrated high and wide. Wanda's a brave woman, but, oh, does she dislike the people's government! I'll tell you what I know about her sometime."

I left Jedynak with the burning desire to be out of the military as quickly as possible. His efforts proved successful. I was taken off active military duty, transferred to the reserves, and promoted to colonel.

Wanda telephoned at the agreed time. We met again; a third meeting was with the children; then she and I met alone a few more times. I could not wait to go back home.

One evening in mid-May I told Zofia that I could no longer live with her, that I loved my family and was going home. She seemed shocked, although she must have guessed that something was in the wind from the way I had been behaving. She wept convulsively, but soon gathered that there was no point. It was over for good. The next day she left on her trip; I packed my clothes and went home.

The children were surprised to see me, not having believed their mother when she told them I would be coming home. They looked at me out of the corners of their eyes, mistrusting my motives. Wanda now seemed independent, decisive. She refused to speak of what she had suffered; the children did, too. My mother-in-law was as warm and kind to me as ever. I was astonished, and thankful. And so we began the summer of 1965.

A Yugoslavian diplomat and friend who lived in our building and knew what was happening in our family offered us a trip to a resort in Dalmatia, near Split. I gladly snapped up the chance to give my family some pleasure. We drove in our little car through Slovakia and Hungary.

The Dalmatian coast, on the Adriatic Sea, is beautiful, and our stay at the resort passed quickly. We then spent an additional two weeks in a rented room by the sea. Our money was dwindling, and it was soon time to return home. At the childrens' request, I drove back through Trieste, so that we could breathe some Italian air, if only for a few moments.

Within me, the worst was at work: I had begun to long for Zofia again. And the desire was driving me mad. I became curt, impatient, I stopped talking, I lost interest in the children. Wanda was anxious, the children were frightened, the atmosphere in the car turned oppressive. Once back in Warsaw, I told Wanda I could not live without Zofia, and shortly thereafter I moved out of the house again. I was at war with myself, and I was bringing my family to ruin.

Autumn came. I lived from one day to the next, without any idea of what was happening to my family. The director of Rapacki's office had defected, Rapacki had grown edgy, and I was buried by a mountain of work. Gomulka had decided that we should support Moscow's moves vis-à-vis the Arab world: plans were being made for our president to visit Egypt and Ethiopia. So I was now deluged with materials for use in preparing for talks. I knew that this would mean burning the midnight oil, and endless revisions and corrections of texts. What in fact occurred exceeded my worst expectations. It began with Rapacki's sending the materials I had prepared to all the members of the Politburo, with a request for their comments. "What could be better," he said, "than the pooled political wisdom of our highest leaders?" I acquiesced and waited. Soon the texts, each with its own deletions and additions, began coming back to me. I was amazed at the banality of some of the corrections, but the worst of it was that they canceled each other out. I was faced with a dilemma. Finally I put all those papers aside, took my originals, rearranged the paragraphs, and had my secretary type clean copies. I then sent them on to Rapacki as the product of our collective thought. He sent me a note to say that collective thought had made a great contribution here. My department joked about it on the sly, saying that I had squared the circle, but I found myself entering a new phase of cynicism.

This second trip to Cairo was made with President and Chairman of the Council of State Edward Ochab, the man who had spoken so disastrously on agricultural matters in Washington. He had replaced Zawadzki, who had died in August of the previous year. Our meetings with President Gamal Abdel Nasser were stiff and conducted strictly according to protocol.

Our visit to Addis Ababa had not been so carefully prepared, because we had been told that the emperor would decide everything on the spot. We were taken to a guest building near the palace; the gardens that surrounded us were fenced and heavily guarded. Our accommodations were luxurious, but nothing could compare with the palace itself. The door handles, the gilding on the furniture, and the cigar and cigarette boxes were made of pure gold. Emperor Haile Selassie, looking very diminutive indeed under his high hat and accompanied by his ever-present little dog, received Ochab hospitably, but before long, his boredom was showing.

That winter I took Zofia and her son to the mountains to ski. The weather in Zakopane was beautiful and cold, the snow was thick, the peaks of the Tatras shone silver in the rays of the sun. I skied alone far into the valleys, trying to delight in the views and the mountain air. It was useless. The more beautiful the landscape, the sharper the pain in my heart and the greater my self-contempt. Sometimes, high on a mountain pass between rocky peaks, I would cover my eyes with my hands and summon up the image of Wanda and the children. Her final words kept ringing in my ears: "Now all is finished between us. We can't depend on you." How could I have done it? Who was I? What was in me that made me so unfeeling?

In the evenings, when I returned to the hotel, I would again try to make the best of it, but my own laughter rang false to me.

One day Zofia began reproaching me. "You're gone for whole days, you're out skiing from morning till night. You've changed. Before Vietnam, you were a completely different person. . . ."

I tried to explain, but that only angered her further.

"You don't treat me the way you promised you would. You're not carrying through with the divorce! You behave strangely. And you're not as young as you think you are."

She went on and on complaining, then concluded that she was disappointed in me. I did not reply, knowing it was that which would infuriate her most. That evening I examined my face in the mirror and saw a nervous tic under one eye. There was something in me I disliked. We returned to Warsaw in a mood far from cheerful.

At the ministry I learned that the Party was mobilizing its forces against the church, readying provocations. I had not read newspapers in the mountains, and my comrades advised me to look through *Trybuna Ludu* to get a feel for the gravity of the situation. I went to the library. Indeed, in mid-January of 1966 Gomulka had announced that the government would celebrate Poland's Thousandth Anniversary. It was obvious that the Party hoped to undermine the celebration of the Millennium of Polish Christianity that the church was preparing. A thousand years before, in 966, Prince Mieszko had adopted Christianity for the tribal nations from which Poland had been formed. A serious confrontation with the church was in the making. Suspicions were confirmed by the next few Party meetings. Lecturers from the Central Committee argued that the Catholic church was engaged in antistate activity. They attacked the Polish bishops, who, in December of the previous year, had sent a letter to the German bishops. In that disgraceful document, said the lecturers, the bishops had forgiven the crimes committed by the Nazis against the Polish people and, in a humiliating fashion, had themselves asked for forgiveness.

"This is a betrayal of our national interests," shouted a young lecturer from the Propaganda Department. "Who gave them the right to forgive?" he cried, glancing at his agitator's notebook. "The church has committed treason."

I looked around the hall. Some Party members seemed excited enough, but no doubt they were only pretending, because in reality they were concerned about nothing and cynical about everything. I did not like the bishops' letter and thought that they should not have forgiven the Germans, but these meetings were too steeped in gross propaganda for my blood.

The Party had decided to play its trump cards. Party activists at the ministry were summoned to the Central Committee building for briefings. In his speeches Gomulka attacked Cardinal Wyszynski by name for trying to move Poland toward the West, even though everyone knew that for twenty years Poland had been, and would always be, a part of the East.

In early March, I asked Wanda to meet me in the Church of the Franciscans, as she had before. I begged her forgiveness, asked her to allow me to come home, and swore that this time it would be for real. Very pale, she heard me out, skeptically. Then she reported that things were worse with Kaytus and burst into tears. I implored her to take me back, and called myself a sinner, although, not being a believer, I could not fully understand the meaning of that word. She said that she would have to think it through and talk with the children. That day I sent her a bouquet of roses and a note: "I believe that together we can save our son and ourselves."

Soon we began seeing each other again. We had long talks about ourselves and what was happening in Poland. As a fervent Catholic, Wanda was suffering from the attacks on the church and on Wyszynski. She kept saying that Moscow wanted us to cease being Poles and, first and foremost, to lose our faith in God. Now I looked on her with love and admiration, wondering at the source of her strength and her faith. A few days later, I returned to my family, for good.

CHAPTER XVIII

I was happy to have returned home and I was grateful to friends who had stood firmly by Wanda and the children during my absence, providing them moral and even financial support. At first I was afraid that some of our friends would not forgive me for what I had done, but even the hardest among them accepted us as a family again and were as warm to me as they had been before. I must admit that at the time I found that surprising, for I had never understood true forgiveness.

I had come back to life, and felt like a new man; I no longer had anything to be ashamed of, no excuses to make. Everything was clear and good. Thanks to Wanda's efforts, bridges were mended with my mother, and the children again began traveling to Milanowek to see their grandmother, who had missed them terribly during the last few years. Wanda's family also began visiting us again, and I learned a great many interesting things from my brother-in-law, Czeslaw, who worked for Polish Radio. He wrote beautifully and spent considerable time traveling around Poland gathering material for his scripts. From his travels he had grown very critical about what was happening in the country. I recall what he told me once.

"I've just returned from Gniezno," he said, "because, as you know, the celebration of the millennium began there." A thousand years ago Gniezno had been the capital of Poland. The first Polish kings lived there; Christian culture had its beginnings there. The first cross was erected there, the first church.

"Many thousands were there for the opening of the celebration. The primate, Cardinal Wyszynski, was there, too, and—can you imagine?—a political scandal was forced even on that holy gathering. During vespers, which was being celebrated by Archbishop Karol Wojtyla, of Krakow, cannon were fired, shaking the old cathedral. It turned out to be a salute for Marshal Spychalski. The authorities had set up a spectacle of their own on the square to compete with the vespers, and they'd brought in people by the truckload from the factories. The crowd around the cathedral stood in silence, prayed, and sang hymns. Eventually, people on the other square, where Spychalski was speaking, joined those around the cathedral. That was how your Party launched the millennium celebration, my brother."

I said nothing. I could sense my son glowering at me.

Thus began the year of the millennium. The world press reported the events as they unfolded in Poland, with the celebration traveling from city to city, and from provocation to provocation. Foreign correspondents tried to judge how many thousand took part in the church's celebration and how many thousand in the Party's, figuring in the number who fled from the latter—quite a complicated process. That made a basis for speculating on the balance of forces within People's Poland. The Polish press kept printing the statements of the so-called patriot priests, that handful of clergy who were co-operating with the government. Things were stepped up in the ministry under the slogan "The battle against the city of darkness." The same veteran debaters spoke at nearly all Party meetings. I listened in silence to that propaganda, never once taking the floor.

In the ministry events kept coming at a rapid clip.

Upon his return from a visit to Afghanistan Rapacki summoned me. Pacing his office, he told me about his talks in Kabul.

"As you may know, we've been having problems with our sheep," he said, staring out the window, and puffing on his cigarette. "The state farms aren't up to the mark, and we're constantly short of wool, which industry needs greatly. I've done my own post mortem in this area. To be brief, there's no wool."

"While I was in Kabul it occurred to me that our sheep could be pastured on those splendid Afghan mountain meadows. You can't imagine the pastureland they have. The grass . . ."

He lit another cigarette and again paced the room, conviction in his voice. "Just picture it—beautiful wool streaming into Poland. The grass of the pastures on the slopes of the Hindu Kush and the Pamirs will be turned into wool that our spinners and weavers will make into cloth. I spoke about this project when I was in Kabul, and the prime minister is very enthusiastic. . . ."

As I made notes, I caught his fervor.

"And I'd like you, Comrade Spasowski," continued Rapacki, in his friendliest voice, "to work out a plan of action. Jagielski's the best one to discuss this with; he's a businesslike person. I'll have a little talk with him. He'll see the point of it right away. He's a very energetic man, you know, the youngest man in the Politburo—an excellent asset for our agriculture."

Mieczyslaw Jagielski had replaced Ochab as minister of agriculture. It was said of him that he was sober minded and realistic, and, most important, was from a family of farming peasants and understood the needs of the rural population.

I had the rather untypical habit of dropping in unannounced at my workers' offices if I needed to see them. One day I went to the Asian Section, but stopped dead at the door. Peals of laughter poured from within. One loud voice was saying, "Sit down, comrades. We have an important assignment! First it was atomic-free zones; now it's sheep zones."

There was another gale of laughter. Now they were laughing at me, too. I walked away from the door feeling sorry for Rapacki. His intentions had no doubt been good, but the absurdity of his plan was painfully apparent. Nevertheless, I decided to keep pushing matters until they came to a standstill by themselves.

Around then, a new employee was sent to my department from Poznan, where he had apparently been a provincial governor. He spoke passable French, and was eminently suited, I decided, to make the investigation trip to Afghanistan. When he returned six weeks later, he strode into my office hale and hearty.

"I have a favor to ask, Ambassador," he began. "Can I give my report standing?"

I looked at him with some surprise.

"I'm sorry, but my rump is still feeling the effects of bounding around in jeeps on horrible roads," he explained. "What mountains! What grass!" he exclaimed after I acquiesced. "I never ate so much mutton in my life. Rapacki is right. . . ." At length and in detail he described his journeys to various valleys in the Hindu Kush mountains. "I'll never forget it. It was the trip of my life. Wonderful mountains, excellent pastureland. The only thing is, there's either no access to it or it's very difficult. And, worse, warring Afghan tribes shoot each others' shepherds and take the sheep."

That was the end of the Rapacki Afghan sheep plan.

Toward the end of June 1966, a few employees in my department simply stopped coming to work. Personnel explained that the Party had delegated them to carry out a very important and secret assignment. The millennium celebration was scheduled to come to Warsaw during this time, and I suspected that plans for antichurch demonstrations were at the root of it.

Within a few days those employees were back on the job, but they had clearly been instructed not to talk. One I knew somewhat better, however, asked to meet me in the city; he promised me an interesting story. We met for lunch in a restaurant on Krakowskie Przedmiescie.

"I want to tell you, Ambassador, what the Party had us do. I trust you in this, because you've never spoken out against the church at meetings and because you're not like some of the others. My family is religious, and though I'm not a practicing Catholic, I have never acted against the church."

"I'm an atheist," I said. "But I don't mind telling you I have no liking for the witch hunts they're up to now."

He looked into my face. "Can I tell you about it then?"

"Please do. I'm curious."

"So. I received instructions from the Central Committee to report to the district committee. The secretary himself told me to bring clothing and things for a few days, but to say nothing to anyone except that I was on an especially important Party assignment. I reported, along with twenty-five or thirty others. An instructor started out by telling us that the people's government was endangered by reactionary forces and that we were to carry out an assignment that could save the whole situation."

My employee looked around and breathed a sigh. "You can imagine how disturbed I was by all this, Ambassador. The instructor gave us an address on Dluga Street, by the Old City, where we were to go in small groups, so as not to attract attention. It's only now that I understand why the government keeps empty apartments all over the city, even though there's such a terrible housing shortage. It turned out that these were to be our temporary quarters; there were mattresses on the floors, chairs. We were fed quite well—sausages, bread, tea—and we were given arm bands marked ORMO, Voluntary Reserve of the Civic Militia. Then we were each issued a heavy oak club and told to wait. At that point it was made clear that leaving was out-and-out forbidden."

"Were there a lot of people in that apartment?"

"It was quite crowded. Fifteen, maybe more. But there were other apartments, so there must have been hundreds of us altogether. We were told to wait for a signal and further instructions. It didn't take me long to realize what we were there to do: we were going to drive people away from the cathedral. With clubs like those"—he gestured to indicate their length and thickness—"you could kill a person!"

"And?"

"We spent the whole time in that apartment. Once, they put us on alert and told us to get ready. A civilian came in and gave us last-minute instructions: we were to beat people on their leg muscles so they'd fall to the ground. But just as he was getting into the details, the alarm was called off. Then it seemed we waited there forever. No one talked; everyone was too afraid. I went out to the courtyard and overheard some men from Security talking. They were saying that the tricky priests hadn't fallen for their provocations. Security hadn't been given the chance it wanted to move in on them. One of them said, 'We would have made it good and hot.' "

"Horrible! Sad." It was all I could say.

"But, Ambassador, the worst of it was that my wife and my oldest boy were at the cathedral that day; they were even in the crowd of people praying out front! The Party expected me to club my own family!"

Soon after this conversation, my brother-in-law confirmed that on Friday, Saturday, and Sunday (June 26) there had almost been trouble in front of the cathedral. Security goons had been accosting the faithful—they had blocked the bishops from passing. Cardinal Wyszynski himself had confronted them.

"Take my word for it," said Czeslaw, "they were a hair's breadth from disaster. You can imagine what the Warsaw people think of that Party of yours now. Gomulka's finished for good."

July 22, the anniversary of the manifesto issued by the Polish Committee of National Liberation in 1944, was always celebrated by the state authorities with great pomp as Poland's national holiday. In the Council of Ministers' palace, Premier Cyrankiewicz gave the usual sumptuous reception. I convinced Wanda that it would be good for us to be seen in public together. So we drove up to the palace in a ministry Mercedes, joining a line of black government, Party, and diplomatic limousines. The guests were received in the drawing rooms and out in the park behind, on a declining series of terraces. It was the first time we had taken part in a gathering of that level in Poland. The weather was fine, and the crowd surged among the tables waiting for the signal that would start the feast. When the strains of our national anthem began, three figures appeared at the top of the terraces. The guests were transfixed. The music died away as Gomulka began descending the stairs with Ochab on his right and Cyrankiewicz on his left. The staging was beyond reproach. Gomulka smiled benignly as they were greeted with deep bows by groups of Party activists. "Just like the tsar's court," I whispered to Wanda. They were clearly pleased with themselves; even puffed-up Ochab had a semblance of a smile as he strutted by. Cyrankiewicz was on the alert, recognizing people in the crowd and pointing them out to Gomulka. When they passed by us, he pointed me out as well, but Gomulka did not acknowledge me. Perhaps he remembered me as the person who had once shouted at him in New York. I had always found bowing repugnant, and this time I made a point of standing straighter than usual.

When the three leaders reached the bottom of the stairs, a signal was given that the tables could be attacked. The Party activists did not prove a disappointment in their zeal. I had considerable experience of receptions in various countries, but that evening the food disappeared with record speed. Diplomats were rudely elbowed away from the tables. The vodka flowed, glasses were clinked, and it was not long before singing started. Then I saw something I had never expected: a drunk collapsed onto a table and shattered all the glasses there. Worse followed. We had had quite enough, and began heading toward the exit. On the way, I spotted Olek Cesarski, who had been in Political Officers School with me. We hugged each other warmly. Olek was now a general.

"Congratulations on the generalship. It's been so many years since we've seen each other," I said, looking him over, unable to believe how he had changed. The broad-shouldered but thin young soldier with the oval face and sharp green eyes had become a dumpy general with a bay window, whose broad face was flushed and unhealthy-looking, dark circles engulfed his eyes.

"Don't exaggerate about me," he replied. "You're the one who's made a terrific career: a diplomat, ambassador to the United States—now that really sounds like something. Remember in 1945 when we studied about the people who represented us in the world? These days they're studying about you."

"I remember, I remember. And I also remember how you criticized the curriculum. What are you doing now?" I asked.

"I'm the head of our antiaircraft defense system. It's a lot of work, and thankless work sometimes, too. What about you?"

"I'm a department director in the Ministry of Foreign Affairs. I was in Vietnam not long ago."

"See! You were always bound for the great world. I saw you once from a car. I wanted to stop, but you were with a woman. Now I see you're with a different one."

"This one's my wife. The other one was someone else," I said candidly. "My life was complicated for a time, but everything's all right now."

We stood for a moment just looking at one another. "Are you happy?" I asked finally.

"Am I happy?" he repeated. "Everyone congratulates me. I live the good life, I have everything I want, but you know . . ." He paused to reflect. "I'll tell you something—those were the best days of my life, back when I knew you, even with those lousy toilets. I believed then. Now, the more I know, the less I believe, the more doubts I have. . . ." His eyes were burrowing into mine. "I'm not living the way I should," he added. "Look what's become of me!"

"I'm glad we can still be frank with each other after so many years," I said. "I had questions even in the old days, but I was sure the foundation was solid. Now . . ."

"You were thin as a rail back then," he interrupted. "The flaming revolutionary, the idealist! I envied you."

We were cut short by some officers, who wanted to be introduced. I never got the chance to tell him what was on my mind. He died a few years later.

My leave time was approaching. Misia, a twenty-year-old university student, had teaching obligations and could not go anywhere with us. Kaytus wanted to go to the Adriatic again.

"We don't have the money for a trip like that, son," Wanda said. "Your father doesn't have dollars, like we did the last time we were there, only the zlotys he gets from his salary."

"Yes, we can go," our fifteen-year-old insisted with conviction. "If you really want to, we can. I have a nest egg, from America. Nearly a hundred dollars."

We were taken aback; he had never betrayed his secret, even when the three of them had needed money desperately.

"I was keeping that money for a rainy day, but I think this is the perfect occasion," he said excitedly. "We'll buy a tent and food. Mama will cook. And all we'll need to buy is gasoline. Let's go! Show us that you really love us. Let's go."

"If Kaytus wants to go so badly, then I do, too," Wanda said, kissing his head.

"We could travel to Italy!" he added.

"To Assisi," I said, surprising myself.

"Assisi! Assisi!" chanted Kaytus.

The decision was made. I rustled up a few dollars, and we set off in our little car with camping equipment and food supplies for a month.

We drove through Czechoslovakia, into Yugoslavia, and stopped on a sandy beach in Budva, south of Dubrovnik. It was the perfect campsite. We ate kasha dolloped with canned Polish goulash and were happy in our little tent home.

One day as Wanda and I sat in front of the tent watching our son swim in the distance, I took her hand and asked, "Tell me what you went through when I was in Vietnam."

"I'm trying to forget," she replied.

"I understand, but I'd like so much to know. Please."

"I went through a great deal," she said after a long silence. "Right after you left for Saigon, I was stopped in front of our building by two strange-looking men in civilian clothes. 'Citizen Spasowska,' one spat out. He was a real hoodlum, with a reptilian face. 'It's been decided to eliminate you. You're doing to die!' "

I looked at her, unable to utter a single word. "That's hard for me to believe," I whispered.

"Oh, that was just the beginning. I was terrified. I felt so powerless, so helpless. The other one added that this was only a warning, and then the two of them marched off. I realized soon enough that they were from Security, the SB. They began following all of us, even Kaytus. They would spew vulgarities at me when I ran into them. The janitor—you know, that brute who drinks all the time and wears a beret all year long—he started taking an interest in us, too. I caught him eavesdropping at our door. Sometimes at night I'd write letters to you telling you all this, but I'd rip them up afterward. You didn't answer any of our letters anyway. I was desperate. Kaytus begged me to take him and Misia and flee Poland. Soon after that, he stopped going to music school. He plastered his entire room with pictures and postcards from America and spent hours looking at his slides and listening to music. He played all alone, read a lot, and longed for the United States. He begrudged me for having brought him to such a hell on earth. It was hard—terribly hard. . . . Only my faith in God kept me going."

"Did you think of me sometimes?"

"Rarely. Any mention of you, and Kaytus would lock himself in his room. I had to hide his key. Do you know what he did? One day I smelled something burning, and I went to see what he was doing. He was burning pages from your father's book over a candle—his book about the Soviets. He confessed immediately. He felt powerless, he said, unable to change his world, but the one thing he *could* do was destroy all the lies his grandfather had filled those pages with."

I thought of that book my father had published in 1936, which I had long tried to forget. It had been written at the height of his blindness, and was based on Soviet propaganda and the rhetoric of the Communist Party of Poland. What would he have said had he seen his grandson, desperate, burning the book page by page over a candle's flame?

"Later, I was summoned to the ministry," Wanda continued. "On the fifth floor, in the Personnel Department, the Vice Director, a horrid man, gave me a tongue-lashing for my irresponsible behavior in appealing for help to the American Embassy in Budapest. He shouted that the scandal had not been confined to Poland, and he threatened me with punishment if I dared contact the American or other embassies in Warsaw. He also reprimanded me for consorting with people from the old underground, and he mentioned Bronek by name. He finished by saying that he supported you in seeking a divorce, and, in fact, was amazed that you had tolerated me for so many years. It was then I exploded. I told him everything right to his face—what I thought about him and the people persecuting me. I also promised him that all of Warsaw would learn of his threats and attempts at intimidation. I knew then that it was I who would have to protect the children. I and my faith."

"I'm so sorry," I murmured. "It never occurred to me that you'd be facing such SB scum." I stroked her hands and kissed her tear-filled eyes.

"I went to General Jedynak," she continued. "He was very decent and tried to calm me. But he let me know it was strictly an SB affair. There was nothing he could do.

"Things were very hard on us. I had no money. We sold everything we had except our dearest heirlooms. Sold them for pennies—to the state store. We bought food on credit. I started looking for a job, but nothing came of that. Friends told me that Security was blocking all my efforts, blacklisting me wherever I went. I couldn't find a lawyer to represent me in the divorce: the ones I knew didn't want to take the case. They said a decision would come from above; I didn't have a chance in the world. I saw for myself that there's no life possible in this country for a person the powerful wish to destroy. It was then I decided we had to leave Poland, even if that meant risking our lives."

Wanda broke off and stared out at the dark blue bay. "But I wasn't the only one who suffered," she said. "You should know what they put Bronek through. They conducted search after search of his place. Even though he's sick and poor, they didn't spare him. They kept bursting in, questioning him, turning his apartment inside out. They confiscated his typewriter and threatened him with a bad end. That was just the beginning. After the bank on Jasna Street was held up, he was arrested and put in jail. He told me later that they had kept hammering away at him, insisting that he was the only one who could have organized that robbery. They accused him of stealing the money for the underground. But he had reliable witnesses; they had to let him go. They didn't stop badgering him, however. They needed a scapegoat.

"Kaytus and I visited him often, and whenever we did, we always noticed someone hanging around the front of his building. But we'd gotten used to that. Kaytus met many wonderful people at Bronek's—Home Army soldiers. He loves those Poles. . . ."

I looked from her to Kaytus, who was slowly walking up the beach.

"We can be proud of our son," Wanda said. "Everything he's been through has made him old, but he has a beautiful heart, and he's good, very good."

My son had clearly changed. He was a big boy now with soft, pensive eyes. In the evenings, in the tent, he would ask what I had done at his age and what life in prewar Poland was like. He asked, too, about his grandfather. Why had he become a communist? I promised to tell him when we returned to Warsaw.

The days passed quickly, and soon we left for Italy. The sun was declining to the west when we caught sight of the outline of Assisi. Rose-colored rays fell on the walls, roofs, and soaring towers. I stopped the car, and we got out to enjoy the view. The sound of church bells reached our ears.

"How beautiful," marveled Wanda. "There's something here that fills me with peace and gentleness."

"Yes. Thanks for bringing us here, Father," Kaytus said simply. "Saint Francis is the most beautiful saint."

Our tent was pitched overlooking a beautiful valley, and the grass around it had a wonderful smell. I listened to my son's even breathing. Soon Wanda, too, was asleep. Despite my fatigue, I could not sleep. My thoughts strayed far and wide with memories of Wanda and the children: my first sight of Kaytus as a baby lying beside his mother in London, Misia and Kaytus in the garden in Buenos Aires and running among the trees on Skyline Drive in Virginia.

A storm was approaching; every so often the tent would be lit up by the lightning. The rumbling quickly intensified and became violent.

"Romek." Wanda woke up suddenly. "What a terrible storm!"

"Don't worry. Everything will be all right."

"Terrible lightning," rasped Kaytus a moment later.

They both cuddled up against me. The wind was tearing at the tent, and it seemed we would be swallowed by the din, by the night itself. Heavy rain battered down. I could feel my wife and son drifting off to sleep again, but I was still wide awake. I began to contemplate why I was there.

Why had I, a Communist, come so willingly to this place, the place Saint Francis had called his home? What did I really know about him? He had led a boisterous life as a youth, had fallen ill and undergone a change. On recovering he had renounced everything, had given all his possessions away, and had lived alone, a beggar preaching God's glory. Seven centuries had passed, nations had risen and fallen, castles and cities had been built and had turned to rubble, but this one man's faith and gentleness still radiated from that place somehow. Even I, an atheist, had been compelled to these thoughts by the greatness of his spirit. I could not remain unmoved. Quite suddenly, I felt his presence. I was a stranger to these feelings and found myself moved to my depths. I began to cry.

In the morning we headed for the basilica, where Wanda and Kaytus prayed, while I sat to one side sunk in thought about my experience the previous night.

Our three days in Assisi passed like a single breath. We returned to Poland penniless, with our last drops of gas, but renewed.

"How are things at home? Everything all right?" Rapacki asked one October day.

"Yes," I could answer. "I'm with my family, and I'm fine."

"Good, *very* good," he replied, with a friendly smile. "In that case, I will ask you: Will you go as our ambassador to India?"

"Of course," I said. "I'll go wherever I'm needed."

"Good then. You'll go after the New Year."

The Council of State approved my appointment to India, and our departure time was established.

I had finished up my affairs at the office when one day the "government" phone on my desk rang. The voice at the other end had a distinctly Russian accent.

"Hello, Comrade Director Spasowski. This is Tolyzhin, of the Soviet Embassy. What's new?"

"Nothing's new," I answered. "What can I do for you?"

"What do you mean, nothing's new, Comrade Director?" he

switched into Russian, speaking with a marked Asian inflection. "You're leaving the country, isn't that so?"

"Yes."

"Well, I'd like to have a talk with you. Can I come see you tomorrow at ten in the morning?"

"Fine."

I hung up and stared down at that modest, black instrument. Whoever had a government phone had power, one of my deputies used to say. It was true. Everyone who had such a phone knew everyone else who did; we were all part of the circle in power. The system—a separate network, operating on a high frequency to prevent anyone from listening in—had been set up by the Soviet secret police for use by our secret police and for the central state and government authorities. To bypass all intermediaries, the person being called had to pick up the phone himself. That went for everybody, Gomulka included. Those phones were limited to a few hundred, whose names were listed in a small brown book—a secret government document. In that respect, Tolyzhin's call was no surprise. Like any diplomat at the Soviet Embassy, he had a government phone. My contact with the Soviet Embassy had been sporadic: in the past year Tolyzhin, who was a counselor, had come to see me once, and another time had sent over an embassy secretary to quiz me on Vietnam. I knew their methods. The Soviet ambassador saw only Rapacki, or, once in a great while, certain of the vice ministers. Most of his contact was with the first secretary, the premier, or other members of the Politburo. The counselors, of whom there must have been ten, often went to see the vice ministers but only certain of the department heads, and I was not one of them.

Tolyzhin appeared the next day. He was of average height, dark-haired, nearly bald, with a cowlick on one side and small, slanted eyes.

"You're heading for an important diplomatic post," he said, wasting no time. "India is an important country. A peaceful country threatened by China. It has an important international position, which we want to make use of. We'd like to discuss these matters with you."

"Go right ahead," I answered.

"Of course, but not here. The office is not the place for that. I'd like to invite you for lunch or dinner, whatever's more convenient for you. Other comrades will be there. We can talk more freely at our embassy, heart to heart. Perhaps next week—Tuesday at one? Or in the evening? Whatever you say."

"One o'clock is fine," I answered, dreading the thought.

The next Sunday I went to visit my mother in Milanowek. She was living by herself in the two rooms of her own villa that had been allocated to her by the Housing Bureau. She greeted me, forever her little boy, with tenderness and love. As usual, we drank tea and ate cakes and jam she had made. Two stray dogs she had taken in lay at her feet, and her favorite cat was curled on her lap.

"I have something for you," she said after a while. "Last time, I forgot. My memory is poor, and I was so happy to see the children. . . . Do you remember when you were at Anielcia's in 1941, just after your father died? I brought you some documents. You looked awful, sitting there still as could be, wearing that threadbare brown sweater. You didn't seem to understand what was being said to you."

"And you say you have a poor memory."

"Well, I told you then I was keeping something else for you. But I forgot all about it, and you never reminded me."

She drew an envelope with blackened corners from under the oilcloth on the table and handed it to me. The envelope did look like it had not seen the light of day for twenty-five years. I opened it and found several sheets of discolored paper fastened by a rusted paper clip. It was a letter from my father to Stalin. I had to strain to read the faded pages of Russian script deftly written in my father's hand. He wrote that he was ending his life at a time when Poland and nearly all of Europe were under the fascist heel, and the bloody Nazi fist was reaching far into the Soviet state. He wished the Soviet Communists success in the fight against fascism. In fiery rhetoric, he wrote that millions of people would be killed in that struggle, but he would die believing that free people would defeat the fascist beast. Then he wrote briefly about himself: that he had been rejected by the Soviets and handed over to be devoured by the Nazis; that by taking his own life he might thereby protect his son. He asked only one thing of Stalin: that he look after his son if the boy managed to survive the storm of history.

It took a long time to read. The lines were blurred and the moldering paper disintegrated in my hands. My mother sat in silence, watching me.

When I finished, I looked up at her and said, "The letter is dated the end of June 1941. By then, German armored columns were already far to the east. They were cutting through the Red Army like butter. There was no hope in sight."

"I remember. I remember it well, as if it were yesterday."

"He wasn't naive any more by then. He knew the Soviets, but he didn't know—he couldn't know—what they were doing to the Poles. He didn't know about the massacre at Katyn, no one knew about it then, except Stalin and his butchers."

"So what will you do with the letter?" she asked.

"I don't know. Perhaps it would be best to destroy it."

"No, you can't do that. Respect has to be shown for everything he wrote. If you're thinking of destroying it, then leave the letter with me; let it stay here. It can die with me."

"Perhaps I really should pass it on to those it was addressed to," I said. "I'll take it with me and think about it."

On my way home I pondered what to do with that letter. Give it to the Soviets? To our Party? The Central Committee did have a department for the history of the Polish workers' movement. But no. Some hack would slather it with lies. They had written so much about my father, but no one had written the truth about him, even though some of the writers had known him well.

Perhaps I should keep it? I couldn't stand the thought of keeping this proof of my poor father's delusions about Stalin. But I would never be able to destroy it. Yes, my mother was right; I had to carry out my father's will.

The Soviet Embassy was located in a monumental new building, erected while the Palace of Culture was under construction. Intended to be imposing in its might and sweep, the building was splendid, palatial, with enormous granite columns; inside were high-ceilinged reception rooms, marble, and great crystal chandeliers. All the same, the building was as cold as an Egyptian pyramid and as impersonal as a bank. There was the traditional enormous portrait of Brezhnev and a few old Russian paintings.

The other people, besides Tolyzhin, at lunch on Tuesday—were embassy employees, none of whom I knew. Drinking vodka and eating appetizers, they praised my diplomatic experience.

"Who can equal your experience as a diplomat?" said one. "You know the German problem—a matter of central importance. You've been in London, South America, six years in America. You were in Vietnam, and now you're going to India."

They oozed insincerity, and I anxiously waited for them to get to the point. And I was all too aware of the envelope in my breast pocket, which I had decided to hand them during the course of this meeting. We sat down at the table.

"Your health," said Tolyzhin lifting his glass. "And your success. But we have to drink it in one gulp, Polish style."

"*Old* Polish style—straight down, not just wetting your lips," said one of the counselors.

"Unfortunately, I don't drink," I said.

They exchanged glances but made no attempt to pressure me.

"Well. We've already informed Piegov," said Tolyzhin, finally.

"Who's Piegov?" I asked.

"Oh, you don't know? He's our ambassador in New Delhi. We wrote to him that a very experienced diplomat would be arriving from Warsaw, one who enjoys great trust . . ."

"And the esteem of our Polish comrades," threw in one of the counselors.

"Piegov is a great ambassador," said Tolyzhin solemnly. "An old Communist, from the time of the revolution, very respected. It's no accident that he's our ambassador to India."

He narrowed his eyes like a crocodile, until only slits remained. "You see, Comrade Spasowski, we didn't forget about you. We value your experience." He peered at me as if checking my reaction. "We informed Piegov because we're counting on your working closely with him for our common cause."

"You understand," explained one of the counselors, "India is of great importance to us. A year ago Aleksei Kosygin invited the premiers of India and Pakistan to Tashkent to settle their differences. It was a resounding diplomatic success. We showed that when we have to, we can also settle differences between capitalists."

Everyone burst out laughing.

He continued. "Prime Minister Indira Gandhi is conducting a peaceful policy. You remember her anti-American speeches against the bombing of Vietnam? Simply an amazing woman, *amazing*."

"The point is to bind India closer to us," Tolyzhin said firmly toward the end of the meal. "Together we will be the anti-Chinese front in Asia, and *that* is one of our highest priorities. You're headed for a very important post, Comrade Ambassador. We wish you success. And a good working relationship with Piegov," he concluded, raising his glass.

I wet my lips with the vodka.

"Drink it *down*, Comrade Ambassador," he insisted, "for our mutual success and eternal friendship."

"Thank you for your good wishes." I set the glass down firmly. "But now I'd like to bring up a certain unrelated matter with you." I reached into my breast pocket. "I want to pass on to you a letter from my father, Wladyslaw Spasowski. He wrote it just before he died. It's addressed to Iosif Vissarionovich Stalin." I placed the envelope on the table. "I'm carrying out my father's will in delivering it to you."

A troubled look rippled across the counselors' faces in a single motion.

"A letter to Stalin?" said Tolyzhin reluctantly. "We can't guarantee that it will be published."

"We don't know anything about that sort of thing," said another face.

"I know you don't," I replied calmly. "But now you'll find out, won't you? I don't expect anything from you. I'm only doing my father's will."

"Well, if that's the case, fine. Does anyone else know about this letter?" asked Tolyzhin.

"No, no one else knows," I said, deciding not to bring up my mother or my wife.

"Good," said Tolyzhin with apparent relief. "The comrades in Moscow will know best how to deal with this."

They turned their attention to the caviar and filled their glasses again.

Kaytus had been in a chronic state of poor health, but during the Christmas holidays he developed acute appendicitis. The case was critical—he had to be operated on at once.

As he was wheeled into the operating room, he took me by the hand and looked at me with pained eyes. "Don't give me away, Father," he said. Seeing his suffering and knowing all he had been through, I was never more aware of how much he meant to me.

The operation and Kaytus's slow recovery meant we had to postpone going to India, and we did not finish packing until the end of March.

Kaytus soon reminded me that I had promised to tell him about his grandfather. We went out into the city. I wanted my son to remember what I told him that day in the context of the Warsaw his grandfather had known. First I took him to the building in which I had spent part of my childhood and youth. I told him how good our life had been until 1939 and what it was like during the first years of the war. We strolled to the Calvinist cemetery along streets I had walked at his age. On Zelazna Street, I showed him where the ghetto wall had been and, farther along, the ruins of my old school. We were to have had a tenth reunion, I said, but nearly everyone had been killed.

Kaytus prayed at the cemetery, kneeling beside the granite slab marked "Wladyslaw Spasowski 1877–1941." I stood and stroked my son's beautiful head.

"All we'd have to do is put my dates under his, and this could be my grave, too," he said as he rose.

"None of us knows when and where he'll be buried," I said, dismissing his morbid thought, "and you will live a long life."

He looked up at me timidly. "I pray for Grandfather, as Mama says I should—we came here even when you weren't living with us—but . . . I dislike him a lot." He blurted it out and waited, wide-eyed.

"Why is that, son?" I asked gently.

"Grandfather fought against God," he said earnestly. "I know it. I read it in his books. He wrote a lot of bad things. He wrote about the Soviets—what a good, just place they live in. And I *know* that isn't the truth."

I could feel he was casting about to resolve something that had troubled him for a long time.

"How could he?" Kaytus erupted. "You always said he was an intelligent man, highly educated. How could he write those things?"

We sat down on a cemetery bench. "He searched for the truth his whole life," I explained. "He searched far and wide, and thought he had found a solution in the Soviets. I, too, thought a better world had come for them. I was nineteen, only three years older than you are now. . . ."

"But for me it's the other way around. I know that 'better' world and I don't ever want to live in it. I'm glad we're going to India."

"You've been through a lot, Kaytus, and I'm sorry for it. I won't lie to you. Your grandfather was mistaken, clearly mistaken. We know that now." It was difficult for me to say those words.

"Father, why was he against religion?"

"I know that religious people like your mother think he was a very sinful man. Still, you should always remember that at the moment of death he showed great fortitude and strength of spirit, and that tells you who a person really is. Do you remember what he wrote as he was dying?"

"I remember," said Kaytus.

"I don't think many people would have been able to do that, and I ask that you never forget it when you're judging your grandfather."

We took a taxi from the cemetery to the Powisle district.

"Know where you are?" I asked as we got out in front of the Polish Teachers' Union building on the street named Wladyslaw Spasowski.

"I know there's a plaque here with my grandfather's face on it."

We stood before it. "Did they put it up because he wrote so well of the Soviets?" Kaytus asked.

"That's just what I want to talk to you about. Let's go down by the Vistula. We can sit on a bench in the sun and have a good talk."

It took only a few minutes to reach the river. Shards of ice were still floating on the water, but it was warm in the sun.

"Polish soldiers crossed this river to the spot where we're sitting now to help in the uprising against the German occupiers," I began.

"But the uprising failed, and the Germans destroyed the whole city."

"Yes, and the soldiers who crossed to the German side were killed. Stalin wanted Warsaw to fall. He used Nazi hands to throttle it. No doubt Stalin wanted to kill your grandfather, too, but your grandfather did the job for him.

"You asked me if they put up that plaque because he wrote well of the Soviets. Listen. After the war all sorts of people were interested in your grandfather's name and works. The first to remember him were his students, who were genuinely devoted to his memory. They formed a union named after him. Mostly they were teachers. They did not forget their professor."

"When you were in Vietnam and Mama and I went to his grave, we never saw anyone there."

"Well, son, maybe it's because they're old now. There are also other people who are using your grandfather to make a career or even money for themselves. After he died, all sorts of people began writing things, obliterating the truth, falsifying. Even the students who had been closest to him libel him in their memoirs: they say the Poland we're living in now is precisely the Poland your grandfather dreamed of. That's a lie. I knew him better than anyone; I know that were he alive today he would not be indifferent to the turn things have taken. I'm afraid he'd end up in prison, even as he did then."

"You think so?"

"I don't think so, I'm sure of it," I replied. "Those opportunists who are using your grandfather's name erased anything that might burden the Soviets with the responsibility for his death. There's nothing in their books about prewar Poland that isn't a glowing tribute to communism and the Soviets. I've simply broken with those so-called followers of Wladyslaw Spasowski. They wrote, for instance, that during the occupation your grandfather tried to go to the Soviet Union but never got there because it was then that the Nazis attacked the USSR. You know what really happened, Kaytus: the Soviets didn't want him; they left him in Nazi clutches."

"Are you a Communist?" asked Kaytus out of the blue.

I found myself taking a moment to think. "I am. But my communism is very different from that of the people in the Party. I traveled the road my father started me on. I was an idealist. I believed in a brotherhood of people liberated from envy and superstition long before it was the thing to do. Only circumstance has made me as privileged as I am today.

"You must know the whole truth about your father, too, Kaytus. You've already seen for yourself how low he can be. Remember, there is no earthly justification for what I did to you. As for the truth about your father and People's Poland . . . the longer I live, the more doubts I have. I feel like I'm in a trap, with no way out. The wall between me and the Party gets higher all the time. I detest their propaganda. I detest their use of force. I think that every person has the right to his own beliefs. If Poland is Catholic, then it has the right to practice its religion, to celebrate its millennium."

Kaytus put his arms around me and kissed my cheek.

"It's good you're like that. I love you. I thought we would never be able to understand each other."

I kissed him back. It felt good to talk openly.

"I feel sorry for Grandfather. He can't say anything now; he can't defend himself," said Kaytus.

"But you and I can do it for him," I said, hugging him close and gazing out at the waters of the Vistula. I had lost much, but I still had my family. "Let's go home," I told him finally. "Your mother's waiting."

CHAPTER XIX

We landed in New Delhi in the early morning, and the heat burst on us as from a stove. I caught a sweetish smell that reminded me of incense. It was a fragrance that hung in the air everywhere in India.

We drove into the city in the embassy car, a large white air-conditioned Chevrolet with tinted windows. Our driver, an Indian who introduced himself as Tarachand, wore an immaculate white suit and kept grinning up at me. Beggars in gray rags lined the road. There was little vegetation on the sun-scorched earth, and the walls of houses were white as chalk. Every so often we would pass a cow wandering freely.

"Are those sacred cows?" asked Kaytus.

"Must be," I replied, seeing how careful Tarachand was to drive around them.

The car came to a stop before a gate marked Tilak Marg 1, and an Indian in a khaki uniform opened the gate and greeted us with a salute. We drove up to a large creamy pink modern villa surrounded by a garden.

The residence was not the property of Poland. It had been requisitioned from some rajah in the fifties and allocated to the Polish ambassador because Nehru had taken a liking to socialist Poland after his visit to Warsaw in June of 1955, a month after the formation of the Warsaw Pact. The floors were inlaid with black marble; long-bladed fans were suspended from the ceilings. There were four bedrooms and a small living room on the second floor; a dining room, a study, a large living room, and two smaller ones on the first. The lovely veranda, also inlaid with black marble, led to a colorful flower garden and a splashing fountain at the rear of the house. A wall overgrown with morning glories enclosed the far end of the garden. Beyond that wall, in very cramped conditions, lived our servants, a dozen families with forty or so children. Tarachand also lived there. I later learned that he was an officer in the Indian army, who had been assigned to the embassy as a driver. "Tara" was to prove a very loyal friend.

My Indian secretary, Peetenbaran, assigned to the embassy by the Communist Party of India, lived in that compound as well. He was an excellent secretary, but reported to someone outside the embassy on everything that passed through his hands. That, of course, was something he had to do; I just did not know precisely for whom he was doing it.

As we came to know these people, our fondness and respect for India increased. Indians seemed honest in word and deed, and attached to traditional values and religion.

Wanda soon changed some of the prevailing customs, however. Unlike her predecessors, she allowed the Indian children to play in the garden. All the families were given a permanent allowance of rice, sugar, and milk. She also taught the children to eat bread with jam or cheese, something new for them.

I paid visits to the socialist embassies, beginning with Soviet Ambassador Nikolai Piegov, their dean. The Soviet Embassy occupied a broad expanse in the diplomatic enclave, but somewhat smaller than the Chinese Embassy's grounds. The compound consisted of a formidable office building and residential buildings. The entire area was surrounded by a fence and guarded on every side by Indians and Russians. When I arrived, the ambassador's secretary ushered me in to Piegov immediately.

"I was informed that you'd be coming," he said. His thick gray hair and kindly light blue eyes gave him a fatherly air. "I know that you're an experienced man, well trained in foreign service. It is precisely people like you who are needed here. What's necessary in India is diplomacy and a constant awareness of the line." He thrust his hand straight out in front of him. "Like that, our Party's unvarying course."

I listened with curiosity as he spoke of India and his work.

"This is an important country, an important post," he said emphatically. "Sometimes our comrades underestimate its importance because they take a narrow view of things. Indian poverty hampers their vision. It's true that there's great poverty here. But this is an enormous country, a subcontinent with half a billion people on it. We have to look to the future—not just at what's in front of our noses, but at what will happen in twenty years—more—fifty."

He poured tea and continued. "India has to be looked at in two ways. First, it's the greatest power in the Third World—it has prestige, influence. And the Third World is our ally in the fight against imperialism. If it's not completely with us today, it will be tomorrow. The sooner they're firmly with us, the better for us and for them. And the easier it'll be to finish off capitalism.

"Second, India offsets Chinese Maoism. Who knows what's going to happen in China, where their adventurism will lead. We need an ally, a strong ally in Asia, and India is the one to have."

"Yes, but it's not a socialist country," I remarked, to have something to say.

"I can see you don't understand," he replied. "They're a long way from socialism. But we are gaining more ground with them than the imperialists are. Imperialists' hands are colonialists' hands, and colonialists' hands are dirty. They pursue only their own interests, they can't see past their own noses. In India you have to be prepared to give more than you take; that's the whole thing. Half a billion poor people and they have no oil, or very little. But we will help them. We have heavy industry, and we will help them."

Piegov spoke with the conviction of an old-time Communist. But just what was our Party's *line?* Did such a line even exist? Piegov had meant the Bolshevik line, established by the Kremlin. Suddenly I was aware of the leagues that separated Piegov and me.

After I presented my credentials to President Sarvepalli Radhakrishnan I made my way to my first meeting with Foreign Secretary T. N. Kaul. Piegov had warned me against him. Hopping nimbly from subject to subject, Kaul convinced me that he was every bit as sharp as Piegov had promised. I admired his brilliance, and in all our future dealings he turned out to be a considerable thorn in my side.

Piegov soon organized a conference for the socialist ambassadors in India. I continued to attend these conferences with reluctance, disliking the distinctly Soviet orientation, and making my own quiet point by never engaging in praise of Moscow. I saw Piegov every few weeks and, aware of the gulf between us, was restrained with him. As I grew to know him better, I began to argue various points with him and express my doubts. That led to heated exchanges at times, but we were arguing on an equal footing. It seemed to me that he enjoyed it, and perhaps even needed to talk with someone like me. We spoke exclusively of India, and only marginally about Poland or the Soviet Union. I even grew to like him.

Soon after we arrived, Misia was accepted by the university to study English. Braving the heat, she set off each day for Old Delhi, for her classes. As the only European there, and a redhead to boot, she enjoyed great popularity. Kaytus was at the American International High School and was happy there.

War broke out in the Near East at the beginning of June 1967. The Israeli air force destroyed the majority of Egyptian planes on the ground, and Israeli tanks reached the Suez Canal. I was instructed by Warsaw to make a clear expression to the Indian Ministry of External Affairs that Poland was outraged about Israeli policy, which posed a threat to world peace. I read the telegram with very mixed feelings. Certainly, I was repelled by the war and especially by the aerial bombardment. On the other hand, never having forgotten the burning ghetto, I was gladdened by Israel's intitiative. I carried out the ministry's instruction formally, expressionlessly.

In mid-June Warsaw broke off relations with Israel. A few days later I received excerpts from a speech Gomulka had delivered at a trade union conference. He condemned Zionism and stated bluntly that he wanted no Zionist fifth column in Poland. His words astounded me. It was a clear attack on Jews. The only good Jews apparently were Jewish Communists who had always followed the Party line.

Kaytus asked me what fifth column meant. I explained by saying that during the civil war in Spain, General Franco's fascist troops had moved on Madrid in four columns; the "fifth" was supposed to create diversionary action inside the capital. Kaytus shook his head, still unable to fathom what Gomulka meant. What sort of fifth column could there be in Poland among the few Jews who had survived the war?

I wanted to discuss these questions with someone wiser than I, but not with a Party slogan spouter. With whom then? I never suspected that it would be in India that I would be given my opportunity.

One day in July of 1967, an appointment was canceled at the last minute, and Tara asked if I would like to take the time to drive outside the city. He wanted to show me something of interest. He took me to Tughlaqabad, a deserted town, buried as far as the eye could see in a sandy landscape. Surrounded by a mighty wall, the city was to have served as a bastion protecting Delhi and other communities on the Yamuna River from attack by savage tribes. It had been built by the prisoners of Tughlaq, a soldier of fortune, who had become king and founded the dynasty that reigned in India during the fourteenth century. Tughlaq had died at the hands of his own son, who, legend has it, deserted the city in despair.

I was struck by the strength of the high walls extending in a circle with a circumference of seven miles. Tara stopped the car where the entrance gate had once been; now only a rubbled path led upward toward the phantom city. The area seemed deserted, but for a chattering little throng of thin beggar children.

"You should go up there, Mr. Ambassador. Nobody's there. The view from the wall is worth seeing. I'll wait here by the car."

I started at the ruined gate and passed towers, ruins of the palace, a deep cistern, passageways that once had been streets, a dark open cellar amid a sea of rubble and stones. I stood on the wall and looked around. The sun was merciless. Desert landscape stretched into the distance, and hot air trembled on the far horizon. I took a deep breath, and the sweet smell of incense filled my head. I sat down on a stone and covered my head with my handkerchief. Centuries ago people had lived here with their dreams and desires, as fervent as my own. And all that was left of them were these stones. And what would remain after me?

I had not indulged in such thoughts since Assisi. Perhaps I had avoided them. Perhaps I was *afraid* of them. Afraid of what? Looking the truth in the eye, a person can deceive everyone but himself. I knew this much: I had been taking what I had thought was a straight path through life. Years ago I would have called it the Communist path. Now I knew too much, had been through too much, to deny that there was an abyss between the idea of communism and the practice. My poor father had wanted to build a bridge between the two, to reconcile idea and practice. He was a philosopher, he knew the idea, and had built the bridge well from his side. But then he had stepped on it, only to have it collapse because the other end was on a swamp. He went under like thousands, like millions, who had believed that communism in practice was what Soviet propaganda proclaimed it to be.

I had taken another path. I had built no bridges, assumed nothing. And yet there was anger in me. What right had the Soviets to treat the Poles the way they had? Polish "people's democracy" boded no good either. I had followed my "ideals" straight ahead, without looking to either side, and had brought my family to the brink of catastrophe. Now what?

I wiped the sweat from my face with my hand. The heat was fierce; the stones burned my fingers. I gazed around the rubble. Why had these reflections come to me in this place and not in my own garden, in a comfortable lawn chair amid the flowers, by the fountain?

"We'll be coming back here often," I said to Tara as we drove away. He smiled.

The monsoon began. Twice a day leaden clouds would fill the sky, and then the rain would come in a steady stream. People came to life. Little boys would race nearly naked through the heavy downpour, and old Indians would walk about, their dhotis sticking to their bodies, a look of relief on their faces. Everything alive drank in the water. Even the sacred cows moved about more briskly.

At this time I learned that Prime Minister Indira Gandhi was considering a trip to Europe, and I began to make efforts to have her invited to Poland. I thought that her visiting Warsaw could result in concrete economic achievements of importance to both countries. I wrote to Warsaw and received Rapacki's permission. I had several talks at the Ministry of External Affairs, and the visit was scheduled for October.

Indira Gandhi invited Wanda and me to a private dinner. I liked her immediately; she was intelligent, pleasant, modest. I sent my recommendations to Warsaw on the basis of that conversation, hoping that the existing co-operation in coal and tractors would broaden as a result of her visit. With the best of intentions, Wanda and I flew to Poland for the occasion. We went via Moscow because it was cheaper.

I met one disenchantment after another. Minister Rapacki was thinner and in poor health, and his mind seemed elsewhere; he was despondent, nervous, his reactions not as lively as they once had been. On orders from his doctor he was smoking less, but his hands trembled. At a meeting he did not look at the people in front of him, but stared off into space, his gaze fixed on the opposite wall. I felt sorry for him.

No one treated relations with India seriously, and my initial conversations confirmed that no one was counting on any actual results. Those I reproached for that attitude only stared at me in astonishment. After Mrs. Gandhi's arrival, things went from bad to worse. The talks with Cyrankiewicz could not have been more inappropriate, an exchange of empty platitudes. The Indian prime minister had not prepared for the visit either, and it produced no tangible results. She met with Gomulka, but I never learned what was discussed. While they met, Wanda and I waited in Belvedere Palace, where Ochab was to host a ceremonial dinner. The meeting with Gomulka lasted considerably longer than expected. By the time Mrs. Gandhi arrived, Ochab was out of patience and wanted to sit down at the table at once, but she confided to Wanda that she would like to wash her hands first. A minute later an angry Wanda was back, to say that all the bathrooms were locked. It turned out that the guards had the keys. Confusion ensued and much running about. A full fifteen minutes later, a major came panting with the keys. Once again the ladies set off. Later, Wanda told me that the bathrooms had long been out of use and were dirty; through the half-open door the officer had handed them soap and a crumpled towel.

Ochab had not changed. At the table, he rose, withdrew a sheet of paper from his pocket, and read a toast, making a few errors. Mrs. Gandhi's reply was brief, a deft improvisation.

I considered the occasion a total failure and made no secret of my opinion.

I visited my mother in Milanowek on that trip. She was still living in two cluttered rooms with her beloved cat and one dog. She complained of poor health and back pains as I stroked her toil-worn hands and gray hair. She would not take anything from me.

"I almost forgot," she said suddenly. "I have something for you." She walked over to the cupboard, bent over, and rummaged around. She drew out a cardboard box and set it down before me.

"Take this with you," she said. "It's the silver Grandmother gave me before the war. I didn't use it much. But you'll have use for it; you entertain. It's very old Polish silver—a sugar bowl, candlesticks, flatware, a salt cellar, saucers. Take them to India, but remember, they've been in our family for many years—so treat them with respect."

I looked through the pieces, admiring their old, classical forms, the masterly work, impossible to duplicate now. That admiration became the start of the only hobby I had in nearly fifty years. From then on, any free time I had was spent studying and seeking out Polish silver in antique stores. Unfortunately, my collection remained a small one: Polish silver, like Poland's people and its monuments, had been ravaged by the storms of war.

Back in New Delhi Wanda told me what she had heard from Bronek Sianoszek.

"He asked me not to tell anyone, but I think this is something you must know about," she said as we sat down with the children for dinner. "Bronek is feeling much better and devoting a lot of time to writing. He has traveled through Poland visiting old friends he made during the war and collecting material for his memoirs. In the Poznan train station he saw two men he had known in the underground. They must have recognized him, too, because they stared at him curiously. They were dressed quite decently, and Bronek noticed they were driving an official car. There wouldn't have been anything special about that encounter were it not for the fact that as the leader of the execution platoon for the Home Army, Bronek was supposed to carry out a death sentence on both of them. They had been working for the Gestapo. But when Bronek went to carry out the sentence, they were nowhere to be found. The Red Army had entered Poland. Everything had changed. The traitors disappeared. Now, more than twenty years later, and purely by chance, he found them."

"Did he let them disappear again?" asked Kaytus excitedly.

"They walked away," answered Wanda. "But through his contacts in Poznan, Bronek determined that they now work for the secret police. One even holds a high position."

"How is that possible?" asked Kaytus, outraged.

"They should be thrown in prison immediately!" added Misia.

"That's not the way things happen, children," said Wanda. "Bronek told me that people like that, dirty hands and all, are very useful to the government. Such people come in handy to a nation that rules by force."

The children turned their questioning faces to me.

"I don't know. . . . The secret police use all sorts of people. That's the way it is everywhere in the world. But I didn't think things were that bad at home," I answered.

"It's disgusting!" said Kaytus. "How can they use scum like that to persecute Poles?"

For a few months we gave no more thought to Bronek.

I had imposed a very strenuous program on myself. First came a trip to the state of Bihar to visit Polish miners working in the two mines there. Then there was one to a hydroelectric station on the Ganges; I traveled to Benares, Budgaya, and immediately after that I was to present my credentials in Ceylon. All my trips were by car. I was getting to know the country well.

I undertook a study of publications on the "green revolution" in India. With aid from the United States, hybrids of wheat and other grains were being produced in India that increased the yield of their harvest. "Backward" India was creating a breakthrough in agriculture that promised to banish the specter of famine. I was very taken with the idea, and decided to obtain wheat kernels that could offer good results in Poland. We were importing great quantities of grain and fodder from abroad, and the food situation remained difficult. Mincing no words with my embassy officials, who, I knew, were well versed in the art of intelligence work, I issued instructions that they acquire the wheat hybrids at once.

While I waited, I learned that not all was well in Poland. Couriers in February of 1968 bore the news. I had known one of them in the United States and invited him to the house.

"Things are bad at home again, Comrade Ambassador," he said, enjoying the tandoori chicken and chapatis. "There's more and more trouble with the young people all the time. They don't write about it in the papers, but the University of Warsaw is in a constant state of pandemonium. Somehow or other reactionary agitators get in there no matter how tight the admissions policy is. The demonstrations at the National Theater have become more frequent and worse. They simply had to forbid any further performances. Our friends took an interest. We had to do it."

"What *friends*?" asked Kaytus.

"Well—I heard that the Soviet Embassy intervened quite firmly, and that was the end of that. I tell you, the tension is incredible."

"What's the news from the ministry?" I asked.

"Aha," he said smacking his lips loudly. "Vice Minister Naszkowski is being persecuted something terrible, and he's such a devoted Communist, too. Minister Rapacki is chronically ill and home most of the time. Winiewicz is running things."

I offered him another helping of tandoori. He tore at it with such gusto that the children exchanged grins.

"How come Polish chickens don't taste this good? Do we have a different sort of chicken, or what?" he asked.

"No. Ours are the same. But there are a great many things we don't know how to do right in Poland," Wanda said.

"These chapatis are delicious," he said, oblivious. "To make a long story short, things are rough at home. But it's what's going on in Czechoslovakia that concerns our comrades—and worries Moscow—more. No one obeys the Party there! They've made a lot of reforms that have nothing to do with a *people's* democracy, and they've elected some guy named Dubcek first secretary. A good Communist like Antonin Novotny wouldn't do for them. I tell you, Comrade Ambassador, nothing good will come of this. And the worst of it is that people in Poland are crazy—happy—about what's happening there; they love it! The students at the university cheer Dubcek like he was a—well, I don't know what."

After the courier left, Wanda snapped at me reproachfully, "How can you bring such Stalinists to our house? I was barely able to keep myself from saying what I really thought of him."

"Forgive me, but I have to know what's going on in Warsaw, especially when we're so far from home."

"I'm fed up with that crew!" she said angrily. "And I never imagined we would be entertaining thugs like that courier here in India. You must have had it with that sort, too. I know you."

The year 1968 did not bode well. Twice now there had been bloody clashes between the police and Warsaw's young. Police brutality was causing widespread indignation, and students in other Polish cities began organizing demonstrations of their solidarity. The wave of police repression spread throughout the entire country. I was not aware that behind the scenes a furious power struggle was on in the Party. A new group was attempting to oust Gomulka and take over the government.

We were anxiously awaiting further reports when I received a coded telegram, for my eyes only, signed by Bejm, the director of the ministry's Communications Department. Speaking on behalf of the Party committee, he informed me that a POP (Primary Party Organization) meeting would take place in a few days. At the meeting the healthy elements in the Party would give a vote of no-confidence to Vice Minister Marian Naszkowski in order to force him to resign. "We have known Naszkowski for a long time, in many different periods," wrote Bejm, "but no one has known him as well as you in recent years." He reminded me that I had reported to Naszkowski at headquarters, had accompanied him on trips to Djakarta, Cairo, and Addis Ababa, and had witnessed the egotistical scenes he had made when he had received government decorations of a lesser rank than ambassadors under him. "In conclusion," he wrote, "and on behalf of the committee and entire Primary Party Organization, I request that you send your opinion of Naszkowski immediately. It will be read at the meeting and included in the minutes."

I spent hours trying to decide what to do. Surely, I had a hearty dislike of Naszkowski. He was a tyrant, a man who had done great harm to the foreign service. I had never written a denunciation. I did, however, have the right and the obligation to speak my mind, especially since I had been asked. I would reply, I decided, but only on condition that my response be read publicly at the meeting. No secret business. But what would happen if I wrote something critical and Naszkowski ended up staying in the ministry and even moved up higher in the Party? No doubt he would throw me out on my ear. To avoid replying then was to be afraid for my own skin, to be an opportunist. I was no opportunist, and I would never be. I decided to write the whole truth as I saw it. I did not *have* to work in foreign service, I did not *have* to occupy any post.

I wrote a scathing report. In it, I said that Naszkowski had never been concerned with the good of Poland; he had always been guided by foreign interests. He had poor relations with his subordinates and was a bad influence on those around him.

I received Bejm's reply the next day. He said that my opinions could not be used; I had gone too far in condemning Naszkowski, and he requested that I write again, limiting myself to Naszkowski's personal qualities. I realized that all my allusions to Naszkowski's Soviet connections had been found unacceptable. Again I had to think what to do and whether or not to reply. Upon deliberation, I wrote again, limiting myself to personality traits.

After the meeting, I received word from Warsaw that it had been stormy and that Naszkowski had been forced to resign. Bejm informed me that my letter had tipped the balance. Rapacki had been opposed to the resignation. Pushed to self-criticism, he said that if everything was not going well at the ministry, his deputy could not be held responsible. He protected Naszkowski, obviously thinking that this was how an honorable man should act. It was like him. Finally, when he could see that all his efforts were in vain, he himself resigned and tore out of the room. I had not foreseen such a turn of events. Rapacki suffered severe heart problems soon thereafter. I felt guilty, since I had been an instrument in the resignation of a man for whom I had utmost respect and great affection. He died in 1970.

A courier who flew to New Delhi shortly after told me that Gomulka had been infuriated by the course the meeting had taken. Apparently the thunder of his displeasure came down on me in particular. Rumor had it that I would either be thrown out entirely or rise very high, depending on which way the wind blew.

What had occurred in the Ministry of Foreign Affairs was a reflection of changes taking place in Poland. Ochab was no longer president, having resigned, like Rapacki, from the Politburo. Spychalski had become president, and his place at the Ministry of Defense had been assumed by General Wojciech Jaruzelski. Winiewicz had become acting foreign minister. Cyrankiewicz remained in his position.

All along, we received troubling news from Warsaw. Young people were suffering. Misia's best friend had been arrested, treated brutally, her head shaved before her release. The worst, however, was yet to come. Bansi, our main servant, came into the dining room one day during lunch and handed Wanda a telegram. She tore open the envelope and then the telegram tumbled from her hands. I jumped up and grabbed it. "Bronek has died tragically."

We were shaken to our foundations. The children wept. Between pangs of conscience for not visiting him during my last trip to Warsaw and great sorrow, terrible suspicions of foul play lurked in my thoughts.

Stefan Klewenhagen, an engineer we had met on the Ganges, and his wife appeared in New Delhi toward the end of that week. We were still feeling the effect of Bronek's death, so Wanda shared news of it with them. Klewenhagen listened closely, asked a few questions, and, when she had finished, said, "Dear Wanda, I don't want to take too bleak a view, but Bronek did not die a natural death. He underestimated an enemy."

"We don't know enough about it," I said, although I felt as he did.

"I have no illusions," said Klewenhagen. "Not after the story about his running into those former Gestapo stooges. . . . It's very rare that we learn the whole truth in this tragic life of ours; the enemy is perfectly capable of wiping out all his traces. What do we know of the innumerable Poles who lost their lives in the East? Only bits and pieces. A last letter from someone, a keepsake brought back by someone else. There's only absolute silence about those who perished there. We know less about the Soviet camps than we do about Auschwitz. If anyone had known for whom those ex-Gestapo people were working, it was Bronek."

"How do you know that?" I asked.

"Listen. Between 1939 and 1941 the Bolsheviks and the Nazis were friends; the Soviets helped the Third Reich as much as they could. The secret police of both countries, the Gestapo and the NKVD, worked closely on their common goal of destroying Poland. I know something about that co-operation, because the meetings took place in Zakopane, and I am from there. I know where they took place and when. The KGB making use of ex-Gestapo informers? That's no surprise. . . ."

"Where do you know those details from?" I asked.

He looked at his wife and spoke earnestly. "We have come to trust you. That probably wouldn't have happened in Poland, but here in India, far from our country, people grow close in peculiar ways. You are a high government and Party official. You must be; otherwise you would not be a Communist ambassador. Still, I trust my instincts about people; they have never failed me. How it happened that you're a Communist, I don't know and won't ask. I'm going to tell you something we never tell anyone—my wife and I have been through too much to talk indiscriminately. During the war I was head of intelligence for the Home Army in the Borderlands. Mostly I was in Lwow. I should add that after the war I was a 'guest' for a long time in Moscow, at the 'Hotel' Lubyanka. It's a miracle I survived. Back in Poland, I visited a few other pleasant 'hotels' of that variety. Not until that butcher Stalin was dead was I released."

He smiled sadly. "I'll tell you briefly what I saw myself in those unfortunate Borderlands. A normal person would not be able to imagine it. The Home Army was growing quickly under the Nazi occupation's General Gouvernement. But in the area under Bolshevik control during the time of Nazi-Soviet co-operation before 1941, the Soviets managed to smash our underground. Their methods were simple and effective. We had documents, exact data on all this. London was informed at every turn about the nature of the Soviet occupation. We sent photographs of the deportations to the East, the prison transports. They always work at night, the Soviets. They abduct people from their houses, pack them into prisons, interrogate and torture them, then send them off deep into Russia's belly. Always at night—as if they feared the light of day."

"And you had photographs?" I asked in surprise.

"Yes. Our people took photographs at dusk, even in the dark."

"Impossible!" I sputtered. "Because even now such light-sensitive film isn't available. I know a little about that."

He smiled. "You're wrong. We were getting special light-sensitive film from Ilford, an English manufacturer. We photographed at night, assembled copious documentation. Our allies were as aware of what Moscow was doing to our people as of what the Nazis were doing."

"Then why didn't you say anything about it?" Wanda scolded him. "To this day, very little is known of what went on under Soviet occupation."

"Yes, unfortunately that's true. As soon as Hitler attacked the Soviets in 1941, the West forgot about all that. They may even have destroyed those awkward, embarrassing documents. What can I say? They sold us out. And I'm afraid they will pay for it. It may cost them their own destruction in the end. I hope I don't live to see it."

After dinner we settled into a conversation about my father, my Communism, my lifelong intransigence.

"Yes," said the engineer, "true faith in an ideal is a powerful force. But you're a Pole first, not a Communist."

I did not respond.

"Do you know Gomulka?" he asked.

"I've met him, and I don't like him," I replied. "He's no statesman. What do you think of what he's said about a Jewish fifth column in Poland? How did he come up with that one? I know Wanda has told Maria a bit about our life during the occupation, our harboring of Jews."

"Yes, my wife did tell me," he said. "I don't think there were many who risked their own lives and lived to see those terrible times end. As for Gomulka's fifth-column notion, I take a straightforward view of the matter: one, there's a power struggle on among the Communists at the top; two, Moscow is behind it. Gomulka is going under and he's grasping at straws on his way down. He's lost all sense of decency. Clearly he's forgotten that he lives in the city that had the largest ghetto in Europe and where the Germans murdered all the Jews, hundreds of thousands of them.

"Remember October 1956, when Gomulka was brought back to the helm? Many of the Jews around him then were fed up with the Soviets, with Stalin, Beria, and Khrushchev, and they stood up for themselves—quite bravely, too. Some showed real character. If it weren't for them, there wouldn't have been any October. There were no patriotic Poles in government posts in those days, and the wounds the Bolsheviks had inflicted on the Home Army were still too fresh. The Poles had no one to lead them. So they put their trust in Gomulka. Now he is calling the Jews a fifth column because the wind has shifted in Moscow."

"So. Thanks to Gomulka, we look like anti-Semites," I exclaimed.

"You've hit the nail on the head, Mr. Ambassador," said Klewenhagen. "That's the Bolshevik method. They play it so that we're always at each other's throats one way or the other. We must realize that the Jewish problem in Poland is the work of Moscow, and only then can we deal with it."

One day I entered my office at the embassy and found a few small gray cloth bags on my desk. Inside were kernels of rare and precious dwarf wheat hybrids. There was no question of their authenticity: the bags were stamped with the red seal of the Indian Institute of Seed Production. The man who had managed this bit of intelligence work was looking at me triumphantly. When I asked him about the cost of the operation, he waved his hands about, saying that he had paid no more than a few rupees. He would charge it to some other, larger, project.

We made arrangements for the next courier from Warsaw to transport the kernels to Poland. He would carry them in his briefcase, thereby avoiding the X-raying of baggage at the airport, which could harm the grain's genetic properties. I informed my ministry that the bags should be taken from the Ministry of Internal Affairs, for whom the courier worked, and passed on to the Ministry of Agriculture for analysis of their potential assistance to Polish grain production.

Kaytus was on vacation from school and asked for my permission to go to Warsaw. Because he would be beginning his studies at the University of New Delhi in the summer, he would not be able to go with us on my leave then. After long discussion, we agreed, but only on condition that he vacation outside Warsaw and behave sensibly. He flew from New Delhi on June 5, accompanied by Julian Janczur, an embassy employee who was taking his family on leave. I recall the date well: it was the day Robert Kennedy was assassinated.

Kaytus returned two months later. We noticed a change in him at once, at the airport. He was still cheerful, active, even energetic at times, but he had a new side: he had become withdrawn, contemplative. I told myself that he was simply more serious, more grown up—he had, after all, turned seventeen in Warsaw. Wanda looked closely at him, trying to divine the meaning of the change.

"First I'll tell you about Bronek," he said when we were home. "Klewenhagen was right; it was a terrible thing. I had no peace after I found out the real facts about his death. I visited his grave a few times. He's in Powazki, the military cemetery, in the Home Army section."

He took a deep breath and went on. "I know exactly what happened. At the end of March, Bronek was supposed to travel to Gdansk in a car a friend had offered to let him use. But on the day he was to leave, someone he did not know appeared with a Volkswagen and said that the friend couldn't make it, and Bronek should go with him. Bronek hesitated, but in the end hopped into the car. They had an accident near Mlawa. According to the police report, the driver was drunk and the Volkswagen hit a tree. The car was damaged very little, and the driver was not injured. Bronek was killed instantly. He had no wounds on the front of his body; only one wound in the back, as if he had been struck with some sharp object. The police closed the case quickly, labeling it an ordinary accident, and the driver was released after a couple of days." Kaytus stopped.

"And that was the end of it?" I managed to stammer.

"No, Bronek's friends from the war—you know he had a lot of them—tried to keep the investigation open, but they came up against a wall of hostility from the authorities. I spoke with one of them—Mama knows him, Tomasz, the judge. A very dignified man. He said to me, 'Tell your mother there is no doubt about it, Bronek was murdered.' "

Kaytus's words were piercing me to the core. Bronek had been the last of my old friends with any fight left in him. German bullets had not killed him, though he had been hit often enough by them. And he had eluded the Soviet roundups, escaped death row. Now, after all those years, that singularly brave Home Army soldier, the man who had come to my family's aid when I deserted them, had been killed by a treacherous blow from the hand of a hired assassin. From behind. I could feel something snap in me. Wanda buried her face in her hands. Kaytus put his arm around her.

"I was at Bronek's grave many times," he said quietly. "I thought about him and wondered if I, too, might die like that."

"What are you saying?" cried Wanda, and grabbed his hand. "How could you say such a thing? You know how much we love you."

I took Kaytus's other hand. "Why do you talk like that?" I asked evenly, though I was angry that he would say such nonsense in front of his mother.

"Don't be angry with me. I have to say this. I don't want to keep anything from you: I received three anonymous death threats in Warsaw."

Wanda and I recoiled in horror with one motion.

"Yes, three of them. They all said the same thing, 'You'll be killed like Piasecki's son!' "

I jumped to my feet. "Can this be possible? What did you do about it? Why didn't you write us about it?"

"Why didn't you come back at once?" demanded Wanda.

"I went to the ministry," said Kaytus calmly, "to the head of personnel. I showed him the letters."

"And what did he say?" asked Wanda.

"Nothing. He said it could be a prank or a joke; on the other hand, it could be serious—hard to tell. One thing was sure: I should be careful. He advised me not to travel in Poland and to return to India. He also asked me to inform him if I noticed anything suspicious. . . . But don't worry. I'm here safe and sound, as you can see," he said to soothe us.

Piasecki. I knew little about Boleslaw, the father—only that before the war he had been a young leader of a chauvinistic and anti-Semitic militant group, that during the war he was in the right-wing underground; that many in his family were killed by Germans and that he himself was arrested by the Soviets. After the war he gained prominence and became chairman of PAX, the largest publisher of religious books, but an organization which many good Catholics and former Home Army soldiers detested as NKVD-sponsored. On January 22, 1957, his son Bogdan was abducted and killed. No one knows who did it. That the terrible fate of such a man's son had been promised to my Kaytus flung me into an abyss of grim conjecture and despair.

In July and August of 1968, the press was full of news about changes taking place in Czechoslovakia. President Tito, of Yugoslavia, and Nicolae Ceauşescu, of Rumania, paid a visit to that country to show support for the democratic reforms being made by Alexander Dubcek, who was now known to want socialism "with a human face." The Soviet army was massing and carrying out maneuvers along the Czech border; the Soviet Politburo was planning to visit Prague. Clearly, Moscow was angry.

On August 20 the world learned that the Soviets had invaded Czechoslovakia. The Prague airport was taken over by Soviet paratroopers while Warsaw Pact armored columns poured into the country to occupy it. I learned of the invasion from wire reports, and was unwilling to believe that Poland had been a part of it. Distressed by the news, my family asked if it were true. I had no answers for them; no information had arrived from Warsaw. It was as if I were reliving August 1938, when, hunched over my map, I had followed that partition of Czechoslovakia.

I did not go to the embassy the next day. Surrounded by newspapers, I tried to pick up European stations on my Japanese radio. But halfway through the day the phone rang. It was Piegov's secretary, requesting that I come see the ambassador at once. I left with a heavy heart.

Piegov received me in his single-story residence, which was attractively inlaid with white marble and graced with stylish Indian furniture. He was in excellent spirits.

"Greetings, Ambassador!" he blared as he came to meet me, his hand extended. "Sit down, sit down. Tea will be here in a minute." He looked relaxed, at ease.

"Well, it finally fell apart over there, but the situation is clear now. Things were bad, very bad. Dubcek is a traitor, no other word for it—a social revisionist. He had surrounded himself with counterrevolutionaries, you know. It's high time . . ."

"But was invasion necessary?" I interrupted.

"Ambassador! You sound like the bourgeois press. What *invasion*?" he said irritably. "It was a case of open counterrevolution. Your own Gomulka assessed the situation correctly, and Polish troops are taking part. Brave boys! And your minister of defense, that general . . . What's his name? . . . Jaruzelski, he's helping. A good soldier and a good Communist." Piegov's face was radiant. "We're back in charge now, rest assured of that."

"What about Warsaw? Have you received instructions yet?" he asked.

"No. I haven't had any word from Warsaw. Perhaps there's a delay in the mail. We don't have radios, like you do; we use commercial telegrams," I said distractedly.

"Don't worry; you'll get your telegrams. We've been working closely with our friends to make sure that everything is clear and that everyone gets what he needs," he said authoritatively.

"They could at least have let me know beforehand," I replied naïvely.

"No, they couldn't," he answered in a decisive voice, a sly smile flickering across his face. "They *couldn't.* No one knew. Were there talks with Dubcek? There were! Were there maneuvers? There were! The world was buzzing with news and speculation, but our advance caught everyone by surprise. They thought we were bluffing! We weren't."

He looked at me twice before he went on, almost in a whisper. "I knew because I myself received a cable from Andrei Andreyevich [Gromyko], a top secret cable, for my eyes only. I was to inform Indira that we would be moving against the counterrevolution. I showed her the cable on the day before the events. You understand, we wanted to demonstrate our respect for her, our trust; friends should not be taken by surprise. Imagine what would have happened if . . ."

"I understand. But that show of confidence was truly a great distinction if she was the only one . . ."

"No, she wasn't," said Piegov. "Andrei Andreyevich sent the same instructions to two other capitals—Cairo and Havana. Nasser and Castro. That was all; no one else. But that's strictly between you and me, Ambassador!"

"Naturally," I replied, feeling that I was made partly responsible for what had occurred. My head was still hammering.

"We've got an important task ahead of us now," continued Piegov. "Dealing with hostile propaganda. The imperialists and reactionaries are slandering our countries and socialism. It's provocative slander. Did those scum really think that we would hand Czechoslovakia over to them? Idiots! Cretins! Wherever our system has been established"—he was loud, emphatic—"*wherever power has ended up in our hands*, that's where it stays forever. Do you understand me? *Forever!*"

I was flabbergasted, repulsed.

"You'll be receiving instructions from Warsaw very soon, today or tomorrow. You'll go to the Indian Ministry of External Affairs. We'll all be going. Only the Yugoslav is breaking ranks. Well, maybe the Rumanian, too—who the hell knows about that one! But we all know where they stand: counterrevolution has taken root in their countries, too. Never mind, their time will come, too; and the later it comes, the more painful it will be. It's very important that it be you, Ambassador, who speaks to the Indians at External. Those bastards there don't always believe *us*. There are a lot of reactionaries and foreign agents among them. It'll be easier for *you* to speak with them, to convince them that we've done the right thing. Poland is popular here, and we must take advantage of that fact. The Indians must be spoken to firmly, decisively. Bang your fist on the table, make them understand what harm the imperialists have been doing, so they realize that our joint collective action was taken to *defend* socialism. This is how we're defending socialism," he said, making a fist, "together! For the good of the Czech and Slovak workers.

"What's wrong, Ambassador? You don't have much to say," he said, taking a long, hard look at me. "Aren't you well today?"

"To tell the truth, I'm worried."

"Worried?" he asked in surprise.

"Couldn't the issue have been handled without force?" I asked before I could stop myself.

Something changed in Piegov's eyes. For the first time I detected a glint of hostility, perhaps even suspicion. "But I explained it to you already. It was a case of open counterrevolution," he said sharply.

At the residence Wanda silently handed me a long telegram that had just arrived from Warsaw. I read that Poland had gloriously fulfilled its international obligation and come to the aid of our Czech brothers. Warsaw reported that the Czech people had welcomed our commanders with flowers, that they were deserving of special honor. I cursed out loud.

Instructions streamed in from Warsaw, just as Piegov had predicted. The new head at the ministry, Winiewicz, sent general guidelines; I was to express displeasure and astonishment at the provocative accusations that had been leveled at Poland and the other Warsaw Pact countries.

The reports of the international press were devastating. Socialism with a human face had been trampled. Later on, I do not remember exactly when, I learned that Dubcek had been tossed like a sack onto a Soviet airplane and flown off to Moscow.

One day, while reviewing old coded cables, I came across the one about the hybrid kernels. Warsaw had never responded to them. I summoned our SB man, Janczur, who was to have checked on the seeds and had recently returned from leave. He arrived with an odd expression on his face. I asked him about the hybrids, but he changed the subject, hardly able to conceal a smirk.

"When did Agriculture receive the seeds?" I asked firmly.

Again he did not answer me directly, but launched into an excited explanation. "I'll tell you, Ambassador, but don't hold it against me, because by the time I arrived in Warsaw and went to the ministry it was all over."

"What was all over?" I shouted, out of patience by now.

"The courier took the wheat to the Ministry of Internal Affairs. The colonel wasn't in, so he gave it to the secretary, who put it somewhere and promptly forgot about it. Then the secretary was replaced. . . ." Janczur began chuckling.

"And then what?"

"Nothing. Someone opened the sacks, and found the seeds. It was summer. There were pigeons in the window sills." Now Janczur, red in the face, stuffed his handkerchief in his mouth.

"They gave all the seeds to the birds!" he ended, all but choking with laughter.

Seeing that I was far from entertained, he regained his self-control and said that when an inquiry was launched, nothing was found—no seeds, no sacks.

I was furious and could not believe that my efforts to help Polish agriculture had come to no more than that.

One night, Kaytus had his own story to tell about Janczur. "I forgot to tell you about this when I came back from vacation. When he and I flew to Poland, we stopped in Beirut. I bought some clothes and went off to look at stones. Janczur raced from one jewelry store to another and bought a great deal of gold. He showed me several dozen rings and tried to talk me into letting him buy some for me; he said he'd even lend me the money if I needed it. When I refused, he was surprised, and when I asked him how he was going to get past customs in Poland with all those rings, he simply shut up. When the plane landed in Warsaw, Janczur and his family were the first off the plane. I watched them through the window. A black limousine was waiting for them. The guards saluted him, and they drove off—out of the airport grounds through a side gate. Their bags were never checked.

"Poland has its own sacred cows, doesn't it?" said Kaytus. "They can beat up students, import gold, you name it, because some bigwig or other gives them carte blanche to. People's Poland," he said, his voice trembling, "I hate it—the hypocrisy, the lies, the violence." He pushed his plate away and strode out of the dining room. Wanda ran after him.

That was the night I truly began to worry about Kaytus. To Wanda and me, he became a kind of obsession.

I found myself climbing up to the ruins of Tughlaqabad soon after that. The city looked entirely different under a cloudy sky.

Dark and gloomy. The leaden clouds seemed to hang above the ruins with grim determination. I looked around and was suddenly struck by the realization of why I was constantly drawn to that place, why it was so easy for me to be with myself there: I was drawn to those ruins because I, too, was in a state of decay. I had come to a dead end—fearful for my son, powerless in the face of Bronek's death. What should I do? What did it all mean? Had I in fact taken a false and hideous path? It was no secret that one cannot make revolutionary progress without sacrifices, but were Bronek and Kaytus those sacrifices? My path was cursed; this is where my ideals had led: my friend, a hero and a patriot, had been murdered; my son, who hated Communism, was faced with an unnamed danger. I had looked on helplessly while Czechoslovakia was smashed and had felt myself to be an accomplice in the invasion. I did not understand what was happening in Poland. And who was this *I* anyway? I was a nothing, a pawn with the title ambassador, moved by someone else at someone else's whims. . . .

I sat there for a long time absorbed in my thoughts, until the sound of footsteps on stone thrust me back into the real world.

Tara came out from behind a wall. "You've been sitting here for a long time, Mr. Ambassador. We should get going," he said, with a look at the sky. "It's not a good idea to sit alone when the vultures are on the watch. Look up there."

High in the sky, large, long-winged birds were circling.

"When they circle like that, it means they've spotted prey. They can tear a dying cow to pieces in a matter of minutes, Mr. Ambassador. Come, let's go."

I didn't argue. With an aching heart, I followed him from that troubled promontory.

Our friend Stefan Klewenhagen and his wife came to New Delhi at the end of September to say farewell to us and to settle their affairs before returning to Poland. Sitting in front of our painting *The Insurgent*, the four of us spoke about the death of Bronek, and the threats that Kaytus himself had received.

"If one assumes they were not malicious jokes, then what was the motive, the point, in writing them?" I asked.

"I don't know," he answered. "The motive could be very complex. Poland is penetrated through and through by Soviet intelligence—political, military, economic, every sort, and by their counterintelligence as well. They recruit people no one would ever suspect, or else they force them to join. You ask me what their motive could be. Well, you told me yourself you attacked Naszkowski, that he was Moscow's man, Rokossovsky's deputy even. Don't you think that was motive enough? Other people attacked him at the meeting, but they were just pawns. *You*—that's a different story; you're well known, you've held important positions. The Soviets put years of work into placing important figures like Naszkowski on the Polish chessboard. You tripped them up."

"Yes, but we're talking about my son," said Wanda, tremulously.

"Forgive me, Wanda, but I think a person has to face the truth. That's the only defense there is. I never forget who I'm dealing with. Of course, the Naszkowski business aside, there might be another motive. Your son went around to his friends and asked questions about Bronek. Do you think that escaped their notice? Not a chance! In Poland you can run up against agents in the most unexpected places."

"What can we do?" cried Wanda. "How can we protect him?"

"You'll have to act very judiciously, unlike Bronek. Your son must be very careful when he goes back to Poland. You told me what the death threats said. The people who murdered Piasecki's son were never found. I think it was a lesson to Piasecki. A clear case of 'the invisible hand.'

"My advice is as follows," he continued. "Remain in India for as long as you can. Don't allow your boy to go back to Poland alone again. He has to be on guard everywhere, even here. And when you all return to Poland, you will have to be watchful."

Fear raced through my mind.

Kaytus asked me one evening, quite out of the blue, if I would find out for him if any Poles were buried in the New Delhi British cemetery. An odd request, but given his fascination with the Polish soldiers buried at Monte Cassino, I understood and obliged. It turned out there was one, and not only did we visit that cemetery to see his grave, but also I found myself accepting an invitation by an official of the British High Commission to attend a ceremony honoring the people of all nationalities buried there.

Despite the fact that a number of our embassy staff had been invited, along with me, not one attended the ceremony. My family and I alone took part in that moving service. My instincts told me that my participation would have repercussions, and, sure enough, at the next reception Piegov appeared before me and greeted me dryly.

"You've been getting a lot of press lately, Ambassador," he said, glaring at me. "Photographs, too."

"Yes, I was at the cemetery," I answered, knowing he was referring to that ceremony. "They took pictures."

"That's just the point, pictures. There was no one there but Westerners. . . . All from the Commonwealth—and then *you!*" His little eyes were burrowing into me.

"A Polish soldier is buried there," I stated simply. When he did not reply, I repeated, "A Pole is buried there. Killed here, in this country. That's why I was there. I didn't attend because the High Commissioners would be there. I attended because of that soldier. It was my duty."

"You say he was a Pole, and well he may have been," said Piegov, sneering. "But the political significance of it—doesn't that concern you, Ambassador? Doesn't it?"

We stood there glaring at one another. One more such remark from him and I would have exploded that he had no right to interfere, that I held his people responsible for what had happened to my father and Bronek. He made a vague gesture of impatience. I nodded and walked away.

The Fifth Party Congress was held in Warsaw in mid-November 1968. People were saying that Gomulka might step down; major changes were expected. I wondered what that would mean for me. After what I had heard about Gomulka, I was expecting the worst, but I was concerned little about myself. On the other hand, I *was* obsessed by the dangers my family might face.

Gomulka's grip on power seemed as tight as ever. Brezhnev's speech at the congress provided considerable food for thought. Moscow had arrogated to itself the right and the duty to "aid" fraternal countries in which it saw socialism endangered by counterrevolution; that posture became known in the West as the "Brezhnev Doctrine."

Piegov was triumphant at the meetings of socialist ambassadors in

New Delhi. I looked over at the Czech chargé. He bore the marks of a man martyred and profoundly afraid. I knew well what was happening in Czech diplomatic posts after the invasion. Many Czech diplomats had refused to co-operate with the new regime; Czech engineers and technicians in India had passed resolutions of protest; and when they all saw that it was hopeless, they had made the difficult decision not to return to their homeland.

I wondered how I would have acted in their shoes, had the invasion been of Poland. Would I have chosen to emigrate? Of course not. Despite everything, I was still true to the idea. I simply condemned the practice, the shabby practice, responsibility for which I placed on the Soviets. For me to stay in the West would have meant a betrayal of myself, my ideals. Though it all come crashing down, I would remain true. There was no changing who I was.

At the end of 1968, Warsaw announced that Stefan Jedrychowski had been named minister of foreign affairs. I did not know him, but intuitively sensed that he was another Naszkowski. It would not be an easy time for me. I found myself wondering if there was a place for me in the foreign service any more.

CHAPTER XX

In 1969 Misia was still at the university, and Kaytus finished secondary school. He planned to study philosophy at the University of New Delhi. We attended the graduation ceremonies at his school and were moved and proud when he was handed his diploma. His marks had been excellent, and he had been chosen "outstanding senior" by his classmates. I wondered what his future would bring. His was an exceptionally quick mind, and he had a kind and sensitive nature. He knew how to win people's friendship, and he had already achieved a measure of wisdom. But those anonymous death threats preyed on my mind; my only comfort was that surely nothing could endanger him here among these gentle people.

The reports from Poland continued to get worse. Food shortages were increasing, and with them, a spreading dissatisfaction. Meanwhile, the Party and government functionaries traveling through India had a completely different story to tell. They maintained that there were improvements in the economy; the effects simply had not made their way down to the workers yet.

Back in Poland on leave, I found for myself that it was the unofficial reports that were true. The ordinary Pole was having to grapple with ever-increasing difficulties. Apart from the shortages of goods, wages could not buy the barest necessities. People were anxious. Wanda had to stand in line for hours to buy food, which often was gone by the time she got to the head of the line. When I wanted to hang a shelf for books, I could find no store that carried wood screws or wire. The most remote corner of India seemed better stocked than Poland's capital. From time to time, driving through India's poorest mud hut villages, I would ask Tara to stop in front of a ramshackle stall so that I could see what they had for sale. They were all alike. An Indian village dweller could obtain all he needed there—primitive tools, hammers, anvils, files, pliers, nails, screws, wire, sheet metal. Bicycle parts, both rubber and metal, were also available everywhere. In the larger towns I saw parts for the cars produced in India under English license. Food stores always had rice, a variety of grains and chapatis. A fabric store would have its stock displayed, and inside an Indian would be busily working at his sewing machine.

And in all of Warsaw no screws, no wire. What was holding up our economy? What excuse would be dredged up this time? The war? It had been over for more than twenty years.

Wanda and I decided not to speak openly in the Warsaw apartment. Diplomats were still living upstairs, and that entire section of the building was probably bugged. After the threats to Kaytus, we thought it better to be cautious. If we wanted to talk freely about what we were witnessing, we went out for a walk.

Friends told us that in Gomulka's opinion socialism had already secured good living conditions for Poles; he would not accept the fact that life was hard. He had apparently lost touch with reality; his contacts were exclusively with high-level Party people, and he was surrounded by secret police who took care that he saw nothing negative. They explained their actions as concern for his health; he was not to be upset.

As I suspected, I was not received well at the ministry. I reported to the new minister, Jedrychowski. From the very start, his manner put me off and I was sorry to see this man at the desk that had once been Rapacki's.

He began with economic affairs, grilling me about production in India, visibly irked that I could not recall exact figures.

"And how much coal does India produce?"

"Last year close to seventy million tons," I answered.

"What do you mean 'close to'? Statistics are *exact*. How much was it—more? Or less?"

He had me. "I don't know," I answered frankly. "Maybe it was seventy and a few decimal points more."

"That won't do, Comrade Spasowski. I can see that a few hundred thousand tons either way has no meaning for you. In fact, it's a very large amount. Clearly, you don't know your way around these things."

I was reminded of my New York run-in with Gomulka about the price of American meat. Stiffening, I said, "Thank you for seeing me, Mr. Minister. I won't take any more of your time." He was surprised to see me rise and he cleared his throat twice, but before he had a chance to speak I had bowed and was through the door.

On the stairs I ran into a man who had once worked with me—the one who had told me about the club squads around the cathedral—and we walked down together.

"I just saw Jedrychowski," I said.

"Oho! They call him the 'pharmacist,' because figures are his passion, decimals especially. He always puts a question mark beside any figure on any paper that comes across his desk. And then we have to write explanations on where we got the figure. We don't do anything here in the department but write memos detailing sources for our figures."

He gave me a look I recognized and leaned in toward me. "They say that Jedrychowski works two jobs—one as our pharmacist; the other as a Soviet stooge."

As usual, I reported to Belvedere Palace and was called in to speak with President Spychalski. The director of the president's office, whom I had known for years, offered me a friendly warning as I waited for my appointment.

"Watch out. He's a hard man. It's rare for an audience to run smoothly. Sometimes he shouts so loudly that I can hear every word through those leather-covered double doors."

"Why do you use that term, 'audience'?" I asked.

"He requires us to. I'm used to it by now," he replied. "Be careful. Believe me. I have a hard time here—you can't imagine. But what can I do? I have no choice."

A bell rang, and he went into Spychalski's office carrying a file. He returned a moment later and said, "He'll see you now. You're lucky. He doesn't seem in too bad a mood today."

Spychalski was pacing his office when I entered. I said hello; he merely pointed to an armchair by an oval marble-topped table.

"What's new in India?" he asked.

I described the presidential election, filling him in on the new president, Varahagiri Ven Kata Giri. I spoke of Indira Gandhi's policies, and told him a decisive battle was probably coming in the Congress Party. Studying me with large, dark eyes, he said nothing. He looked like a man constantly exhausted. Every once in a while his eyes gleamed with impatience.

"Do you *know* Giri?" he asked, interrupting me.

"No, not personally," I replied, "but I know a lot about him."

"What did he do before?"

"For the last two years he was vice president; before that he was governor of several states, most recently in southern India. I heard that he's supposed to be coming to Europe next year. It might be worth our while to invite him to Poland. India is an important country."

Spychalski's face twitched. "What *for?* What do we need a visit like that for?" he said, almost shouting. Dumbfounded, I said nothing, and then he really did begin to shout. "What do we need those visits *for?* You send all sorts of people here, and we have to put up with them. I've had enough of that. Do you understand me? What do you think you're doing?"

I clenched my teeth as he continued at the top of his voice.

"Soon you'll be inviting the whole world here. We've had enough, *enough!* Do you understand?" Silence, and then a snarled "How long have you been there?"

"Two and a half years," I answered numbly. "And I've had . . ."

"And so? What have you accomplished there? Be specific. Tell me—well, tell me. What have you *done* for People's Poland?" he demanded.

"First and foremost, India has become our strongest economic partner in the Third World," I began, my self-control in tow somehow. "We sell them products from our machine and chemical industries, and they sell us fodder and linseed."

"Be specific. *What,* tell me *what.*" He was shouting again. "Don't tell me about any linseed oil!"

I could feel my body go rigid. The foreign minister was strange, the president was a psychopath, a group of psychopaths was running the country.

"I don't see any point in continuing this conversation," I said dryly and rose to my feet.

"Drivel, drivel, you're talking *drivel*!" he shouted from his chair, waving his arms.

"Good-bye!" I shouted so that he could hear me and turned away from him. He was still shouting, "Drivel, drivel!"

The office director was at his desk; he had probably heard everything.

"You're right, Franek," I said. "Your boss is insane; he's an idiot."

"Quiet, quiet!" he cried, muffling his voice and putting a finger to his lips, "He might hear you! Sometimes he comes out of his office after a row, sometimes he listens at the door," he hissed.

"I couldn't care less," I said, offering him my hand.

We spent time in Warsaw fixing up the apartment, seeing family and friends, visiting Bronek's grave. It was only toward the end of our stay that we traveled to Zakopane to see the Klewenhagens. On our way back to Warsaw, our train swayed so much that I complained about it to the conductor. He explained that the railroad ties were beyond repair and should have been replaced long ago.

My entire leave in Poland had been a bitter confirmation.

In November, Wanda and I returned to India alone, Misia having decided to stay in Poland. Kaytus had taken excellent care of the house. The residence was spotlessly clean, and the family silver gleamed on the table, set out to celebrate our return. He seemed more independent and enterprising.

He was now at the university, but he did not have many friends there yet. Most of the people he knew had left India. Often he attended receptions with us, and he gave the impression of being quite a bit older than he was. A great many letters came for him, and he wrote a lot, but it was rare for him to discuss them. And although he and I took walks and swam together, he shared more of his intimate feelings with Wanda than with me. I knew well he did not want to return to Poland; his dream was to study in the United States or in England. That, however, was beyond our means. And even if I had been able to afford it, the ministry would never have granted permission.

Kaytus was aware of this and said frequently that he saw no way out for himself. Wanda held that we should do everything possible so that he could go to America regardless of the consequences, but it was my view that to do that would spell catastrophe for us all.

I presented my credentials in Singapore and planned an official visit to Calcutta. I decided to take Kaytus along. The two of us left by car with Tara in January 1970, taking the now familiar road toward Nepal, to which I was also accredited. Wanda remained in New Delhi and was to fly to join us in Calcutta in two weeks.

We talked a great deal along the way, both happy to be traveling together. I spoke openly with him, treating him as an equal, but whenever the conversation touched on Poland, he grew cautious and weighed his words.

One night, in Clarks Hotel in Benares, he grew talkative as he spoke over dinner of his varied interests; philosophy was now his passion. At times he reminded me of my father. Like him, Kaytus spoke with strong feeling, thought out loud, with an air of concentration, and had pensive eyes and a thick head of hair. Only his face was not my father's. He did not have his grandfather's sharp eyes; his were gentle and kind. I looked on him with love and pride as he told me that he wanted to study the history of philosophy in India. He was interested, too, in geology and mineralogy, in the origin of the earth.

I was surprised to hear Kaytus speak Hindi with the waiters. He seemed fluent; I myself could not speak the language at all. We were served our favorite dish—tandoori chicken and chapatis—and we ate with gusto.

At my mention of Poland he seemed to draw inward, recede. He was on the verge of saying something, but lapsed into silence instead. I pressed him, and finally he blurted, "I can't stand what's happening in Poland, Father. The country is run by false, evil people. They persecute young people, they wipe out true patriots." He said it all in one breath and then looked anxiously at me. "How can I forget Bronek? And how could they . . ." He rested his head on the palm of his left hand and lowered his eyes, his emotion evident. He sat like that for some time, perfectly still.

I took his hand. "I know those are painful things," I said. "They're painful for me, too. And it's all because of me . . . because of the form my life took. . . . You're almost a grownup now, even though you're only—let's see—eighteen years and seven months old. When I was your age, before the war, I thought that the whole world was mine. Little did I know dark clouds were gathering over Poland then. You have a better future ahead of you. I won't try to talk you into forgetting the tragedies you've lived through," I said gently.

"On the contrary, you should remember them well, but keep looking bravely ahead. That's what I always did, even though I lived through terrible, painful times."

Kaytus lifted his head and looked at me as he stroked my hand. "I know what you're like; I know what your life's been like," he said quietly. "I wouldn't have been able to take all that. You must be tough as nails. I'm not. And I envy you for that. You were tough when you left us, too. You were able to cross us out and leave us to the mercy of fate. I wanted to forget you then. I had suffered too much and couldn't understand why. Something happened to me then; something broke inside me and I've never felt the same since," he said in a soft, unhappy voice. He glanced at me again with eyes that made me think my heart would break.

"You're very tough," he repeated. "After all we've seen, you're still on the same path you started on after the war. But me—I can't take it any more. . . . I don't know how to keep my lips sealed; I don't want to know how. I can't pretend when I know that all of them, all your embassy people, the whole ministry, the whole party, are bad, hypocritical, selfish people who care only about themselves."

"Who, for instance?" I asked.

"All of them. They pretend to be Communists but they lust for gold."

"They're not all like that," I responded, somewhat defensively.

"*I don't want to live there!*" he said suddenly and resolutely. "I don't want to see them. I don't want to be near them. . . . I feel helpless there. Do you understand?" he asked, despair tearing at his voice.

I nodded calmly that I understood, but I was alarmed. Were these, then, the feelings he held in the depths of his heart?

"In India, despite the poverty, despite the heat, I feel at home. I'm a free person. But there . . ." His voice trailed off and fell silent.

It was very late, and we went to bed, but for a long time I sat awake thinking of him. What could I do to help him? Was I really so tough? The questions plagued me. But it was good that he and I were traveling together; there would be time to talk and time to confer with Wanda.

It was still dark when we got up the next day to see the sunrise on the Ganges. As our boat left shore, pushing against the current, the first rays of light appeared; Benares itself was still shrouded in darkness. The sky slowly changed to rose, and the color was caught in the river's calm waters. The splash made by the Indian boatmen's oars took me back in time for a moment to the Bug River and my distant youth, and I shuddered. Kaytus sat in the bow spellbound by the sight of the sun rising over the city, the ghats running down the steep shore and joining city and river, the temples large and small. Benares seemed a thicket of temples. We both marveled at the city unfolding before our eyes, like a stage set rising above the smooth surface of the water. The steps began slowly filling. The people of Benares, pilgrims, and beggars were descending together for their morning ablutions, to wash away their sins in the holy waters. Slowly we returned. On the shore we could see the smoldering ashes of bodies that had been cremated the day before; today the ashes would be gathered and thrown into the river.

We drove east from Benares on a road I now knew well. Kaytus shared my fascination with the mountains.

It was not until we reached the Hotel Annapurna in Katmandu that the conversation we had begun in Benares was resumed.

"What do you intend to do when you graduate?" I asked Kaytus one night.

He shrugged his shoulders. "I don't know." After a moment he asked, "How about you? What do you intend to do when your time in India is up? That must be coming fairly soon."

"I'll go back to the ministry. What else can I do? You know I have no friends there. We'll see what happens. But you, you have your own life to live. . . ."

"In Poland?"

"Let's talk about that," I said. "I'll tell you what I think. I think you should finish your studies in Poland. Then the world will be open to you. I won't try to talk you into anything. You can go wherever you like, but you'll be able to go with a diploma in your pocket, and, most important, some real knowledge in your head."

He looked at me, unconvinced. "Real knowledge, from Poland?" he asked. "But you know they've closed all the philosophy departments. There's only a little something left in Krakow. . . ."

"Of course that's a problem," I replied. "But you can study related fields. Who says you have to agree with everything they teach you? You know what you want to know; you read a lot, think, and that requires time. You're still very young. You have your whole life ahead. It's the most sensible, most intelligent move." I could see that he thought otherwise. He looked at me as he had in Benares, with a look of desperation I could not fathom. What had happened to him? He had always been so cheerful, energetic, enterprising, his resourcefulness envied by others.

"I already told you . . . I don't want to live in that place, with those people."

"According to you, all Poles are *those* people," I said bridling.

"Don't pretend you don't know what I mean. I mean the people in power, the Party, the SB, everyone in uniform," he replied pointedly. "I don't want them after me, following me, accosting me. I want to be free." He repeated that last phrase with a tone of insistence. "I want to be *free*."

A bit later he asked, "Do you know the people who work for you well, Father?"

"I think so," I replied. "I mean I know who they are. Nearly all of them are with the secret police. Why do you ask?"

"No special reason. When you were in Poland, they kept trying to get me to go to the Soviet Embassy. One time they managed to talk me into it. But I'll never go back there again. And last year they tried to question me about school, what goes on there. Not only that, but they wanted me to make friends with the Russian diplomats! What do they *want* from me?"

I was about to ask him more, but just then August Lindt, the Swiss ambassador to India, a tall, thin man considerably older than I, walked over to us and sat down. Kaytus said good night and went off to bed. I stayed and talked, the conversation with my son left dangling.

It was well after midnight when we said good night. The restaurant was deserted, and the sleepy waiter was impatient for us to leave. When I went to our room, Kaytus was sleeping peacefully, his breathing even. It took me a long time to fall asleep. Perhaps I really was a hard man and would never understand my son.

Calcutta left its mark on us. Poverty, suffering, and hopelessness seemed to reach their depths in that place. I wondered what effect it would have on Kaytus. As soon as we were back in New Delhi, Wanda and I had a talk about him, and I learned that since our return from Warsaw she had been even more worried about him than I. Her instincts had told her things I had failed to notice: that seeming confidence, that beard, were covering up a great deal. I told her about our talks, about his refusal to go back to Poland. That came as no surprise to Wanda, who said that lately she had noticed a stubbornness and determination that were out of character for Kaytus. We discussed bringing his only Polish friend, Andrzei, to India so that they could attend the university together. His parents were having problems with the boy at home, so we thought this a workable solution for all concerned. Kaytus was very enthusiastic when we told him about the plan, and we began the paperwork right away. It was as if Wanda and I knew we had no time to lose.

In mid-March 1970, Franciszek Szlachcic, the vice minister of internal affairs, stopped in New Delhi en route from Tokyo. He was a big, well-built, long-faced man with shrewd, laughing eyes. He was coarse in his speech, self-confident in his manner. I had not known him before, but had heard that while chief of police in Silesia he had distinguished himself by his personal courage in averting a clash between miners and police by going to face the demonstrators himself. The new SB man asked me if Szlachcic could stay in my residence. I said that he could.

That evening Szlachcic and I went for a walk in the garden. He immediately fell into using the familiar with me. He questioned me about India and seemed to want exhaustive information. When I asked him about Poland, his answers were brief and to the point.

"You did a good job on Naszkowski last year," he said quite suddenly. "You were right that he was a plant, and a dangerous one at that. But you shouldn't have put that in writing. The people on the other side of the Bug have long memories."

"How could we have taken part in the Czech invasion?" I asked, feeling comfortable with the man.

"It's not so simple," he replied. "That was very important to the Soviets, but they didn't have to exert any pressure. Gomulka wanted to do it himself. He was in trouble and knew that ganging up with the people on the other side of the Bug would save his skin. He's a sly one."

He stopped and stretched his arms out to the side like a scale. One hand went up, the other down. "Moscow gained, Poland lost.

But, you'll see, Gomulka will be having serious trouble soon enough."

All in all, Szlachcic made a fairly good impression on me. He was the first I had met who made no attempt to beat around the bush; he called things by their name. And his critical attitude toward the Soviets was to my liking. Wanda, too, said that he was not as hypocritical as the others, but she had not been able to learn much from him about the student disturbances or the tensions between church and state. Kaytus put things more simply: he held it against me that I had allowed a policeman responsible for sordid affairs into our home.

The heat wave started again. We were all worn out; even I, who had had little trouble with the climate, felt weak and weary. Life slowed down. Memories of Warsaw continued to gnaw at me. I spent more time at home, and Wanda noticed that I was not at peace with myself. How could I be of any help to my son when I did not even know what would become of me?

One day as I sat at my desk, my head in my hands, Wanda placed a small brown cloth-covered edition of the New Testament in front of me.

"I know you're at your wit's end," she said stroking my head. "You're starting to see what it all means. I'd like to help you. If you read this book, the greatest book of all, you might free yourself from things that are small and unimportant and catch a glimpse of something truly great."

I picked it up and began glancing through it. I had studied the history of the church, but I had never read the New Testament. I came across the Sermon on the Mount right away and read it through, wondering how much it related directly to me. I read it through a second time, lingering over Christ's final words: "And everyone who hears these words of mine, and does not do them will be like a foolish man who built his house upon the sand; and the rain fell, and the floods came, and the winds blew and beat against that house, and it fell; and great was the fall of it." Was that to be the fate of my house, my life? I could not elude the question. I had been tossed by so many winds, there was no more left of me; I was a ruined man.

Wanda and I made a point of spending time with Kaytus. In the evenings the three of us would listen to our records of classical music. He was very fond of those "concerts" and would show his love for us freely at those moments.

The university was in Old Delhi, and he usually rode his bicycle there, though Tara gave him a lift from time to time or, since he had learned to drive, occasionally he used the Polish Fiat Warsaw had sent. But he preferred his bicycle, because he had heard complaints at the embassy that he was a privileged person. The university had no cooling system, but like a native, he had grown accustomed to the heat. He also fasted now and again, which worried Wanda because he was already so thin, but Kaytus said that his mind worked much better after fasting. He was, however, becoming increasingly less communicative, and we could only attribute that to fatigue. If I was weary, how could I be surprised at his growing despondence. I attended receptions only out of a sense of duty. The air conditioning in my office broke down frequently, and as I sat at the open window wiping the sweat from my brow I would think of my son doing the same at the university.

It was well known that President Giri intended to go to Europe; Piegov had been aware of the trip for quite some time. What I wrote to Warsaw was limited to the strictly informational, because after my first conversation with President Spychalski on the topic of Giri's visit, I had lost all desire for any sort of active role. The ministry sent no response.

Eventually, I heard at External that Giri would indeed be paying a visit to Poland during his European trip. They took it for granted that I was aware of the arrangements made by the Indian Embassy in Warsaw. I immediately cabled my ministry a reproach, but again received no reply. Some days later the Indians presented me with a number of questions concerning Giri's trip, evidently having been unable to get answers from Warsaw. They asked me when I was leaving for Warsaw and were surprised to learn that I had not fixed a departure date. I sent another cable, and this time I received a reply that said there was no reason for me to attend. All right, I thought, reading that humiliating message in the presence of the cryptographer, but what will I say to the Indians?

I discussed the matter with Wanda, and we decided to say nothing about it to Kaytus, especially since his spirits had taken a sudden turn for the worse, for reasons unknown to us. Bansi told Wanda that Kaytus had received a telegram that had caused him to weep, but when we asked him about the telegram he did not want to discuss it. Only when pressed did he admit that a close friend of his had been killed in Vietnam.

At times he seemed to be speaking in riddles. "Father, if things are going badly for you at the ministry, it's no accident. We only think we'll be able to live a different sort of life, but we don't have a chance."

"Kaytus! Why are you talking like this?" I said, reacting strongly.

"That's my business," he answered softly. "I know something, something I won't tell you." He hesitated. "Something I can't tell you. They're all watching you; they think you're their enemy now, just like Mama and me. . . ."

Giri's departure for Europe was approaching. The only possibility of saving face before the Indians was a "diplomatic illness." So I took to my bed, and our help was informed that I was ill. I found that I was in fact in poor health. Useless, helpless, I began to shudder as if suffering from malaria. A doctor friend who came was unable to discover my ailment or how to treat me. The Indians sent expressions of sympathy.

On June 8, the day Giri left, I suffered convulsions. Wanda and Kaytus were very concerned about me. Kaytus looked in on me often and, seeing the New Testament by my bedside, would smile with tender approval and delicately stroke my hand. At that time Wanda gave me another book to read, *The Second Coming*, by Giovanni Pappini. It was the portion of his autobiography in which he described how he moved away from the philosophy of atheism and became a Catholic. I was struck by Wanda's ability to quietly, unassumingly help me.

I was still sick in bed when Giri returned. This was no diplomatic illness any more; it was debilitation, though the trembling stage had passed. There had been no word from Warsaw, and it was only from the press that I had any information about Giri's visit. But by then Polish-Indian relations had ceased to be of the slightest interest to me.

Toward the end of June, I got out of bed and began walking around the residence. The days were hot—above one hundred degrees—and the nights offered no relief. One day a wind sprang up and ruffled through the trees in our garden. We thought a storm and cooler weather were coming, but the sky began turning brown. The Indians covered their mouths with rags and hid in their houses. A sandstorm was blowing through Delhi. A gusting west wind brought clouds of desert sand from Rajasthan, which infiltrated every house, every throat, and covered the ground with a rust-colored layer. Electrical discharges rumbled high above.

The Indian External Ministry sent me a note concerning Kaytus. The note stated that the Polish ambassador's son had brought a sick Indian to the hospital and ordered that he be given treatment. Kaytus explained that while out driving he had found the man lying on the road. The ministry requested that he not act in this manner in the future, because the hospital had no facilities for treating patients of that sort. I showed Kaytus the note. He only shrugged his shoulders.

"I can't change, Father," he said. "Don't be surprised if you receive other notes like that. I gave that hospital all the money I had with me, almost a hundred rupees. That's a huge amount of money to a poor Indian. They should have treated him."

"You can't take care of everyone," I said by way of argument.

"I know that," he answered. "But if I come across someone, I can't just pass him by. Don't you understand that? Can't any of you understand that? Those rich Indians pretend that they don't see the beggars, because otherwise they'd have to help them, as their religion tells them to."

Seeing that he was troubled, I put my arms around him and pressed him to my heart.

We were pleased when we heard from him that he wanted to see Italy again. At least it showed spirit. He disappeared frequently and was reluctant to say where he had been. This worried us, but it turned out he had been saying farewell to friends. One night I awoke from a bad dream bathed in sweat. I had dreamed that Kaytus and I were walking through an enormous field of rubble, not unlike the ruins of Tughlaqabad. I was looking at the wide expanse before me when suddenly I felt a touch and turned around. Kaytus was right behind me, holding a large rock and preparing to throw it at me. Had it not been Tughlaq who had died at the hands of his own son? I was frightened, not by the danger, but because it was he trying to harm me. We looked at one another, and after a while he let the stone fall from his hand and smiled sadly at me. I told Wanda nothing about that dream and struggled to find what it meant. Perhaps it meant nothing at all, was the product of my sick imagination, but it had had such realistic detail. I could not get it out of my mind, could not understand why I had imagined Kaytus, my wonderful, beloved son, wanting to hurt me.

Indian days are most sweltering at that time of year, and that year was no exception. The air hung burning hot over the city. The air conditioners in the windows droned endlessly, and it would take us a long time to fall asleep at night. Mornings we would rise from bed exhausted. Kaytus would get up very early and drive out to the Yamuna River to watch the sun rise. He always left notes saying where he was going and when he would be back. It made us happy to see him return in good spirits.

On July 1, we had the Indian minister of health, Chandresekar, and his daughter to dinner. Our families were close, a friendship that had initially begun between Wanda and the minister's wife, Anne, who was American. We talked until late. Chandra spoke of the disturbing rise in the Indian population, which had exceeded five hundred fifty million that year. He described the tragic future in store for millions for whom there would not be enough food if the monsoon was not up to expectations. Kaytus took part in that conversation, expressing himself freely, astutely. I was already in bed at midnight when he came into our room to kiss us good night, as he usually did. Before leaving he looked at us tenderly, with a delicate smile as warm as it was mysterious.

We slept badly that night. It was very hot and the drone of the air conditioner was unbearable. I was tired when I got up and went to the office after a quick breakfast. I came home around ten o'clock. The newspapers in the dining room had not been touched; Kaytus had obviously not read them yet. Bansi explained that, the night before, Kaytus had asked him not to wake him that morning. He wanted to sleep late. I went upstairs. The door to Kaytus's room was closed. I opened it and saw him lying in bed, his face to the wall, still sleeping. I glanced down at my watch. It was late.

"Kaytus, it's well past ten," I said, walking toward him, talking to the shock of hair above the sheet. He did not move. Maybe he had not got much sleep during the night. I touched his hair with my hand, but he did not respond. Why was he so still? I tried to turn him onto his back, but could not. He was heavy, stiff. Panicking, I tore the sheet off him. Colored pills and powder capsules skipped and hopped about the bed. I recognized Librium. Oh, God, not this! I thought. I seized my son by the shoulders and heaved him around to face me. He was completely inert, his eyes half closed, a little saliva at the corners of his mouth.

"Kaytus! Kaytus! *Kaytus!*" I cried at the top of my lungs, shaking him hard. He gave no sign of life. Only a frozen, immobile face where one full of life and feeling had always been. Desperate, I jumped onto the bed, grabbed his hands, and began giving him artificial respiration. He gave no sign of life, but I didn't stop. I kept at it with all the strength I had.

"Kaytus . . . wake up! Kaytus! Son, wake up, I beg you!" I cried looking at his face, hoping for the slightest spark of life. There was no sign of anything. In a moment of horror I thought I could see the trace of a smile on his deathly face, as if he were saying that it was too late, that all my efforts were in vain.

I did not cease trying, hoping, to force the breath of life back into him, to wake that rigid, inert body. I do not know how long it was, but I kept at it until the last of my strength was gone. I raised my head and saw Wanda, as if through a mist. She was beside me, choking with sobs. I came back to my senses.

"Call Chandra! Tell him to bring doctors immediately!" I shouted.

Wanda ran from the room while I threw myself at Kaytus again, thrusting his arms back and forth and breathing air into him. Nothing helped. There was a stone in my throat; my heart was hammering. I slumped down beside my son and delicately stroked his hair, his beautiful head. Overcome by sobs, I let the tears stream from my eyes.

"Why? Kaytus, son, how could you?" I whispered. I could not bear to look at him, but with my hand I felt his well-loved face, his eyes, nose, lips, his bright golden hair. I do not remember when Wanda returned. She knelt beside the bed, took Kaytus's hands, and began to pray aloud. Every few minutes she would press herself to Kaytus and burst into an agonizing wail. I do not know whether it was minutes or hours before Chandra and Dr. Kosla arrived. They examined Kaytus, spoke briefly to one another, then went off and stood together, their heads lowered. Everything seemed to be taking place in a dream. Kosla's words reverberated as if they were deep within a tunnel: "Death must have occurred a few hours ago."

I turned to Wanda. She clasped me to her, her entire body trembling, and I was sucked backward in time, back to the death of my father. Time passed. Through my tears I saw Kaytus on the bed and Wanda kneeling beside him, weeping, sobbing, praying fervently. I knew no prayers, but, for the first time, I asked the one who had preached the Sermon on the Mount to have mercy on my son. He had always been good, I kept saying, always. It was I who had let him down, who had wronged him. Why was I alive and he dead?

I lost all sense of reality; I could see, but I wasn't there. After a while other people came into the room and spoke with Chandra. White specters, our servants, moved about the room soundlessly. Someone led Wanda out, and someone else took me by the arm and moved me away. I was utterly indifferent to where I was going.

What followed, too, was dreamlike. Wanda and I agreed to everything, to the plans that were proposed for our son's body. But we did not want to be apart, even for a moment; we seemed fused by pain. Only I could feel what she felt, only she could feel what I felt. That night we sat together, silent, hand in hand.

The next day many people came to express their condolences, since the news of Kaytus's death had spread through Delhi. We received those people, nodding our heads, thanking them, looking at them without seeing them. Their words of consolation and encouragement seemed inappropriate, incomprehensible. They came into the main drawing room to look into the coffin where Kaytus lay—there in his black suit as if he were about to leave for a reception with us. His face was serene, but his eyes were closed. His hands, crossed on his chest, held a cross of white ivory Wanda had taken from the wall in his room and placed in his hands. The coffin was cold; it had been packed around with ice. Surrounding it were flowers that either the servants had picked in the garden or our visitors had brought. I remember, too, that a priest who had known Kaytus recited prayers beside the coffin, that I knelt down with Wanda and the others who prayed with the priest. I was told that many ambassadors and several ministers from the Indian government came, that Piegov stood for a long while by the coffin, staring pensively at the cross in Kaytus's hands. He left precipitously, mumbling something to himself.

When everyone had left and we were alone again, Wanda knelt beside Kaytus, kissing and stroking him. She could not bring herself to leave. I stood beside her looking at my son. Was this the cross I would have to bear? Would I ever be able to understand? We stayed beside our son as night fell and then we sat together there in the darkness. I remember the light being turned on in the hall and hearing a soft knock at the door before Bansi came in. At a whisper he said that the bedroom was all made up for us, and Kaytus would not be alone; he would sit with him until we came back. Our servants lavished us with kindness and consideration. They tiptoed about and anticipated our every need.

A variety of people, including friends of Kaytus, some of whom we did not know, offered us their help. They asked what we intended to do, where our son would be buried. With cutting pain we grew aware that we would soon have to part with his body. We both wanted him to be buried in Poland, in the same cemetery as his grandfather, and with searing recall we remembered that Wanda had once given Kaytus a good scolding for saying that he would be buried there someday, that his first and last names were the same as his grandfather's, so only a new set of dates would need to be added.

Before leaving for Warsaw, Wanda and I went into Kaytus's room to say good-bye to his things and to the air he had once breathed. Our good servants had left everything untouched. The pills were still strewn about the sheets on his bed; the things he had placed on his night table that final night were still there. Then I noticed that his watch was missing. I searched the room. None of the valuable things I had bought him in Singapore, including the gold nugget that was part of his mineral collection, were to be found. His old Polish coins were missing, as were a great many other things. On the table by his bed were a pipe, a leather wallet, a red Air France calendar, a notebook, pens, and a small box; beside them was a rusty crescent-shaped piece of iron. We picked up all the objects and notebooks and scoured them for a note, a sign, anything. We found nothing. But the little piece of iron intrigued me. Suddenly I remembered: Monte Cassino. The soldier's boot tap Kaytus had pried out of the dirt. It was clear he had taken one last look at it before going to sleep.

It was difficult for us to leave his room. We looked around again. In the fireplace we found freshly burned paper; the sheets crumbled to ashes in our hands. Had he written something and then at the last moment thought it better for his reasons to remain forever a mystery to us?

On July 5 the entire diplomatic corps, except for those on leave, and our friends gathered at Palam Airport to see Kaytus and us off. By that time we were aware of the genuine warmth we were being shown. That day the embassies accredited in New Delhi received the following note:

> The Embassy of the Polish People's Republic presents its compliments to the Diplomatic and Consular Missions in New Delhi and has the honor to convey the following from Mr. and Mrs. Spasowski: "We are leaving New Delhi today for Poland to accompany humbly the body of our most beloved and only son. To all those who knew him and who are with us in our sorrow, we extend our most heartfelt gratitude."
> *New Delhi*
> *July 5, 1970*

Wanda and I sat holding hands on the Aeroflot flight. We were both thinking the same thing—that Kaytus was with us. I opened my eyes. No. He was not there. He was somewhere else in the plane, in the hold. I wanted to scream, I wanted to crash against the stony Himalayas and be reunited with him, forever. But the engines' even hum was bearing us further into life. The more time went by, the further we were from Kaytus. My thoughts were whirling. From time to time Wanda was shaken by a sob, and her hand squeezed mine all the tighter. The flight was smooth, long, terrible.

We landed in Moscow. Wanda had once said that she would never return to Moscow, and here she was walking beside me, holding my hand tightly, asking the same question I was: Where is Kaytus now? Someone walked over to us, probably an official from our embassy, because he spoke Polish. I did not recognize him, did not remember him. We sat down to wait for our connecting flight to Warsaw. We were not sure when it would leave. Suddenly Wanda cried, "Where is Kaytus? I must be with him. Take me to him!"

The Aeroflot people shrugged their shoulders. The one in charge said stolidly, "The box is being sent to Warsaw. What's all the fuss about? If it's being sent, it'll be on the plane. Calm down. Passengers are not allowed into the cargo room."

Wanda sobbed in Polish, "I want to be with Kaytus! I can't stay here. Can't they understand that?"

The embassy official translated, but the Aeroflot representative was unmoved. Curtly, he replied, "It's not allowed. We have our rules. You need special permission to get in there."

It took me a long while to persuade her that we should leave the airport, since we still had a few hours to wait. We walked a short distance and sat down on the grass behind some bushes. It was a beautiful sunny day. Wanda wept softly and kept repeating that Kaytus would never see any of this again. After a while she dozed off, leaning against my shoulder.

It was evening before we left Moscow. During the short flight, Wanda asked again and again if Kaytus was definitely on the plane with us. I assured her that he was, even though at moments I feared that they might have forgotten to load the coffin on. "The Bolsheviks are horrible," Wanda kept saying. "I hate them every bit as much as *he* did."

Relatives, friends, and acquaintances were awaiting us at Okecie Airport. Our daughter, pale and changed, was the first to run up to us. She threw her arms around her mother. Vice Minister Winiewicz had also come. People surrounded us, each one with something to say, each one trying to give us heart. We had to wait quite a long time for the formalities to be completed. It was with a sigh of relief that we heard an official from the ministry whisper that the coffin was being unloaded. With Kaytus at our side, Wanda grew somewhat calmer.

The streets of Warsaw seemed small, narrow. As we drove up to the chapel at the Calvinist cemetery, I saw that it was still gashed by bullets, its walls still cracked; it had survived the uprising by a miracle. The coffin was placed on a catafalque surrounded by flowers and wreaths from India; their strong aroma filled the chapel. We sat there for hours every day until our son was buried.

A few days later I wrote an obituary notice for the press. A friend later told me that there had been problems with the newspapers. At first they had not wanted to run the obituary, because of its unusual wording. They had needed to be convinced. Apparently they had not liked the words "A boy with a great heart—rare in our times—

a student of philosophy at the university in New Delhi, departed from us forever on July 2, in the land of India, having first given all his possessions to the needy. . . ."

Wanda stopped praying. She even refused to attend the Mass said for Kaytus's soul.

"What's wrong?" I was astonished.

"I can't pray and talk with God as I used to. I don't understand anything any more. I don't know . . ." she answered bitterly.

"What don't you understand?"

"I don't understand what God is doing, what He wants, why He took Kaytus like that . . . having him take his own life . . . so that he would be damned," she said, bursting into tears. "Look how many bad, despicable people there are . . . and he was so good . . . so noble. . . . What did God punish him for?"

I pressed her to me and stroked her hair. "God knows what He's doing," I said, all of a sudden, surprising myself. That was the first time I tried to explain to her how we should bear the cross that had befallen us so unexpectedly, but my words were to no avail. Once again she repeated stubbornly, "I don't want any explanations. I don't want to live without him. I have to die. . . . I must be with him."

The way she looked and what she said broke my heart. I could only hope time would ease her pain.

A large crowd came to the cemetery the day of the funeral, faces familiar and unknown. Some were total strangers, perhaps people who had been intrigued by the unorthodox obituary. Klewenhagen walked over to us, kissed us, and whispered, "So, it happened!" That was the last we saw of him.

The Calvinist minister emerged from the chapel, and old friends, officers from the British zone of Germany, carried the coffin out on their shoulders. A boy in a surplice raised a black cross above his head and began moving toward my father's grave. The rest of us followed. Wanda faltered, and Czeslaw and I supported her. The coffin was placed by the tomb. There were no eulogies, only a brief prayer. The iron doors were opened, and I caught sight of my father's coffin in the dark interior. Wanda fell to her knees, put her arms around Kaytus's coffin, and pressed her face against it, remaining in that position until we succeeded in getting her back to her feet. The sun was shining and the air smelled of flowers as Kaytus was slowly lowered into the grave. I gazed mutely at the inscription on the granite: Wladyslaw Spasowski. The name served for both. The tears flowed freely from Wanda's eyes, but not a single tear welled in mine. I had turned to stone.

Within days Wanda was in the hospital under a physician's care, but I was functioning normally. I was surprised by my own willingness to go to the ministry and deal with an assortment of stupid business. I moved about like an automaton, disturbed only by the state of Wanda's health. The doctors were divided in their opinion on whether she should return to India. Some held that her nerves would not stand the strain; others thought it was precisely there that she would become herself again. Weeks passed, and Wanda decided she wanted to return. More than anything, she had to be where Kaytus had been alive to attempt to unravel the mystery of his death.

Our entire Indian staff and their families were in the house to welcome us, clearly glad that we had returned. This time they had not made the customary wreaths of flowers to put around our necks; they knew there was no joy in our hearts.

The residence was in perfect order. Only Kaytus's room was closed. Bansi unlocked the door, and we went in. Everything was as we had left it.

"I would like to say something," he said quietly.

"Please do, Bansi," said Wanda. "Sit down. We can sit right here, on these three chairs."

He hesitated, but did as she said.

"A few days after sab and memsab left," he began, "that tall man from the embassy came and went directly to Kaytus's room. The door was locked. He told me to open the door right away and to give him the key. I told him that I did not have the key, because memsab had taken it with her. He shouted at me, said I was lying, and threatened to throw me out on the spot."

Wanda and I exchanged glances, both of us aware that the person mentioned was a frequent visitor to the Soviet Embassy.

"You did the right thing, Bansi," I said, praising him. "That key wasn't to be given to anyone. Only a bad person would ask for someone else's key and try to intimidate the holder."

"He went through the house and demanded the key to the safe that holds the silver," said Bansi. "I told him the same thing again, that memsab had taken the key with her, and again he shouted."

This business was troubling me more and more. "Bansi," I asked one day, "was that the first time anyone asked for those keys?"

He smiled. "No. When sab went to Nepal with Kaytus and memsab flew to Calcutta, people came here and started going through all the rooms. I don't know what they were doing, because they closed the doors behind them. They asked for the key to the safe, too, but I told them I didn't have it. They didn't shout at me that time. They just said that the rooms were dirty and should be repainted."

"Thank you, Bansi," I said. "Thank you very much. Don't worry about anything."

"We're not worried now," he replied, "but we were worried that sab and memsab might not come back to us. We were very worried about that."

He rose, and at the door turned and added, "No outsiders were in this room. Just me. I brought a mattress in here at night and slept by the door. No question, no one was in here," he said.

"I don't like this at all," said Wanda slowly.

"I don't like it either," I agreed. "We have to gather up all the threads. . . . I must know everything."

She nodded. "There's no bringing Kaytus back to life, but I want to know who was party to his death. . . . But then, we already know, don't we?"

We set about inspecting the room, in detail this time, everything in turn, item by item. No letter, no note. It was clear that before his death Kaytus had divested himself of everything he owned of value. We looked through numerous notebooks, notes, date books, photographs. But the mystery remained determinedly a mystery.

We were visited by many of Kaytus's friends, Indians and diplomats, who shared their memories of him with us. Gradually, we began to piece together the events of his final days. He had bid his friends farewell as if he were leaving on a trip, but he had done it so discreetly that they had not realized what he was actually talking about. On June 27, his last birthday and five days before his death, he had written in the guest book at a party given for him by some American friends: "Life is a small island of pain in a sea of indifference."

We also spoke with one of his teachers from the American school who had been very close to Kaytus. He was a big, middle-aged man who had a wife and several children; Kaytus had stood godfather to his youngest daughter. It was clear that he felt the loss of Kaytus. "I noticed a change in him at the end of last year. He said that he didn't want to go to Poland, that he was afraid."

"Did he say why?" I asked.

"No. Only that it was a police state and that he didn't feel safe there."

"Did he say where he would have liked to live and what he would have liked to do?" asked Wanda.

"Oh, yes. We spoke about the United States rather often. He was very fond of reminiscing about his time there. He said that the best years of his life had been there. He also spoke about England. He thought that because he had been born on British soil, he should be allowed to be a British citizen. He mentioned that he was going to speak to the high commissioner about this." The teacher lapsed into silence, wiping tears from his eyes. "How could I know? The poor boy was looking for something. He wanted to tear himself free, and I was of no help to him."

"We always thought we were so close to him, but we had no idea either," I said with difficulty.

"He was always such a cheerful boy, always ready to help others. Who could ever have foreseen it? . . . Oh, yes," he said, recalling something, "just before his death, he did tell me that there was no way out for him, that his life had taken a strange turn because he was going to have to do the same thing for his father that his grandfather had done. I asked him what his grandfather had done, but he didn't want to say. Later, the whole thing slipped my mind. Now I can see that there must have been another tragedy there."

I froze. Could there be a mysterious shadow hanging over my son's tragedy? I strained to remember it all—the anonymous death threats, the unfinished conversation in Katmandu, his constant anxiety, Klewenhagen's suspicions, Szlachcic's remarks, what the faithful Bansi had told me. I was unable to halt the rush of thoughts and associations. It was nearly thirty years ago that my father had departed. I knew full well who had driven my father to suicide, but could the blame for Kaytus's be laid on them, too? I had never been a superstitious man, but suddenly I regretted that my son had borne my father's name. The shadow that lay over my son's tragedy would never cease to haunt me.

Soon enough a telegram arrived from Jedrychowski recalling me from India. Wanda was pleased to be returning to Poland, because her mother was seriously ill.

Tara seemed able to read my mind. We were driving home from my office one afternoon when he looked around and asked, "Shall we drive out there?"

"Yes," I replied.

He turned around and drove out to the ruins of Tughlaqabad. I climbed to the top and stood in my usual spot. The weather was beautiful, the sky blue, the visibility excellent. It was all the same; only I was different. I felt empty, no longer the man I had been, no longer struggling with myself. My thoughts seemed to have congealed around a core of pain.

I cast my eyes about, the ruins sparking no rumination, no memories, as dead and hollow as I was. I returned to the car.

"Shall we go there, Mr. Ambassador?" asked Tara, pointing to a red sandstone building on the other side of the road. "Kaytus used to go there often."

"Yes," I answered. I had been there before. There was a Moslem chapel and a marble tomb inside. I stood by Tughlaq's white sarcophagus; beside him lay his son—his killer. Who knew what had really happened? It, too, was a mystery. Perhaps the father had wronged the son as surely as I had wronged Kaytus. If only I could lie beside my son in a stone sarcophagus in the hush of a dead city until everything turned to dust! I wanted no immortality; I wanted oblivion! It was Kaytus who should have lived forever. The memory of the good lives on, I told myself; he won't be forgotten. That much I had learned in Assisi.

The farewell with our servants was emotional. They came with their entire families weighed down with flowers. They said goodbye to us as if we were one of them, repeating that we should return to them, that our place was there. And indeed we thought we would return there someday; Wanda felt she had left her heart there, as Kaytus had.

On the December day we left New Delhi, Palam Airport was crowded with the people who had come to bid us farewell. The airplane lifted off the runway, and we were borne away. But Kaytus's mystery remained behind in India, forever unresolved.

Visiting my mother on one of my trips from England, 1952

Czeslaw Sikorski, Wanda's brother and a relentless critic of my ideology

Wanda in Hyde Park with Misia and Kaytus

WASHINGTON NEWSFOTO

With Wanda in Washington, D.C., 1955

Meeting Juan Perón in the presidential palace in Buenos Aires, my first post as chief of a diplomatic mission

The family in 1956

ADAMS STUDIO

Minister of Agriculture Edward Ochab visiting Washington in 1959

ACKAD

With Premier Piotr Jaroszewicz and his wife in 1960

Bronek Sianoszek, Home Army hero and our dearest friend

1964, during the time I left my family

Misia

With Kaytus in 1969

Kaytus, Wanda, and I before a reception in India, January 16, 1970, six months before the death of Kaytus

Czeslaw, Wanda, and I at Kaytus's funeral

Sitting with the coffin

The burial stone that served for both my father and my son

As deputy foreign minister in Warsaw with U.S. Ambassador Richard Davies

The Hungarian, Bulgarian, and Czechoslovakian ambassadors, Anatoli Dobrynin, and I at the Soviet Embassy's dacha in Maryland, May 1, 1979

WHITE HOUSE PHOTO

Meeting President Ronald Reagan after his inauguration, when I told him Poland was in danger and asked for his help

Paderewski's piano at the embassy

In our Warsaw apartment during a visit home

WHITE HOUSE PHOTO

Secretary of State Alexander Haig, Vice Minister Mieczyslaw Jagielski (foreground), Vice President George Bush, and I at the White House

PONTIFICIA FOTOGRAFIA FELICI

With Pope John Paul II during our confidential visit to the Vatican in December 1980

WHITE HOUSE PHOTO

With President Reagan at the White House three days after my defection

BOOK THREE

The Ideal Abandoned

1970–1981

CHAPTER XXI

We returned to Warsaw via London, for Wanda had an irresistible desire to visit the place where Kaytus had been born. That first evening in London I recall well was December 14, 1970. It was then we learned about the disturbances in the shipyards of Gdansk. Fighting between the police and the workers had raged in the streets of Gdansk throughout the day. Every few minutes British programs were interrupted for the latest reports from Poland.

On the nineteenth we flew to Warsaw on the Polish airline. There were only a few passengers aboard. Okecie Airport seemed deserted; no one was checking passports or baggage. Menace was in the air.

The next day it was reported that Gomulka had stepped down and that Edward Gierek had been made first secretary. I sat at home in front of the television one evening soon after that and listened to him speak. Gierek's face inspired confidence, and his words had a new ring to them. He spoke not in Party jargon, but as any other human being would have. Still, after his speech was over, I knew I had had enough of promises and generalities. The changes and promises had been wrung from and paid for by the workers whose blood had flowed on the streets of Gdansk.

My mother-in-law had been paralyzed by a recent stroke and required constant care. Watching Wanda with her, I thought that this misfortune, like everything in life, had its other side: Wanda seemed to be holding on. She was made to feel useful. Misia lived with us and helped take care of her grandmother a little, but she had finished her studies and was working now. A bleak new chapter in our life had begun.

I visited my mother in Milanowek. She was still living alone with her dog and cat—her best friends, she called them. She did not even want to come to see us in Warsaw for Christmas. Solitude had become her way of life.

Despite the coming of Christmas, Warsaw was as dark and as dismal as our hearts. The days were overcast. Long lines of frostbitten people stood in front of stores whose windows gaped with their emptiness. Mounds of filthy snow crowded the sidewalks and contrasted starkly with our memories of India's sunlit landscape.

On the day before Christmas Eve, Wanda and I went to the cemetery to visit Kaytus. We took him a little festively decorated Christmas tree. "He loved Christmas so much . . ." whispered Wanda through her tears. "We can't leave him all alone in the cold like this."

We stood there a long time.

Wanda's brother, Czeslaw, and his wife came to see us on Christmas Eve, as did some friends who had a son the same age as Kaytus. They tried to cheer us, but words failed them and they ended up sharing our sorrow.

In the evenings Wanda and I would sit in silence on Kaytus's fold-out couch by his desk and be transported to the past. Wanda wept constantly. Sometimes I wondered where her tears came from. All I could feel was a stone where my heart had once been.

I began going to the ministry after Christmas. I had not expected compassion, but was surprised by the chill I encountered. There were no signs of friendliness, no attempt to speak with me. Utterly indifferent, I sat at my desk and dealt with the routine.

On the last day of December I received a note from the minister saying that I would be running the Asian Department temporarily. I had not been appointed director, not a good sign. Many of my fellow employees who had known me for years now pretended not to notice me.

I decided to distance myself from all that and pondered what to do with my life. Only now did I fully realize that I had but a single profession, the foreign service, and that there was no other position for me. I was already fifty and it would be hard to start again from scratch. I castigated myself for not having changed direction earlier. Had I done so, perhaps I would not have lost my son, perhaps I would now be at peace with myself. In conversations with Wanda I struck on an idea: I would finish my current work, withdraw deep into the provinces, to a gamekeeper's cottage in the woods, and begin a new life. Wanda doubted this was possible, but she understood me and was weary of our life; she said she would agree to anything. In confidence, I divulged my plans to her brother and our closest friends, but they only tried to dissuade me. Czeslaw saw my plans as pure fantasy. "Here's my advice to you, Romek: sit on your ass, wait, and see what happens. Gomulka stunk things up—that much is fact—but there seems to be a fresh breeze coming in with Gierek. Let's see how long it lasts. Maybe in a couple of years we'll be able to breathe again, and then, *then,* you'll know what to do next. One step at a time. Running away to the forest is always an option. Perhaps you'll be able to accomplish something positive at the ministry. Who knows? One thing is sure: if you leave your post, it'll be taken at once by some bastard who'll only bring harm to the country. Think it through."

I decided to take his advice and wait.

From Gdansk we began hearing more and more news that had been concealed by the authorities. The truth of what had happened in December along the Baltic coast revealed a sorry picture. Two hundred workers had been killed—five times more than had been reported officially—more than a thousand had been wounded, and a few thousand had been jailed. From Party people I learned that Politburo members Stanislaw Kociolek and Zenon Kliszko had played a vile role in those events. It had been Kliszko, whom Gomulka had sent to Gdansk on the sly as his plenipotentiary, who had ordered the police to use force to suppress the shipyard workers. Neither he nor Kociolek had tried to speak honestly with the workers; they had seen only counterrevolution in the wind.

I did not know the new people Gierek had brought in to the eleven-man Politburo. Edward Babiuch, Stefan Olszowski, and Jan Szydlak meant nothing to me at the time. All I knew was that the real power rested in the Party secretariat, composed of Gierek and six secretaries. Of those, I knew only one, Mieczyslaw Moczar, former minister of Security. I also knew Szlachcic, his successor, whose frankness in our talks in New Delhi had been to my liking. That was all—not very much—that I knew about the new team.

One day at the beginning of February, I ran into Kazimierz Sidor in a corridor at the ministry. We had known each other for twenty-five years, since the Berlin days, and were glad to meet again. The last time I had seen him was in Cairo, where he had been ambassador. His face was still youthful, but his thoroughly gray hair bespoke a sudden aging; he was only five years older than I. He told me that after returning from the Cairo post he had been sidetracked at the ministry, and was still sitting in his little office in the African Department waiting to see what would happen to him. I detected bitterness in his voice; surprising from him, for we did not have many people there with a past like his. He had been the leader of the "partisans," the Communist People's Guard, in the Lublin district from 1942 on, and after the entrance of the Soviets he had become the first governor, as it was called then, of the first scrap of "liberated" Polish territory. He had also belonged to that small group of Communists who had been summoned to Moscow in 1944 for talks with Stalin. I wondered how a person like him could have ended up so bitter. He paced back and forth between door and window. Every once in a while he would stop and gaze out at the snow in the courtyard.

"How could Gomulka have allowed what happened on the coast?" I asked after a while.

Sidor spun around and looked at me with surprise. "It was worse than you think," he said after a moment, "but we'll discuss that some other time. That was a black page for Gomulka, though there were bright ones, too. He prevented bloodshed in 1956, don't forget, and at the beginning of December last year he signed a treaty with the German Federal Republic. That's important. Just think of it! Our western border is now permanently fixed. Poland's borders are now accepted by everyone. And Moscow won't use the Germans to scare us any more. Very important," he repeated.

"Excuse me, but I don't agree. It is important, but I see it differently. Moscow wasn't thinking about Poland when it pushed into Central Europe. On the contrary, they were murdering Poles and deporting them to the Arctic Circle," I said, feeling my voice grow tense.

"You've become a sharp one." Sidor's eyes flashed. "I like to talk with people who have opinions of their own. Still, be careful," he said, with a significant look around the room. "Perhaps we should go to the dining room?"

We went down to the basement. Sidor must have been a frequent customer there, because they let us in although it had not opened yet.

"Could we have some music on the speaker?" he asked the woman in the white apron who opened to door for us. "We're both music lovers." Only then, sure of the sound barrier created by the music, did he feel comfortable enough to talk.

"I'll be brief," I said, "Remember Naszkowski? Remember how much it mattered for him to have Sukarno recognize the Oder-Neisse border? Who do you think was the beneficiary there? You wouldn't say Naszkowski was a good Pole, would you?"

"No, I wouldn't say that about that son of a bitch," said Sidor with a laugh. "But you're sharp as a razor. What happened?"

"Everything. My whole life. I can't stand deceit, hypocrisy, force. I'm getting more and more like my son. . . . In India I had time to do a lot of thinking." We had a long and free conversation.

"Just be careful," he admonished at the end of it. "Don't talk like this to anyone, not in their offices, at least. The walls have ears."

Two days later Moczar was made a member of the Politburo. He was, at once, the secretary of the Central Committee responsible for the army and for Security. A great deal of power now lay in his hands.

One day Sidor dropped by my office looking quite pleased. We made our way to the dining room, where he again asked for music.

"I told you there was unfinished business," he said softly. "The new people can't manage without Moczar. He's in the Buro now because he was supported by people who proved themselves during the war, People's Guard who risked their lives and deserve their good name—the partisans."

"You think the partisans will ever do better than one Moczar on the Buro?" The words came flying out of me, and I regretted them at once.

Sidor was regarding me with a reproachful eye. "How can you say that? The partisans fought here on Polish soil. Our Polish blood was shed here. We come from the people; we didn't arrive here wearing Soviet army coats."

"I know that you fought, I know your record, but, forgive me, you partisans weren't the only ones who fought. What about the entire Home Army? The Warsaw uprising? The people who fought in the Borderlands . . . ? What's happened to them? Is there any justice for them? Or is it only for you?"

"You don't think we have the power coming to us?" I could see that my words had angered him, and he had put me on edge, too.

"It's not important whether or not you have it coming," I said after a moment, weighing my words. "Big Brother will always be against you, because for him anyone who talks like you about the nation, the soil, blood, and Soviet army coats is an enemy. I know them. I know those Soviet ambassadors."

Back in my own office I regretted causing him pain, but that's the way I had become. I could not hide my thoughts if asked to speak.

In mid-February a strike broke out in the Ursus tractor factory, which, like the shipyards on the Baltic coast and Nowa Huta, served as a barometer for the workers' morale in Poland. People in the large industrial enterprises had become aware of the details of how the government had persecuted the workers in Gdansk; that those killed on the streets had been slipped into sacks and buried at night in places unknown.

Gierek was still going about the country, making promises, trying to calm the workers. He kept asking, "Will you help?" And he kept receiving a resounding "We will!"

Sidor spoke with courage at the next Primary Party Organization (POP) meeting, and even seemed to have our conversations in the dining room in mind when he criticized the Party's role in Poland. But his speech met with reserve. It had been, perhaps, too bold a speech for ministry officials who wanted careers in diplomacy and still were not sure which way the wind was blowing. I could not resist requesting the floor. I spoke briefly, saying that Sidor had addressed matters directly, that no good was served by whitewashing the harm the Party had done to the nation. If, I continued, we are to accomplish anything of value in the future, we will need a rebirth, a breaking with the evils of the past, fully and uncompromisingly. I looked at Sidor, who was beaming with pleasure. Some faint-hearted applause rippled through the membership when I was through.

This was my final Party and public statement in Poland. I never said a word at any meeting after that. I was often invited to speak on television and write for the papers, but I always refused, despite pressure from the ministry and the Central Committee. I spoke only at meetings at the ministry on matters of foreign policy, at small conferences of the ministry's board, and at the Central Committee when the secretary was present and mostly on matters concerning the United States.

Sometime after the POP meeting Sidor and I talked in his apartment, which was large and nicely furnished. We sat on beautiful period furniture and drank tea.

Noticing my surprise at the furniture, he said, "They're antiques from Alicja's family. She has a lot of them, and, as an art historian, she's an expert on them."

"You were going to tell me about Gomulka's role in the suppression at Gdansk," I said. "Was it he who ordered that the workers be fired on?"

"No. But when he learned that things were getting hot, he appealed to Brezhnev to send in Soviet divisions."

I was speechless. I had heard a lot, but this surpassed all else.

Sidor looked at me, measuring the impression his words had made. "Unfortunately, it's true," he said after a moment. "I have firsthand information, from Moczar. He was taken aback, too; he couldn't believe it. He had always been loyal to Gomulka; they had been in prison at the same time. Gomulka trusted him, made him minister of Security, secretary of the Central Committee. But as soon as Moczar learned that Gomulka had invited Soviet tanks in, he took action against him. To ensure their safety, the Seventh Plenum was called in a hurry, and held, not in the Central Committee building, but outside Warsaw, in Natolin. That was Moczar's idea and his ministry made sure that the Central Committee members were taken there quickly and without incident. You know Natolin?"

"No."

"Well, the old palace, the former seat of the Lubomirski princes, is surrounded by a dense forest. And that forest in turn is surrounded by fields, so you can see anyone approaching. It makes defense easy and surprise out of the question. It was an ideal place to meet in dangerous times. But the important thing about this plenum occurred before it ever convened. The Soviet ambassador passed on the word that Moscow would never agree to Moczar's election as first secretary, but they did say they would accept Gierek.

"Right after the plenum, Moscow summoned Gierek and Jaroszewicz to hammer them into shape. The people, however, weren't appeased by having only Gomulka go. They want big changes."

"I heard that they're also demanding that Moczar be removed."

Sidor glanced over at me with a look of astonishment. "He does have a lot of enemies—that's true—but his greatest enemy is the Soviets, and so that's mostly their work."

"Possibly, but it was Moczar who paved the way here for the Soviets, along with the others."

Sidor bridled at that remark. I could see that it had wounded him. "And what about you? What about both of us? Weren't *you* paving the way, too?" he shouted indignantly.

I spoke slowly and deliberately, as I always tried to when emotions rose. "I was a tool. I don't deny it. I paved the way. But I've had enough deceit by now, especially self-deceit. I lost my father because of *them,* and still I paved the way. I convinced myself that I was carrying out my father's will. What did it lead to? To the loss of my son!"

"What do you intend to do now?" he asked somberly. "You have no faith in the Party, in the people's government. . . ."

"I'll see. I'm in a sort of state of suspension. Right now I'm acting as director. My friends tell me I can do some good for the country if I stay on. But I've changed, maybe even more than you think. I learned a lot in India, you see. It's a good place to see how transient life is. The mystery of millennia is in the air there. You learn that everything passes, the power of the sword, prison, slavery. Chains break, shackles crumble, castles turn to dust. You can see how one frail man can make a difference."

"You've become a mystic," he said softly.

"No, not a mystic. I've just rejected evil." Stirred by my own words, I covered my face with my hand. Sidor said nothing; I have no idea what went through his mind. Perhaps he was surprised and thought I really had begun moving toward mysticism. Perhaps he felt sorry for me. Perhaps he thought I had gone mad. Perhaps he agreed with me, but found it difficult to admit it to himself.

I rose. "I have to be going now."

He offered me his hand, and we put our arms around one another.

My fate took a different turn from what I had anticipated. At the beginning of March, Minister Jedrychowski called me in. I went thinking I might quit the ministry there and then. To my surprise, he greeted me with a friendly smile.

"I want personally to hand you your appointment as director of the Asian Department."

I left stunned. Maybe it was a good thing I hadn't rushed into anything. Maybe I could accomplish something positive here.

Events developed rapidly. Jedrychowski pressed for the earliest possible visit to Japan, and after a few weeks our delegation was on its way.

Our group flew to Moscow first, since we were to make the rest of our trip on Aeroflot. The responsibility for things in general, the agenda, the arrangements with the Japanese, and the political materials, rested with me.

We were in Moscow only a few hours, but in that time Jedrychowski went alone to the Ministry of Foreign Affairs to meet with Gromyko. The meeting must have gone well, since he was in considerably better humor when we boarded the Soviet plane.

The IL-62 was flying nonstop to Tokyo. Night fell quickly, but dawn came even quicker. This was my first flight over Siberia. Visibility was excellent, and the immensity of this land extended far and wide beneath us. I spotted the great rivers. A range of large, snow-covered mountains appeared in the distance, and peaks beyond them disappeared somewhere between earth and sky. I opened my briefcase and withdrew a map of northern Asia. Yes, right there past the Lena River the ridges of the Verkhoyanskiy Mountains began, and far past them, not visible, were the Yana, the Indigirka, and the Kolyma rivers. I froze. Camps were located there, within the Arctic Circle. It was there Home Army Poles had been sent toward the end of the war. I stood up and peered into the distance, at the blue mountains vanishing on the horizon. Perhaps a few rags of what had once been Polish people were still alive there. I felt my heart constrict; a pain stabbed at my larynx. There I was, in a Soviet plane, flying over them, not even shouting, silent. *Silent.* And what good would my shouting do? They would say I was mad. But a madman with honor, not a sane criminal!

"What are you staring at, Comrade Director?" Jedrychowski asked me. I turned my head; he and his wife were looking at me with curiosity.

"Beautiful view, isn't it? The Soviet Union is an immense country. Boundless space," he added, clearing his throat.

"Yes, immense," I answered, turning back to the window and straining my eyes into the distance where the Kolyma River flowed.

"The view from the right side is even better. We saw Lake Baykal a little while ago," said Jedrychowski, a Russian inflection invading his voice.

I did not reply. I was lost in thought again.

The meetings with Foreign Minister Fukuda were businesslike and courteous. I made my own transcript of the talks. It was during Jedrychowski's speech that I realized the true purpose of his visit. Glancing at his black notebook, he said: "Mr. Minister, like Japan, Poland is a country that suffered greatly during the Second World War. However, our position in the world has changed now. Before the war we were weak and assailed from every side, but now we are part of the powerful socialist community and bound indissolvably in friendship with the Soviet Union. And as a neighbor and friend of the Soviet Union we are best able to assess its policies and actual intentions.

"Please believe me, Mr. Minister," he continued after a moment of silence that was to accentuate the gravity of his words, "our friend and neighbor strives for peace. All the Chinese accusations concerning its hegemonism in Asia are groundless, a fabrication that contradicts common sense. It is the Chinese who are conducting a dangerous policy and threatening world peace."

Fukuda looked at him without so much as blinking an eye. When it was his turn to speak, he focused on Polish-Japanese affairs. His only comment on the Soviet Union was toward the end of his speech. "As far as the Soviet Union is concerned, Japan wants good relations and a correct assessment of Soviet policy and its intentions, but that is not enough. The Soviets have taken some small islands from Japan. Until those islands are returned to us, there can be no question of good relations."

I wracked my brain to figure out what Jedrychowski's purpose was and why the trip had been made to seem so urgent. I had no success. A year later the rest of the pieces were added to the puzzle. Moscow must have had early access to secret information that Washington and Tokyo were undertaking a practical normalization of relations with Peking. I had heard that the Soviets would not allow a powerful triangle of forces—Washington-Tokyo-Peking—to arise in the Far East. Obviously, Moscow was not able to prevent the creation of such a triangle, but it tried every means to counter the process. Moscow's secret information was correct. In February of 1972 President Richard Nixon traveled to Peking. And when Japan's premier, Kakuei Tanaka, was in Peking in September he agreed to establish diplomatic relations with China. Thus the purpose of Jedrychowski's visit had been to indispose the Japanese toward the Chinese and to praise the Soviet Union's policy of peace, which had supposedly nothing in common with hegemonism. It was, no doubt, a naive attempt.

After Japan, I went on to Australia and New Zealand to establish diplomatic ties with those countries. In Wellington, I met a man who had headed a campaign during the war to take in five thousand orphans, children of Polish prisoners who had escaped from the Soviet Union with the help of General Anders's beleaguered soldiers. I found myself thanking that old gentleman on behalf of Poland.

I returned to Warsaw to find Wanda in ill health. She had been caring for her sick mother and taking breaks only to visit the cemetery. We both seemed to be teetering on the edge of nervous breakdowns. To give her some respite from our noisy apartment, a doctor friend took Wanda to a sanatorium outside the city.

Back at the ministry, I learned that control of the army and the secret police had been taken from Moczar, and that his functions as secretary of the Central Committee had been suspended. Weeks later, I went with Sidor for a walk in Lazienki Park and asked him what had happened to Moczar.

"Gierek simply pushed him aside," he replied. "The Russians obviously ordered him to get rid of Moczar. It was repayment for that plenum in Natolin. You were right to say that Russians will never trust Poles who fought for Poland on Polish soil. People like Moczar are dangerous to the Russians—they have their own opinions."

"Let's be frank," I interjected. "Otherwise it makes no sense to talk. Moscow may have removed Moczar, but there were plenty of other people who didn't like him either. We've already spoken of that. The workers demanded he step down. I've also heard people say he was a rabid anti-Semite."

"That's the Soviets' doing!" cried Sidor, coming to a stop. "You see, even you are repeating that rubbish. They know how to start rumors and destroy the people they don't like."

"But what happened in March 1968? Weren't the students beaten? I know from my son and from friends what happened in Warsaw, and Moczar was at the head of it."

"Moczar did what Gomulka ordered him to. . . ."

"Never mind where his orders came from, he was minister of Security during a time when bones were broken and blood was shed."

"So even you think it's good he's out."

"I don't know. The new people on top . . ."

"What do you mean 'new'? They only seem new because you've been far away in India and don't know who's been coming up through the Central Committee machine. Take a closer look at them, at those *new* people. They were all working in the Central Committee before; some of them were secretaries. They're Gierek's people, or people who were quick to catch the new wind in their sails and were kicked upstairs. I'll tell you one thing: it's no accident that they ended up in power. None of them ever smelled gunpowder. None ever knew prewar Poland. Take a good look at them. They're all from the youth movement. They were all still in school during the war."

We headed for the park's gate. Sidor got on a bus, and I walked home. I did not realize then that Moczar's removal from the secretariat was the beginning of the second round, which Moscow had started by playing the Polish Communists off against each other. The first round had been the removal of Gomulka and his October men. Moczar was a symbol. The Soviets wanted to destroy the partisans and their myth, the few who remained of those Communists who had fought the Germans. Moscow had already settled accounts with the Home Army and others, using partisans in large measure to accomplish that task for them.

New developments soon arose. A rumor spread that Gierek had caught Moczar in a conspiracy. Toward the end of May, Gierek had returned unexpectedly from Prague and gone immediately to Olsztyn, a little town about a hundred and ten miles north of Warsaw. There, he supposedly found Moczar plotting a coup with other partisans. I immediately suspected a false rumor had been put into circulation. Even if Moczar had been there with his old cronies from the People's Guard, did that necessarily mean they were hatching a plot? They might have been discussing what they saw in store for themselves. Surely Moczar had sufficient experience of both power and prison to know that a conspiracy had no chance with the Soviets at our necks, and that any coup would be crushed with force. There was no doubt that this was a provocation designed to serve a definite purpose.

Soon the partisans began to be removed from all the more important central Party and government posts. Sidor was holding on because he had been in the diplomatic service for many years; everyone knew that he had no other ambitions. After many months of neglect, he was finally named ambassador to Rome. The Soviet-inspired scenario was over only at the end of the year, at the Sixth Party Congress, when Moczar was removed from the Politburo and the purge of partisans was complete. All those who had fought during the war, with the obvious exception of those who had come from the East, were thus eliminated.

That summer a check was run on Party members; Party cards had to be turned in, and new ones were issued. At my ministry that was a mere formality, but the Party committee invested the proceedings with a certain pomp and solemnity. To my surprise, I read on my new ID that I had been a member of the Polish United Workers' Party since 1948, when the fictional union of Communists and socialists had occurred under the auspices of Cyrankiewicz. At first I was outraged. What right did they have to cancel out three years of my life? Had they done that in the fifties, I would have been at their throats. Now, however, my calm returned quickly. I had graduated to a certain numbness. I only thought that that alteration had been no accident. It was always said that it was length of service that counted most in the Party, and that you could always tell an opportunist by how long he had been a member. I made inquiries, and the explanation was that this had been done so that the socialists would feel equal to the others in terms of length of service. That sounded fine but it smelled false. A few years later I unraveled the sense behind it. There had been two reasons for the changes. The first was the partisans. They had had long periods of service, dating back to the struggle against the Germans. In this move, their past, and the best part of it, was clipped off, amputated. Second, the new group, men in their forties, had joined the Party only in the fifties or even later. They were clearly untainted by any involvement in the war. Both for them and for Moscow, having such people in the highest positions of power—people with no memory—had been a favorable move.

One day, I was visited by the ambassador from Iran. He arrived in a sullen mood and launched into a tirade.

"It's unheard of. In no other capital are conditions like they are here. I will have to inform His Highness the Shah personally. Warsaw can drive a person to distraction. . . . Nothing works at our residence. Everything's always breaking down. Imagine this," he said, looking reproachfully at me. "The residence had just been redone, and I was giving a dinner for members of the diplomatic corps. Everything was very nice. Then the waiters turned on the chandelier . . . and I noticed water dripping from it onto the table. Can you imagine that? *Water dripping from a chandelier!*"

He proved eventually to be a pleasant, cultured man, and I later helped him obtain a new residence. But that day, I remembered my father telling me about Poland's excellent craftsmen, who were demons for work and could handle any job. Alas, that had been long ago and before the war.

In helping the Iranian, I talked to the director of the Office of Residential and Administrative Services.

"You know," he said chummily, "they don't give us enough material. The people in Security do nothing but give orders: hire this one as an electrician; don't touch that residence, God forbid! And then you have to fix the pipes leaking at some minister's place. It could drive you nuts. And then all the diplomats start shouting. The only good thing is that I only understand Polish."

While he was unburdening himself, a wonderful idea flashed through my mind. "Can apartments be switched through your office?" I asked.

"Of course they can," he answered, with some swagger. "We're always swapping little ones for big ones."

"I have a large apartment. Can you swap it for a smaller one?"

"Was it officially allocated?"

"Yes, it was," I said, and told him where it was.

"Oh, that's a very good address. We have a lot of diplomats there. Come see me; we'll talk."

So it was that we exchanged our more "official" apartment for one that was half its size in a little building, 39 Filtrowa Street—a quiet neighborhood. We knew there would not be much room for us, Wanda's bedridden mother, and our grown daughter in those three little rooms, but we were attracted by the peace and quiet and the green leaves just beyond the windows.

The move gave us new life. The windows could be left open at night, the neighborhood was peaceful, Stalin's Palace was far away. We lived there for seven years. It was there, later, that everything we owned was lost when, in December of 1981, the authorities of People's Poland declared war on the Polish people.

In the fall of 1971, the Party was struggling to paste Polish society together. The Sixth Party Congress was scheduled to be held at the beginning of December, and as that date approached, the number of meetings increased. Even non-Party people were excited. They wanted to know what was coming, what Gierek's program would be. I gave in to this mood and, despite my skepticism, tried to persuade myself that some improvement had to occur, since a return to the old way would spell disaster for the country. Things were clearer since Gierek had taken over, I said to Wanda. His actions seemed to make sense.

On the other hand I found the slogans disturbing. The "strategy of dynamic development" had a proud ring when spoken from a Party organization lectern, but it said nothing to me.

I also heard frequently that from now on the Party would act on the principle that "the Party leads, the government governs." It seemed a salutary formula for guarding against mistakes. But once again I saw no difference between "leading" and "governing." The Politburo was a complicated affair, because, apart from Gierek and a few others, its members had key posts in the government. They would "lead" in one building as Party members and then go off to other buildings to "govern."

At the Twenty-fourth Soviet Party Congress, which had taken place in Moscow six months before, it had been stated authoritatively that the Soviets had already reached the stage of a "developed socialist society." No one had any idea what that meant. Speakers argued foggily that this was connected to their splendid economic achievements and the Soviet people's high level of political consciousness. They preached that we Poles had to work and study much harder to achieve their level of social development.

On December 6 Wanda and I sat in front of the television to watch the opening of our Party Congress. Congress Hall in the Palace of Culture was crammed with delegates. Once the members of the Politburo and the secretaries of the Central Committee had filed onstage, Gierek entered, to thunderous applause, followed by the foreign delegations.

"Comrades," began Gierek, "before these proceedings begin, allow me to welcome a worthy Communist, the Nestor of the Polish Communist and workers' movement, a fighter for People's Poland—Dr. Alfred Fiderkiewicz."

The camera zoomed in for a close-up. Fiderkiewicz sat in a large armchair to one side. His bald head was nodding, perhaps from emotion, perhaps from old age—he was eighty-five. It was the same old Dr. Fiderkiewicz, the Communist from Milanowek whose death sentence by the Home Army Bronek had not carried out. We sat still as the hall again roared with applause. Our thoughts were now elsewhere, at a modest grave in the Powazki military cemetery where Bronek had been laid to rest in the section for Home Army soldiers. Tears welled in my eyes.

"No mention of the people murdered in the name of Communism," whispered Wanda, wiping her cheeks. I was unable to speak. I could hear Kaytus's voice, deep, distant, reproachful.

Thus did the Sixth Congress begin for us. But for everyone in Congress Hall euphoria reigned. Edward Gierek was unanimously reelected first secretary of the Central Committee. The congress approved two documents: one on the continuing socialist development of People's Poland and one on security and co-operation in Europe. Of the newly elected Central Committee, fewer than half were former members. Cyrankiewicz and Jedrychowski were removed from the Politburo. Moczar, too, was removed; in that one move, the partisans were completely eliminated. The second round was over. Of all who had fought in the war, only the group from the East, from the Soviet Union, now remained on the field of battle—and that group was led by Premier Jaroszewicz. Another group was the new team brought in by Gierek. They were mostly from Silesia. The rest no longer counted for much. Thus, both Party and country were now being ruled by two groups facing off against each other.

One of the people on Gierek's team was Stefan Olszowski, who had been a member of the Politburo for a year and a Central Committee secretary for a few years. He had been appointed minister of foreign affairs, to replace Jedrychowski. On his first day of service, the directorship of the ministry assembled to welcome the new chief. A large, stocky man appeared in the doorway. He looked much older than the forty-odd years he was. He spoke briefly but well, appealing for co-operation and help from the seasoned veterans at the ministry. Wine was served; a few toasts were made. Then Olszowski walked around with glass in hand greeting his staff. I stood off to one side in order to observe him, but before long he was at my side.

"Comrade Romuald?"

"Yes," I replied, taken aback, because we had not met.

"I recognized you. I was told you'd be the tall one with the reddish blond hair," he said, with a friendly smile. "Maybe we can go off for a bit. I'd like to talk with you."

We stepped away from the crowd, closer to the wall.

"Here's the thing, Comrade Romuald," he said, assuming a dignified official tone. "I want to nominate you for the post of vice minister, if, of course, that would suit you."

Surprised, I said nothing and tried to gather my thoughts.

"As you can imagine," he added, "I've already worked this out with Secretary Franciszek. We want to put you in charge of American affairs." He was referring to Franciszek Szlachcic, who was now a member of the Politburo and the Central Committee secretary responsible for foreign affairs.

"You've been in Washington. No one has experience like yours." He waited, but I remained silent.

"I can see that you're giving it some thought, Comrade Romuald. You don't have to give me your answer immediately," he said, with no little surprise. "But I can't wait very long either."

"Fine," I said. "I'll give you my answer tomorrow, after I think it over and discuss it with my wife. In any case, I thank you for your confidence."

The half-hour walk home allowed me to do more thinking. The air was frosty, there was snow on the ground, the weather was beautiful.

Wanda and I sat at the little table that took up nearly half of our tiny kitchen. She did not look well, and the sadness in her eyes had not diminished. I told her about Olszowski's offer.

"You didn't accept, did you?" she asked apprehensively. "You *can't* accept. Kaytus couldn't stand those people."

"I agree with you," I said, weighing my words. "I've been fed up with them for a long time, too. So much, that I've often thought of quitting. But one must be consistent. After all, when I wanted to quit, everyone was against it."

"Because you weren't being realistic about that gamekeeper's cottage in the country," she replied.

"Maybe I wasn't. But I want to be realistic about the ministry. Either we go to a gamekeeper's cottage and away from all this or we stay and I put myself in the position of doing something tangible."

Wanda was surprised. "So, you want to accept?"

"I'll say it again: I want to be consistent. Either, or."

"And what would you do as vice minister?"

"They want to put me in charge of American affairs."

"Really?" A note of interest crept into her voice. "But what if they want you to make statements that would go against our conscience, that would have made our son ashamed, what then?"

"I'll simply refuse. I'll never make any statements of that sort. I never have."

"But what if they force you to? What if there is no way out?" she said, pressing the point.

"I'll say to hell with it all, and that'll be that."

Wanda looked at me closely. "I won't try to talk you into anything. It has to be your decision. But swear to me, on the memory of our son, that we won't ever have to compromise our consciences."

"I swear."

The next day I called on Olszowski and accepted the post.

CHAPTER XXII

In mid-January 1972 I was officially installed in my new post as vice minister. I returned from a trip to Vietnam and walked into my spacious new office at the ministry. There was a crystal vase full of flowers on a small round table in one corner and a still life on the wall. My secretary, Comrade Janina, showed me in and informed me that she and another secretary, Barbara, would work alternate shifts to keep the work flowing smoothly. I sat down at my large, freshly lacquered desk, beside which was a cabinet containing a telephone installation with many buttons and lights that could be used for all possible types of communication—local, intercity, government, special high frequency, and direct lines to the minister, the vice ministers, and several Central Committee secretaries. On the other side of the room, in a niche, was a large, wood-covered safe for secret documents. As my eyes moved along those attributes of power, I asked myself how it all would end.

From my first day in my new post, I was involved in the work of the ministry's leadership team, known for short as "the leadership." It comprised the minister and three vice ministers—Stanislaw Trepczynski, the former director of Gomulka's secretariat, Jozef Czyrek, who had been promoted from department director, and me. The other two had been vice ministers for a year. Each vice minister directed his own division. My division included three territorial departments: North and South America, Asia, and Africa—that is, the entire world apart from Europe. Czyrek was in charge of Western Europe, and Trepczynski of the socialist countries. The leadership met once a week, usually on Tuesday, and worked for three or four hours at a time according to a set agenda approved by the minister.

The four of us established a good working relationship. Olszowski was not a trained diplomat and allowed his deputies considerable freedom. He never interfered in my duties; on the contrary, he often repeated that he had empowered me to act independently, especially in matters concerning the United States.

By that time the foreign service no longer held any riddles or mysteries for me; I had amalgamated my long experience in Warsaw with things learned at my posts in different corners of the world. I had more years of diplomatic service than the other members of the leadership combined, and so found my opinions given close attention and often prevailing in the making of decisions.

Working independently suited me. I had always liked making decisions and had no fear of taking responsibility. Now I had greater leeway for that sort of action. I was aware that to have the best ideas was not enough; a great deal depended on form, on the manner in which one handled things—more precisely, on deft usage of the ministry's "urgent notes." Those notes served as a sort of transmission belt to the authorities that made the final decisions—the Politburo, the Secretariat, and the Presidium of the government. Through urgent notes our ministry could transcend the bureaucracy and pass on information and submit proposals for approval quickly. Merit aside, it was important that these notes be succinct and to the point. They were to be distributed at once to a list clearly marked on the note itself, and recopied on special forms with borders whose color indicated their degree of secrecy and urgency. The "top's" decision would then be communicated by telephone to the minister or the vice ministers. Proficient in the use of that machinery, I set to work with a will.

My first efforts were ill-starred but instructive. While familiarizing myself with the state of Polish-American relations, I learned that four delegations, from various economic ministries, were about to leave for Washington, D.C., at the same time. Knowing from experience that such a confluence was bound, at the least, to baffle the Americans, I wrote an urgent note expressing my disapproval and recommending that a more sensible schedule be established. The next day, after work hours, I was at my desk when the government phone began to ring and its light to flash. I turned on the speaker.

A deep, resonant voice filled my office. "Spasowski?"

I recognized Jaroszewicz's voice at once. He must also have been using his speaker phone, because he sounded as if he were in a well.

"Listen, Spasowski, what's going on here? What do you mean by sending out an urgent note recommending that visits be postponed!"

"Comrade Premier, I sent out that recommendation . . ."

"By what right?" he shouted. "Who authorized you? Who are you to start scheduling the government's activities?" He fell silent.

I, too, said nothing. Then I heard a whisper, which became audible when I turned the volume on the speaker up to maximum. "This cannot be tolerated! He's allowing himself too much right from the start. . . . I gave the permission for those trips myself. He's known for sticking his nose in where it doesn't belong. . . . Put a stop to it."

"Why aren't you answering me?" roared the premier again.

Now angry myself, I did answer, and did so slowly and distinctly. "Things were not co-ordinated; the schedule is a mess. First no one was going, and now they are all going together."

"Don't lecture us! This had better be the last time!" The speaker crackled as he switched off.

A botched beginning. Lucky that I had the attitude I did. But who was that whispering to him, telling him that I had been butting in for a long time? Suddenly I knew that voice: of course, it was Mieczyslaw Jagielski, whom I had known since the sixties, when he had been minister of agriculture. Rapacki had at first sung paeans to him, but ceased to mention him at all after a time. Now Jagielski was terribly important—a full member of the Politburo, a vice premier, the head of the Planning Commission, and, as if all that were not enough, the permanent chairman of the Executive Committee of the Council for Mutual Economic Assistance (Comecon). He had taken the last position over from Jaroszewicz when the latter had become premier. Since that appointment, Jagielski had always been either coming from or going to Moscow.

I had had experience in the ministry, but before now I had had no clue as to how the power was really distributed. Two people obviously held the reins: the first secretary of the Party and the premier. Gierek, as the head of the Party, seemed to have considerably more say than the premier, who, they said, "governed" but did not "lead." I knew that there were three centers of power: the Politburo, the Secretariat, and the government. Those were teams, not individuals. I had no illusions about the Sejm. It was nothing more than a rubber-stamp parliament acting as directed by the Party, with the exception of a few—a dozen or so—independent and courageous delegates, chiefly Catholics. But over time I became convinced that the organizations were merely façades concealing the fact that the real power was held by only two people. And each of those two had his own trusted assistant to advise him, to relieve and replace him during absences. Gierek's was Franciszek Szlachcic; Jaroszewicz's was Mieczyslaw Jagielski, the man I had heard whispering to him.

I was, in the next few years, to observe the quiet but ruthless struggle between Jaroszewicz and Gierek. Jaroszewicz had an expanded state machine at his disposal and exercised his power from the large Council of Ministers building. Gierek was the head of the Party bureaucracy, which he directed from the formidable Central Committee building. Each had his base in Moscow, but each in a different way. There was a seeming paradox in this confrontation. But ruling the satellite countries is a highly refined art in the Kremlin. That art is based on using competition between two elements precisely in order to weaken both, and to learn, in the process of a given struggle, as much as possible when each side dutifully reports on the other to Moscow. The ancient method of *divide et impera* thus finds full and perhaps even improved application in the USSR's developed socialist society. The Kremlin can, for example, settle the internal problems of a satellite country, can assume the role of arbiter; it knows everything it needs to. I was to learn more of the ins and outs of this situation with the passage of time.

There was an essential difference between Jaroszewicz's and Gierek's forces that I initially failed to notice. Premier Jaroszewicz had complete authority over the country's economic affairs. In the Party Secretariat there was not even one secretary permanently or partially responsible for economic affairs, and those appointed later were mere figureheads. This was no accident. The most important thing to realize, however, was that Moscow was behind Jaroszewicz. He had inherited that backing from his predecessor, Cyrankiewicz, and, like him, was an agent, though in a different guise. Cyrankiewicz had been known to be a socialist, even a liberal. Jaroszewicz was more likely to strike a patriotic pose, as a former soldier and liberator of Poland. Moscow was able to effect its long-range plans for Poland through Jaroszewicz because the country's economy, including foreign commerce and finance, were in his hands alone.

Gierek and Szlachcic, I soon learned, were suspicious of Moscow and of Jaroszewicz. They were Communists, and thus had to have Moscow's support, but they were aware of Moscow's hypocrisy and deceit. They remembered Stalin and Gomulka. No doubt they hoped that by removing Moczar they had won Moscow's favor to some extent, but that was only an illusion. Moscow treated them the way it treats all Poles—as potential enemies. For Moscow, the only good Communist is an obedient one, and even then he is good only as long as he is useful. Thus it sought from the beginning to weaken Gierek's team by stripping it of the people most devoted to him. Round three of Moscow's purge of Poland had begun.

On entering the ruling circle, I was not aware of many of the system's little mechanisms. In the course of a talk at the Ministry of Foreign Trade, a veteran there sensed my ignorance and offered me some friendly, practical advice. "The most important thing is for Janusz to think well of you," he said.

"Janusz? Who's Janusz?" I asked.

"I can see you're a green one," he replied in surprise. "Janusz Wieczorek, in the Council of Ministers."

"What can he do?" I asked.

He shook his head, clearly dismayed by my inexperience. "Anything! You should only know. He can arrange *anything* for you or for me and for all the other ministers, even for the first secretary, the members of the Politburo, the Central Committee secretaries. This is the first time I've run into anyone like you. Didn't you ever use a government hospital?"

"Not really."

"What kind of people are you anyway? You should know that if your family needs to use a government hospital, Janusz is the man to see. You go to him if you want to change apartments. He'll sell you a car at the official rate. He's the man if you want a vacation in a government resort. He gives you hard currency to fly to France in the summer, or to Italy. Whatever you want, he takes care of it. You want a lot outside the city to build a villa or a bungalow? Ask Janusz! He's very important. He's the one, after all, who gives out the envelopes . . . You don't know about that either? My God! Those are the bonuses for doing good work that we get every three months, sometimes every six months, from the premier. Janusz calls people in one by one. He asks you what's new. Finally he gives you a sealed envelope with your name on it and the amount penciled in lightly on one side. You sign a receipt, or sometimes you don't even do that—he just checks you off his list. Then you say good-bye very politely, take your money, and go. The amount varies, twenty thousand zlotys, sometimes even up to forty. Our minister happens to be an old war buddy of the premier. He won't admit it, but he probably gets around thirty-five. Recently I got an extra fifteen thousand from Janusz to fix up my apartment."

"We are allotted money for that?" I asked.

"Just write a nice letter and ask for it. He'll give it to you."

"What do you mean? Either we have it allotted to us or we don't. There have to be rules."

"No. There aren't any. That's just the point. I'm telling you, it's all up to Janusz. That's why it's important that he like you. People who go abroad bring him back nice presents. He likes that a lot. . . ."

I could feel my anger rising. What does that make the Polish government, then, Janusz's private farm?

"Last year he allocated me money so my wife could shop for clothes in West Berlin," he continued, blithely ignoring my ire, and boasting now. "This year we're flying to France. I've already asked for an allocation, but he made no promises. He only says, 'Come by! We'll have a little talk.' That means he'll give me five hundred dollars, maybe more. Full ministers get more, and the Central Committee secretaries and Politburo members get even more. He knows everyone, he knows who gets what. No bureaucracy, no delay. He writes 'To be paid' on your request, signs his name, and the cash is in your pocket. He also allocates apartments, which are always in short supply. The cost runs into the millions there. . . ."

"How does he decide who gets what? Who tells him?"

"I don't know. No one does. He and the premier probably make up a list of who gets the most. You'll meet him soon, no doubt, and you couldn't meet a nicer guy, although he can be gruff and arrogant and tell you bluntly that he has nothing for you and good-bye. At a meeting of the Council of Ministers, just watch. Everyone bows to him first, even the vice premiers, and his return greeting depends on your standing with him. Sometimes he bows his head deeply and smiles, and sometimes so little you can barely see it."

It was my first practical lesson on how to live the comfortable life under people's socialism.

When I filled Wanda in on the conversation later, she said, "Those methods remind me of absolute monarchies, medieval tyrannies. But at least back then they never sounded off about Communism and bragged about being people's democracies. It's getting harder and harder for me to live with all that."

"What do you mean?" I asked.

"I've noticed the people on our street looking back over their shoulders when the black ministry limousine pulls up for you at the house or brings you home. And that tall woman who lives alone across from us—the one who takes her dog out for walks and lives on the top floor—sometimes I see her in her window sitting on the windowsill with her dog. She doesn't walk down our side of the street any more. Since you've become vice minister, I'm well aware what people think. But I feel the worst when I go to buy meat, to that special store for high government officials. It's always filled with wonderful things, but the regular stores have nothing, just people standing in line, waiting, waiting. . . ."

"But you use that meat to help so many people. You give it away, we eat very little of it ourselves. The ability to do that must give you some satisfaction."

"Yes, it gives me satisfaction, but at what price?"

There was no doubt that we were among the ruling elite, living considerably better than the overwhelming majority of Polish society. My salary was now twice what it had been before.

"Yes, it's too high a price," I replied, thinking of another cost that was being exacted of me: my personal time. I was getting home later and later and being called on the government phone at all hours of the night.

Of course our duties also included attending the diplomatic receptions given by the ambassadors whose countries were within the purview of my division. These receptions were entirely different from those given abroad, where we had usually been the only Poles. Here we often found ourselves in the company of high Party and government officials.

The most sumptuous receptions were held in Jablonna, about ten miles north of Warsaw. We were there frequently, at the eighteenth-century palace that had once belonged to the primate. It was there that I heard more than one ironic remark from foreign ambassadors to the effect that the Polish Communists surround themselves with palaces and are able somehow to reconcile sumptuous receptions with revolutionary ideology. That paradox amused them, and our people laughed along with them. I found the ironies deplorable and cringed at the thought of hearing them tossed about in frivolous quips over drinks. But the ironies were even more excruciating if one stopped to think about them. The palace was reminiscent of old Poland, after all, a Poland that had once been rich, powerful, independent; one of the largest states in Europe. That state had been ravaged by its neighbors, robbed of its wealth, stripped of its power. All that remained of it were buildings, often in ruins. Those few that had been restored were quiet reminders of our glorious past.

After one reception at Jablonna, Minister Olszowski invited his three deputies and their wives to travel by sleigh to Jadwisin Palace, which was run by the Council of Ministers, that is, by the infamous Janusz Wieczorek. At a distance we seemed to be approaching a forest, but it was a large park surrounded by concrete posts and chain-wire fencing. Soldiers from the Internal Security Corps were at the gate and checked all our documents closely before we were allowed in. The paved road wound through the trees in the park; the greenery, the freshness of the air, and the tranquillity were all enchanting. As we drove into a large clearing, a lovely period building came into view, the palace of the Radziwills. On each side, prefab wooden houses imported from Scandinavia were set among the trees. Olszowski's was one of these. I spent a moment enjoying the trees and the air, but my colleagues immediately got out the whiskey and began heavy drinking, their tongues and manners loosening. Wanda and I returned at once to Warsaw, swearing that we would never allow ourselves to be talked into attending another such function. Indeed, it was at once our first and our last time at an interoffice gathering.

Elections to the Sejm were held in March. Wanda did not want to vote, but I argued that since I had agreed to become a vice minister we had to. I was aware that I was participating in a fiction by voting for the Front of National Unity candidates—all of them proposed by the Party—but like most Poles I read the election as a referendum. It was an opportunity to voice our hope for a better future, one that was, in our minds, connected with Gierek. We were not voting for the authorities, the Party, or the Front, but for Edward Gierek. The press reported that twenty-two million people turned out and ninety-nine percent of the vote went to the Front. Czeslaw sneered that it was all too reminiscent of Soviet elections. For him it was a rigged election; for him no Communist regime had real support in Poland, no matter who headed it.

At the beginning of April, I went to see Olszowski to discuss Vietnamese affairs, but he had other plans for me.

"Szlachcic called. He wants to talk with you immediately."

"Any idea what it's about?" I asked.

"I don't know. Maybe Vietnam. You were just there, weren't you? In any case, get right over there; it's urgent."

I had not been to the Central Committee building for quite some time. Only people with passes were allowed in, but my ID proved sufficient. I was pointed toward a courtyard, through which I would have to pass. There my papers were checked again. I took the staircase in the marble hall to the second floor. My papers were checked for a third time when I entered a corridor there. Szlachcic was just finishing a briefing session in his office. The massive doors opened, and out trooped several Party secretaries.

Szlachcic greeted me warmly. "So, you're working on American affairs now?" he began.

"Yes, and not only American affairs. Asian and African, too."

"They're not important. The United States is what counts. It's a world power and friendly to Poland. But you know America; I don't have to tell you. Did you know that President Nixon will be visiting Moscow?"

"Yes. But has it been confirmed?"

"It has. I have it on good authority." Polish intelligence was, after all, under Szlachcic's jurisdiction. "Listen carefully. This is why I called you in, and it's for your ears only. Remember that. Number One wants Nixon to visit Warsaw as well."

I was flabbergasted. "I think that's a very good idea. We'll talk with the U.S. ambassador about it."

"It's not that simple," he replied. "Listen closely. The Americans should propose the idea of a visit *themselves.* Not us. Understand?"

My eyes must have widened.

"Yes, it must be their initiative. How you arrange this is your business. But it has to be their idea, and that's that," he repeated emphatically.

"Aha, I see. It'll need some thought."

"I'll be frank with you," he said, lowering his voice to a whisper. "Not everything is as simple as it looks here. Jaroszewicz and his people want to run things their way, the old way, but we don't think that the Soviets have to know *everything*." With that he struck his desk with his fist. "When did they ever tell *us* the truth? You weren't born yesterday; you know what I mean! In any case, this is what Number One wants and *he's right!*"

"I understand perfectly," I replied. "And I share your views one hundred percent. You don't have to explain Soviet policy and diplomacy to me. They only do what they think is good for them. Everyone else gets trampled."

"Exactly."

"I'll think about the Nixon visit. Do you want to know how I do it or are you giving me a free hand?"

"Do as you see fit. You have a free hand. But remember that this is a very important and delicate matter. No one outside the three of us—Number One, you, and me—is to know that it's we who want it. The fewer people involved the better."

I left his office with a great sense of satisfaction. At last I would be able to make a genuinely positive contribution toward bringing Poland closer to the United States.

The official phone was ringing as I returned to my office.

"What did Szlachcic want?" asked Olszowski.

"He wanted to hear my thoughts about Vietnam," I replied, lying without hesitation.

How was I to go about such a delicate mission? It was not so simple. In the first place, I did not trust my office at the ministry. I knew there were listening devices in the telephones. Second, how could I be sure the Americans would keep it a secret? They might not realize the issue's relevance. Or perhaps they would use it to play Warsaw off against Moscow. I could not take that risk. I came to the conclusion that I would have to delude both Olszowski and the American Ambassador Walter Stoessel.

Fate was on my side: Stoessel requested an appointment. As it happened, I had been meeting with him quite often during that time, usually at his request, in connection with reuniting Polish-American families. During this conversation, I asked innocently, as if to satisfy my curiosity, if it were true that Nixon was going to Moscow. He said that there were such plans but that he had no further information. Judging by the glance he cast me, he had made a mental note of my question. As usual, I wrote an urgent note stating that the subject of Nixon's visit to the Soviet Union "to which the Americans attach great significance" had come up during my meeting with Stoessel.

I spoke with Stoessel again a few days later and asked if he knew any more "on the subject we discussed earlier." At this point he must have realized that he was not dealing with my personal curiosity alone; he said a little something about the preparations but was still restrained. In my next urgent note I indicated that Stoessel had returned to the subject he had raised previously and was probing our interest in a visit by Nixon to Warsaw. After reading his copy, Olszowski said to me that my reports were important, that he had spoken about them with Szlachcic, and that it was clear Number One had also taken an interest in the subject.

A few days later Stoessel came to see me with the information that Washington was considering a visit to Warsaw immediately after Nixon's visit to the Soviet Union. I replied in a loud voice that I would pass the American initiative on to the highest leadership. I said the same in my next urgent note, which I passed to Olszowski for his initials. He summoned me at once.

"Comrade Romuald," he began, a serious expression on his face, "Comrade Franciszek [Szlachcic] has instructed me to inform you that Number One will raise this issue at the very next session of the Politburo."

"But the note hasn't been sent around yet," I said, astounded.

"Yes, but I read it to him over the phone," he replied. "And he informed Gierek at once, and Gierek called back to say he'd be bringing it up to the Politburo. But keep all this to yourself."

A short while later I was authorized to pass on our invitation to President Nixon.

I went back over my urgent notes to be sure that anyone reading them would have the impression that the subject had arisen spontaneously and that the initiative had been the American ambassador's. The most important thing was that all this match up with any possible Soviet bugging of our conversations. There had to be nothing contradictory, nothing suspicious.

It was to be the first time a U.S. president had visited Poland. Therefore it sparked the interest of everyone, although reactions varied greatly. Some people in the ministry congratulated me, saying that here I had just assumed my post and had already arranged a "Polish-American summit meeting." But some hard-liners in the Party Central Committee were critical: What's he coming here for? We have no use for a superimperialist of his stripe! The people in Security grumbled: The reactionaries will be raising their heads soon enough! We just got finished with them in December 1970 and now they're starting up again! Colonel Gorecki, chief of the Office of Government Security (BOR), was miserable. "It's not enough we have to protect our own people; now we have to protect that son of a bitch, too! Whose idea was that?" he asked, giving me an evil look. His long dislike of me had inspired him to suspect that the visit was my doing.

Szlachcic and Olszowski made me chief co-ordinator of the preparations. Not only would I be responsible for working up the political background information, but I would have to establish the agenda with the Americans, write the final communiqué, chair the groups formed to make the preparations, and report on it at Central Committee conferences. I would return home at night, my head packed with problems, horrified by how difficult it was to get anything done with a Party-state bureaucracy as dogmatic as ours.

One day Szlachcic said to me abruptly, "Let's go see Number One."

Security wanted to check my documents at the entrance to the corridor where Gierek's office was located, but Szlachcic waved the guards away. I was never asked for my papers again after that. Szlachcic strode into Gierek's office without knocking.

"Here I am," he said simply. "Let me introduce Comrade Spasowski."

Gierek's face was ruddy, appeared healthy; his hair was short and bristly. His steel gray suit, beautifully tailored, fit him perfectly, complemented by a pearl gray tie. He was in patent leather shoes. I was surprised and put off, thinking a dandy's attire out of keeping with Gierek's position.

"We've already met, Comrade First Secretary," I told him. "We were on the same plane to London a few years back."

Gierek thought for a moment, then confirmed it with a smile. "That's right. I remember. We talked about the United States. Well, here we are doing the same thing again." He was in a good mood and completely at ease.

I briefed him on the preparations, telling him that we were making good progress in all areas except economic affairs. The Ministry of Foreign Trade was hiding behind the premier and saying that the Council of Ministers would handle economic and financial affairs independently, that the Ministry of Foreign Affairs had nothing to do with it. The glances that Gierek and Szlachcic exchanged when I said this seemed to indicate they were long familiar with this sort of thing.

"We know what the situation is, Comrade Spasowski. Don't be discouraged. Keep at it. Piotr is a difficult person, stubborn, and has all sorts of people lurking around him," he said, with a wave of his hand. "We'll come to terms with all of them little by little. Right now the most important thing is to have the visit run smoothly, so that a good climate is created in Polish-American relations." He eyed me, and I nodded in full agreement. "This is just a beginning," he continued, satisfied with my show of affiliation. "Life moves on. We need an eye on the future. New possibilities are opening up; we're moving onto the world stage. *The world stage!* A nation of thirty million people can't be stopped. Don't be discouraged by Jaroszewicz's obstinacy. Keep at it at your end. You see, Poland has to defend its own interests. If we don't, who will?" I returned to the ministry bursting with hope.

On the day Nixon flew to Moscow, May 22, Szlachcic phoned me with instructions to gather any press response to Nixon's visit to the Soviet Union and to the bombing of Hanoi and to pass it on to him before Nixon arrived in Warsaw. Four days later word came that Nixon and Brezhnev had signed an important agreement on the limitation of strategic weapons. The Polish press gave the story a lot of play, saying that the world was on the road to peace and security, thanks to the Soviet Union. That enthusiasm was shared at the ministry, and again I was congratulated and told that Nixon's visit could not have been at a more auspicious time, despite the bombing raids in Vietnam.

Those were my thoughts as well. I did not know that the world had entered a period of détente, that the years 1972 and 1973 would later go down in Soviet-American diplomatic history as nothing more than a few euphoric years. I thought that the agreement in Moscow signaled the end of the nuclear threat.

"I'll tell you what I think about that," Wanda's brother Czeslaw said to me. "Nixon's visit to Moscow must be the eighth Soviet-American summit, not counting the one in Paris in 1960 that fell apart because a U-2 spy plane was forced down over the Soviet Union. What have those summits achieved? One: the Teheran Conference, with Stalin, Churchill, and Roosevelt, only strengthened the Soviet Union, which two years before had allied itself to Nazi Germany. The initial agreements that eventually determined Poland's borders were made there. Two: Yalta. The Soviets were made a gift of Central and Eastern Europe. Three: Potsdam made the betrayal at Yalta official and promised that East Germany would be democratized—Soviet-style, that is—and that the Nazis would be punished. As a result, Stalin's criminals were at Nuremberg with the other Allies to try Hitler's criminals, and all with the full majesty of international law. Four: Geneva in 1955 produced nothing either, because the Soviets were interested only in confirming their possessions and, as we know, they had stolen more than they could digest. Five: the so-called spirit of Camp David in 1959, another illusion; nothing came of it. Six: in Vienna in 1961 they only talked and issued a communiqué—about Laos. Seven: Glassboro, 1967—they only talked; nothing was done. What good was any of that? The Soviets were interested only in having the world recognize what they had actually stolen and maintained with force. On what basis am I to believe that this summit in Moscow will not serve the same ends as the previous ones? I don't recognize you," Czeslaw said. "You were always a Communist but you used your head, you thought critically. Now you're a goddamned minister and you've started believing their rubbish about agreements, summits. . . . Hah!"

A few days before Nixon's arrival I received a call from Ryszard Karski, the vice minister of foreign trade.

"I wondered whether there are any moroccan leather folders over at your ministry?"

"Moroccan leather? You must mean plain leather. What do you need them for?"

There was a moment of silence before Karski said, "I have instructions from the premier to put the financial memorandum for Nixon in a *moroccan* leather folder."

"I'll check on it right away," I said, intrigued. "But do me a favor. Bring me the memorandum so I can read it."

Karski paused. "All right, but just to read. Check on the folder. I'll be right over."

Within fifteen minutes Karski was in my office. "I can't leave this with you," he said, handing me the paperbound memorandum. "But go ahead and read it. Did you get the moroccan leather folder?"

"My secretary's checking on it," I replied, turning to the memorandum. The more I read, the greater my astonishment grew. The Polish People's Republic was asking the United States for a loan of several billion dollars.

"Premier Jaroszewicz is going to give this to Nixon?" I asked. Karski nodded. "How did he arrive at that figure?"

Karski shrugged his shoulders. "I don't know. I guess he worked it out with Jagielski. How should I know? They tell us to write something, we write it."

"But that's an enormous amount of money! Even if Nixon wanted to lend us that much, they wouldn't be able to budget for it."

"That's what I think, too," he answered. "They can't expect that kind of money from the American budget. Maybe they're thinking of private capital. Who knows with them? They told us to write it up, and that's what we did."

I returned the memorandum to Karski just as my secretary came in to announce that we had no moroccan leather folders.

Karski rose. "I showed you the memorandum because you asked to see it. But it was only for you. Remember, don't say anything to anyone on top about it, or anyone below you either. Jaroszewicz would kill me."

"Don't worry; it won't get beyond me."

I kept my word. No one learned of the memorandum from me, either then or later. Jaroszewicz handed it personally to Nixon, and that was the last anyone heard of it. The Americans never responded, as far as I know, and I soon forgot about it.

I remembered it a few years later, however, when, after the Seventh Party Congress, it became plain to me that Jaroszewicz was "governing" but Gierek was not "leading." The power had clearly gone into Jaroszewicz's hands. I asked myself if Jaroszewicz and his man Jagielski could have drawn up a memorandum of that sort without approval from Moscow. Obviously not. The contents had to have been co-ordinated with the Soviets. The year 1972 was one of euphoric détente, and Moscow plainly had wished to turn the general good will to its financial advantage. Poland had been used before to initiate various political actions. Why not have Poland sound out the West to see just how willing it was to pay for peace and cooperation, and, if it was, how much? A crude probe, but a calculated one. Jaroszewicz had carried out his assignment obediently, dutifully reaching for the moon with his leather folder. What a good laugh Moscow must have had at the sight: the Polish premier dangling as if he were a hook poised to catch the golden American fish.

Stoessel insisted that the schedule for the visit be spelled out before Nixon set foot in Poland. One question, a delicate one, had dragged on since the beginning; Nixon wanted to meet with the Polish primate, Stefan Cardinal Wyszynski, whom the Polish government considered a troublesome anti-Communist thorn in its side. At several briefings at the Central Committee and with Szlachcic, I was informed that our position was inflexible on this point—a meeting was out of the question. We were at an impasse for weeks. The issue kept going back and forth. Stoessel argued that on the way into Warsaw, by the route already fixed, the president could enter St. John's Cathedral, where I had once sought refuge from the Germans, and meet with the cardinal there. That proposal seemed to me worthy of consideration. I presented the idea to the Central Committee secretaries. Their reaction was more than simply negative; they became verbally abusive and criticized me for my naïveté. With spirited invective, they said that the ambassador had slyly managed to sell me an old proposal in a new package.

With all that pressure, I took a more rigid position in my talks with Stoessel. As usual, he was polite, but I could sense irritation in his voice.

"We're talking about the cathedral now, not the meeting," he argued.

"Unfortunately, he cannot go in," I replied.

"Even for a look?"

"I've told you what the official decision is, Mr. Ambassador. I personally cannot arrange this for you." It was left hanging in the air. I had tremendous respect for Stoessel, and was sorry to disappoint him.

My final meeting with the ambassador took place as Nixon was flying in on Air Force One. We met in the conference room usually reserved for interministry talks. Stoessel was accompanied by advisers from the "advance party," and I by department directors.

"At this very moment," he said, "the plane is over the Ukraine on its way to Poland. It's high time we finished discussing the schedule. What is going to happen with St. John's Cathedral?"

"I share your desire to conclude these points once and for all," I replied. "But I have nothing new to add."

"Mr. Vice Minister"—Stoessel's face was hard, and he was speaking in an official tone—"we have just received an inquiry about this point from the president's plane. It's very important to the president that this matter be clarified now. Will he or will he not be going into the cathedral?"

"I have nothing to add," I replied.

Stoessel did not answer, and our silence lasted quite some time.

Suddenly I heard a metallic voice that seemed to be coming from a tin can. "Well, how come he's not saying anything?" It sounded like Donald Duck.

I looked around in amazement. There was an air of consternation at the table, and then suddenly everyone burst into laughter. Stoessel glanced reproachfully at the man sitting beside him. Clearly the voice had come from under his jacket. Stoessel asked me to disregard this minor incident, and we moved on to other matters. Only later did Stoessel tell me what had happened. Our conversation was being relayed live to President Nixon's plane. Losing patience with our silence, someone on the plane had piped up.

On the day before the president's arrival, a briefing had been called for all ministries and departments involved. Secretary Stanislaw Kania had outlined the security measures for specific points of the schedule.

"Around five hundred people have been assigned to welcome Nixon at the airport," he announced, "a few from Security and the rest from among Party activists. They've been instructed to be friendly, to smile, to wave white-and-red flags, but to do so with a sense of moderation . . . and dignity. The police will be thick along the route in from the airport. Our people will be at all the intersections and turns. At one point they will even stop the car so the people can be seen greeting Nixon spontaneously."

Szlachcic nodded in approval.

"Traffic will be barricaded throughout the city so that the motorcade can pass by quickly and so no random crowds can gather. We're bringing in a lot of people from other cities to make up the crowds. Our own people from Security have been instructed to take the first row along the streets. They'll work with the Party people to keep hostile and rabble-rousing elements away. They know that if there's any insubordination or too enthusiastic cheering, they're to call the police . . . to protect the president's security, that is."

Everyone agreed.

"Nixon's walk through the Old City will make for the biggest problem, because there could be spontaneous demonstrations there if people suddenly start coming out of their houses. What's more, we can't be certain that Nixon won't go into the cathedral. So far, our people haven't detected any unusual preparations there on the part of the church, but the responsibility for seeing that he doesn't go in rests with Comrade Spasowski. Our people have orders to block his way if he tries to go in and to inform him that the cathedral could be a security risk because it has not been checked out."

"Well done," said Szlachcic. "The most important thing, Comrade Kania, is that walk through the Old City. You must be sure that good, responsible Party activists are positioned in the doorways and stores along the way. People *must* be restricted to their houses. Nobody is to go out. After all, our task is to protect a head of state—that's nothing to be ashamed of. Understand that, all of you: we're protecting the president of the United States! Clear out the market. Fill it up with young people from Security, in civilian clothes naturally. They should sit at the café tables under the umbrellas. Issue them money; let them eat pastries and ice cream, drink juice, whatever they want. And they should be with the prettiest girls from Security in their most colorful clothes. They should be laughing; spirits should be high. But *naturally,* not forced, to make the right impression on Nixon. Understand?" he concluded.

"Yes, I understand," replied Kania obediently.

I was ashamed to be part of that circus. I thought about the thousands, the hundreds of thousands of Poles who sincerely desired to welcome the president of the United States.

I must have been called by the entire top that day, but I remember only one call clearly. I picked up the receiver and heard a screechy voice say, "Comrade Minister Spasowski, this is the administrative director. I've been instructed by Comrade Premier Piotr Jaroszewicz to ask you for a decision . . ." He broke off for a noisy drag on his cigarette. "Comrade Premier wants a decision about tomorrow's banquet: should beef be served, first-class beef of course, or quail? Comrade Premier places the responsibility for the decision on you, Comrade Minister. It's a very important matter; we want to make the right impression. . . ."

I covered the receiver with my hand, cursed foully, then shouted, "Quail will do!" and hung up.

President Nixon's visit lasted a mere twenty-four hours. And it went off like clockwork. At the airport it was people from Security and Party activists who were waving the little flags; I do not know if Nixon had any idea whose hands he was shaking as he walked past. A great many ordinary people came out to line the roads, but the activists kept them away from the front rows. The president drove by Zygmunt's Column and then went on foot to the Old City market. To my extraordinary relief, he did not stop in front of the cathedral. The young people sitting at the cafés beneath yellow and green umbrellas were so absorbed in cheerful conversation that they paid little attention to him. In Victory Square he laid a wreath at the Tomb of the Unknown Soldier, and it was there, immediately after the ceremony, that a spontaneous demonstration occurred. People broke through the police cordon to cheer the president. There was an uproar as the crowds ran toward Nixon and the police blew their whistles. At one moment I thought I saw the president's figure rise above the crowd, lifted by the arms of the cheering throng, everyday Poles, not Party activists and Security men. The Central Committee and the Soviet Embassy expressed their acute displeasure afterward, and Kania was reprimanded.

Late that evening—after Nixon's meeting with Gierek and the banquet honoring President and Mrs. Nixon (at which, to my dismay, I saw everyone gnawing with difficulty at their quail)—Stoessel came to my office to prepare the final document, the Joint Polish-American Communiqué to be signed by Nixon and Gierek.

The next day, President Nixon met with Premier Jaroszewicz. I never learned what was said, but I did come to know that Jaroszewicz handed Nixon that leather folder.

At last, after the plenary talks and after a lunch hosted by Nixon, his motorcade headed for the airport. I was elated. The talks had been businesslike and friendly. The final document was good, constructive. It expressed support for the European Conference on Security and Co-operation, announced that bilateral relations would be developed, and established a Joint Polish-American Trade Commission. Polish-American relations had moved on to a new level. My only source of anxiety was Jaroszewicz's secrecy and his folder. Of his intentions I knew little; in fact, apart from generalities, I had handled only one matter for him: the decision in favor of quail.

CHAPTER XXIII

Not five days after the U.S. president's departure, Fidel Castro flew to Warsaw.

"We came to see friends, and what do we see?" asked Castro, straight out in the conference room, his eyes darting in all directions. "Nixon's been here! An imperialist whose planes are bombing Hanoi! *You had that criminal here.* And I've heard about the welcome he got," he said, with another defiant look around the room. "Where's your internationalism? He's bombing our Vietnamese comrades and you have him as a guest! And you want me to talk with you, as one Communist to another!" He was shouting.

I leaned forward to peer over at Gierek. His chin was trembling with anger.

"Comrade Fidel!" Gierek began, his voice quivering, "We want to talk reasonably. You've begun with that point, and we can explain it—but not in this sort of tone."

"I don't need explanations!" cried Castro. "Your actions speak for themselves."

"Comrade Fidel, we cannot discuss things in this way," said Gierek, attempting to be conciliatory. "And besides, you're aware that we were not the only ones to receive Nixon while Hanoi was being bombed. We weren't the *only* ones, Comrade Fidel!" he repeated emphatically. "We understand that you're upset. It wasn't easy for us either. We told . . . *I* told Nixon what I thought of all that."

"What you said to Nixon is of little concern to me," snorted Castro. "And don't compare yourselves to *others.* They're not you!"

he said gruffly, glancing wildly about the room. He was about to add something else but was interrupted by Szlachcic's fist, which came slamming down on the table.

"Comrade Fidel!" Szlachcic roared. "We also know how to hand out insults! Don't forget that. You're going too far."

Castro stared furiously at Szlachcic. Clearly he had not expected a threat of that sort. An icy atmosphere descended over both delegations, and we sat across from one another in silence.

Castro did not leave Poland right away, but went to Lansk for private talks with Gierek. I, too, was there, to negotiate the joint declaration with the Cubans.

It was my first trip to Lansk, a "resort" area where confidential high-level talks were frequently held with other "fraternal" parties. Only twenty people had access to the place, members of the Politburo and Central Committee secretaries. Run by the secret police, it was on no map, and there were no road signs to it. Our cars sped for nearly two hours down highways and then suddenly turned onto a narrow forest road. We came to a barrier guarded by Army Security Corps (KBW) sentries armed with submachine guns. We drove then onto a paved road. KBW patrols were posted among the trees; a metal fence and small telephone booths attached to the trees were testimonies to the high degree of security.

Minutes later our cars pulled into an open space surrounded by large trees and a number of luxurious buildings. In the near distance I could see a silver lake, its surface gleaming; there was a dock and several prefab wooden houses. It was clear that Lansk was a paradise, a well-appointed one.

Gierek later told me that Castro's anger had eventually subsided at Lansk, and that he had asked for us to schedule a talk at which he could address an audience of Polish youth. Within twenty-four hours I was on a Tutka, a little Soviet-built plane, headed for Krakow with Castro at my side.

Castro spoke in the newly constructed university square. The young people listened to the translation sentence by sentence, under the spell of his histrionics. He was practiced at speaking through an interpreter, and knew when to gesture and when to stop. Whenever the word "Poland" was mentioned, he would wait for the obligatory roar of approval.

"I know whom I'm talking to: you're Poland's future!" he shouted, to applause from every side. "The revolutionary future of your country will depend on you, the young people of Poland!"

There were cries of "Bravo, Fidel!" and from one group came the chant "*Fi*-del . . . *Fi*-del . . . *Fi*-del!"

"You don't need to be taught to look to the future. *There* is where a revolutionary instinctively looks! Looking backward is not your way. All of capitalism's rotten temptations don't matter to you, the automobiles, the flashy poison!"

He broke off. There was an angry whistling from the windows, and the crowd on the square had begun to boo.

"But we do want cars!" shouted a student standing nearby.

"We want to live like anyone else!"

Castro was struck dumb. The interpreter whispered in his ear. He had clearly been caught by surprise, his notions of Polish youth were dispelled.

The secretary of the provincial committee leaned over to me and hissed in my ear, "What humiliation! They've done it to us this time. It's always like that with our young people, comrade. You never know with them."

I returned to the hotel hoping that Castro would sleep and forget, but the next day I learned from a security officer that Castro had not slept at all. He had ordered that he be taken around the city, nearly until morning.

"I'll tell you about it," said the officer. "It was a warm night, and you could say that he went for a walk. Old Krakow is impressive, the medieval walls, the stone buildings, the big market, the little market, Cloth Hall, moonlight. It was beautiful, and even I, an old Krakovian, was moved by the sight. Fidel wanted to go to a bar, but it was too late. Krakow goes to bed early, and they were all closed. And I couldn't very well take him to one of our cabarets. The streets were empty, not a soul in sight. Castro walked over to an old man sitting on the steps of a building and called over the interpreter.

" 'Tell him I'm Fidel Castro.'

"The old man did not understand. 'Who are you?' he asked.

" 'My name is Fidel Castro, and I'm the first secretary and premier of the revolutionary government of Cuba.'

"The old man still could not make heads or tails of him. 'Sorry, never heard of it.'

"Castro began explaining to him what Cuba was and what revolution was.

"The old man heard him out and then rasped, 'Cuba? Good, so there's a Cuba. But I'm in Krakow, and we've had it up to here with revolution.' "

Despite an air of activity at the ministry I began for the first time in my life to feel physically weak. When I complained of this to Wanda, she said that I was overtired, which did not surprise her, because, as she said, I was not just working but was "plowing uphill."

My birthday came. Wanda and I planned to go to the cemetery after work and then spend a quiet evening at home together. But that day I was barely able to drag myself to the ministry. I was examined by a doctor there and then taken home. After a difficult night, Wanda called an ambulance to take me to the Ministry of Health Hospital. I collapsed on arrival and lost all sense of time. When I regained consciousness, I was flat on my back in a bed covered with a white quilt. A rigid pain rammed its way from my larynx to my heart, like a stone pipe, and another deep band of pain circled my stomach. I soon realized there were wires and tubes plugged into my body, that I was hooked up to a life-support system. Shudders coursed through me now and again. All the parts of my body seemed to be working separately, dissonantly. Only my mind operated normally, and in my clearest moments I was certain that they were my last.

The room was nearly dark, the curtains drawn tight. There was a soft groan beside me. Straining my eyes, I could make out another bed, another person lying as motionlessly as I. Somewhere in the corridor a bell rang, and the surprise of it sent a shiver and a sharp pain shooting through my body. My mind was working constantly, fitfully, summoning image after image—the streets of New Delhi, the residence, Kaytus, Wanda, ruins, then suddenly the airport, Nixon, Gierek . . . Another shudder shot through me. Everything seemed to lose importance, size; nothing mattered. And then, quite suddenly again, everything mattered. I cried out for my wife, my daughter, my mother. I was overcome by despair, by the realization that I was leaving life as a man without hope. Kaytus's face passed slowly before me; his words came softly, "Don't leave me, Father!" Oh, God, I had betrayed my son and now it was my turn to die. My father appeared at a desk before me looking downcast as he reached for a carafe of water. "Nein!" spat a taut voice. Wanda appeared again, holding Misia by the hand. She called out to me, but I could not understand what she was saying. Wanda, come back! But she dissolved into thin air. I was leaving the two of them to the mercies of fate in a cruel world that I had helped create. Everything went black.

I awoke to see the glass wall that was behind my head reflected in a mirror in front of me. Past the glass, lights were flashing on green screens. Heartbeats. Suddenly I was afraid of the pain, afraid of death. Oh, to die quietly. But did I deserve an easy death? Neither my father nor my son had been so fortunate.

And where would I go? To the next world? What did I know of all that? Surely something would have to remain of me. Something—my mind, my center, perhaps my soul. Wanda was always saying that Kaytus had such a good, pure soul. And mine? Better not think about it. I had wanted death to come before, but it had not shown itself. Now, when I wanted to live, it was making its undeniable approach. Why had I not frozen to death on the Bug River? Why had I not been killed by German bombs? Why had the Gestapo not put a bullet through my head?

I had lived through so much and understood so little. Only once, in Assisi, with my family asleep beside me and a thin tent over my head, had I understood, known anything remotely spiritual. Until then I had considered justice the most important thing and thought I was walking a straight path. How crooked my way had been!

Suddenly the white outline of a nurse appeared before me. She bent over me, looked into my face, then stepped to one side. A second nurse appeared, and, behind her, Wanda, at the foot of my bed gazing lovingly at me, smiling through her tears. I could not speak, but managed to move one hand in recognition. I tried to memorize the way she looked at that moment so that I would be able to summon her image in my last minutes. She made the sign of the cross over me and walked away. Time passed. Wanda came every day. She stood by my bed for a moment and then left. Later I learned that a nurse whom friends of ours knew had allowed her briefly into intensive care. Each time she gazed at me with eyes so full of love that they gave me the strength to fight for my life. I was determined not to leave her alone in the world.

A week passed. The pain in my chest and stomach eased; I could even move a little. The cardiologist informed me that the crisis had passed, but added that I would have to stay on the life-support system; they had not yet been able to diagnose my illness. Wanda set two books on my table: the Old Testament, the brown-covered edition I had read in India, and a second book, its cover orange. Intrigued, I picked it up and read the title, *Roads Leading to Rome*, by Jan Gawronski, a Pole from Volhynia. The first line read, "Every civilized person has two countries, his own and Italy." I began leafing through the book, attracted by its remoteness to my way of thinking, by the unexpected connections it made. The nurses tried to take it from me, saying that I was overdoing it, but I refused to give it up.

Wanda's instincts had been right again. That book transported me to another world, which, at that time, I needed every bit as much as I needed air to breathe. Its opening pages evoked the origins of the eternal city. I could see it all in my mind's eye: the streets of Rome, the vast squares, the magnificence. I read aloud, drinking in every word. Illustrious men, great virtues, great deeds. But why had so many Romans taken their own lives? Rome was great, but its cruelty was as great, and it had not known mercy and goodness.

I tore myself away from the book, from the sounds of Latin throbbing in my ears. It had been no accident that my father, probably the greatest Polish atheist of the century, had written in a trembling hand that he was a *civis universitatis,* a citizen of the world. Perhaps it had also been no accident that he had read Plutarch aloud to me. Was my poor dear father regarding me now from the next world?

I reflected apprehensively on the effects reading about the birth of Christianity would have on me. The news of Christ's birth had come to Rome as a revelation, as something the world had not known previously—love, goodness, faith in one God, redemption, salvation. The first to accept the teaching were the least important of people—the poor, the slaves, the oppressed; to all appearances, a modest start. The Gospel took root in the capital of the empire amid fire and crime, amid the terrible persecution of the Christians. But the strength of the spirit lived on, grew, in the catacombs, that vast underground city. Their faith would not be stopped. For the first time in human history the spirit and the sword were doing battle.

I stopped reading, aware that I had known all these facts for a long time but had understood nothing of their significance. It was only then, in my fifty-second year of life, lying in bed and listening to my stony heart beating, that I understood the life of the spirit.

The spirit and the sword had not ceased to oppose one another since the days of the catacombs. I recalled the ghetto in flames, the Warsaw uprising. Of these events I knew. But there were events of which the world was unaware, which history did not record; events in which people perished for their faith and their love of country. In Siberia, in the Gulag, broken and bereft of everything, people faced their last with only Christ as their refuge. I, too, had felt that fear of imminent death, of the oppressor's boot, of hiding places underground. I had seen fear in people's eyes more than once. I returned to the book with no little thirst to learn something of faith.

Finally one day my doctor said to me, "We're taking you out of intensive care, Mr. Minister. I think you're feeling strong enough." He glanced at the book in my hand. "You're reading too much. Still the same book?"

"Yes. This illness has been an education for me."

"Really? And what have you learned?"

"A great deal: about life, about myself . . ." I spoke without watching my words, absolutely indifferent to what he must think. "I finally understand the great spiritual power of Christianity." The doctor shook his head, confused as to how he should react to such words from a high-level government official.

"It's a question of goodness and love," I continued, oblivious. "Take Poland, for instance. Do you see what's happening here? Tell me, do you?"

After a moment of perplexity, he replied, "I don't know. You're in a better position to judge, Mr. Minister. You have access to the top. You know our leaders, you know Gierek. What do you see?"

"From the top—nothing good," I answered. "Don't take me wrong. I like Gierek. I think he wants to do the right thing for Poland, as I do, as you do. But the system we live under is based on force. Do you ever come across words like 'goodness,' 'love,' 'truth,' 'nobility,' or 'honor' in the press?"

There was obvious consternation in the doctor's voice. "Please, Mr. Minister, I must ask you not to occupy yourself with such weighty problems. *Don't read so much.* If you do, I can see I will have to keep you here longer."

I was moved to a single room on the third floor and was visited at once by Wanda, flowers in hand, smiling with joy. She bubbled over with gaiety, saying that it was clear God had some plans for me. I had the feeling there was something to those words, but I did not respond to them, thanking her instead for her love, her care, and, abstractly, for the two books.

After a month in bed and several weeks relearning how to get around on my own, I was transferred to a sanatorium in Konstancin, outside Warsaw. Wanda accompanied me.

It was October by then, and the weather had turned cool. When we went for walks, I felt barely able to drag myself along, an old man. Every so often I would become aware of my heart, which seemed to have grown palpably harder.

But Konstancin's beautiful woods were putting on their display, doing their magic; gold, bronze, red leaves were falling from the trees. The stately, prewar villas were mostly neglected now, like Villa Rose in Milanowek, and the natural beauty of the place was dimmed by disrepair, by impoverished people.

We walked one day to a forest of oaks, birches, pines, and alders that shimmered with breath-taking color.

"Look," I said, pointing, "this forest has been divided into lots; the stakes have already been driven. I heard that they were allocating the plots. You know, I'd like living here. It's so peaceful and quiet. Maybe we could build a little wooden house, over there, say."

"How?" said Wanda. "We don't have the money."

"I've heard that a little wooden house, one room with a kitchen, isn't expensive at all. We can afford . . ." I stood at the edge of the forest, gazing stubbornly at the lots.

"And what would we live on?" Wanda insisted.

"I could write; I've always wanted to write. But nothing connected with politics. You can't imagine how sick I am of politics. Novels, historical novels, something human. . ."

"I feel sorry for you, Romek, very sorry," said Wanda in her quietest voice, "but that was the road you yourself chose. The later you leave it, the harder it will be. If you were to write—honestly, that is—who in Poland would publish it?"

The discussion was over.

Toward the end of the year I returned to my post as vice minister in charge of American affairs, and at the beginning of 1973 the newly arrived U.S. ambassador, Richard Davies, came to see me. I liked him. He knew Poland, had married after the war in Warsaw, and had a feeling for the country. An excellent diplomat, he was always specific, knew how to listen and how to make his points with clarity and precision. Although he understood our situation and did not demand the impossible, he could be a tough, formidable negotiator. I think he realized quickly that I was sincere in aspiring to closer relations between our countries and that what mattered to me was not appearances but concrete achievements.

I noticed, once, his interest in my father's bronze gladiator, which had become my constant desk companion since I returned from the hospital. I saw myself in that dying gladiator—my futile struggle, my tragic losses, the victory of the spirit over death. But in spite of Davies's obvious curiosity, the statue was a symbol of a new inner life, and that I shared with no man.

Our ambassador to the United States, Witold Trampczynski, was also a welcome associate. He was a serious, educated man. Like me, he hailed from a family with old traditions, but, unlike me, he had started as a fervent nationalist and evolved into a faithful Communist. I had done just the opposite. Nevertheless, our collaboration was based on respect, and we worked excellently together. With Davies on one side and Witold on the other, my work environment was most favorable.

Soon I realized that I, along with the rest of the ministry's leadership, was part of a mirror that distorted reality. We studied the entire world—America, Vietnam, New Zealand, Iceland, the German problem—everything but the Soviet Union. There was a taboo on looking too deeply into anything Soviet, including Soviet foreign policy and Polish-Soviet relations. And yet we were all keenly aware that it was precisely the Soviet Union that had the final say in Polish affairs, that Polish-Soviet economic relations were at once a drain and a burden on our country, and that Moscow's foreign policy left its mark not only on us but also on the entire European and world situation. By all logic it was the Soviet Union we should have been analyzing.

An amusing sight in retrospect was eight men at a table in a beautiful conference room, the most important and powerful man, Minister Olszowski, at the head of the table, running the fingers of his delicate hands over the black glass tabletop and lowering his voice to a whisper in order to impart nuggets of information or instructions from Moscow, the others straining their heads in his direction. I would look around that table in disbelief, but none of the others seemed to share my frustrations.

I sat in the same place at that table for five years. On the wall across from me was a Gobelins tapestry depicting figures from mythology. Gazing at it, I would wonder which had more in common with Polish reality, what was being said or the myths.

Once, when we were discussing German affairs, I interjected a question about East Germany's foreign policy. Olszowski passed it by in silence, but when I repeated it, he remarked that the question was out of place. And he was right in the sense that East Germany's foreign policy was entirely under Soviet control and therefore an untouchable subject. We then spoke of the Balkans, and again I asked inappropriate questions about divergences between the Rumanians and the Soviets. That seemed to be too much, and Olszowski spoke sharply to me. But then Czyrek spoke up in support of me, saying that we had the right to know what the Rumanians were after. That infuriated Olszowski. He lost his self-control and resorted to crudeness. I could only conclude two things from that exchange: Olszowski and Czyrek were not as friendly as they seemed to be, and I was to mind my own business.

The ban on looking into Soviet affairs was, of course, an unwritten one, but it had been in effect since the birth of People's Poland. As early as 1945 the Soviets had their man, Vice Minister of Foreign Affairs Jakub Berman, in our ministry to see that policy was carried out to their liking. Berman was the *éminence grise* of the government, and Stalin's and Beria's agent. The taboo on investigating Soviet policy had been born with him. All Polish ministers since had learned to keep the appearance of being masters of a sovereign state's foreign service. Olszowski was an exemplary servant of the Soviet will; he had been well trained on the Central Committee, had learned to obey instructions, and had developed an instinct for what was permissible and what was untouchable.

It was under the umbrella of détente in the seventies that Poland's usefulness to the Soviet Union reached full flower. The Consular Division, which boasted detailed information on various organizations and figures in Polish émigré communities abroad, was suddenly demanding increased funds to penetrate such communities in the United States, France, and Great Britain, to exploit the opportunities created by détente. I knew full well that nearly all of the directors of that division reported to political intelligence at Security.

I soon realized that the principal task of our diplomacy was to help make the Western countries subscribe to détente, in a supposedly peaceful, broad, and irreversible process of mutual rapprochement. This ostensibly political framework actually promised a measure of economic co-operation, too; that is, in exchange for our role in promoting détente, we could expect to be granted Western credits under particularly favorable conditions, as well as broad access to the West's latest technology. Peace and co-operation had a beautiful, progressive ring. They were heady dreams of a bright future. I came to know, however, that they were only a screen concealing the harsh reality of Soviet goals, and I knew well that the Bolsheviks' main goal was a single-minded one: world subjugation. The Soviet ambassadors I had known all would have had the same response to my feelings of guilt about the manipulation of détente: The end justifies the means. But I felt sullied, humiliated, ashamed of my complicity in the deception. That was in 1976, though. In 1973, détente was still ahead, and I had reason to hope.

As détente flowered throughout the world during that summer and was crowned by Brezhnev's visit to the United States in June, the world saw ten agreements on co-operation signed and intense consultation conducted in Europe on security issues and Mutual Balanced Force Reductions (MBFR). At ministry meetings Olszowski reported that the Soviet Union was now encouraging the development of broad economic, trade, and technological relations with the West. West Germany, which had always been regarded as a black sheep for its revisionism, was now an exemplary partner, who had granted us our first large credits. Those had been followed by a stream of others from Western Europe, and by 1973 the United States was granting Poland grain credits. We were buying modern technology right and left. For us, détente had truly come to mean bonanza.

One day I was visited by Vice Minister Aleksander Kopec, who was in charge of the electric industry. He was just back from a trip to the United States, where he had signed an agreement concerning electronic technology.

"They showed me a lot of interesting things," he said, obviously infatuated. "The place is a gold mine of modern patents." He extended his hand and waved his gold watch; its dark ruby red dial had neither hands nor numbers. I had never seen anything like it before. "Take a look at this little electronics miracle. It works on transistor circuits. It would have taken thousands of the old vacuum tubes to do the same job. The manufacturer gave it to me as if it were nothing but a trifle."

He pressed a button. Bright digits lighted up on the dial. "No moving parts, with the exception of the electrons, that is."

"Wonderful," I marveled.

"Well, now! That's why I'm here today. I was told that you appreciated technological progress. We must acquire this technology for our own electronics industry. It's a matter of greatest importance, Spasowski. It can put us in the forefront of the world at one stroke. You can't imagine how important this is!"

"You're referring to integrated circuits?" I asked.

"Yes, the *technology* for producing integrated circuits. And it's all at Fairchild in California." They have the latest in everything. I told our Soviet comrades about it, and I had their mouths watering. They'd give us a fortune for that information." He glanced at me and hesitated. "But this is strictly between you and me. I've said too much already."

"I understand," I replied.

"You see, the problem is that things aren't progressing very quickly through ordinary channels. We've been at it for a few months now. They say they want to sell us the technology, and we're ready to pay good money for it, but somehow we can't seem to make a deal. And time's wasting. Maybe that new U.S. ambassador could be of some help. You have good relations with him. Well . . . maybe it's worth telling him, as a friend, that if he wants to make a good impression with us, he should help us acquire the technology. That won't be a big deal for him."

There it was: the Soviets pressing Poland to help them acquire electronics technology, technology that would be of enormous significance for weapons systems!

"I understand," I said. "But we'll have to be careful. Everything could be ruined if it's not presented right."

"Very true. We have to be careful." He acknowledged my apparent collusion.

Integrated circuit technology for Poland? We did not need it. We lacked a million more important things. And that it was the military purposes of the Soviet Union that would be served was plain. I wanted no part of it. Nevertheless, the name Fairchild was in the air, on the premier's lips; it had become something of an obsession and I kept hearing the magic word "Fairchild, Fairchild" wherever I turned.

Soon enough I discovered that we were already producing integrated circuits, in a special closed department, under army guard, at the Rosa Luxemburg Factory in Warsaw. We had purchased the technology secretly in Japan, and Japanese specialists were supervising the work. But Japanese technology was proving insufficient for certain "special" Soviet purposes.

I did not discuss this subject with Ambassador Davies. What we did discuss was the reuniting of Polish and Polish-American families. It was an important issue for him, a question of human rights, and one to which the United States was attaching increasing importance. He began by bringing me the names of individuals, then lists of dozens, and later hundreds.

I acknowledged the justice of his requests, but it was not in my power to grant people the right to leave. I wrote an urgent note appealing to the authorities to grant permission for passports to be issued to the people in question in the name of good relations with the United States and in our own economic interests. When it was clear my requests were getting bogged down in the Central Committee I had a series of talks with Olszowski and requested that he intervene. He spoke with Gierek on my behalf, but then nothing happened. Olszowski lashed at me angrily. If the Americans were going to make the progress of Polish-American relations dependent on that particular issue, he said, they were on a road to nowhere.

There were forces at work here that could counteract the highest authority in Poland and do as they pleased—a state within a state. It was the first time I had come up against that situation so palpably. Our secret police clearly had ties with the Soviet secret police, and it was by that route that it received guidelines from Moscow. The opposition I encountered in the reuniting of families had originated in the East.

My life had become something of a paradox. Just as my doubts were increasing, Olszowski presented me with a certificate acknowledging my twenty-five years of diplomatic service. I was considered a senior man in the foreign service, and the lower officials called me the "conscience of the ministry," because I often stood up for victims of injustice. I had succeeded in preventing the dismissal of a number of people, including both department directors and ambassadors. It turned out that my voice carried some weight.

Nevertheless, fundamental doubts gave me no peace. Wanda and I went off to Jadwisin in the summer of 1973. There we read aloud to each other and were temporarily transported from the present to other places, times, ideas. Only now and then were we reminded of where we actually were—in a beautiful park surrounded by cement posts, iron fences, and barbed wire patrolled by armed soldiers of the KBW, the Internal Security Corps.

Stanislav Pilotovich, the Soviet ambassador, had never come to see me, but as soon as I returned from that brief vacation, his deputy, Yuri Ragulin, dropped by without an appointment, as he did every other week or so.

"Hello, Comrade Vice Minister," he bubbled in Polish. "I just need a moment of your time. I have another question from Moscow. The comrades in the highest leadership want to know Warsaw's reaction to West Germany's admission to the UN. It's an important event and of course it interests them."

Why was it that he always came with questions not direcly related to my line of work? "The minister can give you the best explanation of that. Or maybe the head of the West European Division," I replied.

"No, Comrade Spasowski. I *know* whom to ask," he said briskly. "We know what *Trybuna Ludu* has to say. We know your Party's position."

"And you expect to hear something different from me?" I said with feigned surprise.

"No, that's not the point," he said, laughing. "Let me explain. I know that you have a mind of your own, Comrade Spasowski. You're a good, honest Polish comrade whose opinion is not always the same as *Trybuna Ludu*'s. Sometimes it's even *at odds* with our comrades' opinions. And that is precisely why your opinions receive high-level attention from us. I'll tell you quite honestly, there have been cases of its receiving attention at the *highest* level."

Amazed and disbelieving, I asked, "The highest level? You mean the Politburo?"

"Right. And I'll tell you something else. You don't say much, but when you do say something, you say what you think. So! Now! What's your opinion of West Germany's admission to the UN?"

"To tell you the truth, I haven't given it any thought. It's too recent. But it's probably good that West Germany was admitted to the UN, good for the UN and good for West Germany." I paused; he was looking at me intently. "Various associations come to mind. Germany now has the honor of being the equal to other countries. But," I said, pointing, "that building over there was Gestapo headquarters once. I was held there. One doesn't forget that. And later on I worked on the War Crimes Mission; one doesn't forget that either. I know how much the Germans have on their consciences, all of them, the West Germans, and the East Germans, too. Perhaps they can be forgiven, but each person has to do it on his own. It will never be forgotten. No crime of such dimensions can be forgotten."

Ragulin was quite oblivious of my emotion. He was bent over his notebook, scribbling.

"For me that's the most important thing—such crimes cannot be forgotten." It was not only the Germans I had in mind. "From the political point of view," I continued, my voice calm again, "I'm well aware that you, the Soviet Union, attach fundamental significance to Germany. It was true when Marxism was first glorified and it's true today. No other country, no other people interests you like the Germans do. But we Poles should remain cautious. The German problem has cost us too much and in more ways than one."

I was about to go on, but Ragulin cut me off. "Exactly! Valuable words!" he said, nearly shouting. "That's Spasowski talking! And what you said at the meeting was right, too."

"What meeting?" I asked in surprise.

"The last meeting of the leadership."

"But that was only yesterday," I said, stunned.

"Yes, it was. And you spoke calmly there on the subject. It was the right thing to do."

"How do you know that?"

"We know, comrade, we know a lot."

"If you know, then why ask?" I said, my displeasure no doubt audible. Had our conference room been bugged? Who had leaked the discussions?

"Don't take offense. There's no harm in checking."

"You're always questioning me, Comrade Ragulin, but as usual you don't say much yourself. Tell me *your* opinion of the Soviet position on Germany. I don't mean about the UN; I mean in general."

Ragulin could not wriggle out of it. "I'll be brief. I think like you," he said. "We've fought the Germans in two world wars. Millions of people died, a lot of blood was shed, but that's history now. The crimes are history, too. Imperialism was and still is our main enemy. Nazism was no more than the spawn of the imperialists, after all. You know Leninism; you understand. Now we have détente, and it's a very good thing. We have to gather our strength, because this isn't the end of the story either, as you well know, Comrade Spasowski! A large segment of the Germans are with us. The point is for them *all* to be on our side."

This time *I* took notes.

Poland's economy was improving in 1973, of that there was no doubt. The first National Party Conference in mid-October ascribed our new rate of development to "the new strategy of dynamic and harmonious growth." It turned out that economists were unable to explain that strategy to me; they pointed only to the new approach to foreign credits and investments: an approach based boldly on attracting credits and making investments under a so-called open planning system. The economists would admit that the plan was not balanced, but the assumption was that the new, dynamic economy would offset the imbalance sometime in the future. That had a definite ring of novelty to it. I remembered how things had been under Gomulka, with his petty shopkeeper's mentality; he had been aware of every dollar of Polish debt. In his last year in power he had made quite an issue of it. Poland's debt had reached half a billion dollars. Now, it was shooting past the four-billion-dollar mark, and no one was doing anything about it. On the contrary, I heard people say that this was a sign of dynamism. Others joked that the people who should be worrying were the ones lending us the money.

But no one could argue with the facts. Even agriculture was prospering. And people were saying that Poland was fast becoming one great construction site. Fiat was building a car plant; Britain's Leyland would be producing a great variety of engines; France's Berliet would produce buses; the German firm Grundig would be supplying us with state-of-the-art electronics. The most ambitious project was the construction—with the help of the Soviet Union—of an immense steel mill. Located in Silesia, the Katowice Steel Works' goal was to produce ten million tons of steel a year. That was the point at which my optimism collapsed. Why on earth did we need the largest steel mill in Europe? Polish steel production already amounted to some fifteen million tons a year. It was said in the Central Committee that the mill had been Gierek's idea and was to serve as a splendid monument to him. Word reached me that the only person who had opposed building this apotheosis of gigantism was Szlachcic, who had been supported by the Party organization in Krakow. I did not know at that time that at the very start of construction, Gierek had given in to Moscow's demand that a wide-gauge railroad line be built from the Soviet border to Katowice, a distance of two hundred forty miles.

At this time the premier and Jagielski made constant references in their speeches to the need for more far-reaching economic integration with the Soviet Union and the other Comecon countries. It was often said at our leadership meetings that the Soviet Union offered a limitless market for our goods; we should speed things up because others were ahead of us there and we were not taking full advantage of those wonderful opportunities.

I recalled the stories my parents had told about tsarist times, when the spinning and textile mills of Lodz had prospered by selling to the Russian market. But in those days the Russians paid in rubles that were worth something. Nowadays, to understand the accounting alone was a challenge. A Polish saying making the rounds seemed to sum it up best: "The Russians get our coal and in exchange we give them our sugar!"

There was no question that the Soviets had given Poland the role of blazing the trail of economic détente. No other socialist country had intruded itself on the West as Poland had. But what would happen if another freeze set in and we were left with our debts and our investments in construction? I drove those black thoughts away with the stupid argument that, after all, "our people" knew what they were doing. That was easier to do because even such pessimists as Wanda's brother were saying that important changes had occurred and the country was moving forward.

But at the end of 1973 an event occurred that made an optimist even out of me. Robert C. Gunness, the president of Standard Oil of Indiana, flew to Warsaw. I took part in the talks he had with Jan Mitrega, the minister of mining and energy. The topic was the exploitation of oil deposits discovered by our geologists on the Baltic coast. The project was specific and highly promising. The terms for co-operation were discussed and a tentative agreement was reached.

Mitrega was delighted. A miner from Silesia, he was a simple, practical man with a good deal of common sense.

"I want to tell you," I said, lingering in his office after the conference, "that I'm very happy to be part of this. It's a great thing and it's given me heart."

"A great thing is putting it mildly," he said with gusto. "Just think of it, we'll soon be mining two hundred million tons of coal a year. That's a big pile, bigger than you can imagine. And if we have oil on top of that, there'll be no holding us back. Just look how fast we're moving now! And this is only the beginning!"

But this year that had brought me such optimism had not been a good one for the Polish church. The Party was using all its power to tear children and young people away from the influence of religion and their parents. There had been clashes. The church had protested the increasing atheistic trend in the new plans for the school system. Even the ceremonies commemorating the five hundredth anniversary of the birth of the great Polish astronomer Copernicus, himself a priest, did not pass without tensions similar to those accompanying the millennium celebration in the sixties. Separate ceremonies were held by church and state, and the state flatly refused visas to foreign visitors who wished to take part in the church's program.

CHAPTER XXIV

The year 1974 was promising. Living conditions had improved. Consumer goods were more available. I heard people say that at last Poland was beginning to live a normal life, nearly thirty years after the end of the war.

Our foreign policy, too, seemed to be doing well. We were developing relations with the West, and it even appeared that relations with the Vatican would change for the better. In November of the previous year, Minister Olszowski had paid a visit to Rome and had been received by Pope Paul VI. This was the first time since the war that a Polish minister of foreign affairs had visited the Apostolic See. I knew well that for Poles relations with the Vatican were incomparably more important than with any other country. In February 1974, Archbishop Agostino Casaroli, secretary of the church's Council on Public Affairs, came to Warsaw at Olszowski's invitation, the first such visit. But it soon became plain that only limited progress had been made. I learned by chance that Olszowski had been coordinating the details of his moves with Moscow all along. It also soon became obvious that the Party was conducting a two-pronged policy: it was talking with the Vatican, and it was sharpening its attacks against the church in Poland, calling it a hotbed of reaction. Gradually it began to make sense to me: Moscow needed improvement in relations between Warsaw and the Vatican as part of its plan for détente. With the Vatican involved, détente was gaining the support of Europe's largest moral and spiritual force.

In the meantime, the idea of purchasing land in nearby Konstancin had reoccurred to me. I went to see the factotum in charge of such allocations—Wieczorek. Short, portly, bald, with an arrogant look, Wieczorek was not overly friendly in his greeting, or at least so it seemed to me.

"We do have some parcels of land in Konstancin," he said. "I don't know how many, but some. It may be too late. We'll see. Write me a short application, a request. We'll give you an answer within two weeks. Here, have some paper; just use my name for a heading."

I wrote out the information and handed the form back. Then I asked an improper question. "Do all vice ministers have plots of land coming to them?"

Wieczorek cast me a glance of surprise. "They don't have anything coming!" he said irritably. "The land was allocated by the comrade premier; it's he who decides who gets land and who doesn't. And those who get it *pay* for it—at the state price, of course, which is considerably lower than the market value."

I did not like what I was hearing and was angry at myself for getting involved in such a thing.

Two weeks later I received written notice that a parcel of land had been allotted to me, and the following Sunday Wanda and I went out to see our first real estate acquisition. It was a lovely plot, thick with trees, especially birches. Construction had already begun on the adjoining plots. The price, around five hundred dollars, came to two months' salary for me: a steal. I breathed the air in deeply, delighting in the fresh aroma of the forest. Wanda was quiet, pensive. It was clear she did not share my pleasure. After some months, I returned my plot of land to Wieczorek. It would be my first and last piece of property in People's Poland.

I was invited to the Planning Commission of the Council of Ministers for a conference on the use of foreign credits.

"My respected comrades," began the chairman, Vice Premier Jagielski, ceremoniously, "you already know the subject under discussion today—the full exploitation of the foreign credits our country has negotiated. I want to hear your proposals." Dead silence.

"I really don't understand this!" he blurted out in an angry voice. "First the comrades complain that there's no money . . ." He glared up and down the table. "But when, after a great deal of effort, the

Party and the government provide funds, it turns out there are no takers!

"*No takers!*" he roared, spreading his hands. "Just what is the meaning of this, comrades? How are we in the Party and government leadership to understand this behavior?" He glanced about theatrically.

"Comrade Ministers! I remind you that we had nearly one hundred and eighty million dollars to apportion and that only one hundred and twenty have been put to use. We have sixty million left. So then, comrades, now's your time. I'm listening." No one said a word.

I was stunned. I had always thought that when funds were being allocated, priorities were set and formalities were observed.

"A cigarette factory wouldn't be a bad idea," said a shrill voice from the end of the room.

"Fine. What will it cost?" asked Jagielski in a businesslike tone.

"Hard to say. Around five million. Maybe less. It depends. . . ."

"Let's say five," said the chairman decisively. "All right, there's five million. Now, who's next?" Again silence.

"But don't you need yeast factories?" asked Jagielski. "I've been hearing complaints of yeast shortages for a long time now."

"We've already put in for them, but things are moving slowly," said another.

"Now's the time for taking, not waiting! Heavy industry and high technology aren't saying a word. Is there really nothing you need, Comrades?" Jagielski asked.

"We're already at the contract stage," said Vice Minister Kopec. "We're trying to obtain a license to produce integrated circuits. That technology could solve a lot of problems for us, put us in the forefront. . . ."

"Now, *that* I understand," said Jagielski, with a smile. "Modern technology. Comrades. We cannot allow ourselves to base our economic expansion on anything but the latest technological methods. Thank you, Comrade Kopec. So, does anyone need anything else? Heavy industry, maybe."

Credits galore and money to spend. "Open" socialist planning, what a wonderful sight! I ceased listening. I went back in time to when Warsaw lay in rubble, to when this Planning building rose from the ashes—black marble within, the ruins without. The Party had insisted that the building had to be large and impressive—it was to house the planning of a socialist economy, after all. And the Party's propaganda machine continued to drum out the message: Only socialism can save Poland. And here we were. These new credits would have to be repaid with interest. Who was going to do that? Surely not the people at this table.

"I've spoken with Number One," said Olszowski one day. "We have the green light for his visit to the USA. He's already co-ordinated it with Brezhnev."

"Co-ordinated?" I asked.

"You know. Consulted with him. That's how it is. Does that surprise you?"

"No. Not really. But what about Watergate?"

"Our Soviet comrades say that the crisis will come to a head in a couple of weeks."

What did come as a surprise to me was that at the Fourteenth Central Committee Plenum, at the end of June, Szlachcic was removed from his position as secretary of the Central Committee. The news came as a bombshell to many members of the Party. A move for Szlachcic had apparently been in the works for several weeks, but had been kept secret. To our even greater surprise, he was immediately appointed vice premier, meaning that he was now a deputy to Jaroszewicz, whom he had long hated. I could not understand how Gierek could let a right-hand man go or why Jaroszewicz would want to take him on. Was it so that the premier could keep a constant eye on him, I wondered.

I soon learned that the "Franciscans"—those connected with Franciszek Szlachcic—had lost their positions in our ministry as well as in other departments and offices. It was an ominous sign. Not that I was concerned about Szlachcic or the Franciscans—I was not bound to them in any way—but the simple fact was that all those critical of Jaroszewicz had been swept out or neutralized. Gierek, too weak even to protect his own man, now stood alone.

Toward the end of the year Jaroszewicz sent Szlachcic to Havana for a session of the Polish-Cuban Commission; he paid a courtesy call on Castro—an ironic twist. Two years before, in Warsaw, Szlachcic had pounded the table and shouted at Castro.

One thing was clear to me: Szlachcic's removal signaled the final purging of the Party and state machinery. Jaroszewicz would meet no further resistance in fulfilling the Soviet plan for the Polish People's Republic. This was not a question of getting rid of enemies of socialism, but of getting rid of the last of those in leadership positions whose independent minds might have stood in the way.

July 22 was approaching, the thirtieth anniversary of People's Poland. I was invited to attend a ceremony at which the "comrades from the government's leadership cadre" would receive decorations. I despised all decorations, but how could I avoid this "honor"?

On the appointed day, a few dozen ministers, vice ministers, and directors of various central bureaus assembled and were positioned along the wall according to our place on a list. Rows of red boxes with silver eagles had been lined up like soldiers on the table in the center of the hall. Taking a closer look, I saw that they were made of moroccan leather.

Jaroszewicz said a few words of greeting in a strong voice, and then his factotum, Wieczorek, began reading out the names, opening the boxes, and presenting the decorations.

When my turn came, the sacramental words were spoken: "In the name of the Council of State of the Polish People's Republic, I decorate you, Comrade Vice Minister Romuald Spasowski, with the Commander's Cross of the Order of Poland Reborn." There I was, a false player on a false stage.

Jaroszewicz and I were the same height, the two tallest men in the room; without bending, he placed the white-striped red sash around my neck. Suspended from it was a gold cross covered by white enamel. *Polonia Restituta,* it said, Poland reborn.

"Thank you, Premier," I replied gravely. Jaroszewicz gave me a look of surprise, having no doubt expected to hear a rousing "For the glory of the Fatherland!" as he had from the others who had served in the military.

Wine was served, and the ceremony was over. But I was to drink that cup of bitterness again: on the same day, the newspaper reported that on the occasion of People's Poland's thirtieth anniversary, Gierek had decorated Brezhnev with our highest military order, the Virtuti Militari—a singular medal given for valor, courage, and dedication in defense of the fatherland. Poland's highest honor!

Wanda's brother all but shouted as he strode across our threshold that night.

"How could he? Gierek's made a mockery of history, tradition, custom. . . . I know his method: Defile what's sacred to the people and that will undermine any attachment they may have to their country, to their traditions, to freedom."

"The premier awarded me a decoration, too, for the thirtieth anniversary. The Order of Poland Reborn."

"A fine thing! The Order of Poland Enslaved! That son of a bitch Gierek decorates Brezhnev, and that other son of a bitch Jaroszewicz decorates you! Nice company you keep!"

Then Czeslaw realized that he had wounded me deeply. "It's all right. You're on a hard and slippery road. Be careful. Gomulka thought he knew everything, too. Now, Gierek is the all-knowing one. You turn on the television, and there's Gierek giving a speech. You buy a newspaper, and Gierek's on the front page. You turn on the radio, and there he is giving you advice. Where I work, people say they're afraid to open a tin can; Gierek might be inside."

At the beginning of August, President Nixon resigned and Vice President Gerald Ford was sworn in as the thirty-eighth president of the United States. Soon Ambassador Davies confirmed that Gierek's visit was still on, although no date had yet been set. Ryszard Frelek, the head of the Foreign Department of the Central Committee and a member of the Party Secretariat, sent me a draft of the document that was to be signed by Gierek and Ford. The "Joint Statement on Principles of Relations" was a political piece full of the "philosophy" of détente that had been lifted from discussions on security and co-operation in Europe. I doubted whether the Americans would sign something like that in a bilateral declaration with us, doubts I shared with Frelek. He insisted that we try to obtain as much as we could; our Soviet comrades had a great interest in our accomplishing this.

I had prepared the other document, the "Joint Statement on Economic Co-operation," and I passed these two umbrella statements, together with seven interagency accords, to Davies at the beginning of September. He was pleased that Poland was coming forward with so many proposals that lent greater substance to the visit. However, after reading them, he voiced doubts that the United States would agree to such a broad interpretation of détente in bilateral statements.

One accord was missing, the one concerning co-operation in the field of health. Polish medical care was at an all-time low and suffering from enormous shortages, but the Ministry of Health kept dragging its feet. It was an enormous disappointment to me.

One day Olszowski phoned me. "Get everything ready. We're going to Lansk. Gierek is calling a conference to discuss the visit. You'll report on our state of readiness, especially on the official documents," he said, all in one breath. "Bring your wife, if you want. She can walk by the lake; it's pretty there."

Looking through the materials, I saw that I was still lacking the agreement on health, so I decided to improvise. I found a suitable model among agreements with West European nations, changed names, rearranged paragraphs, made a few corrections, and ordered a clean copy typed. The new creation read well as a general call for co-operation. I sent it to the Ministry of Health and to the U.S. Embassy, feeling that even a general agreement would help improve the state of Polish medical care.

In Lansk, I left Wanda by the lake and went to Gierek's residence, which was right on the water. He welcomed me with a broad smile, in excellent spirits.

"Comrade Spasowski! We haven't seen each other for a while. How are you feeling? I heard you were sick."

"Yes, but I feel fine now," I said, trying to keep my tone polite and my memory from crashing back to Brezhnev's Virtuti Militari.

"Good, good. Let's get going. Give us your report, please, Comrade Spasowski."

I reported on the state of our preparations and on the arrangements made thus far with the Americans. There were no comments, so I moved on to discuss the documents, stating at the outset that we had ten.

When I said this, Jagielski leaned over to Szydlak and whispered loudly, "That many?" Szydlak shrugged his shoulders.

But Gierek seemed to be satisfied. "Have things been settled with the Americans in this area?" he asked.

"Oh, yes," I replied. "All our drafts have been passed on, and they have agreed to sign. Of course, the texts will be negotiated further and polished."

Gierek nodded approval. I reported on each document in turn, clarifying their main points. All went well until I began speaking of the financing of scientific and technological co-operation, at which point Gierek interrupted.

"No. I don't agree with you here. I remember that we have a

different sort of agreement with France, better terms. This one ought to be redone."

I was quite familiar with the subject and knew he was wrong. It was a technical point, but one requiring explanation. "No, Comrade First Secretary, you're mistaken. It's not like that," I countered in a decisive tone and began to give my reasons.

"Comrade Spasowski, *you are wrong,*" said Gierek, interrupting again, but in a sharper tone of voice. He went on to argue that a completely different approach was necessary.

I shook my head. "No, no, I really know this in detail." I looked around and saw fear and amazement on the faces at the table. Apparently, on this team, saying no to Number One was unthinkable, not to mention saying it more than once.

"Comrade Spasowski is talking pure nonsense," said Jagielski. "It's obvious that Comrade Edward is right. The error should definitely be corrected. This was a grave oversight. And no way to work."

I looked at Olszowski, hoping that he would come to my aid, but he said nothing, only stared down at the floor.

"You are wrong," I said to Jagielski.

"There is no argument here," he retorted. "You weren't prepared. Don't try to talk us into things you don't know anything about."

"This sort of thing cannot go on," seconded Szydlak.

"That's right. That's *no way to work,*" repeated Jagielski.

The room fell silent. Feeling their censure, I began to lose my self-confidence. It's an inquisition, I thought, a Party inquisition. I despised these people; they disgusted me.

Suddenly Gierek's voice broke the silence. "But, you know, maybe Comrade Spasowski is right. I think I may have mixed this up with another matter. . . ." He paused to search his memory, then continued. "Yes, of course! Comrades, he's right. You're right, Comrade Spasowski. I confused the issue with something else."

I sighed, but still said nothing, my eyes probably brimming with gratitude for Gierek's charity. He did not have to admit he was wrong, after all.

Jagielski spoke up again. "I remember now, too. Yes, in this case he *is* right. Comrade First Secretary has clarified the situation."

"Yes, the situation's clarified now. Edward has set things right," seconded Szydlak.

I looked around to see the rest of them nodding their heads in agreement, Olszowski included.

The final agreement concerned health. I noticed a look of surprise on Jagielski's face. He asked, "Was that draft co-ordinated with the Ministry of Health?"

"Yes," I lied shamelessly. "There was a lot of back-and-forth with them, but we finally worked it out."

"So, how many documents do you have?" he asked a second time.

"Ten. And the agreement on copper will no doubt be signed in Warsaw before the visit. That will create a good atmosphere."

"It's an awful lot," he said with disapproval. "We've never concluded that many agreements at one time, especially with the United States." He glanced meaningfully at Gierek.

"There's no harm in that, comrades. I'd even say it's right on the mark," Gierek responded with animation. "After all, every one of those agreements is beneficial to us. And that's just what the agreements are designed for. Isn't that so, Comrade Spasowski?"

"Of course," I replied, nodding my definite affirmation.

Gierek paused and then said, "We still have a lot to learn about the world. America can be of great benefit to us—in science, technology, many fields. And we, as you all know well, need money. If the Americans lend us money, it will be that much easier to borrow from the Europeans. That is precisely why our relations with them are so important to us.

"I am speaking not only for myself, comrades," he continued. "Comrade Leonid takes the same view of these matters and fully appreciates our efforts. There's nothing to be afraid of, comrades. Our opening to the West should be a bold one. That's the only way to gain anything. There's every indication that there will be an all-European agreement. And we'll continue to play no small role there as well. The joint statement I'll sign in Washington will contribute to this, blaze the trail for it. Comrade Leonid encourages us to be bold in blazing the trail for détente, in taking Western credits. What we're doing will be of greatest service in building socialism in Poland.

"You've worked very hard, Comrade Spasowski, and we thank you. Keep on with the preparations for my visit and come see me directly if there are any problems."

"There's one other thing," I said. "Of a different nature, but important. I'd like to talk with you about it." Gierek waited for me to go on, but I added, "I'll come see you Monday, if I may."

Now delighted, Olszowski offered me his hand and whispered, "Very good."

That Monday I went to see Gierek to inform him in private of a problem that was troubling me. In a beautifully cut suit and gleaming black patent-leather shoes, he was pacing his office when I entered.

"I know from Minister Olszowski that you are well aware of the problem of reuniting Polish and American families," I told him. "I find the whole issue disturbing, and I'd like to clear it up before your visit to Washington."

Gierek nodded. "Yes, I'm familiar with the situation. And so? Is Ambassador Davies still pressing for everyone to be given passports?" I thought I saw a hint of impatience cross his face.

"Yes. He assures me that the subject will have a great bearing on our relations with the United States. I think it's my duty to inform you of the seriousness of the problem; it must be solved."

Gierek looked at me with surprise. "It means that much to them?" he asked. "How many families can there be? Twenty? A few dozen?"

"Oh, many more than that. Hundreds. Soon it will be five hundred."

"Really. That many?" he asked with disbelief.

"The number is not the point. To the Americans every outstanding case is a violation of human rights and proof of our bad will. It would be irresponsible, wrong, and against our own interests to belittle the problem."

"Well, in fact, Comrade Spasowski, I would gladly settle all those cases. What do we care about five hundred or even a thousand malcontents? But our comrades in Security are quick to remind me that the people in the East—" he jerked his head to the side—"are leaning on them *not* to give in to American pressure. That's the whole point. But I agree with you that the problem must be resolved. It's good you came to see me. I'll try to deal with as many cases as possible."

There is something wrong about Gierek, I reflected on my way back to the ministry. He understands what's at stake and seems to want to do the right thing, but he simply doesn't have the strength of a leader any more. He's reluctant to risk confrontation with Security.

I flew to Washington in September to conclude preparations with the State Department, Gierek's visit having now been scheduled for October 8 and 9. To my surprise, the Americans accepted both our drafts for joint statements, with only one minor change. In the new wording both leaders hailed progress in the relaxation of tensions between countries with different socioeconomic systems and stressed the importance of making that progress irreversible.

I should have been happy that everything had been concluded so favorably, but I was not. I could see that the United States of 1974 was not the country I had left in 1961. Something tragic had happened. People were afraid to walk the streets of the capital after dark, and I myself had a close call one night. Buildings near our embassy had been burned down; the charred walls were a frightening sight. Our embassy grounds were now surrounded by an metal fence, something I would never have allowed in the fifties. I was disappointed, disturbed. I had great affection for this country. The six best years of my family's life had been spent here. It was here on American soil that I had felt a free man for the first time since the war.

"America is in the grip of a psychosis," Ambassador Trampczynski told me. "Things are better now than they were a few years ago. There were riots at universities; blacks were burning the cities. And then Watergate. Television brought Vietnam to Americans in living color, and the country is completely exhausted. They're not the people you once knew."

Old memories returned as I walked through the embassy, looking at the paintings, stroking the objects. The place looked neglected, worn. I lifted a loosened metal grate over a heating vent and found a broken vodka bottle, a sorry sight. It was not only America that had changed.

I had seen myself how the State Department had changed. Before, they had looked down on me, superior because they were free. They were convinced of the justice of U.S. policy and of the immorality of a totalitarian system that had subjugated the nations of Eastern Europe. Dulles had been condescending with me as a representative of an oppressive regime. Murphy had been ironic, scoffing.

Now, the State Department people seemed almost too friendly, too polite. They agreed too easily. Ford was willing to place his signature by Gierek's on a document full of the demagoguery of détente, as if he believed that the ten principles of peaceful coexistence now related to us all. The first of them, ironically, concerned sovereign equality; the seventh, the observation of human rights and fundamental freedoms. They had also agreed all too quickly to the irreversibility of détente, even though they probably did not know what that meant. How I would have liked to have found myself sitting across from tough Americans who rejected everything that was suspicious and unconfirmed by experience. Then, perhaps, I would have been able to hope the truth might win out.

Paradoxically, back in Warsaw I found the propaganda of success—the constant repetition that we were number ten in the world in industrial production or that we were building a "second Poland." The Party was dizzy with gigantism, and those who had reservations were seen as killjoys. Critics were told again and again a Pole can do anything! I chewed out employees who repeated such nonsense in my office. The stupidity of it was staggering: bragging of achievements while holding out our hands for new loans, new food shipments. In 1974–75 we received one hundred twenty-five million dollars in U.S. grain credits and were promised more in the years to come because our own agriculture was unable to feed us. It was not agriculture that was at fault. It was the Party's policy toward individual farmers. Any thinking person knew this, yet we were all helpless to do anything about it. The economic euphoria was accompanied by political euphoria: We are the Soviet Union's number-one ally and Brezhnev is our best friend.

At the beginning of October an agreement was signed in Warsaw with U.S. and Canadian banks for three hundred and fifty million dollars to develop Poland's copper industry. Thus Gierek's visit to the U.S. began in an atmosphere of co-operation. A few days later we were in Washington, being welcomed at a ceremony on the White House lawn. Ford's speech made mention of the first Poles who had come to Jamestown in 1608. Gierek, of course, spoke of détente and peace.

Gierek excelled in his role. The speeches the Central Committee man, Frelek, had written for him were eloquent, magisterial. They showed Number One as a statesman in charge of his country and of the key points in European affairs.

I took no part in the talks and was present only at the signing ceremony and the banquets. The full Washington schedule was over after two days, and Gierek and the official party flew to Pennsylvania and Texas. I remained in Washington. A few days later he flew to New York, where I joined him, a passive participant in a luncheon given by David Rockefeller and a special session of the UN General Assembly, which crowned the successful visit.

On the day before our return flight we gathered for a purely Polish meeting. Gierek was in excellent spirits, wine was served, toasts were made. Olszowski and Frelek were beaming with satisfaction. As Gierek began saying good-bye, Olszowski said a few words to him. Gierek spun around, took a good look at me, and walked over.

"Comrades! I want to thank Comrade Spasowski, who did more than anyone else to make my visit a success," he boomed. "To your health," he added, clinking glasses with me.

"And I'd like to make a toast," I replied. "May our visit serve Poland well. . . . To Poland!"

In retrospect, I saw that visit as something of a watershed for me. My hopes were at their highest, despite the many difficulties and the myriad deficiencies. It was after the visit that I began abandoning hope that a Communist Poland could progress.

In Warsaw I learned that former Vice Premier and Minister of Mining and Energy Jan Mitrega had been "removed" from his post. I had heard earlier about corruption in his ministry, but had had no idea that he would be saddled with the responsibility for it.

One day I ran into one of his closest co-workers and proposed a quick walk in the park to talk.

He looked crestfallen. "He was removed unexpectedly. Just as I was," he said. "They *wanted* to get rid of him, and the rest of us got swept out at the same time."

"But the newspapers said there was corruption."

"Corruption? What corruption? You tell me, what ministry *is* free of corruption, if you want to look for it."

"Yes, but people are saying the losses in coal are enormous."

"Nonsense. Coal may be chemically the same as diamonds but you can't hide it. They wanted to strike and they struck. They'll kick everyone out, there'll be a lot of noise about it, the little people will be punished, but Mitrega will come out of it in one piece. The point was," he said, lowering his voice as if by reflex, "they wanted Mitrega out of mining—to break up the group that had plans up its sleeve. I know this. Do you recall the conference on oil, how tremendously promising the oil reserves looked? Well, obviously there were people in the government who didn't like the smell of success at all. Whenever I mentioned the question of oil, I was always told 'It's with the Politburo.' I don't have to explain what that means."

I said nothing, overcome by forebodings.

"Do you know what Vector is? As vice premier, Mitrega supervised an important control system known as Vector. It's a computer system that keeps track of two hundred of the largest investments. It's very important. That system's already been dismantled. And do you know where the computers are now? In Security. Now they have an improved method for controlling the citizenry. I tell you, nothing good will come of this."

"And what about you?" I asked.

"Oh, me, I don't know. They'll toss me out in the provinces somewhere."

I did not see him again. But in a short while I saw that he had been telling the truth. People in mining simply were unwilling to discuss oil and, after a time, Mitrega was shuffled off to Prague as our ambassador.

At the end of November President Ford traveled to Vladivostok to meet with Brezhnev. *Trybuna Ludu* reported glowingly that thanks to our best friend a historic agreement on intercontinental missiles had been achieved. Détente was here.

CHAPTER XXV

I began 1975 with my work cut out for me. Number One was to travel to Havana on January 10, and President Jablonski and Premier Jaroszewicz were to follow at the end of the month. Surely Moscow had "requested" this trip to Havana so that Fidel Castro would not feel neglected by his socialist brothers. The request had to have been quite emphatic if all the highest officials were preparing to travel in great haste.

At the first of our meetings, Castro greeted Gierek with an effusive welcome, calling him a splendid representative of a people whose tradition of struggle for independence was known to the entire world. It was ironic, that stream of praise coming from the lips of one of Moscow's satellites who either did not understand the meaning of freedom or was jibing at Poland's two centuries of struggle with tsarist Russia and the Soviets.

Gierek seemed unaware of the bitter paradox. His remarks were truly those of the leader of a country that had been building socialism for thirty years. He sketched out the beginnings of People's Poland, then moved on to the thirtieth anniversary and a stirring vision of the future. It all had a proud ring to it.

At any rate, Castro was impressed. He rolled his eyes and made notes in pencil on long sheets of paper. No doubt he saw himself achieving similar "successes" in another fifteen years.

Gierek went on to discuss Poland's dynamic strategy for development, describing the enormous investments, bandying figures in the billions of zlotys. He did not mention the Western credits, ascribing all our success to the excellence of the socialist system and to the fraternal aid of the Soviet Union.

Finally, Castro interrupted. "I like figures I can understand," he said waving his pencil. "Unfortunately, zlotys don't mean anything to me. Tell me, Comrade Gierek, how large are those investments in terms of dollars?"

"Comrade Fidel, those are *investment zlotys.* And so they should be divided by four, with a slight margin, a few points more or less," Gierek said confidently, as if the fine nuances of economics were second nature to him.

When Castro began dividing, the man at my elbow, a Planning Commission deputy, groaned to himself, "Oh, not good. What's he doing?" Then he whispered to me, "Comrade, tell him to divide by fourteen or twenty-four, *not* by four."

But Castro had arrived at a figure. "I don't understand!" he shouted. "Your investments come out much larger than the Soviet Union's!"

Now it was Gierek's turn to be surprised. "Impossible," he said. He grabbed a pencil and began figuring. Everyone at the table scribbled, checking the numbers. Castro's mathematics, however, proved correct.

Suddenly the secretary of our Central Committee, Edward Babiuch, said, through the interpreter, "Of course, it's all very clear. Comrade Edward gave you a figure that includes the totality of our investments, including military spending. The figure the Soviet Union provides does not include the military."

Castro barked back, "*What*? Are you saying that my Soviet comrades didn't tell me the truth?"

"They never provide figures on military investment," insisted Babiuch.

Great uneasiness descended, for Castro now felt offended.

Gierek lost his composure and began discussing the zloty's dollar value with Babiuch and Olszowski. I caught snatches. "We've always divided investments by four, and that worked fine. Those are investment zlotys, after all."

"They divided wrong," said the man beside me. "It's time to put a stop to this. It's a disgrace."

Soon Castro raised one hand and said to Gierek, "Let us put this matter aside and move on. Our Polish comrades can inform us later what number to divide by." I thought I detected a tone of mockery.

Unnerved and flustered, Gierek finished quickly, his voice changed, his hands nervous. The meeting closed awkwardly.

Our ambassador to Cuba, Marian Renke, kept shaking his head in the car and saying, "What bad luck, what stupid miscalculation! Absolutely unbelievable!"

I never learned whether we clarified the dollar value of our investments for the Cubans. Even if the Party had attempted to do so, there was no one in Poland who would have been able to determine the exact amount. Gierek's miscalculation revealed the fictions of our financial system. Only investments based entirely on hard currencies could be calculated accurately, since the official exchange rate for dollars in Poland was always greatly inflated—four zlotys, give or take a few points, per dollar. At that time the black-market value in Warsaw was over a hundred zlotys per dollar.

The Polish fiction was modeled on the Soviet Union's. The ruble is always portrayed as stronger than the dollar. The concept of "investment zlotys" was an extension of that fiction and was mainly for the use of the highest leaders. But the method in that madness was that those ridiculous figures helped blur and conceal the truth.

The first thing I learned when I returned to Warsaw in mid-February was that Jaroszewicz had recently "consulted" with Kosygin, and the latter's instructions were grim news indeed. A vice minister of foreign trade filled me in.

"Kosygin wouldn't agree to any further co-operation with Western companies. The 'joint ventures' we were pursuing so hotly have all died a sudden death."

"But we've been discussing these matters with the West for two years now!" I lamented. "How's that going to make us look?"

"Well, it's even worse than you think. Now we have to pretend to continue the negotiations as if nothing's changed. We just can't make any agreements. How do you suppose *that* will go over?" he asked bitterly.

"But what about securing Western credits? Are we to drop that, too?" I asked.

"Oh, no. On the contrary," he replied. "Apparently Kosygin encouraged Jaroszewicz to continue negotiating credits, but with no strings attached. We'll use them to help develop our industry, especially heavy industry and mining, and to buy modern technology and licenses." He shrugged his shoulders. "I guess they want complete control over us. One more thing: we're not allowed to drill for oil on the Baltic shelf."

"Impossible!" I spat out angrily. "We're *not allowed*?"

"Oil is a dead issue, and that's that."

I learned soon thereafter that a joint Polish–Soviet–East German enterprise called Petrobaltic had been created to drill for oil on the Baltic shelf. Only Petrobaltic would be allowed to drill. Dreams of Poland fueling itself had been killed.

For me, this latest blow left no doubt that Moscow was closing a noose around our economy. Gierek and Ford had just put their names to a document touting the universal principles of détente, including sovereign equality, nonintervention in internal affairs, and the fulfillment in good faith of obligations under international law. Détente, I was learning, was to be binding only on the West.

Jaroszewicz had proved he wielded the power and could do whatever he wished with Poland's economy, and Gierek was reduced to the level of garnishing, used only for the sake of appearances.

There were other signs that the screws were being tightened. The so-called white sheets, which were marked "secret," and included monitorings of Radio Free Europe suddenly stopped appearing on my desk. The Communications Department was unable to explain the matter, but when pressed, they admitted that the order had come directly from the minister. I took the issue to Olszowski.

His eyes flashed with displeasure at my question. "You're not the first one to ask about that. You're not reading them any more, and that's that," he replied stiffly.

"I'm not asking to read them, I'm asking you to tell me the reason."

"You all read too much of that nonsense, that mud they're always slinging at us," he snorted.

"I'm surprised at you. In the first place, I don't read too much of it; I was receiving only extracts concerning Polish-American affairs. In the second place, all of Poland listens to those programs. Are we supposed to pretend we don't know that?"

"You can do without that sort of information. You don't have to know what colors they're painting us in," he said, standing and clearly upset. "*None of you will be receiving any more of that filth.* No more propaganda jokes. We've had enough of that."

"And the rest of Poland? How do you expect to stop them?"

"Let them listen. When the time comes, we'll jam, and they won't be able to hear a thing," he sputtered.

I remembered that Frelek had once said that for a laugh you could not beat Radio Free Europe's quips about our leaders, and that *all* the members of the Politburo started each day by reading those transcripts, if only to see if there was anything about them.

At the end of 1974 Olszowski had placed me in charge of scientific and technical co-operation with foreign countries. I had seen this as an important assignment and accepted with pleasure. Unfortunately, that area was in utter chaos. I set about creating some order.

Soon, Miroslaw Milewski, a vice minister of Security, invited me to bring letters concerning the reuniting of families, which we had discussed earlier. I had known Milewski since the sixties. He was a short man with a bald head and a sly expression.

"You're handling scientific and technical co-operation with the West now, isn't that so?" he asked.

"Yes. I'm trying to put some order into the chaos," I replied.

"Lately, you've been touching on matters that are in our domain," he said point-blank. "Look, I'll be frank with you. You should know that scientific and technical affairs fall entirely within our domain. That was clearly decided by the premier. For understandable reasons it's a secret. But not a word of this to anyone, hear? Just be aware of it and be careful."

"My job is to put things in order," I insisted. "I can't work in that pigsty."

"Of course you can't. And if you can't, well, that suits us fine. We're getting the state everything it needs to develop industry, and more. . . . Jaroszewicz is delighted. I'm talking about technology, licenses, and instruments that are kept under the strictest ban by the NATO countries. We're getting it all. We just had to establish an access, and the rest has been easy."

"You pay money for them?" I asked.

"Of course we pay, but not all that much, considering what we get. Those capitalists would sell their mothers and fathers for a little money. I'm telling you, it's a gold mine. You just have to know your way around these things." Milewski scrutinized my face to see if I had understood clearly. "So! Now will you leave these matters alone?" he asked.

"It's a jungle—everything gets lost; you can't tell who's running things. And, as you know, my ministry is supervising this and is responsible."

"We'll have to find another way to persuade you, then," he said stiffly. "But let's talk about reuniting families."

I handed him a list with a dozen or so names. "These are cases that have been dragging on for months now."

He read through the names. "Yes, I remember; all of them keep coming up again and again. Difficult cases. This one here once worked in a secret printing house of ours. We don't let people like that go."

"That was twenty years ago," I remarked. "If he knew any secrets, he could have told them long ago. Ambassador Davies constantly reminds me of this case."

"That's his business, that's what he's paid for. We won't let this one go. People like this need to be taught a lesson."

"But Davies tells me that the question of reuniting families will have an important bearing on bilateral relations."

"And you believe that? Hah! They have short memories. Don't be naive, Comrade Spasowski. You're trying to tell me that if that Polish printer is not reunited with his wife Polish-American relations will collapse and we'll lose our shirts? I'm telling you, it's the other way around. If we show some muscle, they'll dance to our tune. That's what our Soviet comrades always do and it gets them good results."

"Settle these cases," I repeated, pleading now.

"We'll see. Maybe something can be done," he said, softening. "Maybe three or four only."

"Settle at least half of them," I urged.

"Half? That's too many. Why are they so important to you?"

"Which ones will you settle?" I avoided his question.

"We'll do the choosing. That's our affair. We have our own policy. We'll examine each case, and the comrades will decide what suits us best. I'll let you know what happens."

At the beginning of March, Olszowski reorganized the ministry and took scientific and technical co-operation away from me.

In June Poland was reorganized into forty-six provinces and three autonomous cities. Previously, a structure based on the prewar model had been in force—seventeen provinces and five autonomous cities. The traditional three-tiered structure of province, district, and community had been abolished, on the ground that a two-level structure favored the democratization of the country because it brought people closer to the central authorities and facilitated dynamic development. I had great doubts about this and wondered about the true aim of this reform, which proved very costly in execution and consequence. Clearly, the point was to weaken the provinces so there would be no repetition of what happened in 1970, when the powerful province of Silesia imposed Gierek on the Party. If Warsaw—and no individual province—ruled Poland, and if Moscow ruled Warsaw, then Moscow ruled Poland.

What was in store for us? Would the country become unstable and be swamped with problems until it finally went under? No state had ever gone under. Something had to force that to happen.

In preparing for a visit by President Ford, the Central Committee created a steering committee, led by Edward Babiuch. A small man with dark, plastered-down hair and a foxy face, he had risen with lightning speed in the youth movement due to his talent for manipulation and intrigue. He now held positions in the Party, the Sejm, and the Council of State, and, as a Central Committee secretary, was in charge of foreign affairs. At the meetings I reported on preparations, and received instructions nearly identical to those for Nixon's visit. Ford would not be able to meet with the primate, Stefan Wyszynski, and security on his route through Warsaw would be extremely heavy to keep contact with the populace to a minimum.

I worked on only one political document, the joint statement. Everything that could possibly be agreed to with the United States had been signed the year before. This time it was fully agreed that political détente in Europe was to be accompanied by military détente, and that "security in Europe be indivisible and remain closely linked with peace and security in the world as a whole." The visit went smoothly.

After a busy two-day schedule covering Warsaw, Krakow, and Auschwitz, Air Force One flew to Helsinki for the Conference on Security and Co-operation. I recall being at the reception in one of the Western embassies on the day when thirty-five leaders of European countries, the United States, and Canada put their signatures to the Final Act in Helsinki. There was excitement in the air. Many sincerely believed that this was an event of historic significance, one that would open the door to peace and respect for human rights in Europe and throughout the world. Our officials, when discussing it with Westerners, stressed this point by referring to Poland's history, which clearly demonstrated that the only path was that of peaceful solutions and international security. That sounded convincing, beautiful, noble. But perhaps I had heard too much empty talk in my life. As always, my mind was working on two levels, aware of what those fine, polished phrases concealed.

Gierek's speech in Helsinki was carried in full by the Polish press. It had a strongly humanitarian ring to it. "Today, for the first time in history, Europe's peaceful order depends on the universal recognition of the sovereign rights and interests of all the states on our continent. . . ." And, toward the end: "As a Communist, I am, of course, in favor of genuine international cultural exchange, on the highest level of noble, humanitarian values, serving man and progress. Our goal is that people in Poland, Europe, and the rest of the world live in peace and freedom, with security, dignity, and abundance."

Gierek did not return to Warsaw empty-handed. After the conference, he met with West German Chancellor Helmut Schmidt, and emerged with three agreements. Poland was to receive one billion marks of credit and 1.3 billion marks in reparations; one hundred twenty-five thousand ethnic Germans were to be allowed to leave Poland—something they had been trying to do for years.

A few days later, Soviet Premier Kosygin, flew to Warsaw, and was awarded the Grand Sash of the Polish People's Republic's Order of Merit. I learned that the very difficult issues of the economy had dominated his visit. The discussions were shrouded in secrecy.

I ordered my secretary to obtain a copy of the Final Act. After a few weeks, she reported that she was unable to find it. The state publishing house had published it under the title *The Great Charter of Peace,* but no copies were available anywhere.

I then ordered a copy from our Research Department and I received a file marked "Secret," which I was requested to return.

"Why are you keeping this in a secret file?" I asked a man in the Research Department.

"Minister Olszowski's orders," he replied. "He has forbidden it to be shown to anyone. Naturally, that doesn't apply to vice ministers like you, or department directors, or for official use."

"That's absurd," I said. "It was published along with Gierek's speech."

"Yes. They did it so we could inform the West that we had published it in Poland."

"So why can't I find a copy in the bookstores?"

"Because only five hundred copies were printed, and the entire edition was reserved for official use. I think a few copies may have been sent abroad. The rest are in storage."

"How come it's being kept secret?"

"This is strictly between you and me," he said, lowering his voice. "Our comrades in Moscow sent the orders directly to our Central Committee. They know best about these things."

If Poles were not reading the document, neither were any of the rest of the peoples of Central Europe. The West is no doubt pleased that this Great Charter contains a good deal about human rights. And Moscow is pleased that the same Great Charter confirms the Pax Sovietica, that is, the political order Stalin imposed on Europe in 1945. My mind was working on a level of dissidence with increasing frequency, and I had to take special care to switch levels before I opened my mouth.

On a Sunday in mid-August, Wanda got a phone call from the tenants who were living on the first floor of Villa Rose. My mother had suffered a heart attack and was dying. The local ambulance had refused to take her to the hospital, because there were instructions that "unproductive" people of advanced age were not to be hospitalized, owing to a shortage of beds and medicine. My mother had just turned eighty-three.

We at once arranged for an ambulance and a doctor to bring my mother to the government hospital in Warsaw and were soon on our way to Milanowek. Wanda sat praying beside me. Fortunately, we found my mother still alive, but with only a weak spark of life left. We took her back on a respirator, and she immediately went into intensive care. The doctors were not optimistic.

The next day I was telephoned at home by Wieczorek, who also allocated medical services. He launched into me for "illegally" and without his permission having placed my mother in the government hospital. He demanded that she be transferred elsewhere immediately. I headed for the ministry, after telling Wanda that I would move my mother to another hospital and quit my job.

Wanda phoned my chief, Olszowski, and said that she was worried about the effect this would have on my heart. Olszowski, indignant about Wieczorek's behavior, assured her that he would personally settle the matter at once with the premier. By the time I arrived at the ministry, everything had been cleared up. The premier had granted my mother the right to make use of the government hospital.

Olszowski's promptness saved my mother's life. The doctors confessed to me later that she would never have survived being transferred again. Of course, his beneficence had another effect: I did not leave the foreign service. My mother slowly returned to life; and, indeed, she is still alive, though I doubt I will ever see her again on this earth.

Strange and ominous events suddenly began to occur in Warsaw in mid-September. Big fires began to break out in one place after another. Although fire-fighting crews made it there in record time, the Central Department Store in downtown Warsaw was razed one night. It looked like wartime. Could a fire really destroy a concrete building so quickly? I soon learned that this had been the work of arsonists; the fire had been started at several points simultaneously. Strangely enough, however, the authorities were silent on the subject.

The next big fire was at the Rosa Luxemburg Factory, and there were several fires after that. Then word came that a fire had destroyed the new steel Lazienkowski Bridge over the Vistula—part of Lazienkowski Thoroughfare, which had been built with great effort between 1971 and 1974 and was the pride of postwar Warsaw. I went to see for myself, and managed to strike up a conversation with a senior policeman, one of many at both ends of the bridge. He escorted me to the site of the fire. A large stretch of the asphalt surfacing had been burned away, and the steel girders had melted. Surely that was not the work of ordinary arsonists. The policeman looked around, then whispered that it had been done with napalm, phosphorus that burns at temperatures high enough to melt steel. Who had done it? He only shrugged his shoulders.

There were seven mysterious fires of that type. "Seven fires for the Seventh Congress!" appeared soon after, scrawled on walls. Everyone was at a loss to explain it all.

I sought answers but encountered only a wall of silence everywhere. No one even wished to speculate on the matter. Someone offered me some friendly advice: Stay away from those fires.

Napalm? So many targets? It was too organized, too large in scope, I thought. Too much like retribution, or a warning . . . I stopped there. Kosygin had been in Warsaw less than a month before. The secret talks, I heard, had been unpleasant. Kosygin must have demanded a great deal, and Gierek must have refused. Moscow! Of course. Moscow had wanted to threaten Gierek, to show just how far his brand of independence would get him if he opposed their demands.

I was frightened by my own conclusions.

At the Central Committee building, I dropped by Frelek's office one day, as I often did to discuss U.S. affairs, and he surprised me with a loud "Congratulations! There's a great distinction in store for you. You can't imagine how great—you're going to be appointed to the Central Committee at the Seventh Congress! I'm not sure yet what your post will be; perhaps member, deputy member."

Wanda was as dumbstruck as I had been. When she recovered her speech, it was to shout that she would never agree to it. The ministry was one thing, but belonging to the Central Committee meant supporting everything that was happening in Poland, and she did not want me to take that responsibility on myself.

Once again we were against a wall. The easiest thing would have been to quit there and then, but that begged the question. What next? The problem became an obsession, a worry.

Then one day before a leadership meeting, Frelek took me aside and said, "I have bad news for you. You're off the list of Central Committee members."

He could see the relief on my face. "It's not something I want," I said.

"Well, you're still on the list for deputy members. You deserve it! I can't imagine why you were taken off the list," he repeated insistently. "It's not right. I know you're modest, but that's not the point here. *You* should be a member of the Central Committee if anyone should."

It wasn't long before I saw him again.

"Unfortunately, I have bad news for you," he said. "It's serious this time. You were dropped from the list of candidates for deputy member. I'm very sorry, but you won't be on the Central Committee."

It was all I could do to keep from bursting with joy. "Never mind," I told him. "The important thing is that it's resolved, and I can be left in peace."

"I just don't understand it. But I'm glad it doesn't make you unhappy. As a delegate to the Party congress, you'll still have a chance to be a member of the Central Review Commission. That's also a central Party body chosen by election, and a prestigious one, too," he said with conviction.

"Me, a delegate? Why?" I blurted out.

"You'll be a delegate as one of the central Party activists, like Gierek, or me. You'll be elected the way all the Central Committee members are—by some large Party organization outside the capital. You'll go out to some large industrial plant or perhaps to some provincial conference and they'll elect you as their delegate. That's how all of us in the leadership are elected. You know that. Why is it I have to explain all this to you? How many years have you been in the Party anyway?"

The question irritated me. "Officially speaking, according to my present card, since 1948. Twenty-seven years."

"What does that mean—'officially'?" he asked.

"According to my previous card, I've been a member since 1945, an even thirty years."

"I don't understand all this business about cards. How long have you been in the Party?"

"I don't know how to figure! *You* tell me. Does work done at the time Stalin outlawed the Polish Party count?"

"You're not yourself today. You're being very difficult," he said.

I was curious to know how the list of candidates for election to the Central Committee was drawn up. That was not easy information to acquire. In principle, it was a simple procedure. The Central Committee's Organization Department drew up a preliminary list. Central Committee people who were also in Security looked at the candidates' personal files and gave verbal assessments of them. During the period of consideration, the list would be shown "privately" to the Soviet Embassy for some "friendly advice." The list would be returned with little check marks in pencil beside some of the names: these were the "friends of the Soviet Union." More often than not, the number of check marks would exceed the number of places, which allowed the Polish comrades to elect the new members in a "democratic" fashion. It was likely that there had been no check mark beside my name. The reports on me from the Soviet embassies—especially the one in India—could not have been flattering. I never learned who had put me forward as a candidate.

A short time later I was summoned to the Central Committee and informed that I should travel to Wroclaw. On "election" day, the hall in Wroclaw was packed with some five hundred delegates, handpicked Party activists who could be counted on to create no surprises. The first secretary of the municipal committee and other secretaries occupied the first row on the stage. The second and third rows had places for newcomers like me. It was ten o'clock. They were waiting for someone. There were two empty places in the third row.

Suddenly the door swung open, and in strode a man in a general's uniform—Wojciech Jaruzelski, the minister of defense—with a colonel at his side. There was a burst of applause. So Jaruzelski would also be elected a delegate to the Congress by the Wroclaw conference.

I sat there filled with self-loathing for being a part of this parody of an election, for playing the fool.

After a few short speeches, interrupted by applause whenever Gierek was mentioned, the election began. The secretary presented the central activists' candidates, beginning with General Jaruzelski. I could not help glancing back at him. He sat stiff as a mummy, staring straight ahead with no expression whatsoever, his eyes little frozen dots.

All candidates from Warsaw had been elected delegates to the Seventh Congress from Wroclaw. The report was greeted with thunderous applause.

I searched the faces. No questions, no apparent cynicism, no doubts. Their duty was done. They would have elected anyone whose name had come to them in a file, as mine had, and rejected anyone they were instructed to. They were Party careerists. And it was they who were electing me as their delegate to the Congress. I was no better.

The Party took pains to lend the capital a festive air on Sunday, December 7, 1975. Government buildings fluttered with red banners with white lettering: "Welcome, Delegates to the Seventh Congress," "Long live the PZPR, the nation's leading force!" Poland's white-and-red flags were few and seemed timid in that company. It was the first time I had seen Warsaw so lit up. The Palace of Culture, where the congress would be held, glowed with thousands of bulbs and was illuminated further by army searchlights. The Party had spared no expense to provide a sumptuous setting for the proceedings marking Gierek's fifth year in power.

In Congress Hall, under its shimmering chandelier, I found my seat with the other delegates from Wroclaw. The one thousand eight hundred delegates were in their places in that great auditorium. On stage, the members of the Politburo and the Central Committee secretaries filed in and took their places in the banked rows. It made for a rather odd impression—two theaters facing each other.

Gierek and Jaroszewicz were the last to appear and were greeted by a storm of applause. I took a deep breath as the foreign delegations began to enter the hall. Each was greeted with an intensity of applause perfectly calibrated to its relative importance.

Finally, the last and most important person, Leonid Brezhnev, appeared, escorted by several men. The applause was earsplitting, and cries rang out from every side. This ovation *had* to be greater than that given Gierek, I thought bitterly; after all, Brezhnev was our "best friend," a man who had shown us he could torch Poland if he so desired.

I studied Brezhnev throughout the proceedings. It was easy enough to—he was at the very center of the speakers' platform. Most of the time he appeared to be dozing, for his eyes were closed. But he managed to hold himself erect, even though his head rolled and fell from time to time. Then he would suddenly wake up, begin mumbling aloud and at length, realize where he was, and regain his composure. The "great friend of the Poles," as Gierek had called him, this hibernating bear—what would he do when aroused?

Gierek welcomed the delegates and addressed Brezhnev with words of warmth. Then he spoke eloquently and loftily about the Polish working class. He placed great value on the achievements of the five-year plan that had proved the "strategy of dynamic development" correct. I listened for a mention of the loans from abroad, but he skirted the subject of foreign credits and debts entirely.

Poles had never lived as well as they were living now, he said.

How could he! It was no secret that prices were rising and workers were grumbling louder. People were buying up sugar, and everyone was aware of the threat of galloping inflation. And, on top of that, we were in debt. But Gierek said in conclusion that we had to work harder so that life would remain as good as it was now; that the Party would evaluate everyone by the contribution of his labor as well as by his moral and ideological commitment.

And who will do the evaluating? I asked myself. Jaroszewicz? Jagielski? I recalled what Szlachcic had said: "We'll be settling accounts." I looked at the row where the highest leaders were seated. Szlachcic was at the far end. Everyone knew that his account would be settled at this congress, that he would be dismissed from the Politburo.

When the applause for Gierek died down, Brezhnev took the podium, and the reception was just short of pandemonium. The hands of the general, beside me, were red. Was I the only one to see how absurd and corroding this servility was? Brezhnev's speech was slurred and faltering, painful to hear. I could barely make out what he was saying. He praised Gierek, the great leader of the Polish working class, and spoke at length of the eternal friendship of our two nations. Then he began to lecture us, saying that Polish agriculture must undergo socialist transformation. When the farmers read that in the papers, I thought, they'll conclude that there are plans to take their land from them, and then there will be no way out of the food problem.

As I sat in that brightly lit hall, I reminisced how I, as a youth, would take the trolley to Zoliborz to meet with workers. How strong my convictions had been then, almost stronger than life itself. It may have been precisely then that the carnage of Katyn was going on: March, April, May 1940; gunfire in the vicinity of Smolensk; ropes tying hands; pistols at the back of heads; prisoners of war gunned down by the thousands.

The man beside me touched my arm and broke my train of thought. "Did you hear that? You've been elected to the Review Commission."

"The commission?" My mind scrambled back to reality.

"You might have missed it; they read the names so quickly. But I clearly heard yours. Congratulations! The Central Review Commission—that's a great honor."

The congress continued. Jaroszewicz's speech echoed Brezhnev's: Poland should be larger, better, greater, higher. By 1980, he said, nearly one-third of Poland's land would be under socialist agriculture.

Sidor and I talked during one of the breaks. We wedged ourselves into a table in the far corner of the Congressional Restaurant.

"Did you hear about the fires?" I asked, knowing he had just come from Italy.

"Yes, but only when I arrived in Warsaw did I realize what they mean."

"What do you think?"

"Probably the same as you do. They rubbed Gierek's nose in it, to show him that he has to do as they say. They're not fussy about their methods," he replied gloomily.

"That's for sure. They probably wanted him to hand over the money the Germans loaned us. I heard that they demanded we invest it in the Soviet Union."

"Moczar told me in confidence that things are really going to hell. And, as head of the Supreme Chamber of Control, he would know about this. Gierek's crew are out to steal all they can for themselves."

"I know they're all building houses. The villas in Konstancin are quite something. I bought some land, but I gave it up. I want no part of that crew. Do you know about the smuggling case?" I asked. "I dealt with the Brazilian part of it. Over the course of twenty years they brought fifteen tons of gold into Poland and used it to buy an estimated *billion* dollars' worth of antiques."

"Who are *they*?"

"Polish crooks were using the Brazilians' diplomatic pouch for twenty years. Think of it! Twenty years and fifteen tons of gold. When I started digging Security only blocked me. I think the chief culprits aren't in prison, but in office."

Sidor nodded thoughtfully. We said nothing for a long while.

"I want to tell you what I think about the last five years from the point of view of those in power," I said finally.

"I'd be very interested to hear. You were close to them."

"Not close enough to know the real secrets but close enough to pick up various pieces and put together my own picture. Here's what I think. As you know, there were three rounds of purges in the Party. What I don't know is whether we interpret them in the same way. In the first round Gierek's people and Moczar gave Gomulka's people the axe, which of course pleased Moscow because some of Gomulka's people had shown their teeth to Khrushchev. In the second round, Gierek's people turned on Moczar and axed him along with his 'partisans' throughout the country; that had to please Moscow, too. But even then there were still people in power with minds of their own. You remember Szlachcic was dead set against building that gigantic steel mill, not to mention that he had always sought a measure of independence for Poland. And don't forget Mitrega was in favor of Poland drilling for oil. But with the third round, the 'Franciscans,' Szlachcic's people, got the axe, and so did Mitrega. There'll be zero oil for Poland now, and heavy industry is going full steam ahead. Who do you think needs heavy industry? Poland? Wrong. The Soviets."

"They don't have enough of their own?" he asked.

"They do, but if they want to conquer the world, it's probably not enough," I replied. "Szlachcic's dismissal is the official end of round three. It was over some time ago. Only the most obedient are left."

CHAPTER XXVI

I had premonitions of trouble as the year 1976 began. My forebodings arose chiefly from things I was hearing from Party and government people who were taking propaganda for reality, falling into a mire of their own slogans, dizzy from their own supposed achievements.

Unfortunately, my premonitions kept proving true. Poland's debt was increasing at the heady rate of three billion dollars a year. We now owed ten billion dollars, the economy was showing no signs of recovery, and the nation—traditionally an agricultural one—was unable to feed itself. But instead of mobilizing its forces to overcome the economic crisis, the Party busied itself with political changes in the constitution. Babiuch, now part of the ruling troika, demanded that the Polish constitution confirm the leading role of the Party, and spell out that we were bound to the Soviet Union with unshakable, fraternal bonds. His efforts encountered determined opposition from Polish society—intellectuals, artists, students, and the church. It was so strong and widespread that the Party withdrew from its position; the amendments passed by the Sejm in mid-February were watered down.

I had not been mistaken in foreseeing that the Party would push to introduce changes that would affect the nation as a whole. At the end of April, three youth organizations were combined into one, the Union of Polish Socialist Youth, modeled after the Soviet Komsomol, and were thus easier to control. Next the authorities tried to get a bill passed in the Sejm allowing the government to confiscate all farms not personally worked by their owners. Poles viewed this as the first step toward collectivizing agriculture on the Soviet model. The government was also constantly pushing for school reform, both to bring education firmly under its power and to make the curriculum atheistic. The authorities here encountered a great wave of public protest. The tense atmosphere was heightened by constant rumors of drastic price hikes in food staples. This threatened to be the last straw.

Within a few weeks I found myself meeting with Cuban First Deputy Foreign Minister René Anillo Capote, to sign a plan for cooperation between our ministries and to hold political consultations. These took place in the Tatra Mountains, at Zgorzelisko, the luxurious Politburo residence. I stayed on after the Cubans left, and was surprised that evening by the unexpected arrival of Stanislaw Kania, a member of the Politburo and the Central Committee secretary in charge of the army and Security. We dined together and then sank into soft armchairs in the main sitting room. Kania ordered three-star brandy and started tossing it down by the glassful.

"I don't like it that you don't drink," he said. "Our Soviet comrades always say you can't trust anyone who doesn't drink."

"But drunkards can be trusted?" I quipped.

"No, they can't be trusted either. But I'd rather them than non-drinkers," he said. "You're a specialist in those American sons of bitches, so tell me, where do they get all that grain from?"

"They plant a lot," I answered. "You have to go there and see for yourself if you want to understand the success of their agriculture."

"We plant a lot, too, but we end up having to import grain."

"Our agriculture is backward. Theirs is modern. And they have a lot of territory," I explained.

"There, you've hit the nail on the head: modern agriculture. But the Soviet Union has modern equipment, and it doesn't have enough grain either."

"What do you mean? We got a million tons from them toward the end of last year," I replied with a hint of mockery in my voice.

Kania gave me a glassy-eyed stare and reached for the bottle. "A million tons, you say? Maybe it was a million. But how much did they *take* from us? Maybe you didn't know that, but they do, they take from us, the sons of bitches."

"What is it they take?" I asked.

"Whatever they want. Don't pretend you don't know. You're a son of a bitch, too. You even look like an American. Tell me, why are those American sons of bitches so rich? Talk! Tell me!"

"They're rich because they know how to work," I said.

"What does that mean? We don't?"

"They know how to count money," I retorted.

Kania took another swig and wiped his wet lips with the palm of his hand. "And we don't know how to count money?" He peered at me maliciously, and I could see that he was drunk. "Maybe you don't really want to answer the question, heh? Those Americans are sons of bitches, all right. Take our Soviet friends. No one knows how to drink better than they do. We drink together all the time. I know them, I trust them. They're our friends, those goddam sons of bitches."

His head bobbed forward. A gurgling sound came from his throat. Then his head fell onto his chest.

I cursed foully, called the house manager, and with his help dragged Kania to his room. Lumbering back to my own room, I could only ponder the fate of Poland.

Elections to the Sejm were held in March. I went with Wanda and Misia to the polling place. Four years before, people had engaged in lively discussion after casting their votes. Now they were in a hurry. We walked home in silence.

It was a bitter day for me; I knew what a cruel farce we had taken part in. The results of the election were as expected. The overwhelming majority "supported" the National Unity Front, which combined the Party, the Peasant Party, the Democrats, and the non-Party people. Days later I was visited by an old friend with contacts in Security. He told me that the ballots had never been counted. They had been taken in sacks to Security's warehouses in Ochota and simply burned.

It was a period of enlightening visits. An old friend of ours from Germany stopped by at my office. He was a man familiar with all our financial dealings with Western countries. First, we reminisced about working together in Germany and then suddenly, quite bluntly, he said, "Give me a piece of paper."

I handed him a pad. He tore out a sheet, placed it on the glass table, and wrote: "The Russians are buying up everything in Poland

and paying in convertible rubles." "How do you know?" I wrote back. "From a good source. A few days ago in Moscow, Jaroszewicz and Kosygin decided that last year's plans would be carried out at an accelerated pace."

After this "conversation," I put the piece of paper into the shredder. I did not realize, though, the full import of what he had told me.

On June 24, the premier presented the government position on price increases to the Sejm. This had been discussed a great deal, so the news came as no surprise. Food prices were to increase thirty to one hundred percent, meat nearly seventy percent. Meetings with workers to discuss the increases would last only one day. Then the Sejm would hold a final debate on the matter on Saturday.

On Friday an acquaintance stopped me on my way out. "Do you know what's happening, Comrade Minister? The enemy has raised his head. Many factories have gone out on strike in answer to the government's actions."

That evening the premier was on the television news. Looking tense, he announced that he had withdrawn the government's proposal to raise prices. Consultation with workers was still in progress, and many points deserving closer study had been raised. The government would reexamine the entire issue, which could take several months. This delay, he argued, proved that the Party and the government are run on democratic principles. This step by the government, dictated by the superior interests of the nation, should be accepted with a sense of responsibility and in an atmosphere of intense and disciplined work.

Late that evening I was able to pick up a few stations on my old Sony. All were broadcasting reports about the events in Poland, listing the cities where strikes were occurring: Warsaw, Ursus, Radom, Plock, Lodz, and others on the Baltic coast. Unconfirmed reports indicated that in some cities violence had erupted in the streets. Radio Free Europe reported that demonstrations involving thousands of workers at the Ursus factory had paralyzed the main railway line. Bloody clashes had broken out in Radom, and the army was not allowing anyone into the city.

In my ministry the strikes were looked upon with aversion. The minister appeared pleased that the police had dealt effectively with the strikers; for him, the chapter was closed and not worthy of discussion. The subject was not broached at our leadership meeting, even though various diplomatic posts were sending us coded cables describing world reaction to the events. As I soon learned, those cables were not distributed; they were sent only to the relevant vice minister. Thus I was apprised only of U.S. comment. The top leadership had a monopoly on truth.

Wanda and I were in Jadwisin soon after that. By some coincidence, one afternoon I ran into the Soviet ambassador's deputy, Ragulin, headed down a tree-lined path in our direction. Wanda immediately wanted to turn back, but I made her stay. I was curious to see his reaction to this chance encounter. He was with his wife, a tall, good-looking, bejeweled, perfumed blond. Together, the four of us walked back toward the cottages.

"So, the reactionaries have raised their ugly heads here again," said Ragulin, getting right to the point.

"It was the workers who rose up, not any reactionaries," I replied dryly.

"The devil knows who they are. Maybe you haven't heard what went on in Radom? I know the details. Simply unbelievable. Open counterrevolution. At the General Walter Weapons and Ammunition Plant. Unconscionable."

"Counterrevolution? You're off the mark. It's a simple case of the workers being fed up with the way they've been treated."

"They have it *too* good!" he shouted. "And it's precisely because of that that they've gone and conjured up those counterrevolutionary ideas! If they had to worry about the next crust of bread, they'd sober up fast enough. The working class has to defend its own interests, not go counter to them."

"No. The workers know what they want. You can't raise prices one hundred percent from one day to the next and give them some paltry one-day consultation, as if they were a pack of fools. *That* was a clear provocation."

Ragulin stopped. "An important deputy minister like you, and you talk as if you had no idea what this is all about. You have to suppress counterrevolution like Dzerzhinski did!" he roared. "You have monuments to him, but you didn't learn a thing from him. You have to learn from your friends, not your enemies."

I was seething. "Friendship! Is that it?" I sputtered helplessly, wanting to shout out that I supposed only friends started fires in neighbors' yards, but I lacked the courage.

"You don't like our friendship?" he asked defiantly.

"If only because you select people like Szydlak to chair the Polish-Soviet Friendship Society."

That took Ragulin by surprise. "I don't understand. Why don't you like Szydlak?"

"Well, if nothing else, because it's difficult to imagine Polish-Soviet friendship being advanced by someone who served in the Wehrmacht on the Eastern Front."

"Maybe we can trust people like him," said Ragulin, raising an eyebrow.

"That's a strange way of gaining trust and making friends. No one here understands that."

"You've changed," he shot out at me.

" 'Comrade Spasowski is such a good, honest comrade'—that's what you said, isn't it? That I had a mind of my own and spoke it? Well, that's what I just did. If you want yes men, you have Szydlak, and scores of others, I assure you."

We parted without another word.

Only two years later did I learn what actually had occurred on June 25 and the following days, so airtight were the silence and lies the authorities drew about those events. Radio Free Europe was jammed heavily.

The true course of events was as follows. On the critical day, June 25, work came to a halt at about a hundred and thirty of Poland's largest industrial enterprises. The premier had good cause to appear shaken and nervous when, on television, he revoked the price increases. He had not, however, been shaken into good sense. It was on his instructions that the police had gone into operation and shown what they were capable of. Vengeance fell on Ursus like a scourge. Security agents moved through the mobs of workers using invisible dye to mark the clothing of those most active. They were arrested immediately. The police ordered them to crawl down the "health path" on their hands and knees, tortured them, and beat them unconscious. Security was more refined: their torture "extracted" confessions about a counterrevolutionary conspiracy. The authorities managed to intimidate everyone in that small town by telling them that any complaints would have grave consequences. People were tried en masse. The lucky ones only lost their jobs or were fined; the unlucky ones were shipped off to prison.

The same thing, but on a larger scale, occurred in Radom, which has a population of two hundred thousand. The city was cordoned off by the army and police and Security reinforcements were brought in by plane. There were mass arrests; two thousand people were imprisoned in the first few days. Many were tortured. It was as if Poland were holding itself hostage.

One victim was Father Roman Kotlarz. Security had received reports that he had blessed workers who had been demonstrating on the streets. Interrogated by Security, the priest explained that, perceiving the danger and fearing accidental deaths, he had granted the workers absolution *in articulo mortis.* A short time later he died in his own apartment as the result of beatings he had suffered.

Foreign sources later estimated that in Radom six thousand people were arrested and twenty thousand dismissed from work. No one was ever able to establish the number beaten and killed. During the occupation, the Nazis had murdered thirty-two thousand Jews from Radom. Now the people's authorities had Radom devouring itself.

The Central Committee building buzzed. Gierek, who had been at a European conference of Communist Party leaders in Berlin, returned to Poland at once, and the high-frequency phones began ringing nonstop in his office. He had no idea what to do. Eventually, he cut himself off from everyone, and soon found himself out of the picture. His name appeared rarely in the press. Operations were co-ordinated in Jaroszewicz's office.

The rank-and-file Party members were not only embittered, but also felt powerless. The Party, two and a half million members strong, had proved to be a passive, frustrated mass. Asked for my opinion, I said that nothing would change in Poland until honest and fully democratic methods prevailed in the Party.

It was clearly Security that had emerged the winner. That preeminence was confirmed by the fact that the rest of the government was treating it with kid gloves. Poland was never the same after that.

During the tense days of June and July, the church acted with great caution, standing up for the workers and sending appeals privately to the government. When that produced no results, it shifted to increasingly pointed public statements. And for Catholics, a majority of the Polish population, it was Stefan Cardinal Wyszynski who was the highest Polish authority, the man most loved. The Party and the government could claim only physical power; the church ruled supreme in the world of feelings, spiritual values, and unfettered thought. Later the bishops demanded that the government grant an amnesty, desist in repression, and return to the workers their jobs and their rights.

As an antidote to the prefabricated government line against the workers and the church, I turned to my old Catholic friend Jan, a patriotic man and former Home Army officer. At one of these occasions, Czeslaw, too, was present.

"The church isn't a political party," argued Jan. "It takes a completely different perspective. The government tries to use the moral authority that the church has. At the beginning of August, for instance, the premier sent the cardinal flowers and a letter congratulating him on his seventy-fifth birthday. They want to use the church's restraint to serve their own hypocritical ends. Everything the Communists do is cunning and deceitful. Gierek's characterization of church-state relations as dispute-free 'except for a priest here and there' is a ridiculous understatement. All done to deceive. The episcopate spoke out in September, appealing for peace and order, as it always does. And what did the authorities do? They censored their statement. The entire press used only the bits that were convenient for them. They deleted the criticisms. Proof positive that Communism and truth are two different things entirely.

"You've heard about KOR, the Workers Defense Committee?" he asked. "It was founded in September by about a dozen people; they set out to aid all those workers who they felt were victims of injustice. KOR is the conscience, the social conscience of Poland."

"Yes, they're brave, exceptional people. Too bad, there are so few of them," remarked Czeslaw.

"The church has a high opinion of them and supports them," said Jan, his eyes shining. All that faith, all that hope.

I had never encountered KOR. In the future I heard of their activities from friends, but seldom saw their publications. Initially, I dismissed their attempts as doomed to failure. Over time, however, they won my admiration; few had their courage, dedication, and nobility of purpose. But the people in KOR were increasingly subjected to harassment; they were blacklisted, fired, persecuted, imprisoned.

Bronek, Klewenhagen, Jan, Wanda. There was something in these people, something I vaguely envied, but did not understand. There was a block in me somewhere. Perhaps it was my rationalism, perhaps my ego. It was not my Communism; that had long since died in me. I looked at Czeslaw, who seemed to have my dilemma. He believed in nothing. A burned-out shell of a man. It was as if I were looking at a strange, paradoxical image of myself.

"Well what are they doing in the central government these days? You're part of it, aren't you?" asked Czeslaw.

I looked down at the floor. The Central Review Commission I knew by now to be sheer mockery. A sterile debate here, a pointless meeting there. They would not believe me if I told them. It was hard enough for me to believe. Nevertheless, overcoming my reluctance, I told them about everything in detail.

When I was through, Jan said quietly, "It's worse than I thought. We're in the hands of fools."

Witold Trampczynski, our ambassador to Washington, arrived home at the end of November. I could speak to him as I could to no one at the ministry. We had a series of private meetings. The blush was off the rose, he reported. Détente was not doing so well. He insisted that President Jimmy Carter was undermining Soviet-American relations by constantly raising the issue of human rights. Soviet Ambassador Anatoli Dobrynin was getting increasingly annoyed.

At our final meeting I noticed that Witold looked tired.

"I don't have the strength any more, Romek," he told me. "I'm sixty-seven, my heart's no good; my wife is ill. I can't take it much longer. My deputy is getting on my nerves, too. He's an overly ambitious type—and, on top of that, he's connected with Security. I think you should start getting ready for Washington."

That caught me by surprise.

At the Fifth Central Committee Plenum in December, it was announced that Stefan Olszowski was no longer the foreign minister. He became Central Committee secretary in charge of economic affairs. I was dumbfounded. He was not an economist, had had no experience with economic affairs, and would have been the first person to admit it.

The plenum had been convoked under an innocent slogan: "The consistent realization of the socioeconomic program of the Seventh Congress and higher economic efficiency." In reality, this meant a full retreat from the program initiated at the last congress: we were spinning our wheels. Gierek, in the most enigmatic of terms, announced an "economic maneuver" by which we would "supply the market" and "limit our investment." In practice that meant halting numerous investments already in progress and squandering much of the credit we had managed to get. Coupled with 1977's plan to import eight million tons of grain and fodder, that only spelled disaster. But Gierek was putting a good face on it all. Our problems were blamed on everything and everybody: the slump in the world economy, disastrous harvests caused by bad weather, low worker productivity, high meat consumption, even the low political consciousness of "part" of the working class.

Within days of that plenum the new minister of foreign affairs, Emil Wojtaszek, was on the job. I did not know him, though in 1972 he had been a deputy minister for a short time, before leaving to be our ambassador in Paris. I had been ill then. Rumor had it that he was a distant relative of Gierek, and that was why he was advancing so quickly. Short, brisk, dark-complexioned, he must have been around fifty. He appeared to be shrewd, self-confident, egotistical.

Our dependence on the Soviets grew increasingly. In mid-December Premier Kosygin took part in the ceremonies at the opening of the great Katowice Steel Works. That giant was to provide additional millions of tons of steel to produce ships and heavy machinery for the Soviets, and it was to supply our own arms industry, which was now in full swing building tanks for the Warsaw Pact countries. In Moscow, Gierek awarded Brezhnev the Great Cross of Poland Reborn on the occasion of his seventieth birthday.

Poland seemed to be on a road of no return.

CHAPTER XXVII

The Party was of no help to Gierek in calming the nation. In mid-April of 1977 he was criticized at the Seventh Central Committee Plenum for excessive leniency toward the enemies of socialism. Soon thereafter members of KOR were subjected to additional persecution. The deliberations at that plenum were widely commented on by the diplomatic corps, which, by splitting hairs, hoped to discover a conservative opposition forming against Gierek.

That April, I was on a plane bound for Moscow. I was to "consult" with Deputy Foreign Minister Georgi Kornienko, who was in charge of relations with the United States. I went armed with a prepared presentation on the state of Polish-American relations.

"Comrade Spasowski," the new minister, Wojtaszek, had said to me, "be frank with them. You can be sure that they're thoroughly apprised of everything. They've got a magnifying glass on America and West Germany. There's no point in concealing anything. You'd only cause yourself and all the rest of us to come under suspicion. Remember that." I accepted this as good advice. I myself fully expected that the Soviets had details that never reached my office.

I was anxious. I would have to pretend to be candid, to laugh, to respond to toasts to Polish-Soviet friendship. But there was a darker, more fearsome consideration. Perhaps I knew too much about them, hated them too much, was too aware of their deceit. And perhaps they knew that, and I was on my way to be chastened.

The welcome was conducted precisely according to protocol. As I walked across the soft carpet into my room at the VIP quarters I felt something hard underfoot. My first reaction was anger; my second was to burst out laughing. I thought of the adventure of a group of our foreign trade officials. Entering his Moscow hotel room, one of them had stumbled as I had on something under the carpet. He had rolled back the rug and found a nut with a large bolt at the end. Intrigued, the Poles had laboriously twisted the nut off, and suddenly the bolt vanished through the hole in the floor and they heard a crash of shattering glass below. They had unscrewed the chandelier downstairs.

I met with Kornienko three times. He did not take his searching eyes off me as we sat across from one another in a conference room. Nor did Lenin, who scrutinized me from a portrait on the wall. I felt that everything I said was being taped. Neither Kornienko nor anyone else in his entourage took notes. I spoke in Polish. An embassy worker translated, but only one way, because I fully understood Kornienko's questions and comments. He was interested in two things: the Americans' seeming obsession with "reuniting families" and our grain purchases. He regarded the former as both an American tactic of harassment and a possible instrument of appeasement. Perhaps "something should be arranged" from time to time, he said, to demonstrate "our good will." He had only positive things to say about the grain purchases. If they give them to you on good terms, take them, he said.

Kornienko then presented a long, detailed, and formal report on Soviet-American relations. It was as deft and as calculated as a chess game, filled with lofty principle and punctuated by strategy. It was as near-perfect usage of Communist dialectics as I had ever heard.

The Polish Embassy's counselor pushed a slip of paper toward me. It said that I should thank Kornienko for being so "frank" with me. The Soviet Ministry of Foreign Affairs apparently had never spoken so openly about U.S. affairs. This was something new. Accordingly, I thanked Kornienko.

"Frankness for frankness!" he said, beaming.

Irony did not stop there. Within two weeks I was in the United States, to consult with the Department of State. I was to meet with Assistant Secretary Arthur Hartman, his deputy John Armitage, and a few other people, depending on the subject under discussion. I was scheduled to see Deputy Secretary of State Warren Christopher at the end of my visit.

In all respects, my talks at the State Department were different from those in Moscow. The atmosphere was free, informal. People came and went, and I was offered the opportunity to speak with a variety of people. I had a constant sense of haste and organizational improvisation. But in conversation, the Americans were well prepared, their knowledge broader and deeper than mine. In contrast, I had little new to offer them. Ambassador Davies had kept them well informed on Poland. As the talks closed, I said that it would be a great pleasure for us to have President Jimmy Carter visit Poland this year, a remark that was carefully noted. I had felt oddly free with the "imperialists" the entire time.

Witold Trampczynski was persistent about my visiting Dobrynin. I conceded finally by suggesting that he be invited for a lunch. If nothing else, the affair was revealing. As soon as Dobrynin entered, it was clear to me that he and Witold were on the closest of terms. Dobrynin was jovial, even lively. He said nothing of substance, confining himself to jokes and banalities. Witold made me uncomfortable with his servility.

As I prepared to leave, Witold brought up once more his longing to return to Warsaw. I left pondering that and carrying a book he had recommended highly—*The History of Soviet Foreign Policy Between 1945–1970.* Airplane reading. It had been published in Moscow in English, and had been compiled under the editorship of Gromyko by a team from the foreign service, among them Kapitsa and Dobrynin. The only mention of Poland was in a question: "Is there any comparison, for example, between Poland's present international position with, as facts show, the constantly menaced and helpless position of bourgeois and landowner-ruled Poland before the Second World War?" Three pages on Papua New Guinea, ten on Cuba. It was mockery. Thanks to the Soviet Union, People's Poland had no position whatsoever in the circles that counted in the world.

Warsaw's economic planners had pinned their hopes on Japanese technology. That much became clear to me when I found myself preparing to accompany Tadeusz Wrzaszczyk, Jagielski's deputy on the Planning Commission, on a trip to Japan. Wrzaszczyk was known in official Warsaw circles as the Engineer. His mission included ministers and deputy ministers in economics, and his official goal was to further co-operation with Japan, to obtain credits.

He thought we could come out of our talks with as much as a few hundred million dollars with which to purchase entire production lines in Japan. But the trip to Japan proved a failure. To my surprise, our delegation tried, among other things, to get the Japanese to take part in a huge agricultural project for which they would provide us with the latest farming and canning technology. They nodded politely and referred us to Premier Nakasone. Listening to us, the premier appeared to be asleep in his armchair. When the Engineer posed the final question, a silence descended over the room, and the premier opened his eyes. "What for?" he asked. We came home with little except for the packages the Japanese had delivered to the airport for us. Each contained a Seiko watch. So much for People's Poland's foray into the twenty-first century.

On May 7, while I was in Tokyo, the body of a student, Stanislaw Pyjas, of Jagellonian University, was found on the street in Krakow. Pyjas was one of the first KOR members in Krakow and had received many threats; someone wanted to intimidate him into resigning. But he had proved unco-operative, and was murdered for it, his body left in a heap near the building where he lived.

A period of mourning was proclaimed. Students hung black bunting and posted death notices. Several thousand students and workers from Nowa Huta attended a Mass at the Church of the Dominicans the following Sunday, and in the evening a procession carrying black banners and candles proceeded from the scene of the murder to the foot of Wawel Hill, on which the Royal Castle sits. There a declaration was read announcing the formation of the Student Solidarity Committee. The municipal authorities were preparing to take repressive measures when Cardinal Wojtyla spoke in St. Anne's Church and appealed to the citizens of Krakow to protect the students. The young people were left alone.

Pyjas's tragedy affected all of Poland. Two days after his body was discovered, several KOR members went on a hunger strike in St. Marcin's Church in Warsaw. Wanda went, and told me later that many people were going up to the grating behind which the hunger strikers were sitting, to give them flowers and other tokens of respect. The church was full, with people praying and secret police on the watch.

At the same time, the World Congress for Builders of Peace was held in Warsaw. Fifteen hundred people from over a hundred countries attended. At the conclusion of the conference, an appeal was passed calling on the nations of the world to struggle for peace, freedom, social justice, and progress. There was an exquisite absurdity in that.

President Carter's visit was becoming a reality, and I had much to talk about with Minister Wojtaszek.

"By the way," he said, throwing me a significant look, "I can tell you that when Witold Trampczynski comes back from Washington, you'll be taking his place as ambassador to the United States. But keep that to yourself for the time being. Do you have any objections?"

"No, that would be a good way to finish up."

"What do you mean, 'finish up'? You're still young."

"In age, perhaps. Not in life," I said.

"I understand. Your son . . . Well, keep the news to yourself. A lot of people would like that job, *important* people. But Number One likes you, trusts you, and that carries a lot of weight."

I rushed to tell Wanda immediately.

"No one understands you like I do, Romek. I admire you for being able to hold out for so long in such God-awful company. I wouldn't have been able to; it would have been all over for me long ago."

"I don't want it any more," I interrupted to say.

"You with your nerves of steel. I know what you're feeling. If I could find good care for my mother, and if your mother was secure, too, then I'd be glad to go to America, but only America, nowhere else."

Surprised, I rose. "But you said you never wanted to act as a representative of People's Poland again. Did you change your mind?"

"Yes. I have a lot of reasons for wanting to go. I think there should be someone in Washington telling the truth about Poland, representing the people as they really are. We can do that together. I have so many fond memories of America, and Kaytus loved it so."

"Yes." I patted her hand. "We'll go. But remember one thing: If for some reason it doesn't happen, I'm going to quit my job, quit the whole thing and be free of it. I can't do it anymore. I don't want to," I said firmly.

A few days later I began to make cautious inquiries about retirement, just to be on the safe side. I found out that after five years of uninterrupted service any vice minister could retire at his own request. His pension would be proportionate to his term of service. That was what I had hoped, for it had been just five years since my appointment.

The preparations for Carter's visit were conducted in an atmosphere of increasing economic deterioration in Poland. His visit seemed to many Poles the only good news.

Wojtaszek told me one day that Gromyko would be arriving in Warsaw and that I was to take part in Gierek's talks with him. This visit was so unexpected that Wojtaszek was unable to free himself of his duties at such short notice and sent me to the airport to welcome Gromyko.

In a small conference room, Gierek and Gromyko sat side by side on a couch, with Soviet Ambassador Pilotovich at Gromyko's other elbow. Babiuch, Frelek, and two or three others from the Central Committee, as well as Wojtaszek and I, sat across from them. Gierek welcomed "our friend," who was in charge of the "great Soviet Union's" foreign policy and who had been sent to see us by our other "great friend, Leonid Brezhnev."

In contrast, Gromyko began with hardly a preamble. "So Carter's coming to see you." His stony face attempted an expression of surprise. "You must realize what's at stake here. This is no ordinary visit. It's his first visit abroad. It must be seen in relation to world events, to the international situation."

Gromyko used no notes and spoke deliberately, evenly, as if his speech were meant to be recorded. "Carter started out with provocations," he continued. "He wants to teach us about human rights! Imperialists wanting to teach *us*. And the Supreme Soviet just passed a new constitution, unanimously; a document that ensures the rights of the Soviet people. They've taken the offensive and are looking for faults in us and in you, but they don't see any in themselves! It's that insolence that tells us what their true aims are. Yes, Carter's conducting a policy of provocation. If he keeps it up, keeps sticking his nose in where it doesn't belong, he'll go down in history as the man who fanned the flames. He won't succeed, of course."

Hearing him speak, I once again was aware of Moscow's policy to polarize: the world is divided into "us" and "them." "Us" is everything progressive, humanitarian, future oriented; "them" is everything bound to the past and doomed to defeat.

"A certain progress has been made in the Near East—Egypt and

Israel—perhaps even substantial progress," Gromyko said. "But don't let yourselves be led astray. The Americans are smooth talkers." He forced a smile that twisted his face. "They talk a good game, but then they go and do as they please.

"They're getting very bad advice, especially on Polish affairs. You know the adviser I mean. Brzezinski. He'll want to take advantage of your . . ." He paused to search for the right words. "Your passing economic problems. Don't deceive yourselves about his goals.

"There are a great many issues to consider in negotiating with a provocateur. You have to decide for yourselves what's important and what's at stake. You have to weigh all the pros and cons. But don't just think about yourselves. Take the whole socialist camp into account."

His purpose was obvious. He wanted to show Gierek and his advisers on foreign affairs that, by receiving Carter, they were entering on a slippery path. They would need the help of the Soviets, who could walk that path with ease and assurance. Perhaps he even figured that Gierek could be persuaded not to receive Carter. Otherwise, why the sudden arrival?

"Comrade Gromyko," said Gierek, "we hold your advice and your friendship in high esteem. We're aware of the problems and the dangers, but nothing's clear-cut and easy in our times. We thank you for your frank advice and the very valuable information you've provided us. We'll attempt to put it to good use. This won't be my first meeting with the United States, will it, comrades?" He turned to us as if for support. "We know what the Americans are like. Two presidents have been to Poland, and I've been there. We're up to date on American policy and on Soviet efforts to lay the groundwork for peace. Relations with the Soviet Union, the unity of our camp, and the entire socialist community, are of fundamental significance to us, Comrade Gromyko. We can see the efforts the Soviet Union is making, and your own personal efforts, Comrade Andrei Andreyevich, for the cause of peace and co-operation among nations. We, too, want to contribute to that process, and I think that our relations with America do in fact serve the cause of peace and détente well. And they will continue to, I assure you."

Number One was in good form. "As you know, we're having our troubles here, but who doesn't have problems? We're trying to solve some of those problems with economic aid from the West, from France, and the United States of course. This is important to us. Grain purchases are a priority issue. We want to buy grain on credit, and that we can do only in America.

"Those are Poland's interests, and we have to see to them ourselves. Carter's visit has a purpose. You know everything; we don't hide anything. And you'll be fully informed of everything before Carter arrives. That's it."

Gromyko's face remained inscrutable. The two men parted with a cordial handshake. Wojtaszek cast me a triumphant glance.

After the Russians left, Gierek took me aside. "Here's the thing, Comrade Spasowski. You'll be going to Moscow again. We have to keep our Soviet comrades well informed about the preparations for Carter's visit, so that they won't have any grounds for suspicion. I have the feeling they're worried."

"If it's necessary, I'll go of course, Comrade First Secretary," I replied weakly, my heart sinking.

"It's necessary. You just saw how necessary. And it should be done in a professional manner. We have nothing to hide. Remember."

Misia was delighted by the prospect of going to Washington with us. But within a few days of our telling her, she announced that she would be getting married. Her news took us by surprise. We had known her fiancé, an economist, for a long time, but they had seemed in no hurry to get married.

A civil ceremony was planned, which came as a blow to Wanda, who had dreamed about a church wedding for her only daughter. But Misia was an adult now and responsible for her own choices.

Misia and Andrzej Grochulski were married on November 5 by a civil servant in an official hall with the state seal on the wall. Misia looked radiant, with her red-gold locks cascading over her shoulders, but the exchange of vows had none of the solemnity and sacrament of marriage that I, a nonbeliever, remembered in mine.

For a long time now, Wanda and I had planned to spend our wedding anniversary in Zukow, where we had married in 1944. November 12 fell on a Saturday. It was a cold but sunny day, not in the least like the stormy day I had walked beside the *britzka* all those years before. The church looked small and poor, but the interior was as lovely as before, with its light blues and darkened gilding. There I began to think about my life. It all seemed lost in the past, carried away by the river of time; something in me longed for permanence, equilibrium. That day in 1944 had entered deep within me, into my heart. Perhaps it was proof that there was a part of me, after all, that had a soul. It was the part that had loved my father and my mother; that had come there that cloudy day to gaze with emotion at the altar; that loved Wanda and had created my family, loved my children; that had suffered greatly. It was the part that loved Poland and my fellow Poles, that had given protection to Jews, that had been with me in Assisi and on the walls of Tughlaqabad. The part that had refused to let go of life in the hospital.

"Come, let's go see the priest," said Wanda, ending my reverie.

He seemed to regard us with mistrust. Perhaps he had seen the black Mercedes with the chauffeur by the gate, a sign that people in power had arrived.

"Today is our anniversary. We were married here. Could we see the entry in the register?" asked Wanda.

The priest nodded. "We have registers dating back to the seventeenth century. It was God's will that this church and all its books survive the war. What is your name?"

"Spasowski. Romuald Spasowski and Wanda Alina Sikorska."

The priest left and returned with a large book under his arm. "Spasowski, you say." He bent over and started leafing through the pages. Finally he straightened up and said, "It's not here. There's no such entry."

"That's impossible!" said Wanda. "The wedding was performed by Father Sienkiewicz. . . ."

"Father Sienkiewicz?" said the priest in surprise. "Oh, no, that's impossible. Father Sienkiewicz did not perform marriages. His name doesn't appear in these registers," he said with conviction.

"What do you mean?" I protested. "We remember that wonderful priest perfectly well."

"Yes, and he told us that the entry would be made so that nobody could find it. My husband was in hiding from the Germans at the time."

"Father Sienkiewicz did not perform weddings," the priest repeated stubbornly.

It was only after we pored over the pages many times that we suddenly came upon our names. They had been inserted under someone else's entry, but other than that, everything was as it should be, including Father Sienkiewicz's signature. There was also a statement that, with the bishop's permission, no announcement of the wedding would be made in view of the circumstances.

The priest leaned over the book and stared at the page in amazement. "Father Sienkiewicz was before my time. He died shortly after you were married."

"He was the chaplain for our boys in the forest, the Home Army," said Wanda. "We heard he died a terrible death."

"I haven't been here long, but there are people in the village who remember how he died. Would you like to speak with one of them?" asked the priest. He left the room, and moments later I saw the sacristan hurrying off. A woman brought us hot tea, but this time there were no cherry preserves.

After a while an old peasant wearing a short jacket, hat in hand, entered the room. We exchanged greetings and he sat down at the table.

"You knew Father Sienkiewicz?" I asked.

"Of course I knew him. I've lived in this village all my life."

"Please tell us what happened to him," I asked.

The peasant looked from us to the priest, clearly frightened by our request.

"They were married by Father Sienkiewicz in 1944; that's why they're asking," explained the priest.

"Aha. He married them . . . in 1944," repeated the peasant, and that loosened his tongue. "He was a respected priest, a holy man. People loved him. He helped them, hid anyone he could. When the Russians came they arrested him right away. Security got people to accuse Father Sienkiewicz of associating with bandits, informing to the Germans, and stealing church money, all sorts of terrible things like that. There were even those who sank low enough to say they'd seen it with their own eyes! Maybe they were scared, maybe they did it for money. I don't know. They put him out in the middle of the road with his hands tied in back. Security people with red arm bands stood by with submachine guns."

"Did you see that?"

"Yes . . . but I couldn't take it. I ran away. He was standing there, crying, his cassock all torn. . . . He's in the Lord's care now."

We drove back in silence, but as we passed Milanowek, Wanda took my hand and asked tenderly, "You don't regret it?"

"How can you ask? I remember that day so well. It's been my

anchor all these years. I remember Father Sienkiewicz standing before us in his old cassock with the tattered sleeves. I remember the cherry preserves. The church. The table. He was my priest," I said firmly.

Anxious to resolve my future, I made an appointment to see Premier Jaroszewicz. He received me in his new office. The windows looked out on an internal courtyard, not onto the main street, as they had before. I had heard that this change had been made for reasons of security; apparently the premier was afraid for his life.

When I told him that I wanted to retire, he was taken aback.

"But you're going to Washington," he said angrily.

"I haven't been appointed yet," I replied. "I'll go, of course, if I'm appointed, but otherwise, I'd like to retire."

"You're not going to tell us what to do," he barked.

"I don't want to tell you anything. I simply wish to retire. If I'm not going to Washington, I want to retire now, and if I am going, I want to retire when I return," I replied dispassionately.

"How old are you?"

"Fifty-seven."

"You're not eligible for retirement yet," he snapped.

"I *am* eligible, I know the rules. I am requesting retirement and here is my written request with my reasons," I said, placing the paper on his desk.

"I'll see about it," he said. Then, changing the subject abruptly, he asked, "What do you hope to accomplish in America?"

I said a few words about our economic interests. Suddenly he exploded. "None of that matters. We can obtain grain and a few other things, but we pay plenty for it. They don't give us anything really valuable. They're imperialists; there's political scheming behind everything they do. They want to split us off from the Soviet Union."

"I've been steeped in U.S. affairs for years, and that's the first I've heard of that. Do you question the desirability of developing good relations? What about peace? What about détente?"

"You have to know," he replied, "who your enemies are and who your friends are. It's only developing relations with the Soviet Union that makes any sense in the long run." He was spouting the Party line. I saw no point in continuing the conversation. Several days later I received Jaroszewicz's letter approving my retirement after my posting in Washington.

The seventh session of the Polish-American Trade Commission, in which I had taken part, had recently concluded in Warsaw. The Americans had proposed agreements that would facilitate economic relations between our two countries and suggested that they be signed during the president's visit. More important was Secretary of Commerce Juanita Kreps's conversation with the premier. He had expressed a desire to reschedule our payments to the United States in the 1978–81 period. I learned of this when Davies passed on a reply in the form of an "oral statement" to the Ministry of Finance. Washington had treated the premier's "desire" very seriously and warned of the negative long-range consequences. People's Poland was now bankrupt, insolvent.

With Carter's visit to Poland firm, I began urgently preparing to go to Moscow, as Gierek wished. It would be the most onerous mission I had ever executed. I was to make excuses for having invited the U.S. president, feign "eternal friendship," and assure the Soviets that we were guided by the principles of Communism just as they were. The person I was to speak with at the Ministry of Foreign Affairs was Nikolai Rodionov, Gromyko's first deputy.

On the train from Warsaw, I waited for the moment when it would rumble over the iron bridge across the Bug River. The border looked no different from the way it had when Hitler and Stalin had divided Poland on a handshake. Their border lived on—a travesty of justice. Who would have suspected that a boy who had nearly drowned not far from there and been saved by the Germans would be traveling to Moscow forty years later as a vice minister? And for what reason? To make "confession" to the Kremlin about Poland's relations with America.

I was soon in the Soviet Ministry of Foreign Affairs, sitting across from Rodionov, a shrewd, bald-headed man, none too pleasant in appearance. He listened to me without interrupting, taking notes from time to time as I explained the Carter visit. I pointed to our alliance with the Soviet Union, our membership in the socialist community, and, of course, our strong affiliation with Communist ideology. I assured him that we had the experience of three summits behind us and that there would be no surprises. I concealed nothing about Polish-American relations except my own deeply hidden rancor at this last-minute check on the loyalty of a "province" of the Soviet empire. Confession lasted more than an hour.

Rodionov spoke for quite some time. "Well, you can see what they're up to in Belgrade," he said opening a folder. "They give when you press them hard, but only for a short while; then it starts up again. When Carter comes to see us, we'll give him an earful. In Warsaw he'll praise Poland, Poles, and Gierek, too. Remember: Carter's visit must not—*must not*—weaken ties between us! It must not weaken Soviet-Polish relations."

He went on to address specific issues. I took notes. No political conditions can be accepted. It might be useful to get your hands on American technology for processing coal. The reuniting of families—that is, of traitors—should be considered only if it gives you advantages. Warsaw can do without an American cultural center. . . .

The preparations for Carter's visit entered the final stages, and controversy about the program reached fever pitch. Warsaw and Washington had assumed inflexible positions on two issues: a large American reception and the president's press conference. Warsaw took a negative position on both, fearing that the reception might include Cardinal Wyszynski and members of the delegalized KOR, and that the press conference might become a platform for anti-Communist pronouncements. Emotions ran high, and Davies and I had little to say to one another. We were one step from calling the visit off entirely.

The Central Committee men accused me of being too soft, but I succeeded in convincing them that a press conference did not pose as great a threat as they might imagine; Carter was not coming to Poland to make public statements that would harm Polish-American relations. Davies soon brought me word that the president had agreed to abandon the reception.

The visit was saved.

December 29 arrived, and Air Force One was met by representatives of the Party and the government, members of the diplomatic corps, and figures from "Warsaw society," who in reality were Security agents. Carter and his party were greeted amid the rain and snow by Gierek and Jaroszewicz and a bevy of children presenting flowers. Security had provided the children, too. After the national anthems, Carter and Gierek walked along the receiving line. When the president stopped in front of me, I introduced myself and said that I had been appointed ambassador to the United States.

"Really?" he said, "And when are you coming?"

"At the end of January. This will be my second time in Washington, and in the same capacity." I said it all in one breath.

"And when was the first time?" he asked.

"In the fifties."

When they moved on, a voice in my row said, "That old hanger-on Spasowski never misses a chance."

Speeches of welcome began. When Carter spoke, I could not believe my ears. The interpreter mixed Russian and Polish words and spoke with a Russian accent. A murmur of surprise ran through the crowd. The group of Security men behind me chuckled.

I rode from the airport with Zbigniew Brzezinski, neither of us in a talkative mood. He had probably been as angered by the interpreter as I had. He did ask me where I was from, and it turned out that in our youth we had lived almost next door to each other in Warsaw, before the war had flung him to the West.

The next morning, Minister Wojtaszek called me. "I just got a call from Security," he said. "The president's wife and Brzezinski are speaking with Cardinal Wyszynski right now. They went to his residence. It wasn't part of the program."

I was not sure whether Wojtaszek's office was bugged, but I knew the phone certainly was, so I told him I would come over right away.

"We shouldn't make an issue of it," I said when I arrived. "Warsaw isn't a prison, after all. We have to make sure no one overreacts. Call Number One right away, tell him what happened, and let him cool things down. It's the only way."

"You might be right. Thanks. I'll call right now."

Things ran smoothly after that. At the official talks, Carter expressed a surprisingly high opinion of People's Poland. I noted his words: "There are no points of divergence in our bilateral relations. We are very pleased by that and are counting on further progress. We understand that the disastrously bad harvests of the last three or four years have caused Poland great problems. We admire you for being able to maintain your normal standard of living despite that. I had previously approved three hundred million dollars in agricultural credits for Poland. I have now offered an additional two hundred million. We appreciate Poland's economic vitality and we will strive to expand credit opportunities as the need arises. . . . We are deeply grateful to Poland for the support which it has shown since the beginning of the Conference on Security and Co-operation in Europe, for paving the way for the Helsinki agreement, and for its part in the area of human rights. That has been our shared position for generations. We believe that Poland will continue to play that role in the future. We want to expand contacts in science and technology. . . . Our relations, built on family ties, can be made even stronger. Mr. Gierek's coming visit to the United States will serve that end. And then we can repay you, in some part, for the hospitality you've shown us!"

I was glad for Carter's friendly tone, the invitation extended to Gierek, the new credits. But I was irritated, too. Rodionov had been right in saying Carter would praise Poland and the Poles. And Carter's exaggerations irked me. Did he really have no idea what shape the economy was in? How people were living? The daily struggle? Had he not heard about Ursus? Radom? The murders?

Gierek's words, on the other hand, contained the quintessence of Polish propaganda that had been drummed into the nation for more than thirty years. At one point he said, "We're at the cutting edge. In a year or two, we'll see the fruits of our investments. I am, of course, a 'nonbeliever,' but here I would like to say that one must have faith that we are on the right path."

That sentence was like a ray of personal truth breaking through the slogans. What he meant was that we were still deluding ourselves that we were on the right path.

That evening, the leadership gave a ceremonial banquet, at which Gierek and Carter exchanged friendly toasts. The premier was pleasant, even cheerful. Everyone seemed to glow with good will. I shared the general mood for a moment, but I felt no sense of satisfaction.

One January day in 1978, Wojtaszek requested that I accompany Jaroszewicz on an official visit to London for the premier's talks with Prime Minister James Callaghan. I was to replace Vice Minister

Josef Czyrek, who had fallen ill. It was only on the plane that I realized the purpose of that trip. The minister of foreign trade, whom I had come to regard as a swindler, was to sign an agreement concerning Poland's purchase of British ships, and I had to sign—on behalf of our ministry—an agreement on cultural exchange.

The thrust of our visit was obvious: money. It was important to the British to sell ships; their shipbuilding industry was going through a sluggish period. The condition we set was that Great Britain provide us with a multimillion loan, and we in turn would buy British ships. The concept was mind-boggling. Our shipyards on the Baltic were working full steam for the Soviet Union, selling ships for rubles, and we were supposed to buy ships for ourselves with English pounds. In reality, what was at stake was getting our hands on some pounds sterling to keep our ship of state afloat a little longer.

I returned to Warsaw in poor spirits and with a crippling pain in my back. The premier's physician told Wanda that I should go straight to the hospital from the airport. I did, and ended up spending almost a month there.

Lying motionless in bed again allowed me a great deal of time for solitary reflection. I gazed at my favorite photographs of Kaytus and the gladiator statue, which Wanda had brought for me, and I thought about Poland. There was every indication that the Soviet Union was sucking us dry and giving no thought to the consequences. I wanted to be honest with myself on that score, for I would base my actions in Washington on whatever I now understood.

Heavy-construction and road-building machinery produced in Poland under a U.S. license was being shipped exclusively to the East. Meat canned in our factories that had been set up by a Chicago company was being exported to the USSR. Poland itself had no machines, no food. Should not the Russians take care that such a disaster not occur? That their ally not be robbed blind? Could it be that they did not know?

Of course they knew. I knew myself that they knew. The Kremlin chess players had weighed the possible results of what was happening in People's Poland with icy premeditation—what gains there would be, what losses. The main question was: Which is more advantageous, an economically strong People's Poland, a vital member of Comecon, but one where people hold their heads high, or a weak

People's Poland, a crippled member of Comecon, its population impoverished, subdued, beaten, with neither the time nor the energy to strive for freedom?

But why destroy Poland? The Poles, with their urge for freedom, had always been a bone in the Soviet throat. The great Soviet Union, reaching from the Baltic to the Pacific, could get by without an economically healthy Poland, without any Poland whatsoever. They could always squeeze whatever they wanted out of our country. We would build ships, dig coal, give them our raw materials, or we would die of hunger.

And what about our army? Did they need us on that score? The truth was that the loss of the Polish army would be no loss at all. They had enough soldiers of their own. I knew well that Polish soldiers were allowed ammunition for only three days, proof that they did not trust them.

As I looked at my father's dying gladiator, I was frightened by my reflections. I could find no error in my thinking. My premises were sound, and were based on my own experience, on what I had seen with my own eyes. There was no doubt in my mind now that a quiet but cruel siege had been laid to Poland, and its objective was to destroy us and rob us of everything the West was willing to place in our hands. Poland was a battlefield again.

I asked myself the question: If that's their strategy, is it a sound one? Can the spark of freedom in man truly be extinguished? After all, even Lenin in his revolutionary days had proclaimed that a flame could rise from that spark!

One day I gave thought to the question of what I would do if the country began to sink into calamity while Wanda and I were in Washington. Battles could break out. Things might even reach the point of a general strike, the country at a standstill. There would be hunger. Surrounded by Soviet troops, Poland would be cut off from the world. What would we do then?

Of one thing I was sure. We would not flee a sinking ship. We had sailed it through many storms for more than thirty years. The captain is a traitor, and so are a good many of his officers, but the people are the crew. We would go down with them.

I reported to Minister Wojtaszek when I was out of the hospital. He pressed me to leave for Washington quickly.

"I'm not giving you any instructions. You're the best hand in these affairs," he said in a friendly manner. "I'll be brief. Just keep on working; that's all we expect from you. You'll have to report at once to Gierek, of course—I'm sure *he* has instructions for you. Do you have any questions?"

"One, concerning communication."

I took a slip of white paper from a plastic box on his desk and wrote: "We're not the only ones who read our cables!"

He read it and smiled, but then his face darkened. "What do you suggest?" he asked, and I could sense his fear that I might want a special code. That was of no interest to me. It would have been the worst idea, one immediately arousing suspicion.

"I don't suggest anything," I replied. "Just an understanding that you and I will only really talk when I'm here or when you're in New York at the UN."

"I agree," he replied, looking pleased. "I wish you the best."

I went to see Gierek on a Monday in mid-February. When I entered, he seemed to be waiting, standing in the middle of his office like a mannequin, beautifully dressed.

"You're leaving for an important post, Comrade Spasowski, a very important one," he began, with a friendly smile.

"I know, and I'm grateful to you for it," I said sincerely. "I want to thank you for your confidence in my knowledge of American affairs."

"Yes, I do have confidence in you. You've done good work. Carter's visit exceeded my expectations. He may understand us better now, and that should help. Brzezinski's presence, too, was a surprising plus, despite all the talk that he is an evil influence and would spoil things. But life doesn't stand still. You know the Americans inside out; use that knowledge to accomplish more."

"I want to ask you for some guidelines, how you see relations developing with America, and what my tasks will be."

"Yes, very important," he said, and paused. "It's crucial that we don't have any enemies there. I keep hearing that there's a 'Jewish lobby' working against us over there. Now I don't know anything about that, mind you, but people keep bringing it up to me, our comrades in 'special' affairs. There must be something to it if *they* say so. Apparently there's some connection with Israel. We broke off relations with them. But I think the day when we resume relations is not far off. It should be done, in my view.

"There are many religions in America," he continued. "You know that better than I. We don't want them to have a low opinion of us. Religious affairs are important. They're connected to people's souls. I don't know if that's the best way to put it, but there's something to it. What do you think?" he asked.

"I agree completely. Man has a soul, even if he thinks he doesn't and calls it by some other name. Religious affairs play a very important role."

"And now for economic relations, the most important task for you. I'd like to see further improvement in our co-operation with the Americans. Set a new standard, and do it in areas basic to us: coal production, synthetic fibers, protein research, the machine industry, food processing. Keep an eye on those areas. Try to get things going. Write to me if you need to.

"And don't forget the new technology, electronics," he added, as if having to remind himself. "You see, they suspect that as soon as they give us something, we'll pass it directly 'east.' And that's not so at all. We're honest people. I know from our comrades who deal with these things that we don't give away anything if the agreement says it's only for us. You can assure them of that with full authority."

I looked him in the eye, knowing that was not so. But he said it with conviction.

"After we've solved the big problems," Gierek said animatedly, "after we've created a base in raw materials, energy, chemicals, we have to take things a step further. In the next five-year plan we'll move on to supplemental investments! Yes, that's right. Time doesn't stand still, and I want Poland to keep developing in the proper direction. The next five-year plan will include the 'finishing stage' of the industrial base, and we'll have to secure 'supplemental investments' to make it all possible."

Could he be so deluded? His fingers were trembling, and there was a nervous twitch under one eye. What could he possibly be thinking? Here we were with everything collapsing about us, and he was speaking as if everything were rosy, as if he refused to believe otherwise.

"Here's my plan," said Gierek. "The next Party congress, the eighth, will take place in two years, in February 1980, and we'll hold elections immediately afterward, in March. I want Carter to come back to Poland right after that, in May or June."

"Fine, but you should visit there first."

"You're right, perhaps in the fall of 1979."

Our talk was winding down, but there was one last thing to clear.

"Just one point of information, Comrade First Secretary. I wanted to tell you that Wojtaszek and I have an agreement about communication."

"I know. He told me. It's the right way," he answered.

He bade me a warm farewell, shaking my hand several times.

Before leaving, I visited my mother in Milanowek. Nothing had changed there. She was still living in the same two cluttered rooms. The rest of the house was occupied by tenants. Villa Rose was a pitiful reminder of all we had been through since the war. I gazed at the peeling walls, the green fungus on the ceilings, the old furniture. It had once been so beautiful.

Mother, who was eighty-five, was bearing up bravely. She lived alone and did everything herself, with her own trembling hands. I kissed her eyes and stroked her gray head. She was always busy with something. She read a great deal, with a special liking for books about the old days; she wrote traditional verse; she cut figures out of bark with a knife, pasted dried flowers on wooden plaques, drew and painted. She made notes on the history of the family and on historical paintings. There was nothing in the world that could move her from there, despite all our attempts at persuasion. She said that it was only there that she could relive her memories of people and the past.

Wanda made sure that neighbors looked in on her, but from a distance. Mother had a keen dislike for intruders. When I called her from the airport, her words of farewell, her blessing, the final click of the phone, were saddest of all.

Wanda bid a tearful good-bye to her own mother, who was to stay on in our apartment under a professional nurse's care. Not completely aware of what was happening, she asked us to come again soon, but when she realized that we were leaving for a long time and traveling a great distance, she wept like a little child.

After an emotional farewell with Misia, we gathered up a few of Kaytus's little possessions, some silver, Grandmother's clock from Lityn, and we set off for America.

CHAPTER XXVIII

As our plane landed in the United States on March 2, 1978, I squinted out the window at snow glistening in sunlight. Twenty-three years and a lifetime had passed since my last ambassadorship in this country.

There was much to do: for Wanda, a permanent residence to buy; for me, a strong bond of Polish-American relations to establish. I promised myself that from the very start the Americans would feel that I was treating them as friends. It was not relations with Americans that worried me; I was certain they would work out well. It was how to play Dobrynin. He and I would clash sooner or later if he wanted me to behave subserviently as Witold had; and a clash would mean the end of my post in Washington. I had no illusions on that score. The thing to do was to establish correct relations with him from the start, businesslike but not too close.

After an inspection of the embassy's rooms, Wanda and I were in despair. It had obviously been of great importance to someone to wipe out all traces of Polish tradition, everything that could serve as a reminder of independent Poland.

I took a good look at the people who worked at the embassy. They were surprised I was making the rounds so quickly. Some hurriedly stuffed papers into their desk drawers when I appeared. Clearly, they were either from Security or Z-II, military intelligence.

Changes to make work "more efficient" had been put into effect. I was informed of them by our "resident," Bronislaw Zych, whom

I had known in New Delhi. In Washington, too, he was in charge of secret police intelligence, the SB. He seemed very sure of himself. One day he took me to the top floor to see his new, strictly guarded secret. After a number of locks on a steel-plated door were opened, we removed our shoes and went through a narrow passageway that led to a small booth. The walls, ceiling, and floor were made of white plastic. As soon as the door closed, a jamming device began to sound. Zych shone with satisfaction and pride.

"I can discuss top secret matters here," he said, gloating. "No bug can penetrate this booth. It's hermetically sealed, as if it were suspended in air. The jamming distorts any sound that could possibly slip out."

"You can't hide anything from modern technology," I remarked skeptically.

"Oh no," he said indignantly. "There are no miracles when it comes to this little booth. Even laser rays can't work here. I can discuss our operational affairs freely here—the ones we can't discuss in the offices. You can use the 'quiet room,' too, Ambassador, if you wish to speak about something that's highly secret—with me, of course."

Not only had the traces of Poland's old independence been erased, but our foreign service had moved in a new direction—spying for the Soviets.

After a visit to the State Department, I learned that I would not present my credentials until April. That being the case, I went to see Dobrynin. The Soviet Embassy had gone through its own changes. There was now a soldier in the reception room; the effect was unpleasant, aggressive. Going up the stairs, I noticed televisions monitoring special areas.

Dobrynin's office was on the second floor, past a screening room dripping with gilt. The way into his office was through a short, dark corridor and past a secretary's office where two men sat behind desks. The roar of a jamming mechanism indicated that Dobrynin worked in a "quiet" room all the time. As I entered, he rose from his desk with a broad smile on his good-natured face. We shook hands.

"Welcome, Ambassador. Please sit; make yourself at home." An instant later, a white-jacketed waiter entered and set a tray before us. The tea service was made of old silver from tsarist times. Flaky pastries, chocolates, nuts, and dates were arrayed in crystal bowls.

"It's tough here among the Americans," Dobrynin began. "It's not easy work. It's very difficult to come to terms with them."

"But you have a great deal of experience," I remarked.

"Yes, that's true. But you know yourself they don't have a uniform position, the way we do. There are divergences within the administration itself. You make an agreement with the State Department and then it turns out that the White House has reservations. Then the administration says one thing and Congress says another. For them its normal. Things drag on, they get bogged down, and often they come to a dead end. It's hard, but not impossible." He was smiling again.

"As you know, Carter is constantly bringing up 'human rights,' " he continued. "He's not a serious person—just an eccentric from Georgia, that's all. He keeps saying the same thing over and over. It's enough to drive you mad. And the situation around him is complicated, too. Brzezinski, for instance, he poisons the atmosphere. He's a bad influence on Carter. You'll see for yourself. Keep that in mind. We'll discuss it later."

I looked around Dobrynin's orderly office; no papers were lying about. There was a portrait of Lenin on the wall. Two large maps hung on the other walls: one of the Soviet Union, one of the United States. The table at which we were taking our tea must also have served for briefing sessions. There were no windows.

"And what about Congress?" I asked.

"Another story entirely. It's always at odds with the Administration. It's a big machine, and a reactionary one, but there are people there worth talking to. But the most important thing in Congress is business, the dollar. That's America's true strength," he said with a laugh. "But you already know everything I'm telling you. You're a man with experience. How are things in Poland? How's Gierek?"

"Nothing new. Poland's in bad shape. The commodities situation is terrible; everything's in short supply . . ."

"Well, the problems are a natural thing. They'll certainly pass. Who doesn't have problems?"

"It's never been this bad before. It's not only a matter of consumer goods. There are hundreds, several hundreds of factories idle. And our foreign debt keeps growing." I was pressing on, well aware of the source of our problems and our poverty.

Dobrynin listened without blinking an eye. I had a sudden urge to leave. "I must go," I said.

"Don't rush away. It's important that we get off to a good working start. We, the heads of the socialist posts, meet once a month. You must come, too."

"I know. I'll take part. I look forward to an exchange of opinion." My words were thick with irony.

On April 5 I presented my credentials to President Jimmy Carter. It was a mere formality: I and five other ambassadors were seen in the space of an hour.

I began meeting with representatives of the administration, Congress, and American business. As always, I took copious notes of all my meetings, apprehensive about being quoted out of context someday. I had worked out my own method: I prepared for every talk by writing out a point-by-point plan entitled "Before." At meetings I would make notes under the heading "During." Final annotations, made once the talks were over, were given the title "After." I used abbreviations known to me alone, constituting something of a personal code. My notes were kept at the embassy, in a safe reserved for my exclusive use. I always sealed the safe with Plasticine even though it was in a small separate room protected by an electronic alarm system installed in the door.

As I began my mission, I felt with increasing clarity that I was walking a tightrope. I could fall into at least three dangers. The first and greatest was linked with my belief that the crisis in Poland would only worsen and lead to a disaster that was beyond my powers to imagine. If that came to pass, I would be left suspended in a void. The second stemmed from my conviction that I had to be truthful and direct with Americans; but how truthful could I be and represent Warsaw at the same time? The third danger concerned the Soviets. My first conversation with Dobrynin had convinced me that his embassy would keep a very close tab on Polish affairs and on me. And sooner or later I was bound to be seen for what I was. I could afford to make no errors, especially in sizing up people. My instincts rarely failed me, but I would rely, too, on Wanda's unfailing intuitions.

I slowly revealed my intentions to two people from the State Department, George Vest, assistant secretary for European Affairs, and William Luers, deputy assistant secretary for Eastern Europe; and, somewhat later, to Kempton Jenkins, deputy assistant secretary of commerce. I was diplomatic and formal in my relations with other representatives of the Administration of various ranks. I considered doing the same with Brzezinski, but after my conversation with Dobrynin, I relinquished that idea. Brzezinski was considered a "hawk" and the most anti-Soviet member of the administration. Contact between him and me would not go unobserved, and the worst suspicions would be aroused in the Soviet Embassy. I had Brzezinski's name removed from the guest list for our receptions, and did so in a way that would reach some of our officers' ears, especially Zych's.

My relations with the State Department quickly grew as close as they had been in the past. The first talk was at a diminutive table at La Provençal restaurant. Luers had barely been able to fit his legs under the table. Asked about Poland, I was straightforward and admitted I was worried by the way things were tending. He was surprised, perhaps even amazed.

"I read your dossier," he said. "You're neither a liberal nor a hard-liner. What do we need a liberal for? You represent your government, and that's the way it should be."

I did not find that a particularly heartwarming remark. "Well, it is true that I owe being here to Gierek," I replied.

I spoke slowly, trying to allow him to read between the lines. "My role is not an easy one. I want to have the closest possible contact with you so that our relations are real ones, and so I can be of help to my country."

"That's what we'll do! We want it, too," he replied.

"There are some very complex matters on my side, you see. The situation in Poland is complicated, to say the least." I looked him straight in the eye. "The point is, we're not alone. Do you know what I mean?"

"I understand very clearly. We know. And I appreciate your sincerity," he said.

"I am worried about my country. I'm well aware of the problems. I know what their causes are. There are bad things happening in Poland."

"What's your view of the situation?" he asked.

"We're sinking. I don't share the optimism typical of the people in high positions in Warsaw. I think our situation will be critical within three, maybe four years. I consider it my duty to do everything to assure Poland's interests to the maximum. Our affairs may be decided over there on the Vistula, but the United States is the only one that can help us."

"You take a very serious view then."

"Yes, I do. I have to figure that the 'external' element is a constant presence and a constant threat," I said.

"Tell me why you think *we're* concerned with Poland?" he asked out of the blue.

"For three reasons," I replied without hesitation. "One, our common traditions. Two, we're completely different from our neighbors to the East. Three, we occupy an important position in Central Europe."

"You sound like one of our position papers," said Luers.

Soon thereafter, I spoke with George Vest. I felt comfortable with him straight off. We spoke about my brief meeting with Carter.

"The president stated that he was pleased with the progress in reuniting families," he said.

"Yes," I answered, "but I didn't report that in my cable to Gierek." Seeing his astonishment, I went on. "Reporting it would only hinder further progress in that area. Not only do all sorts of people read those cables, but if Gierek read it, he'd think that we'd obviously already done enough—so much, in fact, that Carter is praising us. There are a great many cases still to be resolved, the so-called difficult cases. I didn't want to jeopardize those.

"I'd like to be more precise with you about what I said to Luers," I continued. "I know what Poland needs. Unfortunately, we have to buy large quantities of fodder and grain. Without it, we'll face hunger and even greater dependence on our neighbor. We need grain credits. But how long can you live by borrowing? Grain credits are only a form of interim aid and don't solve the problem. I'd like to bring Gierek here for a visit next year and use that occasion to do something meaningful and real for Polish agriculture. Not get more credits to buy food, but work on aid to increase production."

He nodded. I felt that he was well disposed toward me but detected disbelief in his eyes about the realism of my plans. Toward the end of our talk, he remarked, "It's good that you present things so straightforwardly, even though they're difficult. We Americans appreciate that; we like that approach."

There were disappointments, too, however. In mid-April I went to see Thomas O'Neill, the speaker of the House of Representatives, whom I had met a few years back in Warsaw. Hoping for a conversation similar to the one I had once had with Sam Rayburn in the fifties, I waited impatiently in his outer office, along with a roomful of Americans. The hour of my appointment had already passed when his secretary assured me that I would be first. Just then the office door opened, and the enormous frame of O'Neill emerged. He greeted me, called a photographer over, and we shook hands as flashbulbs went off. He then said it was a pleasure to meet me and, summoning one of the waiting groups, walked off toward his office. I was stunned and angry. Later, that memory haunted me. I did not go to see him again and when some well-meaning Americans advised me to seek his support for grain credits for Poland, I rejected the advice on the spot.

I devoted a great deal of time and energy to seeking aid for Polish agriculture. I spoke with various people and hit on the trail of something potentially important: with the application of modern methods, potato harvests could be significantly increased. The annual potato yield in Poland was about fifty million tons, the second highest in the world. Even a slight increase could be of great importance. I found out that the Food Machinery Corporation (FMC)—whose chairman of the board and chief executive officer, Robert Malott, was also the U.S. chairman of the Polish-American Economic Council—specialized in increasing potato and vegetable yields. Moreover, I learned that this method had already been tested successfully in the Soviet Union. I discussed it with Malott, held a series of talks in Chicago, and then sent Gierek a memorandum.

While preparing for consultations in Warsaw, I decided to leave caution behind and speak with a few people. I called Dobrynin, who invited me to lunch on June 5. We spoke for two hours in his private dining room on the top floor of the Soviet Embassy. He was exceptionally friendly and talkative, even confiding in me.

"I'm curious about your opinion—what do you think causes the greatest difficulties for a post chief in Washington?" he asked.

"Probably the fact that our people at home don't understand America."

"Precisely!" he said emphatically. "My main problem is explaining things in Moscow. Not in the Ministry of Foreign Affairs, but up top, in the Politburo. They don't understand how incredibly complicated conditions here are."

"In Warsaw they also don't understand how the Administration operates, what it can do and what it can't," I added.

"Right! Soviet people can't understand that either," agreed Dobrynin.

We spoke on a great variety of subjects before he asked, "And how's Brzezinski?"

"I haven't been seeing him."

"You haven't been seeing him?" he said with surprise. "You're not meeting with him? He's not coming to see you?"

"No. I haven't invited him," I replied casually, and changed the subject.

That was the freest and most relaxed conversation I ever had with Dobrynin. Later on, events cast a shadow on our relationship.

Two days after that, on the day before my departure for Warsaw, I visited Brzezinski in the White House. Our meeting was formal. We spoke in English. Only toward the end did we switch to Polish. I told him my reasons for going to Warsaw. He wished me success and invited me to come by for a talk after my return.

In official Warsaw, wherever I turned, I met the same questions: How much money are the Americans giving us, and how much grain are we getting on credit? The questions came from the same Party and government people who vied with one another to criticize the United States.

A short time after I returned to Washington, a delegation from our Ministry of Agriculture arrived. I was gratified that my potato project initiative had moved so quickly. However, after reading their instructions, my satisfaction vanished. The delegation's principal task was to present Poland's request for grain and fodder, and only at the very end, in the point on "scientific and technical co-operation," was there a mention of "exploring the possibilities" of purchasing the know-how required to increase the vegetable and potato crops. Nevertheless, I did succeed in steering the delegation so that it spent most of its time at FMC in Chicago and Minnesota. Unfortunately, I could see that the delegation was ill-disposed to the idea and seemed to have been so instructed. The talks produced nothing concrete apart from a statement that they would be continued. The potato project had been nipped in the bud.

A similar fate met our co-operation with International Harvester, which died a slow death over the next few years. Interestingly enough, heavy-construction and road-building machinery, produced under license from that company, was sent to areas where work was being done for the Soviet Union.

At the beginning of August, I learned that Jan Szydlak, a member of the Politburo, a stout, bald man with simian features, was to travel to New York. I heartily disliked the man, and it was with great reluctance that I went to welcome him on instructions from the Central Committee. After the formalities, our consul took him on a tour, and I returned to Washington. My usually talkative chauffeur was silent, and I asked him why.

Suddenly he exploded. "It drives you wild. To hell with that Party! I brought Szydlak an envelope full of money; the POP secretary ordered me to. He reminded me to be careful, because there was close to a thousand dollars of Party dues in the envelope. And that Szydlak went and, goddam him, bought diamond jewelry. A pendant! *With our dues!* A diamond pendant!" he repeated indignantly. "He paid for it right out of the envelope. The hell with people like that! A big shot, a member of the Politburo, a vice premier, the chairman of the Polish-Soviet Friendship Society, and what does he do? He uses our dues to buy jewelry! How do you explain it?"

"I can't," I replied. "The man is simply a scoundrel!"

"A member of the Politburo and a scoundrel?" he asked. "A fine sight we must make."

On October 16, I was in my office writing when my secretary steamed into the room without knocking.

"I just heard on the radio," she said, trying to catch her breath, "a Pole has been named pope."

"A Pole, pope?" I repeated in amazement. "Impossible."

I turned on the radio. After a time, the program was interrupted with the report that Karol Cardinal Wojtyla, of Krakow, had been elected pope and would take the name John Paul II. A Polish pope! Seized by immense and irresistible emotion, I grabbed the phone and called Wanda. She was weeping with joy. Soon my senior officers trooped in, confused looks on their faces. They wanted me to hold a meeting to establish some guidelines for what to say about the matter. I called a conference, and as I looked around saw nothing but long faces. I gave the floor to our press counselor, who reported that the embassy was being bombarded with questions by the press, radio, and TV. I gave each of the other counselors the floor. One advised closing the office for a while and just letting the phone ring. Another said that I should go off somewhere and that those who remained in the embassy should say "No comment." A third thought it was not our business, since it concerned the church and the Vatican. Everyone was agreed on one point: we had to lie low and wait for instructions from Warsaw.

The meeting was nearing its end when the cryptographer came in with a cable from Warsaw telling us to refrain from comment and promising that instructions would arrive without delay. That caused a sigh of relief.

Wanda phoned when I was back in my office. The Apostolic delegation had called to inform her that a Mass would be said that afternoon in St. Matthew's Cathedral for "our Pope."

We met an hour later in front of the cathedral. On our way up the steps, we were stopped by a reporter and asked for a comment. "I'm pleased to be here today," I said. A priest escorted us to the front row. I felt oddly at home.

To my simultaneous satisfaction and embarrassment, the Apostolic delegate greeted Wanda and me from the pulpit. I knew only too well that as ambassador I represented Poles only in a formal sense. Many of them would not have shaken my hand. I was in Washington as Gierek's man and as a representative of a regime that was hardly representative of our nearly entirely Catholic nation. Who was I representing at that Mass? Myself? The regime? No. I was standing in for all those Poles I loved so well—Kaytus, Kazik, Bronek, Tadeusz, Father Sienkiewicz, my father-in-law, all the believers, even my own father. Through my tears I could see the archbishop raise the chalice. I knelt down for the first time.

After the Mass a man walked over to me and asked if I would consent to a television interview. I gave no thought to what I would say. I heard a reporter announce that the Polish ambassador was standing beside the Apostolic delegate. "How do you feel about a Pole being elected pope?" he asked me. I was proud to be Polish, I said; this was a great event in Poland's history.

The telephone in our apartment rang late into the night. Americans from all corners of the land called, introduced themselves, and congratulated us and Poland. A Pole from California expressed his appreciation for my words at St. Matthew's and ended by saying I was a truly Polish ambassador.

People at the embassy had also seen me on television, and they were not pleased. Cables from Warsaw soon confused them entirely. We received copies of messages sent to the pope by Gierek and Jaroszewicz. And excerpts from the Polish press poured in. The Party weekly, *Polityka,* argued that the pope was a representative from a nation that was today building a developed socialist society, that atheists and Catholics in Poland lived in creative and productive coexistence. These lies were particularly insidious in the face of the battle waged constantly against the church. These blandishments were indicative, however, of the outright fear official Poland felt for the power of Polish faith.

I received invitations to High Mass at St. Matthew's Cathedral and the National Shrine, which contains a Polish chapel. I attended, and made no effort to conceal it. A short while later, I observed that Dobrynin was taking a different view of me.

Standing by my side at a reception, he said, in a guileless voice, "You've been making public statements."

"About the election of the pope, you mean?" I said.

"Yes. Are they necessary?" he asked pointedly.

"Of course. The pope is a Pole, after all. Didn't you see the congratulatory telegram Warsaw sent?"

"No." Certainly he had. "But I suppose if it had to be done, that's another story." He never brought up the subject again.

The eighth session of the Joint Commission on Trade, attended by Vice Premier Jagielski, took place in Washington at the beginning of November. It was not so much the session that was important as the related talks. I did not recognize Jagielski on U.S. soil. In Warsaw he thundered; here he was pleasant, affable. Flinging about the most outrageous facts and figures wherever he went, Jagielski argued that Poland's economic situation was on the mend and that the worried reports circulating in the West were both groundless and harmful. This he did very eloquently, winning my admiration for his skill in wielding that lie. Nearly everything he said went against what I knew to be fact.

In Michael Blumenthal, secretary of the treasury, he met a formidable match. "But your balance of payments shows a gap of six billion dollars!" said Blumenthal firmly at one point.

"We're taking two paths," replied Jagielski, unflustered. "The first path is to increase exports, the second is to change the structure of our imports."

Blumenthal shrugged his shoulders. "Will you have to reschedule the payment dates for the credits you've received?"

"Absolutely not, absolutely not! We always pay right on time. We're like Swiss watches!"

The discussion turned to agricultural affairs, and I found myself hearing Jagielski say that Poland had had five bad harvests in a row. "We're counting on those Commodity Credit Corporation grain credits, all five hundred fifty million dollars' worth." He then proceeded to paint a critical picture of Polish agriculture. But it had been Jagielski who, for many years as minister of agriculture, had caused its decline, destroying individual farms to fit the Soviet model and collectivizing the countryside by force. It had been Jagielski, along with Jaroszewicz, who had brought our one tractor factory, Ursus, to ruin. Now he was complaining about the state of Polish agriculture without so much as batting an eye. Disaster, disaster, disaster, I thought, will there never be an end to our begging, wriggling, lying?

News from Warsaw was increasingly more depressing. Wanda and I decided to put up a good front, however. With great effort, she had brought the embassy's reception rooms back into shape, and we began entertaining officially. In keeping with our old custom, we let no chance slip to arrange concerts. I gave awards; we held dinners. We did not invite the heads of the other socialist embassies except on Poland's national holiday and Polish Army Day.

At the beginning of January 1979 I was summoned unexpectedly to Warsaw. A coded cable explained that an important meeting of the Central Committee was to be held and I was scheduled to speak. I informed the State Department that I was leaving the country for a few days, and was invited in for a talk with Under Secretary David Newsom. I was surprised to find seven officials from State and Agriculture in the room. Newsom informed me officially of the president's decision to grant Poland a further three hundred million dollars in CCC credits for agricultural purchases. That brought the total for the current fiscal year to half a billion, the same as it had been in 1978. He then stated that further credits would depend on whether we furnished Washington with economic and political information about the troubling situation in Poland.

"You have to take steps to bring that deteriorating situation under control," Vest said over lunch a few days later. He reminded me that at the end of last year our medium and long-term debt to the West exceeded fifteen billion dollars. "You must take firm steps. Disseminating propaganda and tossing figures about do not make a good impression. I'm not saying this to you personally, you understand. I'm saying it to Warsaw."

Warsaw greeted us with snow and piercing cold. The temperature was close to freezing in our apartment, and I waded through the knee-deep snow on my way to the Central Committee meeting.

In the conference hall I listened to the first speaker, Central Committee Secretary Stanislaw Kania. He read a report on the step-up of forces hostile to socialism. "Our enemies are not in prison. There are no political trials here, but we can always move in that direction. At this point we're only harassing them, making their lives miserable. The church is a hotbed of reaction, and we've known about the pope for years. He's even farther right than Wyszynski! The cult of Mary isn't enough for him; now he wants to make a cult of Stanislaw, the bishop of Krakow." Apparently, the new pope was planning to celebrate the nine hundredth anniversary of the martyrdom of Poland's patron saint, and it was being seen as a provocation.

Kania continued. "He is a pope intent on intellectual sabotage; and he's a moralizer with views similar to Carter's people."

The conference lasted three days, frightening me with its slogans and oversimplifications. Economists spoke, but not one so much as mentioned the country's debts. Evidently that subject was still taboo. Only the Central Committee secretary of press and propaganda said it was nothing to worry about, it could be covered by half of what the country produced annually. My pen fell from my hand when I heard that.

I spoke with Gierek's secretary, Jerzy Waszczuk, after the conference and learned that the First Secretary's staff, unlike their boss, did not delude themselves at all. "There's no way out," he said. "More than seventy percent of our earnings from exports go to service our debts."

"Tell me something," I asked him, "Mieczyslaw Rakowski [the editor of *Polityka*] was recently in Washington. He came unexpectedly, apparently to speak with Brzezinski, and left after his talks at the White House. Why wasn't I notified of this? That was no private visit."

Waszczuk only laughed. "You're not the first to complain about that, and you won't be the last. Rakowski keeps appearing suddenly in Bonn, too; he goes directly to see the chancellor and then is just as suddenly gone. It drives our ambassador there wild."

"What's the story?"

"Rakowski has *access.* Even the Central Committee can't do a thing about it. Neither your foreign minister nor Gierek can do anything, don't you understand yet?"

"The East?"

"Who else?"

That afternoon I visited Witold Trampczynski. He seemed in bad shape.

"I heard you've become Number One's personal adviser," I said.

"Yes," he said with a nod. "What of it?"

"You had definite ideas of what needed to be done."

"Are you trying to insult me?" he asked despondently. "Things are bad, very bad. The premier muddles along. I can't understand how he can be so blind."

"Blind?" I said incredulously. "He's just doing his job!"

Witold's eyes filled with fear. "What are you talking about?"

"Witold, you're an intelligent, educated man," I said. "You must know that Big Brother keeps a very close eye on everything that goes on here. Gierek's watching us go under without so much as lifting a finger."

"I don't know, I don't know. I can't make any sense out of what I see. There are new investment projects all the time, and yet we're well beyond our means, well beyond," he said, and opened his hands in a childlike gesture. They were trembling.

"You say you can't make any sense of it," I said with a bitter laugh. "But you just don't want to look the truth in the face."

"I don't understand Gierek any more. I don't think he reads the reports. He's living in another world. He doesn't like making decisions, and when he has to make one, he does it on the basis of some fantastical picture of things."

We parted, our views as different as ever, but with a sharper sense of what was happening to our country.

I had the difficult cases of reuniting families still to resolve. Vest had sent me a list and asked me to speed things up. I headed for Security to see Miroslaw Milewski, the only man who could help me.

The first words out of his mouth caught me by surprise. "The reports from Washington have not been good, comrade. You've managed to antagonize your people there."

"Is this in connection with the pope?" I retorted.

"Yes, but not only that. We hear that you've been neglecting security as well. That you often read coded cables aloud. You know that cannot be tolerated. We discovered microphones in our embassy in Ottawa; the entire building had been wired by the Canadians! And who knows if that isn't true of your embassy as well?"

"I absolutely deny it. I may have said a word or two aloud, but that's all. Those were irresponsible reports."

"Your predecessor was able to handle the job."

"Possibly. But I'm a different sort. I will not be led by the nose. Here is the case list. It's very important to me that these cases be dealt with."

He looked through the list intently. "We'll do what we can. Maybe a few can be arranged, but not all. Does this matter a lot to the Americans?"

"It does, although I don't know to whom it should matter more, us or them. After all, we've gotten another half a billion dollars out of them," I remarked tartly.

"All right, we'll do what we can."

While I was there, I decided to look in on the Department of Criminal Investigation's director, whom I knew from the Brazilian affair. He was glad to see me and as curious to hear about America as I was interested in what he had to say about Poland.

"The political opposition is getting stronger," he said. "Two years ago we had ten people on our list of active enemies; now there are three thousand five hundred."

"That many?" I said, astonished. "Where are they?"

"Generally speaking, until recently there were centers—KOR, the nationalists, and the church. The last is, of course, very strong; the others can't compare. Then last year the so-called free trade unions began. They're becoming increasingly active in Silesia and on the Baltic coast. It's so bad now that if we wanted to be rid of the dissident element, we'd have to jail at least a thousand of them."

"Put a thousand in jail?"

"Yes, no fewer than that, Comrade Ambassador."

I returned to the ministry nervous and anxious.

Wanda was terribly depressed. In December, Misia had placed Wanda's mother in a home for the chronically ill; she had been unable to find a replacement for her nurse. Wanda's brother, Czeslaw, was suffering from leukemia. Our friends and acquaintances were having a rough time. Winter had made the hardships and shortages only more severe. Bitterness was everywhere, and Gierek was coming in for harsh criticism. People had begun to see their poverty as connected to the "monument" he had erected to himself in Silesia, the enormous Katowice Steel Works. I learned, too, about the great obligations we had assumed in providing goods for the 1980 Olympics in Moscow.

My time in Warsaw was almost over, and I reported to Gierek. He seemed old, vacant. He told me his trip to the United States would not be possible until the spring of 1980.

"It's important that it take place before then," I said to him. "The Americans are worried about us. They gave us half a billion dollars for food, but they made it plain that it would be the last if we didn't furnish them with hard information on how we're doing." Gierek looked at me impatiently, but I continued. "They want economic information, specifics."

"We'll take care of it. Anyway, they don't have to worry about us. We can take care of ourselves. And you take care of my trip there. I want concrete achievements. Right now the most important thing for us is the German problem. Those West Germans are after atomic weapons, and that's no joke. As you recall, I myself told Carter that we could also have atomic weapons if we wanted to." He gave weight to those words, then leaned across his desk to tell me in a confidential tone, "I can tell you, Comrade Spasowski, that Comrade Brezhnev's health is a cause of concern. They don't know what to do over there, but the international situation requires *active* measures. Someone has to take up the scepter, and it can't be Ceausescu or Tito."

There was no doubt that Gierek saw himself as a man of the moment. And that alarmed me.

We left Warsaw exhausted. All I had to show for the trip was permission to reunite between ten and twenty families. The irony was that these reunions had been arranged by Security, the same people who were preparing lists of thousands to be jailed in the future.

I flew to Warsaw again in May, for a session of the Polish-American Economic Council. And I prolonged my stay in order to be there when the pope arrived. I had promised Wanda I would do this, for she had been unable to accompany me—we simply could not afford it.

Warsaw changed from one day to the next. Religious pictures and symbols appeared in windows; from balconies hung rugs, flags—Poland's white and red and the Vatican's white and yellow. Something out of the ordinary was occurring. The city where I had been born and raised, a city that had been rebuilt from ruins, its population hand-picked to serve the purposes of the Communist regime, was now showing its true face, its soul. On the Friday before the pope's arrival, candles burned in windows all day and night; people walked the city until late, in a mood of festive anticipation. Others poured into the capital from everywhere in the country. On Victory Square, workmen labored around the clock. A mighty wooden cross rose above the podium.

I saw the pope's arrival on television on the morning of June 2. And in the early afternoon, I went into the city to catch a glimpse of him as his car passed on its way to Belvedere Palace, where he was to meet Gierek. "Long may you live!" the crowds cried, wiping away tears, as the white-canopied car went by. These were not types Security would have trucked into the city.

Moving through a human sea, I made my way to Victory Square, where the pope would say Mass at four o'clock. Young people in white caps with papal and boy scout insignia were checking passes. I stood in line, but seeing that people without white passes were not being allowed in, I walked off to the side. I could see the podium, the white altar, and the wooden cross towering over it. Religious hymns were sung, then words of greeting boomed out across the square. The words were hard to make out. "A human being cannot fully understand himself without Christ. . . ." I strained to hear through the echoing boom of the speakers to the words of the man.

Finally, my ears adjusted. "Without Christ, one cannot understand the history of the Polish nation, that great thousand-year-old community, of such deep importance to me and to each of us. One cannot understand this city, Warsaw, the capital of Poland, which in 1944 resolved to enter into unequal battle with the invader, a battle in which it was abandoned by its allies, a battle that would leave it in rubble. Christ, too, lay beneath that rubble!"

I could see the Warsaw of January 1945, a stone wasteland gripped by ice and snow. I recalled the two monuments among the snow and cobblestones. I had stopped by both of them—Christ and King Zygmunt. I had not cried then. Hungry and frozen to the bone, I was more concerned about stepping on a land mine. It was only now that I cried, standing alone by a streetlight, unable to see, barely able to hear. After many words and much applause, the last of the homily seemed to echo from a great depth, and engrave itself on memory: "May Your Spirit descend on us! May Your Spirit descend on us! And renew the face of the earth. This earth! Amen!"

I remained in Warsaw a few days, and Jerzy Waszczuk handed me a letter to pass on from Gierek to Senator Edmund Muskie. I knew that the senator had recently been in Warsaw and had spoken with Gierek, but the State Department had been oddly vague in explaining the purpose of his trip. I assumed that the Administration was using this means to acquire firsthand knowledge of our situation, since their ambassador, William Schaufele, was not being given access to the top. I read the letter. Gierek thanked the senator for his interesting conversation and, in connection with the subjects they had discussed, he was enclosing a list of the technology we needed and were willing to purchase. The list contained eighteen items. The first three, evidently the most important, were videotape, sound tape, and color film for home movies.

Pale with fury, I shouted, "What kind of letter is this? Who wrote this nonsense?"

"It came from the Planning Commission, straight from the Engineer."

"But this is compromising! I can't deliver this letter."

"I'm giving you the letter to deliver, that's all. Do as you wish, but the responsibility is yours."

I ran my eye down the list again. "Not a single item has anything to do with agriculture. Has Gierek seen this?" I asked.

"Yes. And Premier Jaroszewicz was consulted."

So that was it.

I went to see Stefan Olszowski, the former foreign minister, who remained the Central Committee secretary in charge of economic affairs.

Things are bad, he told me bluntly. "Carter. Our 'friends' don't like him. They don't like him at all," he remarked. "That human rights policy of his is more than they can bear."

"And you think Moscow wants to come to terms with Washington?"

"Of course, very much so. But on an equal footing. Not with Carter interfering in their internal affairs."

"And if they came to terms, then what?"

"Then things would progress according to the laws of Marxism-Leninism."

"Meaning America would fall?"

"What else? You see, the worst of it is that there's been no contact between Gierek and Brezhnev for quite a long time now."

"They're not talking to each other?"

"Well, there hasn't been anything since the pope's visit. Literally, not a word. Nothing. Everything now goes through the premier, who refused in a rage to take any part in the visit. And now, to add to the discomfort, Moscow's putting on the pressure. You know what a severe winter we had. We appealed to Moscow for five hundred megawatts of energy. Do you know what their response was? They cut off nearly all the current. We suffered enormous losses. The Czechs cut off their current to us, too. Those were political decisions made at the highest level."

"Meaning that the worse things are for us, the better for them?" I asked.

"Don't oversimplify. They're not communicating with Gierek. They consider receiving the pope a serious error. Our Soviet friends know what's going on here; they know what the mood is. It's rough."

"What do you plan on doing? Staying on here?"

He gave me a sharp glance, as if I had touched on a sensitive subject. "I've got time," he wheezed. "I'll tell you one thing, if they offer me the premiership, I'll refuse. It's all or nothing for me!"

I understood. He wanted the first secretary's position. He wanted both positions perhaps; absolute power in his hands.

"I'll give you some good advice," he offered. "Stick close to Dobrynin. He's the only one who'll be able to get you through what's coming next."

CHAPTER XXIX

I returned to Washington at a loss as to how to proceed. The tasks I had set myself had misfired. Ambassadors are expected to be in the "know" and able to do a great deal as the representatives of their governments. With me, it was the reverse. Moreover, all my life I had been impelled toward conscious action. I might not agree, I might criticize, but I had to know first. Now I did not. One thing was clear: I had to make the embassy a positive representation of Poland. I decided to work on substantive contributions: programs like Project Hope, the American Children's Hospital in Krakow, grain credits.

Wanda shared my drive and worked unsparingly. The embassy pulsed with life. Some evenings were devoted to music, with performers from Poland participating. Then, Wanda was in her element. During the course of one year, twenty-nine functions took place in the embassy. That was no easy matter. Our funds were limited, and we had only money enough to purchase food and drink. We never used a caterer. Everything was done by our own people, mainly the wives. Wanda supervised the official entertainment and the food, often spending time in the kitchen herself. I oversaw the reception rooms.

We happened on a fine house on Albemarle Street that, after repairs, promised to be suitable for a residence. After long haggling with Warsaw and the owner, I reached an agreement and purchased it.

During the summer, Wojtaszek paid an official visit to Washington. I saw him again in New York in September when he came for a session of the United Nations. We went for a walk in Central Park. The weather was beautiful. He was in a good mood. Apparently Number One's talks with France and West Germany were going well. They had agreed to lend us support, so there was no cause for worry this year or the next. The situation in the Central Committee had also taken a turn for the better. "The comrades see light at the end of the tunnel," said Wojtaszek, "and Gierek clearly has the situation under control." It was the sort of sunny optimism appropriate to a Sunday walk in Central Park.

As October approached, Wanda and I looked forward to the pope's visit to Washington. We anticipated with great feeling seeing the Pole who now walked in "St. Peter's shoes." When the day finally arrived, we made our way to the Apostolic Delegation, where the diplomatic corps was to meet John Paul II. In one hand Wanda clenched her bag, which contained a letter for the pope written the night before. I assured John Paul that I was doing the best I could for the good of Poland, and Wanda said that her religion had been the great force of her life since childhood. He asked if we might like to wait a while and speak more, but I thanked him and refused, seeing that he was very tired. He told us he would be glad to see us if we were ever in Rome. Wanda withdrew her envelope quickly and handed it to him. The prelate standing behind him reached out to relieve him of it, but John Paul thrust the envelope deep into his pocket.

The Soviet invasion of Afghanistan at the end of December 1979 did not surprise me. The assassinations and purges in Kabul had demonstrated that a violent overthrow was in the making. To my mind, the events there were closely connected to the situation in Iran.

Warsaw's position on this issue was disturbing. Our permanent UN representative, Henryk Jaroszek, thundered in defense of the Soviet invasion, which had supposedly come at the invitation of the "legal government in Kabul." He waved his arms about excitedly and pounded his fist on the lectern.

I was asked to the State Department again. Robert Barry, Luers's successor as deputy assistant secretary for Eastern European Affairs, said that "Teheran and Afghanistan" were making it difficult for them to detect any differences between the Soviets and their satellites. My only defense was our lack of independence, but that cut two ways. If we were not independent, why were they listening to me at all. Fortunately, Gierek did take some action that allayed the bad impression Poland had made: apparently furious at our UN delegate, he demanded his recall.

For me, 1980 began with the Eighth Party Congress. I was in Warsaw by the end of January and strolling the corridors of Joseph Stalin's gift to Poland—Congress Hall in the Palace of Culture.

This time I had an even stronger sense of being seated in a theater. The actors sat in a long row on stage: the rulers, those responsible for everything that was taking place outside that great theater. The next act in the drama was about to begin. Perhaps it would be a tragedy, perhaps it would be a farce. There was something heavy in the air that had not been there during the last act four years before. And I, too, was not the same person. I looked on the players with a cold cynicism that went against my nature.

In his address, Number One attempted to unite patriotism and Communism, the traditions of the Polish army and uprisings with the prewar and contemporary Communists. His ghost-writers had outdone themselves. I could not listen calmly to all that falsity and megalomania, those words "peace," "relaxation of tensions," "détente"; his call for a European disarmament conference.

On the second day, the first speaker was the Kremlin's *éminence grise* and chief theorist, Mikhail Suslov, the chief guest of the congress. He spoke about the United States, although the country was not referred to by name. He painted an idyllic picture of nations striving for peace and freedom—Iran and Afghanistan, for example—and of an evil superpower that had assumed the role of gendarme and was possessed with a malevolent desire to punish, as it had a few years back in Vietnam and as it was doing presently in Iran. I looked about the auditorium at that obedient group. They knew nothing of the world. My eyes ran along the upper, somewhat recessed balcony where I caught sight of Moczar. Immobile, stony, he stared at the long row of people at the speakers' table. There seemed to be something predatory in his gaze.

I stopped attending, but went to the final session to see who the new ruling team would be. After a protracted "discussion," the results of the Politburo "elections" were read. Premier Jaroszewicz's was not among the names. That news afforded me some satisfaction. Good riddance. Over a period of ten years that Soviet superagent had become such a fixture in the top leadership of People's Poland that it seemed he would be there forever. In the lobby, during the break, all those in the know gossiped about the scandal that had been played out behind the scenes. The superagent had not wished to step down. He had shouted and made threats; he had called on Suslov for help. Gierek had been about to break. Some strange bargaining had gone on. But Gierek's people were fed up with the premier and knew that Poland had been brought to ruin while he continued to assure everyone that all was well. They thought that in removing the premier from office they would be removing the responsibility from themselves as well.

Olszowski was not elected to the Politburo either, and many wondered why. I recalled his saying, "All or nothing!" He did not want to share power with Number One in a period of deterioration. He knew he would be blamed for it, too. He was still a young man and preferred to yield for the moment. Shortly after the congress, he was appointed ambassador to East Berlin. There he waited until Gierek fell; then he returned to Poland to assume an influential position in the "new" Politburo.

Soviet influence on Poland's government sustained a certain limitation, because there was no one to replace the superagent who had held the reins for ten years. Soviet influence had not, however, been weakened in the Party.

I wondered who the next premier would be and, while scanning the list of the new team, my eye fell on the name Edward Babiuch, who had remained in the Politburo but had not been given a place in the Secretariat. Could that mean that he would be assigned other duties? I was not mistaken. He was named the new premier. He had always been on close terms with the Soviet Embassy, but he would not be able to play the same role for the Soviets that his predecessor had. His appointment was clearly a temporary one.

On the last day, I read through the "foreign" resolution, which called for a European conference on military détente and disarmament. "The Congress warmly supports the readiness voiced by

Comrade Edward Gierek to host that conference in our heroic capital—a city of peace—Warsaw." Thinking back, I recalled that Moscow had already assigned us various initiatives in the areas of peace and disarmament. This latest initiative had come in Suslov's briefcase, which meant that the conference in Helsinki had been viewed as only a first stage by the Kremlin's planners. Now at issue was the disarmament of Western Europe. As always, Germany was the key to achieving that end, and the immediate target now was Germany's armed forces.

After the congress no one from the Ministry of Foreign Affairs or the Central Committee would seriously discuss the unfair position Poland had taken on Iran and Afghanistan. I claimed this spoke ill of us and damaged our interests with America. Wojtaszek and others dismissed my concerns as exaggerations.

One task remained. A year before, a few rabbis from New York had requested that I check on the progress of the Warsaw synagogue. In the fifties Jews in the United States had appealed to me to promote the rebuilding of this synagogue, the only one not utterly destroyed during the war. I had done so. Now, twenty years later, the question had been raised again.

I went to see the synagogue for myself. What stood before me was a sad sight. The walls were cracked and stripped of their plaster, the windows were boarded up, and the roof had collapsed. The square looked as if it had been barely cleared of the rubble of war.

I saw Kazimierz Kakol, the minister in charge of the Office of Religious Affairs. He grew serious when I told him about the synagogue. "Have you been there? Have you seen it with your own eyes?" I asked.

"Yes," he said. "You see . . . there are problems. Why don't you go see the Central Committee secretary, Comrade Kania?"

I did not have time to see Kania. But I promised myself to see him the next time I was in Warsaw.

I returned to Washington at the end of February, and my suspicions were aroused on the first day. They began with my safe. I had cast only a careless glance at the seal and quickly dialed the combination. It was as I pulled the door open that I noticed the seal had been smeared. But broken now, the seal would not show conclusively that the safe had been opened in my absence. There was nothing missing; my notes were complete. Nevertheless, I could not shake the suspicion that someone had been going through my things.

"That doesn't surprise me in the least," said Wanda. "They're capable of anything. I forgot to tell you that lately letters that come for us to the embassy are being opened."

She brought me letters addressed to us at the ministry and forwarded to Washington by diplomatic pouch, the normal practice. I examined them carefully. Wanda had opened the envelopes with a letter opener, but it was obvious they had been steamed open before that.

"They're not the only only ones that have been opened," she said, handing me the letters mailed to us within the United States. They, too, had been steamed open.

I brought all my notes home that same day and from then on used the safe solely for my official correspondence with the ministry and the Administration. In my spare time I also began inventing records of conversations, which came to quite a stack over a period of time.

At that time, my secretary was Justyna, the wife of a consulate employee who had arrived in Washington the previous year. She seemed pleasant and was very efficient. Unfortunately, my opinion of her changed rapidly when I saw what her innocent looks and smiles concealed. She made daily reports on me to the Security resident and, during working hours, often ran up to see him on the floor above. I could see that if I really wanted to elude Security, I would have to make my own appointments and keep her in the dark.

Outwardly, nothing changed at the embassy. Every Tuesday morning, I held a meeting at which the counselors and secretaries reported on their activity; at the end I would sum up and issue them instructions for the coming week. We usually sat at the long table in the dining room. I would open my notebook in such a way that it could be read by those beside me.

One morning I found the resident waiting for me, his expression uncertain. "Comrade Ambassador, I want to report an accident that took place during the night in the embassy," he began. "Around midnight one of the guards lost his balance. It was dark, he was leaning over the banister, and he fell from the second floor to the first."

"He fell?"

"Yes, he landed on the banister downstairs. An ambulance came for him. I've already issued instructions for them to be more careful in the future. That's all."

I did not believe a word he had said. At the time, there were three guards at the embassy. They were on duty at night, armed, and made rounds through the building; by day they mostly slept. They were not allowed to go outside alone. It had been drummed into their heads that they could be abducted or fall victim to some provocation designed especially for them by the FBI, "the most perfidious secret police in the world." All of them had been recruited from among the officers in the Internal Security Corps. They were inclined to engage in drinking bouts, and tried to keep these secret from me, since some of the "diplomats"—Security majors and colonels—also participated.

The truth soon came to light. I learned that a bout had ended in a brawl. The guard had not fallen, but had simply been thrown downstairs by Security officers.

Not much time passed after the Eighth Party Congress before I began receiving coded cables inquiring insistently whether the Administration would grant us any further credits that year. I replied that it was not the time for such questions; we had not yet fully availed ourselves of the existing credits. At the end of March, I was instructed to request an additional one hundred seventy million dollars and, with a heavy heart, discussed it with Secretary of Agriculture Bob Bergland. It was a pleasant conversation, because Bergland was a pleasant person, but I soon felt that the Administration was ill-disposed to the idea.

Then, one evening I received a call from Bob Barry, with whom I had established a friendly association. He sounded concerned. "We've received some very disturbing reports. American grain is being transferred from ships . . ."

"Where? From whose ships?"

"From your ships to others, belonging to another country," he said.

"You're sure of this?" I asked.

"There's more to it. The technology you've been getting from us is also being transferred to another country." I felt that my worst misgivings had come true: the Soviets were no longer even trying to maintain appearances.

I soon heard from the State Department that Afghanistan was encumbering Polish-American relations and that the current year would not be suitable for a high-level visit. Gierek's visit was out.

The meeting of the ambassadors from the socialist countries took place regularly once a month, with the exception of summer. They began with a dinner, attended by the wives. The host made a speech at the table, praising the unity of the socialist camp and the leading role of the Soviet Union, its Party, and its first secretary, Leonid Brezhnev. The Czech and the Bulgarian were especially adept at this. Then Dobrynin, our dean, spoke, usually confining himself mainly to jokes and witticisms. It was obvious he enjoyed hearing Moscow and himself praised.

After dinner the men would go off for their meeting. At the Soviet Embassy, the women were shown short propaganda films; in others, the national dessert was served. Those were trying occasions for Wanda. She always felt alien. It cost her great effort to restrain herself when Irina Dobrynin spouted propaganda reviling Americans, and all the others obediently agreed. For the most part, she said nothing at all. Only when her patience was exhausted would she make remarks, which often outraged the others. She was all too well known for her candor.

The men met in rooms offering the best possible protection against bugging. In the Soviet Embassy this was Dobrynin's office. Apart from the Soviets, only the Hungarians had a small "quiet" room that was air-conditioned and large enough for us all. In the other embassies, ordinary rooms were used. The host chaired the meeting. Over tea, coffee, drinks, and dried fruit, the others made their reports. Dobrynin always summed up. The reports followed a pattern: bilateral relations were treated first and in detail, the more important conversations with the State Department being cited, followed by general observations on the United States and its foreign policy. It was rare to hear anything new or interesting. Judging by the boredom I read on his face, Dobrynin must have felt the same, though he was usually adept at concealing his emotions.

I often wondered why Dobrynin was so insistent about those meetings. I quickly concluded that there were at least three good reasons to hold them. First, they would demonstrate the cohesive unity of the socialist camp, not only to the socialists themselves, but also to the Americans. It was of particular importance to Moscow that the partners in the Warsaw Pact and Comecon create a monolithic impression. Second, they afforded Dobrynin a constant view of bilateral relations and allowed him to rein in anything that had gone too far out of line with Moscow. Third, the meetings served as a monitor of random business opportunities. For example, if the Hungarian ambassador began an account of interesting conversations with an industrialist wishing to do business with Budapest, Dobrynin would interrupt him, remarking that such matters were "too specific" for discussion at the meeting. That did not mean he was not interested. Quite the contrary. He would ask detailed questions later in private.

He was extremely well informed about Poland. Once in a great while he would ask me about one detail or another. He never reacted negatively, which confirmed my belief that this or that had been part and parcel of the Soviets' calculations all along.

The Socialist dinner of April 23 took place at the Bulgarians' residence, the most modest of all, not counting mine. I noted down nothing of interest at the meeting although I did hear jokes about America being so stymied by the fanatic Khomeini that Carter was considering a "military operation" to rescue the U.S. hostages in Iran.

Two days later Wanda and I watched Carter on television report that a secret military expedition to rescue the hostages had ended in a fiasco. It seemed a repetition of the defeat in Vietnam, although on a microscopic scale. Had the American army lost its combat ability? Why? When?

Secretary of State Cyrus Vance resigned in protest against the rescue operation. As his successor the president appointed Edmund Muskie, whom I had known for a long time.

It was in May 1980 that I suddenly realized that a certain unique constellation now existed for Poland and its aspirations for freedom, so cruelly tried by history. The papal throne was now occupied by a Pole. The new secretary of state was Edmund Muskie, an American of Polish descent. The president's national security adviser was Zbigniew Brzezinski. Clement Zablocki was chairman of the House

Committee on Foreign Affairs. Other influential figures were Congressman Dan Rostenkowski, and Edward Derwinski. Those men could not be indifferent to the fate of Poland. And one did not have to be of Polish descent to see the truth, be of good will, and want to help. There were many Americans who were aware that the Poles had been the first to take up arms during the war and had known no peace since. A certain energy possessed me. The hour for action had come. Only my dying gladiator did not seem to share my hopes.

I soon learned how treacherous diplomacy could be. My first instructions from Gierek after Muskie's appointment arrived. I was to meet with him at once to convey Gierek's message, which contained nothing new. He merely said that, for Poland, East-West relations—especially those between Washington and Moscow—were of utmost importance. But the instructions came late, and Muskie was headed for a meeting in Vienna with Gromyko. Gierek's objective was obvious: to influence Muskie before that meeting. Then something else dawned on me. I had spoken with Dobrynin earlier and noted his interest in Muskie. In fact, he was surprised to learn that I knew him personally. Putting that conversation together with Gierek's cable and calculating how much time had elapsed between the two, I could see that this was no coincidence. Dobrynin must have sent instructions to the Soviet Ministry of Foreign Affairs to have Gierek send Muskie "his" views on Soviet-American relations. In an upside-down sort of way, Moscow was trying to exploit the constellation for itself.

And there were obstacles from the American side. One day at the State Department, Bob Barry picked up a paper and began to read aloud about the illegal activities of the military attaché's staff at my embassy. One of them had been buying up electronic components, disregarding the ban on their export. Over a period of some twelve months, he had purchased one hundred forty thousand dollars' worth, paying in hundred-dollar bills which he carried in his briefcase. The State Department demanded that an end be put to this practice, claiming that it would have influence on bilateral relations.

Immediately upon returning to the embassy, I summoned the military attaché, Colonel Henryk Krszeszowski, and handed him the State Department's "non-paper." He read it through and, to my surprise, burst into laughter. He then made a gesture indicating that we should talk where there could be no surveillance. Then, bending close to my ear, he whispered, "The way those scum watch us is awful, and still they don't know all that much."

"A hundred forty thousand dollars isn't all that much? Don't you realize how this complicates bilateral relations?" I scolded him.

"It's nothing, I tell you, just the tip of the iceberg! By now we've bought a good couple of million dollars' worth."

I stared at him in amazement.

"You don't believe me?" he asked. "One just has to know *how.* Not like him," he said, with a nod at the non-paper, "going around New York stores. We have our ways. Here they would skin us, but in Europe we can get whatever our hearts desire from America."

That conversation returned my sense of reality. My best hopes for Poland's unique constellation in the United States quickly receded.

On May 5, U.S. Secretary of Commerce, Philip Klutznick, flew into Warsaw for the ninth session of the Joint Commission. I took part in the talks. Our side used every possible argument to demonstrate that our terrible economic situation was the result of extenuating circumstances. Warsaw appealed to Klutznick for U.S. support in our talks with the banks and asked for CCC credits amounting to six hundred seventy million dollars for 1980–81. Listening to the exchange, I did not know whether to laugh or to cry.

I sat beside Klutznick during his talk with Gierek. Number One gave the impression of a man cut off from reality and transfixed by a vision of his own. Perhaps he had some basis for it; a week before, Brezhnev and Giscard D'Estaing had met in Warsaw at his invitation.

"Nothing happens all by itself," remarked Gierek. He raised his head as if seeking inspiration. "We want to play a helpful role for the great powers, and we probably are. . . . I'm not suggesting anything . . . and there's no point in saying too much here—but a bridge is needed between East and West. *Of course I'm not suggesting anything,* Mr. Secretary," Gierek repeated, "But your reaction to the situation in Afghanistan has been very harmful."

"We had no choice," replied Klutznick. "I can tell you that we debated the issue for three days. We took two extreme reactions under consideration and we chose to send a definite signal. A warning, sanctions. After all, that was an outright invasion."

"That's no way to accomplish anything with Moscow," observed Gierek.

"It's true that a solution must be found."

I chatted with Gierek briefly after Klutznick left. It was only a social exchange. I was not to see him again.

I thought of what he had said about a bridge. He would have been finished if he said anything of the sort in Moscow. Moscow did not require any intermediaries, any bridges, and considered such ideas heresy.

Wanda and I were frightened by the Poland we now saw. There was nothing to be bought in the store nearest us, which formerly had been supplied decently enough with necessities. It was closed most of the time. People took their places in endless lines at night to buy a piece of meat. Young mothers were at their wit's end trying to find powdered milk. Where were the enormous amounts of grain that had been imported? Where were the extraordinary sums of money that had been loaned to Poland? We met with the same answer everywhere: It had all quietly vanished east. But the West was not saying a word! The West was not raising a hue and cry! I could not fathom why.

Czeslaw was now seriously ill, his leukemia having advanced to the point where he required frequent blood transfusions. In Warsaw, however, blood was not available for ordinary people, and it was only through connections and with the aid of our doctor friends that he was finally able to receive a small amount of blood. We spoke with many people in medicine and were appalled by the picture they painted. Everything was in short supply. Leading surgeons had no rubber gloves, no surgical thread. Hospitals were without disinfectants.

Saddest of all were our meetings with young people, our friends' children, people the same age as Misia, or as Kaytus would have been. They were crushed by the situation and by the lack of any hope. Some of them even said straight out that Kaytus had done the right thing, that this sort of life had no meaning. They asked if an East-West confrontation was brewing; they viewed that alone as a change for the better. We suffered for those young people.

"How could we allow ourselves to purchase a house?" Wanda reproached me. "That money could buy so much medicine! You can see what's going on here. People can't even get aspirin."

"But the money would never go to medicine! Do you know how many millions are spent for embassies in the socialist countries?" I asked Wanda. "Have you heard how much those goddamned Olympic Games in Moscow are costing us? We've built more than thirty tourist inns there, and we're supplying them with food. Yet there's no paint in all of Poland. As for the residence, we didn't do it for ourselves. We're putting a lot of work and our own money into it. It's only right that Poland have a respectable representation in America."

Wanda had to agree, even if it was through her tears.

We began preparing to return to Washington at the end of the month. I still had not dealt with the list of families to be reunited, hesitating about whether to go see Milewski. In the end I overcame my aversion. As always, he was reluctant to accept the list, and, as always, I reminded him we wanted large amounts of U.S. credits in the coming year.

"In any case, it's a good thing you dropped by," he said. "I want you to get off to a good start with our new Security resident, who'll be arriving in Washington soon. You know him, don't you?"

"I do know Slawomir Lipowski, yes. He was in Washington in the fifties."

"Yes, he's a good worker and a good man," said Milewski. "Try to make his job easier. He acquitted himself excellently in Tokyo, and we're banking on him. What's new in the embassy?"

"A lot of work, not much else," I replied.

"We're still receiving bad reports on you," he observed. "Concerning your isolation. You may be working hard but you're keeping too aloof. It bothers people. And then there's the residence . . ."

"What's wrong with the residence? No one's lifting a finger to help with it. My wife's taking care of everything."

"Yes, but some people find it upsetting. It cost so much money, and they complain there's no club, nor is there a decent preschool for the staff's children."

"Excuse me, but an embassy is not a club. Is there anything else?" I asked calmly.

"Yes. Apparently your wife is always in church."

"That's her business. She's always gone to church and always will. No one can forbid her that," I replied, seething.

"It's not her business alone. She's the wife of an ambassador. People view her as an example, and people talk."

"Let them talk. It would be better if they spent their time working instead of spying. I'll tell you one thing: my mail is being opened and read."

"Impossible. We don't monitor ambassadors. But I'll tell you something, comrade. So much is reported about you that if you didn't have the past you have, there'd be trouble for sure. I notice, by the way, you've been writing fewer political cables lately."

"I'm pursuing Poland's interests. Political cables don't produce bread to eat," I replied.

"That's true. And, besides, I suppose you have to be careful when writing. The French crack ninety percent of the cables sent through the embassies in Paris."

"That much? How do you know?"

"We know. From a good source. And we draw the proper conclusions. There are no secrets in the West. That Brzezinski calls the Vatican quite often. His phone bill must be sky high!"

He must have noticed my surprise, for he repeated, "We know! We really know! No secrets!" He snickered.

We returned to Washington and plunged back into work on the residence with a maniacal sort of energy. What for? What was I trying to prove? We were both exhausted, and, after all, in two or three years, we would be leaving Washington, this time forever. I would have the retirement I had asked for years before. Yet I had just brought the works of an old clock from Poland to place reverently on the mantel of a fireplace. Could it be because everything I had clung to throughout my life was now collapsing and I had a need to leave something tangible behind, however small?

I telephoned Brzezinski as soon as I returned. We met soon thereafter, but I was inhibited by the formal atmosphere and by the presence of his coworker, and I departed from the scenario I had prepared. We spoke about Afghanistan and the U.S. elections instead of about Poland. Brzezinski was apprehensive that the Republicans might win, and we reflected on what could be done to help Carter. I, too, wanted a Democratic victory, primarily because it fitted in with my notion of a constellation for Poland. A solution to the problem of Afghanistan would certainly have been of help to the president.

There was not much going on at the embassy, as was usually the case in summer. We waited each day with bated breath for news from Poland. The wave of dissatisfaction after the price hikes in July had grown greater and various incidents were beginning to crop up. I was receiving few coded cables. As usual, Warsaw was not keeping me informed. One day the cryptographer placed a cable on my desk. I read: "Spasowski. Washington. For your eyes only. Komorowski, the secretary of the Central Committee of the Communist Party USA, has been in touch with me. They are collecting information against Brzezinski but have very little. They would like whatever we have, especially about him and his family exploiting peasants. Speed is of the essence. I request instructions. Cias."

Kazimierz Cias was our consul general in New York and had been authorized by Warsaw to maintain contact with U.S. Communists. Despite many rebukes from the Foreign Department of the Central Committee, I had never met any of them, and had no intention of doing so. My memories of collusion with the British Communists stuck like a bone in my throat. I sat down at my desk and wrote a reply: "Cias. New York. For your eyes only. Inform Komorowski that our posts do not gather information against members of the American government. Spasowski."

A few days passed. From the reports of foreign correspondents and people coming from Poland it was clear that the wave of unrest was sweeping through the cities and industrial centers. In Lublin, striking workers had stopped a train carrying a shipment headed east. The cars had been opened, as had their contents. In the cans of "paint" going to the USSR the workers had found ham. At the beginning of August strikes had spread to Lodz and the large textile factories and gradually penetrated Silesia and the Baltic coast, key areas because of miners and shipyard workers. Time was running out.

I telephoned Brzezinski on August 5, and we agreed to meet and talk "off the record." He suggested a restaurant, Maison Blanche, near the White House. When I arrived, I spotted a number of Secret Service people by the entrance. Brzezinski came late, saying that something urgent had come up.

"We were talking about how to help Carter last time. Maybe we should start there, and then move on to Poland. The two are connected," I said.

"Fine, right. Afghanistan," he began animatedly. "Do you see any possibility of Warsaw helping to find an honest solution, one we'd be able to accept?"

"I've been thinking about that. There may be only one way to a solution—through Gierek. He wants to play a role; he might even pull something off. You know that Brezhnev and Giscard met in Warsaw on May 19 on Gierek's initiative. He sees himself as a 'bridge.' So we can try," I continued as Brzezinski nodded. "I have my doubts about what it'll produce, but there's no harm in trying."

"Would you write to Gierek?"

"Oh, no!" I replied at once. "That would produce the opposite result. My cable would be read in Moscow before it even arrived in Warsaw. And the Soviets would treat it as a provocation. There can't be any cables or any letters."

"They read everything?" asked Brzezinski.

"Of course. They have direct access to our entire communications system."

"So what do you intend to do?" he asked after a moment.

"I'll speak with Gierek the next chance I have. The only question is how should it be presented?"

"We want an honest solution. They should be able to save face; that's very important to them. I'll give it some thought, too. . . . Now for Poland. How could we help Poland?" he asked.

"I learned a lot from my last trip home. Something very important, something that may even be of historic significance, is beginning to happen in Poland. I could be wrong, but I think not. Gierek is not in control; people are absolutely fed up with him. But there's no alternative to Gierek. Everyone else is worse. He's supposed to meet with Schmidt again around the twentieth of this month and with Giscard in September. I don't know what'll come of it. People are exhausted. You have no idea how hard things are."

"We know. But what do you propose?"

"Poles shouldn't go hungry. That's very important. And they should feel they're supported by the free world. That means further credits to purchase grain. I know that some of it has been taken by the Soviets . . . but they don't take all of it. Some gets through to the people. Health care is also important—medicine, powdered milk for children. There's a shortage of everything. The hospitals are grappling with enormous difficulties. I'm asking for this type of help on a humanitarian level."

Brzezinski looked closely at me. "Are you a Communist?"

"I'm a member of the Party. There are probably few people in Poland who have been in it as long as I have. So, yes, officially, I am. The reality is something else, but that's not important. It's a long story. My father was an ardent communist."

"Is he dead?"

"Yes, he died in 1941. Excuse me, but I truly want nothing for myself," I said all of a sudden. "I love that poor unfortunate country . . ." I did not finish the sentence. Tears were flooding my eyes. Not wishing Brzezinski to notice, I wiped my nose with my handkerchief.

Brzezinski glanced at his watch. "It's late, I have to go."

"One moment," I said, taking out my notes. "Two things . . . The American Communists have requested that our post provide information to be used against you."

He smiled, unsurprised. "And so?"

"I've told them we don't collect information against members of the American government."

"This is a democracy. Anything's possible here," he remarked philosophically. "And the other thing?"

"When I was in Warsaw I learned that they were aware of your telephone conversations with the Vatican. Apparently you're talking with the Vatican a great deal." That caught his interest. "I don't know how they're listening in, but they are. I have it on good authority. Be careful. That's all."

"Maybe we should make arrangements to see each other again," replied Brzezinski. "Can you come to my office in two days, at five o'clock?"

"Fine. Please inform them at the entrance that I'll be coming."

We rose, and the Secret Service people rose as well. I felt weary, dissatisfied with myself. I had not succeeded in expressing what I felt, and what I had said had sounded flat. Besides, who can understand us? I thought.

Our conversation two days later was brief. Brzezinski said that the president knew and approved of our talk. The rest depended on when I would see Gierek and on the further course of events. I appreciated the good sense of that position, since there were too many unknowns in the equation we had worked out. At the end, I reminded Brzezinski about the grain.

As ambassador, I did not meet with Brzezinski again. But I did learn that not only were the Soviets using U.S. Communists to act against him, but also a campaign was on in Bonn to influence Carter to get rid of him. Evidently the Soviets thought that, as a Pole, he was too aware of their methods.

There was constant news from Poland of strikes. Apparently, as in 1970, the Lenin Shipyard in Gdansk had begun to play the key role. It was reported that the free trade unions were operating there. Soon, I came across the name Lech Walesa for the first time. He was the head of the strike committee. Both he and a woman welder, Anna Walentynowicz, had been fired for their union activities, but the workers had forced management to rehire them. Later on I was to read Walentynowicz's words about herself: "I was born in Volhynia. When the war broke out, my father went to the front, my brother was deported, and my mother died of a heart attack!" Hers was a thoroughly Polish story.

The strike in the shipyard was peaceful. Nevertheless, the authorities cut the shipyard off from the rest of the country, and Gierek rejected the strikers' demands. The Party must have acknowledged that the situation was serious, because they sent Vice Premier Tadeusz Pyka to Gdansk. A narrow-minded dogmatist, he was unable to mollify the workers. He was replaced by Jagielski. This was a development I found disturbing. Not only was Jagielski an agent of Moscow, but also, to my mind, he was the shrewdest and most cunning of them all.

As soon as these talks began in Gdansk, I received instructions to explain to the Administration what was happening in Poland. I carried out those instructions with pleasure in a conversation on August 22 with Warren Christopher. Warsaw made assurances that the authorities wanted an agreement, that the talks were progressing in an atmosphere of calm and responsibility, and that the government was resolved to employ peaceful means only, since the only solution to the problem lay in dialogue.

I spoke with Christopher again three days later. There had been rumors that Gierek was about to resign. I assured Christopher that the Baltic coast was peaceful and that the dialogue was continuing. In accordance with my instructions, I stated that Gierek intended to carry out major reforms in the trade unions and in the economy. And I informed him of the changes in the government that were now official: Premier Babiuch, Vice Premiers Wrzaszczyk (the Engineer) and Pyka had stepped down; the new premier was Jozef

Pinkowski. I knew him and did not think much of him, though I did not mention that. Jozef Czyrek was the new minister of foreign affairs. I had sat beside him at the ministry's leadership meetings for five years. My old boss, with his own designs for power, Stefan Olszowski, had returned from Berlin and was now again a member of the Politburo.

When the miners came out in support of the shipyard workers, the authorities began to yield. An agreement was signed in Gdansk on August 31. On behalf of the government, Jagielski agreed to all twenty-one of the demands advanced by the workers. On their television screens, all Poland and all the free world saw Walesa, representing the workers, and Jagielski put their signatures to the document announcing the birth of Independent, Self-Governing Trade Unions (NSZZ). The bulletin issued by the strikers in the shipyard was called "Solidarity," and two weeks later that name—NSZZ Solidarity—was adopted for all trade unions.

Something dormant in me for years awoke as I watched the workers on television: the warmth for them that I had adopted from my father, a warmth long smothered in demagoguery. They were not being addressed by some staff propagandist from the district committee, but by one of their own. They had their own tribune, Lech. He was all I had once wanted to be. The workers listened to him, believed in him. In forty years the Polish worker had changed. He had been taught atheism assiduously, but he held it in contempt. A look of deep concentration covered the faces of the praying workers. I felt the passion and power of that prayer: full of resolve, ready to sacrifice.

As a young man delivering lectures to workers, I had offered my audiences the consolation that man would triumph in the end. I had believed in the liberation of man. But the liberation I had preached had brought the Polish worker only coercion, exploitation, and deceit. I found myself being brought closer to the church, and I remembered the pope's invitation to visit him in Rome. After much discussion, Wanda and I began planning a trip to Poland with a stop in Rome. It was the only way that we could visit the Vatican with any confidentiality.

The Party seemed to want to march in step with the people at the beginning of September. The Fifth Plenum had confirmed the agreement concluded with the workers in Gdansk, Szczecin, and Silesia.

The Sixth Plenum, held on September 6, suspended Gierek from his duties. The Americans had been expecting that development for several days, but it came as a surprise to me, for I was absolutely unable to see any replacement for him. Gierek had been the best of the worst. His resignation could only bring a period of constant change. It also extinguished the faint hope for his role as a bridge in the problem of Afghanistan.

Stanislaw Kania became the new first secretary.

The situation grew more tense. Jagielski went to Moscow on the tenth, supposedly in an attempt to obtain economic aid, but I felt certain that he was merely reporting in person to the Kremlin on his talks with the Polish workers. Later, Warsaw Pact troops conducted maneuvers in East Germany, Carter increased Poland's CCC credits to six hundred seventy million dollars, meeting the needs I had presented more than halfway, and Washington changed ambassadors in Warsaw, sending Francis Meehan there from Prague. On the eleventh Wanda and I finally moved into our new residence, but we did so numbly, absorbed by the events in Poland. The workers had won their confrontation with the government—a new situation in the Soviet camp. There was no doubt that this was only act one. Big Brother would hardly stand for a discredited Party.

Suddenly, on the thirteenth, I was summoned to an important conference in Warsaw. There a few ambassadors from the more important posts heard from Emil Wojtaszek, now Central Committee secretary in charge of foreign affairs. He said that confidence in the authorities had been impeded, but meetings with the workers were continuing; that it was not easy, because they argued on a high level and their criticisms were devastating; that far-reaching changes, difficult to fathom, had occurred in the Polish mentality. We had had to take a step "to the right" to avoid the abyss.

This analysis was hard on him. He was edgy. A busy workday was crucial for the Party, and the workers were ruining that. They had turned their attention to the uncomfortable, to politics. Our opponents were the Solidarity leaders, KOR people, and others who wanted to destroy our system.

"We've made three agreements—in Gdansk, Szczecin, and Silesia. And it's a good thing that there are three of them and that they're all different. That allows us some elbow room. We'll drag things out, postpone, delay. In the meantime, they'll start bickering with each other and we can marshal our forces." It was "us" and "them," the regime and the workers.

"And now about our 'friends,' " he said, at last. "Tensions have eased in the fraternal countries. Our friends are most afraid of a general strike, just as we are. They think we should be evasive, yield, sign agreements, so long as there's no nationwide strike."

Immediately after that, I attended talks between Minister Czyrek and Secretary Muskie in New York. Following the Party line, Czyrek assured him that the Polish government had the situation in hand. Muskie was not convinced. He balked at the fact that the unions had been required to register with the courts.

"Mr. Secretary," Czyrek said with conviction, "we are keeping our obligations to the workers one hundred percent. We will honor our promise to the independent trade unions ensuring them the right to strike. We will be introducing democratic changes and are engaged in intense dialogue. A commission has been convened to prepare appropriate law. What is important here is that the law correspond to the workers' rights, including the right to strike, of course."

Such a smooth talker, such a glib liar, and he was taking the Americans for fools.

In Washington, I heard our SB men murmuring among themselves. "We should have grabbed them by the throat long ago, but it's too late now. Everything's lost."

"How can you grab a whole factory by the throat when the stupid workers are on strike and have pickets all over the streets?"

"Don't worry. Our comrades will help us out. They've dealt with this sort of thing before."

My main source of information on Poland was, paradoxically as ever, the American press. At the beginning of November, the entire country came to a standstill during a one-hour warning strike. A few days later the first National Congress of Solidarity opened, at which Walesa was elected chairman. The authorities were yielding, but were doing so by creating obstacles, delays and postponements.

I began receiving chaotic, senseless instructions, which I feared would mar the credibility of Polish-American relations. At the end of October I had been instructed to see Muskie on several important matters, one of which was a request for long-term financial credits amounting to three billion dollars. Muskie's reaction was calm but tart. "We know that things are difficult in Poland and that's why you're seeking loans, but the scope of your needs is puzzling and frustrating." I felt like a madman representing the insane.

Ronald Reagan and the Republicans won the elections held in November. The days of Carter and his team were numbered. I was overcome with depression. The unique constellation to which I had attached such great hopes was coming apart, and the contacts I had so carefully cultivated would soon be gone. The Americans did not give up on Poland, however, and made efforts in Warsaw to determine what the three billion I had requested would be spent on. After a few weeks, the embassy in Warsaw received an explanation: "Ambassador Spasowski treats his ministry's instructions too seriously."

Meanwhile, tension surrounding Poland continued to increase. There was no word from Warsaw. But every once in a while *Polityka*'s editor, Rakowski, would speak out about the possibility of a Soviet armed invasion and the dark vision of a Soviet-German collusion against Poland. Had I known nothing about him, I would have wondered whether those were the warnings of a patriot. Knowing who he was, I had no doubts. He was using a tried-and-true Soviet method, exploiting his own reputation as a Party liberal to confuse Poles and frighten Solidarity out of nationwide action. I was forced to admit that he did so shrewdly.

At the beginning of December the border between Poland and East Germany was sealed, and the nation became even more isolated. The Party's Seventh Plenum, held in Warsaw, adopted a resolution holding former First Secretary Gierek and former Premier Jaroszewicz personally responsible for the errors and distortions of the seventies. Instead of initiating reforms, the plenum singled out the culprits, a cheap trick to keep attention from the real problems. An unexpected development was the reinstatement of Mieczyslaw Moczar to the Politburo. I was certain that the mysterious hand had replaced that brutal suppressor of the 1968 student demonstrations on the chessboard of Warsaw.

At this time President Carter made a public statement on the unprecedented concentration of troops around Poland's borders, and the White House added that the Soviets were prepared to intervene in Poland. The embassy underwent a diametric change of mood.

Euphoria reigned among the staff. I think they had received comforting information and instructions from Security through their own channels. In addition, they could read reports about an approaching Soviet invasion in the press. The Security agents, once resigned and depressed, now changed beyond recognition. "Those scum wanted power," someone yelled. "Now we'll teach them to eat stones!"

Malicious remarks began to be directed at me as well. My statements at meetings were termed revisionist. Derisive remarks were made, people saying that my chief occupation was "collecting" food aid.

Our turn to host a dinner for the socialist ambassadors' meeting fell on December 5, 1980. In spite of Wanda's seeing to all the details, the food was served cold and only after great delay, which caused merriment and mockery at the table. Dobrynin and the others made jokes at our expense. Our replies were received with indulgent smiles. Irina Dobrynin was playing queen bee.

"Solidarity is nothing but a bunch of spies. It's counterrevolution!" she spat out.

"There are a million workers in Solidarity," Wanda said, "Ten million, the whole nation!"

"Right!" Irina snapped back. "Ten million spies!"

I had been prepared for controversy with my fellow socialist ambassadors, but my own staff's provocative behavior caught me off guard. In more normal times, I would have sent them all back to Poland, but now I could only grit my teeth. I had more important matters to deal with.

Wanda and I continued to work toward our meeting with the pope. I wanted to hear from his own lips what had to be done to help the Polish people. I also wanted to be certain that my assessment of the situation was correct. I was not counting on anything good from Warsaw, and the embassy had become alien to me.

We began preparing to go in November, aided by the fact that Warsaw had summoned me for another conference. And thus our little conspiracy began.

"Do you think they'll keep us in Warsaw? Not let us out?" asked Wanda solemnly.

CHAPTER XXX

We prepared for our trip amid reports that a Soviet invasion was imminent. The embassy people were aware that we were flying via Rome at our own expense and did not hide their surprise. So I made no secret of Wanda's desire to pray in St. Peter's and let it be known that she was treating the trip as a pilgrimage. Secrets would only have aroused suspicion.

During the few hours we spent in a pensione waiting for our audience with the pope, I thought about what I would say to him. But what would he say to me? I was, after all, an ambassador for the regime.

I saw him in a vast, vaulted chamber; a solitary figure in white. As I greeted him—not kissing his ring—John Paul smiled slightly and pointed to a table by the wall. I could see he was treating me unofficially. We sat in armchairs and bent in close to talk, almost head to head.

"I want to thank you very much for seeing me, Holy Father," I began, having difficulty controlling a slight quaver in my voice. He nodded.

"I have come a long way. I am sixty years old, I was a Communist. Now, near the end, I have realized how very mistaken I was." Emotion made my voice unsteady. "I was seeking something that doesn't exist. I was blind. I never wanted anything for myself. . . ."

I turned, and our eyes met. His were gray-blue, kindly, encouraging.

"What matters is Poland, the people. Washington is a very important place. I'd like to help as much as I can, so that our nation can live in freedom. Poland has earned this; it exists only by its struggling, its will to endure, its dedication and attachment to the Catholic church," I was departing wholly from my original plan.

The Pope listened without interrupting.

"I was in Warsaw, Holy Father, when you held mass on Victory Square. I saw the people, their faith, their desire for freedom. I heard the homily; I understood a great deal. You know Poland better than I do. You listen to people who are wiser and better than I. But there aren't many among them who know Communism from the inside. What can I do to help? I have good relations with the American government. Unfortunately, I cannot make good use of those relations because I'm in a sort of void. Genuine aid does not matter to Warsaw. They'd prefer to borrow money, a great deal of money, obtain technology, financial relief, and large quantities of grain on credit, all of which sinks into that economic sinkhole of ours while the Soviets happily loot away. Holy Father, I think it is the people we must concern ourselves with."

"You are right, Mr. Ambassador," he began after a stretch of silence. I was pained that he used that official form of address. "Our nation has been through great suffering. . . . And is going through it still. We are living in difficult times. Man has the right to live with dignity and truth. It's so hard to be at once the pope and a Pole," he said, his gaze distant. He spoke of life and destiny, man's hope, labor and justice. He neither criticized nor condemned. Neither did he tell me what to do. Listening with rapt attention, and looking deep into his good face, I was not aware of the time passing. In all my life I had never been spoken to like that.

After our talk, Wanda entered and we were both blessed by the pope and given rosaries and mementoes. I was very happy as we left the Vatican. I knew one thing: I must exert myself to the fullest. What would become of my work depended only on me and on God. "On God." It was the first time any such thought had entered my mind.

In Warsaw, despite a certain weakness, a recurrence of my heart disease, I set about making a plan of action. I had to make the fullest possible use of my time there in order to know what to do in Washington. I put my reluctance aside and initiated conferences with highly placed people whose advice or information could aid me. In the back of my mind was always the possibility that Warsaw would not allow me to return to Washington. I was prepared for that eventuality and reconciled to it.

We spent Christmas Eve with Misia, her husband, and my mother, whom Misia had brought from Milanowek for the winter. We spoke of Poland. Wanda recounted her impressions of the home for the chronically ill, where she had visited her mother. All the health service staff had worn Solidarity pins. Morale had changed; there was an air of hope.

Misia told us about the ceremony at the unveiling of a monument in Gdansk to honor the shipyard workers killed in 1970. The workers had demanded that a monument be raised to their dead, and now all Poland could see it: three enormous crosses with anchors at their tops. Thousands of shipyard workers, representatives of the church, Solidarity, and the authorities had looked on together at the unveiling. It was in Misia's telling of all this that I learned that she was active in Solidarity.

Solidarity, Solidarity. It was a Solidarity Christmas. Even the nativity scenes had Solidarity symbols on them: Walesa approaching the Christ child; the dead workers of 1970 lying on the snow. Friends from the Baltic coast told us about the incidents that had occurred in August: the discipline and self-sacrifice, the faith and hope, the talks, the signing of the agreements. The workers had begun and ended each day with prayer and the singing of patriotic songs. Never before had a workers' protest possessed such depth, power, and eloquence. The authorities had recognized that, they said, and had been forced to yield in Gdansk. Not a single window had been broken. Listening to them, I felt it really was a new Poland.

I soon learned what the authorities were thinking. On December 31, Minister Czyrek called a conference at the ministry. He reported on a trip a Polish delegation had made that month to Moscow, and spoke of his own conversation with Brezhnev, employing this honor to great dramatic effect.

I asked Czyrek about Solidarity, and he spoke of his three-hour conversation with Walesa, who had sought advice on how to present Polish affairs abroad, since he was going to Japan.

"It's good that they ask our advice," said Czyrek, "but it doesn't change anything. We have to keep an eye on them."

"There have been a lot of changes in Warsaw," I said. "With whom do you think I should confer?"

"Only one person counts," he replied. "Wojciech Jaruzelski."

I did not go see Jaruzelski. But Czyrek knew what he was talking about. Two months later, in February, Jaruzelski became premier and, in October, first secretary as well. Czyrek became his principal political arm.

On the evening of December 31, we went to Czeslaw's to celebrate New Year's Eve with him. His leukemia caused him to spend most of his time in bed. He said very little, and in the end I fell silent, too. Wanda and Czeslaw's wife spoke in hushed voices in the other room.

"You remember," said Czeslaw at last, "there was a gloomy day during the war when I had a terrible attack of despair. I didn't want to go on living! The Germans were rounding up people in the streets like dogs. I recall sitting at the table with you, looking at some German illustrated weeklies my father had brought from Warsaw, pictures of Germans fighting in sunny Sicily. I envied them being able to die under palm trees or cypresses with the blue sea in sight. Not the way Poles were dying, up against a wall, mouth bandaged shut. You comforted me. You said that we *had* to survive. . . ." He was breathing heavily and speaking with great effort. "Well, we survived. It was a miracle. You ended up seeing the world, and I virtually never set foot outside of Poland. I never will. It won't be long now. . . ."

Tears sprang into my eyes. I had always loved Czeslaw despite our different beliefs, despite ideals, despite careers.

"I've brought you something from sunny Italy," I said, offering him the box containing the silver medal I had been given by the pope.

"Our pope?" he asked wanly, seeing the Vatican seal.

"Yes. He gave me this medal himself, and now I'm giving it to you." Until that moment the visit had been a secret.

Czeslaw suddenly came to life. "You got it from the pope?"

"Yes. I had a long conversation with him just days ago. He gave me that medal."

Czeslaw examined it, turning it over. Then he lay back and closed his eyes, the medal firmly in his hand. Raised a Catholic, he had lost his faith as an adult, and, to a large extent, I had been the cause of that. Now I had been the one to bring him a blessing from the pope. He did not live much longer.

On a cold January morning, I met with Stanislaw Kania, now first secretary of the Party's Central Committee. His eyes looked weary. Our conversation went quickly to the point.

"The Americans are constantly asking me if we've worked out a plan to get out of our economic crisis. What should my answer be?" I said.

Kania shook his head and leaned across his desk. "First, you must understand the *heart* of the matter, the *dimensions* of the crisis. There are, in fact, many lesser crises, any one of which would be enough to bring down a state."

"I understand. But what are we doing to solve the situation?"

"First, the Party has to emerge from its own crisis," he interrupted impatiently. "We've got to deal with Solidarity."

"It's a powerful movement," I remarked.

"Yes, a big missile," he replied, after a moment's thought, "but its fins are small. And," he said, sneeringly, "Walesa's nothing but an ass."

I realized that no enlightenment would come from this conversation, and I quickly ended it. There was no point in bringing up the question of the synagogue.

I spoke with Security's Miroslaw Milewski that same day. This time he had no interest in embassy affairs. He took the list of families seeking to be reunited and set it aside without saying a word. I asked him for his opinion of Poland's situation.

"We've got millions of people against us," he replied glumly. "Who knows, maybe even ten million! How can we use force? And yet, we have to prepare to come to grips with it. Do you know how many people would have to be put in jail just to regain control of the situation? Forty thousand. That's the active core of Solidarity now. We have them all on computer. They'd all have to be locked up, neutralized, and then we could deal with the other millions. . . ."

At that moment I knew Wanda and I need not worry that we would be kept from returning to Washington. The entire top was so absorbed in the confrontation with Solidarity that there was no time for anything else. It was bitter comfort.

I went to see the new premier, Jozef Pinkowski, that day, too. Credits were the only thing that interested him. He had nothing to say, and grinned at me stupidly from time to time. But he was not to be premier for long.

At eight o'clock in the morning of January 8, I spoke with Moczar in his apartment. The odd time and place were the result of his full schedule. We sat alone at the table, Moczar serving breakfast. I observed a self-confidence in him that I had not seen in any of the others. He was now a full member of the Politburo and chairman of the Supreme Chamber of Control, which had brought to light the abuses committed by government and Party people.

"We're in a total crisis," he told me. "The Party's in crisis, there's a crisis of confidence, the economy's in crisis. But that's not all. Demoralization has crept into the Party to a frightening degree, and it's mostly from the top down. Everything has to be put in order from the foundations up. Lots of people are in trouble—accused of fattening themselves on the state's money. We have thick files." He cast me an inquisitive look. "And what about you? Is there anyone finding fault with you? I haven't heard anything, but you never know."

"No, I'm not being criticized," I replied. "I never bought anything in People's Poland. We have a house from before the war in Milanowek; strangers live there now. That's all I have."

"That's good. You're an exception, maybe even the only one. You really don't own anything? How about your apartment in Warsaw?" he asked with evident interest.

"I rent it privately. I have a few pieces of antique furniture that belonged to my mother before the war, and a few old paintings, from before the war, too."

Moczar seemed almost incredulous.

"You see, I treated my principles seriously. I *lived* by them. Even so, that didn't stop me from going astray."

"In what sense?"

"In the sense that it all turned out to be a mistake, a misfortune." I had let my tongue go too far. But Moczar did not react; he hurried off to another meeting.

My last appointment that day was with Stefan Olszowski, at the Central Committee. I sat in the waiting room watching people come and go in a hurry. When Olszowski finally had a free moment, we sat down at a conference table. His complexion was unhealthy, his eyes steely cold.

"Just tell me about the situation in Poland," I said.

"You can see what's going on here, can't you? Solidarity's gotten a taste of power and now they want to topple everything. And worst of all, they don't want to work," he snorted. "I'll be brief. There's no avoiding a confrontation. Things could get hot. This is counter-revolution. Our kind they're out to hang. There won't be enough lampposts for us all! Maybe not right now, but the time will come. Do you know how much they hate us? Have you heard what they're saying in the city? They're calling for people to be removed from office. The gall! I don't think we'll be able to get out of this in one piece without *help*. Do you understand me?"

That was my last "official" conversation in Warsaw. But we did arrange meetings with acquaintances of ours who knew the episcopate and Solidarity well. I wanted to learn all I could. With them, I discussed possibilities for charitable aid that would go directly to people. The regime required that all such activities be directed solely through three agencies: the Polish Red Cross, the Committee on Social Aid, or the Catholic association Caritas. I asked about funneling aid through those, but my question was met with disapproving glances.

"The three organizations you mention are controlled by the secret police. Does that tell you enough?" They advised that medicine go through the Ministry of Health. Solidarity was strong there and would not allow any theft. As for other aid, especially food and clothing, they suggested that it go directly to the church. There it would reach the truly needy.

Wishing to confirm our feelings about Solidarity, Wanda and I met with some of its supporters in a small kitchen, with the radio turned on. I was asked whether America's support could be counted on. I confirmed that it could, with reservations about the extent, since I did not know Reagan.

"Solidarity arose of its own, from the bottom, from among workers, and it has now reached every corner of society," we were told. "It has embraced writers, artists, intellectuals, and young people, of course. It has become a mighty movement that has swept the country like wildfire, reaching into the army, the police, and even your ministry. Like every spontaneous mass movement, it has its weaknesses. Its leaders have talent but little experience. They're better able to inspire genuine emotion and sacrifice than practical judgment. And so they're open to provocation and penetration by the secret police."

Toward the end of our stay, we went to Milanowek. Villa Rose was now a sorry sight. In a few years those cracked walls, which had witnessed an epic of life at the brink of death, would be gone.

For the return trip, I tracked down my father's and my old notes, documents, and photographs. Wanda wanted to take more things with us, especially those connected with Kaytus. I told her no, that we could not allow ourselves to think that we would never come back again.

My safe had been opened in my absence. The seal had been tampered with, and the little telltale markings I had placed there, anticipating just such an eventuality, were gone. Nothing else was missing. As before, I made no mention of the fact. I shared the information about Poland with my staff as if nothing had happened, although I could see the news about Solidarity did not please them at all.

I also filled Bob Barry in, although I did not tell him I was convinced no changes or reforms would occur, or that there would be no plan for extricating ourselves from our economic problems. I was apprehensive lest Washington wash its hands of Poland.

We had arrived in time for the presidential inauguration, and on January 27 President Reagan held a banquet for all ambassadors. I would be meeting him for the first time and decided to make good use of the opportunity. As Wanda and I were introduced, she hung back to allow me a moment with him alone. "Mr. President," I said, "Poland and the United States are connected by a long tradition of friendship. Now my country is in danger. I am asking you to support and to aid the Polish people. We Poles are counting on the United States."

A look of amazement came over his face. I could see that he was thinking these words odd from the ambassador of the Polish People's Republic.

"Thank you. I wish you all the best," he replied, pressing my hand.

Three days later he warned the Soviets against invading Poland. I did not of course make any direct connection between this and what

I had said, though perhaps a few of my words had stuck in his memory. Encouraged, I set vigorously to work organizing aid for the people of Poland. I took the advice I had received in Warsaw and sought help through the church, through the Catholic Relief Services. Only after great insistence on my part did official Warsaw accept this charity. Independently, a relief program was conducted by the Polish American Congress, and medical assistance was rendered by Project Hope through its president, William Walsh.

On February 9, General Wojciech Jaruzelski, until then minister of defense, was named premier. It did not bode well, a military man in that position.

The war of nerves grew more acute in March. On the eighteenth, the Soviets launched military maneuvers around Poland's borders. The next day, Polish authorities committed brutalities in the city of Bydgoszcz, in in the Vistula valley. Representatives of the workers and peasants, demanding that Rural Solidarity be registered, were beaten unconscious by uniformed and plain-clothes police. Poles beating their fellow Poles was a rare occurrence in Polish history. But it had become the norm. Protest strikes erupted, and, as usual, the government flaunted the threat of a Soviet invasion in order to intimidate the people. Thus the few weeks of relative calm that had followed Jaruzelski's appointment came to an end, and it was clear a new phase had begun.

A few days after the events in Bydgoszcz, I paid my first visit to the new Assistant Secretary for European Affairs Lawrence Eagleburger, who struck me as energetic and businesslike. Bydgoszcz came up at once. I condemned the violence and assured him that a thorough investigation had been launched, for that was my information from Warsaw. And I did harbor a sliver of hope that Jaruzelski might uncover and punish the guilty, not wishing to stain his honor as a military man. It soon became apparent that he was only preserving appearances and prevaricating like all the rest; proving himself more loyal to People's Poland than to Poland's people.

Toward the end of the month, things reached such a state that Solidarity carried out a nationwide warning strike. Four million stopped working. A test of strength appeared to be in the making. As became clear later, this was to be Solidarity's greatest show of strength. I received an urgent cable from Czyrek saying that the situation might require the use of extraordinary means. On that day the U.S. Senate passed a resolution stating that the United States would not remain indifferent to Soviet intervention.

I will not forget the events of March 30. Wanda and I were sitting on the porch watching television for reports of Poland when we learned the devastating news that there had been an attempt on President Reagan's life. We stayed by the television for news of his condition, but I was called away when the cryptographer arrived at my door with an uncoded cable informing me that the general strike had been called off at the last moment. An agreement had been reached between Walesa and Mieczyslaw Rakowski, the nation's new vice premier. I was relieved: dialogue had prevailed over confrontation. My relief was immediately followed by the realization that Solidarity had relinquished its only weapon—a strike. Either Rakowski had blackmailed Walesa, using the Soviet threat, or he had made Walesa yet another promise. "They'll be drinking champagne in Warsaw and Moscow for sure today!" I said to Wanda. Reagan had been shot, Walesa had been defused. Late that afternoon an urgent coded cable reported that Warsaw had ordered a state of alert—the kind that precedes a declaration of war.

The Warsaw Pact countries have top-secret instructions concerning the steps for mobilization preceding the outbreak of war. The first is a state of alert. The diplomatic posts must mobilize their staffs and prepare them to evacuate or to carry out special assignments. Finances are to be protected by withdrawing money from bank accounts before they are frozen. Secret documents are to be destroyed. In every embassy there is a sealed envelope containing another, which in turn contains a third, which is sealed with string and wax. The head of the post is to withdraw from that final envelope a carefully folded newspaper-size sheet of paper printed in black and red. These are the detailed instructions on what is to be done at once during each phase.

I went immediately to the embassy and called for the envelope. I unfolded the sheet before me on my desk and, in compliance with instructions, ordered the withdrawal of large sums of money from the bank.

Anxious thoughts crept into my mind. There could be no doubt that this was in preparation for settling accounts with Solidarity in the event the authorities failed to prevent a general strike. But why was a state of readiness necessary outside the country? Only in one case would this seem justified: if Jaruzelski had called for the aid of the Soviet army, as Gomulka had in 1970. And if the Soviet army crossed into Poland, the West might act on the assumption that the Polish state no longer existed. It would therefore freeze Poland's accounts. Those were frightening conjectures.

That evening there was to be a regular socialist dinner, at the Czechs'. Wanda thought it properly should have been called off, in view of the attempt on the president's life. All the same, we dragged ourselves to the affair at the appointed time. The Eastern Bloc ambassadors were in an exceptionally good mood. Merrily, they counted how many American presidents had been shot. I did not speak about the events in Poland. Nevertheless, it seemed to me that Dobrynin knew what was going on. In any case, the next day I received a reassuring cable from the ministry. The immediate pressure was off. But for the next few weeks, we kept more than one hundred thousand dollars in our safes. The alert had not been officially called off; it was in effect throughout that year.

At that time, Vice Premier Jagielski arrived in Washington. He was no longer negotiating with Solidarity, having been replaced by Rakowski, but was back to putting our economy in "order." At the State Department on April 2 Secretary of State Alexander Haig did not mince words. "Unfortunately, we can see your neighbors in various stages of military preparedness in relation to Poland. I spoke about this yesterday with Dobrynin. The American government and American people are of the firm opinion that Poland's problems can only be solved by the political process and by the Poles themselves."

Jagielski assured him that Poland was in control of itself, smiling good-naturedly as he delivered the lie. "I'd like to add," he said, taking a new tack, "that the socialist renewal that has begun as a result of all this will be carried forward consistently. We will not return to pre-Solidarity ways. I have full authority to say this to you." He underscored his words with vigorous gestures of the hand. "It's this very transformation that will enable us to avoid crisis."

I could feel sweat beading my forehead. I knew full well there was no renewal, no change in store; it was only a lie to support another lie.

The comedy was repeated in its entirety for Vice President George Bush, and then again for Representative Clement Zablocki. To Zablocki's direct accusations, Jagielski offered assurances that the Soviet Union was a friendly state. "In proof of their friendship, they have given us 4.2 billion dollars' worth of aid, nearly half a billion of which does not have to be repaid." It was the first time I had heard that figure. Our economic relations with the Soviets had always been "black magic" and taboo.

In all his talks, Jagielski made use of the same big lie that Moscow employs in its policy toward the nations under its yoke: that the Soviets do not interfere in their internal affairs. On his lips, this was not ignorance so much as cynical duplicity. After all, it had been Jagielski and Jaroszewicz together who had carried out Moscow's instructions to subjugate our economy to the Soviets'. Now the whole world could see Soviet armies closing their iron ring around Poland. Was that not interference at its most brutal?

One matter was settled. With the personal intervention of Haig, the Administration agreed to sell us thirty thousands tons of butter and the same amount of powdered milk, not for dollars but for Poland's own unexchangeable currency. They were the very products I had been making strenuous efforts to obtain since my return from Warsaw. Jagielski agreed to the proposal but without enthusiasm. He had been counting on new financial arrangements and further CCC credits amounting to hundreds of millions of dollars.

Jagielski spent several days in our residence. He spoke contemptuously and with outright hatred of Solidarity. Wanda succeeded only once in drawing him out on that subject, over lunch one day. I was not present.

"We've had it up to here with Solidarity. Much less Rural Solidarity! And, besides, who in the world ever heard of a peasants' trade union?"

"I don't understand," protested Wanda. "Surely if our peasants formed a union and saw that they had a future, we wouldn't need to be importing grain from abroad."

"You don't know a thing about what's happening in Poland," Jagielski replied irritably. "You're just repeating what the American press says. I'm surprised your husband doesn't explain these things to you. We'll never agree to the formation of a second Solidarity. You can get that out of your head right now. We have enough trouble with one as it is. We went as far as to make an agreement in Gdansk because there was no way out."

"But you signed with Walesa! Everything would be fine if you just put those points into effect. People would go to work, and there'd be peace."

Jagielski jumped out of his chair and began pacing the room. "Don't you understand anything? Walesa humiliated me! In Gdansk he insulted me, our government, our Party. Those people are riffraff. And those advisers, they're subversives. The time will come when they'll pay for what they extorted from us."

Two weeks later, on April 17, Warsaw did recognize Rural Solidarity. Perhaps it had felt backed into a corner yet again. A week passed and I learned that the Soviets' big ideological gun, Suslov, had arrived in Warsaw. It was clear the recognition of Rural Solidarity had earned Moscow's wrath. Suslov had been abusive and made threats. Afterward, the Soviet news agency, Tass, reported that there were revisionists in the Polish Party. At the Tenth Plenum, held a week later, heads rolled: Wojtaszek and Pinkowski were removed from the Party leadership.

On the afternoon of May 13 I was in my office, with the radio playing quietly. I was listening, as usual, for news from Poland. Suddenly the program was interrupted for a special bulletin: an attempt had been made on Pope John Paul II's life in front of St. Peter's. I felt myself grow weak and angry in turn. Had the mysterious hand reached out for him, too?

Without saying a word, I went home. Wanda was unconsolable. "Those Soviet killers again!" she cried.

As we followed the news from Rome, we learned that the Polish primate, Stefan Cardinal Wyszynski, was seriously ill. The assassination attempt on the pope must have worsened the Cardinal's condition, because he died on the twenty-eighth. Poland went into mourning, and the funeral became a great patriotic demonstration.

Wanda and I were both in particularly low spirits on June 2 when we attended the next in the series of socialist dinners, at the East German ambassador's residence. No one asked us how we were or said a word about the recent events in Poland and Rome: the primate was dead, the pope was struggling for his life. During dinner, Dobrynin was merrier than I had ever seen him, literally overflowing with jokes.

At the meeting, when my turn to report came, I was brief. "I don't have much to say. Unfortunately, the economic situation is becoming more complicated. It looks like we won't be receiving any further CCC credits, since we are not able to fulfill the conditions required. All that we have left now is the tail end of the old credits. I'm making strenuous efforts to obtain food."

"You're trying to obtain food, you're negotiating, but don't you know what suspension of the CCC credits means?" asked Dobrynin sharply.

"I don't understand your question," I replied. But I understood it perfectly well: the Americans were suspending credits to the Polish government; anything I could get would go directly to the people, to Solidarity, and bypass the official Warsaw-Moscow shuttle.

"I asked if you knew what suspension of CCC credits means?"

"We can't meet the conditions, the initial payments," I explained.

"Don't you understand? Don't you *understand* the Americans!" said Dobrynin, pressing the point, in a jeering tone of voice.

"I think I understand the Americans, but I don't see what you're driving at," I said.

"You don't? Come on, Ambassador, where's your political sense? We all know what the point is; we are political animals, after all."

He was intimating that the United States, by denying credits to Warsaw, was undermining the government and so interfering in Poland's internal affairs. Cold anger gleamed in Dobrynin's usually good-natured eyes, and my own expression must have been none too pleasant.

When we finally returned downstairs, I found Wanda pale and overwrought. It was only when we were home that I learned what had happened.

"It began with Irina Dobrynin," said Wanda. "She asked me to tell her some Polish jokes, which she had heard were very good. When I refused, she suggested we dance. They put on some raucous jazz and began dancing alone or in twos, stopping only to drink and devour the desserts. Then they'd start in dancing again, screeching wildly, undulating vulgarly, lifting their skirts above their heads, especially the wives of the Cuban and the Bulgarian ambassadors, though the Czech's wife wasn't far behind. I'd never seen anything like it. And with that demon Mrs. Dobrynin leading them all! They carried on like a witches' sabbath, taking pleasure in our suffering. It was all arranged to hurt, humiliate, and depress me."

That was a turning point in my relations with the socialist ambassadors. I could no longer bear them. I knew that I was not free to break officially with them and that I would have to continue participating in those meetings, but from that evening on I purposely avoided them at every occasion.

At my own embassy, all my actions were being held under a magnifying glass. The Soviets had their eyes and ears among us. Our SB chief Lipowski was in regular contact with the Soviet KGB resident; our economic adviser was in touch with his Soviet counterpart, and our military people with theirs. To preserve appearances, the Soviet diplomats would come to our embassy on days when our private canteen was open, and then, after conversations that often took place in the quiet room, they departed with bulging shopping bags. In addition, there was a Czech connection that went through our first secretary, a Pole of Czech origin. He was often at the Czech Embassy, effecting the conduit through which Dobrynin was informed in detail of everything that went on at the Polish Embassy.

By the summer of 1981, Poland's food-supply situation was tragic. The stores were completely bare. The grain elevators in our ports were full of U.S. grain, and ships lay at anchor week after week waiting to be unloaded. The large state mills, built after the liquidation of many private ones, were undergoing repair, so large shipments of U.S. wheat had to be sent by train to Czechoslovakia for milling. And where it could, the mysterious hand was destroying our food and medicines. The press partially controlled by Solidarity reported horrendous acts of sabotage. Grain was discovered in sewers, coffee in the river, imported cheese in lakes, and massive amounts of grain rotted in storehouses to which Solidarity had no access. People were seething, but there was nothing they could do; the storehouses were guarded by government soldiers. It was at this time that the first shipments of U.S. butter began to arrive in Polish ports. This cheered me, since butter had not been available for a long time.

On June 8, however, I received a teletype from Warsaw. "Please pass on this telegram to the Department of Agriculture in Washington. Re contract no. 7253-1 dated April 17, 1981—30,000 tons of butter. Butter delivered by the MS *Zyrardow* does not conform to the contract as far as the chemical analysis and net weight are concerned. The chemical analysis of 10 samples taken at random has shown a fat content between 76.82 and 79.86 percent, not a single sample was found with the correct content which should be 80 percent. Meantime have to put the whole above mentioned consignment to disposal for inspection at Gdynia cold storage."

I sent coded cables, hoping to create a stir and have the affair exposed. I never did learn where the butter was finally unloaded, nor what eventually became of it. I knew only that acute shortages of butter continued.

Other scandals took place. Within days I was informed of the disastrous situation of our fishing fleet in the northeast Pacific. Thirty Polish ships were anchored off Vancouver without a drop of fuel and without so much as a cent to pay for refueling.

At the embassy, the Party organization, controlled by Security, began to attack me. A meeting of the Party executive took place in mid-June. Such meetings are conducted in secrecy, and to prevent any bugging, take place in the basement of the embassy. I expected criticism, surely, but I had underestimated the diplomats from Security. Lipowski was the first to attack; he was, of course, the most truculent. He was so defiant and showed such unconcealed hatred that I began to laugh at the childishness of it. That infuriated him.

"Comrades, it turns out that it's darkest right under the lamppost, if you know what I mean. We've been observing this for a long time now, and we're well aware who's doing what and why. We won't settle accounts here in a foreign post. We have a long memory, and we know all. Not all of us realize that the United States is our enemy! There are people among us who even consider them our friends! . . ."

Most likely he had counted on provoking me into a row, which would be the beginning of the "Spasowski affair." He had, however, miscalculated. I glanced at my watch. "I think we've exhausted that subject," I said in a calm, almost carefree tone and rose. "Time for me to go. I have more serious duties to attend to."

A few days later we had dinner with Walter Stoessel, now under secretary for political affairs. He assessed the situation in Poland as extremely serious and asked for my comment. I responded that the people who had recently been in Warsaw had seen clear signs of preparation for a Soviet invasion; Soviet staff officers kept appearing in Warsaw for meetings with our General Staff, and KGB groups were conferring with our secret police.

I told him without hesitation that the Polish people were in mortal danger. I caught myself speaking my mind without any regard for the diplomatic considerations. I had crossed the line.

"The only thing that can help us now is if effective pressure is brought to bear on the Soviets," I said. "No more aid to the government in Warsaw—it's clearly against the people. Aid should be focused on the people themselves and be moved through charitable organizations. That's what I've been working on for some time now."

We talked until midnight.

An extraordinary Party congress took place in Warsaw July 14 to 20. Moscow sent a low-ranking delegation as a sign of its displeasure. There were extensive changes of personnel, but the congress mainly ratified decisions made at previous Central Committee plenums. Kania remained first secretary. Jaruzelski, Olszowski, and Barcikowski, the former minister of agriculture, joined by Czyrek and Milewski, made up the top of the Politburo. The Western press was delighted; they reported that for the first time Party elections had been democratic. I did not believe that for a moment, but I did not want the United States to lose interest in Poland. I played along with the myth, and even used these "democratic elections" as proof of our "renewal."

I was disturbed by Rakowski's performance at the congress rostrum. He spoke like a Pole, a Party reformer, and even allowed himself to polemicize with Moscow, to great applause. It appeared that he was gaining in popularity, and that would serve him well in future showdowns with Solidarity. No matter that he had deceived Walesa in March, that he had intimidated Solidarity by saying that our allies were losing their patience with Poland, now he was playing the liberal to good effect.

Nothing changed after the congress. Reports were issued, and wool was pulled over people's eyes, but there were no reforms. Warsaw still wanted credits, and Washington still wanted to know what was going on.

At the end of the month I spoke with Senator Charles Percy, chairman of the Senate Foreign Relations Committee. We had met before. With him was his adviser on foreign affairs, Diana Smith, who took notes. I thanked him for the fifty million dollars' worth of corn credits we had been granted and told him about the grave hunger crisis in Poland.

"Mr. Senator, strikes are breaking out in my country, people are organizing hunger marches. I'm appealing to you for help. We need food to feed our people. Charitable aid is coming in, but it's not enough. I'm asking for help from the Administration, for American aid. I'm not speaking to you on behalf of my government, but, if I may, on behalf of the Polish people." My voice broke. I turned to Diana Smith and said, "Please stop taking notes for a moment. . . . Mr. Senator, they want to starve us into subjugation, into abandoning the just demands of Solidarity, the agreements they signed. I'm asking for all possible aid and support. There's not much time. The world should know the truth. It has to be revealed that there is despair in Poland. I'm asking for an appropriate resolution from you. The banks must be used to force the government in Warsaw to join the International Monetary Fund. Only then can there be any movement toward a sensible economy."

"I understand," he said, nodding in agreement. "Tell me more."

"We are not the masters in our own house. We are surrounded and we are infiltrated. That must not be forgotten. The Party congress that just took place was supposed to be one of historic significance. It would have been if the principle of democratic elections had been observed and if Solidarity had been given its rightful place. But none of that can solve the problems. People are just as hungry now, after the congress, as they were before it. The economy has come apart. The authorities have no plan. They don't want and can't introduce changes because of the Soviets. You have to understand the complexity of our situation. As I said, we're not alone in our house. If that's not taken into account, the whole situation can seem irrational, surreal." My voice broke again. I was unable to control myself in front of the two of them, and I was mortified.

Later that day, I spoke to Jack Scanlan, Barry's replacement as deputy assistant secretary for Eastern Europe. My trust in Jack had been immediate. On July 31, he phoned me to say, "Haig has been told of the situation. We're considering an airlift."

I was delighted. Quickly, I suggested some political preparations: a Senate resolution on hunger in Poland and an official statement to me in Washington and one to Warsaw by Ambassador Meehan. I told him publicity was essential. Poles who were surrounded, cut off, and hungry had to be made aware who it was that was coming to their aid. And the food had to move far beyond butter and milk. Scanlan agreed. Percy phoned that afternoon to inform me that the resolution had passed in the Senate.

Ironically, the next day I received a brief coded cable from Czyrek: "We are interested in any amount of food products. Confirm. Arrange." And to add to the surrealism, the new, "democratically" elected Politburo issued its first statement: a warning to Solidarity that it was inflaming the situation and an assertion that there was no hunger in Poland.

A few days later Scanlan informed me that, upon reflection, the State Department had changed its mind and would move to lend aid through U.S. and West European charitable organizations. I was truly disappointed. The airlift, though difficult and costly, would have been a dramatic show of American will to aid Poland and to show the world in a peaceful and humanitarian way that Soviet arrogance had its limits. The charitable programs were good and important ones—Care, for example, undertook the feeding of one million children in schools—but these were not the dramatic efforts I had hoped for.

Soviet military maneuvers took place in the north of Poland and in Soviet Byelorussia. At the Second Plenum on August 12 and 13, Kania cautiously warned of a national tragedy, using a sure euphemism for invasion, so that sensitive ears in Moscow would not be offended.

Much to our relief, Misia and Andrzej, who had obtained a position at American University, arrived in August. They both looked thin, undernourished.

Looking around the embassy she had known in her childhood, Misia was struck by the change in atmosphere. "Why does everyone scowl at us?" she asked. "What did we do to them?"

"They don't like your father and me," Wanda told her sadly. "It's not the same place you remember."

Misia was quick to understand that it was Security running the embassy these days. "This place has turned into a bunker!" she cried one day in my office. "A car can't even come in through the front entrance. They've cut down the bushes out front to keep Americans from hiding in them. They're simply paranoid."

"Pst!" whispered Wanda, placing a finger to her lips and pointing to the door. She tiptoed over and swung it open. Behind it stood the embassy's first secretary. Under his arm was a file and on his face a sheepish grin.

The long-awaited National Congress of delegates of Solidarity opened in Gdansk on September 5. I followed intently the reports by foreign correspondents and the Polish press. This was the first general assembly of the nearly nine hundred deputies from the world of Polish labor, certainly the first in postwar Poland. The ceremonies began with a service in the historic cathedral in Oliwa, outside Gdansk. Wyszynski's successor as Polish primate, Archbishop Jozef Glemp, called for peace in his sermon. The mood was both exalted and agitated. As if purposely to inflame the situation, the authorities chose this time to halt the investigation into the beatings in Bydgoszcz. I could guess the motive: Warsaw wanted ammunition for its argument that Solidarity endangered People's Poland and the Warsaw Pact. That ammunition could be obtained by adding fuel to the fire of Solidarity's most active wing. If that group could be edged toward a general strike, the ultimate form of intimidation—Soviet invasion—could be used.

But Solidarity's congress seemed to be in a euphoric mood. Instead of solidifying their own power, the delegates addressed the workers of the Soviet Union, Czechoslovakia, East Germany, and the other Warsaw Pact countries. They had felt the entire nation behind them and seemed carried away.

On the sixteenth the authorities attacked Solidarity with unprecedented severity, claiming that the Gdansk agreement had been violated. An echo of the condemnation was immediately heard from Moscow.

There were other signs of trouble. The State Department was now deeply concerned about Poland. Scanlan argued that our lack of a plan for stabilization made it impossible for the United States to provide any broader aid. God helps those who help themselves, he said. He pointed out that if we wished to reach agreement with U.S. banks concerning a rescheduling of payments, we had to come forward with reforms. They are well inclined toward you, he explained, as if to a child, but every one of the six hundred forty banks that made loans to you is constantly asking: Where's my money? He was right, of course.

John Roberts, the U.S. chairman of the Economic Council, also raised the question of finances. On his initiative, and with my support, a bilateral finance group was created, headed by William Miller. There could have been no better candidate for the position; in the Carter Administration, Miller had headed the Federal Reserve and also been secretary of the treasury. Both Roberts and Miller felt that Poland's joining the International Monetary Fund was the only way out of debt and chaos.

Czyrek arrived in New York for a UN session. On September 22, he and I met with Secretary Haig, who opened by saying, "Your economic needs are great. I'd be grateful for comments and suggestions on what we and our partners can do for you."

Czyrek responded that Poland's goal was now socialist renewal and democratic reform. Having established that deception, he went on to attack Solidarity. "We thought Solidarity was interested in sharing responsibility for the country, but it has proclaimed a policy of confrontation and is jeopardizing our relations with our friends. They're doing this despite the principle they've espoused—noninterference by our neighbors. This has caused tension, as we know, and the Soviet Union has had to speak out on the subject. We've tried to reach agreement in various ways. . . . We've spoken with the church, with representatives of Solidarity. We in the government are being understanding, but there are limits. We certainly don't want a national tragedy. We also don't wish to encumber the world situation with our problems. Things are difficult enough as they are."

From there he moved on to economic affairs. We needed raw materials, he said. Fertilizer, farm machines, pesticides . . . What he means, I thought, is that we need everything. And not a word about changes, reforms, or concrete plans. Words, empty words.

Now it was Haig's turn. "What I've heard here today leads me to think," he started amiably, "that you have a deep understanding of the realities . . . and the risks. We've given you a great deal of aid this year; there's been a great deal of effort on our part. We think that Russia should take on some of the weight of your difficult situation. I want to point out to you the constant line taken by Soviet propaganda: supposedly, we're interfering in your internal affairs; on the other hand, *they're* 'magnanimously helping' you. This doesn't make things any easier. We're keeping a close eye on all Soviet reaction. But I'd like to hope that your government is striving to find positive solutions. . . . We would warn you that were you to use martial law as a means of stabilizing the situation, that would have a direct influence on aid from us. And the same applied to the entire Atlantic Community. I assume you will appreciate this point."

Czyrek's response was cautious. "We're trying to act positively, but it's not a 'one-way street.' We don't want to employ any extraordinary means, and this year will prove that. If we are forced to, it will only be because of a 'higher necessity.' "

"That would create great danger, and I don't know where it would lead," said Haig severely.

I met again with Czyrek in New York on the twenty-seventh. He seemed less formal and suggested that we go somewhere for dinner. We went to a Chinese restaurant on the same block as our consulate. The place was empty, but for privacy's sake we took a corner table on the second floor.

"I just had a very tough meeting with Gromyko," Czyrek confided in me, seeming to need to talk. "I've never seen him like that before. Booming at me! Giving me a real tongue-lashing! And the language! It was there in their delegation, their bunker. One curse after another!"

"What about?"

"I'll tell you exactly. Gromyko shouted, 'You're in Lenin's Party, aren't you? Poland is crawling with counterrevolution. What do you propose to do about it? Don't you *know* counterrevolution has to be smashed? They'll have you hanging from the lampposts if you don't settle accounts like we did in 1917. And what are you Poles doing? Tell me, what are you *doing*?' "

Here was Poland's foreign minister looking around a nearly empty restaurant, frightened and shattered, speaking to me in a whisper. "Then Gromyko mocked me, interrogated me, and started shouting all over again. 'What's the government doing? What's the Party doing? What are *you* doing to combat Solidarity, that reactionary slime!' I've had enough," Czyrek said. "I'll be leaving the ministry soon."

He looked at me. "And how are things with you?"

"Very bad. First of all, the situation at the embassy is a disaster."

"I know something about that. We're intending to recall you. There have been a lot of complaints about you, going to church and all that. Apparently, you made no secret of it."

"No. I did what I thought was right. When will you recall me?"

"At the end of the year."

"Oh, no, no," I said. "I won't agree to that. The ministry always has me going back in midwinter, and I've had enough of that. My health is not good. The move is hard."

"All right, all right. We'll extend it two or three months, to early spring."

"One other thing: could you please inform me of the recall by letter? I don't want the whole embassy learning of it at the same time I do. They're all with Security."

"Fine. I'll inform you by courier. Your relations with Security are that bad?"

"Yes, they are. The embassy is no post of the Ministry of Foreign Affairs, you know, but a Security espionage unit. Quite literally. With the exception of me and a few others, they're all Security officers, ranging from captain to colonel. The atmosphere's awful. Suspicion, intimidation, even savage beatings. *I'm* under surveillance, though Security denies it. They open my mail. My secretary works with the resident. Whatever I say at our meetings is reported at once to the Soviet Embassy and the KGB. They even have a stooge who reports to the Czechs. They're all SB—*swine.*"

Czyrek's expression suddenly changed, and his manner became chilly. I had gone too far. I had forgotten that he had come to the ministry after a career at Security. But I was off and running, not to be stopped.

"I'll tell you something else. I'm worried about our staff. This is the sort of atmosphere that causes defections. You know about the cryptographer at our UN delegation and the two consuls who defected. I warn you, I cannot be responsible for the situation at our posts here. I never thought I'd find myself in a position like this at the end of my career. You know that before I left Poland I had arranged to retire." I leaned toward him. "There's a limit to everything," I hissed.

"I'll try to arrange to have you recalled in March," he said.

"Good. I won't come in the winter."

The second session of the Solidarity congress had begun. Once again agitation ran high, this time because the attorney general in Warsaw had upheld the previous decision concerning the beatings in Bydgoszcz. Security and the police could now commit acts of violence with impunity. There could be no doubt that Jaruzelski was behind this decision. As for the "liberal" Rakowski, he was now saying that nothing remained of the possibility for co-operation between the government and Solidarity, and he feigned regret, claiming to have been very attached to the idea. There could be nothing more cynical.

During this session of the congress, the activist group KOR, believing that it had accomplished its mission, dissolved itself. I was struck by the calm and intelligence of Walesa's speech, in which he said, "I realize that this struggle is very hard and that we have very minimal chances of winning if we use unconsidered action. I'm not trying to intimidate anyone but the chances are truly minimal because we underestimate the people we're dealing with. We underestimate them, we fail to see that they can subdue us very easily, very quickly, with hunger!"

Solidarity was now the great majority of the adult population in Poland.

Wanda and I spent whole nights talking about our second, and final, farewell to America. It would be hard for Wanda; she had had enough of People's Poland. For me, my attachment to memory, to people, to the land itself had always proved strong. But even that strength was beginning to erode. I had reached my limit, perhaps. Looking back on my life, I saw myself wading blindly through a monstrous swamp. And to sink in that mud for the rest of my days was too horrible to imagine. To return to Poland would mean I would never be able to tell the truth about myself, my father, my son. At the same time I could not bear the thought of deserting a sinking ship. I was trapped.

I met with Jack Scanlan on October 1. "I'll be recalled soon," I told him. "I just learned that."

"You? Recalled? After all you've done for them?" Jack shook his head. "Things will get only more complicated for Warsaw now."

I told him that once I returned, I would retire. I also revealed to him what I was harboring deep in my heart—the hope of speaking out for Poles who could not speak for themselves. He saw my desperation, and was sympathetic.

On October 6, President Anwar Sadat was assassinated in Cairo. I could not help but see a long shadow behind his death.

I held the usual Tuesday meeting that day. My people sat around scoffing cynically at the events in Egypt. After the meeting, resident Lipowski—in an exceptionally good mood—walked beside me through the Blue Room.

"You know, Ambassador, I'm not as simple as I might seem," he remarked.

"Could be. I don't know, and I'm not interested," I replied and turned toward my office door, but he took me by the arm.

"I'm like a bulldog," he said, with a wink. "When I get my teeth into somebody's ass, I never let go."

"Very nice. Yes, you really are a bad dog," I remarked, and I closed the door on him. The insolence of that psychopathic policeman was beyond endurance.

At this time I was again instructed by Warsaw to request further large grain credits. But by now our debt to the West exceeded twenty-five billion dollars, and thus there was serious question whether the credits already contracted would ever be repaid to the banks. The New York banker Lee Kjelleren, representing a group of American banks, was looking around desperately for someone to speak to in Warsaw. On one occasion he even proposed that the banks be allowed to send a delegation to speak to Jaruzelski himself.

In recent months our residence had been turned into a second office for aid to Poland. Americans seeking advice or help in clearing the way for aid would appear at our door—experts on agriculture and co-ops, representatives of charitable organizations, financiers, presidents and owners of large companies. One of the most active figures was Edward Piszek, an American of Polish descent, whose generosity was unmatched. At times State Department people and even members of Solidarity who happened to be in Washington would take part in those meetings. Wanda was indefatigable in her various roles as hostess, cook, and waitress, since we still allowed no one from the embassy to work in domestic service for us.

On October 18, fresh disturbing news arrived from Warsaw. Stanislaw Kania had stepped down at the Fourth Plenum, and the Central Committee had "elected" Wojciech Jaruzelski first secretary. The general now had all power in his hands; none of the usual Soviet efforts to maintain appearances was being made. The model was now that of a fascist state. Jaruzelski was the commander in chief of the armed forces, the minister of defense, the premier, and the head of the Party. The first congratulatory telegram to arrive was Brezhnev's.

Conditions were continually worsening in Poland as winter approached. Everything had disappeared, and the tension had not abated. A few thousand miners in Katowice clashed with police. Wildcat strikes broke out. The general sent "military troikas," groups of three army officers, into all areas of the country to solve local problems more effectively. The move had a terrifying aspect: armed soldiers policing the villages.

The next meeting of the socialist ambassadors in Washington took place at the Bulgarians'. The new ambassador, Stoyan Zhulev, had just purchased a large residence.

We were received coldly, Dobrynin pretending not to notice me. The speakers were more general and cautious than usual. Less than an hour into the meeting, Zhulev's chauffeur entered the room and said something to him. Understanding enough Bulgarian to know that what he said concerned Wanda, I ran out to the corridor. I was directed to a small drawing room, where I found her lying on a couch, eyes closed, very pale. As I sat down beside her, she whispered, "I've had enough. It's made me sick. . . . Let's go home."

I went back to the other ambassadors and said good-bye. No one inquired how Wanda was. No one even showed us the door.

Back at our residence, Wanda told me the ambassadors' wives had gone to the basement to see a film. They had eaten, drunk, and smoked, reveling all the more when Wanda, for lack of air, sat off to one side by herself. The more Wanda languished, the more the women created an uproar. Somewhere in all this, she asked for a glass of water, but was ignored, laughed at. Finally, she managed to raise herself and go back upstairs, feeling quite shaky. When she lay down in the small drawing room, the ambassador's chauffeur apparently came in by chance. It was he who had brought her water, and he who had had the compassion to call me out.

The dinner at the Bulgarians' had its effect. The next day, Wanda and I were on a train to New York for a meeting with William Cardinal Baum. We spoke about Poland and ourselves. I appealed to the church for help in my plans to give testimony of my life.

"I cannot be muzzled," I told him. "Only in the free world will I be able to fulfill my moral obligation."

"The decision has to be yours," said Baum. "If that is what you truly desire, the church will consider the question."

"It is what I wish, Your Eminence," I said unwaveringly.

"In that case, I'll speak with Cardinal Cook. When the need arises, he'll do what's required. When do you foresee this happening, Mr. Ambassador?"

"I don't know, Your Eminence. Probably not this year. I don't know if I will even need the church's help, but we want to rest assured that we can count on it."

"You can," he said unequivocally.

In November Scanlan provided me with the latest information on the situation inside and around Poland. On the fourth, an incident that seemed of historic significance had occurred. Walesa, Glemp, and Jaruzelski had met for the first time. The Polish press agency had issued an optimistic bulletin stating that views had been exchanged on ways to surmount the crisis and to create a constant dialogue; substantial consultations were to follow. Despite the predictable détente gibberish, I was cheered by the very fact that there was any dialogue at all.

Two days later, I received two coded cables in connection with the IMF. The first stated that we were considering joining; the second, that we *were* joining. At this time Czyrek was in Moscow at a conference of Communist Party secretaries, and thus I assumed that he had secured instructions there. The dates confirmed this. I was also aware that until now Moscow's attitude had been decidedly negative about our joining the IMF. I sensed some trick in this switch.

Our financial people arrived from Warsaw soon after, and talks with the IMF opened on the tenth. The director general, Jacques de Larosiere, expressed his pleasure at our willingness to join the fund and his surprise that we had come to our conclusion with such haste.

Poland seemed to be entering a new phase of dialogue and realism. The new vice premier, Zbigniew Madej, presently in charge of the Planning Commission, was to pay a friendly visit to the United States. Quite separately, I had arranged for a group of agricultural experts from Rural Solidarity to come to Washington at the end of the month.

On Friday the thirteenth, I received a cable from Czyrek. "Pursuant to our conversation in New York, I am informing you that, by decision of the leadership, the time for your return has been set at the end of January." I was astounded. He had agreed not to send a cable and to effect my recall in March. Something had gone awry. Perhaps my recall had been sealed on his trip to Moscow, at Dobrynin's insistence. Wanda and I decided to take advantage of Cardinal Cook's presence in Washington and met with him for breakfast. He already knew about me and, after hearing what I had to say, promised help if I found myself in need.

The next meeting of the Socialist ambassadors was to be held at our embassy. Wanda urged me to postpone, and I considered it, but the reality of our situation prevailed. I could act in no way that would prompt talk that the Poles were breaking with the Warsaw Pact. In the end she admitted that I was right and that it would be better if it was they who refused to attend. In fact, Dobrynin did not attend, nor did the Rumanians. The dinner was stiff, unnatural; the meeting brief and formal. It was our last meeting with them.

That same day, November 24, disturbing news arrived from Poland. Jaruzelski had met with Soviet Marshal Victor Kulikov. People returning from Poland told us that Warsaw was inundated with Soviet officers and KGB.

On December 2, the police, backed by the army, broke up a sit-in by cadets at the Fire Academy in Warsaw. The cadets had demanded that the academy no longer be under Security's authority, but under the Ministry of Higher Education. Solidarity responded to the army's action by announcing a day of protest. A clash seemed in the offing.

Within days, Vice Premier Madej was in Washington extending his hand for sizable credits. In a meeting with Secretary of Commerce Malcolm Baldridge, he was absurd. He said the Polish government was willing to support "joint ventures" on condition that the main political forces, the Party, Solidarity, and the church, were moving in the same direction. An odd thing to say, particularly when the next day the Polish primate appealed for a dialogue to prevent what was developing into a serious clash between government and populace.

To Stoessel, he said that force would be used only as a last resort, but added that there was no place for consensus in chaos. To Bush, he said that consensus would include three forces: the church, the government, and Solidarity. "Solidarity is young, and there are firebrands among them. Winter will teach them a lesson. If Solidarity continues to refuse to co-operate we might all be in danger of a feminist revolution—the women will end up kicking us all out." He was grinning. "The young people don't know what they want. The government does. It wants law and order. And that's the purpose of the antistrike bill, a temporary, provisional thing, effective for only three months. You must realize that the government will use force only to maintain order."

That evening at the embassy, when everyone had left, I sat down at my desk and began to write the things that were on my mind.

> For many months now the whole world has had its eye on Poland. Historic events are taking place in my country. What hangs in the balance is whether the Polish people will find a peaceful way to secure enough independence and freedom to be able to decide their own nation's fate.
>
> For centuries the history of Poland has run with blood. The last war is proof of that, and of the power and indomitability of the Polish nation's spirit—its love of freedom. That spirit was still alive and growing in strength after the war despite the country's sacrifice and suffering. That spirit has seized the entire nation with unexpected force. And it is due to that spirit that the Polish people have shown such fortitude, sacrifice, and discipline in these last two years. In its battle for a free and independent Poland, the people have used determination and persistence, not physical means.
>
> People are cold and hungry. But they want to be free, and they will be. Only peace and co-operation supported by the entire nation can bring that freedom to Poland. This means co-operation among three forces: Solidarity (for nearly the entire society, and especially the workers and peasants, make up Solidarity), the authorities (who should be objective in drawing conclusions about their own tragic guilt from the past), and the church (the traditional mainstay of the Poles, and, as the conscience of the Polish people, part of our soul and history).
>
> Those who reject this arrangement and who would wish once again to impose a foreign yoke on us, do not deserve to be called Poles. They are simply foreign thorns festering in the living body of the nation.
>
> This sort of Poland, and only this sort of Poland will base its

relations with its neighbors—especially the Soviet Union—on principles of equality and good-neighborly coexistence. This sort of Poland and only this sort of Poland will be an agent of peace and co-operation in Europe. A nation of thirty-five million, rich with a thousand years of history, the nation of Copernicus, Marie Curie, Pilsudski, and Walesa, the nation which gave the world Pope John Paul II, will fight until it has that sort of country for itself. We do not want anything from anyone. But we want, and we shall have, a free home that Poles can feel is their own. A place they can inhabit in keeping with their traditions, where they can believe freely in God in keeping with the injunctions of the Catholic religion or any other religion, for tolerance has always been our guiding light.

It was the first draft of my protest manifesto.

On Wednesday, December 9, a few hours after Madej's plane had lifted off, I received a coded cable from the ministry. Warsaw was considering a moratorium, that is, considering declaring bankruptcy if the West refused to furnish us with further credits.

The next day, an important meeting of Solidarity's National Commission opened in Gdansk. Lech Walesa stated publicly that "Solidarity could not retreat any further."

By the evening of the twelfth, news reports began saying that Poland was cut off from the rest of the world. The tragedy had begun. War had been declared on Solidarity. And that meant war against the entire nation.

We did not sleep that night, trying, as we were, not to miss any reports from Poland, and discussing the event for hours. The picture grew grimmer and grimmer.

The press appeared at our residence early Sunday morning wanting information. The phone rang nonstop. I knew no more than they did. I began writing a new statement, this time in English.

Finally, on December 14 the American press reported that Walesa had been taken to Warsaw, and Solidarity was making dramatic appeals for help. There were armed troop carriers and freezing people on the streets. I was struck by the Administration's cautious reaction and by the fact that West Germany's Chancellor Schmidt had not broken off his talks in East Germany.

I received an urgent call to appear at the State Department. Scanlan assumed an official tone when I got there and declared that for the time being the United States government was suspending all aid as well as all financial relief. Events would be monitored and a final decision would be made on the basis of an appraisal of Warsaw's actions.

I immediately sent a coded cable from the embassy. I was on my way out the door when I was stopped by my secretary. She had a telephone in her hand. "Ambassador Dobrynin has summoned you to his embassy at eleven o'clock, Mr. Ambassador."

"*Summoned* me?"

"I mean, he's asked you to *come*," she said, correcting herself. "What should I say?"

"Say I'm busy."

I waited as she spoke. She cupped her hand over the receiver and told me, "The ambassador's secretary has asked me to wait a moment. I think he's gone to talk to the chief." Then, "Ambassador Dobrynin insists that you be there at eleven o'clock. Should I confirm?"

"No. Say that if he has a reason to see me, he should come here. Eleven o'clock. If he can't make it, then maybe for lunch."

"Ambassador Dobrynin invites you to come to lunch with *him*," she said finally.

"Say I invited him first," I said and went upstairs. A minute later she told me Dobrynin's secretary had hung up on her.

The next day the press reported that no one had seen anything of Walesa. I thought of Dubcek tossed like a sack onto a plane. Although martial law was in effect, and the nation was paralyzed, Solidarity's truncated leadership continued to function. Jaruzelski was now heading the Military Council of National Salvation (WRON), a junta of twenty generals and colonels—a new twist to "developed" socialism, I thought. At the State Department, Scanlan expressed his anxiety at the growing number of people interned. What was happening in Poland, he said, was in glaring contradiction to the obligations of the Polish government under the Final Act of the Helsinki conference. Aid and future relations would depend on whether the Polish government displayed appropriate moderation. Warsaw should be made fully aware of this. Lech Walesa was alive, but he was not a free man. As he spoke, I felt an unbearable weight descend on my shoulders.

On the sixteenth, the press reported new strikes and a growing number of arrests. Solidarity's message was: Be with us in our dark hour!

West European ambassadors continued to visit me at the residence. I appealed to them to help us. Sir Nicholas Henderson, the British ambassador, was especially concerned. In a meeting with Count Wilhelm Wachmeister, the Swedish ambassador, I asked him to convey my gratitude to his minister of foreign affairs, Ola Ullsten. At the UN General Assembly session in September he had said that Sweden was well aware of the Soviets' brutal demands to have Poland's democratic changes reversed.

On December 17, I was called urgently by the State Department. With a grave tone, Scanlan communicated his government's position to me. The United States had hoped that the military regime would display a sense of measure. Unfortunately, that had not proven to be the case. There had been excessive use of force. Thousands of workers and intellectuals had been interned. There was nothing to indicate that the regime intended to undertake serious efforts to negotiate a political accommodation with the social, spiritual, and political elements of Polish society. That would have been the only way to ensure peace and economic recovery. If the regime begins moving toward genuine accommodation by establishing free conditions in which free people can negotiate, the United States would hail that process and be prepared to grant further economic aid. Until then, as I understood it, there would be no U.S. government money through Polish government channels.

"My days as ambassador are numbered," I told Jack. "Wanda and I want to do everything we can. Before my post is up, I would like to meet with the secretary of state and the president. Yesterday, I spoke with fellow ambassadors to Washington; I begged for their help on behalf of the Poles, too. I beg you to do everything possible to avoid bloodshed. There could be fighting if the Soviets invade. The Poles need to be helped in offering passive resistance. I'm asking for all the world's help, but especially for the United States'. The Poles have great affection for Americans and are counting on them."

The press was waiting for me as I went out. I stopped and said, "Martial law has been declared. You know the facts. I won't be offering any comment. I'll say one thing only: the ancient historian Plutarch once said that silence in the proper season is wisdom and better than any speech. The Poles are facing tremendous odds. Listen! Can't you hear their silent scream all about you?"

They made way for me, and as I passed some of them patted me on the back. I was powerless to say what I really felt.

Derisive smiles waited for me at the embassy. The "diplomats" were now making no secret of their delight. "Now we'll give them a whipping!" I heard someone say. In my mind's eye were images of half-frozen Poles facing tanks, gas, cannon, clubs with only their bare hands. It was more than I could stand. Wanda and I telephoned Cardinal Cook and said that we would come to New York to see him the next day.

We traveled by train and, like a couple of fugitives on the streets of New York, kept looking around to see if we were being followed. In a New York paper, we read that Polish miners had been killed and wounded. Walesa's fate remained unknown. A show of force was being made in the streets of Warsaw, with columns of armored vehicles ready for action. Gas had been dropped from helicopters on Gdansk; tanks had smashed down the gates and entered the shipyard. There, they had found a sign that read, "There is no just Europe without an independent Poland."

We headed straight for St. Patrick's Cathedral, and then to see the cardinal. I told him briefly that my hour was coming soon, but that I would like to remain in my position for as long as possible.

"You are right," he said. "I don't think you should hurry. Take the long view. We want to help and we will."

I was relieved. Our action was now officially in motion. The one thing that lent us strength was that we were with the people, not physically, but in our hearts and souls, and with each other as we approached the next, and possibly the greatest, turning point in our lives.

In Washington, I went directly to the embassy. My chauffeur said that there was great commotion in the office because the diplomatic pouch, which had to go to Warsaw the next day, needed my approval and no one knew what had happened to me in New York, since I had contacted neither the consulate nor the UN mission.

The atmosphere in the embassy was grim, the eyes unfriendly. Most people had ceased to deal with me, fully aware—thanks to Czyrek's cable—that I was being recalled. The cryptographer brought me the cables. Czyrek instructed me to make it firmly and convincingly clear to the American government that Poland was on its way to normalization and that only in a few places were irresponsible elements continuing to disturb the peace. More comprehensive instructions would follow.

As I was on my way out, my glance fell on the gladiator on my desk. Instinctively, I stuffed him into my coat pocket.

On December 19, I was at the embassy before eight. It was a Saturday, and the guard who opened the door was surprised to see me. I phoned the cryptographer, who came reluctantly and placed the newly arrived cables on the table. Life in Poland was nearly back to normal, wrote Czyrek. Typical Communist dialectics, a shrewd assembly of empty statements designed to cloud the mind. I read them through twice and started to fold them.

"Coded cables cannot be taken!" the cryptographer suddenly snapped.

"Can't be taken by whom?" I replied.

"I have orders not to let you keep coded cables, Comrade Ambassador," he answered coldly. "Lipowski has forbidden it."

I was seething. I had been dealing with coded cables for more than thirty years and had written thousands of them, and now this cryptographer was telling me what I could not do because those were the orders that the Security resident, a thug, had given him.

"Take your cables!" I shouted, all self-control lost. "Do all of you think that I don't know whom I'm dealing with, that I don't know who you are, what you do, and what you think of me? You're informers! Scum! Get out of my sight! You make me sick!"

I left the embassy and went to the State Department. Because it was a Saturday, there were no cars in front. Save one—a dark car with diplomatic plates and two men sitting inside. Soviet Embassy employees—I recognized them at once.

I told Scanlan of Czyrek's instructions to reassure the United States that things in Poland were on an even keel. He burst into bitter laughter, having just received reports of savage police brutality. Apartment doors had been smashed in during the night; people had been dragged half-clothed into the freezing cold, beaten, and abducted. At Wujek, miners had been killed.

"Romek," Scanlan said as I rose to go, "I want to warn you, as a friend. We've picked up signs that people from the Soviet Embassy are following you. We have proof."

"Who?"

"Military attachés. They're driving around your residence and tailing your car. Be careful!"

To my alarm, Wanda was not at the residence when I got home. We had agreed that if any of us ever had to go somewhere suddenly, we would leave a note in the hall. There was none there. Things were in disarray in the bedroom, which was unlike Wanda. Could she have gone and done something reckless? Had she been abducted? As I was about to call the police, she walked in. Sue Block, the secretary of agriculture's wife, had stopped by unexpectedly, she explained, and they had driven out to Bethesda for a quiet talk. There had been heavy traffic on the way back.

We were to be allowed no peace. My secretary called to ask when I would be back at the embassy to approve the diplomatic pouch. My deputy showed up to discuss his return to Poland, for he, too, had been recalled. I asked him to deal with the pouch. Then I hurried Misia out to inform my driver that I would not need him any longer that day. Again, my secretary called, *demanding* that I come to the embassy immediately. For a moment I pondered what to do. Why were they so determined to have me come to the embassy? I dismissed her angrily.

"I don't want you to go there any more," whispered Wanda, reading my mind. "I'm afraid. I have bad premonitions. They want to harm us."

Time went by, the telephone rang again and I snatched it up. My secretary insisted vehemently that I come at once, everyone was lined up waiting to see me. Cursing at her now, I slammed down the receiver.

"The time has come for truth," I said to Wanda.

She understood at once and cried, "At last we'll be free, even if it's in our old age! God help us."

I stood in the middle of the room, my mind in turmoil, images whirling: my mother in Poland, my father's burning eyes . . . the telephone. Quarter past two—Scanlan would still be in his office. I reached out and lifted the receiver. It seemed as heavy as sixty years.

Epilogue

Four years have passed since I raised my voice in protest, but the war declared on the Polish people continues. Solidarity, the beautiful flower of freedom that took root in Polish soil, is blighted. Brute force has triumphed. The workers are powerless again, the peasants helpless, the intellectuals cogs in the machine.

This war has no equal in history. On one side, a nation of nearly forty million people, and, on the other, a handful of reprobate Communists whose power is based solely in the police. Under normal circumstances, the nation would sweep that handful away, even the police would renounce them. But the circumstances are not normal. The handful are backed by Moscow. It is Moscow that assures the handful impunity and enables them to propagate the myth that People's Poland is an autonomous country; that there is a parliament, an executive branch, a judiciary; that parliament passes or repeals laws in accordance with the constitution; that the government uses the powers granted to it; that there is law and order. It is a lie. The parliament represents no one, the handful receive their instructions directly from Moscow, and the courts carry out orders from the secret police. The situation in Poland confirms once again that Communists are morally bankrupt, that they would rather see a nation annihilated than see power slip from their hands.

This war has no equal in history. One side has all the military technology for subjugation. Wanton atrocities are committed. But there are other ways of spreading the terror. Artists and intellectuals are oppressed, democratic institutions are disbanded, universities are deprived of all autonomy. Television, radio, and the press serve the forces of deceit. People are stripped of their livelihoods, and of the fruits of their own labor. The economy of this pseudo-state does not work for the people, but for the alien goal of world conquest. A terrible poverty prevails. A Pole earns in a month what an American worker makes in a day. People go hungry, disease spreads, there is the grind of daily despair.

This war has no equal in history. The target is a nation with crosses in its hands and a thousand-year-old faith in its hearts. Its people make crosses on the streets out of flowers. They pray and speak of reconciliation. It is a nation that has not fired a single shot in return. The spirit against the sword, as it was centuries ago.

This war has no equal in history. Children take part. In downtown Warsaw, Grzes Przemyk, age nineteen, was beaten to death at a police station. There have been scores like him. The young are sent to prison, persecuted, brutalized.

This war has no equal in history. The nation has gone underground. Like the first Christians, they inhabit catacombs—the catacombs of faith, truth, and fraternal aid. The churches are full. People learn the truth from the underground press, from the free world's radios. Solidarity lives on, if only in hearts and minds. Those who write the truth are beaten cruelly within their own four walls, and carried out with hoods over their heads. In that dark night they continue a quiet and solitary battle for freedom and human dignity. How many are murdered is not known, because whole families are intimidated into silence. We do know the names of close to one hundred members of Solidarity who have been murdered, among them the farmer Piotr Bartoszcze, thirty-four, of Rural Solidarity, and the magnificent Father Jerzy Popieluszko, thirty-seven, priest to Warsaw's steelworkers. Fragile child of a Polish village, Popieluszko was a passionate preacher of God's love and truth about his homeland. Such are the people force fears most. Such are the people who must be eliminated.

As a Pole, I am proud. Mine is the nation that produced Father Jerzy, mine is the nation that lives by the spirit of Solidarity.

As a European, I am sad. The countries of Western Europe have not rejected the lie spread by Moscow that Poland's war is an internal affair. They have based their relationship with the Polish people on a fiction, and the real culprit has not been held accountable. An entire nation is held hostage, and life in Europe goes on as if nothing had happened. Poles are alone. Europe's solidarity with Poland failed again. It seems that the countries of Western Europe do not understand, or do not wish to understand that their continent can only have one of two possible futures: either all Europe will be united in freedom or all Europe will be sunk into Communism.

As a citizen of the world, I am troubled. Soviet colonialism—that exploiter of nations and killer of souls—has met only silence from the world's governments. Silence is evil's ally. We should remember that the crime of the Holocaust, the disgrace of our century, was committed in silence.

Not only is the free world silent, but it has a short memory. My generation of Poles came to know Red terror in 1939, when it spilled over the borders and, in 1945, took control of Central Europe. Now that it reaches around the world, only its scope and scale have changed. Its essence remains unchanged: the end justifies the means. The end is world domination. Neither the learned reflections of political scientists nor the good will of the naive can do anything to stop it. Only free man with all his resources and all his determination will turn the tide.

The story of my life was played out in a People's Poland where one communist team after another fell amid upheaval and suffering. First Bierut, then Gomulka, then Gierek and Jaroszewicz: theirs is a tragic legacy. Under each, Poland was a Soviet colony. Jaruzelski's team is no different. It has already distinguished itself for its crime and perfidy. Yet after forty years of oppression, Poles remain Poles in their fight for freedom.

Soviet tyranny is long-lived and thriving, not because it is strong, but because the free world has no solidarity of its own to combat it. Had the West maintained the glimmer of solidarity with the Polish people it expressed in January of 1982 in the program "Let Poland Be Poland," things might have been different. Poles were truly grateful for that sign of the West's support.

My fate is not devoid of its irony. In the fall of 1982, a military court of the Warsaw junta sentenced me to death. In so doing, the court ranked me with the Wujek mine workers who were sentenced to death in their own way—machine-gunned by the people's government. When I heard of the sentence, I felt relief in my heart. My burden of guilt for many years of service to Communism was lightened. Later, the junta's spies, operating in the United States, harassed my daughter. Their reminders that we still had family in Poland was a threat meant to discourage me from writing this book. I would have thought the Warsaw junta knew me better than that.

The greatest day of my life came on April 9, 1985, when I was received into the Catholic church at the age of sixty-four. As I was baptized by John Cardinal Krol in Philadelphia, I asked myself whether I deserved the grace of forgiveness and reconciliation with Him who liberated man's greatest hope. In joining myself to Christ, I felt at last at one with Poland's martyred people.

Index